Nezmija Begic

Nedz mija
Begic

Booooy

Reading Literature

Reading Literature

The McDougal, Littell English Program

Orange Level

McDougal, Littell & Company
Evanston, Illinois
New York   Dallas   Sacramento   Raleigh

Authors

Staff of McDougal, Littell & Company
Marilyn Sherman

Consultants

James Dedes, Teacher, Holmes Junior High School, Mount Prospect, Illinois

Yvonne Fasold, Teacher, Sheldon High School, Eugene, Oregon

Richard H. Gray, Chairman, English Department, Enfield High School, Enfield, Connecticut

Denis M. Hennessy, Teacher, English Department, Delaware Academy Junior-Senior High School, Delhi, New York

Patricia West Jeffries, Teacher, Bethune-Cookman College, Daytona Beach, Florida, and Manatee County Schools, Brandenton, Florida

Neeta Lewis, Teacher, Richardson Junior High School, Richardson, Texas

Sandra J. Nash, Teacher, Beverly Hills Junior High School, Huntington, West Virginia

Lois Samuels, Teacher, Chandler Junior High School, Chandler, Arizona

Mary Theiss, S.S.S.F., Coordinator of Curriculum, Archdiocese of Milwaukee, Milwaukee, Wisconsin

Van White, Department Chairman, English, Walker Junior High School, La Palma, California

Frontispiece: *Portrait of Berthe Kristosser,* 1916, DIEGO RIVERA. Instituto Nacional de Bellas Artes, Museo Casa Diego Rivera, Guanajuato, Mexico. Photograph: IBM Gallery of Science and Art, New York.

ISBN: 0–8123–5400–1

Copyright © 1989 by McDougal, Littell & Company
Box 1667, Evanston, Illinois 60204
All rights reserved. Printed in the United States of America

2 3 4 5 6 7 8 9 10 11 12 13 14 15 / 90 89

CONTENTS

Fantasy and Science Fiction   *150*

■ *Chapter 1 Review*   *194*

CHAPTER TWO
How Writers Write   *197*

Using the Process of Writing   *198*
Prewriting, Drafting, Revising, Sharing

Using the Sounds of Language   *211*
Rhyme, Rhythm, Onomatopoeia, Alliteration, Assonance

CHAPTER FOUR
Greek Myths and Legends 287

CHAPTER FIVE
Poetry 373

CHAPTER SIX
Nonfiction 439

Dear Student,

You are about to embark on an adventure—the adventure of reading fine literature. You will travel through time and space, visiting cities of the past and worlds of the future. You will meet fascinating characters who face exciting challenges. This book and your imagination will guide you.

Reading Literature will introduce you to a wide variety of literature. You will read stories, poems, plays, and works of nonfiction in their original forms. These works have been written by world-famous authors such as Leo Tolstoy, Joan Aiken, Isaac Asimov, Anne Frank, Langston Hughes, Rosemary Sutcliff, Mark Twain, and Margaret Walker. Some of the works may make you laugh and others may make you cry. All of them should make you think.

Literature is your inheritance. Great writers of the past and present have left you a wealth of ideas, experiences, and feelings. Through reading, you can share and enjoy these riches.

Reading Literature can stretch your mind, sharpen your senses, and enrich your life. You will improve your reading, thinking, and vocabulary skills. You will discover how professional writers write, and you will learn to use a similar process for your own writing. Most of all, you will have the thrill of losing yourself in literature and finding there the wondrous challenge that is life.

Sincerely,
The Authors and Editors

CHAPTER ONE

Short Stories

Reading Literature

Short Stories

A **short story** is a work of fiction that develops a single idea and can be read in one sitting. Because the story is brief, each detail counts.

Any definition of the short story must cover a wide variety of stories. Some short stories are concerned with adventure. Others explore the workings of people's minds. Some stories are realistic, while others are highly imaginative.

The History of the Short Story

The telling of stories is not new. Myths and legends were told more than ten thousand years ago. Bible stories have been told for centuries. During the 1300's, great storytellers wrote tales in verse.

The modern short story, however, began only in the 1800's and shortly became one of the most widely read kinds of literature. Great writers from all over the world contributed to this form. In this chapter you will find stories by writers from North America, Russia, Ireland, England, and South America.

The Elements of a Short Story

Setting. The time and place where the action occurs is called the **setting.** In some stories the setting is very important. For example, "A Crown of Wild Olive" must be set in ancient Greece. In other stories the setting is less important. The events in "After Twenty Years" could happen in almost any country and almost any time.

Character. A person or animal who takes part in the action of a story is a **character.** In most short stories the reader gets to know only one or two characters well. For example, the first story of this chapter, "A Spark Neglected Burns the House," focuses on only one character, a Russian peasant named Ivan. The reader learns about Ivan and his motivations, or reasons, for acting.

The important characters in a story are called **main characters.** A main character often changes in some way during the story. In "A Spark Neglected Burns the House" Ivan learns a lesson about revenge. Everyone else in the story is a **minor character.** Minor characters, such as Ivan's father, play important roles.

Plot. The action or events of a story make up its **plot.** Usually the plot grows out of a **conflict,** or struggle, which develops and is settled. In many stories the plot follows these steps.

Exposition: This first part, or introduction, gives the background that the reader needs to know. The exposition introduces the characters and the setting. It may tell what has happened in the past.

Rising Action: In this part, the conflict builds as the main character struggles to solve a problem.

Climax: The climax is the turning point in a story. The main character usually makes a decision or changes in some way.

Falling Action: This part shows the effects of the climax.

Resolution: The resolution tells how the struggle ends. It ties up any loose ends of the plot.

Theme. The **theme** of a short story is the writer's message presented through the characters and the plot. The theme is often the lesson learned by the characters.

How to Read a Short Story

1. Try to read the story in one sitting. Give yourself a chance to experience the single effect that the writer is trying to create.
2. Become familiar with the characters' names, feelings, and motives.
3. Think about how the main character's struggle develops and is resolved.

Comprehension Skills

Inferences

A writer may give information in a story directly or indirectly. For example, a story might begin with this direct statement.

A girl named Deborah woke up early one morning.

The story could give the same information with this sentence.

The sky was changing from a deep purple to a pale pink as Deborah sleepily opened her eyes and looked out her bedroom window.

In the second example the writer depends on the reader to make connections. When the sky gets lighter, the sun is rising; when a person is sleepy but opening her eyes, she is waking up. The reader can combine this knowledge with the facts in the sentence and figure out what is happening. A reader who applies his or her knowledge to the facts of a story in this way is making **inferences.**

Writers have many reasons for using indirect statements. First, limiting a story to direct statements makes it boring. Second, a reader feels insulted to be told everything. Even more important, a writer who counts on the readers to make inferences can say a great deal in a few words. For example, from the second sentence, you could guess that the day was clear and that the sun was just rising. You could not infer these ideas from the first sentence, a direct statement.

In order to understand a short story, it is necessary to make inferences. Here is a sentence from one of the stories in this chapter. What can you infer about the story "After Twenty Years" from the sentence?

His scarfpin was a large diamond, oddly set.

First, you might infer that the character is wealthy or showy. Next, you might guess that the setting of the story is not modern, since men do not wear scarfpins today. So far, you have made inferences about character and setting. From other sentences, you might make inferences about the plot or other elements. Like a detective, you should be alert for clues from which you can infer meaning.

Predicting Outcomes

If you know the ingredients in a recipe, you may be able to guess how the dish will taste. Similarly, if you understand the characters in a story, you may be able to predict their next moves. Depending on how carefully you read, you may even be able to predict the ending of a story. As you read, pause every so often and predict possible outcomes. Don't expect to be right all of the time, of course. A writer can always introduce a new fact that will affect the plot. If you have made predictions, however, you will more easily identify the new fact. This will help you keep track of what is happening in the story.

Exercise: Making Inferences and Predicting Outcomes

A. For each statement below from the stories in this chapter, make one inference about character.

1. Laurie said, noticing his father, "Hi, Pop, you old dust mop!"
2. If things get too rough, I run. And as anybody can tell you, I'm the fastest thing on two feet.
3. Then he saw how thin and pale she was growing.
4. He came in without a word. When I recognized him I started to shake.

B. In the following passage from "The Third Wish," Mr. Peters saves a swan tangled in thorn bushes. Then the swan changes into a little man. After reading the dialogue between them, predict whether Mr. Peters will choose reasonable wishes. Then explain how you made your inference.

"Well, Sir," the little man said threateningly, "I see you know some of the laws of magic. You think that because you have rescued the King of the Forest from a difficulty, you should have some fabulous reward."

"I expect three wishes, no more and no less," answered Mr. Peters, looking at him steadily and with composure.

Vocabulary Skills

Context Clues

When you first began to speak, you learned new words by paying attention to how other people used them. In the same natural way, you can learn the meanings of new words in your reading. You can figure them out by paying attention to the way writers use them.

The words and sentences that surround a word are called the **context** of that word. Often you can figure out the meaning of a word by studying the general context, or the sentences and paragraphs around the word. Other times, there are specific **context clues** in the sentence or nearby sentences that give you an idea of a word's meaning.

Most context clues can be grouped into the following types.

Definition or Restatement Clues. Sometimes a word will be followed by its definition. Study this example.

> Leita baked wonderful <u>meringues</u>, which are dessert toppings or shells made of beaten egg whites and sugar.

A definition or restatement clue is often set off by dashes, commas, a semicolon, or parentheses.

Synonym Clues. A word can also be found in context with its synonym. **Synonyms** are words that have the same or almost the same meaning. You can figure out the meaning of a new word if you can recognize another nearby word as its synonym. Study this example.

> The policeman twirled his club with <u>intricate</u> movements, and "Silky" Bob watched the complicated actions.

By studying the context of this sentence, you can figure out that *complicated* refers to the word *intricate* and so must have a similar meaning. Notice, too, from the example that the two synonyms are the same part of speech; they are both adjectives.

Comparison Clues. Often an unfamiliar word occurs in a comparison with a familiar word. Your understanding of the familiar word may unlock the meaning of the unfamiliar one. Here is an example.

The <u>thatch</u> in the roof was as likely to burn as any other straw.

The sentence compares two materials, thatch and straw. The words *as likely . . . as any other straw* imply that thatch is a kind of straw.

Contrast Clues. In a comparison clue, you learn that an unfamiliar word is like a known word. In a contrast clue, you learn that an unfamiliar word is the opposite of the known word. Here is an example.

At night the street was <u>pacific</u>, unlike the crowded, noisy chaos it was during the day.

In this sentence the word *pacific* is contrasted to *crowded, noisy,* and *chaotic.* From this, you can guess that *pacific* means "peaceful."

Examples in Context. You may find an unfamiliar word in a list or series with a familiar word, or you may find the familiar words listed as examples of the unfamiliar word.

I had several <u>rationalizations</u> for not studying—I had a headache, it was too late, I wouldn't do well on the test anyway.

From the examples that follow *rationalizations,* you can guess the word means "reasons" or "excuses."

Exercise: Using Different Types of Context Clues

For the following sentences based on stories in this chapter, write the definition of the underlined word as you understand it from the context clues.

1. He can make the journey by mulecart, train, or another <u>conveyance</u>.
2. The policeman examines the <u>vicinity</u>, or area.
3. He is a <u>stalwart</u> fellow, not at all cowardly.
4. Her new <u>sidekicks</u> are just as silly and loud as her old companions.

Stories of Action

Have you ever read a story that you didn't want to end? Some stories are so packed with action that you stay involved from start to finish. Others have such surprise endings that you may find yourself going back through them to look for clues you missed the first time. Details of plot are important to the stories in this section. As you read the stories, pay close attention to what happens. Notice the conflict that builds in each story. Try to predict how the stories will end. Most important, enjoy these strong plots and the impact they have on you.

Court Street Fruitstand, 1985, KATHRYN FREEMAN. Photograph: Tatistcheff Gallery, New York City.

A Spark Neglected Burns the House

LEO TOLSTOY

This story is about a senseless, petty feud between two families. What clues to the outcome can you find? Try to predict how the story will end.

There once lived in a village a peasant named Ivan Shcherbakov. He was comfortably off, in the prime of life, the best worker in the village, and had three sons all able to work. The eldest was married, the second about to marry, and the third was a big lad who could mind the horses and was already beginning to plough. Ivan's wife was an able and thrifty woman, and they were fortunate in having a quiet, hard-working daughter-in-law. There was nothing to prevent Ivan and his family from living happily. They had only one idle mouth to feed; that was Ivan's old father, who suffered from asthma and had been lying ill on the top of the brick stove for seven years. Ivan had all he needed: three horses and a colt, a cow with a calf, and fifteen sheep. The women made all the clothing for the family, besides helping in the fields, and the men tilled the land. They always had grain enough of their own to last over beyond the next harvest and sold enough oats to pay the taxes and meet their other needs. So Ivan and his children might have lived quite comfortably had it not been for a feud between him and his next-door neighbor, Limping Gabriel, the son of Gordey Ivanov.

As long as old Gordey was alive and Ivan's father was still able to manage his household, the peasants lived as neighbors should. If the women of either house happened to want a sieve or a tub, or the men required a sack, or if a cart wheel got broken and could not be mended at once, they used to send to the other house and helped each other in neighborly fashion. When a calf strayed into the neighbor's thrashing ground, they would just drive it out and only say, "Don't let it get in again; our grain is lying there." And such things as locking up the barns, hiding things from one another, or backbiting were never thought of in those days.

That was in the fathers' time. When the sons came to be at the head of the families, everything changed.

It all began about a trifle.

Ivan's daughter-in-law had a hen that began laying rather early in the season, and she started collecting its eggs for Easter. Every day she went to the cart shed and found an egg in the cart, but one day the hen, probably frightened by the children, flew across the fence into the neighbor's yard and laid its egg there. The woman heard the cackling but said to herself, "I have no time now; I must tidy up for Sunday. I'll fetch the egg later on." In the evening she went to the cart but found no egg there. She went and asked her mother-in-law and brother-in-law whether they had taken the egg. "No," they had not, but her youngest brother-in-law, Taras, said, "Your Biddy laid its egg in the neighbor's yard. It was there she was cackling, and she flew back across the fence from there."

The woman went and looked at the hen. There she was on the perch with the other birds, her eyes just closing, ready to go to sleep. The woman wished she could have asked the hen and got an answer from her.

Then she went to the neighbor's and Gabriel's mother came out to meet her.

"What do you want, young woman?"

"Why, Granny, you see, my hen flew across this morning. Did she not lay an egg here?"

"We never saw anything of it. The Lord be thanked, our own hens started laying long ago. We collect our own eggs and have no need of other people's! And we don't go looking for eggs in other people's yards, lass!"

The young woman was offended and said more than she should have done. Her neighbor answered back with interest, and the women began abusing each other. Ivan's wife, who had been to fetch water, happening to pass just then, joined in too. Gabriel's wife rushed out and began reproaching the young woman with things that had really happened and with other things that never had happened at all. Then a general uproar commenced, all shouting at once, trying to get out two words at a time, and not choice words either.

"You're this!" and "You're that!" "You're a thief!" and "You're starving your old father-in-law to death!" and "You're a good-for-nothing!" and so on.

"And you made a hole in the sieve I lent you, you jade! And it's our yoke you're carrying your pails on—you just give back our yoke!"

Then they caught hold of the yoke and spilt the water, snatched one another's shawls off, and began fighting. Gabriel, returning from the fields, stopped to take his wife's part. Out rushed Ivan and his son and joined in with the rest. Ivan was a strong fellow; he scattered the whole lot of them and pulled a handful of hair out of Gabriel's beard. People came to see what was the matter, and the fighters were separated with difficulty.

That was how it all began.

Gabriel wrapped the hair torn from his beard in a paper and went to the District Court to have the law of Ivan. "I didn't grow my beard," said he, "for pockmarked Ivan to pull it out!" And his wife went bragging to the neighbors saying they'd have Ivan condemned and sent to Siberia. And so the feud grew.

The old man, from where he lay on the top of the stove, tried from the very first to persuade them to make peace, but they would not listen. He told them, "It's a stupid thing you are after, children, picking quarrels about such a paltry matter. Just think! The whole thing began about an egg. The children may have taken it—well, what matter? What's the value of one egg? God sends enough for all! And suppose your neighbor did say an unkind word—put it right; show her how to say a better one! If there *has* been a fight—well, such things will happen; we're all sinners, but make it up and let there be an end of it! If you nurse your anger it will be worse for you yourselves."

But the younger folk would not listen to the old man. They thought his words were mere senseless dotage. Ivan would not humble himself before his neighbor.

"I never pulled his beard," he said, "he pulled the hair out himself. But his son has burst all the fastenings on my shirt and torn it. . . . Look at it!"

And Ivan also went to law. They were tried by the Justice of the Peace and by the District Court. While all this was going on, the coupling pin of Gabriel's cart disappeared. Gabriel's womenfolk accused Ivan's son of having taken it. They said, "We saw him in the night go past our window towards the cart, and a neighbor says he saw him at the pub offering the pin to the landlord."

So they went to law about that. And at home not a day passed without a quarrel or even a fight. The children, too, abused one another, having learnt to do so from their elders, and when the women happened to meet by the riverside, where they went to rinse the clothes, their arms did not do as much wringing as their tongues did nagging, and every word was a bad one.

At first the peasants only slandered one another, but afterwards they began in real earnest to snatch anything that lay handy, and the children followed their example. Life became harder and harder for them. Ivan Shcherbakov and Limping Gabriel kept suing one another at the Village Assembly and at the District Court and before the Justice of the Peace, until all the judges were tired of them. Now Gabriel got Ivan fined or imprisoned; then Ivan did as much to Gabriel; and the more they spited each other the angrier they grew—like dogs that attack one another and get more and more furious the longer they fight. You strike one dog from behind, and it thinks it's the other dog biting him and gets still fiercer. So these peasants, they went to law, and one or other of them was fined or locked up, but that only made them more and more angry with one another. "Wait a bit," they said, "and I'll make you pay for it." And so it went on for six years. Only the old man lying on the top of the stove kept telling them again and

Conservative

A Spark Neglected Burns the House 11

Almighty

again, "Children, what are you doing? Stop all this paying back; keep to your work and don't bear malice—it will be better for you. The more you bear malice the worse it will be."

But they would not listen to him.

In the seventh year, at a wedding, Ivan's daughter-in-law held Gabriel up to shame, accusing him of having been caught horse stealing. Gabriel, unable to control his anger, gave the woman such a blow that she was laid up for a week. Ivan was delighted. He went to the magistrate to lodge a complaint. "Now I'll get rid of my neighbor! He won't escape imprisonment, or exile to Siberia." But Ivan's wish was not fulfilled. The magistrate dismissed the case. The woman was examined, but she was up and about and showed no sign of any injury. Then Ivan went to the Justice of the Peace, but he referred the business to the District Court. Ivan bestirred himself to the Elder of the District Court and got Gabriel condemned to be flogged. The sentence was read out to Gabriel by the clerk. "The Court decrees that the peasant Gabriel Gordeev shall receive twenty lashes with a birch rod at the District Court."

Ivan, too, heard the sentence read and looked at Gabriel to see how he would take it. Gabriel grew as pale as a sheet and turned round and went out into the passage. Ivan followed him, meaning to see to the horse, and he overheard Gabriel say, "Very well! He will have my back flogged, that will make it burn, but something of his may burn worse than that!"

Hearing these words, Ivan at once went back into the Court and said: "Upright judges! He threatens to set my house on fire! Listen, he said it in the presence of witnesses!"

Gabriel was recalled. "Is it true that you said this?"

"I haven't said anything. Flog me, since you have the power. It seems that I alone am to suffer, and all for being in the right, while he is allowed to do as he likes."

Gabriel wished to say something more, but his lips and his cheeks quivered and he turned to the wall. Even the officials were frightened by his looks. "He may do some mischief to himself or to his neighbor," thought they.

Then the old Judge said, "Look here, my men, you'd better be reasonable and make it up. Was it right of you, friend Gabriel, to strike a woman? It was lucky it passed off so well, but think what might have happened! Was it right? You had better confess and beg his pardon, and he will forgive you and we will alter the sentence."

The clerk heard these words and remarked, "That's impossible under Statute 117. An agreement between the parties not having been arrived at, a decision of the Court has been pronounced and must be executed."

But the Judge would not listen to the clerk.

"Keep your tongue still, my friend," said he. "The first of all laws is to obey God, Who loves peace." And the Judge began again to persuade the peasants but could not succeed. Gabriel would not listen to him.

"I shall be fifty next year," said he, "and have a married son, and have never been flogged in my life, and now that pockmarked Ivan has had me condemned to be flogged, and am I to go and ask his forgiveness? No, I've borne enough. . . . Ivan shall have cause to remember me!"

Again Gabriel's voice quivered, and he could say no more but turned around and went out.

It was seven miles from the Court to the village, and it was getting late when Ivan reached home. He unharnessed his horse, put it up for the night, and entered the cottage. No one was there. The women had already gone to drive the cattle in, and the young fellows were not yet back from the fields. Ivan went in and sat down, thinking. He remembered how Gabriel had listened to the sentence, and how pale he had gone, and how he had turned to the wall; and Ivan's heart grew heavy. He thought how he himself would feel if he were sentenced, and he pitied Gabriel. Then he heard his old father up on the stove cough and saw him sit up, lower his legs, and scramble down. The old man dragged himself slowly to a seat and sat down. He was quite tired out with the exertion and coughed a long time till he had cleared his throat. Then, leaning against the table, he said, "Well, has he been condemned?"

"Yes, to twenty strokes with the rods," answered Ivan.

The old man shook his head.

The Gardener, 1912, ALEX VON JAWLENSKY.
Milwaukee Art Museum Collection, Gift of Mr. and Mrs. Harry Lynde Bradley.

"A bad business," said he. "You are doing wrong, Ivan! Ah! it's very bad—not for him so much as for yourself! . . . Well, they'll flog him, but will that do you any good?"

"He'll not do it again," said Ivan.

"What is it he'll not do again? What has he done worse than you?"

"Why, think of the harm he has done me!" said Ivan. "He nearly killed my wife, and now he's threatening to burn us up. Am I to thank him for it?"

The old man sighed and said, "You go about the wide world, Ivan, while I am lying on the stove all these years, so you think you see everything and that I see nothing. . . Ah, lad! It's you that don't see; malice blinds you. Others' sins are before your eyes, but your own are behind your back. 'He's acted badly!' What a thing to say! If he were the only one to act badly, how could strife exist? Is strife among men ever bred by one alone? Strife is always between two. His badness you see, but your own you don't. If he were bad, but you were good, there would be no strife. Who pulled the hair out of his beard? Who spoilt his haystack? Who dragged him to the law court? Yet you put it all on him! You live a bad life yourself; that's what is wrong! It's not the way I used to live, lad, and it's not the way I taught you. Is that the way his old father and I used to live? How did we live? Why, as neighbors should! If he happened to run out of flour, one of the women would come across. 'Uncle Trol, we want some flour.' 'Go to the barn, dear,' I'd say. 'Take what you need.' If he'd no one to take his horses to pasture, 'Go, Ivan,' I'd say, 'and look after his horses.' And if I was short of anything, I'd go to him. 'Uncle Gordey,' I'd say, 'I want so-and-so!' 'Take it, Uncle Trol!' That's how it was between us, and we had an easy time of it. But now? . . . Why, there's war between you! Is that living? You are a man, and master of the house; it's you who will have to answer. What are you teaching the women and the children? To snarl and snap? Why, the other day your Taraska—that greenhorn—was swearing at neighbor Irena, calling her names, and his mother listened and laughed. Is that right? It is you will have to answer. Think of your soul. Is this all as it should be? You throw a word at me, and I give you two in return; you give me a blow, and I give you two. No, lad! . . . Why don't you speak? Isn't it as I say?"

Ivan sat silent and listened.

The old man coughed and, having with difficulty cleared his throat, began again. "Ivan, my boy, hear your old father! Go and harness the roan and go at once to the Government office; put an end to all this affair there, and in the morning go and make it up with Gabriel in God's name, and invite him to your house. Have tea ready and put an end to this wicked business so that there should not be any more of it in future and tell the women and children to do the same."

Ivan sighed and thought, "What he says is true," and his heart grew lighter. Only he did not know how to begin to put matters right now.

But again the old man began, as if he had guessed what was in Ivan's mind.

"Go, Ivan, don't put it off! Put out the fire before it spreads, or it will be too late."

The old man was going to say more, but before he could do so, the women came in, chattering like magpies. The news that Gabriel was sentenced to be flogged and of his threat to set fire to the house had already reached them. They had heard all about it and added to it something of their own and had again had a row in the pasture with the women of Gabriel's household. They began telling how Gabriel's daughter-in-law threatened a fresh action. Gabriel had got the right side of the examining magistrate who would now turn the whole affair upside down, and the schoolmaster was writing out another petition, to the Tsar himself this time, about Ivan, and everything was in the petition—all about the coupling pin and the kitchen garden—so that half of Ivan's homestead would be theirs soon. Ivan heard what they were saying, and his heart grew cold again, and he gave up the thought of making peace with Gabriel.

In a farmstead there is always plenty for the master to do. Ivan did not stop to talk to the women, but went out to the threshing floor and to the barn. By the time he had tidied up there, the sun had set and the young fellows had returned from the field. They had been ploughing the field for the winter crops with two horses. Ivan met them, questioned them about their work, helped to put everything in its place, set a torn horsecollar aside to be mended, and was going to put away some stakes under the barn, but it had grown quite dusk, so he decided to leave them where they were till next day. Then he gave the cattle their food, opened the gate, let out the horses Taras was to take to pasture for the night, and again closed the gate and barred it. "Now," thought he, "I'll have my supper and then to bed." He took the horse collar and entered the hut. By this time he had forgotten about Gabriel and about what his old father had been saying to him. But just as he took hold of the door handle to enter

the passage, he heard his neighbor on the other side of the fence cursing somebody in a hoarse voice. "What the devil is he good for?" Gabriel was saying. "He's only fit to be killed!" At these words all Ivan's former bitterness towards his neighbor reawoke. He stood listening while Gabriel scolded, and when he stopped, Ivan went into the hut.

There was a light inside; his daughter-in-law sat spinning, his wife was getting supper ready, his eldest son was making strips for bark shoes, his second sat near the table with a book, and Taras was getting ready to go out to pasture the horses for the night. Everything in the hut would have been pleasant and bright, but for that plague—a bad neighbor!

Ivan entered, sullen and cross, threw the cat down from the bench, and scolded the women for putting the slop pail in the wrong place. He felt despondent, and sat down, frowning, to mend the horse collar. Gabriel's words kept ringing in his ears: his threat at the law court, and what he had just been shouting in a hoarse voice about someone who was "only fit to be killed."

His wife gave Taras his supper, and having eaten it, Taras put on an old sheepskin and another coat, tied a sash round his waist, took some bread with him, and went out to the horses. His eldest brother was going to see him off, but Ivan himself rose instead, and went out into the porch. It had grown quite dark outside, clouds had gathered, and the wind had risen. Ivan went down the steps, helped his boy to mount, started the foal after him, and stood listening while Taras rode down the village and was there joined by other lads with their horses. Ivan waited until they were all out of hearing. As he stood there by the gate he could not get Gabriel's words out of his head. "Mind that something of yours does not burn worse!"

"He is desperate," thought Ivan. "Everything is dry, and it's windy weather besides. He'll come up at the back somewhere, set fire to something, and be off. He'll burn the place and escape scot free, the villain! . . . There now, if one could but catch him in the act, he'd not get off then!" And the thought fixed itself so firmly in his mind that he did not go up the steps but went out into the street and round the corner. "I'll just walk round the buildings. Who can tell what he's after?" And Ivan, stepping softly, passed out of the gate. As soon as he reached the corner, he looked around along the fence and seemed to see something suddenly move at the opposite corner, as if someone had come out and disappeared again. Ivan stopped and stood quietly, listening and looking. Everything was still; only the leaves of the willows fluttered in the wind, and the straws of the thatch rustled. At first it seemed pitch dark, but when his eyes had grown used to the darkness, he could see the far corner and a plough that lay there and the eaves. He looked a while but saw no one.

"I suppose it was a mistake," thought Ivan, "but still I will go around," and Ivan went stealthily along by the shed. Ivan stepped so softly in his bark shoes that he did not hear his own footsteps. As he reached the far corner, something seemed to flare up for a moment near the plough and to vanish again. Ivan felt as if struck to the heart, and he stopped. Hardly had he stopped when something flared up more brightly in the same place, and he clearly saw a man with a cap on his head, crouching down with his back towards him, lighting a bunch of straw he held in his hand. Ivan's heart fluttered within him like a bird. Straining every nerve, he approached with great strides, hardly feeling his legs under him. "Ah," thought Ivan, "now he won't escape! I'll catch him in the act!"

Ivan was still some distance off when suddenly he saw a bright light, but not in the same place as before, and not a small flame. The thatch had flared up at the eaves, the flames were reaching up to the roof, and standing beneath it, Gabriel's whole figure was clearly visible.

Like a hawk swooping down on a lark, Ivan rushed at Limping Gabriel. "Now I'll have him; he shan't escape me!" thought Ivan. But Gabriel must have heard his steps, and (however he managed it) glancing around he scuttled away past the barn like a hare.

"You shan't escape!" shouted Ivan, darting after him.

Just as he was going to seize Gabriel, the latter dodged him, but Ivan managed to catch the skirt of Gabriel's coat. It tore right off, and Ivan fell down. He recovered his feet and shouting, "Help! Seize him!

Thieves! Murder!" ran on again. But meanwhile Gabriel had reached his own gate. There Ivan overtook him and was about to seize him, when something struck Ivan a stunning blow, as though a stone had hit his temple, quite deafening him. It was Gabriel who, seizing an oak wedge that lay near the gate, had struck out with all his might.

Ivan was stunned; sparks flew before his eyes, then all grew dark and he staggered. When he came to his senses Gabriel was no longer there. It was as light as day, and from the side where his homestead was,

something roared and crackled like an engine at work. Ivan turned around and saw that his back shed was all ablaze, and the side shed had also caught fire, and flames and smoke and bits of burning straw mixed with the smoke were being driven towards his hut.

"What is this, friends? . . ." cried Ivan, lifting his arms and striking his thighs. "Why, all I had to do was just to snatch it out from under the eaves and trample on it! What is this, friends? . . ." he kept repeating. He wished to shout, but his breath failed him; his voice was gone. He

The Flying Carriage, 1913, MARC CHAGALL. Solomon R. Guggenheim Museum, New York City, Photograph by Robert E. Mates.

wanted to run, but his legs would not obey him and got in each other's way. He moved slowly but again staggered and again his breath failed. He stood still till he had regained his breath and then went on. Before he had got around the back shed to reach the fire, the side shed was also all ablaze, and the corner of the hut and the covered gateway had caught fire as well. The flames were leaping out of the hut and it was impossible to get into the yard. A large crowd had collected, but nothing could be done. The neighbors were carrying their belongings out of their own houses and driving the cattle out of their own sheds. After Ivan's house, Gabriel's also caught fire, then, the wind rising, the flames spread to the other side of the street and half the village was burnt down.

At Ivan's house they barely managed to save his old father, and the family escaped in what they had on. Everything else, except the horses that had been driven out to pasture for the night, was lost; all the cattle, the fowls on their perches, the carts, ploughs, and harrows, the women's chests with their clothes, and the grain in the granaries—all were burnt up!

At Gabriel's, the cattle were driven out, and a few things saved from his house.

The fire lasted all night. Ivan stood in front of his homestead and kept repeating, "What is this? . . . Friends! . . . One need only have pulled it out and trampled on it!" But when the roof fell in, Ivan rushed into the burning place, and seizing a charred beam, tried to drag it out. The women saw him and called him back, but he pulled out the beam and was going in again for another when he lost his footing and fell among the flames. Then his son made his way in after him and dragged him out. Ivan had singed his hair and beard and burnt his clothes and scorched his hands, but he felt nothing. "His grief has stupefied him," said the people. The fire was burning itself out, but Ivan still stood repeating: "Friends! . . . What is this? . . . One need only have pulled it out!"

In the morning the village Elder's son came to fetch Ivan.

"Daddy Ivan, your father is dying! He has sent for you to say good-bye."

Ivan had forgotten about his father and did not understand what was being said to him.

"What father?" he said. "Whom has he sent for?"

"He sent for you, to say good-bye; he is dying in our cottage! Come along, daddy Ivan," said the Elder's son, pulling him by the arm, and Ivan followed the lad.

When he was being carried out of the hut some burning straw had fallen on to the old man and burnt him, and he had been taken to the village Elder's in the farther part of the village, which the fire did not reach.

When Ivan came to his father, there was only the Elder's wife in the hut, besides some little children on the top of the stove. All the rest were still at the fire. The old man, who was lying on a bench, kept turning his eyes towards the door. When his son entered, he moved a little. The old woman went up to him and told him that his son had come. He asked to have him brought nearer. Ivan came closer.

"What did I tell you, Ivan?" began the old man. "Who has burnt down the village?"

"It was he, father!" Ivan answered. "I caught him in the act. I saw him shove the firebrand into the thatch. I might have pulled away the burning straw and stamped it out, and then nothing would have happened."

"Ivan," said the old man, "I am dying, and you in your turn will have to face death. Whose is the sin?"

Ivan gazed at his father in silence, unable to utter a word.

"Now, before God, say whose is the sin? What did I tell you?"

Only then Ivan came to his senses and understood it all. He sniffed and said, "Mine, father!" And he fell on his knees before his father, saying, "Forgive me, father; I am guilty before you and before God."

The old man moved his hands. "Praise the Lord! Praise the Lord!" said he, and again he turned his eyes toward his son. "Ivan! I say, Ivan!"

"What, father?"

"What must you do now?"

Ivan was weeping. "I don't know how we are to live now, father!" he said.

The old man closed his eyes, moved his lips as if to gather strength, and opening his eyes again, said, "You'll manage. If you obey God's will, you'll manage!" He paused, then smiled, and said, "Mind, Ivan! Don't tell who started the fire! Hide another man's sin and God will forgive two of yours!" And the old man folded his hands on his breast, sighed, stretched out, and died.

Ivan did not say anything against Gabriel, and no one knew what had caused the fire.

And Ivan's anger against Gabriel passed away, and Gabriel wondered that Ivan did not tell anybody. At first Gabriel felt afraid, but after awhile he got used to it. The men left off quarreling, and then their families left off also. While rebuilding their huts, both families lived in one house, and when the village was rebuilt and they might have moved farther apart, Ivan and Gabriel built next to each other and remained neighbors as before.

They lived as good neighbors should. Ivan Shcherbakov remembered his old father's command to quench a fire at the first spark, and if any one does him an injury he now tries not to revenge himself, but rather to set matters right again. And if any one gives him a bad word, instead of giving a worse in return, he tries to teach the other not to use evil words, and so he teaches his womenfolk and children. And Ivan Shcherbakov has got on his feet again and now lives better even than he did before.

Leo Tolstoy *(1828–1910)* is considered to be one of the greatest Russian writers. He was an important moral thinker and social reformer of the nineteenth century. He often praised the simple values and strong faith of the Russian peasants. Translated into many languages, his works include stories and novels of military exploits, essays on religious themes, and humorous folk stories. One of Tolstoy's most famous novels, *War and Peace,* has been made into a movie in both the United States and Russia.

Developing Comprehension Skills

1. How does the feud between Ivan's and Gabriel's families begin?

2. Who tries to stop the quarrel from becoming a feud? In your own words, tell what that person says about the first quarrel.

3. Why does Ivan pass up a chance to stop the fire in the shed? Why does his decision turn out to be a mistake?

4. What clues suggest the outcome of the fire?

5. Who do you think is responsible for the fire? Who could have stopped it? Give reasons for your answers.

6. Did Ivan do the right thing in not telling who started the fire? Explain.

Reading Literature: Short Stories

1. **Explaining a Title.** The title of this story has more than one meaning. One neglected spark is the one that sets fire to Ivan's shed and spreads to burn down half the village. Another "spark" does not refer to fire at all. What small incident in the story is like a spark that touches off other events? What very serious situation results?

2. **Understanding Character.** Ivan is the main character in this story. What kind of person is he? How does he change during the story? How does his life change as a result? How is his father important in the story?

3. **Diagraming Plot.** A **plot diagram** is a drawing that shows the five parts of a story's plot. The diagram shows the climax as the peak of the action.

   Copy the following plot diagram onto a sheet of paper. Then read the list of statements.

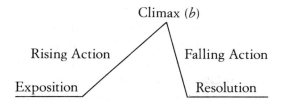

Climax (*b*)

Rising Action   Falling Action

Exposition   Resolution

a. The two families start feuding.
b. Gabriel sets the shed on fire.
c. Ivan admits his own guilt and does not tell anyone that Gabriel started the fire.
d. Gabriel and Ivan rebuild their houses next to each other and live as good neighbors.
e. The Shcherbakov family lives near the Ivanov family in a Russian village.

Mark the letter of each action in its proper place on the diagram. The correct position of statement *b* has been marked for you. It describes the climax.

4. **Identifying Theme.** The **theme** of a story is the writer's message. Which of the following most closely states the theme of this story? Give two details from the story to support your answer.
   a. Homes need to be protected from fire.
   b. Revenge blinds people and causes destruction.
   c. Love binds people together.

Developing Vocabulary Skills

Using Synonym Clues. The following sentences contain words from the story. Figure out the meaning of each underlined word by looking for a synonym clue. Write the synonym clue. Then use the underlined word in an original sentence.

1. If the men needed a <u>sack</u>, they sent to the other house. They soon received the needed bag.
2. The young woman answered sharply because she felt <u>offended</u>—insulted by her neighbor's comment.
3. The old man tried to prevent the <u>feud</u>. He said, "If there has been a fight between the families, make up."
4. Ivan had Gabriel condemned to be <u>flogged</u>. The idea of being whipped made Gabriel furious.
5. If one side is bad and the other side is good, there will be no <u>strife</u>. It takes two bad wills to create conflict.
6. The fire flared up into the <u>eaves</u> of the shed. There, beneath the overhanging edge of the roof, Ivan saw Gabriel.
7. When the village was <u>restored</u>, the two homes were rebuilt side by side.
8. "I only needed to <u>trample</u> on it! Oh, why did I not stamp out the fire?" Ivan asked.

Developing Skills in Study and Research

Using the Card Catalog. The **card catalog** lists alphabetically all the books in a library. Each book has three cards: a subject card, a title card, and an author card. Some libraries have computerized card catalogs with instructions on how to use them. You can find the location of a book by looking up its subject, its title, or its author.

Review the introduction to the card catalog on page 649 in the handbook. Then use the card catalog in your school or local library to do the following research.

1. Author cards are filed alphabetically by last name. In your library's card catalog, find the author cards for Leo Tolstoy. On a sheet of paper, write the titles of books by Tolstoy.

2. "A Spark Neglected Burns the House" takes place in a small Russian village during the second half of the nineteenth century. To learn more about life in a Russian village at that time, look through the subject cards or the subject section of a computerized card catalog under the heading *Russia*. Find at least three books that might have the information you are looking for. On a sheet of paper write down the title, author, and call number for each book. Then go to the shelves and find these books. Look through the table of contents for each book to see what information it covers. On your sheet of paper indicate which book or books would give you information on what life in a nineteenth-century Russian village was like.

Developing Writing Skills

Supporting an Idea. In the story, Ivan's father speaks out against revenge several times. Finally Ivan learns that his father's advice is good. Write two paragraphs showing the truth of the lesson Ivan learns, that revenge destroys people and their friendships. You might write about an event in your life, or you might make up an event.

Prewriting. List the series of events that you experienced or made up. Think about how the situation began. Were you the person mainly responsible? What did you do to make the situation better or worse? What finally happened? Write down details describing the event. Then write a statement about the lesson you learned from this experience.

Drafting. In the first paragraph, write about the events in the order in which they happened. In the second paragraph, tell what you learned.

Revising and Sharing. Read your paragraphs aloud to someone else. Ask the person if you have supported the idea that revenge is foolish. Ask if your writing is clear and convincing. Your listener's comments may suggest changes to make. Rewrite until both of your paragraphs are logical and clear.

After Twenty Years

O. HENRY

Loyalty is an important part of friendship. However, what happens when another important value conflicts with loyalty? Read to discover how two friends deal with this conflict.

The policeman on the beat moved up the avenue impressively. The impressiveness was habitual and not for show, for spectators were few. The time was barely ten o'clock at night, but chilly gusts of wind with a taste of rain in them had well nigh depeopled the streets.

Trying doors as he went, twirling his club with many intricate and artful movements, turning now and then to cast his watchful eye down the pacific thoroughfare, the officer, with his stalwart form and slight swagger, made a fine picture of a guardian of the peace. The vicinity was one that kept early hours. Now and then you might see the lights of a cigar store or of an all-night lunch counter, but the majority of the doors belonged to business places that had long since been closed.

Then about midway of a certain block, the policeman suddenly slowed his walk. In the doorway of a darkened hardware store a man leaned, with an unlighted cigar in his mouth. As the policeman walked up to him, the man spoke up quickly.

"It's all right, officer," he said, reassuringly. "I'm waiting for a friend. It's an appointment made twenty years ago. Sounds a little funny to you, doesn't it? Well, I'll explain if you'd like to make certain it's all right. About that long ago there used to be a restaurant where this store stands—'Big Joe' Brady's restaurant."

"Until five years ago," said the policeman. "It was torn down then."

The man in the doorway struck a match and lit his cigar. The light showed a pale, square-jawed face with keen eyes and a little white scar near his right eyebrow. His scarfpin was a large diamond, oddly set.

"Twenty years ago tonight," said the man, "I dined here at 'Big Joe' Brady's with Jimmy Wells, my best chum and the finest chap in the world. He and I were raised here in New York, just like two brothers, together. I was eighteen and Jimmy was twenty. The next morning I was to start for the West to make my fortune. You couldn't have dragged Jimmy out of New York; he thought it was the only place on earth.

Well, we agreed that night that we would meet here again exactly twenty years from that date and time, no matter what our conditions might be or from what distance we might have to come. We figured that in twenty years each of us ought to have our destiny worked out and our fortunes made, whatever they were going to be."

"It sounds pretty interesting," said the policeman. "Rather a long time between meets, though, it seems to me. Haven't you heard from your friend since you left?"

"Well, yes, for a time we corresponded," said the other. "But after a year or two we lost track of each other. You see, the West is a pretty big proposition, and I kept hustling around over it pretty lively. But I know Jimmy will meet me here if he's alive, for he always was the truest, staunchest old chap in the world. He'll never forget. I came a thousand miles to stand in this door tonight, and it's worth it if my old partner turns up."

The waiting man pulled out a handsome watch, the lid of it set with several small diamonds. "Three minutes to ten," he announced. "It was exactly ten o'clock when we parted here at the restaurant door."

"Did pretty well out West, didn't you?" asked the policeman.

"You bet! I hope Jimmy has done half as well. He was kind of plodder, though, good fellow as he was. I've had to compete with some of the sharpest wits going to get my pile. A man gets in a groove in New York. It takes the West to put a razor-edge on him."

The policeman twirled his club and took a step or two.

"I'll be on my way. Hope your friend comes around all right. Going to call time on him sharp?"

"I should say not!" said the other. "I'll give him half an hour at least. If Jimmy is alive on earth, he'll be here by that time. So long, officer."

"Good-night, sir," said the policeman, passing on along his beat, trying doors as he went.

There was now a fine, cold drizzle falling, and the wind had risen from its uncertain puffs into a steady blow. The few foot passengers astir in that quarter hurried dismally and silently along with coat collars turned high and pocketed hands. And in the door of the hardware store the man who had come a thousand miles to fill an appointment, uncertain almost to absurdity, with the friend of his youth, smoked his cigar and waited.

About twenty minutes he waited, and then a tall man in a long overcoat, with collar turned up to his ears, hurried across from the opposite side of the street. He went directly to the waiting man.

"Is that you, Bob?" he asked, doubtfully.

"Is that you, Jimmy Wells," cried the man in the door.

"Bless my heart!" exclaimed the new arrival, grasping both the other's hands with his own. "It's Bob, sure as fate. I was certain I'd find you here if you were still in existence. Well, well, well!—twenty years is a long time. The old restaurant's gone,

Rainy Night, 1930, CHARLES BURCHFIELD. San Diego Museum of Art, Gift of Misses Anne R. and Amy Putnam.

Bob; I wish it had lasted, so we could have had another dinner there. How has the West treated you, old man?"

"Bully; it has given me everything I asked it for. You've changed lots, Jimmy. I never thought you were so tall by two or three inches."

"Oh, I grew a bit after I was twenty."

"Doing well in New York, Jimmy?"

"Moderately. I have a position in one of the city departments. Come on, Bob; we'll go around to a place I know of and have a good long talk about old times."

The two men started up the street, arm in arm. The man from the West, his egotism enlarged by success, was beginning to outline the history of his career. The other, submerged in his overcoat, listened with interest.

At the corner stood a drugstore, brilliant with electric lights. When they came into this glare, each of them turned simultaneously to gaze upon the other's face.

The man from the West stopped suddenly and released his arm.

"You're not Jimmy Wells," he snapped. "Twenty years is a long time, but not long enough to change a man's nose from a Roman to a pug."

"It sometimes changes a good man into a bad one," said the tall man. "You've been under arrest for ten minutes, 'Silky' Bob. Chicago thinks you may have dropped over our way and wires us she wants to have a chat with you. Going quietly, are you? That's sensible. Now, before we go on to the station here's a note I was asked to hand you. You may read it here at the window. It's from Patrolman Wells."

The man from the West unfolded the little piece of paper handed him. His hand was steady when he began to read, but it trembled a little by the time he had finished. The note was rather short.

> Bob:
> I was at the appointed place on time. When you struck the match to light your cigar I saw it was the face of the man wanted in Chicago. Somehow I couldn't do it myself, so I went around and got a plain clothes man to do the job.
>
> *Jimmy*

O. Henry *(1862–1910)* is the pen name of William Sydney Porter. Before he achieved success as a writer, O. Henry worked as a bank teller, store clerk, and journalist. He served a prison term for bookkeeping irregularities at the bank but always claimed innocence. Two popular collections of O. Henry's stories are *The Four Million* and *Cabbages and Kings.* His stories often have surprise endings.

Developing Comprehension Skills

1. Why is the man from the West waiting in front of a closed store at night?

2. What kind of job does Jimmy Wells, the man who stayed in New York, have? When did you find this out?

3. Has Bob, the man from the West, made his living honestly? Give evidence from the story to support your answer.

4. Why does Jimmy Wells send a plain clothes man to deal with his friend? What does this action tell you about Jimmy?

5. The story contains hints about the ending, but they are disguised so that you will not suspect how the story will turn out. Go back through the story to find clues to the surprise ending.

6. Do you think that Jimmy Wells is fair to his friend? Do you admire his actions or not? Give reasons for your answer.

Reading Literature: Short Stories

1. **Understanding Exposition.** The part of the plot that gives background information is **exposition.** It introduces setting and the main characters. In this story the first six paragraphs are exposition. What do they tell you about the two men? What do they say about the setting? What background information do the paragraphs give you?

2. **Analyzing Conflict.** The main **conflict,** or struggle, in the story takes place inside Jimmy Wells. What two loyalties does Jimmy feel? Why do they conflict?

3. **Understanding Plot.** The events of this story describe what happens on that dark, chilly night when the two friends meet again. What happened in the past is revealed through the characters' dialogue. List the events that happen during the time of the story. Then list, in order, the events that happened at an earlier time.

Developing Vocabulary Skills

1. **Using Comparison and Contrast Clues.** Comparison clues show how an unfamiliar word is like something else. Some words that signal comparison clues are *like, as, same* or *same as, similar to,* and *other.*

   You have also learned that contrast clues show how an unfamiliar word is unlike something else. The following words signal contrast clues: *although, though, but, on the other hand, however, yet, unlike, different from, in contrast to, as opposed to,* and *not.*

   The following sentences contain words from the stories you have read. Write the definition of each underlined word as you understand it from the comparison or contrast clue.

   a. The policeman's actions were <u>habitual</u>, as regular as on any other night.

   b. Jimmy twirled his club with movements as <u>intricate</u> as difficult ballet steps.

   c. His voice was steady when he began to speak, but it was <u>tremulous</u> when he finished.

   d. A <u>trifle</u> started the feud between the families. In the same way, small incidents start big quarrels in many families.

   e. The <u>malice</u> Ivan felt toward Gabriel was like Gabriel's bad feeling toward Ivan.

2. **Using Context Clues to Define Colloquial Expressions.** A **colloquial expression** is an informal word or phrase used in everyday

conversation. Writers may use colloquial expressions when they suit the setting of the story and the characters' experiences. You can often learn the meaning of these expressions from context. For example, look for clues in this sentence that tell you what *to spill the beans* means.

Although Jimmy tried to get information about Bob's life, he was careful not <u>to spill the beans</u> about his own identity.

Although signals a contrast to the phrase *to get information*. So you can guess that *to spill the beans* means the opposite, or "to give away information."

The colloquial expressions in the following sentences are from the story. Use context clues to figure out their meanings. Then explain the meaning of each underlined word or phrase as you understand it from the context clues.

a. The West is a pretty big <u>proposition</u>, and I'm making the most of the opportunity.
b. I'm competing with sharp wits to get my <u>pile</u>. That money wasn't easy to come by.
c. A man gets lazy in New York. It takes the West <u>to put a razor-edge</u> on him.
d. Going <u>to call time on him sharp</u> or wait a little longer for him to show up?
e. Living out West has been <u>bully</u>. It has given me everything I asked it for.

Developing Skills in Study and Research

1. **Understanding Types of Newspaper Articles.** If this were a true story, information about "Silky" Bob's crimes would have been reported in the newspaper.

In a newspaper there are three main types of articles. **News stories,** the most common type, present facts about current events. These articles should tell *who, what, when, where,* and *why* about an event. **Editorials** and **editorial columns** present people's ideas on issues in the news or of interest to the local community. Editorials also include reviews of books, movies, plays, TV shows, and restaurants. Usually the name of the writer of an editorial column is given. A third type of newspaper article is a **feature.** Features can be written on just about any topic. For example, features include interviews with important people, such as government officials or well-known writers. Features can include serious articles on current events or light-hearted pieces meant purely for entertainment.

Get a copy of a recent newspaper from your city or region. If you cannot find one, use a copy available in the library. Notice that the newspaper is divided into different sections. Then skim through each section. Find one news story, one editorial article, and one feature. List the titles or headlines for these articles on a sheet of paper.

In what kind of article would news of "Silky" Bob's arrest be reported? Do you think a newspaper would print an interview with Jimmy Wells? Why or why not?

2. **Using the Newspaper.** Skim the sections of a newspaper to find an example of each of the following. For each editorial or editorial column, write the writer's name, if available.
a. a news story about a world news event
b. an editorial about a national issue
c. a review of a movie or restaurant
d. a feature about a famous person
e. a column about sports

Developing Writing Skills

Writing a Character Analysis. A character's actions in a story should fit with his or her character. Even though a character does something surprising, the motivation, or reason, for such an action must be clear and understandable. In this story Jimmy and Bob have been good friends. They each keep a twenty-year-old promise to meet. Something even stronger than friendship must motivate Jimmy to turn in his friend. What motivates Jimmy Wells? Decide whether or not Jimmy Wells's actions are in keeping with his character. In two paragraphs explain your ideas, following these steps.

Prewriting. First, try to describe what Jimmy Wells is like. Make a list of details given by the writer to describe Jimmy and how he feels about being a police officer.

Next, think about Jimmy's actions in having Bob arrested. Is it difficult for Jimmy to decide to turn his old friend over to the police? Why doesn't Jimmy make the arrest himself? Look for clues that the writer gives to suggest the answers to these questions.

Drafting. In the first paragraph, describe Jimmy Wells before his meeting with Bob. Tell what he looks like and how he acts. In the second paragraph, explain Jimmy's decision to have Bob arrested. Tell why this is a logical or illogical action. Show how Jimmy's character supports or does not support the decision he makes.

Revising and Sharing. Read your first paragraph again. Does it present a clear description of Jimmy Wells as a police officer? Read the second paragraph. Does the second paragraph flow smoothly from the first? Do the ideas build on one another? Does the explanation have unity? If not, revise your writing.

A Man Who Had No Eyes

MacKINLAY KANTOR

In this story a chance meeting takes place between two characters. Each quickly forms an impression of the other. As you read, notice how they learn more about each other. How do their impressions gradually change?

A beggar was coming down the avenue just as Mr. Parsons emerged from his hotel.

He was a blind beggar, carrying the traditional battered cane and thumping his way before him with the cautious, half-furtive effort of the sightless. He was a shaggy, thick-necked fellow; his coat was greasy about the lapels and pockets, and his hand splayed over the cane's crook with a futile sort of clinging. He wore a black pouch slung over his shoulder. Apparently he had something to sell.

The air was rich with spring; sun was warm and yellowed on the asphalt. Mr. Parsons, standing there in front of his hotel and noting the *clack-clack* approach of the sightless man, felt a sudden and foolish sort of pity for all blind creatures.

And, thought Mr. Parsons, he was very glad to be alive. A few years ago he had been little more than a skilled laborer; now he was successful, respected, admired. . . .

Insurance. . . . And he had done it alone, unaided, struggling beneath handicaps. . . . And he was still young. The blue air of spring, fresh from its memories of windy pools and lush shrubbery, could thrill him with eagerness.

He took a step forward just as the tap-tapping blind man passed him by. Quickly the shabby fellow turned.

"Listen, guv'nor. Just a minute of your time."

Mr. Parsons said, "It's late. I have an appointment. Do you want me to give you something?"

"I ain't no beggar, guv'nor. You bet I ain't. I got a handy little article here"—he fumbled until he could press a small object into Mr. Parsons's hand—"that I sell. One buck. Best cigarette lighter made."

Mr. Parsons stood there, somewhat annoyed and embarrassed. He was a handsome figure with his immaculate gray suit and gray hat and malacca stick. Of course the man with the cigarette lighters could not see him. . . . "But I don't smoke," he said.

"Listen. I bet you know plenty people who smoke. Nice little present," wheedled the man. "And mister, you wouldn't mind helping a poor guy out?" He clung to Mr. Parsons's sleeve.

Mr. Parsons sighed and felt in his vest pocket. He brought out two half dollars and pressed them into the man's hand. "Certainly. I'll help you out. As you say, I can give it to someone. Maybe the elevator boy would—" He hesitated, not wishing to be boorish and inquisitive, even with a blind peddler. "Have you lost your sight entirely?"

The shabby man pocketed the two half dollars. "Fourteen years, guv'nor." Then he added, with an insane sort of pride, "Westbury, sir. I was one of 'em."

"Westbury," repeated Mr. Parsons. "Ah, yes. The chemical explosion. . . . The papers haven't mentioned it for years. But at the time it was supposed to be one of the greatest disasters in—"

"They've all forgot about it." The fellow shifted his feet wearily. "I tell you, guv'nor, a man who was in it don't forget about it. Last thing I ever saw was C shop going up in one grand smudge and gas pouring in at all the busted windows."

Mr. Parsons coughed, but the blind peddler was caught up with the train of his one dramatic reminiscence. And also, he was thinking that there might be more half dollars in Mr. Parsons's pocket.

"Just think about it, guv'nor. There was a hundred and eight people killed, about two hundred injured, and over fifty of them lost their eyes. Blind as bats—" He groped forward until his dirty hand rested against Mr. Parsons's coat. "I tell you, sir, there wasn't nothing worse than that in the war. If I had lost my eyes in the war, okay. I would have been well took care of. But I was just a workman, working for what was in it. And I got it. You're so right I got it, while the capitalists were making their

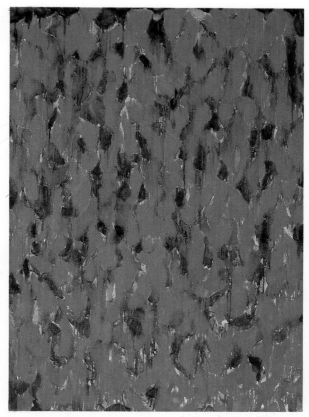

Red No. 1, 1953, SAM FRANCIS. Collection of Marie-Hélène and Guy Weill, Scarsdale, New York.

dough! They was insured, don't worry about that. They—"

"Insured," repeated his listener. "Yes. That's what I sell—"

"You want to know how I lost my eyes?" cried the man. "Well, here it is!" His words fell with the bitter and studied drama of a story often told, and told for money. "I was there in C shop, last of all the folks rushing out. Out in the air there was a chance, even with buildings exploding right and left. A lot of guys made it safe out the door and got away. And just when I was about there, crawling along between those big vats, a guy behind me grabs my leg. He says, 'Let me past, you—!' Maybe he was nuts. I dunno. I try to forgive him in my heart, guv'nor. But he was bigger than me. He hauls me back and climbs right over me! Tramples me into the dirt. And he gets out, and I lie there with all that poison gas pouring down on all sides of me, and flame and stuff. . . . " He swallowed—a studied sob—and stood dumbly expectant. He could imagine the next words: *Tough luck, my man. Awfully tough. Now I want to—*

"That's the story, guv'nor."

The spring wind shrilled past them, damp and quivering.

"Not quite," said Mr. Parsons.

The blind peddler shivered crazily. "Not quite? What do you mean, you—?"

"The story is true," Mr. Parsons said, "except that it was the other way around."

"Other way around?" He croaked unamiably. "Say, guv'nor—"

"I was in C shop," said Mr. Parsons. "It was the other way around. You were the fellow who hauled back on me and climbed over me. You were bigger than I was, Markwardt."

The blind man stood for a long time, swallowing hoarsely. He gulped: "Parsons. I thought you—" And then he screamed fiendishly: "Yes. Maybe so. Maybe so. But I'm blind! I'm blind, and you've been standing here letting me spout to you, and laughing at me every minute! I'm blind!"

People in the street turned to stare at him.

"You got away, but I'm blind! Do you hear! I'm—"

"Well," said Mr. Parsons, "don't make such a row about it, Markwardt. So am I."

MacKinlay Kantor *(1904–1977)* grew up in Iowa, where he helped his mother edit a newspaper. During World War II, he joined the Royal Air Force in England, flew combat missions, and was given an award for his courage. He wrote about the Civil War in novels and stories for young people, such as "Lee and Grant at Appomattox" and "Gettysburg." His novel *Andersonville,* about a confederate prison camp in Georgia, won a Pulitzer Prize in 1956.

Developing Comprehension Skills

1. Mr. Parsons seems quite satisfied with his life. Tell at least two reasons he gives for feeling this way.

2. In your own words describe what happened in the Westbury chemical disaster. How were Mr. Parsons and Mr. Markwardt injured?

3. What can you infer about Mr. Markwardt from the story he makes up about the chemical disaster?

4. At what point in the story do you think Mr. Parsons recognizes the beggar as Mr. Markwardt? How does recognizing the beggar affect Mr. Parsons's attitude toward him?

5. Do you feel sympathy for Mr. Markwardt? Why or why not?

Reading Literature: Short Stories

1. **Diagraming Plot.** Copy the following plot diagram onto a sheet of paper, and read the list of statements that follows it.

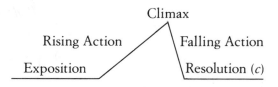

Climax

Rising Action

Falling Action

Exposition

Resolution *(c)*

a. Mr. Parsons interrupts the blind man's story to correct him and to reveal his own identity.

b. A poor, blind man asks the successful Mr. Parsons to buy a cigarette lighter.

c. Then Mr. Parsons reveals that he is blind, thereby showing the different ways each man has gone since the accident.

d. The blind man begins to tell the story of how he lost his eyesight.

e. The blind man gets angry.

Label the diagram with letters to show the five parts of "A Man Who Had No Eyes." The correct position of statement *c* has been marked for you. It describes the resolution.

2. **Understanding Theme.** A short story reveals a **theme,** or message, about life. In this story, Parsons and Markwardt have similar handicaps. Think about how each character deals with his blindness. What message is suggested by their reactions?

3. **Finding Differences Between Characters.** Mr. Parsons and Mr. Markwardt are both blind as a result of the chemical explosion. That is where any similarity between them ends, however. Go back through the story and look for ways the two men are different. For example, how are their appearances different? How did their actions differ during and after the disaster? What differences in their characters can you infer about the two men from their actions?

Make a chart like the one shown below in which to write the differences between the two blind men. Down the left side of the paper, write categories of differences such as "appearance," "attitude," "actions during the disaster," "actions after the disaster." Your chart might start out looking like this one:

Categories	Characters	
	Parsons	Markwardt
appearance		
attitude		

Fill in your chart with as many differences between the two characters as you can find in the story.

Developing Vocabulary Skills

Finding Meaning from General Context. Sometimes you can determine the meaning of a word by using the general context of the surrounding sentences or paragraphs. Read this sentence from "A Man Who Had No Eyes."

His hand splayed over the cane's crook with a futile sort of clinging.

From the words *hand, cane,* and *clinging* you can figure out that the man must be holding tightly to a cane. If the man's hand is "splayed over the cane's crook," his fingers must be spreading out and covering the entire crook. From this context you can understand that splayed means "spread out or covering completely."

Use the general context to determine the meaning of the underlined words in these passages from the story. Write the definition of each word as you understand it from the context. Then use each word in an original sentence.

1. "Certainly. I'll help you out. As you say, I can give it to someone. Maybe the elevator boy would—" He hesitated, not wishing to be boorish and <u>inquisitive</u>, even with a blind peddler. "Have you lost your sight entirely?"

2. "I tell you, guv'nor, a man who was in it don't forget about it. Last thing I ever saw was C shop going up in one grand smudge and gas pouring in at all the busted windows."

   Mr. Parsons coughed, but the blind peddler was caught up with the train of his one dramatic <u>reminiscence</u>.

Developing Skills in Study and Research

Using Encyclopedias. You can get information on research topics by using encyclopedias. Most sets of encyclopedias have one volume at the end that includes the index. All the topics covered in the encyclopedias are listed in alphabetical order in this index volume. The index tells which articles discuss each topic and in what volume or volumes to look for them.

Use at least two different encyclopedias to learn more about the causes of blindness. You might begin by looking up *Vision* and *Blindness* in each encyclopedia's index. Then read the articles on these topics to find out the causes of blindness. Be sure to find an explanation for what caused the blindness of Parsons and Markwardt. On a sheet of paper, list the facts reported in each encyclopedia. Compare these lists of facts, and decide which encyclopedia gives the most information.

Developing Skills in Critical Thinking

Identifying Facts and Opinions. In this story, Mr. Markwardt tries to persuade Mr. Parsons to give him money. Mr. Parsons, however, realizes that Mr. Markwardt's argument is not based on fact.

A **fact** is a statement that can be proved to be true. Here is an example:

> MacKinlay Kantor wrote the story "A Man Who Had No Eyes."

Unlike fact, an **opinion** is based on a person's beliefs. Although an opinion cannot be proved, it may be supported by facts or reasons for holding that opinion. For example, the following sentence states an opinion.

> "A Man Who Had No Eyes" is an uplifting story.

This statement can be supported with reasons. However, because it is an opinion, it cannot be proven true as can a fact.

Some advertisements use opinions to convince you to buy products. Some use opinions supported by facts. Find a magazine or newspaper advertisement for a product. Read the ad carefully. What reasons does it give for buying the product? Which of these are facts?

Developing Writing Skills

Supporting a Prediction. The dramatic meeting between Markwardt and Parsons probably has an impact on both men, but what kind of impact? Do you think the meeting will inspire Markwardt to change? Do you think it will make him feel ashamed? Do you think the meeting will anger or sadden Parsons? Will it make him feel more proud of himself? From what you know about the two characters, try to predict the impact that the meeting will have on each of them. Write your predictions in two paragraphs, following this process.

Prewriting. Review how each character is portrayed in the story. Notice the reactions of the two men at the end of the story when they find out about each other. Based on your understanding of the situation and the two characters, predict the outcome of the meeting, or how it will affect each man. Write down your predictions. List your reasons, as well as any details or quotations from the story that help you to make your predictions. Organize your notes, separating information about Markwardt and Parsons.

Drafting. Using the notes you have made, write two topic sentences. One should predict Markwardt's reaction to the meeting, and the other should predict Parsons's reaction. Support each statement with details from your prewriting notes. Use quotations to support your ideas.

Revising and Sharing. Read your paragraphs. Does each prediction fit with the character as he is drawn in the story? Is each topic sentence clear? Is it supported with quotations and details from the story? If not, you may need to state more reasons for your predictions and look for more details to use as support. Read your paragraphs aloud to check for logical organization and clarity.

Little Dog Lost

JEAN McCORD

Can you think of one day that you wish had never happened? Do you know what you would do differently if you had the day to live over? Read to discover why Jim wishes he could relive and change one summer day.

That summer I was fifteen. My feet had grown so big they tripped me up, and they were always stepping on other people's toes.

I jumped when anyone spoke to me suddenly, and there was a nagging feeling inside that made me want to run away somewhere to be alone.

It seemed as though my pa had turned against me, and even my mother got mad at me awfully easy.

Then something happened that really fixed my wagon. I didn't realize at the time how much it mattered, how a person can be all scarred and torn by the happenings of one day. Somehow it still seems unfair. Even now, all it takes to remind me, to stir up the old, ragged feelings, is the sight of a little white dog switching itself down the streets.

Or to see my sister's fingers.

In those days we went swimming every Sunday at a lake at the city limits.

Timmy, my eight-year-old brother, would race me to the bathhouse where we changed into our suits. We pretended not to see the big, black, crooked sign that said, DRESSING OR UNDRESSING IN HERE STRICTLY FORBIDDEN. Timmy would wander over to the carnival area. He liked to sit on the fence and listen to the people screaming on the rides.

The rest of the family would settle themselves on the beach, my mother watching over the younger kids: two little girls and the baby. She kept an eye on Cutie, too.

Cutie, our old poodle-and-something, wasn't really supposed to be along, but I always helped her sneak into the back of the car and hide down on the floor. She didn't like the hot beach, but she hated to be left behind. She would jog away, the sand so fiery it burned her feet, to find a cool spot of shade. Then she'd fling sand around until she made a hole, and she'd flop there to wait for us to go home.

I was the only one who went swimming.

My ma always warned me, "Be careful, Jim!" and I always answered, "Sure, sure!"

Then I'd run the length of the pier in big leaps, take a flying jump into the satiny, clover-green water, and spend my time horseplaying with the other fellows.

I had played and dived all that day, halfway watching the sun grow bigger and redder as it sank quietly into the far end of the lake. I knew vaguely it was time to quit, or maybe even past time, but I kept on practicing a dive.

Then Timmy came running out on the pier and hollered at me, "Jim! Hey, Jim! Come on! Pa's going to leave without you."

The other fellows all laughed. I glared at Timmy, wishing he knew a little more. I took one more dive and swam slowly all the way to shore.

On the beach I scuffed through wet sand while my brother Timmy danced beside me urging me to run, but my pride wouldn't let me. I just took bigger strides, my long feet smacking into the sand and kicking up spurts behind.

When we reached the car, Pa glared at me and said, "Well, took your own sweet time, didn't you?" Because I knew he was

The Swimming Hole, 1937, ADOLPH GOTTLIEB. Oil on canvas, 25½" x 34¾". © 1979 Adolph and Esther Gottlieb Foundation, New York City.

right, I climbed into the back seat and grabbed furiously at the door, closing it with a great slam.

Instantly there was a high-pitched scream from my little sister Dilly.

I swung around and stared at her in amazement, for she was turning blood-red in the face and her mouth was open in one black screeching hollow. I couldn't see what was wrong with her and looked to my folks both twisting around in front.

Out of nowhere my father fetched me a crack across the head that set my brains to spinning, and I still didn't know what was wrong with everybody. Only then did he reach over behind me and open the door that had caught Dilly's pink baby fingers in a smashing trap.

Dilly continued to scream. Her face was now a horrible purple.

The Old Man cocked his arm to aim me another, but I dodged into a corner and, picking up the rigid little body, handed her over the seat to my mother.

Mother laid the baby down and took Dilly on her lap, "There now, there now," trying to start her breathing again.

I tried to shrink small, like a rat in a corner, as the Old Man jammed gears and wheeled the car around.

Before we finished turning, with Dilly still pealing out screeches, Timmy yelped, "Wait! Hey, wait! We forgot Cutie!"

The Old Man shouted, "We can't wait if she ain't here," and he drove off leaving her, my dog for seven years, leaving her behind at the lake.

I said in a squeaky voice, "Lemme out! I'll go back for her."

But the Old Man growled, "Shut up, you! We got to get this kid to a doctor."

We didn't take her to a doctor. The little fingers didn't seem broken, just kind of flattened out, and after a while Dilly fell into a sleep and no one wanted to wake her up again.

When we pulled up to our house, it loomed empty and silent, a hostile, accusing place. All the way back I had felt like a terrible criminal who should be going off to jail instead of home with decent folks.

I sneaked down to the basement and hid behind the furnace. Three hours later, when the footsteps and voices had quieted, I dragged myself upstairs. I was miserable over losing Cutie, whom I'd fed and brushed and played with as long as I could remember. And I couldn't wipe out of my mind a horrible vision of my sister's fingers turning black and dropping off her hand.

My mother looked at me and then at my feet that were tracking coal dust. She opened her mouth to say something about it, but only said mildly, "You'd better get out of that suit before you catch a cold." Her words sounded so kind after all the rotten names I had called myself that my nose and eyes exploded, and I stumbled upstairs to my room.

I put on dry clothes and went down again. Pa had gone out somewhere and I was grateful for that.

My mother fixed me some food and I forced it down my throat that was squeezed as tight as if a rubber band had been clamped around it.

I knew I had to do something. I couldn't sit around feeling like a criminal, so I said, rough as I could, "I'm goin' out to look for Cutie."

My mother looked astonished and said, "Here?"

"Sure, why not? She's a smart little dog! She ought to know her way home and be here pretty soon."

"Jim." My mother had her back turned and her voice was pinched the way mine felt. "Jim, Cutie's out at the lake. It's late now. Tomorrow morning I'll give you the <u>fare</u>, and you can ride the streetcar out. . . ."

Something boiled over in my brain. "What makes you think she won't come home? Just 'cause some people in this family are dumb. . . ."

I threw on a cap and left. Behind me my ma called; I closed my ears.

We were ten miles from the lake. How could a little short-legged dog who had never been lost in her life trek that distance back? I didn't know, but I fiercely believed. I reminded myself of stories I'd read of dogs walking across whole continents, and I decided Cutie could make at least two miles an hour and should be home just about now.

A block away I started calling, "Here, Cutie! Here I am! Here, Cutie!" thinking she'd come running and I could pick her up and carry her home . . . come into the house with her in my arms and somehow things would straighten out and be all right after all. So I called, throwing my voice on the wind till it echoed from all directions. I bellowed till a skinny guy with kangaroo-pockets under his eyes stuck his head out and yelled, "For goodness sake, kid! Go somewhere else and do yer bellyaching!"

I went a few blocks and started whooping there. Doors and windows flew open and people peered out, trying to see what was happening. I knew if I didn't lower my voice, someone would call the cops. I gave one more big, loud call and a siren started up in the distance; I was dead sure they were coming for me. I legged it away fast toward home.

Creeping beneath our windows, I peered in through the curtains to see if Cutie had slipped by me to her box in the corner. Then I saw it was as empty as a dead baby's cradle. I knew she wasn't coming home; a nasty little voice told me a truth I didn't want to hear.

"Yes, she ain't never comin' back on account of you. Big jerk!" The voice sounded like my father's, but it was my own.

I went off again up and down the streets calling in a hoarse, quiet tone, but it was useless. After seeing the empty box, I knew it was.

It was now eleven o'clock and starting to rain. The rain running down my face felt and tasted like lake water, made me feel as if I were back there again and this afternoon had never happened and maybe never would if I was careful and mended my ways.

At twelve o'clock I knew I had to go home. As slow as my legs would go I dragged along, trying hard to see Cutie in every little white thing showing in the night.

I shinnied up the back porch and crawled in through my window. The bedsprings creaked and my ma came in and felt around for me. I gave a loud snore but I knew I wasn't fooling her. "Jim! Where've you been?" she whispered.

"Out gettin' drunk," I said as mean and low as I could. She stood a minute looking at me, then left.

The next morning she said in a very reasonable voice, "Jim, go out to the lake today. Take Tim along. I'm sure you'll find Cutie there. Here, I'll give you the carfare."

"Leave me alone, will ya?" I sprang up from the table. "Quit rubbing it in!" I rushed out, jumped down the porch steps, and stayed away all that day. I found some guys who didn't know anything about the whole affair, and I forgot it because it seemed so good not to remember.

And the next day was the same. I left before anyone else was up.

On Wednesday I started searching our neighborhood again, looking down every street for Cutie to appear. I told myself in a hard way that she was bound to come home and justify me. I ground my back teeth, willing her to come by herself, because I wanted it that way so badly. Every once in a while the corner of my eye would see something white, and I'd whirl around with this lump in my throat, thinking before I could stop myself, "Cuss you, Cutie, old girl. I knew you could do it." But then it would be something not even resembling a dog, like a girl in a white coat or a newspaper scudding up an alley.

Still I fooled myself, telling myself a lie, hour by hour, until I was truly convinced. If I just waited . . . she would come home by herself.

By Saturday morning no one was mentioning her name anymore. They all thought she was gone for good. I knew tomorrow the family would go out to the lake again, and I became mortally afraid of what they might find there. In my mind hung a picture of a little white dead body cast up on the shore. Perhaps she'd tried to swim home.

Finally I could stand it no longer. I crept upstairs and stole two dimes out of my ma's purse and sneaked out. I hurried to the car line. The ten miles seemed like a hundred. Once I almost got off, wanting to run; I changed seats a dozen times; nothing hurried this lazy elephant.

At the end of the line I had a mile to walk. Sweating and thirsty, I reached the bathhouse. I walked around it twice, swinging my head as if it were on hinges: no dogs; just people sprawled on the sand.

The water smelled cool, inviting. I was slippery-hot but hadn't even thought to bring a suit. That's how stupid I was. It cost a dime to rent one; then I wouldn't have carfare.

I sat on the sand and leaned against the

bathhouse, moping and trying to think of what to do next.

When I pushed up, my head was dizzy from the sun. That had never happened to me before.

I went in, to the locker room's musty dark and wet sand grittiness.

When my eyes could see, I edged up to this big hairy fellow who sold suits and kept your clothes. I felt guilty even talking to him, because I never had rented one of his baggy old moth-bitten suits or one of his tin boxes to bury my clothes in.

So I said loudly, "Hey, mister. You seen a little white dog around here lately?"

He looked me up and down as if I was some freak, or as if he maybe knew how cheap my family was about renting his stuff. He shifted a fat, brown cigar to the other side of his face, mouthing, "Yeah. I seen one around, three, four days ago."

I felt like a pillar of salt inside. I couldn't talk, only stare at him till he said, "She hung around the place like she's lost. I finally drove her away." He turned back to his paper, and running his fat finger up and down a column he said, sounding as if he didn't care a whit, "Yers?"

Swallowing six times, I squeaked out, "Was it a little old lady dog with kinda brown whiskers?"

He grunted, "Yeah. That was her," and moved the paper up. I turned, all sick and dying, and went outside in the hot, yellow, dry air.

I saw her then, running around the lake, going up to people and sniffing them.

Clear as day, there she was, a sad, lonely, lost little dog getting hungrier by the minute. I saw her as if I could reach out and pick her up—but I could see right through her, so I knew it was her ghost, and that was that.

There wasn't going to be any more Cutie. I had waited too long to do what I should have done right away. My mother had been right, and I had been terribly wrong. It'd been too easy to put off this trip, to keep saying, "Wait. Just wait. She'll come home by herself."

All it would have taken was a streetcar token and a ride on the cars. Back when it would have counted. All it would have cost me was to admit I was wrong and set about doing something right. My sister's fingers were healing; she was going to be all right. The one who wasn't ever going to be the same again was me, though I had only an inkling of it then.

I walked back into the locker room and slammed my other dime on the dirty counter. "Here, mister," I said, "I owe you this." And then I spun around and got out of there and walked all the way home to teach myself a lesson. "That'll show you," I said to my inside self.

The next day I wouldn't get in the car with the family. I didn't tell them I'd been to the lake. I said to my ma, "I'm sick of going with you guys all the time. I got things of my own to do." She let me go.

After that, I never went with them again. I wasn't being a martyr. I just knew it wouldn't be any good.

All that was a long time ago.

My family forgot about the door-slamming and the flattened fingers, and the little kids forgot all about Cutie. Everyone forgot except me. And even I forget sometimes. Except that all it takes to remind me again is a little white dog switching itself down the streets, or when I really examine my sister's fingers. They're not bad, only the slightest bit knobby and flat on the ends.

When my sister sees me staring at them, she hides them behind her back self-consciously. She thinks they're ugly, but that's not what I'm thinking. My mind goes into the past like a curtain slowly unfurling. What I see then are all the things I've lost in my whole life. Images of loss roll forth like little play-actors taking a bow, and I sit there and endure the pictures of a girl I loved and almost got and didn't; of good things that came near me and were nearly mine (but when I reached for them, they scooted out of my hand); of bad things said, and lost friends who look at me reproachfully, and things I should have done and didn't.

My sister thinks I'm nuts and moves out of the room, while bitterness floods up inside me. But I have to sit there waiting for the final picture. It's always a little lost dog snuffling round an empty, hot lake, crying softly to itself, until a big, hairy man comes out and drives us both away.

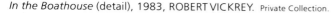

In the Boathouse (detail), 1983, ROBERT VICKREY. Private Collection.

Jean McCord (*born 1924*) lists forty-five different occupations in her biography, including time served in the Women's Army Corps. Her novels include *Deep Where the Octopi Lie* and *Bitter Is the Hawk's Path*. Her short stories have been published in *Seventeen* magazine and in *Best American Short Stories*.

Developing Comprehension Skills

1. How does Jim lose his dog Cutie? How does he try to find the dog?

2. Jim tells about his lost dog many years after it happened. Why is this retelling so many years later important to the story? What does it tell you about Jim's character?

3. How does Jim feel about himself after he loses his dog?

4. Why doesn't Jim go back to the beach the next day to look for Cutie as his mother suggests?

5. Jim never forgives himself for losing Cutie, and he stays bitter. If you could talk to Jim, what would you say to help him get over his bitterness and forgive himself?

6. This story presents a fifteen-year-old boy going through a difficult stage in his life. His relationship with his parents is troubled. Do Jim and his family seem real? Explain why or why not.

Reading Literature: Short Stories

1. **Analyzing Character.** In this story Jim, the main character, is also the one who tells the story. Jim's comments provide clues to his character. What can you infer about Jim from each of these statements that he makes in the story?

   a. I jumped when anyone spoke to me suddenly, and there was a nagging feeling inside that made me want to run away somewhere to be alone.

   b. All the way back I had felt like a terrible criminal who should be going off to jail instead of home with decent folks.

   c. I knew I had to do something. I couldn't sit around feeling like a criminal, so I said, rough as I could, "I'm goin' out to look for Cutie."

   d. I told myself in a hard way that she was bound to come home and justify me.

2. **Understanding Exposition.** At the beginning of a story, the writer usually gives back-

ground information and introduces the characters. This part of the plot, as you know, is called the **exposition.** In this story much of the exposition is given in the first five paragraphs. What does this exposition tell you about the troubled time Jim is going through? Which characters are introduced, and what do you learn about them?

3. **Identifying the Climax.** The **climax** of a story is its turning point. In the first part of this story, Jim holds out a hope that Cutie will return. At the climax, Jim feels both hopeless and angry at himself. At what point does the climax occur? Why is Jim angry?

4. **Understanding Falling Action and Resolution.** The **falling action** of the plot shows how the climax affects the main character. The **resolution** tells how the struggle ends. How is Jim affected by what happens at the climax of the story? Is there a resolution to this story? Explain why or why not.

5. **Analyzing Comparisons.** In their description, writers often use comparisons. That is, they describe one thing by showing how it resembles something else. For example, Jim says that his throat "was squeezed as tight as if a rubber band had been clamped around it." How does this comparison help to describe how Jim feels? Later Jim says that Cutie's box is "as empty as a dead baby's cradle." What feelings does this comparison convey?

Developing Vocabulary Skills

Using Context Clues to Define Colloquial Expressions. The sentences below contain **colloquialisms,** or informal expressions, from the story. Use the synonym and antonym clues in context to learn what each underlined word means. Then write the definition of the word as you understand it.

1. Jim's father fetched him a crack across the head, but even after the blow Jim didn't understand what was happening to his sister.

2. When Jim kept complaining loudly, a man told him to quit his bellyaching or leave.

3. Although the rest of the family hurried to the car, Jim took his own sweet time, and his father yelled at him.

4. Jim legged it away fast toward home, hoping that Cutie would be running toward home too.

5. His sister thought he was nuts when he lost himself in his unhappy thoughts, but Jim knew he was all too sane.

Developing Skills in Speaking and Listening

Taking Notes on an Oral Presentation. At times, you will need to take notes on what a speaker says. Taking notes can help you to remember important information. When you take notes, pay attention to the speaker's words. Listen for the main idea. Write down that main idea on a sheet of paper. For more detailed notes, listen for how the speaker supports his or her main idea. Write these subpoints too.

The writing assignment on the next page tells you to read aloud your completed paragraph. As your classmates read their paragraphs aloud, make notes on their main ideas. Afterward, ask the speakers if your notes accurately reflect what they said.

Developing Skills in Critical Thinking

Evaluating Generalizations. A **generalization** is a broad statement based on particular facts. A generalization is faulty when it is not supported by enough facts or when it is applied too widely. For example, it would be faulty to say, "Cleveland is always cold in January." Since some winters in Cleveland are mild, a safer generalization would use the word *usually* instead of *always*.

Based on this story, evaluate the following generalization: "It is better not to put off until tomorrow what you can do today." What evidence in the story supports this generalization? Do you think the statement can be applied to *all* situations in life? Can you think of one or two instances when it might really be better to put something off? If so, how would you reword the generalization?

Developing Writing Skills

Explaining an Idea. In this story, Jim learns from a mistake. What error in judgment keeps Jim from finding his dog? What lesson does Jim learn from his experience? In one paragraph explain the lesson that Jim learns. Follow these steps.

Prewriting. Reread the part of the story where Jim realizes that he is responsible for Cutie's loss. Think about how Jim could have found Cutie. Then jot down your ideas about the lesson Jim learns. Make notes on how Jim learns this lesson. Copy quotations from the story that identify what he learns. Decide on a logical order for presenting your ideas.

Drafting. Begin with a topic sentence stating the difficult lesson that Jim learns. Go on to give details of how Jim learns this lesson. Include quotations from the story that support or develop your explanation.

Revising and Sharing. Read your paragraph aloud, and listen for sentences that are repetitive or too general. Rewrite these. Make sure that your explanation is clear. Try setting your paragraph aside for a time and rereading it later. Look for weaknesses to correct at that time.

When you are satisfied with your writing, read it to a group of classmates. Read slowly and loudly enough so that your listeners can understand your ideas. Stress your points to be convincing.

The Weapon

FREDRIC BROWN

There are two weapons in this story. The title refers to both of them. As you read, try to identify the weapons. Look for clues that point out how those who control the weapons are alike.

The room was quiet in the dimness of early evening. Dr. James Graham, key scientist of a very important project, sat in his favorite chair, thinking. It was so still that he could hear the turning of pages in the next room as his son leafed through a picture book.

Often Graham did his best work, his most creative thinking, under these circumstances, sitting alone in an unlighted room in his own apartment after the day's regular work. But tonight his mind would not work constructively. Mostly he thought about his mentally arrested son—his only son—in the next room. The thoughts were loving thoughts, not the bitter anguish he had felt years ago when he had first learned of the boy's condition. The boy was happy; wasn't that the main thing? And to how many men is given a child who will always be a child, who will not grow up and leave him? Certainly that was rationalization, but what is wrong with rationalization when—the doorbell rang.

Graham rose and turned on lights in the almost-dark room before he went through the hallway to the door. He was not annoyed; tonight, at this moment, almost any interruption to his thoughts was welcome.

He opened the door. A stranger stood there. He said, "Dr. Graham? My name is Niemand. I'd like to talk to you. May I come in a moment?"

Graham looked at him. He was a small man, nondescript, obviously harmless—possibly a reporter or an insurance agent.

But it didn't matter what he was. Graham found himself saying, "Of course. Come in, Mr. Niemand." A few minutes of conversation, he justified himself by thinking, might divert his thoughts and clear his mind.

"Sit down," he said, in the living room. "Care for a cup of coffee?"

Niemand said, "No, thank you." He sat in the chair; Graham sat on the sofa.

The small man interlocked his fingers; he leaned forward. He said, "Dr. Graham,

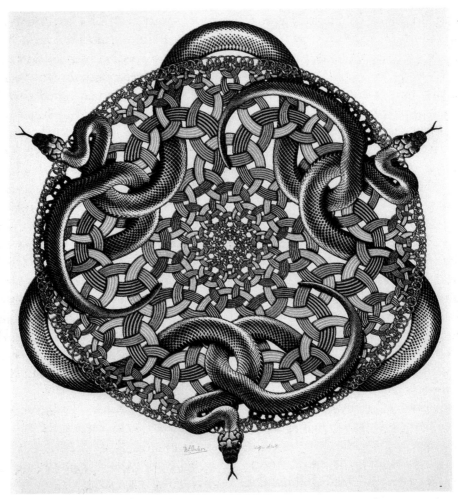

Ring Snakes, 1969, M. C. ESCHER. National Gallery of Art, Washington, D.C., Cornelius Van S. Roosevelt Collection, 1982.

you are the man whose scientific work is more likely than that of any other man to end the human race's chance for survival."

A crackpot, Graham thought. Too late now he realized that he should have asked the man's business before admitting him. It would be an embarrassing interview—

he disliked being rude, yet only rudeness was effective.

"Dr. Graham, the weapon on which you are working—"

The visitor stopped and turned his head as the door that led to a bedroom opened and a boy of fifteen came in. The boy didn't notice Niemand; he ran to Graham.

"Daddy, will you read to me now?" The boy of fifteen laughed the sweet laughter of a child of four.

Graham put an arm around the boy. He looked at his visitor, wondering whether he had known about the boy. From the lack of surprise on Niemand's face, Graham felt sure he had known.

"Harry"—Graham's voice was warm with affection—"Daddy's busy. Just for a little while. Go back to your room; I'll come and read to you soon."

" 'Chicken Little'? You'll read me 'Chicken Little'? "

"If you wish. Now run along. Wait, Harry, this is Mr. Niemand."

The boy smiled bashfully at the visitor. Niemand said, "Hi, Harry," and smiled back at him, holding out his hand. Graham, watching, was sure now that Niemand had known: the smile and the gesture were for the boy's mental age, not his physical one.

The boy took Niemand's hand. For a moment it seemed that he was going to climb into Niemand's lap, and Graham pulled him back gently. He said, "Go to your room now, Harry."

The boy skipped back to his bedroom, not closing the door.

Niemand's eyes met Graham's and he said, "I like him," with obvious sincerity. He added, "I hope that what you're going to read to him will always be true."

Graham didn't understand. Niemand said, " 'Chicken Little,' I mean. It's a fine story—but may 'Chicken Little' always be wrong about the sky falling down."

Graham suddenly had liked Niemand when Niemand had shown liking for the boy. Now he remembered that he must close the interview quickly. He rose in dismissal.

He said, "I fear you're wasting your time and mine, Mr. Niemand. I know all the arguments, everything you can say I've heard a thousand times. Possibly there is truth in what you believe, but it does not concern me. I'm a scientist, and only a scientist. Yes, it is public knowledge that I am working on a weapon, a rather ultimate one. But, for me personally, that is only a by-product of the fact that I am advancing science. I have thought it through, and I have found that that is my only concern."

"But, Dr. Graham, is humanity ready for an ultimate weapon?"

Graham frowned. "I have told you my point of view, Mr. Niemand."

Niemand rose slowly from the chair. He said, "Very well, if you do not choose to discuss it, I'll say no more." He passed a hand across his forehead. "I'll leave, Dr. Graham. I wonder, though . . . may I change my mind about the coffee you offered me?"

Graham's irritation faded. He said, "Certainly. Cream and sugar?"

"Please."

Graham went into the kitchen. He got the coffee, cream, and sugar.

When he returned to the living room, Niemand was just leaving the boy's bed-

Hand with Reflecting Sphere, 1935, M. C. ESCHER.
National Gallery of Art, Washington, D.C., Rosenwald Collection, 1960.

room. He heard Niemand's, "Good night, Harry," and Harry's happy, "Night, Mr. Niemand."

Graham poured the coffee. Later, Niemand declined a second cup and started to leave.

Niemand said, "I took the liberty of bringing a small gift to your son, Doctor. I gave it to him while you were getting the coffee for us. I hope you'll forgive me."

"Of course. Thank you. Good night."

Graham closed the door; he walked through the living room into Harry's room. He said, "All right, Harry. Now I'll read to —"

There was sudden sweat on his forehead, but he forced his face and his voice to be calm as he stepped to the side of the bed. "May I see that, Harry?" When he had it safely, his hands shook as he examined it.

He thought, *only a madman would give a loaded revolver to a retarded child.*

Milwaukee Journal Photo

Fredric Brown *(1906–1972)* began his writing career as a journalist for a Milwaukee newspaper. Born in Ohio, Brown attended college in Indiana and then lived in Wisconsin, New York, and New Mexico. Brown's specialties are science fiction and mystery stories. Two of his works, *Martians Go Home* and *The Lights in the Sky Are Stars,* have been translated into French.

Developing Comprehension Skills

1. What is wrong with Dr. Graham's son?

2. How does Dr. Graham justify his working on a weapon that could destroy the world?

3. What are the two weapons referred to in this story?

4. Like the title of this story, the last line—"only a madman would give a loaded revolver to a retarded child"—has a double meaning. Who could be considered the madmen? What connection is made between Harry, a retarded child, and humanity, the people who control the weapon?

5. Do you think Dr. Graham gets Niemand's point? Do you think Dr. Graham will change his mind about creating the weapon?

6. Whose opinion of "the weapon" do you agree with—Dr. Graham's or Niemand's? Explain your answer.

Reading Literature: Short Stories

1. **Examining Plot.** The **exposition** of a plot, as you remember, gives background information and introduces characters. Identify the exposition in this story. On a sheet of paper, list at least two details from the exposition.

   The climax of the story occurs in the last sentence of the story. What are two events of the rising action?

2. **Understanding Conflict.** What is the main **conflict,** or struggle, in this story? How

do the characters represent this conflict? Is the conflict resolved at the end? Why or why not?

3. **Analyzing Character.** Harry is a minor character, but he plays an important role in the story. For example, Harry helps to show part of his father's character. What can you infer about Graham from the way he treats Harry? Harry also reveals Graham's ability to rationalize, that is, to think of excuses for things. "What is wrong with rationalization?" Graham thinks. How does Graham rationalize not only about Harry but also about the weapon?

4. **Understanding Theme.** The **theme,** or message, of this story is about dangerous technological inventions. What does the story say about these technological inventions? Who is the "madman" in the story? Whose side does the story support—Dr. Graham's or Niemand's? Explain how you know.

Developing Vocabulary Skills

Using Synonym and Antonym Context Clues. You have learned to look for synonyms as context clues for words you may not know. Sometimes a word is used in context with its antonym. **Antonyms** are words that have opposite meanings. For example, *bright* and *dark* are antonyms.

The following sentences use words from "The Weapon." Each sentence contains a synonym or antonym clue. Write the definition of each underlined word as you understand it.

1. Harry, Dr. Graham's only son, was mentally <u>arrested</u>. Graham found it difficult, yet re-

warding, to live with a retarded child.

2. The visitor distracted him, and he could not afford to be <u>diverted</u> from his work.

3. His thoughts about his son were <u>rationalizations</u>, but Graham saw these excuses as harmless.

4. Niemand <u>declined</u> the coffee although he accepted Graham's invitation to sit down.

5. When Graham opened the bedroom door, <u>anxiety</u> overtook him. But he forced his face and voice to express a calmness until he retrieved the gun from his son.

Developing Skills in Critical Thinking

Classifying Characters. The following is a list of some of the characters you have met so far in this chapter.

Ivan	Jim
Ivan's father	Jim's mother
Gabriel	Jim's father
"Silky" Bob	Mr. Niemand
Jimmy Wells	Dr. Graham
Mr. Markwardt	Harry
Mr. Parsons	

Classify these characters into two groups: main characters and minor characters. Make a list of the main characters and a list of the minor characters.

You might classify these same characters in several other ways. For example, you might group them according to which are adults and which are children. You might also classify them according to which characters change and which ones remain the same. Think of two other ways to classify the characters. Make appropriate lists for these classifications.

Developing Writing Skills

Developing an Argument. It is easy to state an opinion. However, it is often difficult to support that opinion. What follows are the two opinions about scientists and their technological inventions expressed in the story.

Scientists should be held responsible for the effect of their work on the world.

Scientists should not be held responsible for future uses or effects of their work.

Select one of the opinions and write an argument to defend it.

Prewriting. Think of reasons to use in writing your argument. List points to support your opinion. Draw ideas from the story and from current news. Take notes on facts that support each statement you list.

Number your reasons in order of importance. You may want to start with the least important and build to the most important.

Drafting. Develop an organized argument. Start with a sentence stating your opinion on the subject of scientists' responsibilities. Present your reasons in order of importance.

Use key words or phrases to introduce each reason. Two types of key words help make an argument clear. Some key words help state the reasons or facts. These include *because, so, since, therefore,* and *as a result.* Other key words help to put the reasons or facts in order of importance. These include *the first reason, second, more important,* and *finally.*

Revising and Sharing. Read your argument to a group. Ask the group members to say whether your argument is supported with good reasons. Change any part of your argument that the group does not find convincing.

Just Try to Forget

NATHANIEL BENCHLEY

How do you think your parents feel when they watch you during a sporting event? Read this story to find out how two parents feel during their son's swimming meet.

Arthur Dobson held open the door of the school gymnasium for his wife, then followed her in. The smell of steam heat and liniment and disinfectant was the same as it had been twenty years before, and he could hear the scurrying, pounding feet of basketball players, punctuated by the sharp *tweets* of the referee's whistle. It never changes, Dobson thought. Every smell and every sound is still the same. He led his wife past the basketball court, then through another door and up a short flight of steps to the gallery above the swimming pool.

The room was of white tile and glass brick, and it was steaming hot and echoed hollowly with a noise of its own. Dobson and his wife sat down behind a railing overlooking the pool, and Dobson took off his topcoat and put it on the seat beside him.

"I'm getting nervous already," his wife said. "Do you think they have a chance?"

"All I know is what Larry said," Dobson replied. "He didn't seem to think so."

"I don't really care, so long as Larry wins his race," she said. "I think he'd die if he didn't win it, with you here and all."

"*He* can't win it or not win it," said Dobson. "He's in the two-hundred-yard relay, so there are three others with him."

"I know, but still . . . ." His wife took off her coat and peered down at the green, transparent water of the pool. "It looks awfully long, doesn't it?" she said.

Dobson looked at the pool and estimated that he could swim about one length—maybe two, if he took it easy. "Long enough," he said.

Two lanky, muscular figures wearing the bright-blue trunks of the rival school walked out of a door at one end of the pool and dived flatly into the water, hitting it with a double crack, like pistol shots. Then more boys in blue trunks came out and followed them, until the whole squad was swimming up and down the length of the pool. At the diving board, two boys took turns doing unbelievably complicated dives, and Dobson and his wife watched them with a kind of uneasy respect.

"It looks as though Larry were right," Dobson said after a while. "They look pretty good."

"I know," said his wife. "Much too good."

Then Larry's team, wearing red trunks, appeared and dived into the water and swam up and down the pool. At first, Dobson had trouble recognizing his son among the twisting, thrashing bodies. The boys all swam alike, with long, powerful strokes, and they made insane-looking, bottoms-up turns at either end of the pool.

Dobson thought back on the summer, many years ago, when he had had some difficulty teaching Larry to swim. As long as Dobson held him, he would splash and paddle gleefully, but the minute Dobson took his hands away he would become panic-stricken and sink. It wasn't until children younger than he had begun to swim that Larry, without any help from his father, took his first strokes.

He's certainly improved since then, Dobson thought. I had no idea he could swim this well. Even last summer, he wasn't swimming like this. Then Dobson looked at the others, in the blue trunks, and they seemed to be swimming just a little better. I guess it always looks that way, he thought. The other guys always look frighteningly good, even if they aren't. But this time they *are* better—there's no getting around it.

When the warmup was over, the two teams retired, and the officials began arranging their lists and checking their watches. It was the final meet of the season, the letter meet, and the gallery was full of spectators, both students and adults. From below came the sounds of more spectators, who were standing or sitting along the edge of the pool beneath the gallery, and the whole place hummed and echoed and rang with noise.

Dobson removed his jacket, put it next to his topcoat, and loosened his tie. He fought down an urge to light a cigarette and locked his hands together in his lap. His wife reached across and clutched them briefly, and her hand was cold and wet. He smiled at her. "It's no good worrying now," he said. "Larry's race isn't until the very last."

There was a patter of applause as the rival team, wearing blue sweat suits, filed out and took places on benches set in three rows at the shallow end of the pool. A moment later, the air was shattered with cheers and whistles as Larry's team, in red sweat suits, came out and sat beside them. Presently, two boys from each team peeled off their sweat suits and dived into the pool, then pulled themselves out, shook hands all around, and waited, nervously flapping their arms and wrists. Dobson looked at his son, who was sitting on the back row of benches, staring straight ahead of him and chewing a thumbnail. I wish I hadn't come, Dobson thought. I wish I'd made up some excuse to stay at home. He remembered a time when he was young and his father had come to watch him play football, and he had spent the entire, miserable game on the bench. Parents should stay away from athletic contests, he told himself. They ought to be barred by law. Larry continued to chew his thumbnail, and Dobson felt sick.

A manager with a megaphone announced the first event, which was the fifty-yard free-style race, and gave the names of the contestants. The starter pointed a blank pistol upward and told the boys to take their marks. There was complete silence as they stood in a row at the edge of the pool, gripping the rim with their toes. The starter said, "Get set," and the boys crouched, their hands on a level with their feet. There was a pause. The pistol banged, and after what seemed to Dobson like an unnaturally long wait, the boys shot forward, cracked into the water, and churned off down the pool.

The crowd shouted and called and cheered and chanted, and the noise swelled to a roar as the swimmers reached the far end of the pool, made their frantic, ducking turns, and headed back for the finish line. They were almost indistinguishable in the boiling spray, but the two in the farthest lane, the ones in the blue trunks, pulled steadily ahead in the final yards and finished first and second. Dobson settled back in his seat.

"That makes the score eight to one already," he said to his wife. "This is going to be murder."

But Larry's team placed first and third in the next event and first and second in the one after that; and somehow, unbelievably, they managed to gain a slight lead. It was never a big enough lead to be safe, and at one point the score was tied, and Dobson saw and pitied the agony of the one boy in each event who failed to score. Some drooped forlornly in the gutter, some cried, and some had to be helped from the pool by consoling teammates, who said futile things to them and patted them on the bottom while they dragged themselves to the benches. As the final event came closer, Dobson looked more often at his son, and it seemed to him that Larry was getting smaller and paler with each race. I wish to God he'd swum first, Dobson thought. I wish it were all over, so he wouldn't have to wait like this. Even if he'd lost, I wish it were all over.

The diving took a long time, with each of the four contestants doing six dives, and the next-to-last event was the medley relay race, which Larry's team won, putting them ahead 37-30. When the score was announced, Dobson's wife gave a little shout and grabbed him. "We've won!" she cried. "They can't possibly catch us now!"

"It looks that way," Dobson replied with a certain amount of relief. "It certainly looks that way."

A student behind him touched his arm. "No, sir," he said. "They can still tie us. The last race counts seven points, and there's no score for second."

"Oh!" said Dobson.

Olympic Backstroke Swimming Trial, 1977, JOE WILDER, M.D. Private Collection.

He saw Larry and his three teammates strip off their sweat suits, jump into the water, then climb out, shake hands, and stand around fluttering their hands and breathing deeply. The boys from the other school did the same, and they looked big and unnaturally husky. They didn't seem as nervous as the boys on Larry's team.

The noise from the crowd was such that the manager had to shout three times for quiet before he could announce the event, and when Larry was announced as swimming third in the relay, Dobson had an odd feeling at the sound of the name. His wife slid her hand into his. "I don't think I'm going to be able to watch," she said. "You tell me what happens."

The first two swimmers took their marks, and a tense silence hung until the crack of the gun. Then, as the swimmers leaped out at the water, the spectators came to their feet and shouted and cheered and stamped, and the noise grew and swelled until Dobson couldn't hear his own voice.

The swimmers thrashed down the pool and then back, and the one in red trunks was slightly ahead as they touched the starting line and two more swimmers sprang out. Dobson didn't watch the second boys; all he saw was Larry, who had moved up to the starting line, breathing in deep gulps, his eyes fixed glassily ahead of him. An official squatted beside Larry's feet, and Larry crouched lower and lower as his teammate in the pool approached him. The red-trunked boy was leading by about two yards when he reached the edge, and it seemed to Dobson that Larry was in the air and in the water at almost the same instant. Then Dobson's throat closed and he couldn't make a sound, but beside him his wife was screaming and pounding the rail, her voice all but lost in the growing pandemonium.

Larry finished his lap three or four yards ahead, but as the two last swimmers raced down and turned, the one in blue trunks began to gain. He closed the gap slowly, and the members of both teams crowded around the finish line, jumping and beckoning and bellowing, and then the red-trunked boy put on a final, frenzied spurt and held his lead to the finish line. Larry and his teammates spilled into the water, hugging one another and falling down and shouting, and the blue-trunked boy clung to the gutter, exhausted and miserable.

Dobson sat back and looked at his wife. "Wow!" he said. And she laughed.

Down below, members of both teams clustered around the officials, and then, suddenly, the ones in blue leaped into the air and shouted, and Dobson saw a boy in red trunks hit the water with his fist. There was some commotion and a lot of noise from the crowd, and Dobson was unable to hear distinctly what the manager said through the megaphone, but he caught the words "Thirty-seven to thirty-seven."

Unbelieving, he turned to a student in the crowd. "What happened?" Dobson asked. "I couldn't hear."

"We were disqualified," the student answered sourly. "Dobson jumped the gun."

For almost a full minute, neither Dobson nor his wife said anything. Then he put on his coat and helped her on with hers, and as they walked slowly down the stairs, she took his arm. "What are we going to say to him?" she asked in a small voice. "What *can* we say?"

"I wish I knew," he replied. "I wish I knew."

They went out to the car and stood beside it while they waited for Larry. Dobson's mind was a jumble of things he wanted to say, but, even as he thought of them they seemed inadequate, and he knew that none of them would do any good. He thought of going in and seeing Larry in the locker room and then quickly decided against it. I guess it's best to wait out here, he thought. He'll come out when he wants to.

After what seemed like an hour, Larry came out of the gym and walked slowly toward them. His hair was wet and slicked back, and his eyes were red—possibly from the chlorine in the pool, Dobson thought, knowing that wasn't the reason. Without a word, Larry opened a door of the car and dropped into the back seat. Dobson got in front, and, after a moment's hesitation, his wife got in back with Larry.

"Do you want to drive around for a while?" Dobson asked as he started the engine.

"Whatever you say," Larry replied. "I don't care."

They drove through the streets of the town and then out into the bleak, snow-spotted country. For several minutes nobody spoke, and then Dobson cleared his throat. "Would you like me to tell you something?" he asked.

"Sure," said Larry, without enthusiasm.

"When I was in school, I wanted to play baseball," Dobson said. "More than anything else, I wanted to make the baseball team. The only trouble was I wasn't good enough. I got in a couple of games as a pinch-hitter, and once they let me play right field, but I dropped the only fly that came my way, and they yanked me out."

He looked into the rear-view mirror and saw the incredulous expression on his wife's face. He continued, "The last game in my senior year—the letter game—we were behind four to three in the ninth inning. We had a man on third, and the coach sent me in to bunt down toward first. On the first ball pitched, I tried to bunt, and the ball hit my right thumb and broke it. Technically, I was eligible for a letter, but I never collected it. I couldn't look at any of the team again."

Larry laughed shortly. "I never heard about that," he said.

"I didn't tell many people," Dobson replied, with another look into the rear-view mirror. "But what I'm getting at is that these things are horrible when they happen—you think you'll never live them down—but sooner or later it gets so you can bear to think of them again. It may take a long while, but eventually it happens."

Larry was quiet for a minute. "I guess I was just trying too hard," he said at last.

NYT Pictures

Nathaniel Benchley *(1915–1981),* author of fifteen novels, many books for teenagers, and several plays, has created his own brand of low-key humor. The son of the famous humorist, Robert Benchley, Nathaniel was educated at Harvard University. After graduation, he worked for the *New York Herald Tribune* and *Newsweek.* He is best known for his novel *The Off-Islanders,* which was made into the film *The Russians Are Coming, The Russians Are Coming.* A New Englander most of his life, he taught his son, Peter, about the islands in the Atlantic and about sharks. Peter grew up to write the best-selling novel *Jaws.*

Developing Comprehension Skills

1. How do Mr. and Mrs. Dobson feel as they watch their son's swim meet?

2. Mrs. Dobson understands how much Larry wants to win the race. She says to her husband, "I think he'd die if he didn't win it, with you here and all." What can you infer about Larry's relationship with his father from this statement?

3. While he waits for Larry's swimming event, Dobson sees his son "getting smaller and paler with each race." What feelings does Dobson imagine his son to be having?

4. How does Larry lose the race for his team?

5. What memories of his own sports experiences does the swim meet bring back for Dobson? Tell what experiences Dobson and his son have in common.

6. Do you think the meet is harder on Larry or on his dad? Which character do you feel more sorry for? Give evidence from the story to explain your answers.

Reading Literature: Short Stories

1. **Recognizing Suspense. Suspense** is the excitement a reader feels about the outcome of a story. In this story the reader is uncertain about how Larry will perform in the

meet. Explain how each of the following elements helps to build the suspense.

   a. Dobson's judgment of the other team
   b. the timing of Larry's event in the meet
   c. the score at the time of Larry's race

2. **Identifying Rising Action.** The first few paragraphs of this story introduce the setting, a high school pool area. The opening exposition also introduces the main characters, Mr. and Mrs. Dobson and their son Larry. Then the rising action builds to the high point of the plot, the **climax,** when the reader learns that Larry jumped the gun. List the main events in the rising action of the plot.

3. **Analyzing Falling Action.** You remember that the **falling action** of a plot occurs after the climax. It shows the effects of the climax on the characters. In the falling action of this story, how does Dobson feel for his son? Find details to support your answer.

   Also during the falling action, Larry is at first terribly ashamed. How does his dad succeed in comforting him?

4. **Understanding Theme.** A theme of this story is the message stated directly in Dobson's anecdote about the baseball game. Reread the anecdote that Dobson tells his son. What is the lesson he has learned that he passes on to his son?

Developing Vocabulary Skills

Inferring Meaning from General Context. A reader can often infer the meaning of a word from the general context in which it is used. Read this sentence from the story:

Then Dobson's throat closed and he couldn't make a sound, but beside him his wife was screaming and pounding the rail, her voice all but lost in the growing <u>pandemonium</u>.

Although no specific context clue gives the meaning of *pandemonium,* you can put together a general meaning from the description of the action. You know that *pandemonium* refers to what is happening: the screaming, the pounding, the excitement. The scene is chaotic, confusing, disorderly. You can then understand that *pandemonium* is similar in meaning to chaos and confusion.

Use this same procedure to discover the meanings of *patter* and *thrashing* in the following paragraphs from the story. Explain the meaning of each of these words.

   There was a <u>patter</u> of applause as the rival team, wearing blue sweat suits, filed out and took places on benches set in three rows at the shallow end of the pool. A moment later, the air was shattered with cheers and whistles as Larry's team, in red sweat suits, came out and sat beside them.

   At first Dobson had trouble recognizing his son among the twisting, <u>thrashing</u> bodies. The boys all swam alike, with long, powerful strokes, and they made insane-looking, bottoms-up turns at either end of the pool.

Developing Skills in Study and Research

Using the Parts of a Book. If you understand the parts of a book, it will be easier to use. For example, the table of contents or the index can help you to find a selection quickly.

Certain parts of a book can help you with your reading too. The glossary, for example, can help you to understand words you do not know.

Look over the following parts of this book: the table of contents, the introductions to chapters, the handbook of literary terms, the glossary, and other material at the back of this book. Use these parts of the book to answer the following questions. Then tell which part provided the answer.

1. What is the definition of *indistinguishable,* as used in the sentence, "They were almost indistinguishable in the boiling spray."

2. What are the five main parts of a plot?

3. One of the study questions for this story uses the term *suspense.* What is the definition of this term?

4. What proofreading symbols could you use during the revising stage for your writing assignment on "Just Try to Forget?"

Developing Writing Skills

Supporting an Opinion About a Main Character. Who do you think is the main character in this story? Decide whether you think it is the father or the son. Then write a paragraph supporting your choice. Follow these steps.

Prewriting. Think of ways that a reader can identify the main character in a story. For example, from which character does the reader see and feel the action of the story? Which character does the reader feel more strongly for? Which character does the reader get to know more about? Around which character does the story revolve? Write down your answers to these questions. Then decide who you think is the main character. Add incidents and sentences from the story that help to support your choice.

Drafting. As a topic sentence, state your opinion about who the main character is. Based on your notes, write sentences to defend that position. Add quotations and details to support your opinion.

Revising and Sharing. Read your paragraph aloud to see if it holds together. Test each sentence to make sure that it supports your opinion about who the main character is. Then read your paragraph to someone else. Ask if the organization is logical and if all the sentences are clear. If not, weed out sentences that do not prove your point. Add sentences to defend your stand with more specific reasons and details from the story. Rewrite sentences to make them clear and logical.

The Trout

SEAN O'FAOLAIN

One sign of growing up is doing something on your own that you think is right. Read to discover what Julia decides to do on her own.

One of the first places Julia always ran to when they arrived in G—— was The Dark Walk. It is a laurel walk, very old, almost gone wild; a lofty midnight tunnel of smooth, sinewy branches. Underfoot, the tough brown leaves are never dry enough to crackle; there is always a suggestion of damp and cool trickle.

She raced right into it. For the first few yards she always had the memory of the sun behind her; then she felt the dusk closing swiftly down on her so that she screamed with pleasure and raced on to reach the light at the far end. It was always just a little too long in coming so that she emerged gasping, clasping her hands, laughing, drinking in the sun. When she was filled with the heat and glare, she would turn and consider the ordeal again.

This year she had the extra joy of showing it to her small brother and of terrifying him as well as herself. And for him the fear lasted longer because his legs were so short, and she had gone out at the far end while he was still screaming and racing.

When they had done this many times, they came back to the house to tell everybody that they had done it. He boasted. She mocked. They squabbled.

"Cry baby!"

"You were afraid yourself, so there!"

"I won't take you anymore."

"You're a big pig."

"I hate you."

Tears were threatening, so somebody said, "Did you see the well?" She opened her eyes at that and held up her long, lovely neck suspiciously and decided to be incredulous. She was twelve, and at that age little girls are beginning to suspect most stories. They have already found out too many, from Santa Claus to the stork. How could there be a well! In The Dark Walk? That she had visited year after year? Haughtily she said, "Nonsense."

But she went back, pretending to be going somewhere else; and she found a hole scooped in the rock at the side of the walk, choked with damp leaves, so shrouded by ferns that she uncovered it

Dry Springs, 1985, GEORGE HARKINS. Tatistcheff Gallery, New York City. Photograph by Rich Sharp.

only after much searching. At the back of this little cavern, there was about a quart of water. In the water, she suddenly perceived a panting trout. She rushed for Stephen and dragged him to see, and they were both so excited that they were no longer afraid of the darkness as they hunched down and peered in at the fish panting in his tiny prison, his silver stomach going up and down like an engine.

Nobody knew how the trout got there. Even old Martin in the kitchen garden laughed and refused to believe that it was there, or pretended not to believe, until she forced him to come down and see. Kneeling and pushing back his tattered old cap, he peered in.

"Be cripes, you're right. How did that fella get there?"

She stared at him suspiciously.

"You knew?" she accused, but he said, "The divil a' know," and reached down to lift it out. Convinced, she hauled him back. If she had found it, then it was her trout.

Her mother suggested that a bird had carried the spawn. Her father thought that in the winter a small streamlet might have carried it down there as a baby, and it had been safe until the summer came and the water began to dry up. She said, "I see," and went back to look again and consider the matter in private. Her brother remained behind, wanting to hear the whole story of the trout; not really interested in the actual trout but much interested in the story which his mummy began to make up for him on the lines of, "So one day Daddy Trout and Mammy Trout. . . . " When he retailed it to her, she said, "Pooh."

It troubled her that the trout was always in the same position. He had no room to turn. All the time the silver belly went up and down; otherwise he was motionless. She wondered what he ate, and in between visits to Joey Pony and the boat and a bath to get cool, she thought of his hunger. She brought him down bits of dough; once she brought him a worm. He ignored the food. He just went on panting. Hunched over him, she thought how all the winter, while she was at school, he had been in there. All the winter, in The Dark Walk, all day, all night, floating around alone. She drew the brim of her hat down around her ears and chin and stared. She was still thinking of it as she lay in bed.

It was late June, the longest day of the year. The sun had sat still for a week, burning up the world. Although it was after ten o'clock, it was still bright and still hot. She lay on her back under a single sheet, with her long legs spread, trying to keep cool. She could see the D of the moon through

the fir tree—they slept on the ground floor. Before they went to bed, her mummy had told Stephen the story of the trout again, and she, in her bed, had resolutely presented her back to them and read her book. But she had kept one ear cocked.

"And so, in the end, this naughty fish who would not stay at home got bigger and bigger and bigger, and the water got smaller and smaller. . . . "

Passionately she had whirled and cried, "Mummy, don't make it a horrible old moral story!" Her mummy had brought in a fairy godmother then, who sent lots of rain and filled the well, and a stream poured out, and the trout floated away down to the river below. Staring at the moon, she knew that there are no such things as fairy godmothers and that the trout, down in The Dark Walk, was panting like an engine. She heard somebody unwind a fishing reel. Would the *beasts* fish him out?

She sat up. Stephen was a hot lump of sleep, lazy thing. The Dark Walk would be full of little scraps of moon. She leaped up and looked out the window, and somehow it was not so lightsome now that she saw the dim mountains far away and the black firs against the breathing land and heard a dog say *bark-bark*. Quietly she lifted the ewer of water and climbed out the window and scuttled along the cool but cruel gravel down to the maw of the tunnel. Her pajamas were very short, so that when she splashed water, it wet her ankles. She peered into the tunnel. Something alive rustled inside there. She raced in, and up and down she raced and flurried and cried aloud, "Oh, gosh, I can't find it," and then at last she did. Kneeling down in the damp, she put her hand into the slimy hole. When the body lashed, they were both mad with fright. But she gripped him and shoved him into the ewer and raced, with her teeth ground, out to the other end of the tunnel and down the steep paths to the river's edge.

All the time she could feel him lashing his tail against the side of the ewer. She was afraid he would jump right out. The gravel cut into her soles until she came to the cool ooze of the river's bank, where the moon mice on the water crept into her feet. She poured out, watching until he plopped. For a second he was visible in the water.

She hoped he was not dizzy. Then all she saw was the glimmer of the moon in the silent-flowing river, the dark firs, the dim mountains, and the radiant, pointed face laughing down at her out of the empty sky.

She scuttled up the hill and in the window, plonked down the ewer, and flew through the air like a bird into bed. The dog said *bark-bark*. She heard the fishing reel whirring. She hugged herself and giggled. Like a river of joy, her holiday spread before her.

In the morning Stephen rushed to her, shouting that "he" was gone and asking "where" and "how." Lifting her nose in the air, she said superciliously, "Fairy godmother, I suppose?" and strolled away, patting the palms of her hands.

Sean O'Faolain *(born 1900)* is an Irish writer who has written many short stories about Irish country life and the War of Independence from England. O'Faolain fought in the war for four years before attending the National University of Ireland. After graduation, he earned a master's degree at Harvard and then taught at Harvard and at Boston College. O'Faolain has also written many biographies of Irish heroes and several travel books.

Developing Comprehension Skills

1. What is The Dark Walk?

2. What explanations do Julia's mother and father give for how the trout might have gotten into the well?

3. Why does Julia remove the trout from the well and put it into the river?

4. After Julia releases the trout, she "flew through the air like a bird into bed." How does Julia feel? Explain the reason for her feelings.

5. How does Julia try to show that she is more grown up than her brother? Find three instances in the story.

6. This story shows Julia at an in-between time in her life. She borders on both childhood and adulthood. In what ways do you think she acts like a child? In what ways does she act like an adult?

Reading Literature: Short Stories

1. **Analyzing Character.** What can you infer about Julia from these passages from the story?

   a. She raced right into it [The Dark Walk]. For the first few yards she always had the memory of the sun behind her; then she felt the dusk closing swiftly down on her so that she screamed with pleasure and raced on to reach the light at the far end.

   b. Passionately she had whirled and cried, "Mummy, don't make it a horrible old moral story!" . . . Staring at the moon, she knew that there are no such things as fairy godmothers and that the trout, down in The Dark Walk, was panting like an engine.

   c. All the time she could feel him lashing his tail against the side of the ewer. She was afraid he would jump right out. The gravel cut into her soles until she came to the cool ooze of the river's bank, where the moon mice on the water crept into her feet. She poured out, watching until he plopped.

2. **Understanding Setting.** The setting plays an important part in this story. For that reason, the writer describes it carefully. His description appeals to several senses. Some details such as "lofty midnight tunnel" and "dark firs" help you to picture the setting in your mind. Other details help you to feel the setting, as in the phrases "damp and cool trickle" and "cool ooze." Still other details of setting appeal to the sense of hearing, such as "she heard the fishing reel whirring." Find three more descriptions of the setting that appeal to each of these senses: sight, touch, and hearing.

3. **Understanding Climax.** The events in a story build to a **climax,** a turning-point that marks the peak of emotion. What event is the climax of this story? What turning-point does this event mark?

Developing Vocabulary Skills

Inferring Meaning and Using a Dictionary. When you come across an unfamiliar word, context clues such as restatement, synonym, or comparison clues might help you unlock the meaning of the word. The general context may also help you to infer the word's meaning. At times, however, you will need to use a dictionary to find out the definition of the unfamiliar word.

For each of the following sentences from the story, tell if the context helps you to define the underlined word or if you need a dictionary. Then write the definition of each word.

1. Before they went to bed, her mummy had told Stephen the story of the trout again, and she, in her bed, had <u>resolutely</u> presented her back to them and read her book.

2. She leaped up and looked out the window, and somehow it was not so <u>lightsome</u> now that she saw the dim mountains far away and the black firs against the breathing land and heard a dog say *bark-bark*.

3. She <u>scuttled</u> up the hill and in the window, plonked down the ewer, and flew through the air like a bird into bed.

4. In the morning Stephen rushed to her, shouting that "he" was gone and asking "where" and "how." Lifting her nose in the air, she said <u>superciliously</u>, "Fairy godmother, I suppose?" and strolled away, patting the palms of her hands.

Developing Skills in Speaking and Listening

Reading Aloud. Choose a passage in this story that you find especially vivid, and think of the feeling it gives you. Then read the passage aloud, trying to convey that feeling. Finally, after you practice reading the passage several more times, read it aloud to a group. Try to make your audience experience the same feeling.

Developing Writing Skills

Writing About an Experience. At the beginning of the story, Julia is both afraid and excited when she is in The Dark Walk. Have you ever felt the same way—say, on a roller coaster or on stage? In one paragraph write about an experience that made you feel both afraid and excited or make up a similar experience. Follow these steps.

Prewriting. Decide on the experience you will write about. Try to picture it in your mind. Jot down information about the experience, including details about the setting, what happened, and how you felt. Go back and add more details. Then organize the events in time order, that is, in the order that they happened.

Drafting. Begin by describing the setting, and then use your notes and outline to write about the experience. Be sure to show how the experience made you feel both afraid and excited. To make the fear and excitement seem real, try to use vivid descriptive details that appeal to more than one sense.

Revising and Sharing. Check to make sure that the events you related are in time order. Read your paragraph aloud, noticing if it flows smoothly. Pay attention to whether all your sentences are clear and complete. When you have a final copy, share it with a friend or family member.

Stories of
Character

In a way, all stories are stories of character, just as all stories have action. The stories in this section, however, let you get to know characters especially well. These characters seem to come alive and become as real as your next-door neighbor. Some of these characters may seem a lot like you. Others may seem surprisingly different. But most of the characters in these stories are hard to forget. As you read these stories, let the characters into your life, and learn from them.

The Blind Singers, 1913, ROBERT HENRI. Hirshhorn Museum and Sculpture Garden, Smithsonian Institution, Washington, D.C.

Reading Literature

More About Short Stories

You have learned about four elements in a short story: setting, character, plot, and theme. You have learned that the plot develops out of the conflicts that the main character faces. Now you will learn more about different types of conflicts and about ways to identify a story's theme. You will also find out about different methods of characterization and about other elements in a story: narrator and point of view.

Conflict. Almost every plot involves a **conflict,** or struggle between two forces. **External conflict** may be between the main character and another character, as in the story "A Spark Neglected Burns the House." External conflict may be a struggle of a character against nature or against society. An **internal conflict** refers to the main character's struggle within himself or herself. For example, in "Little Dog Lost" Jim's internal conflict is between his stubborn need to be right and his desire to find his dog.

Theme. The **theme** of a story is the writer's message about life or about human nature. A theme applies not just to one story but also to situations beyond the story. For example, the theme of "The Weapon" is that it is unwise—even insane—to entrust human beings with dangerous technology.

Some stories have more than one theme. In "A Spark Neglected Burns the House," for instance, one theme is that revenge is destructive. Another theme concerns the need to respect older people.

Various clues in a story can help you identify one or more of its themes. Notice the title, the beginning, and the ending of a story. These often highlight the story's theme. In addition, look for what the main character learns through the conflict in the story.

Characterization. Characterization refers to the methods a writer uses to portray a character. One method of characterization is direct description. For example, here is a description of Parsons from "A Man Who Had No Eyes":

> He was a handsome figure with his immaculate gray suit and gray hat and malacca stick.

A second method of characterization is to present a character's actions and words. Parsons, for instance, always treats Markwardt politely. The reader can judge him to be both kind and fair. A third method of characterization is to reveal what a character is feeling and thinking. The reader learns that Parsons feels "somewhat annoyed and embarrassed" by the blind man's pleadings, although his actions and speech do not betray such emotions.

A fourth method to portray character is through the responses of other characters. One character in a story will talk to or about another character and reveal important information.

Narrator and Point of View. The one who tells a story is called the **narrator.** The term **point of view** refers to the narrative method used in a story. If the narrator is a character in the story, the story is told from the **first-person point of view.** A first-person narrator uses first-person pronouns, such as *I, me, us, we, our,* in telling the story. "Little Dog Lost" is an example of a story told from a first-person point of view. Jim is the narrator and the main character.

If the narrator is not a character in the story but only a voice outside the action, the story is told from the third-person point of view. A third-person narrator uses third-person pronouns, such as *she, he, them, their,* to tell the story.

Third-person narrators are of two main types. If the narrator reports what is going on in all the characters' minds, then the narrator is omniscient, or all-knowing, and the story is told from an **omniscient point of view.** "A Man Who Had No Eyes" is told from an omniscient point of view. The narrator tells what's going on in both characters' minds. If the narrator tells only one character's thoughts, then the story is told from a **third-person limited point of view.** For example, in the story "The Weapon," the reader learns Dr. Graham's thoughts and feelings but not Niemand's.

Charles

SHIRLEY JACKSON

Laurie starts kindergarten and comes home with tales of a horrid boy named Charles. Look for clues in the story that point to who Charles is.

The day Laurie started kindergarten, he renounced corduroy overalls with bibs and began wearing blue jeans with a belt. I watched him go off the first morning with the older girl next door, seeing clearly that an era of my life was ended, my sweet-voiced nursery-school tot replaced by a long-trousered, swaggering character who forgot to stop at the corner and wave goodbye to me.

He came home the same way, the front door slamming open, his cap on the floor, and the voice suddenly become raucous shouting, "Isn't anybody *here?*"

At lunch he spoke insolently to his father, spilled Jannie's milk, and remarked that his teacher said that we were not to take the name of the Lord in vain.

"How *was* school today?" I asked, elaborately casual.

"All right," he said.

"Did you learn anything?" his father asked.

Laurie regarded his father coldly. "I didn't learn nothing," he said.

"Anything," I said. "Didn't learn anything."

"The teacher spanked a boy, though," Laurie said, addressing his bread and butter. "For being fresh," he added with his mouth full.

"What did he do?" I asked. "Who was it?"

Laurie thought. "It was Charles," he said. "He was fresh. The teacher spanked him and made him stand in a corner. He was awfully fresh."

"What did he do?" I asked again, but Laurie slid off his chair, took a cookie, and left, while his father was still saying, "See here, young man."

The next day Laurie remarked at lunch, as soon as he sat down, "Well, Charles was bad again today." He grinned enormously and said, "Today Charles hit the teacher."

"Good heavens," I said, mindful of the

Lord's name, "I suppose he got spanked again?"

"He sure did," Laurie said. "Look up," he said to his father.

"What?" his father said, looking up.

"Look down," Laurie said. "Look at my thumb. Gee, you're dumb." He began to laugh insanely.

"Why did Charles hit the teacher?" I asked quickly.

"Because she tried to make him color with red crayons," Laurie said. "Charles wanted to color with green crayons, so he hit the teacher, and she spanked him and said nobody play with Charles; but everybody did."

The third day—it was Wednesday of the first week—Charles bounced a seesaw onto the head of a little girl and made her bleed, and the teacher made him stay inside all during recess. Thursday Charles had to stand in a corner during storytime because he kept pounding his feet on the floor. Friday Charles was deprived of blackboard privileges because he threw chalk.

On Saturday I remarked to my husband, "Do you think kindergarten is too unsettling for Laurie? All this toughness and bad grammar, and this Charles boy sounds like such a bad influence."

"It'll be all right," my husband said reassuringly. "Bound to be people like Charles in the world. Might as well meet them now as later."

On Monday Laurie came home late, full of news. "Charles," he shouted as he came up the hill; I was waiting anxiously on the front steps. "Charles," Laurie yelled all the way up the hill, "Charles was bad again."

"Come right in," I said, as soon as he came close enough. "Lunch is waiting."

"You know what Charles did?" he demanded, following me through the door. "Charles yelled so in school they sent a boy in from first grade to tell the teacher she had to make Charles keep quiet, and so Charles had to stay after school. And so all the children stayed to watch him."

"What did he do?" I asked.

"He just sat there," Laurie said, climbing into his chair at the table. "Hi, Pop, y'old dust mop."

"Charles had to stay after school today," I told my husband. "Everyone stayed with him."

"What does this Charles look like?" my husband asked Laurie. "What's his other name?"

"He's bigger than me," Laurie said. " . . . and he doesn't ever wear a jacket."

Monday night was the first Parent-Teachers meeting, and only the fact that Jannie had a cold kept me from going; I wanted passionately to meet Charles's mother. On Tuesday Laurie remarked suddenly, "Our teacher had a friend come to see her in school today."

"Charles's mother?" my husband and I asked simultaneously.

"Naaah," Laurie said scornfully. "It was a man who came and made us do exercises. Look." He climbed down from his chair and squatted down and touched his toes.

Michael Rothschild, 1968, ALICE NEEL. Photograph: Robert Miller Gallery, New York City.

"Like this," he said. He got solemnly back into his chair and said, picking up his fork, "Charles didn't even *do* exercises."

"That's fine," I said heartily. "Didn't Charles want to do exercises?"

"Naaah," Laurie said. "Charles was so fresh to the teacher's friend he wasn't *let* do exercises."

"Fresh again?" I said.

"He kicked the teacher's friend," Laurie said. "The teacher's friend told Charles to touch his toes like I just did, and Charles kicked him."

"What are they going to do about Charles, do you suppose?" Laurie's father asked him.

Laurie shrugged elaborately. "Throw him out of school, I guess," he said.

Wednesday and Thursday were routine; Charles yelled during story hour and hit a boy in the stomach and made him cry. On Friday Charles stayed after school again and so did all the other children.

With the third week of kindergarten, Charles was an institution in our family. Jannie was being a Charles when she cried all afternoon. Laurie did a Charles when he filled his wagon full of mud and pulled it through the kitchen. Even my husband, when he caught his elbow in the telephone cord and pulled telephone, ash tray, and a bowl of flowers off the table, said, after the first minute, "Looks like Charles."

During the third and fourth weeks there seemed to be a reformation in Charles. Laurie reported grimly at lunch on Thursday of the third week, "Charles was so good today the teacher gave him an apple."

"What?" I said, and my husband added warily, "You mean Charles?"

"Charles," Laurie said. "He gave the crayons around and he picked up the books afterward, and the teacher said he was her helper."

"What happened?" I asked incredulously.

"He was her helper; that's all," Laurie said, and shrugged.

"Can this be true, about Charles?" I asked my husband that night. "Can something like this happen?"

"Wait and see," my husband said cynically. "When you've got a Charles to deal with, this may mean he's only plotting."

He seemed to be wrong. For over a week, Charles was the teacher's helper. Each day he handed things out, and he picked things up; no one had to stay after school.

"The P.T.A. meeting's next week again," I told my husband one evening. "I'm going to find Charles's mother there."

"Ask her what happened to Charles," my husband said. "I'd like to know."

"I'd like to know myself," I said.

On Friday of that week things were back to normal. "You know what Charles did today?" Laurie demanded at the lunch table, in a voice slightly awed. "He told a little girl to say a word, and she said it; and the teacher washed her mouth out with soap, and Charles laughed."

"What word?" his father asked unwisely, and Laurie said, "I'll have to whisper it to you; it's so bad." He got down off his chair and went around to his father. His father bent his head down, and Laurie whispered joyfully. His father's eyes widened.

"Did Charles tell the little girl to say *that?*" he asked respectfully.

"She said it *twice,*" Laurie said. "Charles told her to say it *twice.*"

"What happened to Charles?" my husband asked.

"Nothing," Laurie said. "He was passing out the crayons."

Monday morning Charles abandoned the little girl and said the evil word himself three or four times, getting his mouth washed out with soap each time. He also threw chalk.

My husband came to the door with me that evening as I set out for the P.T.A. meeting. "Invite her over for a cup of tea after the meeting," he said. "I want to get a look at her."

"If only she's there," I said prayerfully.

"She'll be there," my husband said. "I don't see how they could hold a P.T.A. meeting without Charles's mother."

At the meeting I sat restlessly, scanning each comfortable, matronly face, trying to determine which one hid the secret of Charles. None of them looked to me haggard enough. No one stood up in the meeting and apologized for the way her son had been acting. No one mentioned Charles.

After the meeting, I identified and sought out Laurie's kindergarten teacher. She had a plate with a cup of tea and a piece of chocolate cake; I had a plate with a cup of tea and a piece of marshmallow cake. We maneuvered up to one another cautiously and smiled.

"I've been so anxious to meet you," I said. "I'm Laurie's mother."

"We're all so interested in Laurie," she said.

"Well, he certainly likes kindergarten," I said. "He talks about it all the time."

"We had a little trouble adjusting, the

first week or so," she said primly, "but now he's a fine little helper. With lapses, of course."

"Laurie usually adjusts very quickly," I said. "I suppose this time it's Charles's influence."

"Charles?"

"Yes," I said, laughing, "you must have your hands full in that kindergarten, with Charles."

"Charles?" she said. "We don't have any Charles in the kindergarten."

Shirley Jackson *(1919–1965)* wrote many warm and humorous stories about family life, such as "Charles" and the story collection entitled *Life Among the Savages.* She is also known for her shocking tales of horror, which include the novels *We Have Always Lived in the Castle* and *The Haunting of Hill House.* Jackson's most famous story, "The Lottery," is a grim tale of ritual death in an otherwise ordinary small town. Many of Jackson's stories have been adapted for stage, film, and television.

Homework

Developing Comprehension Skills

1. What are some of the things that Charles does at school?

2. What are some of the things that Laurie does at home that show he is like Charles?

3. What seems to be Laurie's attitude toward Charles and his activities? Give evidence to support your answer.

4. Who is Laurie really talking about when he describes Charles's activities?

5. At what point did you figure out who Charles is? What clues helped you decide?

Reading Literature: Short Stories

1. **Recognizing Foreshadowing.** In the first paragraph of the story, Laurie's mother sends him off to school in jeans and sees her "sweet-voiced nursery-school tot replaced by a long-trousered, swaggering character." This statement turns out to be **foreshadowing.** That is, it gives a hint about how Laurie will approach school. What later action or actions does the statement foreshadow?

2. **Identifying Narrator and Point of View.** The **narrator** of a story is the one who tells the story. Who is the narrator of "Charles"?

Is the story told from a first- or third-person point of view? How would the story be different if Laurie were the narrator?

3. **Understanding Characterization.** A common method of characterization is to present a character's words and actions. In "Charles," for example, Laurie says, "Hi Pop, you old dust mop." Laurie's words show that he is playful and disrespectful toward his parents. Find three other comments or actions by Laurie that help to show his character. What does each reveal about Laurie?

4. **Understanding Surprise Endings.** In this chapter you have read four short stories with unexpected endings: "The Weapon," "After Twenty Years," "A Man Who Had No Eyes," and "Charles." Which of these endings was most surprising to you? Which did you like best? Which did you like least? Give reasons for your answers.

Developing Vocabulary Skills

Using Examples as Context Clues. In some example clues, a familiar word may be given as an example of the unfamiliar word. In others, the unfamiliar word is given as an example of a familiar one. Some key words that point out example clues are *for example, such as, especially, for instance, like, other, such,* and *one kind.* The following sentence gives example clues for the word *arachnids:*

He is afraid of spiders, scorpions, and other arachnids.

Read the following sentences. Each uses a context clue to define a word from the stories you have read. Some sentences use example clues. Others use definition or restatement clues. Decide which type of clue is used in each sentence. Write the definition of the word as you understand it from the context clue.

1. During olden times, one kind of punishment was <u>flogging</u>.

2. The <u>anguish</u>, guilt, and other painful feelings that Graham had experienced were in the past.

3. To the teacher, school days were <u>routine</u>. That is, they did not vary from day to day.

4. "Silky" Bob's tone of voice revealed excessive pride, <u>egotism</u>, and other self-centered attitudes.

5. Mr. Parsons did not want to seem <u>inquisitive</u>, or curious, about the man's handicap.

Developing Skills in Study and Research

Refining a Research Topic. The story you have just read centers on the behavior of students in the classroom. You may want to do research on this topic. One resource to check for information is an encyclopedia. Another way to find information about students and education is to use *The Readers' Guide to Periodical Literature.* This index lists magazine articles by subject. Under the general heading of "Education" in any source, you might look for subheadings such as "Discipline in the Classroom," or "How Teachers Guide Learning." Make use of cross references as you research.

When you look up a subject in an index, you may find subheadings or cross references. A **cross reference** is a reference to a closely related topic. Since "Education" is a broad topic, its listing in *The Readers' Guide* or in an encyclopedia index is likely to have subheadings or cross references.

Using either an encyclopedia index or *The Readers' Guide,* look up the subject *Education.* Read through the list of articles. Also check the articles listed under any cross reference topics suggested. Use the information you find to answer the following questions:

1. Suppose your teacher asked you to write a report about education. What specific topics within the general subject of education might you select? List five possible report ideas.

2. Choose one of the report topics you suggested. Identify at least three articles that you think would provide information about the topic. Write the article titles. For encyclopedia articles, list the encyclopedia, the volume number, and page numbers. For magazine articles, list the magazine title, volume number, date, and page numbers.

Developing Skills in Speaking and Listening

Reading a Dialogue. Select one of the following passages. Then work with one or two partners. Prepare to read the dialogue aloud. Adjust your speed of reading to sound like a natural conversation. Try to express the characters' feelings through your voices.

1. Laurie tells his mother about his first day at school. (page 72)

2. Laurie talks with his mother about his second day of school. (pages 72–73)

3. Laurie tells his parents about Charles staying after school. (page 73)

4. Laurie tells his parents about the visitor who does exercises. (pages 73–74)

5. Laurie tells his father about the girl who says a bad word. (page 75)

Developing Writing Skills

Changing the Point of View. In the story "Charles," the narrator is Laurie's mother. She cannot reveal anything about the teacher's thoughts or Laurie's thoughts. Select one of these two characters. In two or three paragraphs, retell part of the story from his or her point of view.

Prewriting. Select one event from the story, such as the P.T.A. meeting or Charles's kicking the teacher's friend. Decide which character will describe the event, Laurie or his teacher, and whether to use first-person or third-person limited point of view. Jot down what happens in that part of the story. Add the thoughts of the character you chose. Do not list other characters' thoughts.

Drafting. Retell the incident. Limit your retelling to two or three paragraphs. Present the thoughts of the character you selected.

Revising and Sharing. Ask another person to read your paragraphs. Can the person identify the point of view in your story? If not, rewrite your paragraphs.

Thank You, M'am

LANGSTON HUGHES

This story opens at the scene of a crime. Do you think the victim does the right thing? As you read, think about how you would react in this situation.

She was a large woman with a large purse that had everything in it but hammer and nails. It had a long strap, and she carried it slung across her shoulder. It was about eleven o'clock at night, and she was walking alone, when a boy ran up behind her and tried to snatch her purse. The strap broke with the single tug the boy gave it from behind. But the boy's weight and the weight of the purse combined caused him to lose his balance, so instead of taking off full blast as he had hoped, the boy fell on his back on the sidewalk and his legs flew up. The large woman simply turned around and kicked him right square in his blue-jeaned sitter. Then she reached down, picked the boy up by his shirt front, and shook him until his teeth rattled.

After that the woman said, "Pick up my pocketbook, boy, and give it here."

She still held him. But she bent down enough to permit him to stoop and pick up her purse. Then she said, "Now, ain't you ashamed of yourself?"

Firmly gripped by his shirt front, the boy said, "Yes'm."

The woman said, "What did you want to do it for?"

The boy said, "I didn't aim to."

She said, "You a lie!"

By that time two or three people passed, stopped, turned to look, and some stood watching.

"If I turn you loose, will you run?" asked the woman.

"Yes'm," said the boy.

"Then I won't turn you loose," said the woman. She did not release him.

"I'm very sorry, Lady, I'm sorry," whispered the boy.

"Um-hum! And your face is dirty. I got a great mind to wash your face for you. Ain't you got nobody home to tell you to wash your face?"

"No'm," said the boy.

"Then it will get washed this evening," said the large woman, starting up the street, dragging the frightened boy behind her.

He looked as if he were fourteen or fifteen, frail and willow-wild, in tennis shoes and blue jeans.

The woman said, "You ought to be my son. I would teach you right from wrong. Least I can do right now is to wash your face. Are you hungry?"

"No'm," said the being-dragged boy. "I just want you to turn me loose."

"Was I bothering *you* when I turned that corner?" asked the woman.

"No'm."

"But you put yourself in contact with *me*," said the woman. "If you think that that contact is not going to last awhile, you got another thought coming. When I get through with you, sir, you are going to remember Mrs. Luella Bates Washington Jones."

Sweat popped out on the boy's face, and he began to struggle. Mrs. Jones stopped, jerked him around in front of her, put a half nelson about his neck, and continued to drag him up the street. When she got to her door, she dragged the boy inside, down a hall, and into a large kitchenette-furnished room at the rear of the house. She switched on the light and left the door open. The boy could hear other roomers laughing and talking in the large house. Some of their doors were open, too, so he knew that he and the woman were not alone. The woman still had him by the neck in the middle of her room.

She said, "What is your name?"

"Roger," answered the boy.

"Then, Roger, you go to that sink and wash your face," said the woman, whereupon she turned him loose—at last. Roger looked at the door—looked at the woman—looked at the door—*and went to the sink.*

"Let the water run until it gets warm," she said. "Here's a clean towel."

"You gonna take me to jail?" asked the boy, bending over the sink.

"Not with that face; I would not take you nowhere," said the woman. "Here I am trying to get home to cook me a bite to eat, and you snatch my pocketbook! Maybe you ain't been to your supper either, late as it be. Have you?"

"There's nobody home at my house," said the boy.

"Then we'll eat," said the woman. "I believe you're hungry—or been hungry—to try to snatch my pocketbook!"

"I want a pair of blue suede shoes," said the boy.

"Well, you didn't have to snatch my pocketbook to get some suede shoes," said Mrs. Luella Bates Washington Jones. "You could of asked me."

"M'am?"

The water dripping from his face, the boy looked at her. There was a long pause. A very long pause. After he had dried his face, and, not knowing what else to do, dried it again, the boy turned around, wondering what next. The door was open. He could make a dash for it down the hall. He could run, run, run, run, *run!*

The woman was sitting on the day bed. After a while she said, "I were young once and I wanted things I could not get."

There was another long pause. The boy's mouth opened. Then he frowned, but not knowing he frowned.

The woman said, "Um-hum! You thought I was going to say 'but,' didn't you? You thought I was going to say, 'but I didn't snatch people's pocketbooks.' Well, I wasn't going to say that." Pause. Silence.

"I have done things, too, which I would not tell you, son—neither tell God, if He didn't already know. So you set down while I fix us something to eat. You might run that comb through your hair so you will look presentable."

Black Manhattan, 1969, ROMARE BEARDEN. Collection of Mr. and Mrs. Theodore Kheel, New York City.

In another corner of the room, behind a screen, was a gas plate and an icebox. Mrs. Jones got up and went behind the screen. The woman did not watch the boy to see if he was going to run now, nor did she watch her purse, which she left behind her on the day bed. But the boy took care to sit on the far side of the room, where he thought she could easily see him out of the corner of her eye if she wanted to. He did not trust the woman *not* to trust him. And he did not want to be mistrusted now.

"Do you need somebody to go to the store," asked the boy, "maybe to get some milk or something?"

"Don't believe I do," said the woman, "unless you just want sweet milk yourself. I was going to make cocoa out of this canned milk I got here."

"That will be fine," said the boy.

She heated some lima beans and ham she had in the icebox, made the cocoa, and set the table. The woman did not ask the boy anything about where he lived, or his folks, or anything else that would embarrass him. Instead, as they ate, she told him about her job in a hotel beauty shop that stayed open late, what the work was like, and how all kinds of women came in and out, blondes, redheads, and Spanish. Then she cut him a half of her ten-cent cake.

"Eat some more, son," she said.

When they were finished eating, she got up and said, "Now here, take this ten dollars and buy yourself some blue suede shoes. And next time, do not make the mistake of latching onto *my* pocketbook *nor nobody else's*—because shoes come by devilish ways will burn your feet. I got to get my rest now. But I wish you would behave yourself, son, from here on in."

She led him down the hall to the front door and opened it. "Good night! Behave yourself, boy!" she said, looking out into the street.

The boy wanted to say something other than, "Thank you, m'am," to Mrs. Luella Bates Washington Jones; but he couldn't do so as he turned at the barren stoop and looked back at the large woman in the door. He barely managed to say, "Thank you" before she shut the door. And he never saw her again.

Langston Hughes *(1902–1967)* was a playwright, poet, lecturer, and songwriter as well as a writer of novels and short stories. He held many other jobs before he achieved recognition for his writing talent. Hughes based much of his writing on his varied experiences, including his travels in Africa. Many of his works reflect the speech patterns and jazz rhythms Hughes heard on the streets of Harlem in New York City. His first collection of poems was called *Weary Blues*. The poems deal with racial prejudice and the struggle for equality.

Developing Comprehension Skills

1. At the beginning of the story, what keeps Roger from stealing Mrs. Jones's purse?

2. Mrs. Jones tells Roger, "When I get through with you, sir, you are going to remember Mrs. Luella Bates Washington Jones." While you were reading the story for the first time, what did you think Mrs. Jones would do to make Roger remember her? What does she actually do to make him remember her?

3. Roger seems frightened of Mrs. Jones at first. What does she tell him in her apartment that changes his fright to surprise?

4. Mrs. Jones doesn't lecture Roger about stealing. Instead, she tells him, "I have done things, too, which I would not tell you, son—" What can you infer about Mrs. Jones's past from that statement?

5. After Roger leaves her apartment, what opinion do you think he has of Mrs. Jones?

Give evidence from the story to support your answer.

6. Do you think Roger will ever try to steal again? Why or why not?

Reading Literature: Short Stories

1. **Analyzing a Character.** Think about the character of Mrs. Jones. Someone has just tried to steal her purse. Does she act the way you would expect? What does her insistence that Roger wash his face, comb his hair, and eat tell you about her? Based on her actions and her words, describe what type of person Mrs. Jones is. Use evidence from the story to support your statements.

2. **Identifying Conflict.** The plot of any story develops because of a conflict. Conflict may be external, between two or more characters, or internal, within the character. What is the external conflict in this story? Which character experiences an internal conflict?

Explain what opposing impulses that character has.

3. **Exposition.** In a story, the **exposition** is the part that gives background information and introduces the characters. In "Thank You, M'am," the exposition is in the first paragraph. What does the exposition tell about the setting of the story? about the characters? What conflict is introduced?

4. **Examining Setting.** Reread the description of Mrs. Jones's city apartment. What is her apartment like? What does it reveal about her economic level? How does that affect Roger's reaction to her generosity?

5. **Understanding Theme.** In this story Mrs. Jones reacts to a violent act with understanding, trust, and generosity. What effect does her attitude have on Roger? What do you think the writer is saying about the way someone might help a young person in trouble?

Developing Vocabulary Skills

Using Context Clues. The underlined words in the sentences below come from the story. Use context clues to determine the meaning of each word. For each underlined word, write its definition and tell the kind of context clue you used: restatement or definition, synonym, antonym, comparison, contrast, or example clues.

1. Roger suspected that Mrs. Jones did not trust him. And he did not want to be <u>mistrusted</u> now.

2. She told him how to look more <u>presentable</u>, suggesting that he wash his face and comb his hair.

3. Mrs. Jones led him to the <u>stoop</u>, or small porch at the front of the house.

4. At this time of day, the street is <u>barren</u>, not crowded and busy as it is during the afternoon.

5. Roger was <u>frail</u> and willow-wild. Because he was so thin, he looked younger than he was.

Developing Skills in Study and Research

Outlining Elements of a Story. Outlining is a good way of organizing information. The following formal outline clearly shows main topics, subtopics, and details. Notice how numerals and letters are used. Notice how the different parts are indented.

Title

  I. Main topic
    A. Subtopic
      1. Detail relating to A
      2. Detail relating to A
    B. Subtopic
 II. Main topic

What follows is an outline with main topics of Setting and Main Characters for the story "Thank You, M'am." Copy the outline on a sheet of paper and fill in the subtopics. Then complete the outline by listing at least two details under one or more subtopics.

  I. Setting
    A.
    B.
    C.
 II. Main Characters
    A.
    B.

Developing Writing Skills

Explaining an Opinion. Think about the way Mrs. Jones treats Roger. Do you think she does the right thing, or do you think Roger should have been punished? Do Mrs. Jones's actions make Roger more or less likely to try to steal again? Write one paragraph defending your opinion of Mrs. Jones's actions. Follow these steps.

Prewriting. After rereading the story, state your opinion of Mrs. Jones's actions. Then list reasons for your opinion. Look for any of Roger's reactions that might support one of your reasons. Write these reactions down. Make a note of quotations from the story that support your opinion. Finally, organize your ideas in a logical order. Save your strongest reason for last.

Drafting. State your opinion as the topic sentence of your paragraph. Defend your opinion by giving reasons and supporting them with examples and quotations from the story. You may want to end your paragraph with a restatement of your opinion.

Revising and Sharing. Check the organization of your paragraph. Make sure that each of your reasons is supported. Ask someone to read your paragraph and point out any sentences that are unclear. Rewrite these sentences. You might share your opinion with the class by reading your paragraph aloud.

The Man Who Was a Horse

JULIUS LESTER

Have you ever really tried to think and feel as another person or an animal feels? In this story a cowboy named Bob becomes part of a mustang herd in order to capture it.

It wasn't noon yet, but the sun had already made the Texas plains hotter than an oven. Bob Lemmons pulled his wide-brimmed hat tighter to his head and rode slowly away from the ranch.

"Good luck, Bob!" someone yelled.

Bob didn't respond. His mind was already on the weeks ahead. He walked his horse slowly, being in no particular hurry. That was one thing he had learned early. One didn't capture a herd of mustang horses in a hurry. For all he knew, a mustang stallion might have been watching him at that very moment, and if he were galloping, the stallion might get suspicious and take the herd miles away.

Bob looked around him, and as far as he could see the land was flat, stretching unbroken like the cloudless sky over his head until the two seemed to meet. Nothing appeared to be moving except him on his horse, but he knew that a herd of mustangs could be galloping near the horizon line at that moment and he would be unable to see it until it came much closer.

He rode north that day, seeing no sign of mustangs until close to evening, when he came across some tracks. He stopped and dismounted. For a long while he stared at the tracks until he was able to identify several of the horses. As far as he could determine, it seemed to be a small herd of a stallion, seven or eight mares, and a couple of colts. The tracks were no more than three days old, and he half expected to come in sight of the herd the next day or two. A herd didn't travel in a straight line, but ranged back and forth within what the stallion considered his territory. Of course, that could be the size of a county. But Bob knew he was in it, though he had not seen a horse.

He untied his blanket from behind the saddle and laid it out on the ground. Then he removed the saddle from the horse and hobbled the animal to a stake. He didn't want a mustang stallion coming by during the night and stealing his horse. Stallions were good at that. Many times he had known them to see a herd of tame horses and, for who knew what reason, become attracted to one mare and cut her out of the herd.

He took his supper out of the saddlebags and ate slowly as the chilly night air seemed to rise from the very plains that a few short hours before had been too hot for a man to walk on. He threw the blanket around his shoulders, wishing he could make a fire. But if he had the smell of wood-smoke in his clothes, he would have been detected by any herd he got close to.

After eating, he laid his head back against his saddle and covered himself with his thick Mexican blanket. The chilliness of the night made the stars look to him like shining slivers of ice. Someone had once told him that the stars were balls of fire like the sun, but Bob didn't feel them that way. But he wasn't educated, so he wouldn't dispute with anybody about it. Just because you gave something a name didn't mean that that was what it actually was, though. The thing didn't know it had that name, so it just kept on being what it thought it was. And as far as he was concerned, people would be better off if they tried to know a thing like it knew itself. That was the only way he could ever explain to somebody how he was able to bring in a herd of wild horses by himself. The way other people did it was to go out in groups of two and three and run a herd until it almost dropped from exhaustion. He guessed that was all right. It worked. But he couldn't do it that way. He knew he wouldn't want anybody running him to

John Stepp on Ole Paint, about 1923. Black American West Museum and Heritage Center, Denver, Paul W. Stewart Collection and the Stepp family.

and fro for days on end, until he hardly knew up from down or left from right.

Even while he was still a slave, he'd felt that way about mustangs. Other horses too. But he had never known anything except horses. Born and raised on a ranch, he had legally been a slave until 1865, when the slaves in Texas were freed. He had been eighteen at the time and hadn't understood when Mr. Hunter had come and told him that he was free. That was another one of those words, Bob thought. Even as a child, when his father told him he was a slave, he'd wondered what he meant. What did a slave look like? What did a slave feel like? He didn't think he had ever known. He and his parents had been the only black people on the ranch, and he guessed it wasn't until after he was "freed" that he saw another black person. He knew sometimes, from the names he heard the cowboys use, that his color somehow made him different. He heard them talking about "fighting a war over the black man," but it meant nothing to him. So when Mr. Hunter had told him he was free, that he could go wherever he wanted to, he nodded and got on his horse and went out to the range to see after the cattle like he was supposed to. He smiled to himself, wondering how Mr. Hunter had ever gotten the notion that he couldn't have gone where he wanted.

A few months after that he brought in his first herd of mustangs. He had been seeing the wild horses since he could remember. The first time had been at dusk one day. He had been playing near the corral when he happened to look toward the mesa and there, standing atop it, was a lone stallion. The wind blew against it and its mane and tail flowed in the breeze like tiny ribbons. The horse stood there for a long while; then, without warning, it suddenly wheeled and galloped away. Even now Bob remembered how seeing that horse had been like looking into a mirror. He'd never told anyone that, sensing that they would perhaps think him a little touched in the head. Many people thought it odd enough that he could bring in a herd of mustangs by himself. But after that, whenever he saw one mustang or a herd, he felt like he was looking at himself.

One day several of the cowboys went out to capture a herd. The ranch was short of horses, and no one ever thought of buying horses when there were so many wild ones. He had wanted to tell them that he would bring in the horses, but they would have laughed at him. Who'd ever heard of one man bringing in a herd? So he watched them ride out, saying nothing. A few days later they were back, tired and disgusted. They hadn't even been able to get close to a herd.

That evening Bob timidly suggested to Mr. Hunter that he be allowed to try. Everyone laughed. Bob reminded them that no one on the ranch could handle a horse like he could, that the horses came to him more than anyone else. The cowboys acknowledged that that was true, but it was impossible for one man to capture a herd. Bob said nothing else. Early the next morning he rode out alone, asking the cook to leave food in a saddlebag for him on the fence at the north pasture every day. Three weeks later the cowboys were sitting around the corral one evening and looked up to see a herd of mustangs galloping toward them, led by Bob. Despite their amazement, they moved quickly to open the gate and Bob led the horses in.

That had been some twenty years ago, and long after Bob left the Hunter Ranch, he found that everywhere he went he was known. He never had trouble getting a job, but capturing mustangs was only a small part of what he did. Basically he was just a cowboy who worked from sunrise to sunset building fences, herding cattle, branding calves, pitching hay, and doing everything else that needed to be done.

Most cowboys had married and settled down by the time they reached his age, but Bob had long ago relinquished any such dream. Once he'd been in love with a Mexican girl, but her father didn't want her to marry a black man. After that he decided not to be in love again. It wasn't a decision he'd ever regretted. Almost every morning when he got up and looked at the sky lying full and open and blue, stretching toward forever, he knew he was married to something. He wanted to say the sky, but it was more than that. He wanted to say everything, but he felt that it was more than that, too. How could there be more than everything? He didn't know, but there was.

The sun awakened him even before the first arc of its roundness showed over the horizon. He saddled his horse and rode off, following the tracks he had discovered the previous evening. He followed them west until he was certain they were leading him to the Pecos River. He smiled. Unless it was a herd traveling through, they would come to that river to drink every day. Mustangs never went too far from water, though they could go for days without a drop if necessary. The Pecos was still some distance ahead, but he felt his horse's body quiver slightly, and she began to strain forward against his tight hold on the reins. She smelled the water.

"Sorry, honey. But that water's not for

you," he told the horse. He wheeled around and galloped back in the direction of the ranch until he came to the outermost edge of what was called the west pasture. It was still some miles from the ranch house itself, and today Bob couldn't see any cattle grazing up there.

But on the fence rail enclosing the pasture was a saddlebag filled with food. Each day one of the cowboys would bring a saddlebag of food up there and leave it for him. He transferred the food to his own saddlebags. He was hungry but would wait until evening to eat. The food had to have time to lose its human odor, an odor that mustangs could pick out of the slightest breeze. He himself would not venture too close to the horses for another few days, not until he was certain that his own odor had become that of his horse.

He rode southward from the pasture to the banks of the Nueces River. There he dismounted, took the saddle off his horse, and let her drink her fill and wade in the stream for a while. It would be a few days before she could drink from the Pecos. The mustangs would have noticed the strange odor of horse and man together, and any good stallion would have led his mares and colts away. The success of catching mustangs, as far as Bob was concerned, was never to hurry. If necessary he would spend two weeks getting a herd accustomed to his distant presence once he was in sight of them.

He washed the dust from his face and filled his canteen. He lay down under a tree, but its shade didn't offer much relief from the heat of high noon. The day felt like it was on fire and Bob decided to stay where he was until the sun began its downward journey. He thought Texas was probably the hottest place in the world. He didn't know, not having traveled much. He had been to Oklahoma, Kansas, New Mexico, Arizona, and Wyoming on cattle drives. Of all the places, he liked Wyoming the most, because of the high mountains. He'd never seen anything so high. There were mountains in Texas, but nothing like that. Those mountains just went up and up and up until it seemed they would never stop. But they always did, with snow on the top. After a few days though he wasn't sure that he did like the mountains. Even now he wasn't sure. The mountains made him feel that he was penned in a corral, and he was used to spaces no smaller than the sky. Yet he remembered Wyoming with fondness and hoped that some year another cattle drive would take him there.

The heat had not abated much when Bob decided to go north again and pick up his trail. He would camp close to the spot where his mare had first smelled the Pecos. That was close enough for now.

In the days following, Bob moved closer to the river until one evening he saw the herd come streaming out of the hills, across the plain, and to the river. He was some distance away, but he could see the stallion lift his head and sniff the breeze. Bob waited. Although he couldn't know for sure, he could feel the stallion looking at

him, and for a tense moment Bob didn't know if the horse would turn and lead the herd away. But the stallion lowered his head and began to drink, and the other horses came down to the river. Bob sighed. He had been accepted.

The following day he crossed the river and picked up the herd's trail. It was not long after sunrise before he saw them grazing. He went no closer, wanting only to keep them in sight and, most important, make them feel his presence. He was glad to see that after a moment's hesitation, the stallion went back to grazing.

Bob felt sorry for the male horse. It always had to be on guard against dangers. If it relaxed for one minute, that just might be the minute a nearby panther would choose to strike, or another stallion would challenge him for the lead of the herd, or some cowboys would throw out their ropes. He wondered why a stallion wanted the responsibility. Even while the horses were grazing, Bob noticed that the stallion was separate, over to one side, keeping a constant lookout. He would tear a few mouthfuls of grass from the earth, then raise his head high, looking and smelling for danger.

At various times throughout the day Bob moved a few hundred yards closer. He could see it clearly now. The stallion was brown, the color of the earth. The mares and colts were black and brown. No sorrels or duns in this herd. They were a little smaller than his horse. But all mustangs were. Their size, though, had nothing to do with their strength or endurance. There was no doubt that they were the best horses. He, however, had never taken one from the many herds he had brought in. It wasn't that he wouldn't have liked one. He would have, but for him to have actually ridden one would have been like taking a piece of the sky and making a blanket. To ride with them when they were wild was all right. But he didn't think any man was really worthy of riding one, even though he brought them in for that purpose.

By the sixth day he had gotten close enough to the herd that his presence didn't attract notice. The following day he moved closer until he and his mare were in the herd itself. He galloped with the herd that day, across the plain, down to the river, up into the hills. He observed the stallion closely, noting that it was a good one. The best stallions led the herd from the rear. A mare always led from the front. But it was only at the rear that a stallion could guard the herd and keep a mare from running away. The stallion ran up and down alongside the herd, biting a slow mare on the rump or ramming another who threatened to run away or to bump a third. The stallion was king, Bob thought, but he worked. It didn't look like much fun.

He continued to run with the herd a few days more. Then came the crucial moment when, slowly, he would begin to give directions of his own, to challenge the stallion in little ways until he had completely taken command of the herd and driven the stallion off. At first he would simply lead the herd in the direction away from the one the stallion wanted to go, and just before the stallion became enraged, he would put it back on course. He did this many times, getting the stallion confused as to whether or not there was a challenger in his midst. But enough days of it and the stallion gradually wore down, knowing that something was happening but unable to understand what. When Bob was sure the herd was in his command, he merely drove the stallion away.

Now came the fun. For two weeks Bob led the herd. Unlike the stallion, he chose to lead from the front, liking the sound and feel of the wild horses so close behind. He led them to the river and watched happily as they splashed and rolled in the water. Like the stallion, however, he kept his eyes and ears alert for any sign of danger. Sometimes he would pretend he heard something when he hadn't and would lead the herd quickly away simply as a test of their responsiveness to him.

At night he stopped, unsaddled his horse, and laid out his blanket. The herd grazed around him. During all this time he never spoke a word to the horses, not knowing what effect the sound of a voice might have on them. Sometimes he wondered what his own voice sounded like and even wondered if after some period of inactivity, he would return to the ranch and find himself able only to snort and neigh, as these were the only sounds he heard. There were other sounds though, sounds that he couldn't reproduce, like the flaring nostrils of the horses when they were galloping, the dark, bulging eyes, the flesh quivering and shaking. He knew that he couldn't hear any of these things—not with his ears at least. But somewhere in his body he heard every ripple of muscles and bending of bones.

The longer he was with the herd, the less he thought. His mind slowly emptied itself of anything relating to his other life and refilled with sky, plain, grass, water, and shrubs. At these times he was more aware of the full-bodied animal beneath him. His own body seemed to take on a new life, and he was aware of the wind against his chest, of the taut muscles in his strong legs, and the strength of his muscles in his arms, which felt to him like the forelegs of his horses. The only thing he didn't feel he had was a tail to float in the wind behind him.

Finally, when he knew that the herd would follow him anywhere, it was time to take it in. It was a day he tried to keep away as long as possible. But even he began to tire of going back to the west pasture for food and sometimes having to chase a

Almost Home, 1966, JOE BEELER. Collection of the Artist.

horse that had tried to run away from the herd. He had also begun to weary of sleeping under a blanket on the ground every night. So one day, almost a month after he had left, he rode back toward the ranch until he saw one of the cowhands and told him to get the corral ready. Tomorrow he was bringing them in.

The following morning he led the herd on what he imagined was the ride of their lives. Mustangs were made to run. All of his most vivid memories were of mustangs, and he remembered the day he had seen a herd of what must have been at least a thousand of them galloping across the plains. The earth was a dark ripple of movement, like the swollen Nueces at floodtime. And though his herd was much smaller, they ran no less beautifully that day.

Then, toward evening, Bob led them east, galloping, galloping, across the plains. And as he led them toward the corral, he knew that no one could ever know these horses by riding on them. One had to ride with them, feeling their hooves pound and shake the earth, their bodies glistening so close by that you could see the thin straight hairs of their shining coats. He led them past the west pasture, down the slope, and just before the corral gate, he swerved to one side, letting the horses thunder inside. The cowboys leaped and shouted, but Bob didn't stay to hear their congratulations. He slowed his mare to a trot and then to a walk to cool her off. It was after dark when he returned to the ranch.

He took his horse to the stable, brushed her down, and put her in a stall for a well-earned meal of hay. Then he walked over to the corral, where the mustangs milled restlessly. He sat on the rail for a long while, looking at them. They were only horses now. Just as he was only a man.

After a while he climbed down from the fence and went into the bunkhouse to go to sleep.

Julius Lester (*born 1939*) writes about the heritage of black Americans. His folk tale collections, *Black Folktales* and *The Knee-High Man,* include stories based on black American folklore and on black history. He has most recently published *The Tales of Uncle Remus: The Adventures of Brer Rabbit,* a retelling of the Uncle Remus tales that includes the trickster Brer Rabbit among other memorable characters. In his nonfiction work, *The Long Journey Home,* Lester presents a collection of slave narratives, stories of the experiences of American slaves. A professional musician as well as a writer, Lester has coauthored a book titled *The 12-String Guitar as Played by Leadbelly.* Lester was born in St. Louis and attended Fisk University.

Developing Comprehension Skills

1. Bob Lemmons has never been to school. In what way is he educated? How does his way of thinking differ from an educated person's?

2. What is Bob's plan for catching the mustangs? How does it differ from the way other people caught mustangs?

3. How does Bob take control of the herd away from the stallion? In what ways does he become like a horse?

4. How does Bob feel about capturing the wild mustangs for cowboys to ride? Give evidence from the story to support your answer.

5. For Bob, mustangs are the best horses, but he doesn't ride one himself. He thinks that "for him to have actually ridden one would have been like taking a piece of the sky and making a blanket." From this quotation, what can you infer about Bob's attitude toward the mustangs?

6. If you were Bob, would you capture the wild things that you love? Explain why or why not.

Reading Literature: Short Stories

1. **Understanding Conflict.** The conflict in this story is external. What does Bob struggle against? Who wins the struggle?

2. **Recognizing Flashback.** A **flashback** is an incident or conversation that happened before the beginning of a story. "The Man Who Was a Horse" begins one morning as Bob Lemmons is searching for a mustang herd. Reread the flashback beginning in the ninth paragraph with "Even while he was still a slave . . ." and ending in the fourteenth paragraph. What information does the flashback give you about Bob's boyhood? Does being freed from slavery change Bob's life? Explain your answer. How does Bob come to chase his first mustang herd?

3. **Understanding Characterization.** The methods of characterization available to a writer are as follows: describing a character directly, presenting a character's words or actions, revealing a character's feelings and thoughts, and showing other characters' reactions. The following passages from the story show some of these methods of characterization. Some include more than one method. What method or methods of characterization are used in each passage? What can you infer about Bob's character from each?

   a. He walked his horse slowly, being in no particular hurry. That was one thing he had learned early. One didn't capture a herd of mustang horses in a hurry.

   b. As far as he was concerned, people would be better off if they tried to know a thing like it knew itself.

   c. Almost every morning when he got up and looked at the sky lying full and open and blue, stretching toward forever, he knew he was married to something.

   d. That evening Bob timidly suggested to Mr. Hunter that he be allowed to try [to bring in the herd]. Everyone laughed. Bob reminded them that no one on the ranch could handle a horse like he could.

   e. Bob felt sorry for the male horse. It always had to be on guard against dangers. . . . He wondered why a stallion wanted the responsibility.

   f. The cowboys leaped and shouted, but Bob didn't stay to hear their congratulations.

4. **Examining Setting.** A story's **setting** is when and where the action takes place. Setting is important to this story because the plot could not occur in another location and the main character is closely involved with his surroundings. When and where does the story take place? Describe the weather and the terrain. How do these aspects of setting affect Bob Lemmons?

5. **Identifying Point of View.** This story is told from the third-person point of view. In this type of narration, the narrator uses *he* and *they,* instead of *I.* In this story the third-person narrator knows the main character's thoughts and feelings. Find three sentences in the story that show the narrator knows what Bob is thinking.

Developing Vocabulary Skills

Determining Meaning from General Context. When no specific context clue points to the meaning of an unfamiliar word, use the general context, or the surrounding sentences, to help you.

Read the following excerpts from the story. Write your understanding of <u>hobbled</u> and <u>dispute</u>. Then use each word in a sentence.

1. Then he removed the saddle from the horse and <u>hobbled</u> the animal to a stake. He didn't want a mustang stallion coming by during the night and stealing his horse. Stallions were good at that.

2. Someone had once told him that the stars were balls of fire, like the sun, but Bob didn't feel them that way. But he wasn't educated, so he wouldn't <u>dispute</u> with anybody about it. Just because you gave something a name didn't mean that that was what it actually was, though.

Developing Skills in Study and Research

Using the Card Catalog. Bob Lemmons is a black cowboy in fiction. The West had black cowboys in fact too. Use the card catalog to locate a book with information about black cowboys. You might try looking up *Black People Who Made the Old West* by William Katz (Harper & Row, 1977). Read about one of these black cowboys, and tell three ways his life is similar to Bob's.

Developing Writing Skills

Writing a Description. This story contains a great deal of information about stallions. From this information, write a one-paragraph description of a stallion. Try to make it so vivid and real that a reader could picture the stallion.

Prewriting. Reread the passages about mustangs, and stallions in particular. List the questions you need to answer in order to describe a stallion well. They might include these:

How big is a stallion?
What does a stallion do in a herd?
What kinds of noises does a stallion make?
What are a stallion's habits?

When you find details in the story that answer these questions, write them down. After you have enough information about stallions, decide how to arrange the details for your description. You might describe first the horse's appearance and then its actions. Or you might describe the horse from front to back. Make an outline to organize your description.

Drafting. Write a general statement to introduce the stallion you will describe. Then, following your outline and prewriting notes, describe what the stallion looks like and how it acts. Include words and phrases that appeal to different senses. Use specific, vivid details.

Revising and Sharing. Read over your description, taking out parts that are vague or dull and adding more vivid details. Search for precise words to describe the stallion. You might read your description to someone and ask if the person can picture a stallion.

Lather and Nothing Else

HERNANDO TÉLLEZ

Imagine that the person destroying your country is suddenly in your power. What would you do? As you read this story, try to predict what the narrator will do to his enemy.

He came in without a word. I was stropping my best razor. And when I recognized him, I started to shake. But he did not notice. To cover my nervousness, I went on honing the razor. I tried the edge with the tip of my thumb and took another look at it against the light.

Meanwhile he was taking off his cartridge-studded belt with the pistol holster suspended from it. He put it on a hook in the wardrobe and hung his cap above it. Then he turned full around toward me and, loosening his tie, remarked, "It's hot as the devil. I want a shave." With that he took his seat.

I estimated he had a four-days' growth of beard, the four days he had been gone on the last foray after our men. His face looked burnt, tanned by the sun.

I started to work carefully on the shaving soap. I scraped some slices from the cake, dropped them into the mug, then added a little lukewarm water, and stirred with the brush. The lather soon began to rise.

"The fellows in the troop must have just about as much beard as I." I went on stirring up lather. "But we did very well, you know. We caught the leaders. Some of them we brought back dead; others are still alive. But they'll all be dead soon."

"How many did you take?" I asked.

"Fourteen. We had to go pretty far in to find them. But now they're paying for it. And not one will escape; not a single one."

He leaned back in the chair when he saw the brush in my hand, full of lather. I had not yet put the sheet on him. I was certainly flustered. Taking a sheet from the drawer, I tied it around my customer's neck.

He went on talking. He evidently took it for granted that I was on the side of the existing regime.

"The people must have gotten a scare with what happened the other day," he said.

"Yes," I replied, as I finished tying the knot against his nape, which smelt of sweat.

"Good show, wasn't it?"

"Very good," I answered, turning my attention now to the brush. The man closed his eyes wearily and awaited the cool caress of the lather.

I had never had him so close before. The day he ordered the people to file through the schoolyard to look upon the four rebels hanging there, my path had crossed his briefly. But the sight of those mutilated bodies kept me from paying attention to the face of the man who had been directing it all and whom I now had in my hands.

It was not a disagreeable face, certainly. And the beard, which aged him a bit, was not unbecoming. His name was Torres. Captain Torres.

I started to lay on the first coat of lather. He kept his eyes closed.

"I would love to catch a nap," he said, "but there's a lot to be done this evening."

I lifted the brush and asked, with pretended indifference: "A firing party?"

"Something of the sort," he replied, "but slower."

"All of them?"

"No, just a few."

I went on lathering his face. My hands began to tremble again. The man could not be aware of this, which was lucky for me. But I wished he had not come in. Probably many of our men had seen him enter the shop. And with the enemy in my house I felt a certain responsibility.

I would have to shave his beard just like any other, carefully, neatly, just as though he were a good customer, taking heed that not a single pore should emit a drop of blood. Seeing to it that the blade did not slip in the small whorls. Taking care that the skin was left clean, soft, shining, so that when I passed the back of my hand over it not a single hair should be felt. Yes. I was secretly a revolutionary, but at the same time I was a conscientious barber, proud of the way I did my job. And that four-day beard presented a challenge.

I took up the razor, opened the handle wide, releasing the blade, and started to work, downward from one sideburn. The blade responded to perfection. The hair was tough and hard; not very long, but thick. Little by little the skin began to show through. The razor gave its usual sound as it gathered up layers of soap mixed with bits of hair. I paused to wipe it clean, and taking up the strop once more went about improving its edge, for I am a painstaking barber.

The man, who had kept his eyes closed, now opened them, put a hand out from under the sheet, felt of the part of his face that was emerging from the lather, and said to me, "Come at six o'clock this evening to the school."

"Will it be like the other day?" I asked, stiff with horror.

"It may be even better," he replied.

"What are you planning to do?"

"I'm not sure yet. But we'll have a good time."

Once more he leaned back and shut his eyes. I came closer, the razor on high.

"Are you going to punish all of them?"

Barilleros, San Felipe, 1780, THEODORE GENTILZ. Collection of Larry Sheerin, San Antonio, Texas.

I timidly ventured.

"Yes, all of them."

The lather was drying on his face. I must hurry. Through the mirror, I took a look at the street. It appeared about as usual; there was the grocery shop with two or three customers. Then I glanced at the clock, two-thirty.

The razor kept descending. Now from the other sideburn downward. It was a blue beard, a thick one. He should let it grow like some poets, or some priests. It would suit him well. Many people would not rec-

ognize him. And that would be a good thing for him, I thought, as I went gently over all the throat line. At this point you really had to handle your blade skillfully, because the hair, while scantier, tended to fall into small whorls. It was a curly beard. The pores might open, minutely, in this area and let out a tiny drop of blood. A good barber like myself stakes his reputation on not permitting that to happen to any of his customers.

And this was indeed a special customer. How many of ours had he sent to their death? How many had he mutilated? It was best not to think about it. Torres did not know I was his enemy. Neither he nor the others knew it. It was a secret shared by very few, just because that made it possible for me to inform the revolutionaries about Torres's activities in the town and what he planned to do every time he went on one of his raids to hunt down rebels. So it was going to be very difficult to explain how it was that I had him in my hands and then let him go in peace, alive, clean-shaven.

His beard had now almost entirely disappeared. He looked younger, several years younger than when he had come in. I suppose that always happens to men who enter and leave barbershops. Under the strokes of my razor Torres was rejuvenated; yes, because I am a good barber, the best in this town, and I say this in all modesty.

A little more lather under here the chin, on the Adam's apple, right near the great vein. How hot it is! Torres must be sweating just as I am. But he is not afraid. He is a tranquil man, who is not even giving thought to what he will do to his prisoners this evening. I, on the other hand, polishing his skin with this razor but avoiding the drawing of blood, careful with every stroke—I cannot keep my thoughts in order.

Confound the hour he entered my shop! I am a revolutionary but not a murderer. And it would be so easy to kill him. He deserves it. Or does he? No! No one deserves the sacrifice others make in becoming assassins. What is to be gained by it?

Nothing. Others and still others keep coming, and the first kill the second, and then these kill the next, and so on until everything becomes a sea of blood. I could cut his throat, so, swish, swish! He would not even have time to moan, and with his eyes shut he would not even see the shine of the razor or the gleam in my eye.

But I'm shaking like a regular murderer. From his throat a stream of blood would flow on the sheet, over the chair, down on my hands, onto the floor. I would have to close the door. But the blood would go flowing, along the floor, warm, indelible, not to be staunched, until it reached the street like a small scarlet river.

I'm sure that with a good strong blow, a deep cut, he would feel no pain. He would not suffer at all. And what would I do then with the body? Where would I hide it? I would have to flee, leave all this behind, take shelter far away, very far away. But they would follow until they caught up with me. "The murderer of Captain Torres. He slit his throat while he was shaving him. What a cowardly thing to do!"

And others would say, "The avenger of our people. A name to remember"—my name here. "He was the town barber. No one knew he was fighting for our cause."

And so, which will it be? Murderer or hero? My fate hangs on the edge of this razor blade. I can turn my wrist slightly, put a bit more pressure on the blade, let it sink in. The skin will yield like silk, like rubber, like the strop. There is nothing more tender than a man's skin, and the blood is always there, ready to burst forth. A razor like this cannot fail. It is the best one I have.

But I don't want to be a murderer. No, sir. You came in to be shaved. And I do my work honorably. I don't want to stain my hands with blood. Just with lather, and nothing else. You are an executioner; I am only a barber. Each one to his job. That's it. Each one to his job.

The chin was now clean, polished, soft. The man got up and looked at himself in the glass. He ran his hand over the skin and felt its freshness, its newness.

"Thanks," he said. He walked to the wardrobe for his belt, his pistol, and his cap. I must have been very pale, and I felt my shirt soaked with sweat. Torres finished adjusting his belt buckle, straightened his gun in its holster, and smoothing his hair mechanically, put on his cap. From his trousers pocket he took some coins to pay for the shave. And he started toward the door. On the threshold he stopped for a moment, and turning toward me, he said,

"They told me you would kill me. I came to find out if it was true. But it's not easy to kill. I know what I'm talking about."

Hernando Téllez *(born 1908)* is a Colombian diplomat and senator, as well as a writer. He has written newspaper articles about social and political matters in South America. Téllez also writes short stories. A well-known collection of his works, *Ashes for the Wind and Other Tales,* reveals his love of justice and sympathy for the underprivileged.

Developing Comprehension Skills

1. Is the barber on the side of the existing regime, or is he on the side of the revolutionaries? On which side is Torres?

2. What does Torres have planned for the people who have been captured?

3. Why is the barber nervous and sweating while he shaves his customer?

4. Why does the barber decide against killing Torres?

5. Do you think the barber makes the right decision? Give reasons for your answer.

6. At the end of the story, what does Torres say was his reason for going into the barber's shop?

Reading Literature: Short Stories

1. **Identifying Conflict.** Torres and the barber are on opposite sides in a political struggle for power. However, the main conflict in the story is not this external one. It is an internal conflict, within the barber. What opposing sides of his character are in conflict? How do these two sides tug him in different directions?

2. **Understanding a Title.** The title of the story comes from this passage in the story: "I don't want to stain my hands with blood. Just lather and nothing else." What does the title emphasize about the barber? How does the title foreshadow the outcome of the story?

3. **Recognizing Descriptive Details.** The writer uses vivid description in this story. For example, he gives clear descriptions of the shaving process. The descriptions are so detailed that the reader can almost see and feel the shave. Find three passages that are highly descriptive. In each passage, which details are most vivid? What effect do these details have?

4. **Understanding a Surprise Ending.** A **surprise ending** is an unexpected twist in the plot at the end of a story. What is the surprise ending in this story? What does Torres's statement at the end of the story show about his character?

Developing Vocabulary Skills

Using Series Clues. Sometimes a word that is unfamiliar to you is listed in a series along with words that you already know. This series can then give you a clue to the new word's meaning.

Each of the following sentences contains an underlined word from "Lather and Nothing Else." Figure out the meaning of the underlined word, using a series clue or one of the other kinds of context clues you have learned. Then write the word and its definition on a sheet of paper.

1. Before he sat down, Torres put his holster, pistol, and cartridges in the wardrobe.

2. Many people in the town thought Torres was an executioner and a murderer.

3. The barber used the razor, the strop, the brush, and the mug of lather.

4. He shaved the captain's cheeks, chin, and nape.

Developing Skills in Speaking and Listening

Recognizing Nonverbal Communication. **Nonverbal communication** refers to the mo-tions and facial expressions that suggest ideas and feelings. For example, a shrug of the shoulders indicates that a person doesn't know something or doesn't care. A twinkle in a person's eyes might indicate excitement. Wrinkling the nose can be a sign of dislike. In this story the trembling of the barber's hands indicates that he is nervous.

For the next few days, observe other people's gestures and facial expressions. Make a list of the ways you notice people communicating without words.

Developing Writing Skills

1. **Changing Point of View.** This story is told from the first-person point of view. The narrator is the barber, and he tells only his own feelings. Retell the story from the point of view of Torres.

   Prewriting. List everything you know about Torres from the story. Include details about how he acts in the barbershop, what he thinks about the revolutionaries, and what he does to his enemies. Consider what Torres thinks about the barber. Torres knows that the barber is an enemy. How does this affect the way Torres acts in the barbershop? Does Torres look down on the barber? Or does he respect him? Why does Torres go to this barbershop? What does Torres guess is going on in the barber's mind from his observation of the barber's actions? Create details to describe how the shave feels. Organize your details and events in time order.

   Drafting. Using the pronoun *I*, have Torres narrate the events. Be sure to include Torres's thoughts, along with details about what Torres sees, feels, and hears. Do not include the thoughts of the barber.

   Revising and Sharing. Read through your story. Remember that Torres is the narrator, so if you find the name *Torres*, rewrite the sentence. You should find references to the barber. If not, add sentences to identify the barber. Be sure your version of the story makes Torres's thoughts clear. Think of a title for your story.

2. **Developing an Argument.** Do you think the barber is a hero or a traitor? Write a paragraph stating your opinion. Be sure to explain your reasons. During prewriting, gather specific examples and quotations from the story to support your opinion. While drafting, state your opinion followed by your reasons and supporting examples. Then revise your writing and share it with a classmate. For further help, refer to Guidelines for the Process of Writing beginning on page 654 in the handbook.

Raymond's Run

TONI CADE BAMBARA

Listen as Squeaky tells her story. What kind of person is she? As you read, look for qualities she reveals about herself.

I don't have much work to do around the house like some girls. My mother does that. And I don't have to earn my pocket money by hustling; George runs errands for the big boys and sells Christmas cards. And anything else that's got to get done, my father does. All I have to do in life is mind my brother Raymond, which is enough.

Sometimes I slip and say my little brother Raymond. But as any fool can see, he's much bigger and he's older too. But a lot of people call him my little brother cause he needs looking after cause he's not quite right. And a lot of smart mouths got lots to say about that too, especially when George was minding him. But now, if anybody has anything to say to Raymond, anything to say about his big head,[1] they have to come by me. And I don't play the dozens[2] or believe in standing around with somebody in my face doing a lot of talking. I much rather just knock you down and take my chances, even if I am a little girl with skinny arms and a squeaky voice, which is how I got the name Squeaky. And if things get too rough, I run. And as anybody can tell you, I'm the fastest thing on two feet.

There is no track meet that I don't win the first-place medal. I used to win the twenty-yard dash when I was a little kid in kindergarten. Nowadays, it's the fifty-yard dash. And tomorrow I'm subject to run the quarter-meter relay all by myself and come in first, second, and third. The big kids call me Mercury[3] cause I'm the swiftest thing in the neighborhood. Everybody knows that—except two people who know better, my father and me. He can beat me to Amsterdam Avenue with me having a two fire-hydrant headstart and him running with his hands in his pockets and whistling. But

1. **big head**—A symptom of Raymond's physical condition, hydrocephalus (hi′ drə sef′ ə ləs), which causes fluid to accumulate in the skull, resulting in an enlargement of the head.
2. **play the dozens**—To trade insults in a joking way.
3. **Mercury**—Roman name for the Greek god Hermes, the messenger god noted for his swiftness.

that's private information. Cause can you imagine some thirty-five-year-old man stuffing himself into shorts to race little kids? So far as everyone's concerned, I'm the fastest and that goes for Gretchen, too, who has put out the tale that she is going to win the first-place medal this year. Ridiculous. In the second place, she's got short legs. In the third place, she's got freckles. In the first place, no one can beat me, and that's all there is to it.

I'm standing on the corner admiring the weather and about to take a stroll down Broadway so I can practice my breathing exercises, and I've got Raymond walking on the inside close to the buildings, cause he's subject to fits of fantasy and starts thinking he's a circus performer and that the curb is a tightrope strung high in the air. And sometimes after a rain he likes to step down off his tightrope right into the gutter and slosh around, getting his shoes and cuffs wet. Then I get hit when I get home. Or sometimes if you don't watch him, he'll dash across traffic to the island in the middle of Broadway and give the pigeons a fit. Then I have to go behind him, apologizing to all the old people sitting around trying to get some sun and getting all upset with the pigeons fluttering around them, scattering their newspapers and upsetting the waxpaper lunches in their laps. So I keep Raymond on the inside of me, and he plays like he's driving a stage coach, which is OK by me so long as he doesn't run me over or interrupt my breathing exercises, which I have to do on account of I'm serious about my running, and I don't care who knows it.

Now some people like to act like things come easy to them, won't let on that they practice. Not me. I'll high-prance down 34th Street like a rodeo pony to keep my knees strong, even if it does get my mother uptight so that she walks ahead like she's not with me, don't know me, is all by herself on a shopping trip, and I am somebody else's crazy child. Now you take Cynthia Procter for instance. She's just the opposite. If there's a test tomorrow, she'll say something like, "Oh, I guess I'll play handball this afternoon and watch television tonight," just to let you know she ain't thinking about the test. Or like last week when she won the spelling bee for the millionth time, "A good thing you got *receive,* Squeaky, cause I would have got it wrong. I completely forgot about the spelling bee." And she'll clutch the lace on her blouse like it was a narrow escape. Oh, brother. But of course, when I pass her house on my early morning trots around the block, she is practicing the scales on the piano over and over and over and over. Then in music class she always lets herself get bumped around so she falls accidentally on purpose onto the piano stool and is so surprised to find herself sitting there that she decides just for fun to try out the ole keys. And what do you know—Chopin's waltzes just spring out of her fingertips, and she's the most surprised thing in the world. A regular prodigy. I could kill people like that. I stay up all night studying the words for the spelling bee. And you can see me any time of day practicing running. I never walk if I can trot, and shame on Raymond if he can't keep up. But of course he does, cause if he hangs back, someone's liable to walk up to him and get smart, or take his allowance from him, or ask him where he got that great big pumpkin head. People are so stupid sometimes.

So I'm strolling down Broadway breathing out and breathing in on counts of seven, which is my lucky number, and here comes Gretchen and her sidekicks: Mary Louise, who used to be a friend of mine

Sunny Side of the Street, 1950, PHILIP EVERGOOD. Collection of the Corcoran Gallery of Art, Washington, D.C., Museum Purchase, Anna E. Clark Fund.

when she first moved to Harlem from Baltimore and got beat up by everybody till I took up for her, on account of her mother and my mother used to sing in the same choir when they were young girls, but people ain't grateful, so now she hangs out with the new girl Gretchen and talks about me like a dog; and Rosie, who is as fat as I am skinny and has a big mouth where Raymond is concerned and is too stupid to know that there is not a big deal of difference between herself and Raymond and that she can't afford to throw stones. So they are steady coming up Broadway, and I see right away that it's going to be one of those Dodge City scenes cause the street ain't that big and they're close to the buildings, just as we are. First I think I'll step into the candy store and look over the new comics and let them pass. But that's chicken, and I've got a reputation to consider. So then I think I'll just walk straight on through them or even over them if necessary. But as they get to me, they slow down. I'm ready to fight, cause like I said, I don't feature a whole lot of chit-chat, I much prefer to just knock you down right from the jump and save everybody a lotta precious time.

"You signing up for the May Day races?" smiles Mary Louise, only it's not a smile at all. A dumb question like that doesn't deserve an answer. Besides, there's just me and Gretchen standing there really, so no use wasting my breath talking to shadows.

"I don't think you're going to win this time," says Rosie, trying to signify with her hands on her hips all salty, completely forgetting that I have whupped her behind many times for less salt than that.

"I always win cause I'm the best," I say straight at Gretchen who is, as far as I'm concerned, the only one talking in this ventriloquist-dummy routine. Gretchen smiles, but it's not a smile, and I'm thinking that girls never really smile at each other because they don't know how and don't want to know how and there's probably no one to teach us how, cause grown-up girls don't know either. Then they all look at Raymond who has just brought his mule team to a standstill. And they're about to see what trouble they can get into through him.

"What grade you in now, Raymond?"

"You got anything to say to my brother, you say it to me, Mary Louise Williams of Raggedy Town, Baltimore."

"What are you, his mother?" sasses Rosie.

"That's right, Fatso. And the next word out of anybody and I'll be *their* mother too." So they just stand there, and Gretchen shifts from one leg to the other and so do they. Then Gretchen puts her hands on her hips and is about to say something with her freckle-face self but doesn't. Then she walks around me, looking me up and down, but keeps walking up Broadway, and her sidekicks follow her. So me and Raymond smile at each other, and he says, "Gidyap," to his team, and I continue with my breathing exercises, strolling down Broadway toward the ice man on

145th with not a care in the world cause I am Miss Quicksilver herself.

I take my time getting to the park on May Day because the track meet is the last thing on the program. The biggest thing on the program is the May Pole dancing, which I can do without, thank you, even if my mother thinks it's a shame I don't take part and act like a girl for a change. You'd think my mother'd be grateful not to have to make me a white organdy dress with a big satin sash and buy me new white baby-doll shoes that can't be taken out of the box till the big day. You'd think she'd be glad her daughter ain't out there prancing around a May Pole getting the new clothes all dirty and sweaty and trying to act like a fairy or a flower or whatever you're supposed to be when you should be trying to be yourself, whatever that is, which is, as far as I'm concerned, a poor black girl who really can't afford to buy shoes and a new dress you only wear once a lifetime cause it won't fit next year.

I was once a strawberry in a Hansel and Gretel pageant when I was in nursery school and didn't have no better sense than to dance on tiptoe with my arms in a circle over my head, doing umbrella steps and being a perfect fool just so my mother and father could come dressed up and clap. You'd think they'd know better than to encourage that kind of nonsense. I am not a strawberry. I do not dance on my toes. I run. That is what I am all about. So I always come late to the May Day program, just in time to get my number pinned on and lay in the grass till they announce the fifty-yard dash.

I put Raymond in the little swings, which is a tight squeeze this year and will be impossible next year. Then I look around for Mr. Pearson, who pins the numbers on. I'm really looking for Gretchen if you want to know the truth, but she's not around. The park is jam-packed. Parents in hats and corsages and breast-pocket handkerchiefs peeking up. Kids in white dresses and light-blue suits. The parkees unfolding chairs and chasing the rowdy kids from Lenox as if they had no right to be there. The big guys with their caps on backwards, leaning against the fence swirling the basketballs on the tips of their fingers, waiting for all these crazy people to clear out of the park so they can play. Most of the kids in my class are carrying bass drums and glockenspiels and flutes. You'd think they'd put in a few bongos or something for real like that.

Then here comes Mr. Pearson with his clipboard and his cards and pencils and whistles and safety pins and fifty million other things he's always dropping all over the place with his clumsy self. He sticks out in a crowd because he's on stilts. We used to call him Jack and the Beanstalk to get him mad. But I'm the only one that can outrun him and get away, and I'm too grown for that silliness now.

"Well, Squeaky," he says, checking my name off the list and handing me number seven and two pins. And I'm thinking he's got no right to call me Squeaky, if I can't call him Beanstalk.

"Hazel Elizabeth Deborah Parker," I correct him and tell him to write it down on his board.

"Well, Hazel Elizabeth Deborah Parker, going to give someone else a break this year?" I squint at him real hard to see if he is seriously thinking I should lose the race on purpose just to give someone else a break. "Only six girls running this time," he continues, shaking his head sadly like it's my fault all of New York didn't turn out in sneakers. "That new girl should give you a run for your money." He looks around the park for Gretchen like a periscope in a submarine movie. "Wouldn't it be a nice gesture if you were . . . to ahhh. . . ."

I give him such a look he couldn't finish putting that idea into words. Grownups got a lot of nerve sometimes. I pin number seven to myself and stomp away, I'm so burnt. And I go straight for the track and stretch out on the grass while the band winds up with "Oh, the Monkey Wrapped His Tail Around the Flag Pole," which my teacher calls by some other name. The man on the loudspeaker is calling everyone over to the track, and I'm on my back looking at the sky, trying to pretend I'm in the country, but I can't, because even grass in the city feels hard as sidewalk, and there's just no pretending you are anywhere but in a "concrete jungle," as my grandfather says.

The twenty-yard dash takes all of two minutes cause most of the little kids don't know no better than to run off the track or run the wrong way or run smack into the fence and fall down and cry. One little kid, though, has got the good sense to run straight for the white ribbon up ahead, so he wins. Then the second-graders line up for the thirty-yard dash, and I don't even bother to turn my head to watch cause Raphael Perez always wins. He wins before he even begins by psyching the runners, telling them they're going to trip on their shoelaces and fall on their faces or lose their shorts or something, which he doesn't really have to do since he is very fast, almost as fast as I am. After that is the forty-yard dash which I use to run when I was in the first grade. Raymond is hollering from the swings cause he knows I'm about to do my thing cause the man on the loudspeaker has just announced the fifty-yard dash, although he might as well be giving a recipe for angel food cake cause you can hardly make out what he's sayin' for the static. I get up and slip off my sweat pants and then I see Gretchen standing at the starting line, kicking her legs out like a pro. Then as I get into place I see that ole Raymond is on line on the other side of the fence, bending down with his fingers on the ground just like he knew what he was doing. I was going to yell at him, but then I didn't. It burns up your energy to holler.

Every time, just before I take off in a race, I always feel like I'm in a dream, the kind of dream you have when you're sick with fever and feel all hot and weightless. I dream I'm flying over a sandy beach in the early morning sun, kissing the leaves of the trees as I fly by. And there's always the smell of apples, just like in the country when I was little and used to think I was a choo-choo train, running through the fields of corn and chugging up the hill to the orchard. And all the time I'm dreaming this, I get lighter and lighter until I'm flying over the beach again, getting blown through the sky like a feather that weighs nothing at all. But once I spread my fingers in the dirt and crouch over for the Get on Your Mark, the dream goes and I am solid again and am telling myself, Squeaky, you must win, you must win, you are the fastest thing in the world, you can even beat your father up Amsterdam if you really try. And then I feel my weight coming back just behind my knees, then down to my feet, then into the earth, and the pistol shot explodes in my blood, and I am off and weightless again, flying past the other runners, my arms pumping up and down, and the whole world is quiet except for the crunch as I zoom over the gravel in the track. I glance to my left and there is no one. To the right, a blurred Gretchen, who's got her chin jutting out as if it would win the race all by itself. And on the other side of the fence is Raymond with his arms down to his side and the palms tucked up behind him, running in his very own style, and it's the first time I ever saw that, and I almost stop to watch my brother Raymond on his first run. But the white ribbon is bouncing toward me and I tear past it, racing into the distance till my feet with a mind of their own start digging up footfuls of dirt to brake me short. Then all the kids standing on the side pile on me, banging me on the back and slapping my head with their May Day programs, for I have won again, and everybody on 151st Street can walk tall for another year.

"In the first place . . ." the man on the loudspeaker is clear as a bell now. But then he pauses, and the loudspeaker starts to whine. Then static. And I lean down to catch my breath, and here comes Gretchen walking back, for she's overshot the finish line too, huffing and puffing with her hands on her hips, taking it slow, breathing in steady time like a real pro, and I sort of like her a little for the first time. "In first place . . ." and then three or four voices get all mixed up on the loudspeaker, and I dig my sneaker into the grass and stare at Gretchen who's staring back, we both wondering just who did win. I can hear old Beanstalk arguing with the man on the loudspeaker and then a few others running their mouths about what the stopwatches say. Then I hear Raymond yanking at the fence to call me, and I wave to shush him, but he keeps rattling the fence like a gorilla in a cage like in them gorilla movies, but then like a dancer or something he starts climbing up nice and easy but very fast. And it occurs to me, watching how smoothly he climbs hand over hand and remembering how he looked running with his arms down to his side and with the wind pulling his mouth back and his teeth showing and all, it occurred to me that

Raymond would make a very fine runner. Doesn't he always keep up with me on my trots? And he surely knows how to breathe in counts of seven cause he's always doing it at the dinner table, which drives my brother George up the wall. And I'm smiling to beat the band, cause if I've lost this race, or if me and Gretchen tied, or even if I've won, I can always retire as a runner and begin a whole new career as a coach with Raymond as my champion. After all, with a little more study I can beat Cynthia and her phony self at the spelling bee. And if I bugged my mother, I could get piano lessons and become a star. And I have a big rep as the baddest thing around. And I've got a roomful of ribbons and medals and awards. But what has Raymond got to call his own?

So I stand there with my new plans, laughing out loud by this time as Raymond jumps down from the fence and runs over with his teeth showing and his arms down to the side, which no one before him has quite mastered as a running style. And by the time he comes over, I'm jumping up and down, so glad to see him—my brother Raymond, a great runner in the family tradition. But of course everyone thinks I'm jumping up and down because the men on the loudspeaker have finally gotten themselves together and compared notes and are announcing "In first place—Miss Hazel Elizabeth Deborah Parker." (Dig that.) "In second place—Miss Gretchen P. Lewis." And I look over at Gretchen wondering what the "P" stands for. And I smile. Cause she's good, no doubt about it. Maybe she'd like to help me coach Raymond; she obviously is serious about running, as any fool can see. And she nods to congratulate me, and then she smiles. And I smile. We stand there with this big smile of respect between us. It's about as real a smile as girls can do for each other, considering we don't practice real smiling every day, you know, cause maybe we too busy being flowers or fairies or strawberries instead of something honest and worthy of respect . . . you know . . . like being people.

Toni Cade Bambara *(born 1939)* is known for her stories, articles, and essays about black Americans. Her works have been included in anthologies and publications such as *The Liberator* and *Massachusetts Review.* Bambara has worked as a welfare investigator, project director for social programs, and a college instructor. She gathered material for two collections, *The Black Woman* and *Tales and Stories for Black Folks.*

© 1984 Jill Krementz

Developing Comprehension Skills

1. What is Squeaky's responsibility in her family?

2. How does Squeaky feel about Raymond? What does she do about people who make fun of Raymond?

3. What is Squeaky's attitude about running? How is her attitude different from Cynthia Proctor's?

4. Why doesn't Squeaky like Gretchen at first? What makes Squeaky change her mind?

5. Why is Raymond's run so important to Squeaky—even more important than her own winning of the race?

6. What is your opinion of Squeaky? Would you want her to be your friend? Why or why not?

Reading Literature: Short Stories

1. **Identifying Setting.** Where and when does this story take place? List three clues to the setting.

2. **Analyzing Character.** The reader learns a lot about Squeaky through her statements

about herself and through her relationship with her brother Raymond. Some words that Squeaky uses frequently in this story are *serious, honest,* and *respect.* How do these words describe Squeaky's character? Find examples in the story that show that she is a serious, honest, respectful person who is also worthy of respect. Then think of other words to describe her.

3. **Understanding Theme.** At the end of the story, Squeaky and Gretchen smile at each other—a "big smile of respect." Then Squeaky explains that girls "don't practice real smiling every day, you know, cause maybe we too busy being flowers or fairies or strawberries instead of something honest and worthy of respect . . . you know . . . like being people." What theme about growing up as a girl is suggested by these last lines of the story? Do you think Squeaky has the right attitude about being a girl today? Explain why or why not.

Developing Vocabulary Skills

Explaining Colloquial Expressions from Context. This story is written to sound like the real speech of a young girl. Squeaky's speech contains many colloquial expressions.

The following list gives examples of these colloquial expressions. Read these expressions once more in context. Then write down the meanings of the expressions as you understand them.

1. from the jump (page 107, column 1)

2. she hangs out (page 107, column 1)

3. the parkees (page 108, column 2)

4. I'm so burnt (page 109, column 1)

Developing Skills in Study and Research

Using *The Readers' Guide.* Reading this story may have made you want to find out more about the sport of running. One way to find information on running is to read magazines, also called **periodicals.** The library resource that can help you to find information in periodicals is *The Readers' Guide to Periodical Literature.* This index lists the titles of magazine articles published each month. Articles are listed alphabetically under subject headings.

Find a recent volume of *The Readers' Guide* in the library. Do the following research:

1. Locate the page at the front of the volume that explains the symbols and abbreviations used in *The Readers' Guide.* Write down the meaning for each of the following symbols and abbreviations.

   a. il   d. Ap
   b. Sat R   e. pors
   c. 6:46–7   f. F'79

2. Look in *The Readers' Guide* under the subject heading *Track and Field.* Try to find the title of an article that gives helpful hints for runners. If you cannot find such an article, choose one on a related topic. Write down the volume and date of *The Readers' Guide* in which you found the entry. Then write down the following information.

   a. the title of the article
   b. the title of the periodical in which the article appears
   c. the volume number and date of that issue of the periodical
   d. the page numbers of the article

Developing Writing Skills

Writing a Character Description. Several times in the story Squeaky mentions her reputation, or how other people see her. The reader also gets to see another side of Squeaky. She tells of how she feels when she is running and of her genuine affection for Raymond. Write two paragraphs in which you describe Squeaky's reputation in her neighborhood and also her innermost feelings as a young person.

Prewriting. Go back through the story and look for references to Squeaky's reputation. Jot down some notes on a sheet of paper and think of words to describe her character from those examples. Then look for references to her innermost feelings about running, about Raymond, and about other girls. Write down notes on these references and think of words to describe that side of her character. Organize your notes so that your descriptions of her character are supported by examples from the story.

Drafting. Begin with a topic sentence that states what kind of girl Squeaky is in a general way. You may choose to write the first paragraph about Squeaky's reputation and the second about her inner feelings. Make sure you have a topic sentence in each paragraph that expresses the main idea about her character.

Revising and Sharing. Check your final copy for grammar, capitalization, punctuation, and spelling mistakes before giving it to a partner to read. Have your partner look for clear descriptions of character that are supported by examples from the story. Ask your partner if your paragraphs are logical and easy to follow. If not, revise again.

Road to the Isles

JESSAMYN WEST

Fourteen-year-old Cress is worried that her parents will do something to embarrass her on her big night. Read to find out what discovery she makes that turns everything around.

It was the last Thursday in January, about nine in the evening, cold and raining. The three Delahantys sat close about the livingroom fireplace—Mr. Delahanty at the built-in desk working on his schedule, Mrs. Delahanty on the sofa reading, and between them, crosswise in the wing chair, their fourteen-year-old daughter, Crescent. Cress was apparently studying the program of the folk-dance festival in which she was to appear the next evening. For the most part, however, she did not even see the program. She saw, instead, herself, infinitely graceful, moving through the figures of the dance that had been so difficult for her to master.

The high-school folk-dancing class was made up of two kinds of performers—those with natural ability, who had themselves elected the class and those who, in the language of the Physical Education Department, were "remedials." The remedials had been sent into the class willy-nilly in an effort to counteract in them defects ranging from antisocial attitudes to what

Miss Ingols, the gym teacher, called "a general lack of grace." Cress had achieved the class under this final classification but now, at midterm, had so far outgrown it as to be the only remedial with a part in the festival.

The first five numbers on the program, "Tsiganotchka," "Ladies' Whim," "Meitschi Putz Di," "Hiawatha," and "Little Man in a Fix," Cress ignored. It was not only that she was not in these but that they were in no way as beautiful as "Road to the Isles," in which Mary Lou Hawkins, Chrystal O'Conor, Zelma Mayberry, Bernadine Deevers, and Crescent Delahanty took part. The mere sight of her name beside that of Bernadine Deevers, Tenant High School's most gifted dancer—most gifted *person*, really—instantly called up to Cress a vision of herself featly footing it in laced kirtle and starched skirts, a vision of herself dancing not only the outward steps of "Road to the Isles" but its inner meaning: what Miss Ingols had called "the achievement of the impossible."

Under the Pomegranate Tree, 1987, CAROLYN FOX. Collection of J. A. Uribe, Inc. Photograph by Ken McKnight/ Jessica Darraby Galleries, Los Angeles.

Cress thought that she was particularly adapted to dancing that meaning because she had so recently come that way herself. If she had been given three wishes when school opened in September, two of them would have been that Bernadine be her friend and that she herself succeed in the folk-dancing class. Both had then seemed equally impossible. Now, not only did she have a part in the festival, but Bernadine was her dear friend and coming to spend the weekend with her. At the minute the evening reached what she considered its peak of mellowness, she intended to speak to her father and mother about the festival and Bernadine's visit. She was exceedingly uncertain about their performances on both these occasions.

The rain suddenly began to fall harder. Cress's father, hearing it on the roof, watched with gratification as the water streamed across the dark windowpanes. "Just what the oranges have been a-thirsting for," he said.

Mrs. Delahanty closed her book. "How's the schedule coming?" she asked her husband.

"OK, I guess," said Mr. Delahanty.

Cress looked up from the festival program with embarrassment. The schedule was one of the things she wanted to speak to her father about. She hoped he wouldn't mention it while Bernadine was visiting them. Every winter, as work on the ranch slackened, he drew up a schedule for the better ordering of his life. And every spring, as work picked up, he abandoned it as easily as if it had never been. Last winter, he had made a plan called "A Schedule of Exercises to Ensure Absolute Fitness," which included not only the schedule of exercises and the hours at which he proposed to practice them, but a list of the weaknesses they were to counteract. He had even gone so far, last winter, as to put on a pair of peculiar short pants and run six times around the orchard without stopping, arms flailing, chest pumping—a very embarrassing sight and one that Cress could not possibly have explained to Bernadine.

This winter, the subject of her father's schedule-making was not in itself so unsuitable. He had bought a new encyclopedia set and was mapping out a reading program that would enable him, by a wise use of his spare time, to cover the entire field of human knowledge in a year. The name of the schedule, written at the top of a sheet of Cress's yellow graph paper, was, in fact, "Human Knowledge in a Year."

There was nothing about this plan that would call for embarrassing public action, like running around the orchard in shorts, but it was so incredibly naïve and dreamy that Cress hoped her father would not speak of it. Bernadine was far too sophisticated for schedules.

"Where are you now on your schedule, John?" Mrs. Delahanty asked.

Mr. Delahanty, who liked to talk about his plans almost as much as he liked to make them, put down his pen and picked up the sheet of paper on which he had been writing. "I've got all the subjects I want to read up about listed and the times I'll have free *for* reading listed. Nothing left to do now but decide what's the best time for what. For instance, if you were me, Gertrude, would you spend the fifteen minutes before breakfast on art? Or on archeology, say?"

"You don't ever have fifteen minutes before breakfast," Mrs. Delahanty said.

Mr. Delahanty picked up his pen. "I thought you wanted to discuss this."

"Oh, I do!" said Mrs. Delahanty. "Well, if *I* had fifteen minutes before breakfast, *I'd* read about archeology."

"Why?" asked Mr. Delahanty.

"It's more orderly that way," Mrs. Delahanty said.

"Orderly?" asked Mr. Delahanty.

"A-r-c," Mrs. Delahanty spelled, "comes before a-r-t."

Mr. Delahanty made an impatient sound. "I'm not going at this alphabetically, Gertrude, cut and dried. What I'm thinking about is what would make the most interesting morning reading, the most interesting and inspiring.''

"Art is supposed to be more inspiring," Mrs. Delahanty told him, "if that's what you're after."

This seemed to decide Mr. Delahanty. "No, I think science should be the morning subject," he said, and wrote something at the top of a sheet—"Science," Cress supposed. "That's better," he said. "That leaves art for the evening, when I'll have time to read aloud to you."

"Don't change your schedule around for my sake, John," said Mrs. Delahanty, who hated being read to about anything.

"I'm not. All personal consideration aside, that's a more logical arrangement. Now the question is, which art?"

This seemed to Cress the moment for which she had been waiting. "Dancing is one of the earliest and most important of the arts," she said quickly.

"Oho!" said her father. "I thought you were in a coma."

"I've been rehearsing," said Cress.

"Rehearsing!" exclaimed Mr. Delahanty.

"In my mind," Cress said.

"So that's what was going on—'Ladies' Whim,' 'Tsiganotchka'—"

"Father," Cress interrupted, "I've told you and told you the T's silent. Why don't you take the program and practice the names? I'll help you." Cress got up and took the program across to her father.

"Practice them," said Mr. Delahanty with surprise, reading through the dances listed. "What do I care how they're pronounced? 'Korbushka,' 'Kohanotchka,' " he said, mispronouncing wildly. "I'm not going to Russia."

"But you're going to the folk-dance festival," Cress reminded him.

"I don't *have* to go. If you don't want—"

"I do, Father. You know I want you to go. Only I don't want you to mispronounce the names."

"Look, Cress," Mr. Delahanty said. "I promise you I'll keep my mouth shut the whole time I'm there. No one will know you have a father who can't pronounce. Mute I'll come and mute I'll go."

"I don't want you to be mute," Cress protested. "And even if I did, you couldn't very well be mute the whole time Bernadine's here. And Bernadine's the star of the program."

"To Bernadine," said Mr. Delahanty, referring to the program once again, "I shall speak of 'Badger,' and 'The Lumberman's Two Step.' I can pronounce them fine and they ought to hold Bernadine. She's not going to be here long, is she?"

"Friday to Monday," said Mrs. Delahanty.

"In that case," said Mr. Delahanty, "maybe I should find another one. How about 'The Irish Jollity,' Cress? Do I say that all right?"

"Now, John!" Mrs. Delahanty reproved her husband.

"It's all right for him to joke about it to me, Mother. But he mustn't before Bernadine. Bernadine's serious about dancing. She's going to be a great artist."

"A great dancer?" Mrs. Delahanty asked.

"She hasn't decided what kind of an artist yet," Cress said. "Only to be great in something."

"Well, well," said Mr. Delahanty. "I'm beginning to look forward to meeting Bernadine."

"You already have," Cress told him. "Bernadine was one of the girls who rode with us to the basketball game."

Mr. Delahanty squinted his eyes, as if trying to peer backward to the Friday two weeks before when he had provided Cress and four of her friends with transportation to an out-of-town game. He shook his head. "Can't recall any Bernadine," he said.

"She was the one in the front seat with us," Cress reminded him.

"That girl!" exclaimed Mr. Delahanty, remembering. "But her name wasn't Bernadine, was it?"

"No," Cress told him. "That's what I wanted to explain to you, because tomorrow's Friday, too."

Mr. Delahanty left desk and schedule and walked over in front of the fireplace. From this position, he could get a direct view of his daughter.

"What's this you're saying, Cress?" he asked. "Her name isn't Bernadine because tomorrow's Friday. Is that what you said?"

"Yes, it is," Cress told him, seriously. "Only it's not just tomorrow. Her name

isn't Bernadine on any Friday."

Mr. Delahanty appealed to his wife. "Do you hear what I hear, Gertrude?"

"Mother," Cress protested, "this isn't anything funny. In fact, it's a complete tragedy."

"Well, Cress dear," her mother said reasonably, "I haven't said a word. And your father's just trying to get things straight."

"He's trying to be funny about a tragedy," Cress insisted obstinately.

"Now, Cress," Mr. Delahanty urged, "you're jumping to conclusions, though I admit I think it's odd to have a name on Fridays you don't have the rest of the week. And I don't see anything tragic about it."

"That's what I'm trying to tell you, only you keep acting as if it's a joke."

"What is Bernadine's name on Fridays, Cress?" asked her mother.

"Nedra," said Cress solemnly.

Mr. Delahanty snapped his fingers. "Yes, sir," he said, "that's it! That's what they called her, all right."

"Of course," said Cress. "Everyone does on Fridays, out of respect for her sorrow."

"Just what *is* Bernadine's sorrow, Cress?" her mother asked.

"Bernadine never did say—out and out, that is. Once in a while she tries to, but she just can't. It overwhelms her. But we all know what, generally speaking, must have happened."

"What?" asked Mr. Delahanty. "Generally speaking?"

Cress looked at her father suspiciously, but his face was all sympathetic concern.

"On some Friday in the past," she said, "Nedra had to say no to someone. Someone she loved."

"How old *is* Berna—Nedra?" Mrs. Delahanty asked.

"Sixteen," Cress said. "Almost."

"Well, it couldn't have been too long ago then, could it?" her mother suggested.

"Was this person," Mr. Delahanty ventured, "this person Nedra said no to, a male?"

"Of course," said Cress. "I told you it was a complete tragedy, didn't I? His name was Ned. That much we know."

"Then the Nedra is in honor of—Ned?" asked her mother.

"In honor and loving memory," Cress told her. "On the very next Friday, Ned died."

Mr. Delahanty said nothing. Mrs. Delahanty said, "Poor boy!"

"I think he was probably more than a boy," Cress said. "He owned two drugstores."

After the elder Delahantys had thought about this for a while Mr. Delahanty asked, "This 'no' Bernadine—Nedra—said, was it to a proposal of marriage?"

"We don't ever ask about that," Cress told her father disapprovingly. "It doesn't seem like good taste to us."

"No, I don't suppose it is," Mr. Delahanty admitted.

"Anyway," Cress said, "that's Bernadine's tragedy and we all respect it and her wish to be called Nedra on Fridays. And tomorrow is a Friday, and it would be pretty awful to have her upset before the festival."

Mr. Delahanty stepped briskly back to his desk. "Don't you worry for a second, Cress," he said. "As far as I'm concerned, the girl's name is Nedra."

"Thank you, Father," Cress said. "I knew you'd understand. Now I'd better go to bed." At the door to the hallway, she turned and spoke once again. "If I were you, Father, I wouldn't say anything about your schedule to Bernadine."

"I hadn't planned on talking to her about it. But what's wrong with it?" Mr. Delahanty sounded a little testy.

"Oh, nothing," Cress assured him. "I think it's dear and sweet of you to make schedules. Only," she explained, "it's so idealistic."

After Cress left the room, Mr. Delahanty said, "What's wrong with being idealistic?"

Cress thought that her friend, in her costume for "Fado Blanquita," the Spanish dance in which she performed the solo part, looked like the queen of grace and beauty. And she said so.

"This does rather suit my type," Bernadine admitted. She was leaning out from the opened casement window of Cress's room into the shimmering, rain-washed air. She tautened her costume's already tight bodice, fluffed up its already bouffant skirt, and extended her hands in one of the appealing gestures of the dance toward the trees of the orange orchard upon which the window opened.

"Is your father a shy man?" she asked.

Mr. Delahanty, who had been working near the driveway to the house when the two girls got off the school bus an hour before, had, instead of lingering to greet them, quickly disappeared behind a row of trees. Now, in rubber boots, carrying a light spade that he was using to test the depth to which the previous night's rain had penetrated the soil, he came briefly into sight, waved his spade, and once again disappeared.

"No." said Cress, who thought her father rather bold, if anything. "He's just busy. After the rain, you know."

"Rain, sunshine. Sunshine, rain," Bernadine said understandingly. She moved her hands about in the placid afternoon air as if scooping up samples. "Farming is an

Ballet, 1983, MARTHA MOOD. Stitchery from *The Sublime Heritage of Martha Mood, Vol. II* by Lester Kierstead Henderson and Shirley Koploy. © 1983 Lester Kierstead Henderson, Monterey, California.

awfully elemental life, I expect. My father"—Bernadine's father, J. M. Deevers, was vice-president of the Tenant First National Bank—"probably doesn't know one element from another. I expect your father's rather an elemental type, too, isn't he? Fundamentally, I mean?"

"I don't know, Nedra," Cress said humbly.

"He's black-haired," Bernadine said. "It's been my experience that black-haired men are very elemental." She brought her expressive hands slowly down to her curving red satin bodice. "You must have a good deal of confidence in your family to let them go tonight," she went on briskly.

"Let them!" Cress repeated, amazed at the word.

"Perhaps they're different from my family. Mine always keep me on pins and needles about what they're going to say and do next."

"Mine, too," Cress admitted, though loyalty to her father and mother would not permit her to say how greatly they worried her. She never went anyplace with them that she was not filled with a tremulous concern lest they do or say something that would discredit them all. She stayed with them. She attempted to guide them. She hearkened to every word said to them, so that she could prompt them with the right answers. But *let* them! "They always just take it for granted that where I go, they go," she said. "There's not much question of letting."

"Mine used to be that way," Bernadine confided. "But after what happened at the festival last year, I put my foot down. 'This year,' I told them, 'you're not going.' "

"What happened last year?" asked Cress, who had not then been a dancer.

"After the program was over last year, Miss Ingols asked for parent participation in the dancing. And my father participated. He danced the 'Hopak,' and pretty soon he was lifting Miss Ingols off the floor at every other jump."

"Oh, Nedra," Cress said. "How terrible! What did Ingols do?"

"Nothing," said Bernadine. "That was the disgusting part. As a matter of fact, she seemed to enjoy it. But you can imagine how I suffered."

Cress nodded. She could. She was thinking how she would suffer if her father, in addition to mispronouncing all the dances, went out on the gymnasium floor and, before all her friends, misdanced them.

"Are your parents the participating type?" Bernadine asked.

Cress nodded with sad conviction. "Father is. And Mother is if encouraged."

"You'd better warn them right away," Bernadine said. "Your father just came in the back door. You could warn him now."

Cress walked slowly down the hallway toward the kitchen. Before the evening was over, her father, too, would probably be jouncing Miss Ingols around and even calling Bernadine Bernadine—then all would be ruined completely, all she had looked forward to for so long. In the kitchen, she noted signs of the special supper her mother was cooking because of Bernadine: the cole-slaw salad had shreds of green peppers and red apples mixed through it tonight to make it festive; the party sherbet glasses, with their long, icicle stems, awaited the lemon pudding. But her mother was out of the kitchen—on the back porch telling her father to hurry, because they would have to have dinner early if they were to get to the festival in time. "Festival!" Cress heard her father say. "I wish I'd never heard of that festival. How did Cress ever come to get mixed up in this dancing business, anyway?" he asked. "She's no dancer. Why, the poor kid can hardly get through a room without knocking something over, let alone dance!"

"That's *why* she's mixed up with it," her mother explained. "To overcome her awkwardness. And she *is* better."

"But is she good enough?" asked her father. "I'd hate to think of her making a spectacle of herself—to say nothing of having to sit and watch it."

"Now, John," Cress heard her mother say soothingly. "You're always too concerned about Cress. Will she do this right? Will she do that right? Stop worrying. Cress'll probably be fine."

"Maybe fall on her ear, too," her father said morosely. "They oughtn't to put so much responsibility on kids. Performing in public. Doesn't it worry you any?"

"Certainly it worries me. But all parents worry. And remember, we'll have the star of the performance with us. You can con-centrate on Nedra if watching Cress is too much for you."

"That Nedra! The only dance I can imagine that girl doing is one in which she would carry somebody's head on a platter."[1]

Cress had started back down the hall before her father finished this sentence, but she had not gone so far as to miss its final word. She stopped in the bathroom to have a drink of water and to see how she looked in the mirror over the washbasin. She looked different. For the first time in her life, she saw herself through other eyes than her own, through her parents' eyes. Did parents worry about the figures their *children* cut? Were they embarrassed for *them,* and did they wonder if they were behaving suitably, stylishly, well? Cress felt a vacant, hollow space beneath her heart, which another glass of water did nothing to fill. Why, *I'm* all right, Cress thought. *I* know how to behave. I'll get by. *They're* the ones . . . but she looked at her face again and it was wavering, doubtful—not the triumphant face she had imagined, smiling in sureness as she danced the come-and-go figures of "Road to the Isles."

She went back to her room full of thought. Bernadine was changing her costume, and her muffled voice came from under all her skirts. "Did you tell them?" this muffled voice asked.

---

1. The dancing of Salome pleased King Herod so much that he granted her one request: the head of John the Baptist on a platter.

"No," said Cress, "I didn't."

"Why not! Won't you be worried?"

"They're the ones who are worrying. About me."

"About you?"

"Father thinks I may fall on my ear."

Bernadine, clear of her skirts, nodded in smiling agreement. "It's a possibility that sometimes occurs to *me,* Cress dear."

Cress gazed at her friend speculatively. "They're worried about you, too," she said.

"Me?" asked Bernadine, her smile fading.

"Father said the only dance he could imagine you doing was one with a head on a platter."

"Salome!" Bernadine exclaimed with pleasure. "Your father's imaginative, isn't he? Sympathetically imaginative?"

"I guess so," Cress said, and in her confusion told everything. "He keeps schedules."

"Schedules?"

"For the better ordering of his life."

Bernadine laughed again. "How precious!" she said.

Then, as if remembering after too long a lapse the day and her bereavement, she said, "Neddy was like that, too."

"Neddy," repeated Cress, pain for the present making Bernadine's past seem not only past but silly. "Oh, shut up about Neddy, *Bernadine!*"

Bernadine gave a little gasp. "Have you forgotten it's Friday?"

"I don't care what day is is," Cress said. She walked over to her bed, picked up a pillow, and lay down. Then she put the pillow over her face.

© 1984 Jill Krementz

Jessamyn West *(1907–1984)* was stricken with tuberculosis at the age of twenty-nine. During the two years she spent recovering, she wrote a series of short stories that used her Quaker background and her memories of Indiana, where she was born. This book, *Friendly Persuasion,* began her long and successful writing career. The book was eventually made into a movie. West wrote the screenplay for that movie. She went on to write sixteen books, many articles and short stories, and to receive five honorary doctorate degrees. "Road to the Isles" is taken from *Cress Delahanty,* a collection of stories about Cress and her family.

Developing Comprehension Skills

1. Why is Cress in the folk-dancing class? How does the inner meaning of the dance "Road to the Isles" apply especially to her?

2. Bernadine changes her name to Nedra on Fridays because of a "tragic" experience with a man named Ned. What can you infer about Bernadine from this action?

3. Mr. Delahanty teases Cress about mispronouncing the names of the dances and about Bernadine's name change. What does this teasing suggest about Mr. Delahanty's relationship with Cress? How is it different from Mrs. Delahanty's relationship with Cress?

4. At the beginning of the story, Cress is worried that her parents will embarrass her at the dance concert and in front of Bernadine. What discovery does she make that changes her attitude?

5. At the end of the story, Cress tells Bernadine, "Oh, shut up about Neddy, *Bernadine!*" Why do you think Cress's attitude toward Bernadine changes?

6. At the end of the story, what is Cress's mood when she covers her face with a pillow? What has she realized about herself?

7. Do you think Cress's worry about her parents embarrassing her is typical for her age? Explain the reasons for your answer.

Reading Literature: Short Stories

1. **Identifying Climax.** The **climax** of a story is the turning point of its plot and the peak of its emotion. In this story, Cress changes dramatically as a result of a single experience. What is this climax?

2. **Understanding Characterization.** Copy the following chart onto a sheet of paper. Make sure you leave enough space in the boxes to write. Then go through the story and find examples of four types of characterization for each character in the story. List each example in the appropriate box.

3. **Recognizing Point of View.** In **third-person omniscient point of view,** the narrator tells what all the characters are thinking.

	Cress	Mr. Delahanty	Mrs. Delahanty	Bernadine
Descriptions				
Actions & Words				
Thoughts & Feelings				
Reactions of Others				

In **third-person limited point of view,** the narrator tells only one character's thoughts. What is the point of view in "Road to the Isles"? Find a passage or passages that explain your choice.

Developing Vocabulary Skills

Definition and Restatement Clues. Look at the definition clue in this sentence from "Road to the Isles."

The remedial dancers, those who had shortcomings ranging from antisocial attitudes to a general lack of grace, were assigned to a special class.

The phrase set off by commas—"those who had shortcomings ranging from antisocial attitudes to a general lack of grace"—is a definition clue telling you specifically who the remedial dancers are.

Look for definition clues in the following sentences based on the story. Write the meaning of each underlined word as it is defined in the sentence. Then use each word in an original sentence.

1. Bernadine, who was classy and aloof, was far too sophisticated for schedules.

2. Mrs. Delahanty would prefer to study ar-cheology, the science of the life and culture of ancient people, before breakfast.

3. Mr. Delahanty promised to be mute, that is, silent, throughout the entire dance program.

Developing Skills in Critical Thinking

1. **Identifying Opinions.** An **opinion** is a statement of a person's beliefs. In "Road to the Isles" the characters hold a lot of opinions about each other. For example, Mr. Delahanty keeps a schedule. What different opinions do Bernadine and Cress have of this activity? What reasons, if any, do Cress and Bernadine have for their opinions? Locate other opinions in the story.

2. **Recognizing Generalizations.** A **generalization** is a statement about a group that should be true of all its members. A generalization is inaccurate or unsound if it is not based on enough facts.

   In "Road to the Isles" Bernadine makes a generalization that black-haired men are "very elemental." Do you think Bernadine's generalization is sound; that is, is it based on enough facts? What generalizations have you heard people make about other people's appearance?

Developing Writing Skills

1. **Writing an Analysis.** Cress is impressed with Bernadine's popularity. As a result she is nervous about Bernadine's visit, and she makes suggestions to her parents about how to behave. Have you noticed different attitudes toward popularity among the young people you know? Does everybody want to be popular? Or do some people value popularity more than others? Write a paragraph analyzing young people's attitudes toward popularity. Follow these steps.

   Prewriting. Think about popularity and how much value different young people place on it. Talk to your classmates about popularity, and observe how they interact. Make notes on their comments and their behavior. Consider how much popularity means to you and how your attitude affects your behavior. Jot down notes on these ideas. Based on your study, draw a conclusion about whether there is one common attitude toward popularity or whether different people have different attitudes. Write down your conclusion.

   Decide how to organize your paragraph. Make an outline that shows your planned organization. Include ideas from your notes.

   Drafting. In your topic sentence state your conclusion about attitudes toward popularity. Explain your conclusion, and support it with incidents you have observed, comments from your classmates, and personal experiences as outlined in your prewriting notes.

   Revising and Sharing. Check to see that your paragraph has a strong topic sentence. Ask yourself if the paragraph is organized logically. Check that you have explained your conclusion as well as given specific support for that idea. Ask a partner to read your paragraph. Have your partner point out weak or unclear sentences.

2. **Writing a Prediction.** What do you think will happen on the night of Cress's performance? Will her parents' fears be realized? Or will Cress shine brilliantly? How will Bernadine do? Use your imagination to predict the outcome of Cress's big night.

   In your prewriting notes write down what you think is most likely to happen during the dance performance. Then write down your reasons. As you draft, write down your prediction supported by your reasons. Share your prediction with a classmate to find out if your prediction is clear and makes sense. Revise your draft, keeping in mind your classmate's suggestions. For further help, refer to Guidelines for the Process of Writing beginning on page 654 in the handbook.

A Crown of Wild Olive: Part 1

ROSEMARY SUTCLIFF

In ancient Greece a truce was called between warring nations so that the Olympic games could be held. Read to discover how the games help to build a friendship between two boys from countries at war.

It was still early in the day, but already it was growing hot, the white dry heat of the Greek summer; and the faint off-shore wind that made it bearable had begun to feather the water, breaking and blurring the reflections of the galleys lying at anchor in Pireaus Harbor.

Half of Athens, it seemed, had crowded down to the port to watch the *Paralos,* the State Galley, sail for the Isthmus, taking their finest athletes on the first stage of their journey to Olympia.

Every fourth summer it happened; every fourth summer for more than three hundred years. Nothing was allowed to stand in the way, earthquake or pestilence or even war—even the long and weary war which, after a while of uneasy peace, had broken out again last year between Athens and Sparta.

Back in the spring the Herald had come, proclaiming the Truce of the Games; safe conduct through all lands and across all seas, both for athletes and for those who went to watch them compete. And now, from every Greek state, and from colonies and settlements all around the Mediterranean, the athletes would be gathering. . . .

Aboard the *Paralos* was all the ordered bustle of departure, ropes being cast off, rowers in their places at the oars. The Athenian athletes and their trainers with them had gathered on the afterdeck. Amyntas, son of Ariston, had drawn a little apart from the rest. He was the youngest there, still several months from his eighteenth birthday and somewhat conscious that he had not yet sacrificed his boy's long hair to Apollo, while the rest, even of those entered for the boys' events—you counted as a boy at Olympia until you were twenty—were already short-haired and doing their Military Service. A few of them even had scars gained in border clashes with the Spartans, to prove that their real place, whatever it might be on the race track or in the wrestling pit, was with the men. Amyntas envied them. He was proud that he had been picked so young to run for Athens in the Boys' Double Stade, the Four Hundred Yards. But he was lonely. He was bound in with all the others by their shared training; but they were bound together by something else, by another kind of life, other loyalties and shared experiences and private jokes, from which he was still shut out.

The last ropes holding ship to shore were being cast off now. Fathers and brothers and friends on the jetty were calling last moment advice and good luck wishes. Nobody called to Amyntas, but he turned and looked back to where his father stood among the crowd. Ariston had been a runner too in his day, before a Spartan spear wound had stiffened his left knee and spoiled his own hopes of an Olympic Olive Crown. Everyone said that he and Amyntas were very alike, and looking back now at the slight dark man who still held himself like a runner, Amyntas hoped with a warm rush of pride that they were right. He wished he had said so, before he came aboard. There were so many things he would have liked to have said, but he was even more tongue-tied with his father than he was with the rest of the world when it came to saying the things that mattered. Now as the last ropes fell away, he flung up his hand in salute and tried to put them all into one wordless message. "I'll run the best race that's in me, Father—and if the Gods let me win it, I'll remember that I'm winning for us both."

Among the waving crowd, his father flung up an answering hand, as though he had somehow received the message. The water was widening between ship and shore. The Bos'n struck up the rowing time on his flute, and the rowers bent to their oars, sending the *Paralos* through the water towards the harbor mouth. Soon the crowd on shore was only a shingle of dark and colored and white along the waterfront. But far off beyond the roofs of the warehouses and the covered docks, a flake of light showed where high over Athens the sunlight flashed back from the upraised spear-blade of the great Athene of the Citadel, four miles away.

They were out around the mole now, the one sail broke out from the mast, and they headed for the open gulf.

That night they beached the *Paralos* and made camp on the easternmost point of the long island of Salamis; and not long past noon the next day they went ashore at the Isthmus and took horse for Corinth on the far side, where a second galley was waiting to take them down the coast. At evening on the fifth day they rode down into the shallow valley where Olympian Zeus the Father of Gods and men had his sanctuary and where the Sacred Games were celebrated in his honor.

What with the long journey and the strangeness of everything, Amyntas took in very little of that first evening. They were met and greeted by the Council of the Games, whose president made them a speech of welcome, after which the Chief Herald red them the rules. And afterwards

Greek ships at sea, 6th century B.C. Black figure kylix. Reproduced by Courtesy of the Trustees of the British Museum, London.

they ate the evening meal in the athletes' mess; food that seemed to have no more taste nor substance than the food one eats in a dream. Then the dream blended away into a dark nothingness of sleep that took Amyntas almost before he had lain down in the narrow stretcher bed in the athletes' lodging, which would be his for the next month.

He woke to the first dappled fingers of sunlight shafting in through the doorway of his cell. They wavered and danced a little, as though broken by the shadows of tree branches. Somewhere farther down the valley a cuckoo was calling, and the world was real again, and his, and new as

though it had been born that morning. He rolled over and lay for a few moments, his hands behind his head, looking up at the bare rafters; then shot off the bed and through the doorway in one swallow-dive of movement, to sluice his head and shoulders in the icy water trickling from the mouth of a stone bull into a basin just outside. He came up for air, spluttering and shaking the water out of his eyes. For a moment he saw the colonnaded court and the plane tree arching over the basin through a splintered brightness of flying droplets. And then suddenly, in the brightness, there stood a boy of about his own age, who must have come out of the lodging close behind him. A boy with a lean angular body and a dark, bony face under a shock of hair like the crest of an ill-groomed pony. For a long moment they stood looking at each other. Then Amyntas moved aside to let the other come to the conduit.

As the stranger ducked his head and shoulders under the falling water, Amyntas saw his back. From shoulder to flank it was criss-crossed with scars, past the purple stage but not yet faded to the silvery white that they would be in a few years' time; pinkish scars that looked as though the skin was still drawn uncomfortably tight over them.

He must have made some betraying sound or movement, because the other boy ducked out from under the water, thrusting the wet russet hair back out of his eyes, and demanded curtly, "Have you never seen a Spartan back before?"

So that was it. Amyntas, like everyone else, had heard dark stories of Spartan boys flogged, sometimes to death, in a ritual test of courage before the shrine of Artemis Orthia, the Lady of the Beasts.

"No," he said, "I am Athenian." And did not add that he hoped to see plenty of Spartan backs when once he had started his Military Service. It was odd, the cheap jibe came neatly into his head, and yet he did not even want to speak it. It was as though here at Olympia, the Truce of the Games was not just a rule of conduct, but something in one's heart. Instead, he added, "And my name is Amyntas."

They seemed to stand confronting each other for a long time. The Spartan boy had the look of a dog sniffing at a stranger's fist and taking his own time to make sure whether it was friendly. Then he smiled; a slow, rather grave smile, but unexpectedly warm. "And mine is Leon."

"And you're a runner." Amyntas was taking in his build and the way he stood.

"I am entered for the Double Stade."

"Then we race against each other."

Leon said in the same curt tone, "May we both run a good race."

"And meanwhile,—when did you arrive, Leon?"

"Last night, the same as you."

Amyntas, who usually found it nearly as difficult to talk to strangers as he did to his own father, was surprised to hear himself saying, "Then you'll have seen no more of Olympia than I have. Shall we go and get some clothes on and have a look around?"

But by that time more men and boys were coming out into the early sunshine, yawning and stretching the sleep out of their muscles. And Amyntas felt a hand clamp down on his shoulder and heard the voice of Hippias his trainer, "Oh no you don't, my lad! Five days' break in training is long enough, and I've work for you before you do any sightseeing!"

After that, they were kept hard at it, on the practice track and in the wrestling school that had the names of past Olympic victors carved on the colonnade walls. For the last month's training for the Games had to be done at Olympia itself; and the last month's training was hard, in the old style that did not allow for rest days in the modern fashion that most of the Athenian trainers favored. Everything at Olympia had to be done the old way, even to clearing the stadium of its four years' growth of grass and weeds and spreading it with fresh sand. At other Crown Games, the work was done by paid laborers, but here, the contending athletes must do it themselves, to the glory of the Gods, as they had done it in the far-off days when the Games were new. Some of them grumbled a good deal and thought it was time that the Priests of Zeus and the Council of the Games brought their ideas up to date; but to Amyntas there seemed to be a sort of rightness about the thing as it was.

His training time was passed among boys from Corinth and Epidauros, Rhodes and Samos and Macedon. At first they were just figures in outline, like people seen too far off to have faces, whom he watched with interest at track work, at javelin or discus throwing or in the wrestling pit, trying to judge their form as he knew they were trying to judge his and each other's. But gradually as the early days went by, they changed into people with faces, with personal habits, and likes and dislikes, suffering from all the strains and stresses of the last weeks before the Games. But even before those first few days were over, he and the Spartan boy had drifted into a companionable pattern of doing things together. They would sluice each other down, squatting in the stone hip-baths in the washing room after practice, and scrape the mess of rubbing oil and sand off each other's backs—it took Amyntas a little while to learn to scrape the bronze blade of the strigil straight over the scars on Leon's back as though they were not there—and when they took their turn at scraping up the four years' growth of grass and sun-dried herbs from the stadium, they generally worked together, sharing one of the big rush carrying-baskets between them. And in the evenings, after the day's training was over, or in the hot noonday break when most people stretched themselves out in the shade of the plane trees for sleep or quiet talk, they seemed, more often than not, to drift into each other's company.

Once or twice they went to have a look at the town of tents and booths that was beginning to spring up all around the Sacred Enclosure and the Gymnasium buildings—for a Games Festival drew many people besides those who came to compete or to watch; merchants and wine sellers and fortune tellers, poets determined to get poems heard, horse dealers from Corinth and Cyrene, goldsmiths and leather-workers, philosophers gathering for the pleasure of arguing with each other, sword and fire swallowers, and acrobats who could dance on their hands to the soft notes of Phrygian pipes. But Leon did not much like the crowded noisy tent-ground; and most often they wandered down to the river that flung its loop about the south side of Olympia. It had shrunk now in the summer heat, to little more than a chain of pools in the middle of its pale dried-out pebbly bed; but there was shade under the oleander trees, and generally a whisper of moving air. And lying on the bank in the shade was free. It had dawned on Amyntas quite early that the reason Leon did not like the fairground was that he had no money. The Spartans did not use money, or at least, having decided that it was a bad thing, they had no coinage but iron bars so big and heavy that nobody could carry them about or even keep a store at home that was worth enough to be any use. They were very proud of their freedom from wealth, but it made life difficult at a gathering such as this, when they had to mix with people from other states. Leon covered up by being extremely scornful of the foolish things for sale in the merchants' booths and the acrobats who passed the bowl around for contributions after their performance; but he was just that shade too scornful to be convincing. And anyway, Amyntas had none too much money himself, to get him through the month.

So they went to the river. They were down there one hot noontide something over a week after they had first arrived at Olympia; Amyntas lying on his back, his hands behind his head, squinting up into the dark shadow-shapes of the oleander branches against the sky; Leon sitting beside him with his arms around his updrawn knees, staring out into the dazzle of sunlight over the open riverbed. They had been talking runners' talk, and suddenly Amyntas said, "I was watching the Corinthian making his practice run this morn-

ing. I don't *think* we have either of us much to fear from him."

"The Rhodian runs well," said Leon, not bringing back his gaze from the white dance of sunlight beyond the oleanders.

"But he uses himself up too quickly. He's the kind that makes all the front running at first and has nothing left for the home stretch. Myself, I'd say that red-headed barbarian from Macedon had the better chance."

"He's well enough for speed; and he knows how and when to use it. . . . What do you give for Nikomedes' chances?"

"Nikomedes?—The boy from Megara? It's hard to say. Not much, from the form he's shown so far; but we've only seen him at practice, and he's the sort that sometimes catches fire when it comes to the real thing. . . ."

There was a long silence between them, and they heard the churring of the grasshoppers, like the heat-shimmer turned to sound. And then Amyntas said, "I think you are the one I have most to fear."

And Leon turned his head slowly and looked down at him, and said, "Have you only just woken to that? I knew the same thing of *you,* three days ago."

And they were both silent again and suddenly a little shocked. You might think that kind of thing, but it was best not to put it into words.

Leon made a quick sign with his fingers to avert ill luck; and Amyntas scrambled to his feet. "Come on, it's time we were getting back." They were both laughing, but a little breathlessly. Leon dived to his feet also and shot ahead as they went up through the riverside scrub. But the next instant, between one flying leap and the next, he stumbled slightly and checked, then turned back, stooping to search for something among the dusty root-tangle of dry grass and camomile. Amyntas, swerving just in time to avoid him, checked also.

"What is it?"

"Something sharp. . . ." Leon pulled out from where it had lain half-buried, the broken end of a sickle blade that looked as though it might have lain there since the last Games. "Seems it's not only the Stadium that needs clearing up." He began to walk on, carrying the jagged fragment in his hand. But Amyntas saw the blood on the dry ground where he had been standing.

"You have cut your foot."

"I know," Leon said, and went on walking.

"Yes, I *know* you know. Let me look at it."

"It's only a scratch."

"All the same—show me."

Leon stood on one leg, steadying himself with a hand on Amyntas's shoulder, and turned up the sole of his foot. "Look then. You can hardly see it."

There was a cut on the hard brown sole, not long, but deep, with the blood welling slowly. Amyntas said in sudden exasperation, "Haven't you *any* sense? Oh we all know about the Spartan boy with the fox under his cloak, and nobody but you Spar-

tans think it's a particularly clever or praiseworthy story; but if you get dirt into that cut, you'll like enough have to scratch from the race!"

Leon suddenly grinned. "Nobody but we Spartans understand that story. But about the dirt, you could be right."

"I could. And that bit of iron is dirty enough for a start. Best get the wound cleaned up, in the river before we go back to the Gymnasium. Then your trainer can take over."

So with Leon sitting on a boulder at the edge of the shrunken river, Amyntas set to work with ruthless thoroughness to clean the cut. He pulled it open, the cool water running over his hands, and a thin thread of crimson fronded away downstream. It would help clean the wound to let it bleed a little; but after a few moments the bleeding almost stopped. No harm in making sure; he ducked his head to the place, sucked hard and spat crimson into the water. Then he tore a strip from the skirt of his tunic. He would have commandeered Leon's own—after all it was Leon's foot—but he knew that the Spartan boys were allowed to own only one tunic at a time. If he did that, Leon would be left without a respectable tunic to wear at the Sacrifices. He lashed the thin brown foot tightly. "Now—put your arm over my shoulder and try to keep your weight off the cut as much as you can."

"Cluck, cluck, cluck!" said Leon, but he did as Amyntas said.

As they skirted the great open space of

the Hippodrome, where the chariot races would be held on the second day of the Games, they came up with a couple of the Athenian contingent, strolling under the plane trees. Eudorus the wrestler looked around and his face quickened with concern, "Run into trouble?"

"Ran into the remains of a sickle blade someone left in the long grass," Amyntas said, touching the rusty bit of metal he had taken from Leon and stuck in his own belt. "It's near the tendon, but it's all right, so long as there's no dirt left in it."

"Near the tendon, eh? Then we'd best be taking no chances." Eudorus looked at Leon. "You are Spartan, I think?—Amyntas, go and find the Spartan trainer. I'll take over here." And then to Leon again, "Will you allow me to carry you up to the lodging? It seems the simplest way."

Amyntas caught one parting glimpse of Leon's rigid face as Eudorus lifted him, lightly as a ten-year-old, and set off towards the gymnasium buildings; and laughter caught at his stomach; but mixed with the laughter was sympathy. He knew he would have been just as furious in Leon's place. All this fuss and to-do over a cut that would have been nothing in itself—if the Games had not been only three weeks off.

He set off in search of the trainer.

In the middle of that night, Amyntas woke up with a thought already shaped and complete in his mind. It was an ugly thought, and it sat on his chest and mouthed at him slyly. "Leon is the one you have most to fear. If Leon is out of the race. . . ."

He looked at it in the darkness, feeling a little sick. Then he pushed it away and rolled over on to his face with his head in his arms, and after a while he managed to go back to sleep again.

Next day, as soon as he could slip away between training sessions, he went out into the growing town of tents and booths, and found a seller of images and votive offerings, and bought a little bronze bull with silvered horns. It cost nearly all the money that he had to spare, so that he would not now be able to buy the hunting knife with silver inlay on the hilt that had caught his fancy a day or two since. With the little figure in his hand, he went to the Sacred Enclosure, where, among altars shaded by plane trees and statues of Gods and Olympic heroes, the great Temple of Zeus faced the older and darker house of Hera his wife.

Before the Temple of Zeus, the ancient wild olive trees from which the victors' crowns were made cast dapple-shade across the lower steps of the vast portico. He spoke to the attendant priest in the deep threshold shadows beyond.

"I ask leave to enter and make an offering."

"Enter then, and make the offering," the man said.

And he went through into the vastness of the Temple itself, where the sunlight sifting through under the acanthus roof tiles made a honeycomb glow that hung high in

Zeus (detail), about 460 B.C. Greco-Roman bronze sculpture. Photograph by David Finn, New York City.

the upper spaces and flowed down the gigantic columns but scarcely touched the pavement under foot, so that he seemed to wade in cool shadows. At the far end, sheathed in gold and ivory, his feet half lost in shadows, his head gloried with the dim radiance of the upper air, stern and serene above the affairs of mortal men, stood the mighty statue of the God himself. Olympian Zeus, in whose honor the Sacred Games had been held for more than three hundred years. Three hundred years, such a little while; looking up at the heart-stilling face above him, Amyntas

wondered if the God had even noticed yet, that they were begun. Everything in the God's House was so huge, even time. . . . For a moment his head swam, and he had no means of judging the size of anything, even himself, here where all the known landmarks of the world of men were left behind. Only one thing, when he looked down at it, remained constant in size; the tiny bronze bull with the silvered horns that he held in his hand.

He went forward to the first of the Offering Tables before the feet of the gigantic statue and set it down. Now, the tables were empty and waiting, but by the end of the festival, they would be piled with offerings; small humble ones like his own and silver cups and tripods of gilded bronze to be taken away and housed in the Temple treasury. On the eve of the Games they would begin to fill up, with votive offerings made for the most part by the athletes themselves, for their own victory or the victory of a friend taking part in a different event. Amyntas was not making the offering for his own victory, nor for Leon's. He was not quite sure why he was making it, but it was for something much more complicated than victory in the Double Stade. With one finger still resting on the back of the little bronze bull, he sent up the best prayer he could sort out from the tangle of thoughts and feelings within himself. "Father of all things, Lord of these Sacred Games, let me keep a clean heart in this; let me run the best race that is in me and think of nothing more."

Outside again, beyond the dapple-shade of the olive trees, the white sunlight fell dazzling across his eyes, and the world of men, in which things had returned to their normal size, received him back; and he knew that Hippias was going to be loudly angry with him for having missed a training session. But unaccountably, everything, including Hippias's anger, seemed surprisingly small.

Developing Comprehension Skills

1. What major differences between Amyntas and Leon are obvious when they first meet?

2. How does the friendship between Amyntas and Leon grow? What do they come to realize about each other for the upcoming race?

3. What happens to Leon? How does this affect his chances in the race?

4. What mixed feelings does Amyntas have about Leon's accident?

5. Amyntas makes an offering at the Temple of Zeus and says this prayer: "Father of all things, Lord of these Sacred Games, let me keep a clean heart in this; let me run the best race that is in me and think of nothing more." What is the "clean heart" that Amyntas asks for? What is the "more" that he doesn't want to think about?

6. Who do you think will win the race—Amyntas or Leon? Do you think they will continue to be friends after the games are over? Give reasons for your predictions.

Reading Literature: Short Stories

1. **Interpreting Setting.** The setting for this story is far away in time and place. Through this story you can learn about the customs and traditions of a different society. What does the story reveal about how early Greeks worshipped? What do you learn about Olympic traditions? What are Spartan and Athenian rituals for boys entering manhood?

2. **Identifying Characters.** Part 1 of this story introduces both main and minor characters. Identify each of the following characters: Amyntas, Ariston, Hippias, Leon, and Eudoras. Which of these characters are main characters? Which are minor characters?

3. **Understanding Exposition and Rising Action.** The **exposition** is the part of the plot that gives background information. It also introduces characters and setting. The exposition of this story is the first five paragraphs. What does the exposition tell about where Amyntas is going and why? about Amyntas's age? The rising action consists of the main character's struggle and the problems the character faces. What are the main events of the rising action as told in this part of the story?

A Crown of Wild Olive: Part 2

ROSEMARY SUTCLIFF

In the first part of the story, you saw how Amyntas and Leon—boys from warring nations—become friends as well as competitors. Read this last part of the story to find out who wins and what happens to their friendship.

Leon had to break training for three days, at least so far as track-work was concerned; and it was several more before he could get back into full training; so for a while it was doubtful whether he would be able to take his place in the race. But with still more than a week to go, both his trainer and the Doctor-Priest of Asklepius declared him fit, and his name remained on the list of entrants for the Double Stade.

And then it was the first day of the Festival; the day of solemn dedication, when each competitor must go before the Council to be looked over and identified and take the Oath of the Games before the great bronze statue of Zeus of the Thunderbolts.

The day passed. And next morning before it was light, Amyntas woke to hear the unmistakable, unforgettable voice of the crowds gathering in the Stadium. A shapeless surf of sound, pricked by the sharper cries of the jugglers and acrobats, and the sellers of water and honeycakes, myrtle and victors' ribbons calling their wares.

This was the day of the Sacred Procession; the Priests and Officials, the beasts garlanded for sacrifice, the athletes marching into the waiting Stadium, while the Herald proclaimed the name and state of each one as he passed the rostrum. Amyntas, marching in with the Athenians, heard his own name called, and Leon's, among names from Samos and Cyrene, Crete and Corinth, and Argos and Megara. And he smelled the incense on the morning air and felt for the first time, under his swelling pride in being Athenian, the thread of his own Greekness interwoven with the Greekness of all those others. This must have been, a little, the thing their Great-Grandfathers had felt when they stood together, shield to shield, to hurl back the whole strength of invading Persia so that they might remain free. That had been in a Games year, too. . . .

Charioteer at the Greek Games, 410–390 B.C. Black-figure painted vase. Reproduced by Courtesy of the Trustees of the British Museum, London.

The rest of that day was given over to the chariot and horse races; and that night Amyntas went to his sleeping cell with the thunder of hooves and wheels still sounding somewhere behind his ears. He seemed to hear it in his dreams all night, but when he woke in the morning, it had turned into the sound that he had woken to yesterday, the surf-sound of the gathering crowd. But this morning it had a new note for him, for this was the Day, and the crowd that was gathering out there around the Stadium was his crowd, and his belly tightened and

the skin prickled at the back of his neck as he heard it.

He lay for a few moments, listening, then got up and went out to the conduit. Leon came out after him as he had done that first morning of all, and they sluiced down as best they could. The water barely dribbled from the mouth of the stone bull now, for with the vast gathering of people and the usual end-of-summer drought, the water shortage was getting desperate, as it always did by the time the Festival days arrived.

"How is the foot?" Amyntas asked.

"I can't remember where the cut was, unless I look for it."

They stood looking at each other, the friendship that they had never put into words trying to find some way to reach across from one to the other.

"We cannot even wish each other luck," Amyntas said at last, helplessly.

And Leon said, almost exactly as he had said it at their first meeting, "May both of us run a good race."

They reached out and touched hands quickly and went their separate ways.

The next time they saw each other, they were waiting oiled and naked for the track, with the rest of the Double Stade boys just outside the arched way into the Stadium. The Dolichus, the long distance race, and the Stade had been run, each with its boys' race immediately after. Now the trumpet was sounding to start the Double Stade. Amyntas's eyes went to meet Leon's, and found the Spartan boy's slightly frowning gaze waiting for him. He heard the sudden roar of the crowd, and his belly lifted and tightened. A little stir ran through the waiting boys; the next time the starting trumpet sounded, the next time the crowd gave that roar, it would be for them. Hippias was murmuring last-minute advice into Amyntas's ear, but he did not hear a word of it. . . . He was going out there before all those thousands upon thousands of staring eyes and yelling mouths, and he was going to fail. Not just fail to win the race, but *fail*. His belly was churning now, his heart banging away right up in his throat so that

it almost choked him. His mouth was dry and the palms of his hands were wet, and the beginnings of panic were whimpering up in him. He looked again at Leon and saw him run the tip of his tongue over his lips as though they were suddenly dry. It was the first time he had ever known the Spartan boy to betray anything of what was going on inside him, and the sight gave him a sense of companionship that somehow steadied him. He began to take deep quiet breaths, as he had been taught, and the rising panic quieted and sank away.

The voice of the crowd was rising, rising to a great roar; the Men's Double Stade was over. He heard the Herald crying the name of the winner and another roar from the crowd; and then the runners were coming out through the arched entrance; and the boys pressed back to let them past, filthy with sweat and sand and oil. Amyntas looked at the face of the man with the victor's ribbons knotted around his head and arms and saw that it was grey and spent and oddly peaceful.

"Now it's us!" someone said; and the boys were sprinting down the covered way, out into the open sun-drenched space of the Stadium.

The turf banks on either side of the broad track and the lower slopes of the Kronon Hill that looked down upon it were packed with a vast multitude of onlookers. Half-way down on the right-hand side, raised above the tawny grass on which everybody else sat, were the benches for the Council, looking across to the white marble seat opposite, where the Priestess of Demeter, the only woman allowed at the Games, sat as still as though she herself were carved from marble, among all the jostling, swaying, noisy throng. Men were raking over the silver sand on the track. The trumpeter stood ready.

They had taken their places now behind the long white limestone curbs of the starting line. The Umpire was calling: "Runners! Feet to the lines!"

Amyntas felt the scorching heat of the limestone as he braced the ball of his right foot into the shaped groove. All the panic of a while back had left him; he felt light, and clearheaded, and master of himself. He had drawn the sixth place, with Leon on his left and the boy from Megara on his right. Before him the track stretched white in the sunlight, an infinity of emptiness and distance.

The starting trumpet yelped, and the line of runners sprang forward like a wave of hunting dogs slipped from the leash.

Amyntas was running smoothly and without hurry. Let the green front-runners push on ahead. In this heat they would have burned themselves out before they reached the turning post. He and Leon were running neck and neck with the red-headed Macedonian. The Rhodian had gone ahead now after the front-runners; the rest were still bunched. Then the Corinthian made a sprint and passed the boy from Rhodes, but fell back almost at once. The white track was reeling back underfoot, the turning post racing towards them.

The bunch had thinned out, the front-runners beginning to drop back already; and as they came up towards the turning post, the first boy from Macedon, and then Nikomedes catching fire at last, slid into the lead, with Amyntas and Leon close behind them. Rounding the post, Amyntas skidded on the loose sand and Leon went ahead; and it was then, seeing the lean scarred back ahead of him, that Amyntas lengthened his stride, knowing that the time had come to run. They were a quarter of the way down the home lap when they passed Nikomedes; the Megaran boy had taken fire too late. They were beginning to overhaul the redhead; and Amyntas knew in his bursting heart that unless something unexpected happened, the race must be between himself and Leon. Spartan and Macedonian were going neck and neck now; the position held for a few paces, and then the redhead gradually fell behind. Amyntas was going all out. There was pain in his breast and belly and in the backs of his legs, and he did not know where his next breath was coming from; but still the thin scarred back was just ahead. And then suddenly Amyntas knew that something was wrong; Leon was laboring a little, beginning to lose the first keen edge of his speed. Snatching a glance downward, he saw a fleck of crimson in the sand. The cut had reopened.

His body went on running, but for a sort of splinter of time his head seemed quite apart from the rest of him and filled with an unmanageable swirl of thoughts and feelings. Leon might have passed the top of his speed anyway; it might be nothing to do with his foot—But the cut *had* re-opened. . . . To lose the race because of a cut foot. . . . It would be so easy not to make that final desperate effort that his whole body was crying out against. Then Leon would keep his lead. . . . And at the same time another part of himself was re-membering his father standing on the quayside at Piraeus as the *Paralos* drew away—crying out that he was not running only for himself but for Athens, his City and his people. . . . A crown of wild olive would be the greatest thing that anyone could give to his friend. . . . It would insult Leon to let him win . . . you could not do that to your friend. . . . And then, like a clean cold sword of light cutting through the swirling tangle of his thoughts, came the knowledge that greater than any of these things were the Gods. These were the Sacred Games, not some mere struggle between boys in the gymnasium. For one fleeting instant of time, he remembered himself standing in the Temple before the great statue of Zeus, holding the tiny bronze bull with the silvered horns. "Let me run the best race that is in me and think of nothing more."

He drove himself forward in one last ag-onizing burst of speed. He was breathing against knives, and the roar of the blood in his ears drowned the roar of the crowd. He was level with Leon—and then there was nothing ahead of him but the win-ning post.

The onlookers had crowded right down towards it; even above the howl of the blood in his head he heard them now, roar on solid roar of sound, shouting him in to victory. And then Hippias had caught him as he plunged past the post; and he was bending over the trainer's arm, bending over the pain in his belly, snatching at his breath and trying not to be sick. People were throwing sprigs of myrtle; he felt them flicking and falling on his head and shoulders. The sickness eased a little and his head was clearing; he began to hear friendly voices congratulating him; and Eu-dorus came shouldering through the crowd with a colored ribbon to tie around his head. But when he looked around for Leon, the Spartan boy had been swept away by his trainer. And a desolation rose in Amyntas and robbed his moment of its glory.

Afterwards in the changing room, some of the other boys came up to congratulate him. Leon did not come; but when they had cleaned off the sand and oil and sweat and sluiced down with the little water that was allowed them, Amyntas hung about, sitting on the well curb outside while the trainer finished seeing to his friend's foot. And when Leon came out at last, he came straight across to the well, as though they had arranged to meet there. His face was as unreadable as usual.

"You will have cooled off enough by now. Do you want to drink?" Amyntas said, mainly because somebody had to say something, and dipped the bronze cup that always stood on the well curb in the pail that he had drawn.

Leon took the cup from him and drank and sat down on the well curb beside him. As Amyntas dipped the cup again and bent his head to drink in his turn, the ends of the victor's ribbon fell forward against his cheek, and he pulled it off impatiently and dropped it beside the well.

"Why did you do that?" Leon said.

"I shall never be sure whether I won that race."

"The judges are not often mistaken, and I never heard yet of folk tying victors' ribbons on the wrong man."

Amyntas flicked a thumb at Leon's bandaged foot. "You know well enough what I mean. I'll never be sure whether I'd have come first past the post, if that hadn't opened up again."

Leon looked at him a moment in silence, then flung up his head and laughed. "Do you really think that could make any difference? It would take more than a cut foot to slow me up, Athenian!—You ran the better race, that's all."

It was said on such a harsh, bragging note that in the first moment Amyntas felt as though he had been struck in the face. Then he wondered if it was the overwhelming Spartan pride talking or simply Leon, hurt and angry and speaking the truth. Either way, he was too tired to be angry back again. And whichever it was it seemed that Leon had shaken it off already. The noon break was over, and the trumpets

were sounding for the Pentathlon.

"Up!" Leon said, when Amyntas did not move at once. "Are you going to let it be said that your own event is the only one that interests you?"

They went, quickly and together, while the trainer's eye was off them, for Leon was under orders to keep off his foot. And the people cheered them both when they appeared in the Stadium. They seldom cared much for a good loser, but Leon had come in a close second, and they had seen the blood in the sand.

The next day the heavyweight events were held; and then it was the last day of all, the Crowning Day. Ever after, Amyntas remembered that day as a quietness after great stress and turmoil. It was not, in truth, much less noisy than the days that had gone before. The roaring of the Stadium crowds was gone, but in the town of tents the crowds milled to and fro. The jugglers with knives and the eaters of fire shouted for an audience and the merchants cried their wares, and within the Sacred Enclosure where the winners received their crowns and made their sacrifices before the Temples of Zeus and Hera, there were the flutes and the songs in praise of the victors and the deep-voiced invocations to the Gods.

But in Amyntas himself, there was the quiet. He remembered the Herald crying his name and the light springy coolness of the wild olive crown as it was pressed down on his head; and later, the spitting light of pine torches under the plane trees, where the officials and athletes were feasting. And he remembered most, looking up out of the torchlight, and seeing, high and remote above it all, the winged tripods on the roof of the great Temple, outlined against the light of a moon two days past the full.

The boys left before the feasting was over; and in his sleeping cell Amyntas heard the poets sing in praise of some chariot team and the applause, while he gathered his few belongings together, ready for tomorrow's early start, and stowed his olive crown among them. Already the leaves were beginning to wilt after the heat of the day. The room that had seemed so strange the first night was familiar now, part of himself; and after tonight it would not know him anymore.

Next morning in all the hustle of departure, he and Leon contrived to meet and slip off for a little on their own.

The whole valley of Olympia was a chaos of tents and booths being taken down, merchants as well as athletes and onlookers making ready for the road. But the Sacred Enclosure itself was quiet, and the gates stood open. They went through, into the shade of the olive trees before the Temple of Zeus. A priest making the morning offering at a side altar looked at them; but they seemed to be doing no harm and to want nothing, so he let them alone. There was a smell of frankincense in the air and the early morning smell of last night's heavy dew on parched ground. They stood among the twisted trunks and low-hanging branches and looked at each other and did not know what to say. Already they were remembering that there was war between Athens and Sparta, that the Truce of the Games would last them back to their own states, but no further; and the longer the silence lasted, the more they remembered.

From beyond the quiet of the Enclosure came all the sounds of the great concourse breaking up; voices calling, the stamping of impatient horses. "By this time tomorrow everyone will be gone," Amyntas said at last. "It will be just as it was before we came, for another four years."

"The Corinthians are off already."

"Catching the cool of the morning for those fine chariot horses," Amyntas said, and thought, There's so little time, why do we have to waste it like this?

"One of the charioteers had that hunting knife with the silver inlay. The one you took a fancy to. Why didn't you buy it after all?"

"I spent the money on something else." For a moment Amyntas was afraid that Leon would ask what. But the other boy only nodded and let it go.

He wished suddenly that he could give Leon something, but there was nothing among his few belongings that would make sense in the Spartan's world. It was a world so far off from his own. Too far to reach out, too far to call. Already they seemed to be drifting away from each other, drifting back to a month ago, before they had even met. He put out a hand quickly, as though to hold the other boy back for one more moment, and Leon's hand came to meet it.

"It has been good. All this month it has been good," Leon said.

"It has been good," Amyntas agreed. He wanted to say, "Until the next Games, then." But manhood and Military Service were only a few months away for both of them. If they did meet at another Games, there would be the faces of dead comrades, Spartan or Athenian, between them; and like enough, for one of them or both, there might be no other Games. Far more likely, if they ever saw each other again, it would be over the tops of their shields.

He had noticed before how, despite their different worlds, he and Leon sometimes thought the same thing at the same time and answered each other as though the thought had been spoken. Leon said in his abrupt, dead-level voice, "The Gods be with you, Amyntas, and grant that we never meet again."

They put their arms around each other's necks and strained fiercely close for a moment, hard cheekbone against hard cheekbone.

"The Gods be with you, Leon."

And then Eudorus was calling, "Amyntas! Amyntas! We're all waiting!"

And Amyntas turned and ran—out through the gateway of the Sacred Enclosure, towards where the Athenian party were ready to start, and Eudorus was already coming back to look for him.

Marathon Youth (detail), about 300 B.C. Greek bronze sculpture. National Museum, Athens. Photograph by David Finn, New York City.

As they rode up from the Valley of Olympia and took the tracks towards the coast, Amyntas did not look back. The horses' legs brushed the dry dust-grey scrub beside the track and loosed the hot aromatic scents of wild lavender and camomile and lentisk upon the air. A yellow butterfly hovered past, and watching it out of sight, it came to him suddenly that he and Leon had exchanged gifts of a sort, after all. It was hard to give them a name, but they were real enough. And the outward and visible sign of his gift to Leon was in the little bronze bull with the silvered horns that he had left on the Offering Table before the feet of Olympian Zeus. And Leon's gift to him. . . . That had been made with the Spartan's boast that it would take more than a cut foot to slow him up. He had thought at the time that it was either the harsh Spartan pride or the truth spoken in anger. But he understood now, quite suddenly, that it had been Leon giving up his own private and inward claim to the olive crown, so that he, Amyntas, might believe that he had rightfully won it. Amyntas knew that he would never be sure of that, never in all his life. But it made no difference to the gift.

The track had begun to run downhill, and the pale dust-cloud was rising behind them. He knew that if he looked back now, there would be nothing to see.

Photo by Mark Gerson

Rosemary Sutcliff *(born 1920)* lives in England and is known for her historical novels and stories for young people. After attending the Bideford Art School, Sutcliff began to write stories that successfully combined actual historical events and the lives of her characters. Although her characters live in the past, they struggle with recognizable problems as they grow from childhood into adulthood. Such conflicts make Sutcliff's books popular with young people of any era.

Developing Comprehension Skills

1. How is Leon's foot before the race? What happens to his foot near the end of the race?

2. Why does Amyntas hesitate in the race when he sees Leon slow down?

3. After he wins the race, Amyntas feels "a desolation" that "robbed his moment of its glory." Why does Amyntas feel that way?

4. Why can't Amyntas ever be sure that he is the better runner? Who do you think is the better runner? Support your opinion with evidence from the story.

5. As Leon and Amyntas part, Leon says, "The Gods be with you, Amyntas, and grant that we never meet again." What does Leon mean?

6. At the end of the story Amyntas realizes that he and Leon have exchanged "gifts of a sort." What "gifts" do they exchange?

7. How accurate were the predictions you made in Part 1 about the outcome of the race and the boys' friendship?

Reading Literature: Short Stories

1. **Identifying Conflict.** This story about friendship has many conflicts—external ones between characters and between countries and internal ones within characters. Identify one external and one internal conflict and tell who is involved in each.

2. **Analyzing the Climax.** The action of a story builds to its **climax,** or the turning point of its plot. The action of this story builds up to the race and the one incident that determines the winner. Find the passage that marks the climax of this story.

What struggle goes on in Amyntas's mind in that moment?

3. **Recognizing Characterization and Understanding Character.** One method of characterization is to describe a character directly. Other methods include presenting a character's words, actions, feelings, and thoughts, and showing another character's reaction to that character. From these methods of characterization a reader can infer what a character is like.

Study the following lines about or spoken by Amyntas. Tell which method or methods of characterization are used in each quotation. Then explain what you infer about Amyntas's character from each sample.

a. Amyntas, son of Ariston, had drawn a little apart from the rest. He was the youngest there, still several months from his eighteenth birthday . . . .

b. So with Leon sitting on a boulder at the edge of the shrunken river, Amyntas set to work with ruthless thoroughness to clean the cut.

c. In the middle of that night, Amyntas woke up with a thought already shaped and complete in his mind. It was an ugly thought, and it sat on his chest and mouthed at him slyly. "Leon is the one you have most to fear. If Leon is out of the race. . . ."

d. His mouth was dry and the palms of his hands were wet, and the beginnings of panic were whimpering up in him.

e. It would insult Leon to let him win . . . you could not do that to your friend. . . .

f. "I shall never be sure whether I won the race."

g. He put out a hand quickly, as though to hold the other boy back for one more moment, and Leon's hand came to meet it.

   "It has been good. All this month it has been good," Leon said.

4. **Understanding Theme. Theme** is a message conveyed through a story. In this story, Amyntas learns what makes a good friend. What lesson does he learn about being a good friend while being true to himself and his own abilities? Expressed in a general way, what Amyntas learns is one theme of the story. State this theme about friendship.

Developing Vocabulary Skills

Inferring Meaning from General Context. The descriptions of setting in this story often contain unfamiliar words. Still, you can infer the meanings of these unfamiliar words through context. For each excerpt below from the story, use the overall context to figure out the meaning of the underlined word. Write a definition for the word as you understand it from the context.

1. He woke to the first <u>dappled</u> fingers of sunlight shafting in through the doorway of his cell.

2. After that, they were kept hard at it, on the practice track and in the wrestling school that had the names of past Olympic victors carved on the <u>colonnade</u> walls.

3. They would <u>sluice</u> each other down, squatting in the stone hip-baths in the washing room after practice. . . .

4. Before the Temple of Zeus, the ancient wild olive trees from which the victors' crowns

were made cast dapple-shade across the lower steps of the vast <u>portico</u>. He spoke to the attendant priest in the deep threshold shadows beyond.

Developing Skills in Study and Research

1. **Checking Information in Two Sources.** You can check the accuracy of information on the early Olympics as presented in the story by doing research in the library. Sometimes it is necessary to check more than one source. First, make up a list of facts that you'd like to research. Try listing them as questions, such as the following.

   How old are the Olympic Games?
   Where were they held?
   What events did the Games have?
   What was the Double Stade event?
   Were there separate events for boys?
   Were women allowed at the Games?
   How important were the Games to the ancient Greeks?
   How important was the God Zeus to the Games?

   Next, look in an encyclopedia for some basic facts about the early Olympic Games. Check the encyclopedia's index for the different volumes where information can be found. Then, look in the card catalog for a book on the subject. Check as many historical facts in the story as you can in those two sources.

2. **Using Maps.** Locate an atlas in your library to find a map of Greece. Use the index or table of contents to find the map. Then answer the following questions:

a. These names are used in the story: Sparta, Athens, Crete, Corinth, Argos, Salamis, Samos, Megara, and Olympia. Where are these places on the map?

b. Cyrene is a city mentioned in the story. Does it appear on the map of modern Greece? What can you conclude about this city?

c. Compare the location of Greece to the location where you live. What can you conclude about how your climate compares to the Greek climate?

d. Trace the route of Amyntas's journey from Pireaus Harbor to Olympia in the valley where the Games are held. How far is this journey? In the story, why do you think this journey takes five days?

Developing Skills in Critical Thinking

Classifying and Categorizing. In this section of the chapter, you have read seven short stories. Which ones are written in first-person point of view? Which are written in third-person omniscient or limited point of view? Make a chart to classify the stories according to their point of view.

Developing Writing Skills

Writing a Definition. Amyntas decides that letting Leon win would not be an act of friendship. Respecting Leon as a friend enough to try his best is an act of friendship for Amyntas. Likewise, for Leon, friendship means unselfishly honoring Amyntas as the best runner, rather than being proud and concerned about his own bad luck. Think about what you know of friendship from your own experience. In a paragraph write a definition of your idea of friendship. Follow these steps.

Prewriting. Jot down a list of qualities that you think are necessary for a good friendship. Think of an example or two of a good friendship that illustrates those qualities. Use your notes to come up with a statement of what friendship means to you. Then organize your ideas and examples in an outline for a paragraph.

Drafting. Begin with a statement of what true friendship means to you. Develop your definition by explaining the qualities that friendship includes. Support your definition by presenting your examples of true friendship.

Revising and Sharing. Reread your paragraph. Is your definition clear? Be sure that you have included specific examples to illustrate your definition. Finally, read your paragraph aloud to someone. Ask whether each sentence is clear and whether the organization of the paragraph is logical. If not, revise your definition again.

Fantasy and Science Fiction

The stories in this section will take you out of this world. Unlike the familiar worlds of the realistic and historical stories you've read so far, the worlds of these stories don't exist on any map. These stories are known as fantasy and science fiction. A **fantasy** story, such as the first one in this section, has a totally imaginary setting where magic can happen and wishes can come true. **Science fiction** refers to fictional stories based on scientific facts or theories. Science fiction is usually set in the future and often on a distant planet.

Man Glowing with Happiness, 1968, RUFFINO TAMAYO. Museo Ruffino Tamayo, Mexico City. Photograph by Jesus Sanchez Uribe.

The Third Wish

JOAN AIKEN

Can you think of stories in which the main character is granted three wishes? How do the stories end? As you read this story, look for clues to the outcome.

Once there was a man who was driving in his car at dusk on a spring evening through part of the forest of Savernake. His name was Mr. Peters. The primroses were just beginning, but the trees were still bare and it was cold; the birds had stopped singing an hour ago.

As Mr. Peters entered a straight, empty stretch of road he seemed to hear a faint crying, and a struggling and thrashing, as if somebody was in trouble far away in the trees. He left his car and climbed the mossy bank beside the road. Beyond the bank was an open slope of beech trees leading down to thorn bushes through which he saw the gleam of water. He stood a moment, waiting to try and discover where the noise was coming from, and presently heard a rustling and some strange cries in a voice that was almost human— and yet there was something too hoarse about it at one time and too clear and sweet at another. Mr. Peters ran down the hill, and, as he neared the bushes, he saw some-

thing white among them that was trying to extricate itself; coming closer he found that it was a swan that had become entangled in the thorns growing on the bank of the canal.

The bird struggled all the more frantically as he approached, looking at him with hate in its yellow eyes, and when he took hold of it to free it, hissed at him, pecked him, and thrashed dangerously with its wings, which were powerful enough to break his arm. Nevertheless, he managed to release it from the thorns, and carrying it tightly with one arm, holding the snaky head well away with the other hand (for he did not wish his eyes pecked out), he took it to the verge of the canal and dropped it in.

The swan instantly assumed great dignity and sailed out to the middle of the water, where it put itself to rights with much dabbling and preening, smoothing its feathers with little showers of drops. Mr. Peters waited, to make sure that it was all right and had suffered no damage in its struggles. Presently the swan, when it was satisfied with its appearance, floated in to the bank once more, and in a moment, instead of the great white bird, there was a little man all in green with a golden crown and long beard, standing by the water. He had fierce, glittering eyes and looked by no means friendly.

"Well, Sir," he said threateningly, "I see you are presumptuous enough to know some of the laws of magic. You think that because you have rescued—by pure good fortune—the King of the Forest from a difficulty, you should have some fabulous reward."

"I expect three wishes, no more and no less," answered Mr. Peters, looking at him steadily and with composure.

"Three wishes, he wants, the clever man! Well, I have yet to hear of the human being who made any good use of his three wishes—they mostly end up worse off than they started. Take three wishes then—" he flung three dead leaves in the air "—don't blame me if you spend the last wish in undoing the work of the other two."

Mr. Peters caught the leaves and put two of them carefully in his notecase. When he looked up, the swan was sailing about in the middle of the water again, flicking the drops angrily down its long neck.

Mr. Peters stood for some minutes reflecting on how he should use his reward. He knew very well that the gift of three magic wishes was one that brought trouble more often than not, and he had no inten-tion of being like the forester who first wished by mistake for a sausage, and then in rage wished it on the end of his wife's nose, and then had to use his last wish in getting it off again. Mr. Peters had most of the things which he wanted and was very content with his life. The only thing that troubled him was that he was a little lonely and had no companion for his old age. He decided to use his first wish and to keep the other two in case of an emergency. Taking a thorn he pricked his tongue with it, to remind himself not to utter rash wishes aloud. Then, holding the third leaf and gazing around him at the dusky under-growth, the primroses, great beeches, and the blue-green water of the canal, he said:

"I wish I had a wife as beautiful as the forest."

A tremendous quacking and splashing broke out on the surface of the water. He thought that it was the swan laughing at him. Taking no notice, he made his way through the darkening woods to his car, wrapped himself up in the rug, and went to sleep.

When he awoke, it was morning and the birds were beginning to call. Coming along the track towards him was the most beautiful creature he had ever seen, with eyes as blue-green as the canal, hair as dusky as the bushes, and skin as white as the feathers of swans.

"Are you the wife that I wished for?" asked Mr. Peters.

"Yes I am," she replied. "My name is Leita."

She stepped into the car beside him and they drove off to the church on the outskirts of the forest, where they were married. Then he took her to his house in a remote and lovely valley and showed her all his treasures—the bees in their white hives, the Jersey cows, the hyacinths, the silver candlesticks, the blue cups, and the luster bowl for putting primroses in. She admired everything, but what pleased her the most was the river that ran by the foot of his garden.

"Do swans come up here?" she asked.

"Yes, I have often seen swans there on the river," he told her, and she smiled.

Leita made him a good wife. She was gentle and friendly, busied herself about the house and garden, polished the bowls, milked the cows, and mended his socks. But as time went by, Mr. Peters began to feel that she was not happy. She seemed restless, wandered much in the garden, and sometimes, when he came back from the fields, he would find the house empty and she would only return after half an hour or so with no explanation of where she had been. On these occasions, she was always especially tender and would put out his slippers to warm and cook his favorite dish—Welsh rarebit with wild strawberries—for supper.

One evening he was returning home along the river path when he saw Leita in front of him, down by the water. A swan had sailed up to the verge, and she had her arms around its neck and the swan's head rested against her cheek. She was weeping,

Summer, 1890, FRANK WESTON BENSON. National Museum of American Art, Smithsonian Institution, Washington, D.C., Gift of John Gellatly.

and, as he came nearer, he saw that tears were rolling, too, from the swan's eyes.

"Leita, what is it?" he asked, very troubled.

"This is my sister," she answered. "I can't bear being separated from her."

Now he understood that Leita was really a swan from the forest, and this made him very sad because when a human being marries a bird it always leads to sorrow.

"I could use my second wish to give your sister human shape, so that she could be a companion to you," he suggested.

"No, no," she cried, "I couldn't ask that of her."

"Is it so very hard to be a human being?" asked Mr. Peters sadly.

"Very, very hard," she answered.

"Don't you love me at all, Leita?"

"Yes, I do, I do love you," she said, and there were tears in her eyes again. "But I miss the old life in the forest, the cool grass and the mist rising off the river at sunrise, and the feel of the water sliding over my feathers as my sister and I drifted along the stream."

"Then shall I use my second wish to turn you back into a swan again?" he asked, and his tongue pricked to remind him of the old king's words, and his heart swelled with grief inside him.

"Who would darn your socks and cook your meals and see to the hens?"

"I'd do it myself, as I did before I married you," he said, trying to sound cheerful.

She shook her head. "No, I could not be as unkind to you as that. I am partly a swan, but I am also partly a human being now. I will stay with you."

Poor Mr. Peters was very distressed on his wife's account and did his best to make her life happier, taking her for drives in the car, finding beautiful music for her to listen to on the radio, buying clothes for her and even suggesting a trip around the world. She said no to that; she would prefer to stay in their own house near the river.

He noticed that she spent more and more time baking wonderful cakes—jam puffs, petits fours, éclairs, and meringues. One day he saw her take a basketful down to the river, and he guessed that she was giving them to her sister.

He built a seat for her by the river, and the two sisters spent hours together there, communicating in some wordless manner. For a time he thought that all would be well, but then he saw how thin and pale she was growing.

One night when he had been late doing the accounts, he came up to bed and found her weeping in her sleep and calling: "Rhea! Rhea! I can't understand what you say! Oh, wait for me, take me with you!"

Then he knew that it was hopeless and she would never be happy as a human. He kissed her goodbye, then took another leaf from his notecase, blew it out of the window, and used up his second wish.

Next moment, instead of Leita there was a sleeping swan laying across the bed with its head under its wing. He carried it out of the house and down to the brink of the river. Then he said "Leita! Leita!" to waken her and gently put her into the water. She gazed around her in astonishment for a moment, and then came up to him and rested her head lightly against his hand; next instant, she was flying away over the trees towards the heart of the forest.

He heard a harsh laugh behind him and, turning around saw the old King looking at him with a malicious expression.

"Well, my friend! You don't seem to have managed so wonderfully with your

Home of the Heron, 1893, GEORGE INNESS.

first two wishes, do you? What will you do with the last? Turn yourself into a swan? Or turn Leita back into a girl?"

"I shall do neither," said Mr. Peters calmly. "Human beings and swans are better in their own shapes."

But for all that he looked sadly over towards the forest where Leita had flown, and he walked slowly back to his empty house.

The next day, he saw two swans swimming at the bottom of the garden, and one of them wore the gold chain he had given Leita after their marriage; she came up and rubbed her head against his hand.

Mr. Peters and his two swans came to be well known in that part of the country; people used to say that he talked to the swans and they understood him as well as his neighbors. Many people were a little frightened of him. There was a story that once when thieves tried to break into his house they were set upon by two huge white birds that carried them off bodily and dropped them in the river.

As Mr. Peters grew old, everyone wondered at his contentment. Even when he was bent with rheumatism he would not think of moving to a drier spot, but went slowly about his work, milking the cows and collecting the honey and eggs, with the two swans always somewhere close at hand.

Sometimes people who knew his story would say to him:

"Mr. Peters, why don't you wish for another wife?"

"Not likely," he would answer serenely.

"Two wishes were enough for me, I reckon. I've learned that even if your wishes are granted they don't always better you. I'll stay faithful to Leita."

One autumn night, passers-by along the road heard the mournful sound of two swans singing. All night the song went on, sweet and harsh, sharp and clear. In the morning Mr. Peters was found peacefully dead in his bed with a smile of happiness on his face. In between his hands, which lay clasped on his breast, were a withered leaf and a white feather.

Joan Aiken (*born 1924*) has been writing stories and poems since the age of five. She was born in England, the daughter of an American poet, Conrad Aiken. When she was seventeen, Aiken sent one of her stories to a radio station. It was accepted for broadcasting. Later, she worked for that station as well as for *Argosy Magazine.* Aiken is known for her imaginative stories and novels, such as *The Whispering Mountain* and *The Wolves of Willoughby Chase.*

Developing Comprehension Skills

1. How does Mr. Peters earn a reward?

2. Why is his new wife unhappy? How does Mr. Peters try to cheer her up?

3. What causes Mr. Peters to turn Leita back into a swan? What does this decision reveal about his character?

4. Why does Mr. Peters decide not to use his third wish?

5. Do you think Mr. Peters uses his wishes wisely? Give reasons for your answer.

Reading Literature: Short Stories

1. **Understanding Mood. Mood** is a feeling or atmosphere created by a story. All the elements of a story contribute to its mood, especially the descriptions of setting and what the characters do and say. In "The Third Wish," for example, the mood is mostly one of calm and peace. The descriptions of the quiet forest scenes help create this mood. Both Mr. Peters and Leita are calm, quiet characters. Even Mr. Peters's death is described as peaceful. Nothing really disturbs the peaceful mood of the story, except the rather irritable King of the Forest.

   Look back through the story and find three samples that help to create the mood. If you were to make a movie of this story, what music would you choose to go with it?

2. **Identifying Foreshadowing. Foreshadowing** is the use of clues to indicate what will happen later in the story. For example, several incidents and descriptions foreshadow the discovery that Leita is a swan. One incident is the quacking and splashing that Mr. Peters hears when he makes his first wish. Other incidents in the story foreshadow that Mr. Peters's wishes will not make him any better off. Find two examples of foreshadowing in the story.

3. **Diagraming Plot.** Diagraming a plot can help you to understand a story. Review the explanation of how to diagram a plot on page 21. Then draw a plot diagram for this story. Include these five parts of the plot: the exposition, the rising action, the climax, the falling action, and the resolution.

4. **Understanding Theme.** Mr. Peters learns a lesson from using two of his three wishes. It keeps him from using his third wish. Identify the sentence spoken by Mr. Peters near the end of the story that directly states the lesson he learns and the main theme of this story.

Developing Vocabulary Skills

Using Antonym Clues. Antonyms are words that have opposite meanings. For example, *neat* and *messy* are antonyms. Sometimes the antonym of a word that is unfamiliar to you is found in context. The antonym may give you a clue to the meaning of the word. In the following sentences the underlined words are from the story. Use antonym clues to determine their meanings. Then write a definition for each word as you understand it from the context. Use each word in an original sentence.

1. Mr. Peters heard strange cries in a voice that was too <u>hoarse</u> at one time and too clear and sweet at another.

2. Mr. Peters <u>extricated</u> the swan that was tangled in the thick thorn bushes.

3. Although the King of the Forest expected Mr. Peters to react with nervousness or fear, Mr. Peters looked at him steadily and with composure.

4. The forester made two rash wishes that he later regretted. Mr. Peters vowed to make only careful, wise wishes.

5. Leita's skin was as white as the feathers of swans while her hair was as dusky as the bushes.

6. Mr. Peters's house was in a remote valley but was still close to the lovely river where the swans swam.

7. Leita's expression was hardly malicious, but neither was it loving.

Developing Skills in Critical Thinking

Organizing Ideas in an Argument. When writers develop arguments, they support opinions with reasons and facts presented in a logical order. One kind of logical order is a listing of reasons from the weakest to the strongest. This order is called **order of importance.** It leaves readers with the most powerful reason fresh in their minds.

In this story, Leita confesses that it's "very, very hard" to be human. Mr. Peters tries various ways to make her happy as a human. Notice on page 154 that he organizes the activities in order of their importance, or what he thinks is their importance: He starts by taking her for drives in the car and ends by suggesting a trip around the world.

What can you think of that might make a character like Leita want to stay human? List four or five ways that you would try in order of their importance. That is, start with the things she might like the least and end with the things you think she would like the most. Compare your suggestions with others in your class.

Developing Writing Skills

Explaining Fantasy Elements in a Story. Unlike the realistic stories you've read in this chapter, "The Third Wish" is a fantasy. Things happen in this story that cannot happen in the real world. For example, magic happens and animals are transformed into people and back again. Write a paragraph explaining the fantasy elements in the story. Follow these stages in the process of writing.

Prewriting. Go back through the story. List all the events and characters in the story that are not realistic. Arrange them in the order in which they occur or are introduced.

Drafting. Write a topic sentence stating that the story is a fantasy. Then explain the events and characters from your notes as examples of fantasy elements.

Revising and Sharing. Read your paragraph. Be sure that it includes examples of fantasy from the story. Look over your sentences to make sure that they are clear and complete. Ask a classmate to read your explanation and offer suggestions or comments.

Future Tense

ROBERT LIPSYTE

What would happen if you wrote a story that turned out to be true? Read to find out whether the story that Gary is writing is scientific fact or science fiction.

Gary couldn't wait for tenth grade to start so he could strut his sentences, parade his paragraphs, renew his reputation as the top creative writer in school. At the opening assembly, he felt on edge, psyched, like a boxer before the first-round bell. He leaned forward as Dr. Proctor, the principal, introduced two new staff members. He wasn't particularly interested in the new vice-principal, Ms. Jones; Gary never had discipline problems, he'd never even had to stay after school. But his head cocked alertly as Dr. Proctor introduced the new Honors English teacher, Mr. Smith. Here was the person he'd have to impress.

He studied Mr. Smith. The man was hard to describe. He looked as though he'd been manufactured to fit his name. Average height, brownish hair, pale white skin, medium build. Middle age. He was the sort of person you began to forget the minute you met him. Even his clothes had no particular style. They merely covered his body.

Mr. Smith was . . . just there.

Gary was studying Mr. Smith so intently that he didn't hear Dr. Proctor call him up to the stage to receive an award from last term. Jim Baggs jabbed an elbow into his ribs and said, "Let's get up there, Dude."

Dr. Proctor shook Gary's hand and gave him the County Medal for Best Composition. While Dr. Proctor was giving Jim Baggs the County Trophy for Best All-Round Athlete, Gary glanced over his shoulder to see if Mr. Smith looked impressed. But he couldn't find the new teacher. Gary wondered if Mr. Smith was so ordinary he was invisible when no one was talking about him.

On the way home, Dani Belzer, the prettiest poet in school, asked Gary, "What did you think of our new Mr. Wordsmith?"

"If he was a color he'd be beige," said Gary. "If he was a taste he'd be water. If he was a sound he'd be a low hum."

"Fancy, empty words," sneered Mike Chung, ace reporter on the school paper. "All you've told me is you've got nothing to tell me."

Dani quickly stepped between them. "What did you think of the first assignment?"

"Describe a Typical Day at School," said Gary, trying unsuccessfully to mimic Mr. Smith's bland voice. "That's about as exciting as tofu."

"A real artist," said Dani, "accepts the commonplace as a challenge."

That night, hunched over his humming electric typewriter, Gary wrote a description of a typical day at school from the viewpoint of a new teacher who was seeing everything for the first time, who took nothing for granted. He described the shredded edges of the limp flag outside the dented front door, the worn flooring where generations of kids had nervously paced outside the principal's office, the nauseatingly sweet pipe-smoke seeping out of the teachers' lounge.

And then, in the last line, he gave the composition that extra twist, the little kicker on which his reputation rested. He wrote:

    The new teacher's beady little
    eyes missed nothing, for they were
    the optical recorders of an alien
    creature who had come to earth to
    gather information.

The next morning, when Mr. Smith asked for a volunteer to read aloud, Gary was on his feet and moving toward the front of the classroom before Mike Chung got his hand out of his pocket.

The class loved Gary's composition.

They laughed and stamped their feet. Chung shrugged, which meant he couldn't think of any criticism, and Dani flashed thumbs up. Best of all, Jim Baggs shouldered Gary against the blackboard after class and said, "Awesome tale, Dude."

Gary felt good until he got the composition back. Along one margin, in a perfect script, Mr. Smith had written:

You can do better.

"How would he know?" Gary complained on the way home.

"You should be grateful," said Dani. "He's pushing you to the farthest limits of your talent."

"Which may be nearer than you think," snickered Mike.

Gary rewrote his composition, expanded it, complicated it, thickened it. Not only was this new teacher an alien, he was part of an extraterrestrial conspiracy to take over Earth. Gary's final sentence was:

    Every iota of information, frag-
    ment of fact, morsel of minutiae
    sucked up by those vacuuming eyes
    was beamed directly into a com-
    puter circling the planet. The
    data would eventually become a
    program that would control the
    mind of every school kid on earth.

Gary showed the new draft to Dani before class. He stood on tiptoes so he could read over her shoulder. Sometimes he wished she were shorter, but mostly he wished he were taller.

"What do you think?"

"The assignment was to describe a typical day," said Dani. "This is off the wall."

He snatched the papers back. "Creative writing means creating." He walked away, hurt and angry. He thought: *If she doesn't like my compositions, how can I ever get her to like me?*

That morning, Mike Chung read his own composition aloud to the class. He described a typical day through the eyes of a student in a wheelchair. Everything most students take for granted was an obstacle: the bathroom door too heavy to open, the gym steps too steep to climb, the light switch too high on the wall. The class applauded and Mr. Smith smiled approvingly. Even Gary had to admit it was really good—if you considered plain-fact journalism as creative writing, that is.

Gary's rewrite came back the next day marked:

Improving. Try again.

Saturday he locked himself in his room after breakfast and rewrote the rewrite. He carefully selected his nouns and verbs and adjectives. He polished and arranged them in sentences like a jeweler strings pearls. He felt good as he wrote, as the electric typewriter hummed and buzzed and sometimes coughed. He thought: *Every champion knows that as hard as it is to get to the top, it's even harder to stay up there.*

His mother knocked on his door around noon. When he let her in, she said, "It's a beautiful day."

"Big project," he mumbled. He wanted to avoid a distracting conversation.

She smiled. "If you spend too much time in your room, you'll turn into a mushroom."

He wasn't listening. "Thanks. Anything's okay. Don't forget the mayonnaise."

Gary wrote:

```
    The alien's probes trembled as
he read the student's composi-
tion. Could that skinny, bespec-
tacled earthling really suspect
its extraterrestrial identity? Or
was his composition merely the re-
sult of a creative thunderstorm in
a brilliant young mind?
```

Before Gary turned in his composition on Monday morning, he showed it to Mike Chung. He should have known better.

"You're trying too hard," chortled Chung. "Truth is stronger than fiction."

Gary flinched at that. It hurt. It might be true. But he couldn't let his competition know he had scored. "You journalists are stuck in the present and the past," growled Gary. "Imagination prepares us for what's going to happen."

Dani read her composition aloud to the class. It described a typical day from the perspective of a louse choosing a head of hair to nest in. The louse moved from a thicket of a varsity crew-cut to the matted jungle of a sagging perm to a straight, sleek blond cascade.

The class cheered and Mr. Smith smiled. Gary felt a twinge of jealousy. Dani and Mike were coming on. There wasn't room for more than one at the top.

House of Death and Life (Study), 1984-85, GABRIEL LADERMAN. Photograph: Jessica Darraby Gallery, Los Angeles.

In the hallway, he said to Dani, "And you called my composition off the wall?"

Mike jumped in. "There's a big difference between poetical metaphor and hack science fiction."

Gary felt choked by a lump in his throat. He hurried away.

Mr. Smith handed back Gary's composition the next day marked:

See me after school.

Gary was nervous all day. What was there to talk about? Maybe Mr. Smith hated science fiction. One of those traditional English teachers. Didn't understand that science fiction could be literature. *Maybe I can educate him,* thought Gary.

When Gary arrived at the English office, Mr. Smith seemed nervous too. He kept folding and unfolding Gary's composition. "Where do you get such ideas?" he asked in his monotone voice.

Gary shrugged. "They just come to me."

"Alien teachers. Taking over the minds

of schoolchildren." Mr. Smith's empty eyes were blinking. "What made you think of that?"

"I've always had this vivid imagination."

"If you're sure it's just your imagination." Mr. Smith looked relieved. "I guess everything will work out." He handed back Gary's composition. "No more fantasy, Gary. Reality. That's your assignment. Write only about what you know."

Outside school, Gary ran into Jim Baggs, who looked surprised to see him. "Don't tell me you had to stay after, Dude."

"I had to see Mr. Smith about my composition. He didn't like it. Told me to stick to reality."

"Don't listen." Jim Baggs body checked Gary into the schoolyard fence. "Dude, you got to be yourself."

Gary ran all the way home and locked himself into his room. He felt feverish with creativity. Dude, you got to be yourself, Dude. It doesn't matter what your so-called friends say, or your English teacher. You've got to play your own kind of game, write your own kind of stories.

The words flowed out of Gary's mind and through his fingers and out of the machine and onto sheets of paper. He wrote and rewrote until he felt the words were exactly right:

```
With great effort, the alien
shut down the electrical panic im-
pulses coursing through its sys-
tem and turned on Logical
Overdrive. There were two possi-
bilities:
```

```
  1. This high school boy was
exactly what he seemed to be, a
brilliant, imaginative, appren-
tice best-selling author and
screenwriter, or,
  2. He had somehow stumbled onto
the secret plan and he would have
to be either enlisted into the
conspiracy or erased off the face
of the planet.
```

First thing in the morning, Gary turned in his new rewrite to Mr. Smith. A half hour later, Mr. Smith called Gary out of Spanish. There was no expression on his regular features. He said, "I'm going to need some help with you."

Cold sweat covered Gary's body as Mr. Smith grabbed his arm and led him to the new vice-principal. She read the composition while they waited. Gary got a good look at her for the first time. Ms. Jones was . . . just there. She looked as though she'd been manufactured to fit her name. Average. Standard. Typical. The cold sweat turned into goose pimples.

How could he have missed the clues? Smith and Jones were aliens! He had stumbled on their secret and now they'd have to deal with him.

He blurted, "Are you going to enlist me or erase me?"

Ms. Jones ignored him. "In my opinion, Mr. Smith, you are overreacting. This sort of nonsense"—she waved Gary's composition—"is the typical response of an over-stimulated adolescent to the mixture of reality and fantasy in an environment dominated by manipulative music, television, and films. Nothing for us to worry about."

"If you're sure, Ms. Jones," said Mr. Smith. He didn't sound sure.

The vice-principal looked at Gary for the first time. There was no expression in her eyes. Her voice was flat. "You'd better get off this science fiction kick," she said. "If you know what's good for you."

"I'll never tell another human being, I swear," he babbled.

"What are you talking about?" asked Ms. Jones.

"Your secret is safe with me," he lied. He thought, *If I can just get away from them. Alert the authorities. Save the planet.*

"You see," said Ms. Jones, "you're writing yourself into a crazed state."

"You're beginning to believe your own fantasies," said Mr. Smith.

"I'm not going to do anything this time," said Ms. Jones, "but you must promise to write only about what you know."

"Or I'll have to fail you," said Mr. Smith.

"For your own good," said Ms. Jones. "Writing can be very dangerous."

"Especially for writers," said Mr. Smith, "who write about things they shouldn't."

"Absolutely," said Gary, "positively, no question about it. Only what I know." He backed out the door, nodding his head, thinking, *Just a few more steps and I'm okay. I hope these aliens can't read minds.*

Jim Baggs was practicing head fakes in the hallway. He slammed Gary into the wall with a hip block. "How's it going, Dude?" he asked, helping Gary up.

"Aliens," gasped Gary. "Told me no more science fiction."

"They can't treat a star writer like that," said Jim. "See what the head honcho's got to say." He grabbed Gary's wrist and dragged him to the principal's office.

"What can I do for you, boys?" boomed Dr. Proctor.

"They're messing with his moves, Doc," said Jim Baggs. "You go to let the aces run their races."

"Thank you, James." Dr. Proctor popped his forefinger at the door. "I'll handle this."

"You're home free, Dude," said Jim, whacking Gary across the shoulder blades as he left.

"From the beginning," ordered Dr. Proctor. He nodded sympathetically as Gary told the entire story, from the opening assembly to the meeting with Mr. Smith and Ms. Jones. When Gary was finished, Dr. Proctor took the papers from Gary's hand. He shook his head as he read Gary's last rewrite.

"You really have a way with words, Gary. I should have sensed you were on to something."

Gary's stomach flipped. "You really think there could be aliens trying to take over Earth?"

"Certainly," said Dr. Proctor, matter-of-factly. "Earth is the ripest plum in the universe."

Gary wasn't sure if he should feel relieved that he wasn't crazy or be scared out of his mind. He took a deep breath to control the quaver in his voice, and said: "I

The House of Glass, 1939, RENÉ MAGRITTE. Museum Boymans-van Beuningen, Rotterdam, The Netherlands.
© 1988 ADAGP/ARS, New York City.

spotted Smith and Jones right away. They look like they were manufactured to fit their names. Obviously humanoids. Panicked as soon as they knew I was on to them."

Dr. Proctor chuckled and shook his head. "No self-respecting civilization would send those two stiffs to Earth."

"They're not aliens?" He felt relieved and disappointed at the same time.

"I checked them out myself," said Dr. Proctor. "Just two average, standard, typical human beings, with no imagination, no creativity."

"So why'd you hire them?"

Dr. Proctor laughed. "Because they'd

never spot an alien. No creative imagination. That's why I got rid of the last vice-principal and the last Honors English teacher. They were giving me odd little glances when they thought I wasn't looking. After ten years on your planet, I've learned to smell trouble."

Gary's spine turned to ice and dripped down the backs of his legs. "You're an alien!"

"Great composition," said Dr. Proctor, waving Gary's papers. "Grammatical, vividly written, and totally accurate."

"It's just a composition," babbled Gary, "made the whole thing up, imagination, you know."

Dr. Proctor removed the face of his wristwatch and began tapping tiny buttons. "Always liked writers. I majored in your planet's literature. Writers are the keepers of the past and the hope of the future. Too bad they cause so much trouble in the present."

"I won't tell anyone," cried Gary. "Your secret's safe with me." He began to back slowly toward the door.

Dr. Proctor shook his head. "How can writers keep secrets, Gary? It's their natures to share their creations with the world." He tapped three times and froze Gary in place, one foot raised to step out the door.

"But it was only a composition," screamed Gary as his body disappeared before his eyes.

"And I can't wait to hear what the folks back home say when you read it to them," said Dr. Proctor.

"I made it all up." Gary had the sensation of rocketing upward. "I made up the whole . . ."

Robert Lipsyte (*born 1938*) was a prize-winning sportswriter for *The New York Times.* Lipsyte is best known to young readers for his first novel, *The Contender,* a story about a young black boxer. Other well-known Lipsyte novels include *One Fat Summer, Summer Rules,* and *Summerboy.* Beside his novels, screenplays, and television scripts, Lipsyte has written two works of nonfiction: *Assignment: Sports* and *Free to Be Muhammad Ali.* He is presently a network television correspondent for NBC News, based in New York.

Developing Comprehension Skills

1. What is Gary's composition about?

2. Why does Gary have to rewrite his composition the first time? How does the composition change with each rewrite?

3. As Gary continues to revise his composition, he gives more detailed information. Which of his ideas turn out to be accurate, and which turn out to be wrong?

4. What happens to Gary at the end of the story? Why does it happen?

5. Based on what Dr. Proctor says, what can you infer will happen to Gary after he disappears?

6. Do you believe that Gary will ever return to Earth? Why or why not?

7. Gary has a "creative imagination." Based on this story and on your own experience, what are some of the positive and negative points of having a creative imagination?

Reading Literature: Short Stories

1. **Recognizing Science Fiction.** Many science fiction stories are based in reality or have realistic elements. Which elements in this story are realistic, and which are elements of science fiction?

2. **Analyzing a Surprise Ending.** What is surprising about the ending of this story? Explain how the writer leads you in one direction through his descriptions of Mr. Smith and Ms. Jones and then surprises you at the end.

3. **Understanding Theme.** Dr. Proctor says, "Writers are the keepers of the past and the hope of the future. Too bad they cause so much trouble in the present." How is Gary "the hope of the future" as a writer? What "trouble" does he cause, and for whom?

4. **Explaining a Title.** Sometimes the title of a story has more than one meaning. Often it gives a clue to a story's theme. Think of all the possible meanings for the words *future* and *tense*.

Developing Vocabulary Skills

Inferring Meaning from General Context. Use the general context of the following paragraphs from Gary's composition to help you determine the meaning of each underlined term. Write a definition for each underlined word or phrase.

1. Every iota of information, fragment of fact, morsel of minutiae sucked up by those vacuuming eyes was beamed directly into a computer circling the planet. The data would eventually become a program that would control the mind of every school kid on earth.

2. The alien's probes trembled as he read the student's composition. Could that skinny, bespectacled earthling really suspect its extraterrestrial identity? Or was his composition merely the result of a creative thunderstorm in a brilliant young mind?

3. With great effort, the alien shut down the electrical panic impulses coursing through its system and turned on Logical Overdrive.

Developing Skills in Speaking and Listening

Reading Dramatically. Hearing an action story read aloud can make the plot and characters come alive for the audience. After you have finished the writing assignment below, practice reading your narration. Slightly speed up or slow down your speech at various points to emphasize action, to build suspense, or to highlight parts of the narration. Practice changing your voice for each character, if your composition has different characters.

When you are ready, present your dramatic reading to a small group or to the entire class.

Developing Writing Skills

1. **Writing a Composition.** In the story, Gary, Mike, and Dani all wrote creative compositions for their writing assignments, "A Typical Day at School." According to Dani, "A real artist accepts the commonplace as a challenge." In other words, what you know best can be the most difficult or challenging to write about. Write your own version of "A Typical Day at School." Try to think of a viewpoint that will make this commonplace topic interesting. Your composition should have from three to five paragraphs.

   Prewriting. Decide on the narrator of your composition. Will it be an average student, an unusual student, or even an inanimate object?

   Next, imagine that you are the narrator. List what you might notice on a typical day at school, what you might do, how you might feel, and how you might react in a variety of situations.

   Drafting. Use your list to write your composition in chronological order. The first paragraph might take place in the morning or be the first incident. Each of the following paragraphs could carry your reader later into the day.

   Revising and Sharing. Exchange compositions with a partner. Check the narration you're reading for the following items:

   a. Are the paragraphs arranged in chronological order? If not, how should they be rearranged?

   b. Is the viewpoint clear? If not, how could it be improved?

   c. Has a typical day at school been described in an interesting or unusual way? How could it be made more interesting?

   Revise your narration keeping in mind your partner's suggestions.

2. **Changing Point of View.** The point of view of a story determines how much the audience knows. Rewrite the last episode of the story from Dr. Proctor's point of view. Remember that Dr. Proctor may offer different ideas and information to the reader.

   In your prewriting notes, list all the things that Dr. Proctor would know about but Gary wouldn't. When you draft, you can follow the original story giving only Dr. Proctor's thoughts instead of Gary's. Refer to Guidelines for the Process of Writing beginning on page 654 in the handbook. Have a classmate read your rewrite for sense and clarity.

All Summer in a Day

RAY BRADBURY

Imagine a time and place with no sun. How would you feel? Would you be satisfied living your life indoors—no sun, no fresh air, no clear sky? Read to see what the sun means to the characters in this story.

"Ready?"

"Ready."

"Now?"

"Soon."

"Do the scientists really know? Will it happen today, will it?"

"Look, look; see for yourself!"

The children pressed to each other like so many roses, so many weeds, intermixed, peering out for a look at the hidden sun.

It rained.

It had been raining for seven years; thousands upon thousands of days compounded and filled from one end to the other with rain, with the drum and gush of water, with the sweet crystal fall of showers and the concussion of storms so heavy they were tidal waves come over the islands. A thousand forests had been crushed under the rain and grown up a thousand times to be crushed again. And this was the way life was forever on the planet Venus, and this was the schoolroom of the children of the rocket men and women who had come to a raining world to set up civilization and live out their lives.

"It's stopping! It's stopping!"

"Yes, yes!"

Margot stood apart from them, from these children who could never remember a time when there wasn't rain and rain and rain. They were all nine years old, and, if there had been a day, seven years ago, when the sun came out for an hour and showed its face to the stunned world, they could not recall. Sometimes at night she heard them stir, in remembrance, and she knew they were dreaming and remembering gold or a yellow crayon or a coin large enough to buy the world with. She knew they thought they remembered a warmness, like a blushing in the face, in the body, in the arms and legs and trembling hands. Then they always awoke to the tatting drum, the endless shaking down of clear bead necklaces upon the roof, the walk, the gardens, the forests, and their dreams were gone.

All day yesterday they had read in class

about the sun. About how like a lemon it was, and how hot. And they had written small stories or essays or poems about it:

I think the sun is a flower,
That blooms for just one hour.

That was Margot's poem, read in a quiet voice and in the still classroom while the rain was falling outside.

"Aw, you didn't write that!" protested one of the boys.

"I did," said Margot. "I *did*."

"William!" said the teacher.

But that was yesterday. Now, the rain was slackening, and the children were crushed before the great, thick windows.

"Where's teacher?"

"She'll be back."

"She'd better hurry; we'll miss it!"

They turned on themselves, like a feverish wheel, all tumbling spokes.

Margot stood alone. She was a very frail girl who looked as if she had been lost in the rain for years, and the rain had washed out the blue from her eyes and the red from her mouth and the yellow from her hair. She was an old photograph dusted from an album, whitened away, and if she spoke at all her voice would be a ghost. Now she stood, separate, staring at the rain and the loud, wet world beyond the huge glass.

"What're *you* looking at?" said William.

Margot said nothing.

"Speak when you're spoken to." He gave her a shove. But she did not move; rather, she let herself be moved only by him and nothing else.

They edged away from her; they would not look at her. She felt them go away. This was because she would play no games with them in the echoing tunnels of the underground city. If they tagged her and ran, she stood blinking after them and did not follow. When the class sang songs about happiness and life and games, her lips barely moved. Only when they sang about the sun and the summer did her lips move, as she watched the drenched windows.

And then, of course, the biggest crime of all was that she had come here only five years ago from Earth, and she remembered the sun and the way the sun was and the sky was when she was four, in Ohio. And they, they had been on Venus all their lives, and they had been only two years old when last the sun came out and had long since forgotten the color and heat of it and the way it really was. But Margot remembered.

"It's like a penny," she said, once, eyes closed.

"No, it's not!" the children cried.

"It's like a fire," she said, "in the stove."

"You're lying, you don't remember!" cried the children.

But she remembered and stood quietly apart from all of them and watched the patterning windows. And once, a month ago, she had refused to shower in the school shower rooms, had clutched her hands to her ears and over her head, screaming that the water mustn't touch her head. So after that, dimly, dimly, she sensed it; she was different, and they knew her difference and kept away.

Red Sun, 1935, ARTHUR DOVE. The Phillips Collection, Washington, D.C.

There was talk that her father and mother were taking her back to Earth next year; it seemed vital to her that they do so, though it would mean the loss of thousands of dollars to her family. And so the children hated her for all these reasons, of big and little consequence. They hated her pale, snow face, her waiting silence, her thinness, and possible future.

"Get away!" The boy gave her another push. "What're you waiting for?"

Then, for the first time, she turned and looked at him. And what she was waiting for was in her eyes.

"Well, don't wait around here!" cried the boy, savagely. "You won't see nothing!"

Her lips moved.

"Nothing!" he cried. "It was all a joke, wasn't it?" He turned to the other children. "Nothing's happening today. *Is* it?"

They all blinked at him and then, understanding, laughed and shook their heads. "Nothing, nothing!"

"Oh, but," Margot whispered, her eyes helpless. "But, this is the day, the scientists predict, they say, they *know,* the sun . . ."

"All a joke!" said the boy, and seized her roughly. "Hey, everyone, let's put her in a closet before teacher comes!"

"No," said Margot, falling back.

They surged about her, caught her up and bore her, protesting and then pleading and then crying, back into a tunnel, a room, a closet, where they slammed and locked the door. They stood looking at the door and saw it tremble from her beating and throwing herself against it. They heared her muffled cries. Then, smiling, they turned and went out and back down the tunnel, just as the teacher arrived.

"Ready, children?" She glanced at her watch.

"Yes!" said everyone.

"Are we all here?"

"Yes!"

The rain slackened still more.

They crowded to the huge door.

The rain stopped.

It was as if, in the midst of a film concerning an avalanche, a tornado, a hurricane, a volcanic eruption, something had, first, gone wrong with the sound apparatus, thus muffling and finally cutting off all noise, all of the blasts and repercussions and thunders, and then, secondly, ripped the film from the projector and inserted in its place a peaceful tropical slide that did not move or tremble. The world ground to a standstill. The silence was so immense and unbelievable that you felt that your ears had been stuffed or you had lost your hearing altogether. The children put their hands to their ears. They stood apart. The door slid back, and the smell of the silent, waiting world came in to them.

The sun came out.

It was the color of flaming bronze, and it was very large. And the sky around it was a blazing blue tile color. And the jungle burned with sunlight as the children, released from their spell, rushed out, yelling, into the summertime.

"Now, don't go too far," called the teacher after them. "You've got only one hour, you know. You wouldn't want to get caught out!"

But they were running and turning their faces up to the sky and feeling the sun on their cheeks like a warm iron; they were taking off their jackets and letting the sun burn their arms.

"Oh, it's better than the sun lamps, isn't it?"

"Much, much better!"

They stopped running and stood in the great jungle that covered Venus, that grew and never stopped growing, tumultuously, even as you watched it. It was a nest of octopi, clustering up great arms of flesh-like weed, wavering, flowering in this brief spring. It was the color of rubber and ash, this jungle, from the many years without sun. It was the color of stones and white cheeses and ink.

The children lay out, laughing, on the jungle mattress, and heard it sigh and squeak under them, resilient and alive. They ran among the trees, they slipped and fell, they pushed each other, they played hide-and-seek and tag, but most of all they squinted at the sun until tears ran down their faces. They put their hands up to that yellowness and that amazing blueness and they breathed of the fresh air and listened and listened to the silence that suspended them in a blessed sea of no sound and no motion. They looked at everything and savored everything. Then, wildly, like animals escaped from their caves, they ran and ran in shouting circles. They ran for an hour and did not stop running.

And then—

In the midst of their running, one of the girls wailed.

Everyone stopped.

The girl, standing in the open, held out her hand.

"Oh, look, look," she said, trembling.

They came slowly to look at her opened palm.

In the center of it, cupped and huge, was a single raindrop.

She began to cry, looking at it.

They glanced quietly at the sky.

"Oh. Oh."

A few cold drops fell on their noses and their cheeks and their mouths. The sun faded behind a stir of mist. A wind blew cool around them. They turned and started to walk back toward the underground house, their hands at their sides, their smiles vanishing away.

A boom of thunder startled them, and like leaves before a new hurricane, they tumbled upon each other and ran. Lightning struck ten miles away, five miles away, a mile, a half mile. The sky darkened into midnight in a flash.

They stood in the doorway of the underground for a moment until it was raining hard. Then they closed the door and heard the gigantic sound of the rain falling in tons and avalanches everywhere and forever.

"Will it be seven more years?"

"Yes. Seven."

Then one of them gave a little cry.

"Margot!"

"What?"

"She's still in the closet where we locked her."

"Margot."

They stood as if someone had driven them, like so many stakes, into the floor. They looked at each other and then looked away. They glanced out at the world that was raining now and raining and raining steadily. They could not meet each other's glances. Their faces were solemn and pale. They looked at their hands and feet, their faces down.

"Margot."

One of the girls said, "Well . . . ?"

No one moved.

"Go on," whispered the girl.

They walked slowly down the hall in the sound of cold rain. They turned through the doorway to the room, in the sound of the storm and thunder, lightning on their faces, blue and terrible. They walked over to the closet door slowly and stood by it.

Behind the closet door was only silence.

They unlocked the door, even more slowly, and let Margot out.

Ray Bradbury *(born 1920)* had a passion for adventure stories, secret code rings, and comic strips as a boy in Illinois. When he was twelve years old, he was given a toy typewriter. Since then, he has written over a thousand stories, as well as novels, plays, movie scripts, and television programs. Two well-known collections of Bradbury's stories are *The Martian Chronicles* and *Dandelion Wine. The Martian Chronicles* and his novel *Farenheit 451* were made into movies.

© 1984 Jill Krementz

Developing Comprehension Skills

1. How long has Margot lived on Venus? Why does she want to return to Earth?

2. What are some of the reasons Margot's classmates dislike her? Name three ways that they show their dislike.

3. Where do the children force Margot to go? What does she miss?

4. How do you think the other children feel about their prank at the end of the story? How do you know?

5. When the children see Margot again, how do you think they will treat her? How do you think Margot will feel?

6. At the beginning of the story, Margot is unhappy because she misses the sun. The other children do not know what they are missing. Do you think it is better to experience something wonderful and then lose it or never to experience it at all? Explain your answer.

Reading Literature: Short Stories

1. **Identifying Setting.** **Setting,** as you know, refers to when and where a story takes place. This story is set on the planet Venus. What is plant life on Venus like? The weather on Venus? Tell when this story is set. How do you know?

2. **Analyzing the Exposition.** The **exposition,** or introduction, of a story gives background information. The first several

paragraphs of this story are its exposition. What information does the exposition give about Margot? What background information does it give about the other children?

3. **Recognizing Science Fiction. Science fiction** stories are based on scientific advances. Often they are set in the future. "All Summer in a Day" was written before scientists knew very much about Venus. We now know, for example, that humans cannot breathe the air of Venus, nor do large plants grow there. Still, this classic science fiction story has a message for our world. What makes it science fiction? What does this story tell us about things in our world that we take for granted?

4. **Understanding Theme.** One of the themes of this story is about how people are sometimes cruel to each other. Margot is a sensitive child. Think about how the other children treat her and why. What do you think their actions say about the reasons people sometimes treat each other cruelly?

Developing Vocabulary Skills

Using a Dictionary or Context Clues. The following sentences use words from the story. For each underlined word tell whether you can figure out the meaning from context or whether you have to look in a dictionary. Then write a definition of the word.

1. Margot thought the children may have felt a rosy warmth like a <u>blushing</u> in the face, in the body, in the arms and legs.

2. Their faces were <u>solemn</u> and pale. The children looked sadly at their hands and feet, their faces down.

3. All of the thundering blasts and <u>repercussions</u> were cut off.

4. They heard the sound of the rain falling in tons and <u>avalanches</u>, like rocks crashing to the ground.

5. The girl <u>wailed</u> with fear when she saw the first raindrop.

6. They breathed the fresh air and listened to the blessed silence. They looked at everything and <u>savored</u> everything.

7. Even though it would mean a loss of money to her family, it seemed <u>vital</u> to Margot to go back to Earth.

Developing Skills in Study and Research

Locating a Short Story in the Library. Finding a short story in the library is not as easy as locating a book, because short stories are not indexed by title in the card catalog. However, you might be able to find a short story by looking up the writer's name in the card catalog. If a collection of short stories by the writer is listed, you can look for the book on the shelves to see if it contains the story. If a collection by the author is not listed, consult the *Short Story Index.* This work, usually found in the reference section of the library, lists the short stories published each year and the collections in which they appear. If you see a listing for a collection that contains the short story you're looking for, check the card catalog to see if the library owns that collection. If so, find the book on the shelves.

Follow the above procedure to find the collection from which "All Summer in a Day" is taken.

Developing Writing Skills

Writing a Description. The Venus that is described in this story is not the Venus that scientists have described. It is an imaginary environment created by the writer. Create your own strange, new environment for another planet. Describe it in one or two paragraphs. Follow the process of writing described in the following paragraphs.

Prewriting. Carefully reread the first long paragraph of this story. It describes in vivid detail the environment on Venus. Decide what kind of environment you will create. You might think of some other unusual weather condition. Let your imagination go. Try to picture the setting in your mind. Jot down specific details about what your imaginary planet is like. Write down exactly what you see. Add information about sounds and smells. Plan how you intend to organize your description. Place the details in that order.

Drafting. One way to begin is to state briefly where your setting is. Then, following your plan, describe details of the environment. If new ideas occur to you as you write, include them in your draft. Use descriptive words, phrases, and sentences that appeal to different senses.

Revising and Sharing. Read your draft aloud. Look for ways of making your description more specific and colorful. Insert more precise words wherever you can. Make sure that the description appeals to more than one sense. Check for clear, complete sentences. Ask a classmate to try to imagine the place you are describing as you read your description aloud. Have the classmate comment on how precise your description is.

All Cats Are Gray

ANDRE NORTON

In this story, you will enter the rough world of the Spaceways. The challenges are dangerous and often mysterious. Find out how Steena uses her weaknesses as well as her strengths to defeat the enemy.

Steena of the Spaceways—that sounds just like a corny title for one of the Stellar-Vedo spreads. I ought to know; I've tried my hand at writing enough of them. Only this Steena was no glamorous babe. She was as colorless as a lunar planet— even the hair netted down to her skull had a sort of grayish cast, and I never saw her but once draped in anything but a shapeless and baggy gray spaceall.

Steena was strictly background stuff, and that is where she mostly spent her free hours—in the smelly, smoky, background corners of any stellar-port dive frequented by free spacers. If you really looked for her you could spot her—just sitting there listening to the talk—listening and remembering. She didn't open her own mouth often, but when she did, spacers had learned to listen. And the lucky few who heard her rare spoken words—these will never forget Steena.

She drifted from port to port. Being an expert operator on the big calculators, she found jobs wherever she cared to stay for a time. And she came to be something like the masterminded machines she tended— smooth, gray, without much personality of their own.

But it was Steena who told Bub Nelson about the Jovan moon rites—and her warning saved Bub's life six months later. It was Steena who identified the piece of stone Keene Clark was passing around a table one night, rightly calling it unworked Slitite. That started a rush which made ten fortunes overnight for men who were down to their last jets. And, last of all, she cracked the case of the *Empress of Mars.*

All the boys who had profited by her odd store of knowledge and her photographic memory tried at one time or another to balance the scales. But she wouldn't take so much as a cup of canal water at their expense, let alone the credits they tried to push on her. Bub Nelson was the only one who got around her refusal. It was he who brought her Bat.

Lunar Disconsolation, 1949, ANTONI TÀPIES. Collection of Jordi Ginferrer, Banyoles, Spain.

About a year after the Jovan affair, he walked into the Free Fall one night and dumped Bat down on her table. Bat looked at Steena and growled. She looked calmly back at him and nodded once. From then on they traveled together—the thin gray woman and the big gray tomcat. Bat learned to know the inside of more stellar bars than even most spacers visit in their lifetimes. He developed a liking for Vernal juice—drank it neat and quick, right out of a glass. And he was always at home on any table where Steena elected to drop him.

This is really the story of Steena, Bat, Cliff Moran, and the *Empress of Mars,* a story which is already a legend of the spaceways. And it's a good story, too. I ought to know, having framed the first version of it myself.

For I was there, right in the Rigel Royal, when it all began on the night that Cliff Moran blew in, looking lower than an ant-man's belly and twice as nasty. He'd had a spell of luck foul enough to twist a man into a slug snake, and we all knew that there was an attachment out for his ship. Cliff had fought his way up from the back courts of Venaport. Lose his ship and he'd slip back there—to rot. He was at the snarling stage that night when he picked out a table for himself and set out to drink away his troubles.

However, just as the first bottle arrived, so did a visitor. Steena came out of her corner, Bat curled around her shoulders stolewise, his favorite mode of travel. She crossed over and dropped down, without invitation, at Cliff's side. That shook him out of his sulks because Steena never chose company when she could be alone. If one of the man-stones on Ganymede had come stumping in, it wouldn't have made more of us look out of the corners of our eyes.

She stretched out one long-fingered hand, set aside the bottle he had ordered, and said only one thing, "It's about time for the *Empress of Mars* to appear."

Cliff scowled and bit his lip. He was tough, tough as jet lining—you have to be granite inside and out to struggle up from Venaport to a ship command. But we could guess what was running through his mind at that moment. The *Empress of Mars* was just about the biggest prize a spacer could aim for. But in the fifty years she had been

following her bizarre derelict orbit through space, many men had tried to bring her in—and none had succeeded.

A pleasure ship carrying untold wealth, she had been mysteriously abandoned in space by passengers and crew, none of whom had ever been seen or heard of again. At intervals thereafter she had been sighted, even boarded. Those who ventured into her either vanished or returned swiftly without any believable explanation of what they had seen—wanting only to get away from her as quickly as possible. But the man who could bring her in—or even strip her clean in space—that man would win the jackpot.

"All right!" Cliff slammed his fist down on the table. "I'll try even that!"

Steena looked at him, much as she must have looked at Bat the day Bub Nelson brought him to her, and nodded. That was all I saw. The rest of the story came to me in pieces, months later and in another port half the system away.

Cliff took off that night. He was afraid to risk waiting—with a writ out that could pull the ship from under him. And it wasn't until he was in space that he discovered his passengers—Steena and Bat. We'll never know what happened then. I'm betting that Steena made no explanation at all. She wouldn't.

It was the first time she had decided to cash in on her own tip and she was there—that was all. Maybe that point weighed with Cliff; maybe he just didn't care. Anyway, the three were together when they sighted the *Empress* riding, her dead-lights gleaming, a ghost ship in night space.

She must have been an eerie sight because her other lights were on too, in addition to the red warnings at her nose. She seemed alive, a Flying Dutchman of space. Cliff worked his ship skillfully alongside and had no trouble in snapping magnetic lines to her lock. Some minutes later the three of them passed into her. There was still air in her cabins and corridors, air that bore a faint corrupt taint which set Bat to sniffing greedily and could be picked up even by the less sensitive human nostrils.

Cliff headed straight for the control cabin, but Steena and Bat went prowling. Closed doors were a challenge to both of them and Steena opened each as she passed, taking a quick look at what lay within. The fifth door opened on a room which no woman could leave without further investigation.

I don't know who had been housed there when the *Empress* left port on her last lengthy cruise. Anyone really curious can check back on the old photo-reg cards. But there was a lavish display of silk trailing out of two travel kits on the floor, a dressing table crowded with crystal and jeweled containers, along with other lures for the female which drew Steena in. She was standing in front of the dressing table when she glanced into the mirror— glanced into it and froze.

Over her right shoulder she could see the spider-silk cover on the bed. Right in the middle of that sheer, gossamer expanse was a sparkling heap of gems, the dumped contents of some jewel case. Bat had jumped to the foot of the bed and flattened out as cats will, watching those gems, watching them and—something else!

Steena put out her hand blindly and caught up the nearest bottle. As she unstoppered it, she watched the mirrored bed. A gemmed bracelet rose from the pile, rose in the air and tinkled its siren song. It was as if an idle hand played . . . . Bat spat almost noiselessly. But he did not retreat. Bat had not yet decided his course.

She put down the bottle. Then she did something which perhaps few of the men she had listened to through the years could have done. She moved without hurry or sign of disturbance on a tour about the room. And, although she approached the bed, she did not touch the jewels. She could not force herself to do that. It took her five minutes to play out her innocence and unconcern. Then it was Bat who decided the issue.

He leaped from the bed and escorted something to the door, remaining a careful distance behind. Then he mewed loudly twice. Steena followed him and opened the door wider.

Bat went straight on down the corridor, as intent as a hound on the warmest of scents. Steena strolled behind him, holding her pace to the unhurried gait of an explorer. What sped before them was invisible to her, but Bat was never baffled by it.

They must have gone into the control cabin almost on the heels of the unseen—

if the unseen had heels, which there was a good reason to doubt—for Bat crouched just within the doorway and refused to move on. Steena looked down the length of the instrument panels and officers' station seats to where Cliff Moran worked. Her boots made no sound on the heavy carpet, and he did not glance up but sat humming through set teeth, as he tested the tardy and reluctant responses to buttons which had not been pushed in years.

To human eyes they were alone in the cabin. But Bat still followed a moving something, which he had at last made up his mind to distrust and dislike. For now he took a step or two forward and spat—his loathing made plain by every raised hair along his spine. And in that same moment Steena saw a flicker—a flicker of vague outline against Cliff's hunched shoulders, as if the invisible one had crossed the space between them.

But why had it been revealed against Cliff and not against the back of one of the seats or against the panels, the walls of the corridor or the cover of the bed where it had reclined and played with its loot? What could Bat see?

The storehouse memory that had served Steena so well through the years clicked open a half-forgotten door. With one swift motion, she tore loose her spaceall and flung the baggy garment across the back of the nearest seat.

Bat was snarling now, emitting the throaty rising cry that was his hunting song. But he was edging back, back toward Steena's feet, shrinking from something he could not fight but which he faced defiantly. If he could draw it after him, past that dangling spaceall . . . . He had to—it was their only chance!

"What the . . ." Cliff had come out of his seat and was staring at them.

What he saw must have been weird enough: Steena, bare-armed and bare-shouldered, her usually stiffly-netted hair falling wildly down her back; Steena watching empty space with narrowed eyes and set mouth, calculating a single wild chance. Bat, crouched on his belly, was retreating from thin air step by step and wailing like a demon.

"Toss me your blaster." Steena gave the order calmly—as if they still sat at their table in the Rigel Royal.

And as quietly, Cliff obeyed. She caught the small weapon out of the air with a steady hand—caught and leveled it.

"Stay just where you are!" she warned. "Back, Bat, bring it back!"

With a last throat-splitting screech of rage and hate, Bat twisted to safety between her boots. She pressed with thumb and forefinger, firing at the spacealls. The material turned to powdery flakes of ash—except for certain bits which still flapped from the scorched seat—as if something had protected them from the force of the blast. Bat sprang straight up in the air with a scream that tore their ears.

"What . . . ?" began Cliff again.

Steena made a warning motion with her left hand. "*Wait!*"

She was still tense, still watching Bat. The cat dashed madly around the cabin twice, running crazily with white-ringed eyes and flecks of foam on his muzzle. Then he stopped abruptly in the doorway, stopped and looked back over his shoulder for a long, silent moment. He sniffed delicately.

Steena and Cliff could smell it too now, a thick oily stench which was not the usual odor left by an exploding blaster shell.

Bat came back, treading daintily across the carpet, almost on the tips of his paws. He raised his head as he passed Steena, and then he went confidently beyond to sniff, to sniff and spit twice at the unburned strips of the spaceall. Having thus paid his respects to the late enemy, he sat down calmly and set to washing his fur with deliberation. Steena sighed once and dropped into the navigator's seat.

"Maybe now you'll tell me what's happened?" Cliff exploded as he took the blaster out of her hand.

"Gray," she said dazedly, "it must have been gray—or I couldn't have seen it like that. I'm color-blind, you see. I can see only shades of gray—my whole world is gray. Like Bat's—his world is gray, too—all gray. But he's been compensated, for he can see above and below our range of color vibrations and, apparently, so can I!"

Her voice quavered, and she raised her chin with a new air Cliff had never seen before—a sort of proud acceptance. She pushed back her wandering hair, but she made no move to imprison it under the heavy net again.

"That is why I saw the thing when it crossed between us. Against your spaceall it was another shade of gray—an outline. So I put out mine and waited for it to show against that—it was our only chance, Cliff.

"It was curious at first, I think, and it knew we couldn't see it—which is why it waited to attack. But when Bat's actions gave it away, it moved. So I waited to see that flicker against the spaceall, and then I let him have it. It's really very simple. . . ."

Cliff laughed a bit shakily. "But what *was* this gray thing? I don't get it."

"I think it was what made the *Empress* a derelict. Something out of space, maybe, or from another world somewhere." She waved her hands. "It's invisible because it's a color beyond our range of sight. It must have stayed in here all these years. And it kills—it must—when its curiosity is satisfied." Swiftly she described the scene, the scene in the cabin, and the strange behavior of the gem pile which had betrayed the creature to her.

Cliff did not return his blaster to its holder. "Any more of them on board, d'you think?" He didn't look pleased at the prospect.

Steena turned to Bat. He was paying particular attention to the space between two front toes in the process of a complete bath. "I don't think so, but Bat will tell us if there are. He can see them clearly, I believe."

But there weren't any more and two weeks later, Cliff, Steena, and Bat brought the *Empress* into the lunar quarantine station. And that is the end of Steena's story because, as we have been told, happy marriages need no chronicles. Steena had found someone who knew of her gray world and did not find it too hard to share with her—someone besides Bat. It turned out to be a real love match.

The last time I saw her, she was wrapped in a flame-red cloak from the looms of Rigel and wore a fortune in Jovan rubies blazing on her wrists. Cliff was flipping a three-figure credit bill to a waiter. And Bat had a row of Vernal juice glasses set up before him. Just a little family party out on the town.

Andre Norton *(born 1912),* the pen name of Alice Mary Norton, has published more than eighty books of science fiction. Born in Cleveland, Ohio, Norton studied at Western Reserve University and eventually became a children's librarian. Her training in research and her love of history led her to write historical novels in the 1930's. With the publication of books such as *Star Man's Son* and *Star Gate* in the 1950's, Norton began her successful journey into the world of science fiction. Her books have been translated into many languages including Danish, German, Japanese, and Arabic.

Developing Comprehension Skills

1. At the beginning of the story, what has happened to the *Empress of Mars?*

2. How does Steena first happen to notice the space creature aboard the *Empress?*

3. Why are Steena and Bat able to see the space creature? How does Steena kill it?

4. What special qualities of Steena's character help her to succeed? Could she have succeeded without Bat? Explain.

5. At the beginning of the story, Steena appears colorless and dull. How does her appearance change? What change in attitude accounts for her change on the outside?

6. In addition to internal changes, in what two ways have Steena's and Cliff's lives changed by the end of the story?

7. Do you find Steena a believable character?

Reading Literature: Short Stories

1. **Recognizing Science Fiction. Science fiction** stories are based on scientific facts or theories. They are often set in the future. What scientific advances are referred to in this story? How do you know the story is set in the future?

2. **Understanding the Narrator.** This story is written in first-person point of view, using the pronoun *I*. Who is the narrator? The first two sentences give you some clues. How is the narrator aware of the story of Steena, Cliff, Bat, and the *Empress?*

3. **Identifying the Climax.** The **climax** of a story is the turning point of the action. The emotion comes to a peak as the main character makes an important decision or changes in an important way. After the climax, the reader usually knows what the outcome of the story will be. What is the climax of this story? Explain your answer.

4. **Understanding Characterization. Characterization** refers to the methods a writer uses to portray characters. These include describing the character directly and showing the character's words, thoughts, feelings, or actions. They also include showing other characters' reactions to the character. A writer often uses a combination of methods in presenting a character. What method or methods are shown by each of the following quotations? What can you infer about Steena or Cliff from each quotation?

a. "Only this Steena was no glamorous babe. She was as colorless as a lunar planet—even the hair netted down to her skull had a sort of grayish cast . . ."

b. "She didn't open her own mouth often, but when she did, spacers had learned to listen. And the lucky few who heard her rare spoken words—these will never forget Steena."

c. "Cliff worked his ship skillfully alongside and had no trouble snapping magnetic lines to her lock."

d. " . . . she watched the mirrored bed. A gemmed bracelet rose from the pile, rose in the air and tinkled its siren song . . . . Then she did something which perhaps few of the men she had listened to through the years could have done. She moved without hurry or sign of disturbance on a tour about the room."

e. "Cliff scowled and bit his lip. He was tough, tough as jet lining—you have to be granite inside and out to struggle up from Venaport to a ship command."

Developing Vocabulary Skills

Inferring the Meaning of Coined Words. Sometimes science fiction writers use **coined words,** or words that are made up. Often you can infer the meaning of these words from context. The sentences below from this story use coined words related to space travel. Infer the meaning of each underlined word, and write its definition as you understand it.

1. I never saw her but once draped in anything but a shapeless and baggy gray spaceall.

2. It was Steena who identified the piece of stone Keene Clark was passing around a table one night, rightly calling it unworked <u>Slitite</u>. That started a rush which made ten fortunes overnight for men who were down to their last jets.

3. I don't know who had been housed there when the *Empress* left port on her last lengthy cruise. Anyone really curious could check back on the old <u>photo-reg</u> cards.

4. "Toss me your <u>blaster</u>." Steena gave the order calmly . . . And as quietly, Cliff obeyed. She caught the small weapon out of the air with a steady hand—caught and leveled it.

Developing Skills in Critical Thinking

Evaluating Stereotypes. A **stereotype** is a fixed idea, often applied to all members of a group without recognizing individual differences. For example, a stereotype of a professor is the idea of a scholarly but absent-minded gentleman. Some characters in literature are stereotypes. Examples are the miser, the witch, and the villain. Stereotyped characters have little substance or special identity. In this story, Steena is a female space traveler. Do you think she is a stereotyped character? Support your answer with evidence from the story.

Developing Writing Skills

Creating a Creature. Cliff asks, "But what *was* this gray thing?" Answer this question by writing a one-paragraph description of the gray space creature as you imagine it.

Prewriting. Review the parts of the story that refer to the space creature. Jot down any information that might help you to describe it. Then try to visualize what Bat sees when he sees the space creature. Let your imagination go. You may create a strange, wild, weird creature. Make notes on the creature's appearance, actions, smells, and sounds. Decide on a logical way to organize your description.

Drafting. In your topic sentence, identify the creature you are describing. Continue with specific details about how the creature looks, acts, smells, and sounds. Follow your plan of organization and your notes. Try to include vivid, specific details that would help a reader to visualize the creature.

Revising and Sharing. Read over your paragraph. Does it have a clear topic sentence that introduces the description? Have you used vivid details that appeal to different senses? Read your paragraph aloud and have someone sketch the creature. If the drawing is accurate, you have written a skillful description.

The Assassin

ROBERT SILVERBERG

If you could change the outcome of one historical event, what would it be, and why? Try to predict what happens when the character in this story uses a time machine in an attempt to change history.

The time was drawing near, Walter Bigelow thought. Just a few more adjustments, and his great ambition would be fulfilled.

He stepped back from the Time Distorter and studied the complex network of wires and tubes with an expert's practiced eye. TWENTY YEARS, he thought. Twenty years of working and scrimping, of pouring money into the machine that stood before him on the workbench. Twenty years, to save Abraham Lincoln's life.

Now he was almost ready.

Bigelow had conceived his grand idea when still young, newly out of college. He had stumbled across a volume of history and had read of Abraham Lincoln and his struggle to save the Union.

Bigelow was a tall, spare, rawboned man standing better than six feet four—and with a shock he discovered that he bore an amazing resemblance to a young portrait of the Great Emancipator. That was when his identification with Lincoln began.

He read every Lincoln biography he could find, steeped himself in log-cabin legends and the texts of the Lincoln-Douglas debates. And gradually, he became consumed with bitterness because an assassin's hand had struck Lincoln down at the height of his triumph.

"Awful shame, great man like that," he mumbled into his glass one night in a bar.

"What's that?" a sallow man at his left asked. "Someone die?"

"Yes," Bigelow said. "I'm talking about Lincoln. Awful shame."

The other chuckled. "Better get yourself a new newspaper, pal. Lincoln's been dead for a century. Still mourning?"

Bigelow turned, his gaunt face alive with anger. "Yes! Yes—why shouldn't I mourn? A great man like Lincoln—"

"Sure, sure," the other said placatingly. "I'll buy that. He was a great president, chum—but he's been dead for a hundred years. One hundred. You can't bring him back to life, you know."

"Maybe I can," Bigelow said suddenly—and the great idea was born.

It took eight years of physics and math before Bigelow had developed a workable time-travel theory. Seven more years passed before the first working model stood complete.

He tested it by stepping within its field, allowing himself to be cast back ten years. A few well-placed bets, and he had enough cash to continue. Ten years was not enough. Lincoln had been assassinated in 1865—Friday, April 14, 1865. Bigelow needed a machine that could move at least one hundred twenty years into the past.

It took time. Five more years.

He reached out, adjusted a capacitor, pinched off an unnecessary length of copper wire. It was ready. After twenty years, he was ready at last.

Bigelow took the morning bus to Washington, D.C. The Time Distorter would not affect space, and it was much more efficient to make the journey from Chicago to Washington in 1979 by monobus in a little over an hour, than in 1865 by mulecart or some such conveyance, possibly taking a day. Now that he was so close to success, he was too impatient to allow any such delay as that.

The Time Distorter was cradled in a small black box on his lap; he spent the hour of the bus ride listening to its gentle humming and ticking, letting the sound soothe him and ease his nervousness.

There was really no need to be nervous, he thought. Even if he failed in his first attempt at blocking Lincoln's assassination, he had an infinity of time to keep trying again.

He could return to his own time and make the jump again, over and over. There were a hundred different ways he could use to prevent Lincoln from entering the fatal theater on the night of April 14. A sudden phone call—no, there were no telephones yet. A message of some kind. He could burn down the theater the morning of the play. He could find John Wilkes Booth and kill him before he could make his fateful speech of defiance and fire the fatal bullet. He could—

Well, it didn't matter. He was going to succeed the first time. Lincoln was a man of sense; he wouldn't willingly go to his death having been warned.

A warm glow of pleasure spread over Bigelow as he dreamed of the consequences of his act. Lincoln alive, going on to complete his second term, President until 1869. The weak, ineffectual Andrew Johnson would remain Vice-President, where he belonged. The South would be rebuilt sanely and welcomed back into the Union; there would be no era of carpetbaggers, no series of governmental scandals and no dreary Reconstruction era.

"Washington!"

Moving almost in a dream, Bigelow left the bus and stepped out into the crowded capitol streets. It was a warm summer day; soon, he thought, it would be a coolish April evening, back in 1865. . . .

He headed for the poor part of town, away from the fine white buildings and gleaming domes. Huddling in a dark alley on the south side, he undid the fastenings of the box that covered the Time Distorter.

He glanced around, saw that no one was near. Then, swiftly, he depressed the lever.

The world swirled around him, vanished.

Then, suddenly, it took shape again.

He was in an open field now; the morning air was cool but pleasant, and in the distance he could see a few of the buildings that made the nation's capitol famous. There was no Lincoln Memorial, of course, and the bright needle of Washington's Monument did not thrust upward into the sky. But the familiar Capitol dome looked much as it always had, and he could make out the White House further away.

Bigelow refastened the cover of the Distorter and tucked the box under his arm. It clicked quietly, reminding him over and over again of the fact that he was in the year 1865—the morning of the day John Wilkes Booth put a bullet through the brain of Abraham Lincoln.

Time passed slowly for Bigelow. He made his way toward the center of town and spent the day in downtown Washington, hungrily drinking in the gossip. Abe Lincoln's name was on everyone's tongue.

The dread War had ended just five days before with Lee's surrender at Appomattox. Lincoln was in his hour of triumph. It was Friday. The people were still discussing the speech he had made the Tuesday before.

"He said he's going to make an announcement," someone said. "Abe's going to tell the Southerners what kind of program he's going to put into effect for them."

"Wonder what's on his mind?" someone else asked.

"No matter what it is, I'll bet he makes the South like what he says."

He had never delivered that speech, Bigelow thought. And the South had been doomed to a generation of hardship and exploitation by the victorious North that had left unhealing scars.

The day passed. President Lincoln was to attend Ford's Theater that night, to see a production of a play called "Our American Cousin."

Bigelow knew what the history books said. Lincoln had had an apprehensive dream the night before: he was sailing on a ship of a peculiar build, being borne on it with great speed toward a dark and undefined shore. Like Caesar on the Ides of March, he had been warned—and, like Caesar, he would go unheeding to his death.

But Bigelow would see that that never happened.

History recorded that Lincoln attended the performance, that he seemed to be enjoying the play, and that shortly after ten that evening, a wild-eyed man would enter Lincoln's box, fire once, and leap to the stage, shouting, "Sic semper tyrannis!"[1]

The man would be the crazed actor John

---

1. **Sic semper tyrannis!**–"Thus always to tyrants!" This is the motto of the state of Virginia.

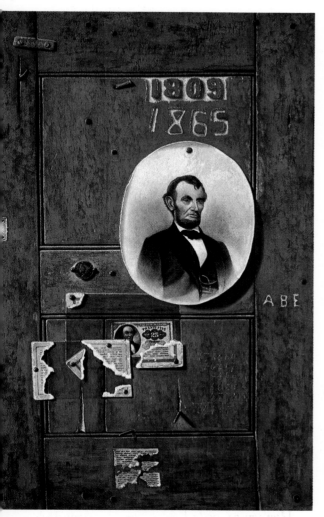

Reminiscences of 1865, after 1900, JOHN F. PETO.
The Minneapolis Institute of Arts.

Wilkes Booth. He would snag a spur in the drapery as he dropped to the stage, and would break his leg—but nevertheless he would vanish into the wings, make his way through the theater he knew so well, mount a horse waiting at the stage door. Some days later he would be dead.

As for President Lincoln, he would slump forward in his box. The audience would be too stunned to move for a moment—but there was nothing that could be done. Lincoln would die the next morning without recovering consciousness.

"Now he belongs to the ages," Secretary of State Stanton would say.

No! Bigelow thought. It would not happen. It would not happen. . . .

Evening approached. Bigelow, crouching in an alley across the street from the theater, watched the carriages arriving for the performance that night. Feeling oddly out of place in his twentieth-century clothing, he watched the finely-dressed ladies and gentlemen descending from their coaches. Everyone in Washington knew the President would be at the theater that night, and they were determined to look their best.

Bigelow waited. Finally, a handsome carriage appeared, and several others made way for it. He tensed, knowing who was within.

A woman of regal bearing descended first—Mary Todd Lincoln, the President's wife. And then Lincoln appeared.

For some reason, the President paused at the street-corner and looked around. His eyes came to rest on the dark alley where Bigelow crouched invisibly, and Bigelow stared at the face he knew almost as well as his own: the graying beard, the tired, old, wrinkled face, the weary eyes of Abe Lincoln.

Then he rose and began to run.

"Mr. President! Mr. President!"

He realized he must have been an outlandish figure, dashing across the street in his strange costume with the Time Distorter clutched under one arm. He drew close to Lincoln.

"Sir, don't go to the theater tonight! If you do—"

A hand suddenly wrapped itself around his mouth. President Lincoln smiled pittyingly and turned away, walking on down the street toward the theater. Other hands seized Bigelow, dragged him away. Blue-clad arms. Union soldiers. The President's bodyguard.

"You don't understand!" Bigelow yelled. He bit at the hand that held him, and got a fierce kick in return. "Let go of me! Let go!"

There were four of them, earnest-looking as they went about their duties. They held Bigelow, pummelled him angrily. One of them reached down for the Distorter.

In terror Bigelow saw that his attempt to save Lincoln had been a complete failure, that he would have to return to his own time and try all over again. He attempted to switch on the Distorter, but before he could open the cover rough hands had pulled it from him.

"Give me that!" He fought frantically, but they held him. One of the men in blue uniforms took the Distorter, looked at it curiously, finally held it up to his ear.

His eyes widened. "It's ticking! It's a bomb!"

"No!" Bigelow shouted, and then watched in utter horror as the soldier, holding the Distorter at arm's length, ran across the street and hurled the supposed bomb as far up the alley as he could possibly throw it.

There was no explosion—only the sound of delicate machinery shattering.

Bigelow watched numbly as the four men seized his arms again.

"Throw a bomb, will you? Come on, fellow—we'll show you what happens to guys who want to assassinate President Lincoln!"

Further down the street, the gaunt figure of Abe Lincoln was just entering the theater. No one gave Bigelow a chance to explain.

Robert Silverberg (*born 1935*) has written over fifty science fiction and nonfiction books. His favorite subjects are archaeology, space exploration, and military history. *Needle in a Timestack* and *Lost Race of Mars* are two of his science fiction works. Silverberg was born in New York and attended Columbia University. He has also written under the pen name of Walker Chapman.

Developing Comprehension Skills

1. What is the purpose of Bigelow's Time Distorter? How long does it take him to develop it?

2. Why does Bigelow want to prevent Lincoln's assassination?

3. Bigelow considers different ways to prevent Lincoln's assassination, most of them violent. He never considers that he might fail. What can you infer about Bigelow's character from these two points?

4. What keeps Bigelow from warning Lincoln? What makes Bigelow seem dangerous to the President's bodyguards?

5. Bigelow's plans for warning Lincoln are quite vague because he thinks he will have several chances. What might Bigelow have done to ensure his success?

Reading Literature: Short Stories

1. **Analyzing Character.** Bigelow is a good scientist and an admirer of Lincoln. He also appears to be extreme and unreasonable. Review the beginning of the story. Find details about Bigelow that show he may be too excessive in his admiration of Lincoln. For example, what is significant about Bigelow's physical appearance?

2. **Identifying Exposition.** The exposition in this story introduces the main character, Walter Bigelow. It also provides background

information about the Time Distorter and why Bigelow develops it. How does Bigelow get the idea to travel in time? Find the point in the story where the exposition ends and the rising action begins.

3. **Understanding Irony.** One kind of **irony** is the contrast between what is expected and what actually happens. For example, Bigelow expects to stop Lincoln's assassin. In fact, what actually happens?

   Another kind of **irony** occurs when the reader understands a truth that a character does not understand. In this story, the bodyguard says to Bigelow, "Come on, fellow—we'll show you what happens to guys who want to assassinate President Lincoln!" What is ironic about the bodyguard's statement?

4. **Recognizing Theme.** The main character in this story tries to change history. However, Bigelow never achieves his goal. What does this story say about our ability to change the course of history?

Developing Vocabulary Skills

Using a Dictionary or Context Clues. Read the following sentences about "The Assassin." Try to use context clues to find the meaning of each underlined word. Then write the definition of the word as you understand it from the context. If you cannot infer the word's meaning from context, look up the word in a dictionary. Write down its dictionary definition and the label *Dictionary.*

1. Bigelow developed a workable time-travel <u>theory</u>, or scientific idea.

2. He admired and identified with Lincoln, the Great <u>Emancipator</u>.

3. The Time Distorter gave Bigelow an <u>infinite</u> number of chances. If he failed, he could return to his own time and make the jump again, over and over, as many times as he needed.

4. Bigelow wanted to prevent the weak and <u>ineffectual</u> Andrew Johnson from becoming President.

5. Bigelow thought of killing John Wilkes Booth before he made his speech of <u>defiance</u> and fired at Lincoln.

6. Bigelow watched a woman of <u>regal</u> bearing, Mary Todd Lincoln, descend from the carriage.

7. Bigelow realized that he was an <u>outlandish</u> figure, racing about in his strange costume with a box under his arm.

8. Lincoln had an <u>apprehensive</u> dream the night before the performance.

9. The bodyguards <u>pummelled</u> Bigelow with angry fists, and he fought back frantically.

10. The soldier ran across the street and <u>hurled</u> the suspected bomb as far as he could throw it.

Developing Skills in Critical Thinking

Evaluating Facts. "The Assassin" presents many facts about Lincoln and his assassination. List the facts presented about Lincoln's assassination. Then check the accuracy of these facts. Use the card catalog to find a book about Lincoln, and read the section about Lincoln's assassination. Try to verify the facts presented in the story. Are there any inaccuracies?

Developing Writing Skills

Comparing Two Characters. In both "The Weapon" and "The Assassin" the main character is a scientist who has worked on a brilliant invention. How are these two characters alike? In two paragraphs, compare these characters.

Prewriting. Review the two stories. Make notes on the characters of James Graham and Walter Bigelow. Answer these questions about each man and see how the answers are similar:

1. What is the scientist's attitude toward his invention?

2. Why does the scientist develop the invention?

Think of other ways to compare the two men. Jot down notes on these ideas. Then look over your notes, and decide on three or four points of similarity to discuss in your paragraphs.

Make an outline to organize these points of similarity from least important to most important. Find quotations or examples in the stories that illustrate each point. Add these to your outline.

Drafting. Follow your outline as you compare Bigelow and Graham. For the first paragraph, write a topic sentence summarizing two similarities between the characters. Explain and illustrate these similarities with specific examples and quotations from the stories. For the second paragraph, write a second topic sentence summarizing the most important similarity or similarities. Explain and support your topic sentence with specific examples and quotations.

Revising and Sharing. Read over your draft. See if you can state your comparisons more clearly. Make sure that you have supported each topic sentence fully with quotations and examples from the stories. Ask a classmate to examine your paragraphs for clarity and unity. Rewrite passages that are vague or confusing.

Chapter 1 *Review*

Using Your Skills in Reading Short Stories

The following paragraph is the exposition from "First Confession," a short story by Frank O'Connor. Read the paragraph. Then explain what you can tell about the story's characters, setting, and conflict.

> It was a Saturday afternoon in early spring. A small boy whose face looked as though it had been but newly scrubbed was being led by the hand by his sister through a crowded street. The little boy showed a marked reluctance to proceed; he affected to be very interested in the shop-windows. Equally, his sister seemed to pay no attention to them. She tried to hurry him; he resisted. When she dragged him he began to bawl.

Using Your Comprehension Skills

Here is a paragraph from a myth that you will read in Chapter Three. Read it and tell what you can infer about the character of the king. Also explain where he is and what he is doing.

> The great king gazed thoughtfully down on the earth below him. He had made the green land that stretched out before his eyes. With the help of the other gods, he had made men and women who lived on that earth, and he felt truly like the All-Father he was called.

Using Your Vocabulary Skills

In each of the following sentences there is a context clue. The clue suggests the meaning of a word you will come across in Chapter Three. For each sentence, write the definition of the underlined word as you understand it from the context. Then tell whether you used the general context or one of the following context clues: definition or restatement, synonym, antonym, comparison, contrast, example.

1. "What have you given up that is dear to you? What have you <u>sacrificed</u>?" asked Mimir.

2. Masa carved a <u>barracuda</u>, a large fish that preys on other fish.

3. Shetu's husband was as <u>obstinate</u> as a child who refuses to go to bed.

4. The baby boy <u>clambered</u> down from his mother's back and went to the well.

5. Instead of a <u>resounding</u> crash, they heard only silence.

6. The woman took pity on escaped prisoners and other types of <u>fugitives</u>.

7. He snatched the bucket from the rim of the well and threw it back into the dark <u>cavity</u>.

Using Your Skills in Critical Thinking

Develop an argument for or against this statement: Scientists should seriously investigate the possibilities of time travel. State your opinion. Then list at least three reasons to support your opinion. Arrange them in order of importance from weakest to strongest.

Using Your Writing Skills

Choose one of the writing assignments below.

1. Choose two stories from this chapter in which setting is an important element. Explain how the setting is essential to the events in each story. Give examples from the stories. Develop your analysis in two paragraphs.

2. Below are listed three elements for a story. Make up details to fit these elements and write a plan for the story either in outline form or in two or three paragraphs. Include information about the characters, setting, and plot.

   Setting: a store near your school
   Characters: a clerk in the store and a mysterious stranger
   Conflict: The stranger wants to buy things that are not available in any store.

CHAPTER TWO

How Writers Write

Using the Process of Writing

"It's impossible to write a good story by carrying a rabbit's foot in your pocket," said Nobel Prize-winning writer Isaac Bashevis Singer. Writers need more than just luck. To create good writing, they must work hard. In this section, you'll learn about the process of writing that professional writers use. You'll be able to use this same process in your own writing.

Gregory in the Pool (Paper Pool 4: A, B, D, G), 1978, DAVID HOCKNEY. Printed and Published by Tyler Graphics, Ltd., Bedford Village, New York. Copyright ©1978 David Hockney/Tyler Graphics Ltd.

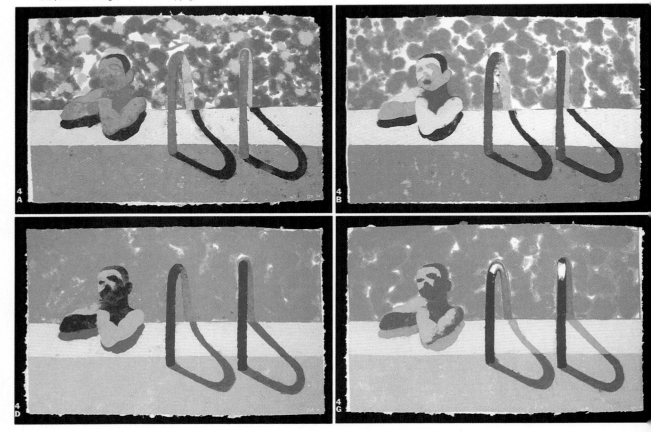

Understanding the Process of Writing

Have you ever seen a sculpture you liked especially well? You can enjoy looking at a sculpture without knowing exactly how the artist cut and chiseled the stone. You can admire its texture and shape without being an expert.

Imagine, however, that you tried to carve a sculpture. You would face the same problems sculptors face. You might try the same techniques. You would begin to see every other sculpture in a new way. As a sculptor yourself, you would appreciate the skill it takes to make a beautiful sculpture.

Reading can be compared to seeing a sculpture. You can enjoy a good poem or story without understanding the skill that went into its writing. However, understanding what went into it helps you appreciate that poem or story even more.

In this chapter you will learn how many professional writers write. You will learn about the techniques writers use. You will practice ways to make your own writing clear and lively. After all, the best way to learn the process and techniques of writing is by writing.

The Stages in the Process of Writing

Like sculptors and artists of all kinds, writers work hard. According to writer Pete Hamill, "Writing is the hardest work in the world not involving heavy lifting." Writing also is in many ways a very personal activity. Every writer has his or her own way of going about it.

The tools of writing have undergone major changes over the past few years. Many writers have traded in their pens and typewriters for word processors and memory typewriters. This new technology affects how writers write.

Most writers agree, however, that the process of writing follows four basic stages:

prewriting—a time of planning
drafting—a time of getting your ideas on paper
revising—a time of rewriting or reworking
sharing—a time of letting others read your work

These stages are not necessarily fixed steps that follow one after the other. The stages describe types of activities that writers use at different times during their writing. Some writers simply start drafting as a way of thinking and sorting out their ideas; then they practice some of the prewriting techniques. Other writers go back and forth between stages—drafting some parts, jotting down notes, revising, drafting some more, and so on to the final draft. Yet, at one time or another, most writers go through each stage in the process.

Prewriting

Before beginning a writing project, a writer needs a starting point, some ideas to get his or her writing going. Prewriting provides just such a starting point. It is the stage of planning and preparing to write. Prewriting can be a time for making lists, brainstorming, jotting down notes, outlining, freewriting, or simply thinking.

Some writers such as novelist Vladimir Nabokov start with an overview of what they want to write:

I always have at the very start a curiously clear preview of the entire novel before me or above me.

Other writers are less clear on how their writing will turn out. Novelist Scott Spender had this to say:

I try to know as much as I can about a book before the beginning, but I never know exactly where it's going to end.

Still other writers begin at the ending. Fiction writer Katherine Anne Porter said, "If I didn't know the ending of a story, I wouldn't begin." Novelist and editor Toni Morrison feels the same way: "I always know the ending; that's where I start."

Prewriting includes just about anything that sets a writer in motion. What writers see, hear, read, and think about may give them ideas for their writing. Many writers believe that their most important work is done before they actually sit down to write.

Just because prewriting is an early stage of the writing process doesn't mean that a writer may not return to this activity at a later point. Because most writers think while they write, they can change their minds about what they're saying and they can think of something new. A bit more prewriting at that time can help bring this new information into the overall plan.

Deciding on a Topic. "A writer's material is what he cares about," according to novelist John Gardner. Writers choose topics that interest them. You should choose topics that interest you too. Although most of your writing projects will be assigned, you'll often have a choice about the specific topic. No matter how different your writing projects are, the following steps can help you decide on a topic.

1. Start by brainstorming possible topics. Make a list of things you're interested in or would like to know more about.
2. Think about the possible topics on your list, and pick one that is especially appealing to you.
3. Think about how long your assignment will be and consider whether your topic will fit the assigned length.

Determining a Purpose. The four main purposes for writing are to express an idea, to inform, to persuade, and to entertain. When you write, ask yourself what you want to accomplish. If you want to make readers laugh, for example, you might think up surprising situations and funny characters. If you want to inform, you may need to research your topic in the library. How and what you write depends on the purpose for your writing.

Choosing a Form. The form of a piece of writing refers to the type of writing it is, such as a story, a poem, an article, or a report. Most of the time the form of your writing will be assigned. You will be asked to write a paragraph, a poem, a story, a report, or an essay.

When you are writing on your own, you can choose the form for your writing. Choose the form that best suits your topic and purpose. For example, suppose your topic is a description of what it's like at a public swimming pool on a hot summer day. You want your description to be entertaining. A funny poem might be a good form for your description. You wouldn't choose a story form for your description unless you had events and characters to tell about. A report wouldn't be a good form either unless you wanted to tell your audience factual information about the pool itself.

Knowing the Audience. A good writer reaches his or her audience as surely as an arrow reaches a bull's-eye. Good writers understand the audiences they write for. They know the level of their audiences' knowledge. They know what their audiences will find appealing and interesting. Colombian novelist and Nobel Prize winner Gabriel Garcia Márquez imagines that his audience is composed of his friends:

> When I'm writing I'm always aware that this friend is going to like this, or that another friend is going to like that paragraph or chapter, always thinking of specific people. In the end all books are written for your friends.

Always think about who your readers will be, and write directly to them. For your writing assignments, your audience will most likely be your teacher and classmates, some of whom may be your friends. Consider what they already know about your topic. For example, if you're writing about a story the entire class has read, then you can assume that the class will understand your references to characters and events. If, however, you're writing a report on jet engines, you may have to explain things the class does not know.

Gathering Information. The kind of information a writer gathers depends on what the audience needs to know in order to understand his or her ideas. It also depends on the form of the writing. A report, an article, or an essay probably calls for research in a library. A story needs characters, a plot, and the other elements of a short story.

Most writers agree that reading is essential to all kinds of writing. French writer André Gide advised writers to read so that "ideas will again begin to stir." The great eighteenth-century writer Samuel Johnson remarked:

> The greatest part of a writer's time is spent in reading in order to write; a man will turn over half a library to make one book.

When you gather information for your writing, be sure to take plenty of notes. What follows are some techniques you can use for gathering information.

Reflecting, or thinking about what you already know, is an important first step in gathering information. You'll probably do quite a bit of reflecting while you are choosing a topic and purpose or are deciding on a form for your writing. Fiction writers usually go through a great deal of reflecting before they begin to write a story. This is how Paul Gallico explains how he creates and then gets to know his characters:

> I spend two or three days writing character sketches, setting down all and everything I know about each of the characters in the story. Like the iceberg, seven-eighths of this material remains submerged and doesn't show, but the characters have now taken on life for me, and I am able to think and speak and act as they might.

Another technique that writers use is called analyzing. **Analyzing** means breaking down a topic into parts to find out what kind of information you need to gather. Then, through a technique called **inquiring,** you can make a list of questions to answer for each part.

Many writers keep a journal or notebook of their thoughts and feelings. Such a journal helps them "catch and keep something of life," as novelist Henry James observed. Try keeping a journal yourself. Writing about an experience in a journal can both help you understand it and give you practice in writing. Then you can review your journal as you gather ideas for each writing activity.

Organizing Your Ideas. Like a winning baseball team or a successful dance troupe, a good piece of writing has all its parts organized into a working whole. Before you start writing your first draft, you need to develop some sort of clear organizational plan to guide you.

Different writers find different ways to organize. Some just jot down ideas or points they want to cover. Other writers make formal outlines. For writer Hugh Auchincloss, an outline is essential to keep on track:

> I work very carefully from an outline. Every time I haven't, everything's had to be destroyed, because the story grows like a freak.

Just as there is no set way to organize information, there is no set time to do the organizing. In fact, you may start organizing as you go about gathering your ideas and facts.

Information should be organized in a logical order. The form of your writing usually dictates what kind of order is logical. For a story, you might choose chronological, or time, order. For an essay or report, you might arrange your information to build up to a conclusion.

As you organize your information in a logical order, keep in mind that all the points must relate to your topic. You may find yourself adding or taking away information as you organize. You may continue to do this when you revise your writing at a later time.

Drafting

You can begin drafting whenever you feel ready. **Drafting** is the activity of getting your words down on paper or into a word processor. They may not be the words you will end up with, but they are a start. The important part is to put words on the page. Why? As many writers say, a blank sheet of paper can be pretty scary. Fiction writer Frank O'Connor explained his drafting this way:

> I write any sort of rubbish which will cover the main outlines of the story, then I can begin to see it.

There are as many different ways of drafting as there are writers. Some writers say they must have peace and quiet so they can concentrate. Fiction writer Eudora Welty is one of these writers. She said:

> When we are in the act of writing, we are alone and on our own in a kind of absolute state of Do Not Disturb.

Other writers feel comfortable writing in a busy cafe or with music playing. For some it is most important to work at a specific time of day or to be in a special place. Certain writers even claim to have a favorite pencil or a favorite chair.

For some writers drafting is a slow process. For others it is done with the speed of lightning. Playwright Edward Albee is one of the fast drafters:

> Usually, the way I write is to sit down at a typewriter after that year or so of what passes for thinking, and I write a first draft quite rapidly.

Notice that for Albee, prewriting—"that year or so of what passes for thinking"—provides the solid foundation that allows him to hammer out a play quickly.

Just because a writer is drafting, doesn't mean he or she stops thinking about or planning a topic. In fact, writers say they scrap or change their plans as they draft. Most writers find that new ideas come to them during the act of writing. These new ideas can steer the writing in unexpected directions according to writer Ernest Hemingway:

> Sometimes you know the story. Sometimes you make it up as you go along and have no idea how it will come out. Everything changes as it moves.

For Hemingway, as for other writers, drafting is a process of shaping and reshaping.

As you draft, let your ideas flow. Follow your organizational plan and your prewriting notes, but remain open to new ideas. If you get stuck or confused, try using prewriting techniques to get yourself started again.

Revising

Revising is as necessary to the writing process as the paper itself. All writers must at some point look critically at what they've written and make changes. Even famous writers make corrections and often rewrite. Revising can be a slow process. Short story writer Sherwood Anderson made this comment about revising:

> I have seldom written a story, long or short, that I did not have to write and rewrite. There are single short stories of mine that have taken me ten or twelve years to get written.

to lecture me again. I said:

"Scat!" ~~and So~~ he darted right ~~back~~ to my knee, put his broad
furry paws on my pants and looked me in the face. I shall never
forget the ~~x~~ fear and ~~xxxxxxxxxfxxxxxxxxxxxx~~ wonder that I felt *at the*
bravery of Baron Weasel. ~~He stood his ground and berated~~ ~~transferred his feelings to me. he scolded~~ me. I
could see by the flashing ~~bright lights of~~ his eyes, and the curl
of his lip that he was ~~terribly indignant~~. *furious at me for trapping him. He couldn't*
talk, but I knew what he meant. ~~He might just as well~~
~~have talked to me. And in a way, he did.~~

~~Wonder~~ *filled* ~~flood over~~ me as I realized he was *absolutely* ~~totally~~ unafraid.
No, *other* animal, and I knew quite a few by now, ~~had been~~ so brave, *in my presence.* ~~and~~
~~Screaming, he~~ *jumped on* ~~darted over~~ me, *This surprised and* ~~and this~~ scared me. He leapt *in* from
my lap to my head, took a moutful of hair and wrestled ~~with~~ it.
~~My~~ goose bumps *rose.* ~~were~~ ~~goose bumps. and~~ I ~~remembered not~~ *was too* ~~frightened~~ *to move.*
~~frozen.~~ A good thing, too, because ~~just as I was about to hit him~~ *I guess he figured I was*
not going to fight back and ~~in self defense,~~ his scream *danger* changed to a purr ~~shutter. it was~~ *of peace. Still, I*
couldn't move. ~~a friendly noise and so I sat perfectly still.~~
Presently, ~~royalty~~
Down climbed the Baron as stately as *"* ~~royalty~~, and off he marched,
never looking back. ~~again.~~ He sunk beneath the leaves like a fish
beneath the water. ~~and~~ *N*ot a stem rippled to mark his way.

And so, the Baron and I met for the first time, and it was the
beginning of a harassing, but wonderful friendship.

Frightful had been watching all this. Her feathers were down.
~~her~~ She was skinny with fright. So young and inexperienced she
knew an enemy when she saw one. I picked her up and whispered into
her birdy smelling *neck* feathers.

" You *wild one* ~~all out here~~ know, ~~too much.~~ "
Since I couldn't go home,
I decided to spend the day in the marsh down the west side
of the mountain. There were a lot of cattails and frogs there,
~~and my supplies were running~~ *for these* low. ~~I kept a lot of frogs in~~
~~the spring for two days.~~

Most writers say that when they revise they study their work objectively, as a reader would. They look for ideas that aren't clear, conclusions that aren't logical, sentences that are dull, and other weaknesses to change. Reading their work aloud helps some writers notice problems. Another technique that works for some writers is to set the work aside for a time and then come back to it later. Try some of these writer-tested techniques and see how they work for you.

Throughout the processes of drafting and revising, writers may make several drafts of their work. With each revision, writers make changes—both big ones and small ones. They may add sections or take away entire scenes. Fiction writer Elizabeth Coatsworth explained how she makes major revisions:

> I begin playing with the shape of the book and the characters, discarding a scene that doesn't help with the progress of the story or adding one that does.

When you revise your work, don't be timid about making big changes. Trim the fat from your draft. Beef it up with muscle. The result will be a stronger piece of writing.

Along with the big changes, make refinements in your draft. Polish sentences. Insert needed details. Replace dull words with brighter ones. Juggle phrases for clarity. Check your facts too. Novelist Jean Craighead George said of her revising, "My notes, *Roget's Thesaurus,* and the dictionary were constant companions." Notice that reference books are as important to George as her own notes when she does a final tune-up on her writing. You can see on page 207 how George changed a page of her first draft.

Here are some questions to ask yourself as you revise:

1. Have I organized the information in the best possible way? Does it hold together as a unified whole? Does it flow smoothly?
2. Have I included necessary information and left out unrelated details?
3. Are my main ideas clear?
4. Could I replace any word with a more precise one?
5. Could I make my writing more interesting to my audience?
6. Have I communicated what I wanted to say about this topic?

While they are revising, some writers like to share their writing with people they trust. They may allow an editor, a relative, or a friend to read a draft of their work and make comments. This kind of feedback can be very helpful in letting the writer know how well his or her ideas are understood.

Proofreading. Proofreading is a final step in revision. When you proofread, your goal is to make your writing clear and correct. Direct your attention to finding and correcting errors in spelling, grammar, usage, and mechanics. Then mark changes on the final draft.

Even changes that are minor can make a big difference to your readers. Writer Ruth Stiles Gannett explains why every period and comma should be in the right place:

> Punctuation can determine both clarity and emphasis, and I check it when I'm reading the story aloud.

Making a Final Copy. With the last proofreading corrections in place, a writer makes a neat final copy. For most writers, this final copy is the one they share with others. This may be the copy that is finally sent to the publisher.

Sharing

Giving your writing to someone else to read is one way of sharing. Another person's reaction can tell you if you really have communicated what you wanted to say. You may even decide to go back and revise your final copy after another person has responded to it.

For you and your classmates, there are a number of other ways to share your writing assignments. You can display them on bulletin boards or put them together in a booklet. You can also try to get your writing published in student newspapers or magazines.

Practicing the Process of Writing

Like the professional writers quoted in this chapter, you too are a writer. Try following their processes and practicing some of their techniques. You may also get help from the Guidelines for the Process of Writing on page 654 in the handbook.

Remember, the three stages of writing discussed in this chapter are not separate steps that you must follow one after the other. Rather, think about prewriting, drafting, and revising and sharing as kinds of activities that writers use in a variety of ways to help them write.

As you continue to exercise your writing ability, your skills will grow. The more you write, the more you may find you enjoy it. Like the French novelist Gustave Flaubert, you may decide someday that "it is a delicious thing to write."

Using the Sounds of Language

Words are the writer's tools. The good writer chooses words both for their meanings and for their sounds. In this section you will learn how writers get the sounds of language to work for them through these techniques:

rhyme	onomatopoeia	assonance
rhythm	alliteration	

Solo, 1979, ROMARE BEARDEN. Private Collection. Photograph: Sheldon Ross Gallery, Birmingham, Michigan.

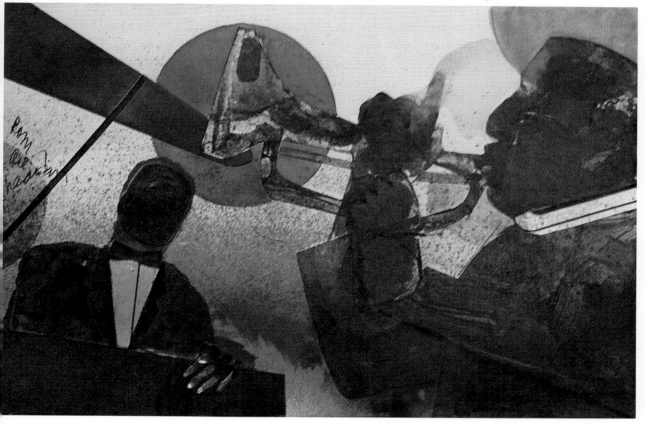

Rhyme

Rhyme is the repetition of syllable sounds at the ends of words. Rhyme may involve one or more syllables.

Examples: rest alive   remember
          best survive September

Rhyme in Prose. Rhyme is not usually used in prose. Some sayings, though, use rhyme to make their ideas more memorable. Here are two examples:

Birds of a feather flock together.
A friend in need is a friend indeed.

Rhyme within sentences makes important words stand out. Occasionally, you may find rhyme in a famous speech.

Let us have faith that right makes might, and in that faith let us dare to do our duty as we understand it.
—Abraham Lincoln, Address at New York City

Rhyme in Poetry. Rhyme helps to create the musical quality of poetry as well as to emphasize key words. Rhyme may occur within a line:

We'll grind and break and bind and take
And plunder ye and pound ye!   —C. S. Lewis, "Narnian Suite"

Usually, however, rhyme comes at the ends of lines. Sometimes lines that come after one another rhyme.

I saw a star slide down the sky,
Blinding the north as it went by,
Too burning and too quick to hold,
Too lovely to be bought or sold,
Good only to make wishes on
And then forever to be gone.   —Sara Teasdale, "The Falling Star"

Sometimes every other line rhymes, as in this example:

> Go quietly; a dream
>> When done, should leave no trace
> That it has lived, except a gleam
>> Across the dreamer's face.   —Countee Cullen, "If You Should Go"

Notice the pattern of rhyme in these lines:

> They are all gone away,
>> The House is shut and still,
> There is nothing more to say.
>>> —E. A. Robinson, "The House on the Hill"

The pattern of end rhyme in a poem is called its **rhyme scheme.** Lower case italic letters are used to show the rhyme scheme. Each line of a poem is given a letter. Lines that rhyme are given the same letter.

Once when the snow of the year was beginning to fall,	*a*
We stopped by a mountain pasture to say, "Whose colt?"	*b*
A little Morgan had one forefoot on the wall,	*a*
The other curled at his breast. He dipped his head	*c*
And snorted at us. And then he had to bolt.	*b*
We heard the miniature thunder where he fled.	*c*

> —Robert Frost, "The Runaway"

Exercises: Using Rhyme

A. Identify the rhyme in the following sentence.

> He that goes a-borrowing, goes a-sorrowing.
>> —Benjamin Franklin, *Poor Richard's Almanac*

B. Identify the rhyme scheme of the following stanza of a poem.

> The day is done, and the darkness
>> Falls from the wings of Night,
> As a feather is wafted downward
>> From an eagle in his flight.
>>> —Henry W. Longfellow, "The Day Is Done"

Rhythm

Rhythm is the pattern of stressed and unstressed syllables in a line of poetry. The pattern is shown by marking syllables with the following symbols:

/ for accented, or stressed, syllables

◡ for unaccented, or unstressed, syllables

Example: Máry had a líttle lámb.

Its fléece was whíte as snów.

Rhythm in Prose. All writing has rhythm. Writers may slow down the rhythm of their prose to describe calm, quiet scenes. They may quicken the rhythm of their writing for fast-paced action. Accented syllables, punctuation, and pauses all change the rhythm of prose. Here is an example of a slow rhythm that builds tension:

> And then, when my head was well in the room, I undid the lantern cautiously—oh, so cautiously—cautiously (for the hinges creaked)—I undid it just so much that a single, thin ray fell upon the vulture eye.
> —Edgar Allan Poe, "The Tell-Tale Heart"

Here is an example of prose with quick, lively rhythm:

> The sled started with a bound, and they flew on through the dusk, gathering smoothness and speed as they went, with the hollow night opening out below them and the air singing by like an organ.
> —Edith Wharton, *Ethan Frome*

Rhythm in Poetry. Rhythm helps to create the effect of poetry. Notice how the strong, pounding rhythm in this example echoes the sound of marching troops.

‿ / ‿ / ‿ ‿ / ‿ /
O what is that sound that so thrills the ear
  / ‿ ‿ / ‿ / ‿ /
  Down in the valley drumming, drumming?
/ ‿ ‿ / ‿ / ‿
Only the scarlet soldiers dear,
  ‿ / ‿ / ‿
  The soldiers coming.

          —W. H. Auden, "O What Is That Sound"

Poets sometimes break their rhythm patterns to emphasize important words. In this verse, note the three heavy beats in the third line.

  ‿ / ‿ / ‿ / ‿ /
When Daniel Boone goes by, at night,
  ‿ / ‿ / ‿ /
The phantom deer arise
  ‿ / / / ‿ / ‿‿
And all lost, wild America
  ‿ / ‿ / ‿ /
Is burning in their eyes.

          —Rosemary and Stephen Vincent Benét, "Daniel Boone"

Exercises: Using Rhythm

A. Read the following excerpts aloud to hear the rhythm. Explain what effect the changes in rhythm have in each one.

1. A quarter of an hour passed, and a half, and a whole. I was alert; I kept watching the riverbank and the rows of mat huts that crowded to the verge of the muck at the bank. I grew weary, tensely waiting for the cook.

          —John Hersey, *A Single Pebble*

2. Well, son, I'll tell you:
Life for me ain't been no crystal stair.
It's had tacks in it,
And splinters,
And boards torn up,
And places with no carpet on the floor—
Bare.   —Langston Hughes, "Mother to Son"

B. Copy the verse in Exercise A above. Mark the stressed and unstressed syllables.

Onomatopoeia

Onomatopoeia is the use of words that imitate sounds.

Examples: tick-tock, crash, plink, wham, tweet

Onomatopoeia in Prose. Writers use onomatopoeia when they speak of sounds. There are many words that suggest sounds, such as *hum, murmur,* and *splash.* Sometimes writers may also invent words to imitate a sound. You might find words such as *wham, pow,* and *zing* in a comic strip.

Find examples of onomatopoeia in the following exerpts. It may be helpful to read the sentences aloud.

> I lay in bed, and at the same time I rode that train to Siberia. I heard the clacking of the wheels, the whistle of the locomotive.
> —Isaac Bashevis Singer, "Growing Up"

> From far below came the whimpering of the raccoon kits, and an occasional mournful howl from Wowser.
> —Sterling North, *Rascal*

> The limes were there, the white thorns were there, and the chestnut-trees were there, and their leaves rustled harmoniously when I stopped to listen, but the clink of Joe's hammer was not in the midsummer wind. —Charles Dickens, *Great Expectations*

Onomatopoeia in Poetry. Poets use onomatopoeia to create lively effects. Onomatopoeia is a way in which the sound of a poem can echo its meaning. Notice the following uses of onomatopoeia.

> Scraw,
> scraw,
> go away!
> Nobody loves the blue jay.
> —Eve Merriam, "Creatures We Can Do Without"

We rush into a rain
That rattles double glass   —Theodore Roethke, "Night Journey"

The doors are twisted on broken hinges.
Sheets of rain swish through on the wind.

> —Carl Sandburg, "Four Preludes on Playthings
> of the Wind"

I'm sitting in the living room,
When, up above, the Thump of Doom
Resounds. Relax. It's sonic boom.   —John Updike, "Sonic Boom"

Exercises: Using Onomatopoeia

A. Find an example of onomatopoeia in each of the following excerpts.

1. From the thick grass at the foot of the bush came a low hiss—a horrid cold sound that made Rikki-tikki jump back two clear feet.
   > —Rudyard Kipling, "Rikki-tikki-tavi"

2. The whing of father's racquet and the whack
   of brother's bat on cousin's ball
   > —Isabella Gardner, "Summer Remembered"

3. You could hear the tinkle of ice in the lemonade pitcher. In a distant kitchen, because of the heat of the day, someone was preparing a cold lunch. Someone was humming under her breath, high and sweet.
   > —Ray Bradbury, *The Martian Chronicles*

4. *See how he dives*
   From the rocks with a zoom!   —William Jay Smith, "Seal"

B. Use onomatopoeia in three sentences to recreate these sounds.

> a school bell   a car engine   an animal's call

C. Invent three onomatopoetic words to imitate sounds. Define each word.

D. Find three examples of onomatopoeia in advertisements.

Alliteration

Alliteration is the repetition of a consonant sound at the beginnings of words.

Examples: <u>d</u>o or <u>d</u>ie   <u>n</u>ow or <u>n</u>ever
                <u>s</u>afe and <u>s</u>ound   <u>s</u>weet <u>s</u>mell of <u>s</u>uccess

Alliteration in Prose. Alliteration in a sentence is fun to say and enjoyable to hear. It has the effect of drawing attention to certain words through sound. This makes them easy to remember. For example, alliteration is found in many familiar phrases such as "down in the dumps" and "turn the tables." Tongue twisters rely on alliteration: "rubber baby buggy bumpers." Alliteration is also found in many sayings, such as these:

He who laughs last laughs best.
Time and tide wait for no man.

In sentences, alliteration tends to emphasize certain words and ideas. Notice how the repetition of beginning sounds draws attention to key words and ideas in the following sentences.

The deep churned. Something was happening far down in the dim, foggy-green depths.   —Paul Annixter, "Battle in the Depths"

Touch each object you want to touch as if tomorrow your tactile sense would fail.   —Helen Keller, "The Seeing See Little"

There is always something left to love. And if you ain't learned that, you ain't learned nothing.   —Lorraine Hansberry, *A Raisin in the Sun*

Alliteration in Poetry. Alliteration is one of the poet's most important sound techniques. It makes particular words stand out. It also creates a sound to carry the meanings of the words. For example, look for the repeated beginning consonant sounds in these lines.

Let us walk in the white snow
In a soundless space   —Elinor Wylie, "Velvet Shoes"

The repetition of *w* in the first line and of *s* in the second gives a hushed sound to the lines. This sound reinforces the idea of quiet expressed by the words.

Often, the sounds and meanings of the words combine to create a mood, or a certain feeling, in a poem. In these lines the repetition of *b* and *t* gives a feeling of urgency.

Hear the loud alarum bells—
    Brazen bells!
What a tale of terror, now, their turbulency tells!
        —Edgar Allan Poe, "The Bells"

Think how different the sound and feeling of the poem would be if the last line read: "What a story of horror their noisy racket tells!"

Exercises: Using Alliteration

A. Identify the alliteration in each of the following excerpts. Tell which consonant sounds are repeated. Explain the effect of the alliteration.

1. Homeless, they have a hundred homes. They flit from furnished room to furnished room, transients forever.
        —O. Henry, "The Furnished Room"

2. In hundreds of houses sleepy women woke sleepier children.
        —Esther Forbes, *Johnny Tremain*

3. They were women then
   My mama's generation
   Husky of voice—Stout of
   Step   —Alice Walker, "Women"

4. I saw lingering, late and lightless,
   A single swan, swinging, sleek as a sequin.
        —W. R. Rodgers, "The Swan"

B. Find five examples of alliteration in headlines, sayings, and songs.

Assonance

> **Assonance** is the repetition of a vowel sound within words.
>
> Examples: fr<u>ee</u> and <u>ea</u>sy   m<u>a</u>ke the gr<u>a</u>de

Assonance in Prose. Assonance has the same effect as alliteration. It emphasizes certain words and helps create a mood, or feeling, in a piece of writing. Assonance can also show connections between certain words. For example, in the following sentences the repetition of the long *o* sound reinforces the connection between *poetry* and *old*.

> Poetry is old, ancient, goes far back. It is among the oldest of living things. So old it is that no man knows how and why the first poems came.   —Carl Sandburg, *Early Moon*

Assonance in Poetry. In poetry, too, assonance stresses words and creates a feeling. In the following lines the many long *i* sounds bring the words *night, life, bride,* and *I* all together in a single repeated sound.

> And so, all the night-tide, I lie down by the side
> Of my darling, my darling, my life and my bride
>   —Edgar Allan Poe, "Annabel Lee"

Exercises: Using Assonance

A. Find examples of assonance in this excerpt and explain the effect.

> Slow things are beautiful:
> The closing of the day,
> The pause of the wave
> That curves downward to spray
>   —Elizabeth Coatsworth, "Swift Things Are Beautiful"

B. Write three sentences using assonance.

Using Figures of Speech

Figures of speech use ordinary words in unusual ways. They force a reader to look at familiar things as if they were new. Figures of speech lead readers to think about things and ideas in a fresh way. In this section, you will learn about these figures of speech:

simile	personification
metaphor	hyperbole

Summer (detail), 1573, GIUSEPPE ARCIMBOLDO. The Louvre, Paris
Photograph: Scala/Art Resource, New York City.

Simile

> **Simile** is a stated comparison between two things that are actually unlike but that have something in common. It contains the words *like* or *as*.
>
> Examples: My kitten is as fierce as a tiger.
> The snow settled on the roof like a
> comforting blanket.

Similes in Prose. By comparing one thing to another, a simile helps readers picture in their minds what someone or something looks like.

He was only a little boy, ten years old, with hair like dusty yellow grass and with shy polite grey eyes, and with a mouth that worked when he thought. —John Steinbeck, *The Red Pony*

The sun rose over Stony Lonesome and hung like a burning balloon in the sky as Danny danced back up the Smokey Creek trail.
—Jim Kjelgaard, *Big Red*

A simile can also give a general impression of someone or something. For example, read this description of how a boy walks:

Johnny stalked out of the kitchen as stiff-legged as a fighting tom-cat. —Esther Forbes, *Johnny Tremain*

The simile compares Johnny to a fighting tom-cat not just in the way he looks but also in the way he acts. Johnny seems at the moment very ready for a fight.

Similes in Poetry. Like similes in prose, similes in poetry help readers picture something in their minds. Similes can work to create impressions. In the following lines, a description of a woman's eyes gives an impression of her stormy feelings.

Eyes like a lake
Where a storm-wind roams
Caught me from under
The rim of a hat.   —Carl Sandburg, "Under a Hat Rim"

A simile can also express an important idea. For example, in these lines the future is compared to a flame.

We have tomorrow
Bright before us
Like a flame.   —Langston Hughes, "Youth"

The brightness and warmth in the simile suggest the idea of hope for tomorrow—a bright future. In the next lines, a simile gives a physical description to explain an idea.

The Truth
is quite messy
like
a wind blown room   —William J. Harris, "The Truth Is Quite Messy"

Exercises: Using Simile

A. Explain each simile in the excerpts below. Tell what things are compared and what impression or idea is given.

1. The stars twinkled down like a million flirting eyes.
                    —Maureen Daley, "Sixteen"
2. What happens to a dream deferred?
   Does it dry up
   Like a raisin in the sun?
   Or fester like a sore—
   and then run?
   Does it stink like rotten meat?
                    —Langston Hughes, "Dream Deferred"

B. Write similes to describe three of the following items.

   1. sand in your shoes   3. when school lets out

   2. a stadium crowd   4. an angry face

Metaphor

Metaphor is a figure of speech that makes a comparison between two unlike things that have something in common. It does not contain the words *like* or *as*.

Examples: The flowers are a carpet of color.
The ship plows the sea.

Metaphors in Prose. Like similes, metaphors help readers to picture something or someone. A metaphor usually gives more than just a physical description. For example, here is a description of what it is like to sail on the Atlantic Ocean:

> We often seemed to be riding under the sky on a billowing mirror; or perhaps the sea was crystal clear and bottomless.
> —Thor Heyerdahl, *The Voyage of Ra*

In these lines the sea is compared to "a billowing mirror." This metaphor creates an idea of the clearness and calmness of the sea.

The following metaphor describes an old driveway.

> The drive was a ribbon now, a thread of its former self, with gravel surface gone, and choked with grass and moss.
> —Daphne du Maurier, *Rebecca*

The narrowness of the driveway is emphasized by the comparison to "a ribbon" and "a thread." The reader gets the impression that the driveway used to be much wider.

An extended metaphor compares unlike things in several ways. Extended metaphors occur in both poetry and prose. The following extended metaphor compares reading to eating.

> I was hungry enough for literature to want to take down the whole paper at this one meal, but I got only a few bites, and then had to postpone.
> —Mark Twain, *A Connecticut Yankee in King Arthur's Court*

Metaphors in Poetry. Metaphors occur frequently in poetry. Often the comparisons are very unusual—even surprising. Such metaphors help readers see things in new ways. Look for what is being compared in these lines:

> A soft sea washed around the House
> A sea of summer Air
> > —Emily Dickinson, "A Soft Sea Washed Around the House"

The "summer air" is compared to "a sea." How is air like a sea? The metaphor suggests that the hot, heavy air of summer can seem as thick and slow as water. In this way, the metaphor gives an impression of what something feels like.

In this poem, a metaphor describes ordinary toads.

> Lumps of mud,
> the toads are jumping
> down the trail in twilight.   —José Juan Tablada, "Haikus"

By comparing toads to "lumps of mud," the metaphor creates a vivid impression in a few words.

Exercises: Using Metaphor

A. Identify each metaphor in the excerpts below. Tell what two things are being compared. Explain how they are alike.

1. A house divided against itself cannot stand. I believe this government cannot endure permanently half slave and half free.
   > —Abraham Lincoln, Second Lincoln-Douglas Debate

2. My heart is what it was before,
     A house where people come and go;
   But it is winter with your love,
     The sashes are beset with snow
   > —Edna St. Vincent Millay, "Alms"

B. Write metaphors to describe two of the following things.

    snake   fire   closet   computer   music   mountains

Personification

> **Personification** is a figure of speech in which human quali-
> ties are attributed to an object, an animal, or an idea.
>
> Examples: The motor coughed.
> The moon gazed down.

Personification in Prose. Personification is a special kind of comparison. It creates a certain impression by making nonhuman things appear human. Notice the use of personification in these two examples:

> The old house was the same, droopy and sick.
> —Harper Lee, *To Kill a Mockingbird*

> It was a clear athletic stream that rushed and ran, and jumped and splashed. —Jean Craighead George, *My Side of the Mountain*

The old house in the first example is compared to a sick person to give a sense of how the house appears to those who see it. The stream in the second example gives the impression of athletic health and vigor. By giving objects human qualities, personification helps readers understand objects in the same way they understand other humans.

Places can be personified, too, as in this example:

> The giant kingdom that was the Reata Ranch lay dozing in the sun, its head in the cloud-wreathed mountains far to the north, its arms flung east and west in careless might. —Edna Ferber, *Giant*

Personification in Poetry. Personification is used frequently in poetry. Like its effect in prose, personification in poetry makes objects and ideas understandable by describing them as human. Try to imagine the human pictures that the use of personification creates in the following examples.

In the evening the city
Goes to bed
Hanging lights
About its head.　　　—Langston Hughes, "City"

The jukebox has a big square face,
A majestic face, softly glowing with red and green and purple lights.
　　　　　—Kenneth Fearing, "King Juke"

In the next example, nature is given human traits.

Spring brings out her baseball bat, swings it through the air,
Pitches bulbs and apple blossoms, throws them where it's bare
　　　　　　—Myra Cohn Livingston, "A Circle of Seasons"

Exercises: Using Personification

A. Identify the personification in each of the following excerpts. Tell what is being compared to humans. How is it like humans?

1. A great door in the side of the vessel whispered out a breath of oxygen.
　　　　　—Ray Bradbury, *The Illustrated Man*

2. Inside the pencil
   crouch words that have never been written
　　　　　—W. S. Merwin, "The Unwritten"

3. The lawnmower
   Grinds its teeth
   Over the grass,
   Spitting out a thick
   Green spray　　　—Valerie Worth, "Lawnmower"

4. The city is so big
   Its bridges quake with fear
　　　　　—Richard García, "The City Is So Big"

B. Use personification to describe two of the following objects, or choose two objects of your own.

　　a pencil sharpener　　a video game　　a skyscraper　　a slide

Hyperbole

> **Hyperbole** is a figure of speech in which the truth is exaggerated for emphasis.
>
> Example: You could have knocked me over with a feather.

Hyperbole in Prose. With hyperbole, a writer makes a point by overstating it. Hyperbole is often used for humorous effect as in tall tales. Look at this example.

> At three weeks, Paul Bunyan got his family into a bit of trouble by kicking around his little tootsies and knocking down something like four miles of standing timber.

Hyperbole can also be found in descriptions. A writer emphasizes the qualities of a person or thing by exaggerating them, as in this example:

> The skin on her face was as thin and drawn as tight as the skin on an onion and her eyes were gray and sharp like the points of two icepicks.　　—Flannery O'Connor, "Parker's Back"

Hyperbole can also be used to describe a person's emotions. In the following example, a boy is pulling a man up from a deep hole. See how the writer uses hyperbole to describe the boy's feelings as he struggles.

> It was not a mere man he was holding, but a giant; or a block of granite. The pull was unendurable. The pain unendurable.
> 　　—James Ramsey Ullman, "A Boy and a Man"

What is exaggerated in the following examples?

> There did not seem to be brains enough in the entire nursery, so to speak, to bait a fishhook with.
> 　　—Mark Twain, *A Connecticut Yankee in King Arthur's Court*

People moved slowly then. There was no hurry, for there was nowhere to go, nothing to buy and no money to buy it with, nothing to see outside the boundaries of Maycomb County.

—Harper Lee, *To Kill a Mockingbird*

Hyperbole in Poetry. Hyperbole is common in humorous poetry. Hyperbole can make a point in a lighthearted way. It can be used to poke fun at someone or something. For example, read this description of a dull town.

It's a slow burg—I spent a couple of weeks there one day.

—Carl Sandburg, "The People, Yes"

A boy's tardiness is exaggerated in this hyperbole:

Why does a boy who's fast as a jet
Take all day—and sometimes two—
To get to school?   —John Ciardi, "Speed Adjustments"

Hyperbole can also emphasize the impact of an event, as in this example:

Here once the embattled farmers stood
And fired the shot heard round the world.

—Ralph Waldo Emerson, "The Concord Hymn"

Exercises: Using Hyperbole

A. Identify the hyperbole in each excerpt. What is being exaggerated?

1. If I read a book and it makes my whole body so cold no fire can warm me, I know that is poetry.

—Emily Dickinson, Letter to Col. Thomas
Higginson

2. He runs a mile in nothing flat.
He can run right out from under his hat

—John Ciardi, "Speed Adjustments"

B. Write hyperboles about being loud, cold, and late.

Chapter 2 *Review*

Understanding the Process of Writing

Review the stages in the process of writing: prewriting, drafting, revising, and sharing. Then read the following statements and identify which stage each writer is talking about. Also identify any overlapping of stages that the writers mention.

1. I make no attempt to correct as I go along because I know I must go over the manuscript word for word later. I am busy telling a story and do not want to interrupt it with clerical details.   —Keith Robertson

2. I discover that I have gotten an idea somewhere. . . . Then over the next six months or a year or two years, it gradually, slowly develops—I think about it occasionally. The characters are forming at that time.
   —Edward Albee

3. With each draft I become more and more concerned with getting the sentence structure and the wording just the way I want it. The story must be paced, and the sentences must read as smoothly and rhythmically as possible.   —Robert M. McClung

Understanding the Sounds of Languages

The following excerpts each contain at least one example of these techniques:

    rhyme   onomatopoeia   assonance
    rhythm   alliteration

For each of the following excerpts, find an example of one of these techniques and explain its effect.

1. Sling your knuckles on the bottom of the happy
   tin pans, let your trombones ooze, and go husha-husha-
   hush with the slippery sandpaper.   —Carl Sandburg, "Jazz Fantasia"

2. He kept his eyes fixed on her, marveling at the way her face changed with each turn of their talk, like a wheat-field under a summer breeze.
   —Edith Wharton, *Ethan Frome*

3. He swings down like the flourish of a pen
   Signing a signature in white on white.

   > —Robert Francis, "Skier"

4. He solved ten problems in trigonometry. His mind cut neatly through their knots and separated them.

   > —John Updike, "A Sense of Shelter"

5. He nested with owl,
   And with bear-cub and possum,
   And knew all his orchards
   Root, tendril, and blossom.

   > —Rosemary and Stephen Vincent Benét,
   > "Johnny Appleseed"

6. She had seemed a pale, quiet woman in the house at Paddington, but in court she had flamed out against the sober background, flaunting herself like a tropical flower.   —Agatha Christie, *Witness for the Prosecution*

7. The pine tree pointed his finger to the sky,
   And the oak spread out his arms,
   The lakes cuddled down in the hollows of the ground,
   The rivers ran down to the sea

   > —James Weldon Johnson, "The Creation"

8. Then, on his back, with his tail lashing and his jaws clicking, the shark plowed over the water as a speedboat does.

   > —Ernest Hemingway, *The Old Man and the Sea*

Understanding Figures of Speech

In the excerpts above and on the preceding page, find an example of each of the following figures of speech:

simile	personification
metaphor	hyperbole

Explain the effect of each figure of speech.

CHAPTER THREE

Myths and Tales from Many Lands

Shang-Yuan Fu-Jen, early 19th century (Edo period), KANŌ NAGANOBU. From the *Scroll of the Chinese Immortals.* The New York Public Library, New York City. Photograph by Otto Nelson.

Reading Literature

Myths and Tales from Many Lands

Long ago, people wondered how the world came to be and why there were such things as thunder and rainbows. Ancient peoples didn't have scientific answers. They explained natural events in myths. A **myth** is a very old story that answers basic questions about the world, such as how the earth and its people were created. The explanations found in myths usually involve gods or godlike beings.

A **folk tale** differs from a myth in that it deals more with people than with gods. Tales often gave people practical lessons about everyday life. For example, the fisherman in "The Story of the Fisherman and the Brass Bottle" finds that being clever is necessary for his survival. Legends, fables, and fairy tales are all folk tales.

Myths and tales were important to ancient societies. First, they were entertaining. The stories were full of adventure and excitement. Second, myths and tales reinforced social and moral values.

Today we can discover the values of ancient peoples by reading their stories. We also have much to learn from these stories. For although they come from different societies, the ideas and values in myths and folk tales are known to people everywhere.

The History of Myths and Tales

Scientists believe that myth-making began about 250,000 B.C. Stories were passed from generation to generation. From this oral tradition, myths and tales were gathered and written down.

Many theories explain how myths develop. One theory says that a myth may be based on a real person or event in the past. For example, myths of many lands tell of a great flood that covered the earth. Hundreds of thousands of years ago there may have been a tremendous flood. Another theory states that ancient people created myths to satisfy inner needs. People have always needed heroes, for example.

The Elements of Myths and Tales

Setting. In myths, the setting is sometimes supernatural, sometimes earthly. Most Norse myths, for instance, take place partly in the heavens and partly on earth. On the other hand, the setting of a tale is more closely tied to a group of people and its way of life.

Character. Characters in folk tales and myths are often less complicated than in short stories. Usually these characters represent a particular quality or type of person. The main character of a myth is often a god or a hero. He shows qualities that the society respects.

Plot. As you know, plot involves a **conflict,** a struggle between opposing forces. The conflict in myths and tales is likely to be **external.** It might be a fight between the hero and someone or something. Sometimes a myth or tale will have an **internal** conflict, such as a character's inner struggle to come to a decision. In addition to a conflict, plot in myths and tales often includes supernatural or magical events.

Purpose. One major purpose of myths is to explain an element of human life or nature. A purpose of both myths and tales is to entertain and to teach the values of a culture.

Theme. Like every story, a myth or tale has a **theme** or message, which is often a lesson about values or about life.

How to Read Myths and Tales

1. Bring a folk tale or myth alive by reading it aloud.
2. Try to identify the theme of each myth or tale. What does each myth explain? What lessons does the myth or tale teach?
3. Compare myths and tales. Notice similarities and differences in such elements as theme, plot, setting, and characters.
4. Think about what the myths and tales reveal about the societies that created them. What values were important in these societies? What was their idea of a hero?

Comprehension Skills

Comparison and Contrast

The myths and tales in this chapter are similar in some ways to the short stories in Chapter One. However, they are quite different in other ways. Finding the similarities between two or more things is called making **comparisons.** Identifying differences is called making **contrasts.** Stories can be compared and contrasted in terms of their settings, characters, plots, and themes.

Read the following opening paragraphs. The first is from the short story "A Spark Neglected Burns the House" in Chapter One. The second paragraph comes from the Norse myth "How Odin Lost His Eye." It appears in this chapter.

> There once lived in a village a peasant named Ivan Shcherbakov. He was comfortably off, in the prime of life, the best worker in the village, and had three sons all able to work. . . . Ivan's wife was an able and thrifty woman, and they were fortunate in having a quiet, hardworking daughter-in-law.

> Once when the world was still very young, Odin sat on his throne in the most beautiful palace in Asgard. His throne was so high that he could see over all three parts of the world from where he sat. On his head he wore a helmet shaped like an eagle. On his shoulders perched two black ravens called Memory and Thought. At his feet crouched two snarling wolves.

These paragraphs are similar in several ways. Both paragraphs introduce main characters and settings. The paragraph from "A Spark Neglected Burns the House" introduces Ivan in his village. The paragraph from "How Odin Lost His Eye" introduces Odin in Asgard.

These two paragraphs differ, however, in several important ways. While both introduce setting, the two settings are quite different. The first paragraph of "A Spark Neglected Burns the House" describes a nineteenth-century Russian village. The paragraph from "How Odin

Lost His Eye" describes Asgard, the grand heaven of the Norse gods. The characters are also quite different. Ivan is a lowly peasant, while Odin is a mighty god. The paragraph from "A Spark Neglected Burns the House" is realistic in its description of characters and setting. In contrast, the paragraph from "How Odin Lost His Eye" has supernatural elements, such as Odin's ability to see the whole world.

Exercise: Making Comparisons and Contrasts

Read the following opening paragraphs. The first is from the short story "Thank You, M'am" in Chapter One. The second is from "The Tale of the Superman" in this chapter. Then answer the comparison and contrast questions.

She was a large woman with a large purse that had everything in it but hammer and nails. . . . It was about eleven o'clock at night, and she was walking alone, when a boy ran up behind her and tried to snatch her purse. The strap broke with the single tug the boy gave it from behind. But the boy's weight and the weight of the purse combined caused him to lose his balance, so instead of taking off full blast as he had hoped, the boy fell on his back on the sidewalk and his legs flew up. The large woman simply turned around and kicked him square in his blue-jeaned sitter. Then she reached down, picked the boy up by his shirt front, and shook him until his teeth rattled.

Once upon a time there was a man who believed he was stronger than anyone else in the whole world. He certainly was strong, for whenever he went to the . . . forest, he would bring back a load ten times as big as most men could carry. Sometimes, when he found a dead tree lying on the ground, he would toss it on to his head with a mighty heave and carry it home in one piece. But he was proud, too; and, when he reached home, he would . . . fling the load down on the ground, and call to his wife: "Come and see what your superman has brought you!"

1. What similar physical quality do the two main characters have?
2. In what different ways do the two characters show their strength?
3. What different settings do the two paragraphs present?
4. "Thank You, M'am" describes realistic actions. How are the superman's actions different?

$\mathcal{V}$ocabulary Skills

Word Parts

As you know, an unfamiliar word may contain a word that is more familiar. For example, suppose you didn't know what *unconquerable* means. However, you recognized the word *conquer* in it. Here, the word *conquer* is the **base word.** The word parts on either side of the base word are called **affixes.** The word part added at the beginning of a base word is a **prefix.** A word part added at the end is a **suffix.**

Prefix + Base Word + Suffix = New Word
un-   + conquer   + -able = unconquerable

To unlock the meaning of a word with affixes, first separate the affixes from the base word. In the example, the prefix *un-* means "not." The suffix *-able* means "capable of being." Unconquerable means "not capable of being conquered." An unconquerable country is one that cannot be taken over by enemies.

If you know the meanings of affixes, you can figure out many unfamiliar words. The following charts list common affixes.

Prefix	Definition	Example
dis-	"opposite of" or "not"	disappear
il-, im-, in-, ir-	"not" or "opposite of"	illegal, immoderate, inexact, irregular
mis-	"wrong" or "wrongly"	misdeed, misuse
non-, un-	"not"	nonresident, unfold
pre-	"before"	preview
re-	"again" or "back"	reappear, repay
sub-	"under" or "less than"	substandard
super-	"above" or "greater than"	superstructure, superhero

Note that adding a suffix sometimes changes the spelling of the base word. It may also change its part of speech.

Suffix	Definition	Example
-able	"capable of being" or "having the quality of"	usable, honorable
-er, -or	"one who does a certain thing"	winner, conductor
-ful	"full of" or "having"	graceful, hopeful
-less	"without"	shapeless
-ly	"in a certain manner"	surely
-ment	"the act of" or "the state of being"	movement, contentment
-ness	"the state of being"	greatness
-ous	"full of" or "having"	courageous
-ward	"in the direction of"	westward

Exercises: Using Word Parts to Find Meaning

A. Each word below is from Chapter Three. Write the base word and identify every prefix or suffix. Then explain the meaning of the word in terms of its word parts.

1. helplessly
2. immodest
3. discourteous
4. wonderful
5. northward
6. thoughtfully
7. mismanage
8. precut
9. approachable
10. achievement
11. uncomfortable
12. nonsense

B. In each sentence, find at least one word with a prefix or suffix from the charts. Identify each word part, and tell what the word means.

1. In Norse mythology, the creator looked down upon ice and darkness.
2. Odin's beautiful horse carried him on dangerous adventures.
3. Odin was unafraid to look upon sorrow and death.
4. The woman refastened the baby on her back and walked homeward.
5. The wrestler told Maru-me that he was a powerful man.

The Beginning of a World

Norse mythology came from the people who originally lived in the area we call Scandinavia today. Compare this Norse story of creation with others you know.

NORSE MYTH
Retold by Catharine F. Sellew

Long, long ago, before there were any days or nights—long before there was any time at all—there was no world, no earth or sky or sea. Only a deep crack yawned in the universe like the mouth of a huge monster. All around were mist and darkness, but deep down in the dark pit of the crack leaped the red tongue of fire.

There, too, a bottomless spring never stopped bubbling and running over. As the water rushed into the cold darkness, it turned into sheets of ice. The great spirit looked down upon this ice and darkness. He saw that nothing grew there. He saw that all was gray and silent. So he made a tremendous man called a giant and placed him on the ice. He made a huge cow which gave the giant gallons and gallons of milk.

The huge cow used to feed on the salt she found in the ice. One day, while she was licking the salt, her rough tongue came upon a golden hair. She licked and licked and found more golden hairs. Soon she found they were growing on the head of a giant frozen in the ice. Day after day she kept licking until she got to his shoulders, then his chest, then his waist. Finally he stood before her free from the ice. He was even taller and more handsome than her master. His name was Bure (by o͞or′ ə).

That was the beginning of a world of giants. It was a cold world with no sunshine, no blue sky, no green grass.

Some of the giants were evil, and they fought and quarreled with the good giants like Bure. Finally the grandsons of Bure conquered the bad giants and drove them far out into the cold gray twilight at the edge of the universe. It was so cold that their breath turned to ice the minute it passed their lips and fell like icicles on the ground.

Then the children of the good giants made for themselves a new world in which they were to be the gods who ruled over everything.

In the center of the universe they created a green land with rivers and lakes and

Ancient Geology, 1987, KAREN KUNC. Woodblock, 24" x 39". Photograph: Jan Cicero Gallery, Chicago.

mountains. That was the earth. Then they carved a man out of a tall ash tree and a woman out of a graceful elm. The gods gave them the power to move and think. And they placed them on the earth to start the human race.

At the top of the world the gods made a beautiful city for themselves. They called it Asgard. It was filled with gold and silver palaces. And because the gods wanted a road from their shining city down to the earth and then beyond to the dark world of the giants, they took fire and water and air and made a wonderful rainbow. The rainbow was so wide and so strong and so long that it stretched like a bridge across the three parts of the universe.

Now there was a new world, but no sky to cover it. Where should the gods place the sun and the moon and the stars? Where should they place the fluffy white clouds or the heavy thunderheads? When they made the sky, how should they hold it over the three parts of the world?

Then they found four very strong and very ugly little men called dwarfs to hold the four corners of the sky on their shoulders. Their names were Nordri, Sudri, Austri, and Westri, which mean North, South, East, and West. And the gods filled the sky with sparks that shone when there was no sun or moon nearby. They called them stars.

In this new world there grew a mighty tree that was ever green. It was so tall that its topmost branches shaded the palaces of the gods and its lower branches shaded the earth and the land of the giants. The tree had three roots, one growing in each of the three parts of the world.

The ruler of this new world was All-Father, king of the gods. He was a great warrior and he called himself Odin (ō′ din). Odin's beautiful gray horse, Sleipner (slāp′ nêr), had eight feet and could run faster than the wind. Sleipner carried his master through many fierce battles and on many long and dangerous adventures. And when the great All-Father galloped across the rainbow bridge, the thundering of the horse's hoofs echoed from the heavens to the deepest and darkest caves of the giants.

Viking wooden harness collars with bronze decoration. Danish National Museum, Copenhagen.

Catharine F. Sellew (*born 1922*) has been interested in mythology since her mother read Greek myths to her as a child. After graduating from college, Sellew began to rewrite both Greek and Norse myths to make them easier to read. Two of her well-known collections are *Adventures with the Gods* and *Adventures with the Giants*.

Developing Comprehension Skills

1. According to this Norse myth, what is the world like before the giants' children create the new world? How is the new world different from the world of the giants?

2. How are the giants and the gods similar? How are they different?

3. Besides the creation of the earth, this myth also explains the creation of several other things. What are three of them?

4. Myths reflect the society that creates them. What seems to have been important to Norse society?

5. Do you think ice is a vital part of this myth? Explain your answer.

Reading Literature: Myths

1. **Diagraming Setting.** The Norse universe has three parts: Asgard at the top, the earth at the center, and the world of the giants at the edge of the universe. Diagram these three parts of the universe, and show how they are connected. Label each part, and write on it the name of its ruler. Then write a sentence or two describing the setting of each part.

2. **Identifying Conflict.** The plot of a story always involves a **conflict,** a struggle between opposing forces. Who is involved in the conflict in "The Beginning of a World"? What is the struggle about? Who wins?

3. **Recognizing Symbols.** A **symbol** is a person, place, or object that stands for something beyond itself. Storytellers often use symbols to represent complicated ideas. For example, a dove represents peace. The color red often stands for anger.

   In this Norse creation myth, ice is used as a symbol of death. Wherever there is ice, breathing and movement stop. For example, before the creation of the world, there was "ice and darkness." The giant Bure comes to life only when the cow licks away the ice from around him.

   Trees are also important in this myth. Go

back through the myth and find some examples of trees in the creation of the world. From these examples, what do you think trees stand for?

Developing Vocabulary Skills

Spelling Changes with Affixes. The spelling of some base words changes when a suffix is added. The following rules explain how to spell words when suffixes are added:

a. When a suffix beginning with a vowel is added to a word ending with silent *e*, the *e* is usually dropped.

change + -ing = changing

Note that the *e* is not dropped when a suffix beginning with a consonant is added.

use + -ful = useful

b. When a suffix is added to a word ending in *y* preceded by a consonant, the *y* is usually changed to an *i*.

lonely + -ness = loneliness

Note that when the *y* is preceded by a vowel, it is not changed.

delay + -ed = delayed

c. Words ending in one consonant preceded by one vowel double the final consonant before adding *-ing, -ed,* or *-er.*

occur + -ing = occurring

Note that when two vowels appear together in the word, the final consonant is not doubled.

cheat + -ed = cheated

Read each of the following sentences about the myth you have just read. On a sheet of paper, copy each underlined word. Next, draw a line between the base word and its ending. If the spelling of the base word has changed, write the letter of the spelling rule beside the word.

1. There, too, a <u>bottomless</u> spring never <u>stopped bubbling</u> and <u>running</u> over.

2. The gods wanted a road from their <u>beautiful, shining</u> city down to the earth.

3. Sleipner <u>carried</u> his master on many long and dangerous adventures.

4. The gods <u>carved</u> a man out of a tall ash tree and a woman out of a <u>graceful</u> elm.

Developing Skills in Study and Research

Using the Library Filing System. To find books on the Norse people and their mythology, you must understand the library filing system. The most commonly used library filing system is the Dewey Decimal System. Skim the list of Dewey Decimal categories on page 648 in the handbook at the back of this book. Decide how each of the following books would be coded. On a sheet of paper, list the number range for each book. For example, a book of poetry would be assigned a number between 800 and 899 in the Dewey Decimal System.

1. a book about Norse mythology

2. a book about the history of Scandinavia

3. a book about ice and ice formations

4. a book about Scandinavian art

Developing Writing Skills

Describing a Setting. This myth describes two settings, one before the creation of the world and one after the creation. The first setting, for example, is "a deep crack" that "yawned in the universe like the mouth of a huge monster." The details that describe each setting help you to visualize it. In one paragraph, write a description of a setting you know well. Use details to help your readers visualize the setting.

Prewriting. Decide on the specific setting you will describe. On a sheet of paper, list two or three details about the setting. Use some details that appeal to more than one sense. For example, the description "roots like tangled knots" appeals to the sense of sight. The detail "swept by howling winds" appeals to the sense of hearing as well as the sense of sight.

Drafting. In a paragraph, describe the setting you chose. Include the details from your list, as well as any others that would help a reader to visualize the setting. Explain what a person in that place might see, hear, touch, taste, and smell.

Revising and Sharing. Read your description to another person. Ask the person to try to visualize the setting, and have him or her make comments about what other information is needed or what is not clear. Use these suggestions to revise your paragraph. Then get together with your classmates and put all of the descriptions of setting in a booklet for everyone to read.

How Odin Lost His Eye

As you read this myth, pay attention to the details about the Norse god Odin. How does he live up to his title of All-Father?

NORSE MYTH
Retold by Catharine F. Sellew

Viking helmet, about A.D. 550–800.
History Museum, Stockholm. Giraudon/Art Resource, New York City.

Once when the world was still very young, Odin sat on his throne in the most beautiful palace in Asgard. His throne was so high that he could see over all three parts of the world from where he sat. On his head he wore a helmet shaped like an eagle. On his shoulders perched two black ravens called Memory and Thought. And at his feet crouched two snarling wolves.

The great king gazed thoughtfully down on the earth below him. He had made the green land that stretched out before his eyes. With the help of the other gods, he had made men and women who lived on that earth. And he felt truly like the All-Father he was called.

The fair elves had promised they would help his children of the earth. The elves were the tiny people who lived between heaven and earth. They were so small that they could flit about doing their work unseen. Odin knew that they were the artists who painted the flowers and made the beds for the streams. They took care of all the bees and the butterflies. And it was the elves who brought the gentle rain and sunshine to the earth.

Even the ugly dwarfs, who lived in the heart of the mountains, agreed to help. They forged iron and metals, made tools and weapons. They dug gold and silver and beautiful jewels out of the earth. Sometimes they even cut the grain and ground the flour for the farmers on the earth.

All seemed to be going well. Odin found it hard to think of evil times. But he knew that the frost giants were only waiting for a chance to bring trouble to his children. They were the ones who brought cold and ice to the world and shook the earth in anger. They hated Odin and all the work of the gods.

From high on his throne Odin looked down beyond the earth deep into the gloomy land of his enemies. He saw dark figures of huge men moving about. They looked like evil shadows. He, the king of the gods, must have more wisdom. It was not enough just to see his enemies. He must know more about them.

So Odin wrapped his tall figure in a blue cloak. Down from his throne he climbed. Down the broad rainbow bridge he strode, and across the green earth till he came to one of the roots of the great evergreen tree. There, close by the tree, was a well full of clear water. Its surface was so still it was like a mirror. In it one could see pictures of things that had happened and things that were going to happen.

But beside the well sat an old man. His face was lined with the troubles of the world. His name was Mimir (mē′ mir), which means Memory. No one, not even the great Odin, could see the pictures in the well unless he first drank some of its water. Only Mimir could give the magic drink.

"Aged Mimir," Odin said to the old man, "you who hold the knowledge of the past and future in your magic waters, let me have but one sip. Then I can know enough to protect the men and women of the earth from the hate of the giants."

Mimir looked kindly at Odin, but he did not smile. Although he spoke softly, his voice was so deep it reminded Odin of the distant roar of the ocean.

"The price of one drink from this well is not cheap," Mimir said. "And once you have drunk and gazed into the mirror of life, you may wish you had not. For sorrow and death as well as joy are pictured there. Think again before you ask to drink."

But once the king of the gods had made up his mind, nothing could change it. He was not afraid to look upon sorrow and death.

"What is your price, aged Mimir?" Odin asked.

"You are great and good, Odin," answered Mimir. "You have worked hard to make the world. Only those who know hard work may drink from my well. Yet, that is not enough. What have you given up that is very dear to you? What have you sacrificed? The price of a drink must be a great sacrifice. Are you willing to pay the price?"

What could the king of the gods sacrifice? What was most dear to him? Odin thought of his handsome son, Balder, whom he loved most in the world. To give up his son would be like giving up life and all that was wonderful around him. Odin stood silent before Mimir. Indeed that would be a high price!

Then Mimir spoke again. He had read Odin's thoughts.

"No, I am not asking for your dear son. The Fates say his life must be short, but he has time yet to live and bring happiness to the gods and the world. I ask for one of your eyes."

Odin put his hands up to his bright blue eyes. Those two eyes had gazed across the world from his high throne in the shining city of the gods. His eyes had taught him what was good and beautiful—what was evil and ugly. Those eyes had also seen his children, the men and women of the earth, struggling against the hate of the giants. One eye was a small sacrifice to win knowledge of how to help them. Without another thought, Odin plucked out one of his blue eyes and handed it to Mimir.

Then Mimir smiled and gave Odin a horn full of the waters of his well. "Drink deeply, brave king, so you may see all that you wish in the mirror of life."

Odin lifted the horn to his lips and drank. Then he knelt by the edge of the well and watched the pictures passing across its still and silent surface. When he stood up again, he sighed, for it was as Mimir had said. He had seen sorrow and death as well as joy. It was only the glorious promise at the end that gave him courage to go on.

So Odin, the great king of the gods, became one-eyed. If you can find Mimir's well, you will see Odin's blue eye resting on the bottom. It is there to remind men and women of the great sacrifice he made for them.

One-eyed Odin (left), Thor, and Freyr, 12th century. Viking Tapestry. Skogs Church, Halsingland. Photograph: Werner Forman Archive, London/Statens Historiska Museer, Stockholm.

Developing Comprehension Skills

1. Why does Odin want to look into the future?

2. What can you infer about Odin from the sacrifice that he makes?

3. What is the difference between Odin's feelings before and after he looks into the future?

4. How does Odin live up to his title of All-Father?

5. How do you think Odin might have used his knowledge of the future to help humans? Explain your answer.

Reading Literature: Myths

1. **Understanding Theme.** Myths, like other stories, contain **themes,** or messages about life. One of the themes of "How Odin Lost His Eye" concerns the importance of sacrifice. What does this myth tell you about when sacrifice may be necessary? What does the myth say about the people or gods who are willing to make a sacrifice?

2. **Comparing and Contrasting Myths.** When you compare and contrast elements of a myth, you look for similarities and differences. The two Norse myths in this chapter introduce the good giant Bure and the god Odin. Compare these two characters. Which character is presented in more detail? What are the similarities between the characters? For example, how are Bure's and Odin's attitudes toward the evil giants similar? What are some differences between the two characters?

3. **Identifying Conflict.** As you have learned, an **external conflict** involves a struggle between the main character and an outside force. An **internal conflict** is a struggle that takes place within a character. An internal conflict usually involves a decision that the character must make. What is the external conflict that worries Odin at the beginning of the myth? What internal conflict must Odin resolve before he looks into the well?

Developing Vocabulary Skills

Identifying Affixes and Base Words. You have learned that an **affix** is a prefix or suffix added to a base word. The letters that form some affixes may also appear in the spelling of other words. For example, the letters r and e in *reach* look like the prefix *re*. However, the letters *ach* do not form a base word, so *re* is part of the word *reach* and not a prefix.

In each of the following words, two or three letters are underlined. On a sheet of paper write whether the underlined letters form a prefix, a suffix, or part of a base word.

1. gener<u>ous</u>
2. <u>un</u>iverse
3. cunn<u>ing</u>
4. <u>mis</u>spell
5. <u>re</u>move
6. soft<u>ly</u>
7. <u>dis</u>tant
8. ug<u>ly</u>

Developing Skills in Critical Thinking

Recognizing Slanted Language. The **denotation** of a word is its literal or dictionary definition. The **connotation** of a word is the sum of the suggested meanings that surround the literal definition. For example, the words

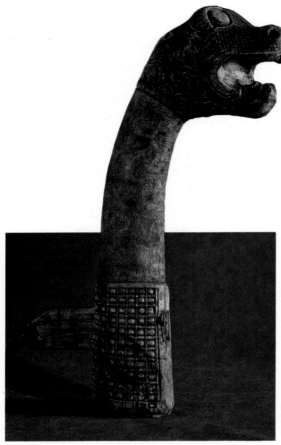

Wooden post, animal head, from the Oseberg ship burial, 9th century. University Museum of National Antiquities, Oslo, Norway.

Read the following groups of sentences. For each group, point out the different connotations of the underlined words and explain how these differences affect the meanings of the sentences.

1. a. Odin was a powerful king of the gods who took care of humans.
   b. Odin was a powerful king of the gods who meddled in the affairs of humans.
2. a. When Odin made up his mind, nothing could change it; he was determined.
   b. When Odin made up his mind, nothing could change it; he was stubborn.
3. a. Odin willingly sacrificed his eye to see what would happen in the future.
   b. Odin couldn't wait to give up his eye to see what would happen in the future.

Developing Skills in Speaking and Listening

Reading a Story Aloud. Myths were originally told aloud to a group of people. Select a section that is several paragraphs long from one of the two myths you have just read. Prepare to read it aloud to the class.

Try to make your voice express the feeling that the myth conveys. Emphasize important words and ideas. Practice an appropriate reading speed, not too fast or too slow. Be sure you can pronounce all the words correctly. Read through the selection several times so that you are comfortable with it. When you are ready, read the selection aloud to the class.

slender and *skinny* have similar definitions. However, the connotation of *slender* is more positive than the connotation of *skinny*. Most people think of a slender person as graceful and healthy, whereas they think a skinny person is too thin and unhealthy. **Slanted language** refers to words with strong connotations that are used to influence someone's thinking.

Developing Writing Skills

1. **Explaining a Prediction.** After Odin peers into the future, he is encouraged only by "the glorious promise at the end" that gives him the strength to go on. What do you think this "glorious promise" is? Will the humans conquer the giants? Will a new kind of world evolve from the struggle? Explain your idea of "the glorious promise" in one paragraph.

   Prewriting. Reread the myth and decide what you think Odin sees as "the glorious promise." Write down your prediction. Then list the reasons why you think your prediction is accurate. If possible, add quotations from the myth to support your explanation.

   Drafting. In the topic sentence for your paragraph, state your prediction of "the glorious promise." Explain your reasons as listed in your notes. When possible, support your explanation with specific quotations from the myth.

   Revising and Sharing. Check your paragraph for complete sentences. Then read it aloud to someone, and ask that person if your argument is clear. You may need to reorder your ideas to make your paragraph flow logically. Make sure that you present a strong case for your prediction of "the glorious promise."

2. **Understanding a Hero.** Odin is a hero in the Norse myths. He has special strengths that were important in Norse culture. He also stands for values that Norse society respected, such as wisdom and self-sacrifice. Write a paragraph describing what makes Odin a hero. Identify the special strengths and the values that he stands for. Use examples from the story to illustrate your ideas. As you compose your paragraph, follow the steps in Guidelines for the Process of Writing beginning on page 654 in the handbook.

The Fish

AUSTRALIAN MYTH
Adapted by Eric and Nancy Protter

This Australian myth explains why fish have certain habits. It also teaches an important lesson. Look for this lesson as you read.

Long, long ago there lived in that region of the world now known as Australia two brothers named Naru and Masa. Now, as it happened, Naru was very clever while his brother was extremely stupid.

One day Naru carved a squid out of wood. It looked so real that he decided to throw it into the sea. Instantly it came alive and swam away. However, to express its gratitude to Naru, from that day on it drove a school of small herrings close to shore so that Naru might catch them easily and have plenty to eat.

After a while, Masa noticed that his brother had more than enough fish to eat for his supper whereas he, Masa, had scarcely any at all. Greatly curious as to how his brother managed to catch so many fish, he decided to question him.

"Where do you find so many fish, brother? Tell me so I may go there, too."

"Masa, I will tell you a secret," replied Naru. "I carved a squid that looked so real that when I threw it into the water it became alive. Out of gratitude it has been driving the herrings close to shore so that I may easily catch them for my supper."

Thinking for a moment, he suggested, "Why don't you carve a fish too? But make *sure* that it is a squid," he warned with a severe tone in his voice.

Masa went home immediately and sat down to carve a fish. But because he was extremely stupid, he greedily carved a barracuda instead of a squid, as his brother had suggested. As soon as it was finished, he threw the wooden barracuda into the water, and, just like the squid earlier, the barracuda became alive. Immediately it swam toward the herrings and devoured them. Seeing this, Masa began to cry.

"What kind of fish did you carve?" demanded Naru angrily.

"A barracuda," sobbed his brother.

"You fool!" exclaimed Naru in despair. "Now your fish will eat up all the others, and in the end he won't even spare us."

And that is exactly what happened.

Even to this day, barracudas attack fish and people.

Melanesian dance mask in the form of a fish, date unknown. Reproduced by the Courtesy of the Trustees of the British Museum, London.

Developing Comprehension Skills

1. According to this myth, who creates the squid and the barracuda? What human qualities does each creator reveal?

2. How are the squid and the barracuda different?

3. This myth teaches a lesson about the consequences of cleverness, stupidity, and greed. What is this lesson?

4. Do you think Masa is an evil person for creating the barracuda? Explain your answer.

Reading Literature: Myths

1. **Identifying Purpose.** A myth can have several purposes: to explain something in nature, to teach cultural values, and to entertain. Think of the purposes of this Australian myth. Explain how the myth achieves these purposes.

2. **Understanding Myths.** A myth reflects the values and way of life of the society that created it. What can you tell about the values and way of life of the original Australian people from this myth?

Developing Vocabulary Skills

Reviewing Context Clues. In Chapter One, you learned how to use different kinds of context clues. The following sentences contain words from "The Fish." Figure out the meaning of each underlined word by using a context clue. On a sheet of paper, write each underlined word and its definition as you understand it from the context.

1. Naru carved a squid, a long-bodied sea creature with many arms.

2. To express its gratitude to Naru, the squid drove herrings close to shore. This act of thankfulness made it easy for Naru to catch fish to eat.

3. Although Naru was usually gentle with his brother, he warned him in a severe tone of voice.

4. The barracuda chased, caught, and devoured the tiny herrings.

5. Naru yelled out with despair because he knew that the situation was hopeless.

Developing Writing Skills

Writing a Story. Although myths have been passed on from ancient times in the oral tradition, you can write a story that has characteristics of a myth. Choose one of your favorite animals. Write a short myth-like story to explain its creation. Explain who created the animal and why.

Prewriting. To write a story, you will need ideas for a plot, a setting, and one or two characters. Use the chart below to help you think of details for each element. Make sure that your details fit together. For example, details about your animal must in some way relate to the reasons or results of the creation, like the squid and the barracuda in "The Fish."

Drafting. Using the ideas in your chart, tell the story of the animal's creation. Use a chronological order to organize the plot.

Revising and Sharing. Read your myth to a classmate or friend. Ask if he or she understands the plot and why the animal was created. Based on the feedback you get, make changes in or additions to your myth. Then give your final copy to a friend or family member to read and enjoy.

Setting	Character	Plot
Place	Description	Reasons for Creation
Time	Behavior	Results of Creation

The Tale of the Superman

AFRICAN TALE

This story from Nigeria describes at least three different superman characters. Look for similarities and differences in the characters as you read.

Once upon a time there was a man who believed he was stronger than anyone else in the whole world. He certainly was strong, for whenever he went to the forest to get firewood for his home, he would bring back a load ten times as big as most men could carry. Sometimes, when he found a dead tree lying on the ground, he would toss it on to his head with a mighty heave and carry it home in one piece. But he was proud, too; and, when he reached home, he would burst triumphantly into the compound, fling the load down on the ground, and call to his wife: "Come and see what your superman has brought you!"

His wife would bend low as she came out of the door of her mud hut, then straighten her back and smile.

"Superman?" she would mock. "If you really saw a superman, you would run away from him. Don't talk to me of supermen! Strong you may be, but superman, no!"

Then the man would get angry and sit down under the cassia tree outside his hut muttering: "It's a lie! I am a superman.

Just show me another who is stronger than I. Then I will believe you when you say I am not a superman."

One day the man's wife, whose name was Shetu, went to draw water. She took a large calabash,[1] put it on her head, and walked along the winding bush path until she came to a well. Now this well was a magic one, and, although Shetu managed to throw the bucket down into the water, she could not pull it up. She hauled and she tugged and she heaved; leaning backwards and digging her heels into the ground, she put her whole weight to the task. She even called upon Allah to help her but all to no avail.

"Alas!" she exclaimed, sinking down on the mud beside the well and wiping the perspiration from her forehead with the hem of her skirt. "Ten men would be needed to raise that bucket from the well today. I must go home without any water."

---

1. **calabash**–A container made from the gourd, the fruit of the tropical calabash vine.

Sadly she rose to her feet and began the journey back along the dusty path that wound in and out between the forest trees. Suddenly, she saw another woman approaching, and they stopped to exchange greetings.

"Why are you returning from the well with your calabash empty?" asked the stranger. "Has the well dried up?"

"Oh no!" exclaimed Shetu, "I have been struggling for a long time to raise the bucket from the water, but it is too heavy and I am not strong enough. It needs at least ten men to bring it to the top."

The other woman smiled and said: "Do not despair! Come, follow me to the well. I will see that you get your water after all."

Shetu was sure that the woman would not be able to help her, but she decided to follow to prove the truth of her words. As the woman led the way back along the path, Shetu noticed a fine-looking baby tied on her back. He turned his head and stared at her with bright, unblinking eyes for so long that she began to feel uncomfortable under his gaze.

At length they reached the well, and Shetu showed the woman the long rope that stretched far down into the well, with the magic bucket on the end.

"See!" she began, "I threw the bucket down but could not raise it up. I fear you will not be able to help either."

The woman laughed, untied the child from her back, and told him to pull the bucket up from the well. Without faltering, the child seized the rope in his little, fat hands and pulled the bucket up as easily as if it had been a feather on the end of a piece of string.

Shetu put her hand to her mouth in amazement. She could not speak, but the other woman did not seem at all disconcerted and told her child to draw more water. He did it again and again, without any sign of strain.

The two women set to work, washing first themselves and then the clothes they were wearing. These soon dried in the hot sun. Then they filled their calabashes with water and began their homeward journey.

After a little while, they came to a place where another path branched off to the east, and the woman with the baby turned up this new track.

"Where are you going?" asked Shetu.

"Home, of course," replied the other.

"Is your home along that path?" said Shetu. "I did not know that it led to a village. What is your husband's name?"

"My husband's name is Superman," said the stranger, and walking quickly along the narrow track she soon disappeared into the forest.

Shetu was too amazed to speak, but as soon as she got back to her hut she told her husband all that had happened during the day. At first he would not believe her, but soon he realized that she was speaking the truth, and anger welled up in him like bubbles rising in a pot of broth.

"Aha!" he exclaimed. "So there is another man who calls himself a superman, is there? Just let me see him, that's all! I'll soon show him who is the real superman!"

"O no!" begged his wife. "Keep away from him, in Allah's name, for I'm sure he will destroy you, and then what will become of me? If you had seen the strength of his infant son, you would realize that the father must be fifty times as strong."

But nothing she could say would persuade her obstinate husband to give up his foolish idea.

"Early tomorrow morning," he said firmly, "you must take me to the path that leads to this man's house."

The next day the husband got up before dawn and, full of confidence, took his hunting weapons from their hiding place. With a quiver of sharp arrows on his back, his bow in his hand, and his trusty sword slung from his shoulder, he felt ready for anything.

Then he shouted to his terrified wife, "Come along, lazy-bones! Come out of that hut and lead me to the place where this impostor lives! No, wait!" he exclaimed. "First of all take me to this magic well, that I may see the bucket for myself."

The woman picked up her calabash, placed it on her head, and led the way to the well. She was far too worried to realize how foolish it was to take a vessel to a well from which neither of them would be able to draw water; but she hurried along the path, with her husband still shouting at her from the rear. Presently she noticed that there was another figure on the path in front of her, and, when she and her husband reached the well, they found the other woman and her baby son there too.

Shetu's husband ignored them and began to peer down into the well, straining to catch sight of the water at the bottom.

"Give me that bucket!" he stormed, and, snatching it from the ground beside the well, he threw it with all his strength down into the dark cavity. They all heard it strike the water with a resounding splash.

"I'll put an end to this nonsense once and for all," he boasted, as he began to haul on the rope. "Ten men, indeed! Watch me pull the bucket up!"

He grunted and groaned, he swore and he sweated, but the bucket would not come up. Frustrated, he leaned further and further into the well, cursing the bucket, the rope, and the water so heartily that he forgot to keep his foot anchored against the rim of the well and all but tumbled in after the bucket. Just in time, the baby boy reached his hand over the cloth that tied him to his mother's back, seized both the rope and the man, and whisked man and bucket safely out of the well with never a word.

The man sat on the ground in dazed surprise, rubbing his head and watching the child, who had clambered down from his mother's back, pull up bucket after bucket of cold, clear water, while his mother filled her water-pot.

Then Shetu turned to him triumphantly. "Now that you have seen what the son of the real superman can do, are you not afraid to meet the superman himself?"

The man had been silently wondering

Crowned head of an Oni, 12th–15th century. Zinc brass. Wunmonije Compound, Ife Museum of Ife Antiquities, Nigeria. Photograph by Dirk Bakker.

and seizing her calabash which the child had filled with water, she placed it on her head and hurried away from the well.

The other woman turned doubtfully to the man. "So you want to see my husband, do you?" she asked. "You'd be far better off if you went home." But he would not listen. Presently the woman fastened her baby on her back again and led the way through the forest.

At last they reached the woman's compound. It looked much the same as any other home. There was nothing to show that it belonged to a superman, so the man's courage began to return.

"My husband, the superman, is away hunting in the forest," explained the woman. "You can hide somewhere until he comes back, and then you can peep out and look at him. But do not let him see you. He eats men like you!"

"Bah!" said the man, "I'm not afraid. There's no need for me to hide."

"What if I tell you that my husband ate a whole elephant for breakfast today, and that he has been known to eat ten elephants at one sitting?" asked the woman. "Are you not then afraid, O foolish little man?"

Then the man let her lead him to a corn bin that stood on the edge of the compound. It was made of mud and looked rather like an outsized water-pot. When the man had climbed in through the opening at the top, he found he could see over the edge only by standing on tiptoe.

"Now, keep quiet if you value your life,"

how he could get out of his visit to the real superman's compound; but, since his wife had shamed him by suggesting he would be afraid, he had to put a brave face on things. So he said stubbornly, still rubbing his bruised head, "I am more determined than ever to go and see this so-called superman."

"Right! Then you go alone," said Shetu,

admonished the woman as she left him. "I must cook my husband's supper."

Towards evening the man in the corn bin heard a sound like an approaching tornado. A great wind began to shake the forest trees and to lift the thatch from the nearby huts. Then into the clearing around the compound came the master of the house. As he spoke, the air throbbed with the power of his voice, and his feet shook the ground like an earthquake.

"Wife! Wife!" he called. "Have you cooked me my elephant?"

"Indeed I have," replied the woman. "Come and see whether this one is big enough for your supper."

The man in the corn bin cowered with fright. So it was true! There was, after all, another more worthy of the name of Superman. How he did hope with all his heart that the elephant the woman had cooked was big enough. He stood trembling while he heard the superman eating his supper and cracking elephant bones like sticks of sugar cane.

"Allah grant that the elephant is a big one," he murmured again and again between his chattering teeth.

Time passed until, when the sky was dark and night had come, the real superman shouted, "Wife! Wife! I smell the smell of man. Where is he, that I may eat him?"

"Good husband, I am the one whom you can smell," she replied. "There is no one here but me." However, she found it difficult to satisfy her husband that there was no one hidden in the compound. He prowled about, shaking the place with his shouts and heavy footsteps, while the man in the corn bin nearly died of fright.

At last the superman left the compound and began to search in the nearby forest land, roaring all the while, "I smell the smell of a man."

As soon as he was gone, the woman crept over to the corn bin and whispered to the terrified man within, "Oh, why did you not believe me from the first? What a lot of trouble we should both have saved."

"Alas! I am truly sorry," said the foolish man. "But how could I believe such a thing unless I saw it with my own eyes? And how can I escape from this place?"

"Now listen," whispered the woman. "Soon my husband will return for the night. Watch the door of our hut, and, when my husband is fast asleep, I will put my little lamp outside. Then you must make haste and escape and never come back again."

"Thank you! Thank you!" said the man, trembling violently as he felt the wind blow across the compound, announcing the return of the superman.

The hours passed slowly, but the man dared not sleep. Then at last, just before dawn, he saw a tiny flickering light, like a firefly, at the door of the hut. Carefully, he swung himself up on to the rim of the corn bin and let himself down to the ground without a sound. Then he began to run, and how he did run! Never had his feet taken such long strides or his heart beat so quickly. Just when he thought he was safe, he heard the roars of the superman in the distance, and his heart sank. He felt sick with fright.

"I smell the smell of a man," shouted the voice he had learned to dread.

The poor man ran faster and faster, until he came to a field where some men were clearing the ground to make a farm. They stopped in their task of uprooting bushes and felling trees and inquired, "Hey! Where are you going? Who is chasing you, that you run so fast?"

"Someone who calls himself Superman is chasing me," panted the runner. "Can you help me?"

"There are several of us here," replied the men. "Stay with us until this so-called superman catches up, and we'll deal with him."

The man crouched, panting, on the ground, when suddenly a mighty wind rose up, so strong that it lifted all the laborers off the ground and dropped them several yards away.

"Here!" they called in fright. "What's happening to us?"

"It's the superman," exclaimed the terrified fugitive. "He puffs and blows so strongly that a great wind precedes him."

"If that's the case, we are no match for him," said the men, now terrified in their turn. "You'd better keep on running."

Again the man leaped to his feet in fear and began his race. Presently he came to another group of men, who were hoeing up the ground in preparation for planting.

They looked at him with amazement.

"Hey! Where are you going? Who is chasing you, that you run so fast?" they shouted.

"Someone who calls himself Superman is chasing me," puffed the man. "Can you help me?"

The men laughed. "There are ten of us here," they said. "Surely we can deal with your so-called superman. Stay with us until he catches up to you."

The man collapsed gratefully onto a heap of earth and tried to get his breath back. Then the men who were hoeing found themselves blown about by a strong wind, which tumbled them higgledy-piggledy all over their farm.

"Here!" they said. "What's happening?"

"It's that superman," said the man despondently. "He puffs and he blows so strongly that a great wind precedes him."

"In that case, we are no match for such a man," said the men who had been hoeing. "You'd better keep on running." They lay flat on their faces, hoping that the superman would not see them as he passed by.

By now the poor man was nearly dead with fatigue, but with a great effort he managed to drag himself to his feet and continued to run away from the superman, even faster than before. Presently he came to another group of men, who were planting guinea corn seed in a patch of ground already cleared and hoed.

"Hey! Where are you going?" they

called in surprise. "Who is chasing you, that you run so fast?"

"Someone who calls himself Superman is chasing me," replied the poor fellow in a weak voice. "Can you help me?"

"Well, there are a dozen or more of us here," replied one of the men. "I don't think a superman would bother us much. Stay with us until he catches up to you."

The man staggered and fell, too exhausted to say more, but after a few moments a mighty wind came. It lifted up the men who were sowing, whirled them round in the air, and cast them to the ground in a heap.

"Here!" they gasped. "What's happening to us?"

"It's that superman," explained the runner in despair, knowing full well what would be the outcome.

"Then you'd better keep on running," said the frightened men, as they dropped their long planting-hoes and handfuls of seed and ran helter-skelter into the forest to hide.

The man thought his end had come, but, rousing himself to make one last effort, he ran on. Suddenly, as he rounded a bend in the path, he saw in the distance what looked like a huge man sitting under a baobab[2] tree, his enormous legs stretched out beside the path.

"I've dodged a wasp, only to run into a hornet," the fleeing man thought, as he tried to hide behind a bush. "But no! nothing can be worse than the fate that will befall me if I stop running."

So he went on his way, with his heart in his mouth.

When he reached the baobab tree, he found that it was indeed a gigantic man sitting there, surrounded by roasted elephants, which he was hungrily eating, and throwing their huge bones away over his shoulder into the forest.

"Stop!" he boomed. "Who is chasing you, that you run so fast?"

The exhausted man fell in a heap at the giant's feet and panted, "Someone who calls himself Superman is chasing me. Can you help me?"

"Of course I can," boomed the giant. "I am Giant-of-the-Forest. Stay with me until he catches up to you."

Suddenly the wind made by the puffings and blowings of the superman lifted our poor man from the ground and twirled him round and round in the air. Then he fell down some distance away from the giant.

"Come back," called Giant-of-the-Forest. "Don't you want me to help you?"

"I couldn't stop myself," explained the man. "It's the breath of that superman."

The giant did not seem at all put out. He laughed kindly and said, "Give me your hand. I will sit on it, and then the breath of this so-called superman cannot blow you away."

There they sat—and the man's arm was almost crushed by the weight of the giant—until Superman came rushing up to

---

2. **baobab**—An African tree with a huge trunk.

them. He was in a fine temper!

"Give me that man," he bellowed to the giant. "He's mine! I want to eat him."

"Come take him then," said the giant, grinning horribly.

Then Superman leaped at the giant, who rose to his feet and began to fight with him. They leaped, they stamped, they struggled and wrestled, twisting their legs together, each trying to throw the other to the ground. Then, with a mighty leap, they endeavored to loosen each other's grip. So mighty was the leap that they rose together far into the heavens and disappeared from sight.

The man could not believe his luck at first, but he soon came to his senses, slipped quietly into the forest, and began another long race to his home.

When he got back, his wife was delighted to see him, for she had never expected to set eyes on him again. He told her all about his alarming adventures, trying to show himself in the light of a hero. But his wife would have none of it.

"Let that be a lesson to you," she said callously. "Never boast about your achievements again. However strong or clever or rich or powerful you are, there is always somebody more so."

The man had to admit that she was right.

As for the real Superman and the Giant-of-the-Forest, to this day they are still up there wrestling in the heavens. When they are tired, they sit on a cloud to recover their strength, but soon they rise up again and continue to struggle. If you listen carefully, you will sometimes hear them fighting. People may tell you it is thunder, but you will know it is really Superman and Giant-of-the-Forest wrestling high above the clouds.

Developing Comprehension Skills

1. Why does the man in the tale call himself a superman?

2. What three people does the man meet who are stronger than he? How does he escape the real Superman?

3. When the man finds the Giant-of-the-Forest, he says to himself, "I've dodged a wasp, only to run into a hornet." Who is the wasp? Who is the hornet?

4. Compare and contrast the Superman and the Giant-of-the-Forest. In what ways are they alike? In what ways are they different?

5. When the man tells his wife of his alarming adventures, she says, "Let that be a lesson to you." What lesson does the man learn?

6. Which character or characters in the tale do you think really deserve to be called Superman? Why? Find details to support your answer.

Reading Literature: Tales

1. **Analyzing Character.** Shetu's husband says, "I am a superman. Just show me another who is stronger than I." After he sees the powerful baby, he still insists on meeting the baby's father. "I am more determined than ever to go and see this so-called superman," he states. What can you infer from these statements about the man's character? How does he get himself into trouble?

2. **Identifying Purpose.** Folk tales became popular and survived through the ages because they were entertaining. Find two or three incidents that you think make this tale entertaining. For instance, what are some incidents that make the tale funny? What other incidents make it exciting and suspenseful?

3. **Examining Setting.** List all the details used to describe the location. Point out two aspects of the setting that are realistic and two that are magical.

4. **Comparing and Contrasting Myths and Tales.** As you know, both myths and tales come from the oral tradition of storytelling. However, there are important differences between them. Myths explain aspects of nature and usually concern gods and supernatural events. Tales deal more with human beings and their failings. Compare and contrast the superman tale with the myth "How Odin Lost His Eye." How are the characters in the myth and the tale alike? How are they different? How is the setting of the superman tale different from the setting of the Norse myth? What similarities and differences can you find in the plots of the myth and the tale?

Developing Vocabulary Skills

Finding Affixes and Base Words. The following paragraph, which is based on "The Tale of the Superman," contains ten words with affixes. On a sheet of paper, write each word that has an affix. Next to it, write the base word separated from the affix. Finally, write the definition of the whole word. For this exercise, ignore words with -ed and -ing suffixes. You may refer to the charts on pages 238 and 239 to find the definitions of common prefixes and suffixes.

Shetu's husband, bragging about his superior strength, called himself a superman.

One day, though, Shetu met a woman with an unusual baby who stared at her with unblinking eyes. As Shetu watched in amazement, the baby lifted a heavy bucket from a well. When Shetu told her husband about the powerful baby, he went to the well to prove his own greatness of strength. The man tossed the bucket into the well, but then could not pull it back up. The baby reached for the rope and whisked the bucket up. The man made a very unwise request; he asked to meet the baby's father. The woman was doubtful, but she finally gave in. She took the man home with her and hid him inside the compound. However, just hearing the returning Superman's loud voice made the man tremble violently. He later escaped and quickly ran away.

Developing Skills in Study and Research

Using the Audio-Visual Catalog. Suppose you wanted to find information that is not available in books. The audio-visual catalog is one library resource that might be helpful. The catalog is organized like the card catalog for books. It lists information about audio-visual materials in the library. These materials include records, tapes, filmstrips, movies, and other sources that you can listen to or view.

You have read stories from Norway, Australia, and Africa. Choose one of these countries to research. Then check the audio-visual catalog for titles of materials on the landscape, climate, clothing, housing, people, and occupations in that country. Finally, write the titles of at least three films, filmstrips, or recordings.

Developing Writing Skills

Contrasting Characters. The idea of a superman has sparked the imaginations of people around the world. In the United States, for example, Superman appears as a hero in comic strips, movies, and TV shows. Read the comic strip that follows and think about how today's comic-book Superman differs from Superman in the African tale. Write one paragraph explaining the differences between these two characters.

Prewriting. Review "The Tale of the Superman" and the comic strip "Superman." List the characteristics of the two supermen. Organize the differences between the men into an outline with examples and/or quotations illustrating these differences.

Drafting. Write a topic sentence summarizing the differences between Superman in the African myth and Superman of the modern-day American comic strip. Then, using your notes, explain the differences between the two supermen. Support these contrasts with examples or quotations from the selections.

Revising and Sharing. Reread your paragraph. Make sure that the differences between the two supermen are clear. Ask someone else to read the paragraph. See if the person gains a thorough understanding of how the two supermen differ. If not, revise your paragraph again.

Three Strong Women

JAPANESE TALE
Retold by Claus Stamm

Like "The Tale of the Superman," this story has a character who is proud of his strength. Read about what happens when he meets other strong people.

Long ago, in Japan, there lived a famous wrestler, and he was on his way to the capital city to wrestle before the Emperor.

He strode down the road on legs thick as the trunks of small trees. He had been walking for seven hours and could, and probably would, walk for seven more without getting tired.

The time was autumn; the sky was a cold, watery blue, the air chilly. In the small, bright sun, the trees along the roadside glowed red and orange.

The wrestler hummed to himself, "Zun-zun-zun," in time with the long swing of his legs. Wind blew through his thin brown robe, and he wore no sword at his side. He felt proud that he needed no sword, even in the darkest and loneliest places. The icy air on his body only reminded him that few tailors would have been able to make expensive warm clothes for a man so broad and tall. He felt much as a wrestler should—strong, healthy, and rather conceited.

A soft roar of fast-moving water beyond the trees told him that he was passing above a river bank. He "zun-zunned" louder; he loved the sound of his voice and wanted it to sound clearly above the rushing water.

He thought: They call me Forever-Mountain because I am such a good, strong wrestler—big, too. I'm a fine, brave man and far too modest ever to say so. . . .

Just then he saw a girl who must have come up from the river, for she steadied a bucket on her head.

Her hands on the bucket were small, and there was a dimple on each thumb, just below the knuckle. She was a round girl with red cheeks and a nose like a friendly button. Her eyes looked as though she were thinking of ten thousand funny stories at once. She clambered up onto the road and walked ahead of the wrestler, jolly and bounceful.

"If I don't tickle that fat girl, I shall regret it all my life," said the wrestler under his breath. "She's sure to go 'squeak' and I shall laugh and laugh. If she drops her bucket, that will be even funnier—and I can always run and fill it again and even carry it home for her."

He tiptoed up and poked her lightly in the ribs with one huge finger.

"Kochokochokocho!" he said, a fine, ticklish sound in Japanese.

The girl gave a satisfying squeal, giggled, and brought one arm down so that the wrestler's hand was caught between it and her body.

"Ho-ho-ho! You've caught me! I can't move at all!" said the wrestler, laughing.

"I know," said the jolly girl.

He felt that it was very good-tempered of her to take a joke so well and started to pull his hand free.

Somehow, he could not.

He tried again, using a little more strength.

"Now, now—let me go," he said. "I'm a very powerful man. If I pull too hard I might hurt you."

"Pull," said the girl. "I admire powerful men."

She began to walk, and though the wrestler tugged and pulled until his feet dug great furrows in the ground, he had to follow. She couldn't have paid him less attention if he had been a puppy—a small one.

Ten minutes later, still tugging while trudging helplessly after her, he was glad that the road was lonely and no one was there to see.

"Please let me go," he pleaded. "I am the famous wrestler Forever-Mountain. I must go and show my strength before the Emperor"—he burst out weeping from shame and confusion—"and you're hurting my hand!"

The girl steadied the bucket on her head with her free hand and dimpled sympathetically over her shoulder. "You poor, sweet little Forever-Mountain," she said. "Are you tired? Shall I carry you? I can leave the water here and come back for it later."

"I do not want you to carry me. I want you to let me go, and then I want to forget I ever saw you. What do you want with me?" moaned the pitiful wrestler.

"I only want to help you," said the girl, now pulling him steadily up and up a narrow mountain path. "Oh, I am sure you'll have no more trouble than anyone else when you come up against the other wrestlers. You'll win, or else you'll lose, and you won't be too badly hurt either way. But aren't you afraid you might meet a really strong man someday?"

Forever-Mountain turned white. He stumbled. He was imagining being laughed at throughout Japan as "Hardly-Ever-Mountain."

She glanced back.

"You see? Tired already," she said. "I'll walk more slowly. Why don't you come along to my mother's house and let us make a strong man of you? The wrestling in the capital isn't due to begin for three months. I know, because Grandmother thought she'd go. You'd be spending all that time in bad company and wasting what little power you have."

Okane, Strong Woman of Omi, about 1830, KUNIYOSHI. The Mann Collection, Highland Park, Illinois.

"All right. Three months. I'll come along," said the wrestler. He felt he had nothing more to lose. Also, he feared that the girl might become angry if he refused and place him in the top of a tree until he changed his mind.

"Fine," she said happily. "We are almost there."

She freed his hand. It had become red and a little swollen. "But if you break your promise and run off, I shall have to chase you and carry you back."

Soon they arrived in a small valley. A simple farmhouse with a thatched roof stood in the middle.

"Grandmother is at home, but she is an old lady and she's probably sleeping." The girl shaded her eyes with one hand. "But Mother should be bringing our cow back from the field—oh, there's Mother now!"

She waved. The woman coming around the corner of the house put down the cow she was carrying and waved back.

She smiled and came across the grass,

walking with a lively bounce like her daughter's. Well, maybe her bounce was a little more solid, thought the wrestler.

"Excuse me," she said, brushing some cow hair from her dress and dimpling, also like her daughter. "These mountain paths are full of stones. They hurt the cow's feet. And who is the nice young man you've brought, Maru-me?"

The girl explained. "And we have only three months!" she finished anxiously.

"Well, it's not long enough to do much, but it's not so short a time we can't do something," said her mother, looking thoughtful. "But he does look terribly feeble. He'll need a lot of good things to eat. Maybe when he gets stronger he can help Grandmother with some of the easy work about the house."

"That will be fine!" said the girl, and she called her grandmother—loudly, for the old lady was a little deaf.

"I'm coming!" came a creaky voice from inside the house, and a little old woman leaning on a stick and looking very sleepy tottered out of the door. As she came toward them, she stumbled over the roots of a great oak tree.

"Heh! My eyes aren't what they used to be. That's the fourth time this month I've stumbled over that tree," she complained and, wrapping her skinny arms about its trunk, pulled it out of the ground.

"Oh, Grandmother! You should have let me pull it up for you," said Maru-me.

"Hm. I hope I didn't hurt my poor old back," muttered the old lady. She called

out, "Daughter! Throw that tree away like a good girl, so no one will fall over it. But make sure it doesn't hit anybody."

"You can help Mother with the tree," Maru-me said to Forever-Mountain. "On second thought, you'd better not help. Just watch."

Her mother went to the tree, picked it up in her two hands, and threw it. Up went the tree, sailing end over end, growing smaller and smaller as it flew. It landed with a faint crash far up the mountainside.

"Ah, how clumsy," she said. "I meant to throw it over the mountain. It's probably blocking the path now, and I'll have to get up early tomorrow to move it."

The wrestler was not listening. He had very quietly fainted.

"Oh! We must put him to bed," said Maru-me.

"Poor, feeble young man," said her mother.

"I hope we can do something for him. Here, let me carry him, he's light," said the grandmother. She slung him over her shoulder and carried him into the house, creaking along with her cane.

The next day they began the work of making Forever-Mountain over into what they thought a strong man should be. They gave him the simplest food to eat and the toughest. Day by day they prepared his rice with less and less water, until no ordinary man could have chewed or digested it.

Every day he was made to do the work of five men, and every evening he wrestled with Grandmother. Maru-me and her mother agreed that Grandmother, being old and feeble, was the least likely to injure him accidentally. They hoped the exercise might be good for the old lady's rheumatism.

He grew stronger and stronger but was hardly aware of it. Grandmother could still throw him easily into the air—and catch him again—without ever changing her sweet old smile.

He quite forgot that outside this valley he was one of the greatest wrestlers in Japan and was called Forever-Mountain. His legs had been like logs; now they were like pillars. His big hands were hard as stones, and when he cracked his knuckles the sound was like trees splitting on a cold night.

Sometimes he did an exercise that wrestlers do in Japan—raising one foot high above the ground and bringing it down with a crash. Then people in nearby villages looked up at the winter sky and told one another that it was very late in the year for thunder.

Soon he could pull up a tree as well as the grandmother. He could even throw one—but only a small distance. One evening, near the end of his third month, he wrestled with Grandmother and held her down for half a minute.

"Heh-heh!" she chortled and got up, smiling with every wrinkle. "I would never have believed it!"

Maru-me squealed with joy and threw her arms around him—gently, for she was afraid of cracking his ribs.

"Very good, very good! What a strong man," said her mother, who had just come home from the fields, carrying, as usual, the cow. She put the cow down and patted the wrestler on the back.

They agreed that he was now ready to show some *real* strength before the Emperor.

"Take the cow along with you tomorrow when you go," said the mother. "Sell her and buy yourself a belt—a silken belt. Buy the fattest and heaviest one you can find. Wear it when you appear before the Emperor, as a souvenir from us."

"I wouldn't think of taking your only cow. You've already done too much for me. And you'll need her to plow the fields, won't you?"

They burst out laughing. Maru-me squealed; her mother roared. The grandmother cackled so hard and long that she choked and had to be pounded on the back.

"Oh, dear," said the mother, still laughing. "You didn't think we used our cow for anything like *work!* Why, Grandmother here is stronger than five cows!"

"The cow is our pet," Maru-me giggled. "She has lovely brown eyes."

"But it really gets tiresome having to carry her back and forth each day so that she has enough grass to eat," said her mother.

"Then you must let me give you all the prize money that I win," said Forever-Mountain.

"Oh, no! We wouldn't think of it!" said Maru-me. "Because we all like you too much to sell you anything. And it is not proper to accept gifts of money from strangers."

"True," said Forever-Mountain. "I will now ask your mother's and grandmother's permission to marry you. I want to be one of the family."

"Oh! I'll get a wedding dress ready!" said Maru-me.

The mother and grandmother pretended to consider very seriously, but they quickly agreed.

Next morning Forever-Mountain tied his hair up in the topknot that all Japanese wrestlers wear and got ready to leave. He thanked Maru-me and her mother and bowed very low to the grandmother, since she was the oldest and had been a fine wrestling partner.

Then he picked up the cow in his arms and trudged up the mountain. When he reached the top, he slung the cow over one shoulder and waved good-by to Maru-me.

At the first town he came to, Forever-Mountain sold the cow. She brought a good price because she was unusually fat from never having worked in her life. With the money, he bought the heaviest silken belt he could find.

When he reached the palace grounds, many of the other wrestlers were already there, sitting about, eating enormous bowls of rice, comparing one another's weight and telling stories. They paid little attention to Forever-Mountain except to wonder why he had arrived so late this year. Some of them noticed that he had grown very quiet and took no part at all in their boasting.

All the ladies and gentlemen of the court were waiting in a special courtyard for the wrestling to begin. They wore many robes, one on top of another, heavy with embroidery and gold cloth, and sweat ran down their faces and froze in the winter afternoon. The gentlemen had long swords so weighted with gold and precious stones that they could never have used them, even if they had known how. The court ladies, with their long black hair hanging down behind, had their faces painted dead white, which made them look frightened. They had pulled out their real eyebrows and painted new ones high above the place where eyebrows are supposed to be, and this made them all look as though they were very surprised at something.

Behind a screen sat the Emperor—by himself, because he was too noble for ordinary people to look at. He was a lonely old man with a kind, tired face. He hoped the wrestling would end quickly so that he could go to his room and write poems.

The first two wrestlers chosen to fight were Forever-Mountain and a wrestler who was said to have the biggest stomach in the country. He and Forever-Mountain both threw some salt into the ring. It was understood that this drove away evil spirits.

Then the other wrestler, moving his stomach somewhat out of the way, raised his foot and brought it down with a fear-

The Grand Champion Onogawa, Followed by Sword-bearing Attendant Named Kusonoki, 1793, SHUNEI. Photograph: Dr. Lawrence R. Bickford.

ful stamp. He glared fiercely at Forever-Mountain as if to say, "Now you stamp, you poor frightened man!"

Forever-Mountain raised his foot. He brought it down.

There was a sound like thunder, the earth shook, and the other wrestler bounced into the air and out of the ring, as gracefully as any soap bubble.

He picked himself up and bowed to the Emperor's screen.

"The earth-god is angry. Possibly there is something the matter with the salt," he said. "I do not think I shall wrestle this season." And he walked out, looking very suspiciously over one shoulder at Forever-Mountain.

Five other wrestlers then and there decided that they were not wrestling this season, either. They all looked annoyed with Forever-Mountain.

From then on, Forever-Mountain brought his foot down lightly. As each wrestler came into the ring, he picked him up very gently, carried him out, and placed him before the Emperor's screen, bowing most courteously every time.

The court ladies' eyebrows went up even higher. The gentlemen looked disturbed and a little afraid. They loved to see fierce, strong men tugging and grunting at each other, but Forever-Mountain was a little too much for them. Only the Emperor was happy behind his screen, for now, with the wrestling over so quickly, he would have that much more time to write his poems. He ordered all the prize money handed over to Forever-Mountain.

"But," he said, "you had better not wrestle any more." He stuck a finger through his screen and waggled it at the other wrestlers, who were sitting on the ground weeping with disappointment like great fat babies.

Forever-Mountain promised not to wrestle any more. Everybody looked relieved. The wrestlers sitting on the ground almost smiled.

"I think I shall become a farmer," For-ever-Mountain said, and left at once to go back to Maru-me.

Maru-me was waiting for him. When she saw him coming, she ran down the mountain, picked him up, together with the heavy bags of prize money, and carried him halfway up the mountainside. Then she giggled and put him down. The rest of the way she let him carry her.

Forever-Mountain kept his promise to the Emperor and never fought in public again. His name was forgotten in the capital. But up in the mountains, sometimes, the earth shakes and rumbles, and they say that is Forever-Mountain and Maru-me's grandmother practicing wrestling in the hidden valley.

Developing Comprehension Skills

1. Where is Forever-Mountain heading when he encounters Maru-me?

2. Why does Forever-Mountain faint after he meets the rest of Maru-me's family?

3. Notice the differences in Forever-Mountain at the beginning of the story and at the end of the story. How does he change in appearance? How does his attitude change?

4. Why do you think Forever-Mountain so easily gives up wrestling and becomes a farmer at the end of the tale?

5. By becoming stronger does Forever-Mountain become a better person? Explain your answer.

Reading Literature: Tales

1. **Comparing Tales.** "The Tale of the Superman" and "Three Strong Women" can be compared in several ways. Both the African tale and the Japanese tale have main characters who are extremely strong. In what other ways are these characters similar? How are the lessons they learn similar? What are the differences in the way the two characters learn their lessons?

2. **Explaining Humor.** One humorous part of this tale is the three women's pampering of their cow, which they carry everywhere and treat like a pet. Identify two other parts of the tale that you find funny. What makes them funny?

3. **Understanding Similes.** A **simile** is a comparison that uses the words *like* or *as*. A simile is used to describe Forever-Mountain at the beginning of the story: "He strode down the road on legs thick as the trunks of small trees." What picture does that simile create in your mind? Find three other sim-

iles used later in the story to describe the physical change in Forever-Mountain. Then find a simile that describes the other wrestlers at the Emperor's palace. Describe the pictures this simile creates in your mind.

4. **Recognizing Irony.** When a character says something and the reader knows that the opposite is true, the statement is an example of **irony.** Explain the irony in this thought of Forever-Mountain's: "I'm a fine, brave man and far too modest ever to say so. . . ."

Developing Vocabulary Skills

Using Affixes. In the following sentences, the underlined words are from the story. Each word consists of a base word with at least one affix. Find the affix or affixes in each word. Then change the meaning of the word by adding a different affix to the same base word. On a sheet of paper, write the base word, then the new word and its definition. You may refer to the chart of affixes on pages 238 and 239.

1. Forever-Mountain trudged <u>helplessly</u> after the girl, who pulled him along.
2. The girl gave a <u>satisfying</u> squeal and giggled.
3. She looked <u>sympathetically</u> over her shoulder.
4. "We are almost home," she said with <u>happiness</u>.
5. The two older women pretended to consider <u>seriously</u>.
6. The court ladies had their faces painted dead white, which made them look <u>frightened</u>.

7. The first wrestler bounced <u>gracefully</u> into the air.
8. He bowed <u>courteously</u> before the Emperor's screen.

Developing Skills in Speaking and Listening

Speaking a Dialogue. Working in a group of two or three, choose the characters and dialogue from one of these scenes:

   a. Forever-Mountain and Maru-me walking to the farm (pages 266–268)

   b. Maru-me arriving home and talking to her mother and grandmother (pages 268–269)

   c. Maru-me, her mother, and Forever-Mountain discussing the gift of the cow (pages 270–271)

Rehearse reading the dialogue to one another. Try to convey the character's feelings by varying the tone of your voice. After you have prepared the dialogue, present it in front of the class. Then, have class members write answers to these questions:

1. Did the students speak loudly enough?
2. Were all the words clear and easy to understand?
3. Did the speakers use tone of voice to help express the characters' feelings?

After the class members have answered the questions, have them make suggestions for improving the reading.

Developing Writing Skills

Writing a Humorous Story. A humorous story often involves exaggerated characters and situations. For example, in "Three Strong Women," the women's strength and deeds are exaggerated. Other humorous stories may deal with ordinary problems solved in ridiculous ways. Write a humorous story of your own.

Prewriting. To help you think of ideas for a story, make a list or chart similar to the one below.

In the first column write problems and solutions that could be used in a story. Ordinary problems are useful because they make the ridiculous solutions stand out more.

In the second column, list characters you could include. Note details about them that would be humorous, such as a tiny hat or a long nose.

In the third column, describe the settings you might use. Include an ordinary setting and an unusual one.

Next, from your chart choose the problem, characters, and setting that you think would make the best story. Sketch out a plot that involves the problem and solution. Think of a dialogue between your characters.

Drafting. Refer to your prewriting notes for plot and dialogue. Present the events of your story in chronological order. Include humorous details to keep your audience interested.

Revising and Sharing. Read your story aloud to a friend or classmate. Ask the person to suggest changes that might improve the humor of your story. If you agree with these suggestions, rewrite parts of the story to reflect them. Then combine your final copy in a booklet with the stories of several classmates.

Problems/Solutions	Characters	Setting

The Story of the Fisherman and the Brass Bottle

TALE *from* The Arabian Nights
Retold by Amabel Williams-Ellis

What would you expect from a genie in a bottle? Read to find out what a poor fisherman gets from a powerful genie.

There was once a certain Fisherman, who had a wife and children. Though he was very poor, it was his custom never to cast his net into the sea more than four times on any one day. One day he went down to the shore, and for the first time that day, he cast his net. He threw it out and waited until it rested quietly in the water, and when he drew it together by its strings, he found that it was heavy, so he naturally began to hope he had got a good catch.

He pulled as hard as he could, but it was so heavy that he could not draw it up; so he took the end of the cord, knocked a stake into the shore, and tied the cord to it. He then stripped off his clothes, swam round the net, and pushed and pulled until he got the whole net into shallow water. But, alas! when he got it right out and could see what he had got, what was his disappointment when he saw that it was only a dead donkey!

Getting rid of the wretched donkey, he wrung out his net and exclaiming, "In the name of Allah!" he cast it again. Once more he pulled, but it was now even more difficult to raise than before. But he was disappointed again, for this time he found in it only a large broken jar clogged with sand and mud. He got rid of the jar, wrung out his net, and went back to the edge of the sea for the third time, and again threw his net. But, alack! as before, it had nothing in it but worthless rubbish.

Upon this he raised his head towards heaven and said, "O Allah, thou knowest that I never cast my net more than four times, and I have now cast it three times!" Then, for the last time, he tried again, and again had great difficulty in getting his net out. This time, however, at the very bottom, was a large and strange-looking bottle made of brass. He pulled it out and, looking at it carefully, saw that its mouth had been closed with an ancient stopper of lead

Genie and the Fisherman, 1909, MAXFIELD PARRISH. Illustration from *Arabian Nights.* Private Collection. Photograph: Charles Scribner's Sons, New York City.

and that, on this lead, had been stamped the magic seal of Solomon the Great. At this the Fisherman began to feel more cheerful, for, said he to himself, "I can sell this old brass bottle in the market. It may even be worth ten pieces of gold!"

When he had put on his clothes again and had picked up the bottle, he noticed how heavy it was and said to himself, "I had better open it and see what is in it.

Whatever it is, I can store it in my fish basket before I sell the bottle."

So he took out a knife and began to pick away carefully at the seal, easing off the lead until he had pulled it all away in one piece. Then he shook the bottle and laid it on the ground, so that whatever was in it might pour out. What was his amazement when there came out nothing but smoke! This smoke seemed never-ending; it rose towards the sky and then it began to spread out. Soon it began to collect together, and at last he could see that it was taking the form of a Jinni[1] so huge that its head was in the clouds, though its feet rested upon the ground. This Jinni's head was like a dome; its legs were like masts; its mouth was like a cavern; its teeth were like stones; its nostrils like trumpets; its eyes like lamps; and it had long, matted, dust-colored hair.

When the Fisherman saw this dreadful sight, he was so much afraid that it seemed to him that the day had grown dark. The Jinni, as soon as it saw the Fisherman, seemed almost as much frightened as he.

"There is no God but Allah, and Solomon is his Prophet!" it exclaimed. "O Prophet of Allah, kill me not, for I will never again oppose you in word or rebel against you in deed!"

"O Jinni!" said the Fisherman, who was shocked at this. "It is not Solomon, but Mahomet who is the Prophet of Allah! Solomon has been dead a thousand and eight hundred years!"

At that the Jinni seemed to be very angry and answered in a voice like thunder, "Here is news for you then, O Fisherman!"

"News of what?" asked the Fisherman.

"Of your being instantly put to death!" the Jinni answered.

"O Master of all the Jinn!" said the unfortunate Fisherman, "I have done you good! Why do you threaten to kill me? For I have let you out of that bottle and rescued you from the bottom of the sea!"

But the Jinni only answered, "Choose what kind of death you will die."

"But what is my crime," said the Fisherman, "that death should be my reward?"

"You will understand when you hear my story, O Fisherman," the Jinni replied.

"Tell it then," said the Fisherman, "but be short, for my soul has sunk down to my feet with fear!"

"Know then," said the frightful creature, "that I was one of the Jinn who rebelled against Solomon the Great. To punish me he called for this bottle and imprisoned me in it and closed it with a leaden stopper, and he stamped the lead with the Most Great Name and gave orders that the bottle should be thrown into the sea. I said in my heart, 'Whoever sets me free, I will enrich him forever.' But a hundred years passed over me and no one liberated me, and then there began another hundred years. Then I said, 'Whoever sets me free, I will give him the treasures of the earth.' But no one came, and four hundred years passed over me. Then I said, 'To whomever sets me free I will give three wishes.' But still no one liberated me. Then I fell into a violent rage and said, 'Whoever sets me free now, I will kill! And I will only allow him to choose in what way he will die.' So now, O Fisherman, choose!"

When the Fisherman heard this, he

---

1. **Jinni**—According to Moslem legend, a supernatural being that can take on human or animal forms and influence human lives. Same as *genie*.

called on the name of Allah and began once more to plead with the dreadful creature, saying that he had acted kindly to it and that it was wrong to reward kindness with cruelty.

But to this the Jinni only shook its great head.

Then the Fisherman began to think. 'Certainly,' thought he, 'this is a most fearful and gigantic Jinni and I am only a man. All the same, with the art and reason that Allah gave to man I will plot against the horrible creature just as it has plotted against me!' So he spoke to it again.

"Very well! If I must die—die I must! But by the Most Great Name engraved upon the seal of Solomon, before I die I charge you to answer one question! Will you answer truly?"

On hearing him speak of the Most Great Name, the Jinni replied, "Ask and be brief!"

"This is my question. How can you possibly have been in this bottle? It is not large enough to hold your hand or your foot; how, then, could it ever have held your whole body?"

"Do you not believe, then, that I was ever in it?" asked the Jinni.

"No!" said the Fisherman. "And I will never believe anything in your story until I see you in it again!"

"See then!" said the Jinni. Then it shook itself and was again turned into smoke. This smoke once more rose to the sky, and then, little by little, it poured back into the bottle.

No sooner was it all inside than the Fisherman snatched up the leaden stopper and, clapping it over the mouth of the bottle, cried out in triumph, "Now, horrible creature! Choose what manner of death *you* will die!"

The Jinni tried to break the seal, but the Name on it prevented this. Then it began to beg for mercy, "Oh set me free! Show kindness and reward evil with good! I vow that I will never do you harm but will show you a marvel which will enrich you forever!"

"No!" answered the Fisherman. "I shall now throw you and your bottle back into the sea, and what is more, I shall build a house here so that I can watch, and I shall warn any other fisherman who happens to come here never to cast a net in this place! I shall tell him that here lives the vilest, filthiest, most ungrateful, and most disgusting of all Jinn!" So saying, the Fisherman took up the bottle and held it as if to throw it.

But still the Jinni begged in a humble voice, "For the love of Allah the Merciful let me out, O most excellent Fisherman! In the next world, those who return good for evil are sure of a reward! And in this world you shall have a reward that will benefit both you and your children."

At last, after making the creature swear by Allah, Solomon, Mahomet, and all the other prophets that it really would do him no harm but give him the promised reward, the Fisherman (though he trembled as he did it) again opened the bottle. Once more the tall column of smoke rose up, once more it collected itself into the form of the monstrous Jinni.

Its first act was to kick the bottle into the sea!

"That is not a sign of good!" thought the poor Fisherman, but aloud he said to it, "Now perform your promise, O Jinni!"

At that the Jinni gave a loud laugh.

"Take your net and follow me," it said, and so saying it set off inland. So the Fisherman took his net and followed, though he still trembled for fear. The creature led him out of the city. They went over a mountain, and beyond that, down again into a flat and desert valley which the Fisherman had never seen before. Beyond were four black mountains and in the middle of the valley, which was wide, was a large lake. When the Fisherman came near, he saw swimming in the water crowds and shoals of strange-looking fish, such as he had never seen before; some were white, some blue, some yellow, and some red.

"Cast your net," said the Jinni. "But, however many fish you catch, take out of your net only one of each color and put the others back. Take the four fish to the Sultan, give them to him as a present, and he will reward you. You can come back, but be careful not to take fish from this lake more than once a day, and never more than one of each color. And now, O Fisherman, that advice is your reward! Excuse me from doing more for you! For remember I have been in that bottle for one thousand and eight hundred years and know very little about the world and have no better ways of performing my promise."

So saying, the Jinni stamped hard upon the ground, which instantly opened and swallowed him up.

Thanking Allah for the fish (and also that he seemed to have got rid of that abominable Jinni) the Fisherman made his way back to the city, went to his house, took a bowl from the shelf, filled the bowl with water, and put the fish into it. They were still lively and splashed about in the water. Then, with the bowl on his head, the Fisherman set off for the Sultan's Palace.

When he saw these four extraordinary fish, the Sultan was astonished and, just as the Jinni had foretold, gave the Fisherman an excellent reward. So that night, having now more money than they had ever had before, the Fisherman, his wife, and his children all sat down to a good supper.

Developing Comprehension Skills

1. Why was the Jinni originally imprisoned in the bottle?

2. How does the Fisherman get the Jinni back in the bottle?

3. Why do you think the Fisherman releases the Jinni from the bottle a second time? What does this tell you about the kind of person the Fisherman is?

4. At the end of the story, does the Jinni believe in revenge? Or does he learn to return good for evil? Support your answer with evidence from the tale.

5. If you were the Fisherman, would you have released the Jinni from the bottle a second time? Explain why or why not.

Reading Literature: Tales

1. **Inferring Cultural Values.** You can often tell which values a society admires by looking at the kinds of actions that get rewarded or punished in its tales. For example, the Jinni was punished for rebelling against Solomon by being imprisoned in the bottle. Therefore, you can infer that rebellion is not approved of by the society. Likewise, at the end of the story the Fisherman's kindness is finally rewarded, so you can infer that kindness is an important value.

Read the following statements of values. Find evidence in the story that proves they are important.

a. It is wrong to repay kindness with cruelty.

b. Return good for evil.

c. Physical strength and power are not as important in life as cleverness.

2. **Analyzing Theme.** In this tale, the Jinni is imprisoned in a bottle for over eighteen hundred years. At first, he generously wants to reward his rescuer. Then, over the centuries he becomes angry and finally vents his rage on the innocent Fisherman. What does the Jinni's unjust action suggest about the results of bottling up feelings for a long time?

3. **Identifying Conflicts.** As you know, the main character in a tale may have both external and internal conflicts. In this tale, one of the Fisherman's conflicts is external. What or who is the opposing force? What is the Fisherman's internal conflict? How is it resolved?

4. **Recognizing Details of Plot.** The idea of a bargain, when two characters agree to make a trade, is often found in tales. In this folk tale, what bargain does the Fisherman strike with the Jinni? Another frequent plot detail of folk tales is a transformation, or a change from one form to another. What transformations occur in this tale?

Developing Vocabulary Skills

Describing Words with Affixes. The word in parentheses within each sentence below is taken from the tale. Add a prefix or suffix to each word so that it makes sense in the sentence. Write the new word on a sheet of paper. Remember to make necessary spelling changes. Refer to the lists of affixes on pages 238 and 239 and the spelling rules on page 244 for help.

1. The Fisherman's net contained nothing but (worth) trash.

2. The Fisherman felt the (heavy) of the bottle in the net.

3. The Fisherman watched in (amaze) as nothing but smoke came out of the bottle.

4. It did not seem (believe) that a Jinni so huge could have come out of such a small bottle.

5. The Jinni repaid the Fisherman's kind act with an (kind) one.

6. The Jinni wanted to punish his (rescue) with death.

7. After being tricked back into the bottle, the Jinni begged the Fisherman to (open) it.

8. The Fisherman was surprised at the (strange) of the fish.

Developing Skills in Critical Thinking

Recognizing Slanted Language. Slanted language refers to the way words are used to influence someone's thinking. Slanted language often relies on words with strong connotations. The **connotation** of a word is the sum of the suggested meanings that surround the literal definitions of words.

Slanted language can make an opinion seem like a fact. For example, a factual statement about a baseball team might be "The team has a 5–5 record and a new coach." A negatively slanted statement about the team might be "The team has lost five games and has an inexperienced coach." In contrast, a positively slanted statement might be "The team has won five games and has an energetic new coach."

Below are some slanted statements about "The Story of the Fisherman and the Brass Bottle." Underline the words with strong connotations that slant the meaning of each statement. Then rewrite each statement to change its slant to either positive, negative, or neutral.

1. In the tale, a poor, innocent Fisherman is at the mercy of a wicked Jinni.

2. Solomon the Great took ruthless revenge on the unfortunate Jinni and imprisoned him in the brass bottle.

3. The scheming Fisherman tricks the unsuspecting Jinni into getting back in the bottle.

Developing Writing Skills

Creating a Creature. One of the main characters in this tale is a frightful Jinni, which is described as "so huge that its head was in the clouds, though its feet rested upon the ground." A series of similes also helps the reader to visualize the Jinni: "This Jinni's head was like a dome; its legs were like masts; its mouth was like a cavern; its teeth were like stones; its nostrils like trumpets; its eyes like lamps; and it had long, matted, dust-colored hair." Create your own scary creature. In two paragraphs, describe the creature and what it does.

Prewriting. Dream up a wildly strange and fearful creature. You may want to draw a sketch of it first. Then list details to describe the way the creature looks. Besides visual details, add details that appeal to the sense of hearing, touch, and smell. Think of similes that would help a reader imagine what the creature is like. Then describe the creature's behavior.

Drafting. Write one paragraph using the list of details about the creature's appearance. In the second paragraph, describe what the creature does. Use specific details from your notes in your description.

Revising and Sharing. Reread your two paragraphs. Have you used vivid details to describe your creature? Does the first paragraph describe how the creature looks? Does the second paragraph describe how the creature acts? Reorganize your paragraphs or add details, as necessary. Then check for complete and clear sentences. Read your description aloud to classmates or friends. If they can visualize your creature, you have succeeded in describing the creature well.

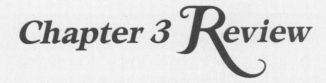

Chapter 3 Review

Using Your Skills in Reading Myths and Tales

Read the following paragraph from a Navajo myth. Then answer these questions: What is the purpose of the myth? What does it explain?

> In the beginning there was First Man. He was a god who had once been an ear of corn. He and First Woman made the sun, the moon, and the stars out of precious stones. They were planning to arrange the stars in an orderly way in the heavens. However, Coyote, always the trickster, scattered the stars about the sky.

Using Your Comprehension Skills

Read the following two paragraphs. The first paragraph is from the Greek myth "The Beginning of the World," which you will read in Chapter Four. The second paragraph is from the Norse myth "The Beginning of a World" in this chapter. Compare and contrast the settings in the two paragraphs. How are the two kingdoms of gods alike? How are they different?

> Zeus chose as his kingdom the very top of a mountain in Thessaly. He called it Olympus. Here, with the exception of Poseidon and Hades, all the gods lived. They were shut off from the earth by a gate of clouds that was guarded by the goddesses known as the Horae. Each god had a palace of his own, but they all assembled daily in a mammoth hall in Zeus's palace.

> At the top of the world the gods made a beautiful city for themselves. They called it Asgard. It was filled with gold and silver palaces. And because the gods wanted a road from their shining city down to the earth and then beyond to the dark world of the giants, they took fire and water and air and made a wonderful rainbow.

Using Your Vocabulary Skills

The following sentences are from Chapter Four. In each sentence, find the word or words that contain one or more affixes. Write the base word separated from each affix. Then write a definition for the whole word.

1. "In this space, a huge, shapeless mass hung."

2. "She was a faithful worshipper of the gods."

3. " 'We dare not treat the remains of our parents with such disrespect as this.' "

4. "The hills re-echoed with the sound."

5. "The Hydra had nine heads, and its middle head was immortal."

6. "The sight was so dreadful that he almost ran from it in terror."

7. "Hera heard the words with some displeasure, yet not enough to make her question the decision of her husband."

8. "For nine days they were hopelessly lost at sea."

Using Your Skills in Critical Thinking

Some of the following sentences from the myths and tales in this chapter are examples of slanted language and some are not. Identify which sentences are examples of slanted language, and explain what makes them slanted.

1. "Shetu was too amazed to speak, but as soon as she got back to her hut she told her husband all that had happened during the day."

2. "The next day they [the women] began the work of making Forever-Mountain over into what they thought a strong man should be."

3. " 'I shall tell him that here lives the vilest, filthiest, most ungrateful, and most disgusting of all Jinn!' "

4. "For the love of Allah the Merciful let me out, O most excellent Fisherman!"

Using Your Writing Skills

Choose one of the writing assignments below.

1. Choose one myth and one tale from this chapter. Compare and contrast the characters of the myth and the tale.

2. Write an original myth-like story. Choose from one of the following topics or make up a topic of your own.

   a. How dogs got their tails
   b. Why the seasons change
   c. What causes lightning
   d. The origin of music

CHAPTER FOUR

Greek Myths and Legends

Ulysses Deriding Polyphemus (detail), 1829,
JOSEPH MALLORD WILLIAM TURNER.
The National Gallery, London.

Reading Literature

Greek Myths and Legends

Like all myths, Greek **myths** are old stories that were passed down in an oral tradition. They explained the beginning of the world and described the gods who ruled it. Myths also helped the early Greeks understand puzzling events in nature and in human life. A wild storm could be explained as the act of an angry god. Falling in love might be caused by the goddess of love.

Legends, like myths, are old stories from an oral tradition. Unlike the heroes in myths, however, the heroes in legends may have really lived. Some experts believe that many Greek legends began as stories about the soldiers who fought in the Trojan War around the thirteenth century B.C. Over the years the storytellers exaggerated the heroes' adventures. The adventures were also used as lessons that taught important Greek values such as bravery and honesty.

The History of Greek Myths and Legends

The earliest versions of the myths and legends in this chapter are about 3,000 years old. The stories of the Trojan War were written as a long poem by the poet Homer who lived about 850 B.C.

Rome conquered Greece around 148 B.C. The Romans then adopted the Greek myths and legends. For the most part, the Romans just changed the names of the gods: for example, Ares became Mars.

Throughout history Greek myths and legends have been important in art, music, and writing. They have inspired paintings, songs, plays, poems, and stories.

The Elements of Greek Myths and Legends

Character. Many of the characters in myths are gods. The Greek gods are much more powerful than human beings. However, the gods often show human faults such as jealousy and spite. Use the chart on page 295 to keep track of the gods as you read.

Heroes in myths are usually half gods. They are braver, stronger, and more clever than other humans. Unlike the hero of a myth, the hero of a legend is only human and does not have supernatural powers. Sometimes a legendary hero is helped by a god or a goddess. Most of the time, however, the hero must use human strength and intelligence to get out of trouble.

Setting. The setting of a myth or legend is not limited to earth. Events may happen in imaginary places, such as the home of the gods. However, many settings in Greek myths and legends were real places in ancient Greece. Some still exist today. Use the map on pages 332–333 to find many of the places named in this chapter.

Plot. Each myth and legend has a **plot,** or series of connected events. The **conflict,** or struggle, may be an **external** one between two opposing forces. The conflict may also be **internal,** such as the inner struggle of a hero making a choice.

Purpose. Greek myths have several purposes. They explain happenings in nature, such as the change of seasons. They also tell about gods and goddesses. Both myths and legends teach the values of a culture. At the same time they entertain the reader.

Theme. The **theme** is a story's message, or the lesson it teaches about life. Like most stories, Greek myths and legends have many themes that apply to people everywhere.

How to Read Greek Myths and Legends

1. Pay attention to the hero in a myth or legend. Decide what that hero tells you about early Greek values.
2. Identify the lesson that the myth or legend teaches.

Comprehension Skills

Relationships

Two important kinds of relationships in stories are relationships between events and relationships between characters. It is important to recognize these relationships in order to understand a story. If you know when one event happens in relation to another, you are more able to understand a story's plot. If you know the relationship between two characters, you will be better able to understand each one.

Understanding Relationships Between Events

There are two main kinds of relationships between events: time order and cause and effect.

Time Order. The term **time order** describes the sequence of events: what happens first, second, third, and so on. Some words that point to time-order relationships are *first, next, then, before, during, now, later, soon, finally,* and *when.*

Cause and Effect. In a **cause-and-effect** relationship, one action causes another, which is the effect. Tracing causes and effects in a story can help you understand why events happen. The following words point to cause-and-effect relationships: *because, since, consequently, therefore, as a result,* and *for this reason.*

Understanding Relationships Between Characters

Understanding relationships between characters can help you make sense of each character's actions and motives, or reasons for acting. What follows are some kinds of relationships that exist in the stories you will read.

Family Relationships. Characters in Greek myths and legends often act to help a family member. Zeus, the king of the gods, is the father of several Greek heroes. This relationship helps explain some of the problems as well as the power of these heroes.

Political Relationships. Political relationships are based on who has power and who does not. The relationships between gods and humans are important in Greek myths and legends. A character can be punished for showing disrespect for a god or a goddess. The ancient Greeks also valued the relationship between a leader and his people. Soldiers were expected to obey their leaders or face terrible consequences.

Social Relationships. Social relationships include both friends and enemies in Greek myths and legends. Fighting fairly is an important part of the relationship between enemies. Often a character is judged by the way he fights. Sometimes an enemy can be overpowered by the hero and become a helpful friend.

Exercise: Understanding Relationships

Read this passage about the Greek god Hephaestos from the first myth in this chapter, "The Beginning of the World," retold by Sally Benson. Then answer the questions that follow.

> Hephaestos was an artist, the son of Zeus and Hera. He had been born lame and, because of this handicap, had learned the art of working in metals. He was architect, smith, armorer, and chariot builder for the gods.

1. How is Hephaestos related to Zeus, the king of the gods?
2. What causes Hephaestos to learn the art of working in metals?
3. What kinds of tasks does Hephaestos do for the rest of the gods?

Vocabulary Skills

Four Ways to Find Meanings

You have already learned two ways to unlock word meaning. You know that when you come across an unfamiliar word, you can use context clues to figure out the word's meaning. You can also look at the word parts. There are two other ways to unlock the word's meaning. One way is to think about the origin of the word. The second way is to use a dictionary.

Context. As you know, the context of a word can lead you to its meaning. **Context** is made up of the words and sentences that surround a word. The following sentence has a context clue that tells you what *sagacity* means:

Odysseus was noted for his sagacity: that is, his good judgment.

Word Parts. You will also remember that breaking a word into its parts can help you learn its meaning. If you know the meanings of the affixes that are added to base words, then you may be able to figure out the meaning of an unfamiliar word. Look at this sentence from "Perseus Slays the Gorgon," retold by Sally Benson.

She was so pale and motionless, that if it had not been for her . . . hair that moved in the breeze, he would have taken her for a marble statue.

The parts of the word *motionless* can lead you to its meaning. The base word is *motion,* meaning "movement." The suffix is *-less,* which means "without." *Motionless* means "without movement" or "still."

Word Origins. Many English words are based on words from other languages. For example, some English words come from Greek words and names. The word *hydra,* referring to a type of sea animal, comes from the name of a creature in Greek mythology, the Hydra. The Hydra was a nine-headed monster killed by the Greek hero Heracles. In this chapter you will learn about words that come from Greek mythology.

The Dictionary. Sometimes you cannot use any of the first three ways to find the meaning of an unfamiliar word. Then you must look up the word in a dictionary. This chapter will help you decide when to use a dictionary.

Exercise: Determining Word Meaning

Read each sentence below. On a sheet of paper write the letter or letters of the way or ways you used to find the meaning of the underlined word.

a. context   c. word origins
b. word parts   d. the dictionary

1. Nessus was a <u>centaur</u>, a creature that was half man and half horse.
2. The captain suspected a <u>ruse</u> was used to get the battle plan.
3. The monster was so ugly that she was <u>indescribable</u>.
4. To find out his son's future, the king consulted the <u>oracle</u> that spoke for the gods.
5. She lived a very <u>Spartan</u> lifestyle.
6. He proceeded <u>stealthily</u> toward the horrible creature.
7. The leader had to deal with the results of his <u>injustice</u>.
8. Antaeus <u>compelled</u>, or forced, all strangers to wrestle with him.
9. Daedalus was an <u>ingenious</u> craftsman who could think of clever inventions.
10. Her <u>odyssey</u> took her all over the world and brought her many adventures.

Greek Myths

Angry gods, superheroes, and hideous monsters—these are some of the characters you'll meet in the Greek myths in this section. As you read, you will see that the Greek gods are powerful but not always kind. The gods have their favorites whom they sometimes help. However, they often take revenge on the humans and on other gods who displease them.

The Idleness of Sisyphus, 1981, SANDRO CHIA. Oil on canvas in two panels. Collection, The Museum of Modern Art, New York City, Purchase.

Greek and Roman Gods and Goddesses

This list identifies the most important Greek gods and goddesses by their Greek names. Their Roman names appear in italic type.

The Titans—giants who sprang from the meeting of the earth and the heavens

Kronos (krō' nŏs), *Saturn,* was the father of the gods.

Atlas (at' ləs) held the heavens on his shoulders.

Prometheus (prō mē' thē əs) created the first man from a handful of earth.

Epimetheus (ep ə mē' thē əs) gave a gift to each animal.

Themis (thē' məs) was the goddess of law and justice.

Rhea (rē' ə) was the wife of Kronos.

Mnemosyne (ne moz' ih nē) was the goddess of memory.

The Rulers—children of Kronos and Rhea

Zeus (zoōs), *Jupiter,* was the ruler of all living creatures.

Hera (hir' ə), *Juno,* was the wife of Zeus and queen of the gods and goddesses.

Hades (hā' dēz), *Pluto,* was the ruler of the Underworld, the Kingdom of the Dead.

Poseidon (pō sī' d'n), *Neptune,* was the ruler of the oceans.

Separate Creations

Athene (ə thē' nə), *Minerva,* the goddess of wisdom, sprang fully grown from Zeus' head.

Aphrodite (af'rə dī' tē), *Venus,* the goddess of love and beauty, sprang from the sea foam.

Dionysus (dī ə nī' səs), *Bacchus,* was the god of wine.

Iris (ī' ris) was the goddess of the rainbow.

Children of Zeus and Hera

Hephaestos (hi fes' təs), *Vulcan,* was the god of fire and metalworking. Aphrodite was his wife.

Hebe (hē' bē), the heavenly wife of Heracles, was the goddess of youth.

Ares (er' ēz), *Mars,* was the god of war.

Children of Zeus and Goddesses Other than Hera

Hermes (hʉr' mēz), *Mercury,* was the messenger god and the god of science, of commerce, and of sports.

Apollo (ə päl' ō), *Phoebus,* was the god of the sun, of the lyre, of archery, and of prophecy.

Artemis (är' tə mis), *Diana,* was Apollo's sister. She was the goddess of the moon, of wild animals, and of hunting.

The Horae (hō' rī), the Hours, guarded the gates of heaven and were the goddesses of time.

The Moirai (moi rī'), the three Fates, spun the thread of human life.

The Charities (kar' ə tēz), the three Graces, presided over social occasions.

The Muses (myoōz' əz), the nine daughters of Mnemosyne, presided over the arts and sciences.

The Erinyes (i rin' ē ēz'), the Furies, punished others for wrongdoing.

The Beginning of the World

GREEK MYTH
Retold from a collection of myths by Sally Benson

This is the ancient Greek myth of creation. Read to find out how the kingdom of gods and goddesses was created as well as how the world began.

A long time ago, more years than anyone can count, there was no earth, no sky, sun, moon, or stars. There was only space. In this space, a huge, shapeless mass hung suspended. It was without color, and it was neither hard nor soft. There was no water on it and no land, not even a blade of grass or the tiniest of living things.

No one knows how long this mass hung, motionless and barren, in the vastness of time. It might have stayed there forever had it not been for an invisible force that existed in the midst of the chaos. The force was Nature, who discovered that millions of seeds lay hidden in the hot, thick bulk. Years passed while Nature, appalled by the dreadful waste, wondered how she could give life to still form. She finally appealed to a god who was so far away that he was scarcely aware of the tremendous mass which seemed no more than a tiny speck to him. He listened to Nature and agreed to help her, and with a word he separated the earth from the sea and the heavens from both. There was a deafening clap of thunder as he spoke the word. Flames leapt high in the air and formed the skies. Beneath them, the air arose, while the earth, being the heaviest, sank to the bottom. The seas boiled and swirled around it, and enormous hot waves, higher than mountains, washed over it. The air would not settle, and the din it made as it rushed madly about was deafening. The heavens were jet black, shot with streaks of fire. Only the earth lay quiet, barren, and dead.

Nature, realizing that the god had not finished his task and that the seas and skies should be tamed if life were to exist, pleaded with another, lesser god to help her once more. They took some of the water from the wild, raging seas and made calm, peaceful rivers. They raised the earth in places and made mountains. Lakes and valleys formed in the hollows. They smoothed the earth's surface for fertile fields. And they left stony plains for sheep to wander and graze. They scattered seeds,

Morning, 1879, THOMAS DEWING. Delaware Art Museum, Wilmington.

and forests grew to shelter the birds, deer, rabbits, and all small timid things.

The Gods and Goddesses

As the earth and heavens met, there sprang into being a race of gigantic gods called Titans. They had as their ruler a cruel god named Kronos (krō′ nŏs), who had many children. Kronos' son Zeus (zoos), with his brothers and sisters, rebelled against Kronos and defeated him. They sentenced him to one of the underground regions under the control of Hades (hā′ dēz), Lord of the Underworld. This was a dreadful place surrounded by three impenetrable walls and the waters of the burning river. Kronos' brother, Atlas, was forced to bear the heavens on his shoulders for eternity.

Zeus and his favorite brothers, Poseidon (pō sī′ d′n) and Hades, divided the world into three parts. Poseidon said he would rule the ocean. Hades, who was a rather melancholy god, chose the Kingdom of the Dead. The earth was to belong to all the gods; and Zeus was chosen to reign over all living creatures: gods, men, and beasts.

Zeus chose as his kingdom the very top of a mountain in Thessaly. He called it Olympus. Here, with the exception of Poseidon and Hades, most of the other gods lived. They got along together as most families do, sometimes quarreling and bickering among themselves and, at other times, dwelling amicably together. They were shut off from the earth by a gate of clouds that was guarded by the goddesses known as the Horae (hō' rī), the Hours. Each god had a palace of his own, but they all assembled daily in a mammoth hall in Zeus' palace. There they talked over the affairs of the day. They dined on nectar and ambrosia, drink and food so delicious that it cannot be compared with anything in the world. It was so miraculous that the tiniest sip or bite would cause the lowliest of humans to become immortal. The lovely goddess, Hebe (hē' bē), served them their food and drink, and Apollo (ə päl' ō) played soft tunes on his lyre.

Apollo, son of Zeus, was the god of the sun. He was also the god of the lyre, of archery, and of prophecy. Every day he drove his flaming chariot across the skies, bringing the day. Apollo's sister, Artemis (är' tə mis), pale and beautiful, was goddess of the moon. She was also the goddess of wild animals and hunting.

All the Immortals had kingdoms over which they ruled. Aphrodite (af' rə dī' tē), for example, was the goddess of love and beauty. She sprang from the foam of the sea. As she was born, a soft breeze carried her along the waves to the Isle of Cyprus. Here she was dressed in flowing robes by the Horae and led to the palace of Zeus. She wore an enchanted sash embroidered in glowing colors, which had the power of inspiring love in all who beheld her. As she bowed before Zeus, all of the gods were enchanted by her beauty. Each one asked to have her for his wife. Zeus finally gave her to Hephaestos (hi fes' təs) as a reward for the service of forging thunderbolts.

Hephaestos was an artist, the son of Zeus and Hera (hir' ə). He had been born lame and, because of this handicap, had learned the art of working in metals. He was architect, smith, armorer, and chariot builder for the gods. He built them houses of shining brass. He designed golden shoes that enabled them to walk on water or air and to move from place to place with the speed of the wind. He shod the steeds that whirled the celestial chariots through the air. Most miraculous of all, he endowed the chairs and tables of his design with self-motion so that they could move themselves in and out of rooms. There is a story that his lameness was the result of a quarrel with Zeus. Angry with Hephaestos for taking Hera's part in a dispute, Zeus flung him from the heavens. He was a whole day falling, and he landed on the Island of Lemnos, which was afterwards sacred to him.

Hera, Zeus' wife, was something of a scold. She was tall and regal-looking, and she was apt to interfere in things. The goddess of the rainbow, Iris (ī' ris), was her personal attendant and messenger. The peacock was Hera's favorite bird, because of its pride and splendor.

Athene (ə thē' nə), the goddess of wisdom and expert in arts and crafts, had no mother. She sprang forth from Zeus' head, fully armed. She was wise and kind and chose the owl for her favorite bird, because of his sage, thoughtful expression. It was one of her tasks to weave the cloth for all the robes worn by the goddesses. Day after day she sat in the shade of the olive trees weaving soft and colorful materials. She was assisted in her work by the three Charities, who personified charm, grace, and beauty. They were frivolous, pretty girls who enjoyed presiding over banquets and other social gatherings. They were very elegant and considered good manners and social arts extremely important.

Hermes (hur′ mēz), tall, lean, and fleet of foot, was the god of all gymnastic sports, commerce, science, and even thieving. He presided over everything that required skill and dexterity. He was Zeus' messenger and wore a winged cap and winged shoes. In his hand he carried a rod entwined with two serpents. He is said to have invented the lyre. Roaming about the earth one day, he found a tortoise. He stripped it of its covering. Then, in the shell he made holes through which he drew nine cords of linen. He gave the lyre to Apollo.

Dionysus (dī′ ə nī′ səs) was the god of wine. He was a peaceful, jovial god, famed as a lawgiver and a promoter of civilization. He liked nothing better than to sit around in the great hall of the palace, eating, drinking, and talking.

The nine Muses (myōz′ əz) were the daughters of Zeus and Mnemosyne (ne moz′ ih nē), who was also known as Mem-

ory. Each one of the nine had chosen one of the arts such as astronomy, history, poetry, and dance as her particular province. They all presided over song and prompted the memory, in honor of their mother. They sang when Apollo played soft tunes on his lyre.

There were the Moirai (moi rī′), the Fates, who spun the thread of human destiny. The life of a person continued until all the thread allotted to that person was spun.

The Erinyes (i rin′ ē ēz′), or Furies, punished secretly. If criminals escaped the law or won unjustified acquittal in the courts, they stung them throughout life. Nemesis (nem′ ə sis), too, was an avenging goddess. She represented the anger of the gods against the proud and insolent.

There were a great many lesser gods and goddesses. Pan, the god of flocks and shepherds, dwelt in Arcadia, a mountainous region where contentment reigned. The Satyrs (sāt′ ərz) were deities of the woods and fields. They were covered with bristly hair, horns grew on their heads, and they had feet like those of goats. Momus (mō′ məs), a grotesque fellow, was god of laughter, and Plutus (plōō′ əs), cold and grasping, was god of wealth.

The First Man

The beginning of the world was a time of great peace and happiness. All over the land seeds swelled and burst, and animals came into being. Horses roamed the plains, chipmunks and squirrels played in the trees, and deer ran through the woods without fear. The cats lay in the sun all day and padded softly through the wet grass at night. Fish appeared in the seas and rivers, and the birds were busy building nests. Only the dog was unhappy, because there was no one on earth for him to love.

Now at this time, there lived a god named Prometheus (prō mē′ thē əs), who was one of the Titans. He had escaped punishment at the hands of Zeus. He was a gigantic creature who could step across riv-

ers as easily as humans can step across brooks. In two strides, he could reach the top of the highest mountain.

Prometheus and his brother, Epimetheus (ep′ ə mē′ thē əs), had been selected to guard the animals as they came to life. Epimetheus decided to give each animal a gift that would help it survive in the new wilderness. He gave wings to the birds, claws to the tiger, and shells to the turtles. To others he gave courage, strength, speed, and keenness of mind. Prometheus had

A computer-enhanced photograph of the Great Red Spot on Jupiter. NASA.

promised his brother that he would approve these gifts after they were given. In the meantime, he had been thinking that something was missing. There was need for a nobler animal than any that had sprung from the seeds that lay in the earth and the sea.

One day, as he was resting on the shore, Prometheus scooped up a handful of earth. To amuse himself, he began to form an image in the shape of the gods. He moistened the image with water from the ocean so that it would hold together. He modeled the figure standing upright, its face uplifted, gazing at the heavens. In the handful of earth, he found a seed. It was different from any seed he had ever seen, larger and more shining. He washed it off in the sea and placed it in the exact center of the statue he had made. The sun beat down on the image, heating it, and a fresh breeze sprang from the sea, cooling it. Like a piece of pottery, it hardened and dried. Inside, the seed grew and gave the image life. The color of the earth faded from it. It took on the reflections of all around it: blue from the ocean for the eyes, gold from the skies for the hair, the color of the pale sand for the skin, and deep red from the sunset for the lips. Prometheus called it Man.

Taking Man by the hand, Prometheus led him to Epimetheus, and asked his brother to bestow a gift, finer and more valuable than any other. Epimetheus hung his head in shame. The last gift, he said, was gone. He had given the giraffe a long

Diadoumenus, 440–430 B.C. Roman copy of a Greek original by Polyklietos. The Metropolitan Museum of Art, New York City, Fletcher Fund, 1925. (25–78.56)

neck so it could reach fruit from the tallest trees. While Man waited, Prometheus and his brother talked over what they should do. They finally decided to ask Athene, goddess of wisdom, to help them. It was quite some time before they found her. They finally came upon her seated at her loom, weaving robes for the goddesses in the heart of an olive grove.

Hearing their problem, she agreed to accompany Prometheus to heaven. There he might find something belonging to the gods that he could give to Man. They rode up into the sky. As they passed the chariot of Apollo, Prometheus dipped his torch into the sun. Turning, he descended quickly to earth. He handed the torch to Man and gave him fire, the most valuable gift of all. With it, humans became the rulers of the world. They heated metals and formed weapons to protect themselves; they made tools to cultivate the fields; they built fires to heat their dwelling places.

When the gods learned that Prometheus, a Titan, had stolen the fire from heaven, they became enraged. He had, they said, made Man too powerful by giving him this divine gift. Zeus, hearing what Prometheus had done, ordered him chained to a rock on a mountain, face upward in the burning sun. There he lay while a vulture gnawed at his liver, which was renewed every time it was eaten.

Now, Prometheus knew a deadly secret which, if he told it, would cause Zeus' downfall. What this secret was, no one today knows. For a moment, Prometheus thought he would reveal it to save himself. Immediately, however, he acknowledged to himself that he had, indeed, stolen the fire from the gods. He accepted his punishment, scorning to tell the secret. He comforted himself with the thought that he had given a divine gift—that is, he had sacrificed himself to Man, whom he had created.

That night, Man slept in a cave. Close to him huddled a dog, growling and twitching in his sleep, while in front of the fire, which crackled and leapt in the hollow of a rock, a cat lay purring.

Sally Benson *(1900–1972)* received an Academy Award nomination for her screenplay of the book *Anna and the King of Siam.* Benson was born in St. Louis, Missouri, and attended school in New York City. A job with the *New York Morning Telegraph* gave her experience as a feature writer, book reviewer, and film critic. She was also interested in mythology, the subject of her book *Gods and Heroes.*

Developing Comprehension Skills

1. According to the myth, what invisible force appeals to the gods to help create the world? How do the Titans come into being? Who rebels against the Titans?

2. Choose any three gods and goddesses in the myth and state what personal quality or power each is noted for.

3. Why are the gods angry with Prometheus for stealing fire and giving it to humans?

4. Arrange the following events in order.

   a. On his way to heaven to get a gift for Man, Prometheus dips his torch into the sun.

   b. Prometheus asks his brother Epimetheus to give Man a valuable gift.

   c. Prometheus scoops up a handful of earth and creates Man in the shape of the gods.

   d. Prometheus is chained to a rock on a mountain.

   e. Prometheus returns to earth and gives Man the fire from heaven.

   f. Epimetheus says that the last gift is gone.

   g. The gods become enraged.

5. Epimetheus and Prometheus give the animals many gifts such as courage, strength, and speed. However, the gods think fire is a much more valuable gift, "a divine gift." Do you agree that fire is a more valuable gift than the others? Explain your answer.

6. Does Prometheus deserve the punishment he receives? Should he have told the secret he knew to save himself? Explain.

Reading Literature: Greek Myths

1. **Identifying Purpose.** The main purpose of a Greek myth is to explain why the world is the way it is. What creations does this myth explain? How does it explain the difference between animals and humans?

2. **Understanding Greek Gods.** For the ancient Greeks, many aspects of human experience could be linked to the gods. For example, if a person seemed very wise, he or she was said to be favored by Athene, the goddess of wisdom. For each of the following statements, name the Greek god, goddess, or group of gods that could be said to be the cause. Look back at the chart on page 295 if you need help remembering the gods and goddesses.

   a. A person falls in love.

   b. Bad luck befalls a family.

   c. A young woman is skilled at hunting.

   d. War breaks out between two countries.

   e. A young man is very good at sports.

3. **Comparing Myths.** In Chapter Three, you read a Norse myth about the beginning of the world. Compare the Norse myth with the Greek myth in this chapter. How are the two explanations of the earth's beginnings different? What do the two myths have in common?

Developing Vocabulary Skills

Recognizing Base Words. As you know, some words are made up of a base word and one or more affixes. Sometimes the spelling of the base word is changed slightly when an affix is added. For example, the base word of *avenging* is *avenge*.

Each of the following words is from "The Beginning of the World." On a sheet of paper, write the base word only.

1. deafening
2. dismount
3. impenetrable
4. lameness
5. unjustified
6. mountainous

Developing Skills in Study and Research

Using Library Sources and Taking Notes. Encyclopedias and nonfiction books on Greek culture and mythology are good sources of information about the Greek gods. The index in an encyclopedia lists the volumes and page numbers that have information on Greek mythology. The table of contents and index in a nonfiction book will tell where specific topics are covered in the book.

When you take notes on a subject, write down main ideas and important facts. Also write down the source of your information. For an encyclopedia article, include the name of the encyclopedia, the date, and the volume and page number where you got the information. For a book, write the title, author, and page number.

Choose one Greek god or goddess to research in two sources: an encyclopedia and a book on mythology. Take notes on the information. Share anything new you learn about the god or goddess with the class. As a group you may want to make a supplementary list of gods and goddesses to include additional information you learn from your research.

Developing Writing Skills

1. **Writing an Explanation.** This myth says that with the gift of fire, human beings became the rulers of the world. In a paragraph, explain why fire made it possible for humans to rule the world.

   Prewriting. Reread the section "The First Man." Think about the kind of creature that Prometheus wanted to create. Then list the kinds of things that fire enables humans to do. Think about the kind of life humans could make for themselves with fire and how much control they could have. Add other activities that having fire would make possible.

   Drafting. Open your paragraph with a topic sentence that explains in general why fire made it possible for humans to rule the

world. Then use the details from your prewriting notes to support your main idea.

   Revising and Sharing. Ask a classmate to read your paragraph. Revise any parts that are unclear or too general. Add supporting details or examples where they are needed. Proofread and prepare a final copy.

2. **Expanding a Myth.** This Greek myth describes the creation of the first human. Imagine that you are the first person created on earth. What would you think and do? How would you feel? Write one or two paragraphs describing the events and your own reactions. Follow the steps in the process of writing: prewriting, drafting, revising, and sharing. For more help, see the Guidelines for the Process of Writing beginning on page 654 in the handbook.

The Flood

GREEK MYTH
Retold from a collection of myths by Sally Benson

Myths around the world tell about great floods. What is the cause of the flood in this myth? Who survives the flood?

The first age of humans was called the Golden Age. It was an age of innocence and happiness. There were no seasons, and perpetual spring reigned. All things that people needed to sustain themselves grew in the fields, and it was not necessary to sow or reap crops. Because the air was so soft and warm, people lived in the open or roamed from place to place, carefree and content.

After a time, Zeus decided to shorten the time of spring and divide the year into seasons. Then houses became necessary to protect the young and aged from the cold. People learned to plow and cultivate their lands and to rob the forest of its trees to build homes. This was called the Silver Age.

With food growing scarcer, people became more grasping. They clung tightly to the lands they had cultivated and guarded their homes. They became suspicious of neighbors who had more than they, and their tempers flared. They began to quarrel

Composition—Storm, 1913, WASSILY KANDINSKY. The Phillips Collection, Washington, D.C.

amongst themselves, and often blows were exchanged. This age of humans was known as the Bronze Age.

Then followed the Iron Age, a period of

horror for the inhabitants of the earth. Crime burst on the world and honor fled. People outwitted their friends and duped them for gain. They built fences around their properties and were proud of their wealth and prestige in the community. They despoiled the forests of wood to build boats, and they sailed out on the sea and robbed it of its treasures. Not satisfied with what the earth produced on its surface, they dug into it and mined ore and metals. They found iron and gold and fashioned them into weapons. With the weapons, they killed their enemies. Wars became common on the earth.

Then Zeus, burning with rage at the stupidity of people, summoned all the gods to a mighty council. They came from everywhere, taking the road to the palace of heaven. The road is still visible on clear nights stretching across the dark blue sky. It is called the Milky Way.

Zeus addressed the assembly in stern, indignant tones. He told them of the frightful conditions that existed on the earth. Then he announced that he intended to destroy every person who dwelt on it and to create a new race that, unlike the first, would be worthy of life. Turning, he seized a thunderbolt in his bare hands. He was about to hurl it to earth and wipe out all life, when he realized that such a mighty conflagration would even set heaven afire. He changed his plan and announced that he would flood the world.

With the help of all the gods, Zeus captured the north wind, which scatters the clouds, and chained it up. The south wind was sent to blow the clouds together, and soon the sky was pitch black and threatening. There was a terrific clash as the clouds met, and rain fell in torrents. Fields were flooded, crops destroyed, and fruit was beaten from the trees.

Zeus called on his brother Poseidon to loose the rivers from their course and rout the ocean from its bed. He implored his brother Hades to rock the land with violent earthquakes. The sea washed over the shores. Cattle, fowl, people, and houses were swept away in the torrent. The temples of the gods, long neglected, fell into the waters. The whole world was a mighty sea. Here and there, for a while, one could see a few people who had taken to their boats or sought protection on a hilltop, but soon these disappeared in the swirl of the angry flood.

Only one mountain rose above the maddened waters, and this was called Parnassus (pär nas' səs). On this mountain a husband and wife found refuge with some of the innocent creatures of the earth. The names of the humans were Deucalion (doo kal'yən) and Pyrrha (pir'ə). They were descendants of Prometheus, who had allowed himself to be tortured through eternity for the sake of humankind. Deucalion and Pyrrha had taken no part in the warfare and hatred that had swept the earth. He was a just, honest man; she was a faithful worshipper of the gods. Looking down from Olympus, Zeus saw them clinging to the rocks on Parnassus, the water already

Paestum, 1982, PHILIP PEARLSTEIN. Collection of the Artist. Photograph: Hirschl and Adler Modern, New York City.

washing about their feet and ankles. Remembering the blameless lives they had led, he unchained the north wind to drive away the clouds, and Poseidon directed his son, Triton, to blow on his shell and sound a retreat to the waters. The sea returned to its bed, and the rivers subsided.

Then Deucalion said to Pyrrha, "O my wife, only surviving woman, you are joined to me first by the ties of kindred and marriage and now by common danger. Would

that we possessed the power of our ancestor, Prometheus, and could renew the race as he first made it! But as we cannot, let us seek yonder temple and inquire of the gods what remains for us to do."

They walked toward the temple, slipping and falling on rocks covered with slime. The temple was almost in ruins, and no fire burned on its altars. There they kneeled and prayed to Themis (thā′ məs), the goddess of law and justice, to help them. The oracle answered, "Depart from the temple with heads veiled and garments unbound, and cast behind you the bones of your mother."

They looked at one another in astonishment. Where could they find the bones of their mother? Also, if they found them, how could they desecrate their mother's bones by casting them to the ground?

Finally, Pyrrha spoke, "We cannot obey," she said firmly. "We dare not treat the remains of our parents with such disrespect as this."

Upon leaving the temple, they sought protection in a nearby wood and talked over what they should do. Then Deucalion said, "Either I am deceiving myself, or the command is one we may obey without impiety. The earth is the parent of all. The stones are her bones. These we may cast behind us, and I think this is what the oracle means. At least, it will do no harm to try."

They veiled their faces, unbound their garments, and, picking up stones, they cast the stones behind them. The stones, striking the earth, grew soft and began to assume shape. Slowly, they showed a vague resemblance to the human form, as a statue does when it is half finished by a sculptor. The moisture and slime that covered them became flesh. The stony part became bones. The veins in the rocks became human veins. The stones thrown by Deucalion turned into men, and those cast by Pyrrha grew into women.

Thus, a whole new race was created. It was a hardy race whose very bones contained stone from the earth, a race that owed its existence to the descendants of the hero who had first made Man.

Developing Comprehension Skills

1. Who in this myth is responsible for dividing the year into seasons?

2. According to this myth, there were four ages of humans before the flood. List these four ages, and describe them in your own words.

3. Why does Zeus decide to destroy the world with a flood rather than with a thunderbolt?

4. What human beings survive the flood? Why does Zeus allow them to live?

5. Why is the oracle's message from Themis so offensive to Deucalion and Pyrrha at first? What do they decide the message means?

6. Deucalion and Pyrrha are direct descen-

dants of Prometheus. How are they like him? What qualities do they have that are important for the renewal of the race of humans?

Reading Literature: Greek Myths

1. **Understanding Theme.** The **theme** of a myth is its message about life or human nature. What does this myth say about the results of hatred and warfare?

2. **Recognizing a Hero.** Prometheus is considered a hero both in this myth and in "The Beginning of the World." Review both of these myths. What actions make Prometheus heroic? What values does Prometheus represent?

3. **Understanding Figurative Language.** **Figurative language** is language that communicates ideas beyond the literal meanings of the words. The words in a figurative expression are not literally true, but they create pictures and ideas in the mind of the reader. For example, this myth describes the earth as "the parent of all" and refers to stones as "her bones." What idea of the earth does this figurative language create? Later, stones turn into humans. The stony part becomes bones, the moisture on the stone becomes flesh, and the veins in the rock become blood vessels. What does this comparison suggest about the strength of the new race? What relationship between earth and humans does this description bring out?

4. **Examining a Myth.** "The Flood" tells about humans fighting and killing each other. It also tells of death and suffering in the great flood. What role do the gods play in causing human suffering and death? What hope about the future of humans does the myth express?

Developing Vocabulary Skills

Using Context Clues. The underlined words in the following sentences are from "The Flood." Use a context clue to figure out the meaning of each word. Then select the best definition from the choices.

1. There was no winter, only perpetual spring. The weather was always sunny and warm; flowers were always in bloom.
   a. lasting forever   c. never
   b. short   d. unhappy

2. People despoiled the forests by chopping down all the trees for wood to build boats.
   a. planted   c. ignored
   b. used   d. destroyed

3. During the meeting with the gods, Zeus spoke in harsh, indignant tones that showed his fury at human beings.
   a. understanding   c. angry
   b. joking   d. friendly

4. Deucalion and Pyrrha did not desecrate, or destroy the sacred memory of, the bones.
   a. dishonor   c. explain
   b. praise   d. break

5. The ancient Greeks did not want to show impiety, or disrespect, for the gods.
   a. courtesy   c. lack of respect
   b. jealousy   d. high regard

Developing Skills In Critical Thinking

Classifying. **Classifying** means grouping according to a common factor. For example, you might classify characters in myths under the two headings of gods and humans. In the two Greek myths in this chapter, you have read about many characters. Classify each character according to the place he or she lived: heaven, earth, or the underworld. First write the three heads, then classify the characters under the appropriate heads.

Developing Writing Skills

Comparing and Contrasting Characters. Compare and contrast the hero Prometheus with the powerful god Zeus. How are the two gods similar? How are they different? Explain your ideas in two paragraphs.

Prewriting. Make two lists, one headed *Prometheus* and the other headed *Zeus*. Refer to your answer for Question 2 under Reading Literature: Greek Myths to review Prometheus' heroic actions. Add other information about Prometheus from the two myths. What do you know about Prometheus' power? What about his relationships with other gods?

Now review the two myths, looking for details about Zeus. What kind of power does Zeus have? How does Zeus use his power? What negative qualities does Zeus display? What heroic qualities does he have? List your answers to these questions under the heading *Zeus*. Also, jot down examples from the myths to support your answers.

Then look for similarities and differences in your two lists. Compare Zeus' and Prometheus' heroic qualities. Compare the extent of their power and how they use it.

Drafting. Begin your first paragraph with a topic sentence that states in general how Zeus and Prometheus are alike. Go on to explain specific ways they are alike. Begin the second paragraph with a statement about the differences between Zeus and Prometheus. Then use your prewriting notes to explain these differences. Use examples from the myths to support your analysis.

Revising and Sharing. Read your paragraphs and check for clear topic sentences. See if any parts of the paragraphs are vague or confusing. If so, make these parts clear. Then share your final copy with a group of your classmates. Discuss the different ideas that each of you came up with.

Perseus Slays the Gorgon

In this action-packed myth, the hero Perseus fearlessly fights his enemies. As you read of his adventures, think about Perseus' reasons for fighting.

GREEK MYTH
Retold from a collection of myths by Sally Benson

Perseus (pur' sē əs) was the son of Zeus and Danae (dan' ə ē). When he was born, his grandfather, Acrisius (ə crē' sē us), consulted an oracle and prayed to know what the infant's fate would be. To his horror, the oracle answered that the child would one day slay him. Acrisius was terrified over this prophecy. He wanted to murder Perseus, but he was too tender-hearted to do the deed himself. He finally decided to shut up Danae and her baby in a chest and set them adrift on the sea. He secretly hoped that they would be dashed to pieces on the rocks.

Clinging to her baby in the dark, hot chest, Danae huddled in terror while the box whirled and dipped in the waves. It seemed like days before they were washed upon the shores of Seriphus (ser' ə fus), where they were found by a fisherman. He took the mother and her baby to Polydectes (po' lē dec' tēs), the king of the country, who took them into his own home and treated them with kindness. Here Perseus grew to manhood.

Not far from Seriphus, there lived a horrible monster named Medusa (mə doo' sə) the Gorgon. She had once been a beautiful maiden whose hair was her chief glory, but she had dared to vie in beauty with Athene. In a rage, Athene turned her into a horrible figure and changed her beautiful ringlets into hissing serpents. Medusa became cruel and so frightful looking that no living thing could behold her without being turned to stone. She dwelt in a foul, dank cavern, and all around lay the stony figures of men and animals that had unfortunately chanced to catch a glimpse of her and had been petrified by the sight.

When Perseus became of age, Polydectes told him the story of the monster and begged him to attempt her conquest. Athene favored Perseus and lent him her shield to take on his journey. Hermes gave him his winged shoes so that he might travel with the speed of the wind.

As he neared the mouth of the cave where the dreadful maiden lived, Perseus turned his back lest he see Medusa and share the fate of others who had tried to kill her. Slowly and stealthily, he walked backwards, holding his shield before his eyes and guiding himself by the reflections in it. He entered the cave. Beholding Medusa's head mirrored in the shining metal, he stopped in horror. Medusa lay asleep. Fastened securely to her scalp by the tips of their tails, snakes with awful breath writhed and twisted about her face and neck. Their eyes winked evilly. Water dropped from the roof of the cave, and the air was dank. In the half-light, Perseus saw hundreds of lizards and giant toads crawl-

Medusa, 1892, ALICE PIKE BARNEY. National Museum of American Art, Smithsonian Institution, Washington, D.C., Gift of Laura Dreyfus Barney and Natalie Clifford Barney in Memory of Their Mother, Alice Pike Barney.

ing over her body. The sight was so dreadful that he almost ran from it in terror. However, remembering his vow to Polydectes who had raised him, he advanced slowly, keeping Medusa's image reflected in the shield. Closer and closer he crept until he stood within reach. And then he struck. Her head fell to the ground.

After the slaughter of Medusa the Gorgon, Perseus, bearing with him her head, flew far and wide, over land and sea. He eventually arrived at the country of the Ethiopians, of which Cepheus (sē′ fə yoōs) was king. Cassiopeia (kas′ ē ə pē′ ə), his queen, had been so proud of her beauty that she had dared to compare herself to the sea nymphs. This roused their indignation to such a degree that they sent a prodigious sea monster to ravage the coast. Fishermen and ships were destroyed by the dreadful monster. Cepheus in dismay consulted the oracle, who directed him to sacrifice his daughter, Andromeda (an dräm′ ə də), to appease the deities. Weeping and sad, Cepheus ordered his beautiful daughter to be chained to a rock where the sea monster could find her and devour her. He kissed Andromeda tenderly and hastened away, fearing to look back.

At this moment, Perseus, flying far overhead, glanced down and saw the maiden. She was so pale and motionless, that if it had not been for her flowing tears and her hair that moved in the breeze, he would have taken her for a marble statue. As he hovered over her, he said, "O maiden, undeserving of those chains, tell me, I beseech you, your name and the name of your country. Tell me why you are thus bound."

At first she was silent, half-frightened at the sight of the hero who floated in the wind above her. But seeing that he was not going to harm her, she told him her name and that of her country, and the punishment that had fallen on the land because of her mother's pride of beauty. Before she had finished speaking, a sound was heard far off on the water. Then the sea monster appeared, its head raised above the surface, cleaving the waves with its broad breast. Andromeda shrieked in terror, and her father and mother who were hiding not far away rushed back to the rock. They stood near, wretched and helpless.

Perseus flew close to them and said, "There will be time enough for tears. This hour is all we have for rescue. My rank as the son of Zeus and my renown as the slayer of Medusa might make me acceptable as a suitor. I will try to win her, if the gods will only favor me. If she be rescued by my valor, I demand that she be my reward."

The parents eagerly consented.

The monster was now within a stone's throw of Andromeda. With a sudden bound, Perseus soared high into the air. As an eagle in flight sees a serpent below and pounces on him, so the youth dropped down onto the monster and plunged his sword into its shoulder. Irritated by the wound, the monster raised himself up and then plunged into the depths. Coming to the surface once more, it tried to attack

Perseus, who was still on its back. Like a wild boar surrounded by a pack of barking dogs, it turned swiftly from side to side. Perseus stuck to its back and struck it time and again with his sword, piercing its sides, its flanks, and its tail. The brute spouted water and blood from its nostrils, and the wings of the hero were wet. He no longer dared trust the wings to carry his weight, and he alighted on a rock which rose above the waves. As the monster floated past, Perseus gave it a death stroke.

The people who had gathered on the shore shouted so that the hills re-echoed the sound. Andromeda's parents, wild with joy, embraced their future son-in-law. Andromeda was unchained and descended from the rock.

At the palace a banquet was spread for them, and joy and festivity ruled the land. Suddenly, a noise was heard and Phineus (fin′ ē əs), who had been betrothed to Andromeda, burst in and demanded the maiden as his own. It was in vain that Cepheus reasoned, "You should have claimed her when she lay bound to the rock, the monster's victim. The sentence of the gods dooming her to such a fate dissolved the engagement, as death itself would have done."

Phineus made no reply and hurled his javelin at Perseus. It missed its mark and fell to the floor. Perseus would have thrown his in turn, but the cowardly assailant ran and took shelter. His act was a signal to his band to set upon the guests of Cepheus. They defended themselves and a general conflict ensued. The old king argued with the fighters trying to stop them, but was ignored. He called the gods to witness that he was not guilty of this terrible outrage on the rights of hospitality.

Perseus and his friends fought on, but the numbers of their assailants were too great for them. Then Perseus thought once more of the Gorgon's head. "I will make my enemy defend me," he said to himself. He called out, "If I have any friend here, let him turn away his eyes!"

He held Medusa's head high. "Seek not to frighten us with your tricks," a man cried, and raised his javelin to throw it. He was instantly turned to stone. Another was about to plunge his sword into the fallen body of his foe when his arm stiffened. Men were petrified with their mouths open as they shouted in anger. The swords of those still alive hit against the bodies of their enemies and broke.

Phineus, still hiding, beheld the dreadful result of his injustice. He called aloud to his friends, but got no answer. He touched them and found them stone. Falling on his knees, he stretched out his hands to Perseus. "Take all," he begged. "Give me but my life!"

"Base coward," Perseus cried, "this much I will grant you. No weapon shall touch you. You shall be preserved in my house as a memorial to these events."

So saying, he held the Gorgon's head in front of Phineus. In the very form in which he knelt with his hands outstretched Phineus became fixed, a mass of stone!

Developing Comprehension Skills

1. Why is Perseus' grandfather afraid after Perseus is born? What does his grandfather do?

2. Who asks Perseus to destroy Medusa? What relationship does Perseus have to this person?

3. How does Perseus manage to kill Medusa without being turned into stone? What help does he get from the gods?

4. Why is Andromeda chained to a rock? How does Perseus rescue her?

5. First Medusa and later Phineus are enemies of Perseus. How does killing Medusa help Perseus defeat Phineus?

6. Perseus turns Phineus into stone as Phineus begs for mercy. Do you think that Perseus should have let him live? Explain your answer.

Reading Literature: Greek Myths

1. **Analyzing Conflict.** Perseus has conflicts with three main opponents in this myth: Medusa, the sea monster, and Phineus. How is the second conflict related to the first? How is the third conflict related to the first two?

2. **Understanding the Relationship Between Greek Gods and Humans.** According to Greek myth, the gods often intervene in the lives of humans. Make a list of the ways that gods intervene in the lives of the characters in this myth. What can you infer about the reasons a god or goddess would interfere in a human life?

3. **Identifying Cultural Values.** Myths, as you know, reflect the values, or goals and ideals,

Girl with Pigeons, 5th century B.C., Relief. The Metropolitan Museum of Art, New York City, Fletcher Fund, 1927. (27.45)

that are important to a culture. One way to identify these values is by looking at those actions that are rewarded and those that are punished in a myth. Perseus is rewarded for

killing Medusa and the sea monster by receiving the beautiful Andromeda as his
wife. Which characters are punished in the
myth and why? What do these rewards and
punishments suggest about the qualities that
the early Greeks valued?

Developing Vocabulary Skills

Deciding When to Use a Dictionary. You
have learned that a context clue can help you
figure out the meaning of an unfamiliar word.
However, sometimes there are no context clues
for an unfamiliar word in a sentence. In such a
case, you'll need to check a dictionary.

Read each pair of sentences below. Note the
use of each underlined word. On a sheet of
paper, write *context* after the letter of the sentence that provides a context clue for the word.
Write *dictionary* after the letter of the sentence
without a context clue.

1. a. Perseus no longer dared trust the wings
to carry his weight, so he underlined(alighted) on a
rock that rose above the waves.
   b. Perseus underlined(alighted) on a rock before he
killed the monster.

2. a. Perseus claimed that he was a son of Zeus
and that he was a underlined(valorous) suitor.
   b. The underlined(valorous) Perseus was rewarded for
his bravery in rescuing Andromeda.

3. a. Phineus became fixed in the very form
in which he knelt with his hands outstretched and face half underlined(averted), a mass of
stone!
   b. Perseus warned his friends to keep their
eyes underlined(averted), for they could be turned to
stone by looking directly at Medusa's terrible head.

Developing Skills in Speaking and Listening

1. **Retelling a Myth.** Choose one of the following three sections of the myth of
Perseus.
   a. the slaying of the Gorgon (paragraphs 3
through 5)
   b. the slaying of the sea monster (paragraphs 6 through 12)
   c. the revenge against Phineus (paragraphs
13 through 19)

Summarize the section in your own words.
Then prepare to retell the section in a way
that brings out the actions and the feelings
of the characters. Pace yourself to speak
quickly to suggest excitement, slowly to
show sadness, or softly to suggest caution.
Practice making your voice show the emotions the characters feel.

2. **Evaluating a Presentation.** Work with a
group of three or four other students. Listen
to each group member retell one of the sections of the myth. Then discuss which
speaking techniques were most successful.
Some questions to consider include the
following.
   a. Did the person speak loudly enough?
   b. Were all the words clear and easy to
understand?
   c. Did the speaker stress words that helped
listeners feel the emotions of the
characters?
   d. Did the speaker pace the retelling to suit
the action of the story?
   e. Did the speaker use different tones of
voice to suggest different feelings?

You may think of other ways to judge speaking techniques.

Developing Writing Skills

Contrasting a Character's Motives. The reasons for a character's actions are called **motives.** Write a paragraph contrasting Perseus' motives for killing Medusa with his motives for killing the sea monster.

Prewriting. First think about why Perseus kills Medusa. Does he act for others or for himself? What does he hope to gain from risking his life? Then decide why Perseus kills the sea monster. How are his motives different from those for killing Medusa? What does he hope to gain from killing the sea monster? Decide what is the main difference between Perseus' motives for killing each monster. Plan how you will develop and support that idea in a paragraph.

Drafting. Begin with a topic sentence that states the main difference between Perseus' motives for killing the two monsters. Then explain how the motives are different. Use quotations or examples from the myth to support your statements. To signal contrasts, you may need to use phrases such as *in contrast, however,* and *on the other hand.*

Revising and Sharing. Read your paragraph to a classmate. Ask him or her to restate the idea. If your classmate cannot state the main idea, your topic sentence may need to be revised. Check to see that the differences in Perseus' motives are clearly explained. If necessary, add signal words.

The Labors of Heracles

GREEK MYTH
*Retold from a collection of myths
by Sally Benson*

The name Heracles means "well-known because of Hera." As you read about the hero, decide why his name is appropriate.

The day Heracles was born, Hera declared war against him. He was the son of Zeus and Alcmene (alc mē′ nə). Hera, always hostile to the offspring of Zeus by mortal mothers, sent two serpents to destroy him as he lay in his cradle. Heracles seized the snakes and strangled them with his own hands.

When all efforts to kill Heracles failed, Hera abandoned attempts to destroy him. Instead, she bound him in service to his cousin Eurystheus (yŏŏ ris′ thē əs), King of Argos. Heracles had to perform all of Eurystheus' commands. The tasks were so dangerous that Hera hoped Heracles would be slain.

Eurystheus ordered Heracles to engage in a series of desperate adventures, which are called "The Labors of Heracles."

At this time, the valley of Nemea (nē′ mē ə) was inhabited by a terrible lion. It was large and fierce and had overcome all the hunters who had been sent to capture it. Eurystheus bade Heracles to bring him the skin of this monster. Heracles went alone and sought the animal in its lair. Calling it forth, he set on the beast with a club, but his blows fell on the lion's thick skull in vain. Then Heracles caught it and strangled it with his bare hands, as he had the serpents. He returned wearing the dead lion's skin on his shoulders. The skin was so tough that arrows could not pierce it. Eurystheus was frightened, not only by the sight of the skin but also by this proof of the awesome strength of the hero. He ordered Heracles to deliver the accounts of his exploits outside the town in the future.

Heracles' next labor was the slaughter of the Hydra (hī′ drə). This monster ravaged the country of Argos and dwelt in a swamp near the well of Amymone (am u′ mō nē′). The well had been discovered by Amymone when the country was suffering from a dreadful drought.

Poseidon, who loved the maiden, had permitted her to touch a rock with his trident, and a spring of three outlets burst

Hercules Leading Cerberus to Eurystheus, 525 B.C. Greek vase.
The Louvre, Paris. Giraudon/Art Resource, New York City.

forth. Here the Hydra took up its position, polluting the clear waters and devouring any person who came to fill a pitcher at the fountain. The Hydra had nine heads, and its middle head was immortal.

Accompanied by his faithful servant Iolaus (i ō lā′ əs), Heracles set forth to vanquish the monster. He found the Hydra lying near the spring, and he attacked it savagely. He struck at its heads with his club, but each time he knocked off a head two new ones grew forth. At length, with the help of Iolaus, he tied up the monster and burned away its mortal heads. Then they buried the ninth and immortal one underneath a rock.

The Labors of Heracles   319

Eurystheus was so enraged that his rival had performed another task successfully that he sent him off quickly to clean the Augean (ô jē′ ən) stables. Augeas (ô jē′ əs), king of Elis (ē′ lis), had a herd of three thousand oxen, whose stalls had not been cleaned for thirty years. Filth lay piled up almost to the oxen's heads and Heracles, seeing the state of the stables, was dismayed. It did not seem possible that he could clean them before nightfall as Eurystheus had demanded. However, two rivers flowed nearby, and Heracles diverted them from their beds and brought them through the stables. The clear rushing waters swept all the dirt before them, and by sundown the stables were washed and in order.

The next labor of Heracles was of a more delicate kind. Admeta (ad mē′ tə), the daughter of Eurystheus, longed to own the magic belt of the queen of the Amazons, and Eurystheus ordered Heracles to go and get it for her. The Amazons were a nation of women. They were very warlike and ruled several flourishing cities. It was their custom to bring up only their female children. The boys were either sent away to neighboring cities or put to death. On this adventure, Heracles was accompanied by a number of young men who had volunteered to aid him on his quest. They finally arrived at the country of the Amazons. Hippolyta (hi pöl′ i tə), the queen, received him kindly, and consented to give him her belt. However, Hera was enraged that the hero was accomplishing his labor so easily. She took the form of an Amazon and persuaded the powerful women of the country that Heracles was carrying off their queen. They armed themselves and came in great numbers down to the ship. There Heracles, thinking that Hippolyta had betrayed him, killed her and took her magic belt back to Eurystheus.

Then, Eurystheus asked Heracles to bring him the oxen of Geryon (jir′ē ən). Geryon was a monster with three bodies who dwelt on the island of Erytheia (er′ē thē′ə) the Red. It lay at the west under the rays of the setting sun.

The oxen were guarded by the giant Eurytion (yōō rit′ē ən) and the two-headed dog, Ortheus (ôr thē′ əs). Heracles strangled the giant and the dog, then crushed Geryon to death, and brought the oxen safely to Eurystheus.

The most difficult labor of all for Heracles was getting the golden apples of the Hesperides (hes per′ ə dēz), because he did not know where to find them. These were the apples that Hera had received at her wedding from the goddess of the earth. She had entrusted them to the keeping of the daughters of Hesperus, who were assisted by a faithful dragon. After searching throughout the world, Heracles finally arrived at Mount Atlas in Africa. Atlas, who bore the weight of the heavens on his shoulders, was related to the Hesperides. Heracles thought that if anyone could, the Titan might be able to find the apples and bring them to him. Yet how could he send Atlas away from his post, and who would bear up the heavens while he was gone? In his mighty strength, Heracles took the burden on his own shoulders and sent Atlas to seek the apples. The giant Titan was only too pleased to be released from his eternal punishment and gladly went on the search. He called to the Hesperides, and they gave him the precious apples. Atlas reluctantly returned and took the heavens on his shoulders once more, and Heracles took the apples back to Eurystheus.

On his travels, Heracles encountered Antaeus (an tē′ əs), the son of Terra, the Earth. He was a mighty giant and wrestler, whose strength was invincible so long as he remained in contact with his mother Earth. Antaeus compelled all strangers who passed through his country to wrestle with him. If conquered, which they all were, they were put to death. Heracles fought Antaeus and found that it was of no use to throw him, for he always rose with renewed strength from every fall. Finally Heracles lifted the giant Antaeus up from the earth and strangled him in the air.

Still another of Heracles' tasks was to bring Cerberus (sər′ bər əs) from the lower world. Cerberus was a gigantic, three-headed dog who guarded the gates of Hades' realm. Hades gave his permission to carry the beast to the upper air, providing Heracles could do so without the use of weapons. Accompanied by Hermes and Athene, Heracles journeyed to the realms of darkness. There, in spite of the monster's struggling, he seized it, held it fast, and carried it to Eurystheus. Afterwards, he took the dog back again.

Worn out by his adventures, which had taxed his strength to the utmost, Heracles became nervous and easily aroused to anger. One day, in a fit of madness, he killed his friend Iphitus (ə fē′ təs). For this offense, he was condemned to become the slave of Queen Omphale (äm′ fə lē′) for three years. While in this service, the hero's spirit seemed broken. He refused to talk of his exploits and was content with the company of the hand-maidens of Omphale, assisting them in their spinning. Heracles even allowed their queen to wear his lion's skin.

When this service was ended, he married Dejanira (dej′ ä nī′ rä) and lived happily with her for three years. Once, when he was traveling with his wife, they came to a river. The Centaur Nessus (nes′ səs), half-man, half-horse, carried travelers across the river for a stated fee. Heracles forded the river himself but gave Dejanira to Nessus to be carried across. Nessus attempted to run away with her. Heracles heard her cries and shot an arrow into the heart of Nessus. The dying Centaur told Dejanira to take a portion of his blood and keep it as a charm to preserve the love of her husband.

Dejanira did so, and before long thought she had occasion to use it. In one of his conquests, Heracles had taken prisoner a fair maiden named Iole (ī′ ō lē). When he was about to offer sacrifices to the gods in honor of his victory, he sent his wife for a white robe to use. Dejanira was jealous of Iole. Thinking this a good opportunity to try her love spell, she soaked the garment in the blood of Nessus. She took good care to wash out all traces of it, but the magic power remained. As soon as the garment became warm on the body of Heracles, the poison penetrated into all his limbs and caused the most intense agony. In his frenzy, he seized Lichas (lī′ kəs), who had brought him the fatal robe, and hurled him into the sea. He wrenched off the garment. It stuck to his flesh, and he tore away whole pieces of his body. In this frightful state, he embarked on a ship and sailed for home. Dejanira, on seeing what she had unwittingly done, hanged herself. Heracles, realizing that he was dying, ascended Mount Etna. He built a funeral pyre of trees and laid down on the pyre, his head resting on his club and his lion's skin spread over him. With a serene face, he commanded his friend Philoctetes (fil′ äk tē′ tēz) to apply the torch to the pyre.

The gods felt troubled at seeing the champion of the earth brought to this end. Zeus addressed them. "I am pleased to see your concern," he said, "and glad that my brave son enjoys your favor. But now I say to you, fear not! He who conquered all else is not about to be conquered by those flames which you see blazing on Mount Etna. Only his mother's share in him can perish. What he derived from me is immortal. I shall take him to the heavenly shores, and I ask of you all to receive him kindly. If any of you feel grieved at his attaining this honor, no one can deny that he has deserved it."

The gods all gave their consent. Hera heard the words with some displeasure, yet not enough to make her question the decision of her husband.

So when the flames had consumed the mother's share of Heracles, the divine part rose from the flames with an awesome dignity. Zeus enveloped him in a cloud and took him up in a chariot drawn by four horses to dwell among the stars. As he took his place in heaven, the shoulders of Atlas bent lower with the added weight. Hera, now reconciled to him, gave him her daughter Hebe (hē′ bē) in marriage. He dwelt, a hero among gods, until the end of time.

Developing Comprehension Skills

1. List the seven labors of Heracles in the order in which they are told in this myth.

2. When does Heracles' marriage to Dejanira take place in relation to his labors?

3. For each action listed below, explain the character's motivation. If the myth does not state a reason, infer a motive from the information given in the myth.

   a. Hera tries to kill the infant Heracles.

   b. Heracles kills Hippolyta, the queen of the Amazons.

   c. Nessus lies to Dejanira, telling her that his blood is a love potion.

   d. Dejanira sends Heracles a robe steeped in the poisonous blood of Nessus.

   e. The gods consent to accept Heracles into the heavens.

4. In the course of his adventures, Heracles kills several innocent people, including Queen Hippolyta, his friend Iphitus, and the messenger Lichas. He is punished for only one of these actions. Do you think he should have been punished for the other killings? Give reasons for your answer.

Hercules Slaying the Lion (detail), 6th century B.C. Attic black-figure amphora. The Art Institute of Chicago, Katherine K. Adler Fund.

Reading Literature: Greek Myths

1. **Diagraming Setting.** One interesting aspect of myths is their wide range of settings. The story of Heracles, for example, takes place not only on earth, but also in heaven and in the underworld. Create a map showing the location of these mythological places. Referring to your answer in question 1 in Developing Comprehension Skills, show in which place each of Heracles' labors occurred.

2. **Understanding a Hero.** Heracles is shown to have both good and bad qualities. Name some good qualities and some bad qualities. Why do you think he is considered a great hero?

3. **Describing the Greek Gods.** Each myth you have read adds information about the gods on Olympus, particularly about Zeus and Hera. Considering all the information given so far, describe either Zeus or Hera. Mention both good and bad qualities.

Developing Vocabulary Skills

Identifying Greek Prefixes. This myth refers to Poseidon's trident, a three-pronged pitchfork. *Trident* uses the prefix *tri-,* meaning "three." Many other English words concerning numbers contain Greek prefixes. The following chart lists several of these prefixes and their meanings. Use this information to define the underlined words in the following paragraph. Use a dictionary as necessary.

Greek prefix	English meaning
mono-	one
bi-, di-, dia-	two
tri-	three
tetra-	four
penta-	five
hex-	six
hept-	seven
oct-, octa-	eight
dec-, deca-	ten
poly-	many

The track meet occurs twice each <u>decade</u>. At the opening ceremonies, the band, an <u>octet</u> of horns and drums, plays several <u>polyrhythmic</u> tunes. The athletes wear <u>monograms</u> of their names on their uniforms. They walk onto the <u>tetragonal</u> field and line up in the shape of a <u>pentagon</u>, which is the contest's symbol. Events include the long jump, the high jump, <u>bicycle</u> races, as well as several running races. Photographers set up their cameras on <u>tripods</u> near the finish line. The scoring uses a <u>decimal</u> system. The winners take home shiny, <u>monochromatic</u> trophies.

Developing Skills in Critical Thinking

Making Evaluations. When you evaluate a retelling of a myth, you look at both the information and the way that it is presented. Comparing two or more retellings of the same myth may also help. To develop standards for evaluation, ask these questions.

1. How much information does the story present?
2. How exciting does the writer make the story?
3. How fully does the writer develop the characters?
4. How effective is the description of setting?

Find mythology books in the library that contain myths about Heracles. The following are recommended books.

Hercules by Bernard Evslin (Morrow)
Greek Myths by Olivia Coolidge (Houghton Mifflin)
Greek Gods and Heroes by Robert Graves (Doubleday and Company, Inc.)
The Golden Treasury of Myths and Legends by Anne Terry White (Golden Press)

Compare two or three versions of the Heracles myth. Decide which one you like best. Explain the standards you used to evaluate the myths.

Developing Writing Skills

Rewriting a Myth. Choose one of the seven labors of Heracles summarized in this myth. In two or three paragraphs, expand the story of the labor, adding your own details.

Prewriting. Jot down or outline the events in the labor you select. Then use your imagination to provide any details not given in the myth. Make sure the following information is included.

1. a description of the setting

2. a description of the appearance of Heracles and of his opponent

3. an explanation of the amount of work involved

4. comments about Heracles' feelings

Drafting. Write two or three paragraphs retelling the labor. Write about events in the order they occur. Select precise words to describe the details of the setting, action, and characters.

Revising and Sharing. Read your expanded account of the myth to a classmate to make sure it is clear and exciting. Then get together with six other classmates who have written about the other labors of Heracles. Combine your final copies in a booklet for others to read.

The Flight of Icarus

GREEK MYTH
*Retold from a collection of myths
by Sally Benson*

*People have always wanted to fly.
What happens in this myth when
that wish is fulfilled?*

King Minos, on the island of Crete, needed a place to house the Minotaur (min′ ə tôr′), a monster with the head of a bull and the body of a man. Daedalus (ded′ ə ləs), the master craftsman and architect, sailed to Crete and designed an intricate labyrinth to contain the Minotaur and his victims. The labyrinth had many twisting turns and dead ends. No one who entered there could escape. Anyone who dared to enter was eventually devoured by the monster. However, a young man named Theseus (thē′ syōōs) relied on his cleverness and strength to kill the Minotaur and escape from the labyrinth.

When Theseus escaped from the labyrinth, King Minos flew into a rage with its builder, Daedalus. He ordered the builder shut up in a high tower that faced the lonely sea. In time, with the help of his young son, Icarus (ik′ ə rəs), Daedalus managed to escape from the tower, only to find himself a prisoner on the island. Several times he tried by bribery to stow away on one of the vessels sailing from Crete, but King Minos kept strict watch. No ships were allowed to sail without being carefully searched.

Daedalus was an ingenious craftsman and was not discouraged by his failures.

"Minos may control the land and sea," he said, "but he does not control the air. I will try that way."

He called his son Icarus to him and told the boy to gather up all the feathers he could find on the rocky shore. As thousands of gulls soared over the island, Icarus soon collected a huge pile of feathers. Daedalus then melted some wax and made a skeleton in the shape of a bird's wing. The smallest feathers he pressed into the soft wax and the large ones he tied on with thread. While his father worked, Icarus played about on the beach happily. He chased feathers that blew away in the strong wind that swept the island and sometimes took bits of the wax and worked it into strange shapes with his fingers.

It was fun making the wings. The sun shone on the bright feathers; the breezes ruffled them. When they were finished, Daedalus fastened the wings to his shoulders and found himself lifted upwards where he hung poised in the air. Filled with excitement, he made another pair for his son. They were smaller than his own, but strong and beautiful.

Finally, one clear, wind-swept morning, the wings were finished. Daedalus fastened them to Icarus' shoulders and taught him how to fly. He bade him watch the movements of the birds, how they soared and glided overhead. He pointed out the slow, graceful sweep of their wings as they beat the air steadily, without fluttering. Soon the boy Icarus was sure that he, too, could fly and, raising his arms up and down, skirted over the white sand and even out over the waves, letting his feet touch the snowy foam as the water thundered and broke over the sharp rocks.

Daedalus watched him proudly but with misgivings. He called Icarus to his side. Putting his arm around the boy's shoulders, he said, "Icarus, my son, we are about to make our flight. No human being has ever traveled through the air before, and I want you to listen carefully to my instructions. Keep at a moderate height. If you fly too low, the fog and spray of the sea will clog your wings. If you fly too high, the heat of the sun will melt the wax that holds them together. Keep near me and you will be safe."

He kissed Icarus and fastened the wings more securely to his son's shoulders. Icarus stood in the bright sun, the shining wings drooping gracefully from his shoulders. His golden hair was wet with spray and his eyes were bright and dark with excitement. He looked like a lovely bird. Daedalus' eyes filled with tears and turning away he soared into the sky, calling to Icarus to follow. From time to time, he looked back to see that the boy was safe and to note how he managed his wings in his flight. As they flew across the land to test their skill before setting out across the dark, wild sea, farmers below stopped their work and shepherds gazed in wonder, thinking Daedalus and Icarus were gods.

Father and son flew out over the sea, passing several islands. Icarus, beating his wings in joy, felt the thrill of the cool wind on his face and the clear air above and below him. He flew higher and higher into the blue sky until he reached the clouds. His father called out in alarm. He tried to follow, but he was heavier and his wings could not carry him. Up and up Icarus soared, through the soft moist clouds and out again toward the glorious sun. He was bewitched by a sense of freedom. He beat his wings frantically so that they would carry him higher and higher to heaven itself.

The blazing sun beat down on the wings and softened the wax. Small feathers fell from the wings and floated softly down,

Violet-Tailed Sylph and Crimson Topaz, 1983, ROBERT LOSTUTTER. Collection of Graham Gund, MA.
Photograph: Dart Gallery, Chicago.

warning Icarus to stay his flight and glide to earth. But the enchanted boy did not notice them until the sun became so hot that the largest feather dropped off and he began to sink. Frantically he fluttered his arms, but no feathers remained to hold the air. He cried out to his father, but his voice was submerged in the clouds.

Daedalus, crazed by anxiety, called back to him, "Icarus! Icarus, my son, where are you?" At last he saw the feathers floating from the sky, and soon his son plunged through the clouds into the sea. Daedalus hurried to save him, but it was too late. He gathered the boy in his arms and flew to land, the tips of his wings dragging in the water from the double burden they bore. Weeping bitterly, he buried his small son and called the land Icaria in his memory.

Then with a flutter of wings, Daedalus once more took to the air. But the joy of his flight was gone and his victory over the air was bitter to him. He arrived safely in Sicily where he built a temple to Apollo and hung up his wings as an offering to the god. Into the wings he pressed a few bright feathers he had found floating on the water where Icarus fell. And he mourned for the bird-like son who had thrown caution to the winds in the exaltation of his freedom from the earth.

Reading Literature: Greek Myths

1. **Understanding Setting.** The setting at the beginning of this myth is the island of Crete. Identify at least three aspects of this setting that affect what happens in the myth.

2. **Recognizing Realistic Details.** In some ways, the story of Icarus seems more realistic than the other myths in this chapter. For example, Daedalus and Icarus seem to have an ordinary father-son relationship. List at least five realistic details about characters or action in the myth of Icarus.

3. **Analyzing Elements of Myths.** As you have learned, a **myth** is an old story from the oral tradition that explains aspects of nature or human life. A myth usually teaches a lesson and shows what is important to a society. Because myths are related to the religion of a culture, they are usually about gods and goddesses. What typical element of myths is absent from this story?

Developing Comprehension Skills

1. Who kills the Minotaur and escapes from the labyrinth? On whom does King Minos take out his anger?

2. Why does Daedalus want to fly?

3. The myth says that Daedalus watches with pride but also "with misgivings" as Icarus flies. From what you know about Icarus, what is the basis for his father's fears?

4. Icarus does not mean to disobey his father when he soars higher and higher into the sky. What causes Icarus to fly so high?

5. What lesson does this myth teach about freedom and good judgment?

6. The myth of Icarus continues to be popular. What human experiences does the myth recall? What human feelings does the myth appeal to?

Developing Vocabulary Skills

Determining the Meaning of a Word. To learn the meaning of an unfamiliar word, you can either use context clues, identify word parts, analyze the origin of the word, or look up the word in a dictionary. Notice the underlined words in the following sentences from "The Flight of Icarus." Decide which of the four methods is best for determining the meaning of the underlined word. On a sheet of paper write either *context, word parts, word origin,* or *dictionary.* You may use more than one method for a word.

1. When Theseus escaped from the underlined labyrinth, King Minos flew into a rage.

2. Daedalus was not discouraged by his failures.

3. Daedalus fastened the wings to his shoulders and found himself lifted upwards where he hung poised in the air.

4. Daedalus, crazed by anxiety, called back to him.

Developing Skills in Study and Research

Using Maps. Some settings described in the myths are based on the actual geography of Greece and surrounding areas. Examine the map of ancient Greece and the Mediterranean area on pages 332 and 333. Then answer the following questions.

1. In what sea is the island named for Icarus?

2. In what direction do Icarus and Daedalus fly?

3. Where is Mount Olympus, the mythical home of the gods, in relation to the rest of Greece?

4. Which locations of Heracles' labors are shown on the map?

5. Where is the mountain where Deucalion and Pyrrha were saved?

6. How does studying the maps help you to understand the myths in this chapter?

Developing Writing Skills

1. **Describing an Experience.** Imagine yourself in Icarus' place, flying above the sea. You are so excited and delighted by flying that you forget your father's warnings. You are aware only of the pleasures of flying. Write one or more paragraphs telling what you sense and feel.

   Prewriting. Make a chart with headings for at least three of the five senses: sight, hearing, smell, touch, and taste. Under each heading try to list two or three details about the flight. For example, you might smell the salty sea air. Expand some details with words that suggest how thrilled you feel during the flight.

   Drafting. Combine the descriptive details into sentences arranged in some logical order.

   Revising and Sharing. Read your description. Does it express the emotions you think Icarus felt? If not, add descriptions of the flight that make it seem more exciting. Then share your final copy with another classmate and compare your descriptions.

2. **Analyzing Relationships.** Think about the relationship between Daedalus and Icarus. How do Daedalus and Icarus treat each other? How well does Icarus obey his father? What conflicting feelings does Daedalus have toward his son? Write at least one paragraph explaining this father-son relationship. Give evidence from the story to support your ideas. Follow the steps of the process of writing: prewriting, drafting, revising, and sharing. For more help, see the Guidelines for the Process of Writing beginning on page 654 in the handbook.

Greek Legends

In contrast to myths, legends are believed to be based on historical events or real people. Another difference between legends and myths is that legends focus more on humans than on gods. In this section you will read legends about Odysseus and the other heroes of the Trojan War. The selections are based on two long poems of Homer, *The Iliad* and *The Odyssey. The Iliad* is based on legends about the Trojan War. *The Odyssey* combines stories about Odysseus with other Greek legends.

The Trojan Horse (detail), 16th century. School of GIUSEPPE ARCIMBOLDO. The National Swedish Portraits Collections, Gripsholm. Photograph: The National Museums of Sweden, Stockholm.

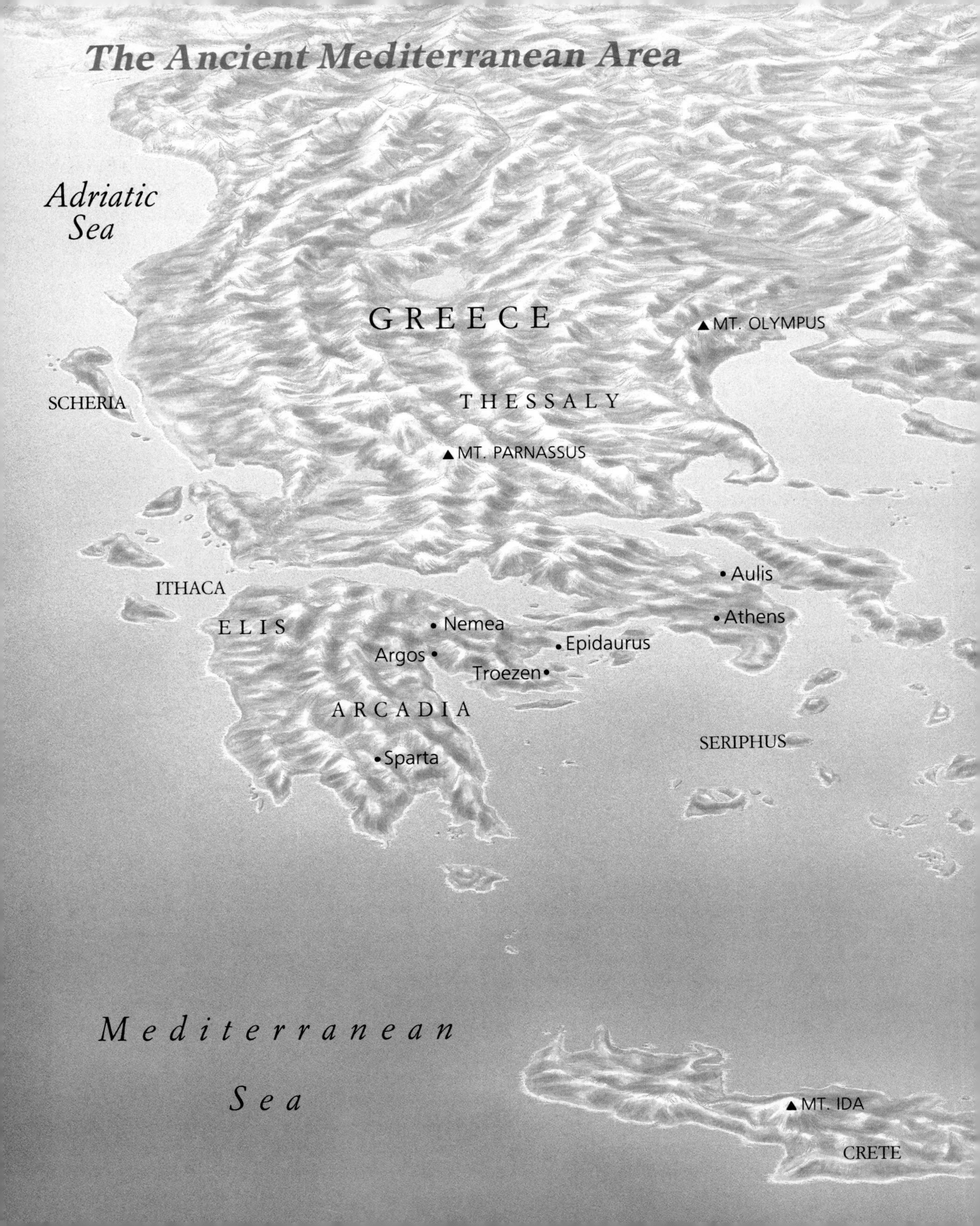

The Ancient Mediterranean Area

Adriatic Sea

GREECE ▲MT. OLYMPUS

THESSALY

SCHERIA

▲MT. PARNASSUS

• Aulis

ITHACA

ELIS • Nemea

• Athens

• Epidaurus

Argos • Troezen •

ARCADIA

• Sparta

SERIPHUS

Mediterranean

Sea

▲MT. IDA

CRETE

Black
Sea

Circe's
Island

ITALY

Rome•

GREECE

TURKEY

Island of
the Sirens

Calypso's Island

MT. ETNA ▲

Scylla and
Charybdis

MT. ATLAS ▲

Country of the
Cyclopes

Thrinacia

AFRICA

Country of the
Lotus-Eaters

Mediterranean Sea

0   100 200 300
Miles

N

© ML & Co.

LEMNOS

•Troy

Aegean Sea

ASIA
MINOR

ICARIA

NAXOS

The Trojan War

Greek gods often cause trouble. Read this famous legend to find out what part the gods play in starting the Trojan War.

GREEK LEGEND
*Retold from a collection of myths
by Sally Benson*

When Peleus (pā′ lē əs) was married to Thetis (the′ təs), all the gods and goddesses were invited to the wedding feast with the exception of Eris (er′ is), goddess of discord. Enraged at the slight, Eris threw a golden apple among the guests. The golden apple bore the inscription: "For the fairest."

Hera, Aphrodite, and Athene each claimed the apple. Soon they were quarreling bitterly. Zeus was not willing to make a decision on so delicate a matter. He sent the goddesses to Mount Ida, where the beautiful shepherd Paris, the son of Priam (prī′ əm), King of Troy, was tending his flocks. Paris was asked to make the decision about the goddesses.

The goddesses gathered around Paris, each extolling her own charms. Each one promised to reward him if he gave her the prize. Hera promised him power and riches. Athene told him that she would see that he gained glory and renown. Aphrodite whispered that he should have the fairest woman in the world for his wife.

Paris decided in favor of Aphrodite and gave her the golden apple, thus making the other two goddesses his enemies.

Under the protection of Aphrodite, Paris sailed for Greece, where he was hospitably received by Menelaus (men′ ə lā′ əs), King of Sparta. Now Helen, the wife of Menelaus, was the very woman whom Aphrodite had destined for Paris.

Helen was the daughter of Zeus and a mortal, Leda. Helen was the most beautiful woman in the world and had been sought as a bride by hundreds of suitors. The young men loved her so devotedly that they swore that no matter which of them she chose to wed, the others would defend her from harm all her life. She married Menelaus and was living with him happily when Paris became their guest.

Paris, aided by Aphrodite, persuaded Helen to elope with him, and he carried her away to Troy. Overcome by grief, Menelaus called upon his brother chieftains of Greece to fulfill their pledge and join in his efforts to recover his wife. Only

Judgment of Paris,
about 1430. Florentine,
unknown artist. Museo del
Bargello (Museo Nazionale), Florence.
Photograph by Francesco Lazzeri, Greve, Italy.

one of them held back. His name was Odysseus (ō dis' ē əs). He had married a woman named Penelope (pə nel' ə pē) and was happy with his wife and child. He had no wish to embark on such a troublesome affair. One of his friends, Palamedes (pal' ə mē' dēs), was sent to beg him to join the quest.

When Palamedes arrived at Ithaca where Odysseus lived, Odysseus pretended to be mad. Seeing Palamedes approaching,

he hastily yoked a donkey and an ox together to the plough and began to sow salt. Palamedes, suspecting a ruse, placed Odysseus' child before the plough, whereupon the father turned the plough aside, showing plainly that he was no madman. After that, Odysseus could no longer refuse to fulfill his promise.

Now, although Paris was the son of Priam, King of Troy, he had been brought up in obscurity because of a prophecy. The oracle had warned that he would one day be the ruin of the state. As he entered Troy with Helen, these forebodings seemed likely to be realized. The army that was being assembled in Greece was the greatest one that had ever been known. Agamemnon (ag′ə mem′ nän), brother of Menelaus, was chosen as the commander-in-chief. Achilles (ə kil′ ēs) was the most illustrious Greek warrior. After him came Odysseus, famous for his wisdom and cleverness.

On the other hand, Troy was no feeble enemy. Priam was now an old man, but he had been a wise ruler and had strengthened his state by governing well at home and keeping peace with his neighbors. The principal support of his throne was his son Hector, a brave, noble young man. Hector

Athena Building the Trojan Horse, 470–460 B.C. Attic red-figure kylix. Archeological Museum of Tuscany, Florence, Italy.

feared danger when he realized the great wrong his brother Paris had done in bringing Helen to Troy. He knew that he must fight for his family and country, yet he was sick with grief at the foolish circumstances that had set hero against hero.

After two years of preparation, the Greek fleet and army assembled in the port of Aulis (ô′ lis). Here they suffered more delays: disease broke out in the camps, and there was no wind to fill their sails. Eventually, they set out for the coast of Troy and plunged at once into a battle with the Trojans. For nine years they fought, neither side winning over the other. The Greeks began to despair of ever conquering the city. Finally they decided to resort to a trick thought of by Odysseus. They pretended to be preparing to abandon the siege, and most of the ships set sail with many warriors on board. They did not head for home, but sailed to a nearby island, where they hid in a friendly harbor. The Greeks who were left in the camp built a huge horse of wood that, they said, was to be a peace offering to Athene. Instead, at night, they filled it with armed men and left it in their camp. The remaining Greeks then sailed away.

When the Trojans saw that the encampment had broken up and the fleet had gone, they threw open the gates to the city, and everyone rushed forth to look at the abandoned camp grounds. They found the immense horse and wondered what it could be. Some thought it should be carried back to the city and put on exhibition as a trophy of the war, but others, more cautious, were afraid of it. One of the people Laocoön (lā äk′ ə wən′), the priest of Poseidon, tried to warn them against it. "What madness, citizens, is this?" he exclaimed. "Have you not learned enough of Greek fraud to be on your guard against it? For my part, I fear the Greeks even when they offer gifts."

As he spoke, he threw his lance at the horse's side. It struck, and a hollow sound like a groan came forth from it. The people were almost ready to take his advice and destroy the horse, when a group of people appeared, dragging a young man with them. He appeared to be a Greek prisoner, and he was brought before the Trojan chiefs. They promised him that they would spare his life on one condition: he was to answer truly the questions they asked him.

He told them that he was a Greek named Sinon (sī′ non), and that he had been abandoned by his countrymen, betrayed by Odysseus for a trifling offense. He assured them that the wooden horse had been made as an offering to Athene and that the Greeks had made it so huge to prevent its being carried into the city. Sinon added that the Greeks had been told that if the Trojans took possession of the horse, the Greeks would lose the war.

Then the people began to think of how they could move the enormous horse into the city. Suddenly, two immense serpents advanced from the sea. The creatures crawled up on the shore, and the crowd fled in all directions. The serpents slithered to the spot where Laocoön stood with his two sons. First they attacked the children, crushing their bodies and breathing their pestilential breath into the faces of the boys. Laocoön tried to drag his children away, and the serpents wound their bodies around his. He struggled pitifully to free himself, but they soon strangled him and his sons. In awe, the people crept back to the camp. They decided that the gods had taken revenge on Laocoön for talking against the wooden horse, which must be a sacred object. They began to move it into the city in triumph. All day, the Trojans feasted and sang around the horse, which they had placed in the main square of Troy. At last, exhausted from the festivities, they went to their homes and fell asleep.

When the city was quiet, the armed men who were hidden in the body of the horse were let out by Sinon. They stole to the gates of the city, which were closed for the night, and let in their friends, who had returned under the cover of darkness. They set fire to the city, and the people, overcome with feasting and sleep, were ruthlessly killed. Troy had fallen.

King Priam was the last to be slain, and he fought bravely to the end.

Menelaus hastened to the palace and found his wife, Helen. Not even Aphrodite could save Paris from the wrath of his enemies. He was killed, and Menelaus carried his wife safely back to Sparta.

Developing Comprehension Skills

1. What does Aphrodite promise Paris if he chooses her as "the fairest"?

2. How does Odysseus try to avoid going to war? What is his reason for not wanting to aid Menelaus?

3. Why do the Greeks resort to trickery in order to conquer Troy?

4. Why do the Trojans believe Sinon and not Laocoön about the wooden horse?

5. How does the wooden horse cause the downfall of Troy?

6. Do you think that Paris is totally to blame for the Trojan War? If not, who should share the blame with Paris?

Reading Literature: Greek Legends

1. **Understanding Character.** Paris is offered rewards by Hera, Aphrodite, and Athene. Why do you suppose he chooses the one he does? What does his choice tell you about his character?

2. **Identifying Conflict.** The struggle that a character faces in a story is called the **conflict.** If the struggle is with another character or an outside force, the conflict is **external.** If the struggle is within the character, the conflict is **internal.** Identify one external and one internal conflict in this legend. Who or what are the opposing forces in each conflict?

3. **Comparing Myths and Legends.** The main difference between a myth and a legend is that legends are believed to be based on events and people in history. In addition, legends tend to be more about humans than about gods. Look up "Trojan War" in an encyclopedia to learn the historical background. Then list the specific elements of "The Trojan War" that make it a legend rather than a myth.

Developing Vocabulary Skills

Deciding When to Use the Dictionary. Each of the underlined words in the paragraph below is from "The Trojan War." For the words that can be defined from context clues, write the words and their definitions on a sheet of paper. For the words that require a dictionary to define, write the words, label them *dictionary,* and write the correct dictionary definition.

The beginning of the Trojan War can be traced to an apple with an inscription that read "For the fairest." Hera, Aphrodite, and Athene all claimed the apple. Each extolled her charms to Paris, who had to decide which goddess deserved the apple. Athene promised Paris renown if he chose her, but he had no need for fame. Hera promised him immense power, but he had no desire to be a great ruler. Paris hastened to choose Aphrodite and her reward, the most beautiful woman in the world. After Paris stole Helen from her husband Menelaus, Menelaus began his quest, the search for his wife.

Developing Skills in Critical Thinking

Evaluating Cause and Effect. The Trojan War begins as a result of several actions and decisions. What are the causes of this famous war? Which of the causes could have been changed or avoided? Which could not have been changed? Is the war the only possible result of the actions that come before it?

Developing Writing Skills

1. **Examining Character Motivation.** A motive is the reason for a character's actions. For example, in "The Trojan War" Menelaus' motive for going to war was to regain his wife Helen. It is obvious that Odysseus has no desire to help Menelaus. Neither does Hector wish to fight for his brother Paris' cause. Yet both heroes join the battle. What do you think are their motives for doing so? Write one paragraph explaining the possible reasons for their actions.

   Prewriting. Review the legend and find the reasons why Odysseus and Hector do not want to go to war. (You may also want to review your answers to Developing Skills in Critical Thinking.) Then consider the pressures on the two heroes to join the fighting. For each character, jot down answers to these questions.

   Why doesn't he want to fight?
   Who expects him to fight?
   Why does he choose to fight?

   Look over your ideas, and organize them in logical order.

   Drafting. Using your notes, develop a paragraph to explain Odysseus' and Hector's motives for joining the Trojan War. Be sure to include the reasons they would rather not fight. Cite examples or quotations from the story to support your reasons.

   Revising and Sharing. Ask another person to read your paragraph. Have the person restate to you each hero's main motive for fighting as expressed in your paragraph. If the person cannot identify your main ideas, ask the person to point out sentences that are confusing. Rewrite those sentences to strengthen your paragraph.

2. **Explaining an Expression.** People sometimes use the expression "Beware of Greeks bearing gifts." Now that you have read this legend, can you explain that expression? Write your explanation in one paragraph. Be sure to refer to the meaning of the expression in the legend, as well as to the more general meaning today. Follow the steps in the process of writing: prewriting, drafting, revising and sharing. For more help see the Guidelines to the Process of Writing beginning on page 654 in the handbook.

The Voyage of Odysseus

GREEK LEGEND
*Retold from a collection of myths
by Sally Benson*

Odysseus is the clever Greek warrior who thought up the trick of the Trojan horse. As you read about his first adventures on his long journey home, you'll see his intelligence in action.

When Troy had fallen, Odysseus with his men set sail for home. No sooner were they out of the harbor than a dreadful storm blew up and drove their ship from its course. For nine days they were hopelessly lost at sea. Finally they sighted the country of the Lotus-eaters. Almost dying of thirst, the men first set out to look for water. When they had refreshed themselves, Odysseus told them to explore the land and find out who the inhabitants were. Soon the men came upon a group of people who received them hospitably and offered them some of their own food, the lotus plant, to eat.

Odysseus' men did not know the power of the lotus leaf. Anyone who ate one immediately forgot all about home and family and wanted to remain with the Lotus-eaters forever. Half-starved and flattered by the attentions shown them, the men from the ship were only too happy to sit down at the table and eat. Odysseus waited a while for his soldiers and then went in search of them. He saw them feasting and saw what they were eating. Knowing what effect the sweet-tasting lotus would have on them, he begged them to come with him. The men, who were by this time in dreamy half-sleep, did not even hear him. By force, he dragged them away and tied them to the benches of the ship until he hoisted the sails and got under way. The sea air soon cleared their heads, and they sailed on.

After many days they sighted the country of the Cyclopes (sī klō′ pēz). These huge giants each had but one eye, which was placed in the middle of the forehead. They lived in caves and tended their flocks, eating whatever roots and wild grasses grew on the rocky shores. Odysseus left the main body of his ships at anchor and went with one vessel to the Cyclopes' island to search for supplies. He and his companions landed, carrying with them a jar of wine

Cyclops, 1947, WILLIAM BAZIOTES. The Art Institute of Chicago, Walter M. Campana Memorial Prize.

for a present. They wandered about until they came to a large cave, which they entered. Finding no one about, they explored it. They found quantities of cheese, pails of milk, lambs and kids in wooden pens, and dried and salted meat. They ate some of the cheese, drank a few pails of milk, and were about to cook a roast of meat when they heard dreadful noises outside of the cave. Peering out, they saw a frightful giant called Polyphemus (päl′ ē fē′ məs). He carried an immense bundle of firewood, which he threw to the ground at the mouth of the cave. Then he drove his flock of sheep and goats into the cavern to be milked, and, when they were safely in, he moved a large stone, closing the entrance. It was so large that twenty oxen could not move it.

As the men quaked with terror, Polyphemus sat down and milked his goats. When he had finished, he turned his great eye around and saw the men who huddled in the shadows of the pens. He spoke to them, and his voice was a dreadful growl that echoed from the dripping walls. "Who are you?" he asked. "And where do you come from?"

Odysseus stepped forward and answered him humbly. "We are Greeks," he said, "returning from a great expedition. We have lately won much glory in the conquest of Troy. We are now on our way home, but we are lost. And, if you will offer us your hospitality, in the name of the gods, we will restock our larders and be on our way."

Polyphemus did not answer. He reached out his great hand and seized two of the Greeks as easily as a man picks a handful of grass. He hurled them against the side of the cave and dashed out their brains. As their companions stood watching in horror, he pulled the men apart and ate them up, clothes and all. Then, having made a hearty meal, he stretched himself out on the floor and went to sleep.

Odysseus drew forth his sword and was about to kill the giant as he slept. Then he remembered the huge rock that blocked the entrance to the cave. He realized that if he killed the giant, he and the rest of his men would be hopelessly imprisoned and would eventually die of starvation. All night, the men huddled in fright in the dark, damp cave. They were unable to decide what to do. When morning came, they were sunk in hopeless despair. The giant awoke, lazily stretched out his hand, and grabbed two more of the men. He hurled them against the walls and feasted on their flesh until there wasn't a fragment left. Then the giant moved the rock away from the entrance, drove out his flocks, and replaced the rock.

When he was gone, the men came out from their hiding places. Odysseus tried desperately to plan how he might avenge the death of his companions and make his escape with his friends. Searching the cave for a weapon, he found a massive tree trunk that had been cut by the Cyclops (sī′ kläps) for a staff. He ordered his men to sharpen the end of it to a fine point. When that was done, they seasoned it in the fire and hid it under the straw on the floor. Then four of the boldest were selected, and Odysseus told them of his scheme.

It was almost evening when they had finished their tasks, and they soon heard the Cyclops approaching. He rolled away the stone and drove his flock in as usual. After milking his sheep and goats, he seized two more men, dashed their brains out, and made his evening meal. After the giant had supped to his content, Odysseus approached him and handed him a bowl of

Ulysses and Polyphemus, 1982, EARL STALEY. Phyllis Kind Gallery, Chicago and New York City.
Photograph by William H. Bengtson.

wine, saying, "Cyclops, this is wine. Taste it and drink after eating your meal of man's flesh."

The giant was delighted with the taste of the wine and called for more. Odysseus gave him bowl after bowl of the heady drink, and this pleased the giant so much that he promised Odysseus that he would be the last of his party to be devoured. He asked his name, and Odysseus replied, "My name is No-man."

When he had drunk the last of the wine, the giant lay down to sleep. Then Odysseus called to his four friends and, lifting the staff, they thrust the end of it into the fire until it was red hot. Then they plunged it into the Cyclops' one eye.

The monster roared in pain. Odysseus and his men sprang back and hid themselves in the cave. Polyphemus bellowed and called out to the other Cyclopes to help him. Hearing his cries, they came from their caves and flocked around his den. "What hurt," they asked, "has caused you to sound an alarm?"

"O friends, I die," he answered, "and No-man gave the blow."

"If No-man gave the blow," they said,

"then you have been killed by a blow from Zeus, and you must bear it."

They turned away from the cave, leaving him groaning on the ground. He was not dead, only wounded, and in the morning he rolled the huge stone aside and let his flocks out to pasture. Although he couldn't see, he stood at the entrance of the cave to feel everything that passed him, so that Odysseus and his men could not escape. Earlier, Odysseus had told his companions to harness the rams of the flock three abreast with willow branches, which they found on the floor of the cave. To the middle ram of each group of three, one of the Greeks hung, protected on either side by the other two rams. One by one, the men swung from the shaggy coats of the rams. As they passed the giant, he felt the animal's backs and sides, but he never thought to feel their bellies. So all the men escaped. Odysseus was the last one who passed.

Once outside the cavern, the men released themselves and ran to the ship, driving the flock before them. They hastened aboard and pushed off from shore. When they seemed to be a safe distance away, Odysseus shouted out, "Cyclops, the gods have repaid you for your atrocious deeds! It is Odysseus to whom you owe your loss of sight."

The Cyclops, hearing this, bellowed in rage and, seizing a huge rock from the side of the mountain, he hurled it with all his might in the direction of the ship. Down it came, just clearing the vessel's stern. The ocean heaved and threw the ship once more toward the land, and it barely escaped being dashed against the shore. The sailors pulled away with the utmost difficulty. Odysseus was about to call to the giant again, but his friends begged him not to do so. He waited until they were far out at sea. Then, unable to resist taunting the Cyclops, he called out again. The giant answered him with curses, but his men pulled at their oars and soon reached the rest of the fleet. At once they set sail again.

Developing Comprehension Skills

1. The following are six important events that happen after Odysseus leaves the country of the Lotus-eaters. Arrange these events in time order.

   a. Polyphemus hurls a huge rock at the ship.
   b. Odysseus and his men escape from the cave.
   c. Odysseus and his men land on the island of the Cyclopes.
   d. Odysseus taunts Polyphemus and identifies himself.
   e. Polyphemus eats several men.
   f. Odysseus gives Polyphemus wine.

2. Contrast what Odysseus and his men expect from Polyphemus when they first arrive and what they ultimately get.

3. Why does Odysseus tell Polyphemus that his name is No-man?

4. How do Odysseus and his men get out of the cave after Polyphemus has been blinded? Who thinks up the plan?

5. Why do you think Odysseus tells Polyphemus his real name at the end? What does Odysseus' action show about his character?

6. Do you think what Odysseus and his men do to Polyphemus is justified by the Cyclops' own actions? Explain.

Reading Literature: Greek Legends

1. **Understanding Theme.** Polyphemus is a powerful giant, but Odysseus and his men escape from him. How do they manage to get away? What lesson does this legend teach about how to overcome a strong opponent?

2. **Analyzing Character.** The early Greeks respected Odysseus as a hero because of his great strength, courage, cleverness, honor, and intelligence. Odysseus also displays weaknesses, just as other humans do. Review the actions of Odysseus in the two legends you have read. Find at least two instances when he shows admirable qualities and two instances when he shows human weaknesses.

3. **Contrasting Mythical and Legendary Heroes.** Greek myths and legends both portray heroes, but they are different kinds of heroes. Think about mythic heroes such as Prometheus, Perseus, and Heracles. Then think about the legendary hero Odysseus. How is Odysseus different from the mythic heroes? For example, how is his relationship with his countrymen different from that of the mythic heroes? How are his conflicts different? What is different about the way he fights?

Developing Vocabulary Skills

Recognizing Greek Word Origins. The name Cyclops comes from the Greek words *kyklos,* meaning "round," and *ops* meaning "eye." (Notice that *k* becomes *c* in English.) Explain how the meaning of each English word listed below is connected to the meaning of one of these two Greek words. Use a dictionary to check word meanings.

cyclone	bicycle	cyclist
cyclometer	optical	optometrist

Developing Skills in Speaking and Listening

Giving a Dramatic Reading. Work with a small group of students to develop a dramatic reading of one scene in "The Voyage of Odysseus." Your group might choose one of these scenes:

1. discovering the land of the Lotus-eaters (paragraphs 1 and 2)

2. meeting Polyphemus (paragraphs 3 through 6)

3. putting out Polyphemus' eye (paragraphs 8 through 11)

4. leaving the island of the Cyclopes (paragraphs 15 through 17)

Work together to decide how to share the reading. You might, for example, assign one person to read the sentences about each character. Practice reading the scene with expression, trying to convey the drama of the scene with your voices. Be sure to pronounce words clearly and speak loudly enough to be heard. When you have practiced enough, present your dramatic reading to the class.

Developing Writing Skills

Writing a Description. In the legend, Odysseus and his men explore Polyphemus' cave. At first, it seems strange to them. It is a new place and they are unsure what to do. Imagine what the cave looks like. In two or more paragraphs, write a description of the cave.

Prewriting. Reread the description of Polyphemus' cave in the legend. List the details that are given. Then try to imagine more details about the cave, including what it looks like, what is in it, and what it smells like. Add these details to your list. Decide on a logical order for presenting the description of the cave.

Drafting. Write your description following your prewriting notes. Use words and phrases that appeal to the senses of sight, hearing, smell, and touch. Use a clear order of details as you move from one part of the description to the next.

Revising and Sharing. Proofread your description for misspelled words and incorrect punctuation and grammar. Then share your final copy with a classmate. Contrast the different ways each of you described the cave.

Circe, the Enchantress

A beautiful goddess soon threatens Odysseus and his men. Read to find out how Odysseus resists Circe's charms.

GREEK LEGEND
Retold from a collection of myths by Sally Benson

Near the island of the Cyclopes lay the island of Aeolus (ā′ ə ləs). Aeolus ruled the winds, and he sent them forth to fill the sails of ships or kept them chained as he chose. Odysseus and his men landed at the beautiful little island, and Aeolus greeted them in a friendly manner. When they were ready to leave, Aeolus gave them a leather bag tied with a silver string. The bag held all the winds that might be harmful or dangerous. Aeolus warned Odysseus not to open the bag until he reached home. Until that time, the god of the winds promised that he would send forth only his pleasantest breezes.

For nine days the ship sped before the swift breezes of Aeolus. All that time, Odysseus stood at the wheel, without sleep. At last, exhausted, he lay down to rest. While he slept, the crew approached him and, seeing the leather bag lying by his side, wondered what it could contain. They decided that it must hold some rare treasure that the hospitable King Aeolus had given their commander. They loosed the string, and the winds rushed forth with a dreadful sound. The ships were driven from their course again, back to the island they had left. Here Aeolus, indignant at the folly of the sailors, refused to help them again. They were obliged to row away from the island.

For weeks they sailed the seas until they came to the isle where Circe (sur′ sē), the daughter of the sun, dwelt. After landing on the sloping beach, Odysseus climbed a high hill and, gazing about, saw no signs of life except in one spot on the center of the island. There he saw a palace, surrounded by lovely trees.

He ordered one half of his crew under the leadership of Eurylochus (yʊ ril′ ə kus) to go to the palace and ask for hospitality. The men set forth, and, as they approached the palace, they found themselves surrounded by wild beasts—lions, tigers, and wolves. These animals were not at all fierce, and the men looked at them in wonder. They did not know that these animals had been men. These men had been changed into the forms of beasts by Circe's enchantments.

The men drew near the palace, and soon they heard soft music and a sweet woman's voice singing. Eurylochus called aloud, and the goddess herself came forth and invited them in. The men gladly followed her, all that is, but Eurylochus, who suspected danger. He hid himself in a tall tree where he could look over the hedges and see what befell his men.

The goddess led them to a banquet table and served them with wine and other delicacies. When they had feasted heartily and were stuffed like pigs with rare food and drink, she touched them with her wand and changed them into swine. Their bodies only were changed; they retained their

The Sirens, 1875, EDWARD BURNE-JONES. John and Mable Ringling Museum of Art, Sarasota, Florida.

human minds. Then she shut them up in sties and supplied them with acorns and other things that swine love.

Eurylochus climbed down from the tree and hurried back to the ship where he told his tale to Odysseus. Angered by the loss of his men, Odysseus determined to go himself and see if he could find any means to set his companions free. He went alone, and, as he walked, he met a youth who addressed him familiarly and who seemed to know all about him and his adventures. He told Odysseus that he was the god Hermes. He warned Odysseus of the magic arts of Circe and of the danger of approaching the palace. Odysseus would not heed the warning. Hermes gave him a sprig of a plant that had the power to resist sorceries. He then advised Odysseus how best to resist the charms of the lovely goddess.

Odysseus thanked him and went on his way. When he reached the palace, he was received by Circe, who entertained him as she had done his companions. After he had eaten and drunk, she touched him with her wand, saying, "Hereafter, seek the sty and wallow with your friends."

Instead of obeying, he drew his sword and rushed at her, furious. She fell to her knees and begged for mercy. He told her that he would spare her only if she swore to release his companions and practice no further arts against them. She led him to the pens and changed the swine back to humans once more. Odysseus was so grateful to her that he accepted her invitation to stay on the island for a while and rest from the tiresome voyage. Odysseus would have forgotten his native land entirely had not his companions reminded him of his duty.

Sadly, Circe saw the Greeks to their ships and instructed them how to pass safely by the Sirens. The Sirens were sea nymphs who charmed unhappy mariners by their songs until the travelers could do nothing else but throw themselves into the sea. Circe told Odysseus to fill the ears of his sailors with wax so that they could not hear the music. Odysseus himself should be bound to the mast with stout ropes.

"Warn your men," Circe said. "No matter how you plead to be released, they must refuse. They must not release you until you have passed the Sirens' island."

It was well that Odysseus followed her advice. When they reached the island, the sea was calm, and over the waters came the notes of music so lovely that Odysseus cried to be set free. The men, obedient to his first orders, bound him still tighter and held to the course. The music grew fainter and fainter and soon faded in the distance.

Developing Comprehension Skills

1. Name three problems that Odysseus and his men have to deal with in this legend.

2. What does Aeolus give Odysseus? Why doesn't the gift help him?

3. What animal does Circe turn Odysseus' men into? Why is this animal appropriate to what the men have been doing in the palace?

4. How does Odysseus resist Circe's sorcery and get her to help him?

5. Odysseus saves his men from Circe, but later they rouse him from Circe's charms and get him back on his journey. What kind of relationship does Odysseus seem to have with his men? How well do they obey him? Explain your answers.

6. Before Odysseus' ship passes the Sirens, he fills his sailors' ears with wax. Why do you think he himself chooses to hear the song, while being bound to the mast?

Reading Literature: Greek Legends

1. **Contrasting Characters.** Polyphemus and Circe both present threats to Odysseus as he journeys home. Contrast the dangers that these characters create for Odysseus and his men. How do the methods of Polyphemus and Circe differ? How does each respond after Odysseus overcomes them? Which of these characters would you rather contend with as an enemy? Why?

2. **Understanding Purpose.** The legends of Odysseus relate his adventures on his way home from Troy. Consider the purposes of these legends. They are not meant only to entertain. They also teach important lessons about life. What values might these legendary adventures teach?

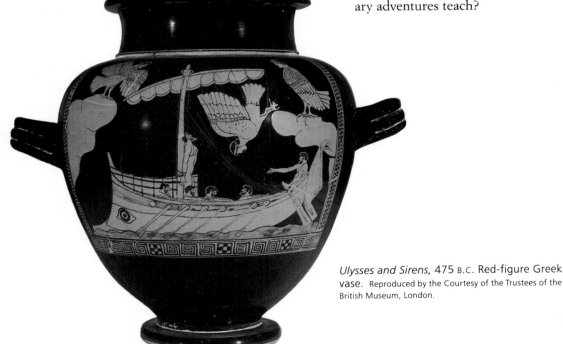

Ulysses and Sirens, 475 B.C. Red-figure Greek vase. Reproduced by the Courtesy of the Trustees of the British Museum, London.

Developing Vocabulary Skills

Using Word Parts. Read the following sentences from "Circe, the Enchantress." In each sentence find one word that contains one or more affixes. Write the word on a sheet of paper. Identify the base word and the suffix or prefix. Remember that the spelling of some base words changes when a suffix is added. Using the charts on pages 238–239 and your knowledge of the base word, write a definition of the word.

1. "The bag held all the winds that might be harmful."
2. "These men had been changed into the forms of beasts by Circe's enchantments."
3. "The men gladly followed her."
4. "He drew his sword and rushed at her, furious."
5. "The Sirens were sea nymphs who charmed unhappy mariners."

Developing Writing Skills

Analyzing Plot. As you have already seen in other myths and legends, both humans and gods can do harm as well as good. These two kinds of behavior produce conflicts and so help to develop the plot. In this legend Circe and Odysseus each act in negative ways and in positive ways. In a paragraph explain how the two kinds of behavior of these two characters help to develop the plot.

Prewriting. Make three lists. Head one *Circe*, one *Odysseus*, and one *Plot Development*. Under the first two heads describe the actions of the two characters. Identify the actions as *negative* or *positive*. Then briefly explain how each action helps to develop the plot. Decide whether you want to discuss Odysseus or Circe first. Also decide the order in which you want to discuss each action and its relationship to the plot.

Drafting. In your topic sentence state that Circe's and Odysseus' negative and positive actions help to develop the plot in this legend. Then present specific examples from the legend to support your idea. Explain how each action produces or relates in some way to the conflicts in the legend.

Revising and Sharing. Have a classmate read your paragraph. Ask for his or her comments about words or sentences that are unclear. Check that you have enough examples from the legend and that you give equal discussion to both Odysseus and Circe.

The Perils of Odysseus

GREEK LEGEND
*Retold from a collection of myths
by Sally Benson*

*More dangers await Odysseus and
his men, but Circe warns them
ahead of time. As you read, find
out whether Circe's warnings can
save them.*

In a cave high up on a rocky cliff, near a narrow passage through which Odysseus' ships had to pass, lived Scylla (sil′ə), who had once been a lovely water nymph. She had spurned the love of Glaucus (glä′ kəs), a sea deity and a favorite of Circe. To punish her, Circe had changed her into a monster. Serpents and barking monsters surrounded her, and, more horrible, they were attached to her, so she could not drive them away. In shame, she turned from the green waters of the sea she loved and hid herself on the lonely rock. As the years passed, she grew into a beast at heart and preyed on the mariners who sailed too near her. She had six heads, and, from every vessel that passed, she seized six of the crew and devoured them.

Near the cave where Scylla dwelt was a bottomless hole named Charybdis (kə rib′ dis). Three times each day the water rushed into it with terrific force, and three times the tide rushed back. Any ship coming near the whirlpool when the tide was rushing in was carried down to the blackest depths of the ocean where not even Poseidon could save it.

Circe had warned Odysseus of these two dangers. As they approached the dreadful places, he kept strict watch. The roar of waters from Charybdis could be heard from a distance, but Scylla could not be seen. While Odysseus and his men watched the dreadful whirlpool with anxious eyes, they were not on guard from the attack of Scylla. She darted her snaky heads down, caught six of his men from the deck of the ship, and bore them away, shrieking, to her den. It was the saddest sight Odysseus had yet seen, as he felt powerless to save them. Soon their cries were stilled, and Scylla, sated with human blood, allowed the ship to pass.

After passing Scylla and Charybdis, the sailors came in sight of Thrinacia (thri na′ sē ə). On this island the cattle of the Titan

Scylla and Charybdis, 1983, EARL STALEY. Collection of the Artist. © 1983 Earl Staley.

Hyperion (hī pir′ ē ən) were pastured, tended by his daughters. Circe had warned Odysseus that these flocks must not be molested, no matter what the needs of the voyagers might be. She cautioned him that if her warning were not heeded and the flocks were touched, destruction was sure to fall on the entire crew.

Odysseus would gladly have passed the island without stopping, but his companions begged for rest and refreshment. As Odysseus yielded, he made them swear that they would not touch one animal of the sacred flock and herds. They would have to be content with the provisions that remained on board the ships. They landed. As long as the provisions lasted, the men kept their oath. However, when their food was gone, they were forced to rely on what birds and fishes they could catch near the shores. Driven reckless by hunger, they killed some of the cattle and tried to make amends for their deed by offering a portion of the kill to the gods.

Odysseus had been overseeing some repairs to his ships when the cattle were slain. When he returned to land, he was horrified at what his men had done. The men were already preparing the meat to eat. Odysseus, looking down at the skins of the animals, saw the hides creep along the ground and heard the joints of meat moaning plaintively as they turned on the spit.

He bade his men make haste to set sail. They hurried away from the island, thinking that they had escaped punishment. No sooner were they at sea than the fair weather changed. A storm blew up. A stroke of lightning shattered the mast and killed the pilot. At last the vessel, beaten by the waves, fell to pieces.

The keel and mast floated side by side, and Odysseus made them into a raft to which he clung. The rest of the crew perished. Through the night Odysseus held to the raft. By morning he had drifted to the island of Calypso (ka lip′ sō).

Calypso was a sea nymph, and she saw Odysseus on the raft just as he was about to be dashed to death on the rocks. She pulled him from the sea and brought him food and drink. For many days he lay near death while she nursed him back to health. She made him a bed of fragrant violets and would have kept him with her, had not Zeus bade her to send him on his way. Together they built a sturdy raft and provisioned it well. Calypso sadly saw Odysseus sail out to sea.

He journeyed for many days and, when he was in sight of land, another storm broke out. His mast fell and great cracks appeared beneath his feet. Calypso, learning of his plight, sent a sea nymph to him who took the form of a cormorant and lighted on his sinking raft. The cormorant gave Odysseus a scarf and told him to bind it around his chest so that it would buoy him up as he swam to land.

Odysseus clung to the raft until it fell apart. Then, plunging into the sea, he began to swim. Athene smoothed the waves before him and sent him a wind that carried him toward shore. The surf beat high on the rocks, but soon he found calmer water at the mouth of a gentle stream where he landed, breathless and nearly dead. He kissed the soil and lay down to sleep.

Developing Comprehension Skills

1. What causes Scylla to be turned into a monster?

2. Circe warns Odysseus and his men about Scylla, Charybdis, and the sacred cattle of Hyperion. In what cases do her warnings fail to help the travelers?

3. Why does Odysseus decide to stop in Thrinacia where Hyperion keeps his cattle?

4. Why do Odysseus' men kill some of Hyperion's cattle?

5. How does the legend explain the cause of the storm that kills Odysseus' men?

6. Do you think Odysseus is responsible for the misfortune that kills all of his men? Does he make any mistakes as a leader in his decision to land on Thrinacia? Explain.

Reading Literature: Greek Legends

1. **Recognizing Suspense.** The **suspense,** or tension, in a story makes readers want to know what will happen next. This legend contains several suspenseful episodes. Identify two episodes and explain how suspense is created in each. What details or actions build the tension and excitement?

2. **Identifying Cultural Values.** In legends, as in all folk tales, actions that a society approves of are often rewarded and actions that a society frowns on are punished. In this way, legends convey cultural values and standards of proper behavior.

   Think about how Odysseus' men suffer in these legends. At one point they are turned into swine. They endure many storms at sea before they ultimately die in a shipwreck. What are the connections between their actions and what happens to them? What do their punishments suggest about the proper behavior of soldiers toward their leader and their gods?

3. **Understanding Legends.** Legends are based on historical events and focus on humans rather than gods. Legends also, however, contain many imaginary events and creatures. Which details in this legend could actually happen? Which ones are imaginary? Give one example of an incident in which the real and the imaginary are mixed together.

Developing Vocabulary Skills

Identifying Meanings of Suffixes. As you know, a suffix is a word part added to the end of a base word that changes the meaning of the base word. Each of the words listed below is from one of the selections you have just read. List each word on a sheet of paper and underline the suffix. Then figure out the meaning of the suffix from the list provided and write the correct suffix definition next to each word.

Words	Suffix Definitions
dangerous	without
friendly	female
traveler	like, characteristic of
blackest	most
goddess	full of
bottomless	a person who does a certain thing

Developing Skills in Study and Research

Outlining Plot. An outline can help you to see the order of events in a legend and the relationships between these events. To make an outline, first list the main events as main topics. Under each of these main topics, list at least two subtopics that give details about the main events.

Make an outline of Odysseus' voyage from its beginning in Troy up to this point. First, review the legends and decide on the main events, or topics. Write each main topic as a sentence preceded by a Roman numeral. Then, decide on the subtopics under each main topic. Write each subtopic as a sentence preceded by a capital letter. The subtopics follow the main topic. The first event is outlined as an example. Remember to write at least two subtopics under each main topic.

I. Odysseus goes to the land of the Lotus-eaters.
   A. Odysseus' men eat the lotus plants and don't want to leave.
   B. Odysseus drags his men away and escapes.

Developing Writing Skills

Writing about Theme. One theme in "The Perils of Odysseus" is that humans cannot always control what happens to them. In his experiences with Scylla and Charybdis as well as with Hyperion's cattle, Odysseus is unable to control his men or their common destiny. Write a paragraph telling how one incident illustrates this theme.

Prewriting. From the legend, select one of Odysseus' adventures and review the details given in the account. Make notes of the answers to questions such as these:

What tragedy occurs?
Is Odysseus warned of the danger?
How does he try to control the situation?
Is the outcome a result of the gods, the forces of nature, or the disobedience of Odysseus' men?

Drafting. Use the ideas in your notes to develop a topic sentence that clearly states the theme you are illustrating. Use details from your prewriting notes to develop the idea stated in the topic sentence. You might include quotations from the legend for additional support.

Revising and Sharing. Show your paragraph to a classmate. Ask the person to find details that support the topic sentence. If the person cannot find any supporting details, you need to add more specific support or to write your sentences more clearly.

The End of Odysseus' Voyage

GREEK LEGEND
*Retold from a collection of myths
by Sally Benson*

Odysseus arrives in a strange land before finally getting home. How are the people of this land different from others he has met? Is Odysseus himself any different?

The land where Odysseus had fallen exhausted was Scheria (sher′ ē ə), the country of the Phaeacians (fē′ ə cē′ ans). These people had originally dwelt very near the Cyclopes. After many quarrels with the savage race, they migrated to another island. They were a peaceful, godlike people, and the gods themselves often appeared among them. Their island was so remote from the wars of the mainland that the Phaeacians had almost forgotten the use of the bow and arrow.

On the night Odysseus swam ashore and while he lay sleeping on a bed of leaves, the daughter of the king of the island had a dream. She dreamed that Athene appeared before her to remind her that her wedding day was not far distant; it would be wise to wash all the family clothes for the great occasion. This was quite a task, as the fountains were far away, and all the garments had to be carried to them.

When the princess awoke, she told her parents about her dream. Her father then ordered grooms to harness a wagon to carry the clothes. Her mother, the queen, packed a lunch of food and wine. The princess climbed into the cart, while her lovely attendants followed on foot. They arrived at the riverside, turned the mules out to graze, and unloaded the wagon. They worked with speed and cheerfulness, and in no time at all the clothes were clean and spread on the shore to dry.

Then the girls bathed themselves and sat down beneath a tree for the picnic lunch. When they had eaten, they amused themselves with a game of ball. Athene, who had been watching them, caused the ball thrown by the princess to fall into the water. At that, they all screamed, and the noise awoke Odysseus.

He looked through the bushes and saw a group of maidens. By their dress and actions, he knew the maidens were of high rank. He needed their help badly. When Odysseus stepped out from the thicket, all the young girls screamed again and fled in

The Garland, 1899, THOMAS DEWING. Private collection. Photograph: David Nisinson Fine Art, New York City.

all directions—all but the princess.

Odysseus told her his story and begged her for food and fresh clothing. The princess promised him her father's hospitality and, calling back her attendants, scolded them for their foolish fears. "This man," she said, "is an unhappy wanderer. It is our duty to cherish him. Phaeacians have no enemies to fear, and the poor and needy are sent to us by Zeus. Go bring him food and clothing from the wagon. You will find my brother's garments there, washed clean and fresh."

Odysseus bathed and put on the clothes the maidens brought him. When the princess saw him clad in the splendid robes, she whispered to her maidens that she wished the gods would send her such a husband. Turning to Odysseus, she asked him to follow them to the city. "But when we draw near it," she added, "wait in a grove, for I fear the remarks that might be made by the people if they see me return with a gallant stranger."

He agreed to hide in the grove and to follow her to the palace later. After allowing her time to reach the palace, he went his way. As he neared the outskirts of the city, he met a young woman who was carrying a pitcher to the well. It was Athene who had assumed this form. Odysseus asked her to direct him to the palace of the king, and the maiden offered to be his guide. Under the guidance of the goddess and, by her power, enveloped in a cloud that shielded him from sight, Odysseus passed among the busy crowd. He looked with wonder at the harbor, the ships, the forum, and the battlements, until he came to the palace. Here the goddess left him.

Before entering the courtyard of the palace, Odysseus stood and gazed about him. The splendor of the scene astonished him. Bronze walls stretched from the entrance to the interior house. The doors were gold. The doorposts were carved out of silver, and the lintels were silver ornamented with gold. Along the walls were seats covered with scarves of the finest texture, the work of the Phaeacian maidens, and on these seats the princes sat and feasted. Golden statues of graceful youths held lighted torches which shed a soft radiance over everything. Fifty women served in the household. Some were employed to grind the corn, others to wind off the purple wool or ply the loom. For the Phaeacian women as far exceeded all other women in household arts as the mariners of their country did the rest of mankind in the management of ships.

A spacious garden lay outside the court, filled with pear, pomegranate, apple, fig, and olive trees. Neither winter's cold nor summer's drought arrested their growth, and they flourished in constant succession, some budding while others were maturing. In one part of the garden one could see the vines, some in blossom, some loaded with grapes. On the garden's borders, flowers bloomed all year, and the air was sweet with their perfume. In the center of the garden, two fountains poured forth their waters.

Odysseus was filled with admiration. He was not observed by the others because he was still enveloped in the cloud Athene had thrown around him. After feasting his eyes on all the beauty, he went into the hall where the chiefs and senators were assembled. They were pouring an offering to Hermes, whose worship followed the evening meal. Just then, Athene dissolved the cloud that surrounded Odysseus. He walked to the queen's throne, knelt at her feet, and implored her to help him to return to his native country. Then, withdrawing, he seated himself in the manner of suppliants, by the hearthside.

For a time, no one spoke. At last an aged statesman, addressing the king, said, "It is not fit that a stranger who asks our hospitality should be kept waiting in supplicant guise. Let him, therefore, be led to a seat and supplied with food and wine."

The king arose, took Odysseus by the

hand, and led him to the table. He dismissed his guests, and Odysseus was left alone with the king and queen. The queen recognized that the clothes he wore were those which her maidens and she herself had made. She asked him from whom he had received these garments. He told them of the wreck of his raft, his escape by swimming, and the help given him by the princess. The royal couple heard his story and promised to furnish him with a ship so that he might return to his native land.

The next day, a ship was prepared, and a crew of stout rowers was selected. Then everyone went to the king's palace, where a great banquet had been prepared. After the feast, the young men of the country showed Odysseus their skill in running and wrestling. They challenged him to show what he could do. He arose from his seat, seized a quoit far heavier than any the Phaeacians had thrown, and sent it farther than the farthest throw of theirs.

After the games, they returned to the hall and the herald led in a blind bard. He took for his theme the story of the wooden horse. Apollo inspired him and he sang so feelingly of the terrors and exploits of that eventful time that Odysseus was moved to tears.

When the king saw his grief, he turned to him. "Why are your sorrows awakened at the mention of Troy?" he asked. "Did you lose a father or brother there? Or perhaps a dear friend?"

Odysseus said that he himself had fought at Troy. Then he recounted all the adventures that had befallen him since his departure from that city. The king was so moved by his tale that he proposed that all the chiefs should present Odysseus with a gift. They obeyed and vied with one another in loading the illustrious stranger with costly things.

The next day Odysseus set sail and in a short time arrived at Ithaca, his own land. When the vessel touched the strand, he was asleep, and the mariners, without awaking him, carried him ashore. They laid him on the chest that contained his presents and then sailed away.

Developing Comprehension Skills

1. What kind of people live in the land of Scheria?

2. Name two ways in which the goddess Athene helps Odysseus in Scheria.

3. The Phaeacians had once lived very near the Cyclopes. How do the Phaeacians differ from the Cyclopes?

4. You have read about many of Odysseus' adventures as he journeys home from Troy. Would you like to trade places with Odysseus and have these adventures? Why or why not?

Reading Literature: Greek Legends

1. **Contrasting Legends.** The legends of Odysseus tell of his long journey home after the war in Troy. Contrast Odysseus' first adventure with Polyphemus with what happens to him on Scheria, the last stop on his journey home. In what condition does Odysseus arrive at both places? What different treatment does Odysseus receive from Polyphemus and from the Phaeacians? Also contrast the way Odysseus acts toward Polyphemus with the sadness and fatigue he displays with the Phaeacians.

2. **Understanding a Hero.** During Odysseus' stay in Scheria, you learn more about him. He demonstrates his great strength by throwing a huge quoit in the games at the king's palace. He also shows a more tender side of his personality. For example, he humbly begs the princess for food and fresh clothing, and he weeps with sadness at the bard's song of Troy. Review the legends of Odysseus that you have read. Think about the qualities he displays during his journey, including those shown in this selection. What qualities are those of a hero? What qualities are not heroic?

3. **Analyzing Cultural Values.** An important social value for the ancient Greeks was hospitality. Think back to some of Odysseus' adventures and find examples of gods and humans who acted hospitably to him and his men. What can you infer from those examples about the importance of hospitality to the ancient Greeks? What meaning does hospitality seem to have beyond just supplying food and shelter?

Developing Vocabulary Skills

Recognizing Greek Word Origins. Several Greek names from legends form the bases for English words. You can use your new knowledge of Greek characters and places to help you understand these words. First, identify the Greek name that is the origin for each word or phrase that follows. Then, use a dictionary to find out the meaning of the English word or phrase. Explain the similarity between the English word and the Greek name.

1. atheneum
2. titanic
3. Atlantic
4. odyssey
5. cyclopean
6. polyphemus moth
7. hermetic
8. calypso

Developing Writing Skills

Analyzing Character. You have seen how Odysseus changes during his adventures. At the beginning of his voyage, he is a victorious warrior returning home with his ship and crew. By the end of his voyage, he is alone and reveals a gentler, more civilized side. In two paragraphs, discuss the two sides of Odysseus' character and how both help him survive his ordeals.

Prewriting. List all of Odysseus' adventures. After each, jot down aspects of his character that Odysseus reveals during the adventure. Note the qualities that help Odysseus to survive the adventure.

Drafting. In one paragraph, describe Odysseus' strengths as a warrior and explain how they help him in his early adventures. Then in the second paragraph, describe Odysseus' humbler, more civilized side and explain how it helps him in his later adventures. Be sure to write a strong topic sentence for each paragraph.

Revising and Sharing. Reread your paragraphs, looking for unclear or confusing sentences. Make sure that you have supported each topic sentence with specific examples from Odysseus' adventures. A friend or family member might be interested in reading your final copy.

The Fate of the Suitors

GREEK LEGEND
Retold from a collection of myths by Thomas Bulfinch

Odysseus has been away from home for a long time. What changes have taken place while he has been gone? What is his homecoming like?

Odysseus had now been away from Ithaca for twenty years. When he awoke, he did not recognize his native land. Athene appeared to him in the form of a young shepherd, informed him where he was, and told him the state of things at his palace. Imagining him dead, more than a hundred nobles of Ithaca and of the neighboring islands had been for years suing for the hand of Penelope, Odysseus' wife. They lived in his palace and ordered its people about as if they owned both. To take vengeance upon them, it was important that Odysseus should not be recognized. Athene accordingly changed him into an unsightly beggar, and, as such, he was kindly received by Eumaeus (yōo mā′ əs), a faithful servant of his house.

Telemachus (tə lem′ ə kəs), Odysseus' son, was absent in quest of his father. He had gone to the courts of those kings who had returned from the Trojan expedition. While he was away on the search, Athene told him to return home. When he arrived,

he sought out Eumaeus to learn something of the state of affairs at the palace. Finding someone with Eumaeus, he treated the stranger courteously and promised him assistance. Eumaeus then went to the palace to inform Penelope privately of her son's arrival. Secrecy and caution were necessary because the suitors were plotting to kill Telemachus.

When Eumaeus had gone, Athene presented herself to Odysseus and told him to make himself known to his son. At the same time she restored his look of vigorous manhood. Telemachus viewed this transformation with astonishment and, at first, thought Odysseus must be more than mortal. Then Odysseus told Telemachus who he was and explained that the disguise had been the idea of Athene.

The father and son planned how they could get the better of the suitors and punish them for their outrages. It was arranged that Telemachus should proceed to the palace and mingle with the suitors. Odysseus

Penelope at Her Loom, 1509, PINTORICCIO. Reproduced by the Courtesy of the Trustees, the National Gallery, London.

would go as a beggar for, in those days, beggars were admitted into the halls of chieftains and often treated like guests. Odysseus reminded his son not to show unusual interest in him.

At the palace they found the usual scene of feasting and disorder. The suitors pretended to receive Telemachus with joy at his return. The old beggar was permitted to enter and was provided with a portion from the table. A touching incident occurred as Odysseus entered the courtyard. His old dog remembered him.

As Odysseus sat eating his portion in the hall, the suitors began to insult him. When he protested, one of them raised a chair and hit him. Telemachus had hard work to restrain his indignation at seeing his father treated unjustly but, remembering his father's directions, said little.

The Return of Odysseus (Homage to Pintoriccio and Benin), 1977, ROMARE BEARDEN.
The Art Institute of Chicago.

Penelope had put off a decision to marry again for so long that she could not delay further. Her husband's return could no longer be expected. She therefore consented to submit the question of her choice of husband to a contest of skill among the suitors. The test selected was that of shooting with the bow. Twelve rings were arranged in a line. He whose single arrow was sent through the whole twelve was to have the queen for his prize. A bow that one of his brother heroes had given to Odysseus in former times was brought from the armory and, along with its quiver full of arrows, was laid in the hall. Telemachus had taken care that all other weapons should be removed.

The first thing to be done was to bend the bow in order to attach the string. Telemachus endeavored to bend it but found all his efforts fruitless. Modestly confessing that he had attempted a task beyond his strength, he yielded the bow to another. The next contender tried to with no better success and, amidst the laughter and jeers of his companions, gave it up. Another tried it, and another. They rubbed the bow with tallow, but all to no purpose; it would not bend.

Then spoke Odysseus, humbly suggesting that he should be permitted to try. "For," said he, "beggar that I am, I was once a soldier, and there is still some strength in these old limbs of mine." The suitors hooted with derision, but Telemachus spoke up for him and let him try. Odysseus took the bow. With ease he adjusted the cord to its notch, then he sped an arrow unerringly through the rings.

Without allowing the suitors time to express their astonishment, Odysseus said, "Now for another mark!" and aimed directly at one of the most insolent of the suitors. The arrow pierced his throat, and the suitor fell dead. Telemachus, Eumaeus, and another faithful follower, well armed, now sprang to the side of Odysseus. The suitors, in amazement, looked around for arms but found none. Neither was there any way of escape, for Eumaeus had secured the door. Odysseus announced himself as the long-lost chief, whose house they had invaded, whose substance they had squandered, and whose wife and son they had persecuted for ten long years. He told the suitors that he meant to have ample vengeance. All were slain, and Odysseus was left master of his palace and possessor of his kingdom and his wife.

Thomas Bulfinch *(1796–1867)* was born in Newton, Massachusetts. He introduced generations of readers to Greek and Roman mythology. He also is known for rewriting Celtic, Scandinavian, and Oriental tales. Bulfinch worked as a banker in Boston for thirty years and did not begin his literary career until the age of fifty-seven.

Developing Comprehension Skills

1. How long has Odysseus been away from his home in Ithaca?

2. Name two things that have been happening at Odysseus' palace while he has been gone.

3. It is necessary for Odysseus to be disguised when he returns to his palace so that he will not be recognized. Why do you think Athene chooses the disguise of a beggar?

4. When Telemachus returns home, he goes directly to Eumaeus for information. What can you infer about the role of Eumaeus in Odysseus' household?

5. Odysseus and Telemachus plan to take revenge on the suitors. List in order of time the steps the two take to rid their home of the suitors and make Odysseus master of his palace again.

6. At the end of the legend, Odysseus kills all of Penelope's suitors. To the ancient Greeks, Odysseus' action was considered heroic. Do you think the slayings are heroic? Why or why not?

Reading Literature: Greek Legends

1. **Contrasting Cultural Values.** As a stranger and a beggar, Odysseus is treated differently by the suitors at his palace in Ithaca than he is by the Phaeacians in Scheria. Describe the difference in hospitality in these two places. In what ways have the values in Odysseus' homeland changed during his long absence? Give examples from the legend.

2. **Understanding Theme.** Each of the following statements is a theme from the legends of Odysseus. Events from the legends are listed below the statements. Match each theme with the event that supports it.

Themes:
   a. Justice sometimes calls for violence.
   b. Humans will be punished for disobeying the all-powerful gods.
   c. Hospitality is an important social value.
   d. Intelligence can overcome strength.

Events:
   (1) The god Hyperion causes a disastrous storm after Odysseus' men kill the god's cattle.
   (2) Odysseus kills the suitors who have overrun his palace.
   (3) Odysseus is taken in and cared for by the Phaeacians.
   (4) Odysseus outwits Polyphemus and escapes from his cave.

3. **Analyzing Minor Characters.** Penelope and Telemachus are interesting minor characters. Penelope waits twenty years for her husband to return, stalling insistent suitors during that time. What can you infer about Penelope's character from these actions? Telemachus was a young boy when his father left. What signs do you see in his character that show he is the son of Odysseus?

Developing Vocabulary Skills

Completing Analogies. In an **analogy** there are two pairs of related words. Each pair is related in the same way. Here are two examples:

Finger is to *hand* as *toe* is to *foot*.
Day is to *night* as *dawn* is to *dusk*.

In the first example, the relationship between *finger* and *hand* is that a finger is part of a hand. In the same way, a *toe* is a part of a *foot*. In the second example, the two words in each pair are opposites.

To complete an analogy, you must figure out the relationship between the first two words. Then find the missing word that will form the same relationship with the third word. Here is an example:

One-eyed is to Polyphemus as six-headed is to _____.

Circe	Scylla
Charybdis	Calypso

One-eyed describes the physical appearance of Polyphemus. *Six-headed* describes the physical appearance of the monster Scylla.

Choose the answer that will correctly complete each analogy. Use a dictionary if necessary.

1. Create is to destroy as originate is to _____.

begin	original
end	start

2. Tetrahedron is to four as octagon is to _____.

ten	six
two	eight

3. Zeus is to gods as Hera is to _____.

Muses	nymphs
Furies	goddesses

4. Priam is to Troy as Menelaus is to _____.

Ida	Sparta
Athens	Ithaca

5. Apollo is to sun as Artemis is to _____.

earth	stars
moon	rainbow

6. Heracles is to Hydra as Perseus is to _____.

Medusa	Minotaur
Cyclopes	Circe

Developing Skills in Critical Thinking

Classifying. There are many ways to work with the information in the legends you read. One way is to classify, or group, the legends according to their elements. For example, you might classify legends according to their settings: the sea, an island, a city. Some legends might be classified in more than one group. For example, in "The Perils of Odysseus" the settings include a cave, a whirlpool, the sea, and an island.

Review the legends you have read in this chapter. Think of three different classifications in which to group the legends. For example, you might consider three characters or forces that the hero is in conflict with. You could also use three different ways conflicts are resolved (help from gods, physical force, and human intelligence). Make a chart with a heading for each classification. Then decide which legends fit in each of the classifications. Remember that the same legend may fit in more than one group. List the titles of the legends in the classifications where they belong.

Developing Skills in Speaking and Listening

Presenting a Dialogue. A conversation between characters is called a **dialogue.** The legends in this chapter do not include a dialogue between Odysseus and Penelope after his return from his wanderings. Odysseus and

Penelope have not seen each other for twenty years. As you can imagine, they must have a great deal to say to each other.

Imagine a dialogue between Odysseus and Penelope after he has killed the suitors. Working in a small group with several other students, decide what should be included in the dialogue. Take notes as you plan what Odysseus and Penelope will say. After you assign parts and rehearse the dialogue, present it to the class.

When you read a part in the dialogue, try to express your character's feelings. Project your voice so that the audience can hear the dialogue clearly.

Developing Writing Skills

Rewriting a Legend. Legends are passed on orally from generation to generation. As they retell legends, storytellers often make changes or add new details. Choose a single adventure, or episode, from one of the legends of Odysseus that you have read. Rewrite the adventure in your own words. Add details that you think will make it more interesting, while still maintaining the basic values and themes of the original legend it came from.

Prewriting. Choose the adventure that you would like to retell. Reread this part of the legend. Make notes on the main events. Then jot down details you would like to add as you retell the episode.

Drafting. Using time order, rewrite the part of the legend that you have chosen. Use your own words, and make the changes you planned in your notes.

Revising and Sharing. Read your draft aloud to yourself to see if the episode makes sense and reads smoothly. If not, revise your version. Then get together with your classmates who have chosen adventures to retell other than the one you retold. Put your final copies together in a booklet for others to read.

Chapter 4 Review

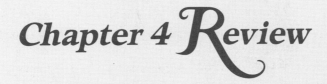

Using Your Skills in Reading Greek Myths and Legends

The following paragraphs are based on a Greek myth about a greedy king named Midas. The god Dionysus had given him the power to change all he touched to gold. Midas soon realized that he could not eat gold. What elements make this myth different from a legend?

> Dionysus felt that the greedy king had learned his lesson and took pity on him. "Go," he said, "to the river Pactolus. There wash away your fault and its punishment."
>
> Midas hurriedly made his way to the source of the river. Obeying the god, he plunged his head and body into the waters. He had scarcely touched the water before the gold-creating power passed into it. The river sands were stained gold, as they remain to this day.

Using Your Comprehension Skills

Read the following excerpt from Robert Hayden's poem "Those Winter Sundays" in Chapter Five. Then answer the questions about relationships.

> Sundays too my father got up early
> and put his clothes on in the blueblack cold,
> then with cracked hands that ached
> from labor in the weekday weather made
> banked fires blaze. No one ever thanked him.

1. What is the family relationship between the man in the poem and the speaker?

2. What does the man in the poem do for his family every morning?

3. What is his family's response to his action?

Using Your Vocabulary Skills

The following lines are from the poems in the next chapter. Tell what method you would use to find the meaning of each underlined word: word parts, context clues, word origins, or the dictionary.

1. The creatures of this star

   —"Southbound on the Freeway" by May Swenson

2. People in the restless street

   —"Faces" by Sara Teasdale

3. In the heel of my thumb
   are whorls, whirls, wheels
   in a unique design

   —"Thumbprint" by Eve Merriam

Using Your Skills in Critical Thinking

The myths and legends in this chapter include gods, monsters, and other characters. Choose any eight of these characters. Group them into two or three classifications of your choice.

Using Your Writing Skills

Complete one of the following writing assignments.

1. Several of the myths and legends in this chapter tell stories of revenge. Choose two incidents involving revenge from two different myths or legends. In two paragraphs, describe the incidents and explain why the character in each takes revenge.

2. Create your own god or goddess, and write a description of him or her in two paragraphs. Include in your description information about the physical appearance, the range of power, the character, and the behavior of your god or goddess.

CHAPTER FIVE

Poetry

Reading Literature

Poetry

Poetry is writing that is arranged in lines. Poets communicate by using all the qualities of words—sounds, meanings, and shapes. Poets also make every word count. At the same time they explore many levels of meaning in what they are writing about. These characteristics make poetry a beautiful and powerful way to share thoughts and feelings.

The History of Poetry

Poetry existed long before written language. Passed by word of mouth from generation to generation, early forms unified groups of people. Chants, songs, and prayers expressed religious beliefs. **Epics,** very long poems, preserved the events of history and celebrated heroic deeds.

Today, poems continue to express experiences, ideas, and feelings of groups of people and of individuals. Modern poets use old forms and also experiment with many new ones.

The Elements of Poetry

Shape. The **shape** of a poem is the way it looks on the page. Poems are arranged in lines, which may or may not be sentences. The lines are often grouped in **stanzas,** separated by space. The shape of a poem often emphasizes individual words and the connections between them.

Rhythm. The **rhythm** of a poem is the pattern of stressed and unstressed syllables. Rhythm brings out the musical quality of language. Rhythm also can create mood and emphasize ideas.

Rhyme. The **rhyme** is the repetition of the same sound at the ends of words—*peek* and *creak,* for example. Many traditional poems contain rhyme at the ends of lines. The pattern of such rhyme is called the **rhyme scheme.**

Speaker. The **speaker** is the voice that "talks" to the reader. The speaker is not always the same as the poet, even in a poem that uses *I* and *me.* In one poem in this chapter, the speaker is a child. In another, the speaker is a space alien observing Earth.

Theme. The **theme** of a poem is the message about life or human nature that is shared with the reader. For example, a poem might point out that there can be hidden beauty in ordinary objects.

Mood. The **mood** of a poem is the feeling that it creates in the reader. For example, the mood can be sad, joyful, angry, or tender.

How to Read a Poem

1. Let yourself get involved in the poem. Try to see, hear, smell, taste, and feel what is described.
2. Read the poem aloud to hear its sounds. Often the sounds of a poem bring out its meaning.
3. Make sure that you understand every word in the poem. Pay special attention to how the words work together.
4. Identify the speaker and the subject. What does the speaker say about the subject?
5. Identify the theme of the poem. Try to express the theme in your own words.

Comprehension Skills

Figurative Language

Figurative language is language in which words communicate ideas beyond the exact meanings of those words. Figurative language is different from **literal language,** which uses only the ordinary meanings of words. For example, "It was raining cats and dogs" is a figurative statement. Its meaning has nothing to do with animals. A literal statement that expresses the same idea is "It was raining extremely hard."

Figurative language links ideas in fresh, often surprising ways. Figurative language also can arouse emotions because of the connotations, or feelings, surrounding words. For example, one poem in this chapter is called "Song of the Truck." By referring to road noises as music, the poet conveys a happy, enthusiastic feeling. (Specific types of figurative language, called figures of speech, are discussed in Chapter Two, How Writers Write, as well as later in this chapter.)

Recognizing Figurative Language

To grasp the full meaning of poetry, you must be able to recognize and interpret figurative language. Read the following line from "Those Winter Sundays" by Robert Hayden.

I'd wake and hear the cold splintering, breaking.

The poet is not using literal language. He doesn't mean that the cold can splinter and break. Rather, he is using figurative language to create a sense of cold.

Read this description of wind blowing through trees.

A line of elms plunging and tossing like horses
—Theodore Roethke, "Child on Top of a Greenhouse"

Notice how the comparison of the wind-blown trees to wild horses creates a vivid picture and conveys feelings of excitement.

Exercises: Understanding Figurative Language

A. Read these lines from poems in this chapter. Following each line are two sentences. Identify which sentence states the literal meaning and which the figurative meaning of the line of poetry. Which meaning fits the line best?

1. I hear America singing, the varied carols I hear.
   —Walt Whitman, "I Hear America Singing"
   a. You must look at leaves closely, noticing every detail about them.
   b. You should be quiet and crawl in between the leaves.

2. You must enter in
   To the small silences between
   The leaves.   —John Moffitt, "To Look at Any Thing"
   a. I am aware of all the people and activities that make America special.
   b. I am listening to Americans singing carols.

B. Read these lines from poems in this chapter. Then tell in your own words what the figurative language in each means.

1. in seeking the universe/with the eyes of another
   —Marcel Proust, "Discovery"
2. each spring the gold young corn/gives us life
   —Aztec, "Song of a Dream"
3. For when dreams go/Life is a barren field
   —Langston Hughes, "Dreams"

Vocabulary Skills

Origins of English Words

Why is the word *land* used in English to describe the solid part of the earth's surface? Why isn't the word *glemp* or *dorf?* Where do English words come from?

Words have become part of the language in several ways. For example, some words are borrowed from other languages and some come from sounds. In this chapter you will study the ways words become part of English.

Beginnings of English

The English language developed in what is now the country of England. The original settlers of the area spoke a language called Celtic, but few Celtic words remain in English. For more than a thousand years the land was invaded by people from all parts of Europe. The Romans invaded first in 55 B.C. Then in A.D. 449, Germanic tribes known as Angles, Jutes, and Saxons began to take over. Later there were invasions by the Vikings and finally by the French, in A.D. 1066.

The languages of all these groups of people contributed to the development of English. The language of the Angles, Jutes, and Saxons replaced Celtic and became the basis of English. Some Latin words came from the early Roman occupation, and many more Latin words came into the language from the spread of Christianity to England. The Viking and especially the French invasions brought further additions and changes. What we call modern English was in use about A.D. 1500. New words continue to enter the language.

Types of Word Origins

Borrowed Words. As mentioned earlier, English words have been borrowed from many other languages. Here are four examples.

Latin—candle	Spanish—plaza
Arabic—algebra	African—gumbo

Words from Names. A new word may be based on the name of a person or place. For example, *pasteurize* comes from the name of the scientist, Louis Pasteur, who invented pasteurization.

Clipped Words. Some new words are shortened forms of existing words. *Phone,* for instance, was clipped from *telephone.*

Combined Words. Words may be put together from two existing words or word parts. *Safeguard* is a compound combining two words. *Retell* combines the Latin prefix *re-,* meaning "again," with *tell.*

Words from Sounds. Words can come from sounds. Such words are called **echoic words.** Examples include *lull, chirp, squeak,* and *hush.*

Exercises: Recognizing Word Origins

A. Figure out the meaning of each underlined word below. (Mars was the roman god of war. The Titans were a race of giants.)

1. The earthquake caused a <u>titanic</u> landslide.
2. The country was ruled by <u>martial</u> law during the uprising.

B. The following words were added to English in five ways. Identify the origin of each word: *Borrowed Words, Words from Names, Combined Words, Clipped Words,* and *Words from Sounds.* Use the clues that you see and hear in the words or use a dictionary.

howl	fan	roadhog
crepe	zeppelin	ad

Observations

Have you ever looked at a thread under a microscope? Have you ever seen a street from the top of a building or from an airplane? If you have, you know that familiar objects can look strange and new. Poetry can also give you a new perspective, a different way of seeing. In the poems in this section, you will discover that such things as everyday work, cars on the highway, and the stem of a plant are much more than they seem.

Urban Freeways, 1981, WAYNE THIEBAUD. Private Collection. Photograph: Allan Stone Gallery, New York City.

Discovery

MARCEL PROUST

Some discoveries are of new lands or even of new stars. How is the discovery in this poem different?

The real voyage of discovery
   consists not in seeking new landscapes,
    but in having new eyes,
     in seeing the universe
      with the eyes of another,   5
      of a hundred others,
    in seeing the hundred universes
     that each of them sees.

Marcel Proust (*1871–1922*) was born in Anteuil, France. He spent most of his life in Paris. After earning a university degree in 1895, he began writing short stories for magazines. From 1908 to the end of his life, he devoted himself to writing his great novel. The seven-volume masterpiece, *Remembrance of Things Past,* explores the idea that reality is no more than each individual's perception of it. The novel is one of the most important works of the twentieth century.

Developing Comprehension Skills

1. According to this poem, what kind of eyes does a person need for the real voyage of discovery?

2. What meanings does the word *universe* have in the poem? the word *seeing*?

3. Does the poem ask the reader to make a literal or a figurative journey? Explain your answer.

4. In order to grow as a human being, a person must be open to many ways of looking at life. How does the poet emphasize this idea in lines 6 and 7 of this poem?

5. What is the "real voyage of discovery," according to the poem? Do you agree that it is a worthwhile voyage?

Reading Literature: Poetry

1. **Examining Shape.** If a poem has an unusual shape, the poet has a reason for it. The first six lines of this poem slope to the right, and then the seventh line abruptly switches back to the left. How does the shape of the first six lines suggest a journey? How does the position of the last two lines connect them to the beginning of the poem? (Think about how lines 7 and 8 explain the meaning of the "real voyage of discovery" in line 1.)

2. **Understanding Theme.** In poetry, as in stories, **theme** is the writer's message about life. The theme of this poem is about discovery. Usually, when you think of discovery, you think of finding a new place or learning a new fact. What kind of inner journey is the poem about? State your idea as the theme of the poem.

3. **Identifying Repetition.** A poet may repeat a word or phrase to emphasize it. What words are repeated in this poem? Why are they emphasized?

I Hear America Singing

WALT WHITMAN

This poem is about ordinary people in their daily work. What feelings about America and its people does the poem express?

I hear America singing, the varied carols I hear,
Those of mechanics, each one singing his as it should be blithe
    and strong,
The carpenter singing his as he measures his plank or beam,
The mason singing his as he makes ready for work, or leaves off
    work,
The boatman singing what belongs to him in his boat, the
    deckhand singing on the steamboat deck,   5
The shoemaker singing as he sits on his bench, the hatter singing as
    he stands,
The wood-cutter's song, the ploughboy's on his way in the
    morning, or at noon intermission or at sundown,
The delicious singing of the mother, or of the young wife at work,
    or of the girl sewing or washing,
Each singing what belongs to him or her and to none else,
The day what belongs to the day—at night the party of young
    fellows, robust, friendly   10
Singing with open mouths their strong melodious songs.

Susan Comforting the Baby (No. 1), about 1881, MARY CASSATT. Columbus Museum of Art, Ohio, Bequest of Frederick W. Schumacher.

Developing Comprehension Skills

1. Name the kinds of workers mentioned in the poem.

2. Most of the people in the poem are not singing actual songs. What does it mean for them to be singing? What figurative meanings does *singing* have in the poem?

3. The title of the poem "I Hear America Singing" suggests that the workers in the poem represent the American people. What ideas does this poem convey about Americans?

4. The speaker says that each of the workers is singing "what belongs to him or her and to none else." What does this line emphasize about each worker?

5. This poem was written during the middle of the nineteenth century. Does the strong, vibrant spirit of the poem apply to the American people today? Explain your answer.

Reading Literature: Poetry

1. **Identifying Rhythm.** This poem is an example of **free verse,** which is poetry written without a regular pattern of rhythm or rhyme. The poem does have rhythm, though, because of its repetition of words and phrases. Give two examples of repeti-

tions that help to create rhythm in the poem.

2. **Recognizing Mood. Mood** is the feeling created in the reader by a literary work. The mood of this poem is cheerful and hopeful. What words help to create this mood?

3. **Understanding the Speaker.** The **speaker** of a poem is the voice that "talks" to the reader. The speaker of this poem is identified as *I*. What can you tell about the speaker's attitudes? Do you have feelings about America that are similar to the speaker's? Explain your answer.

Walt Whitman *(1819–1892)* had to pay for the printing of his first book of poetry. Publishers were not interested in the new free form and rhymeless style of the poems. Later, however, the book *Leaves of Grass* brought Whitman the recognition he deserved. It is considered by some to be the greatest single book of American poetry. During the Civil War, Whitman volunteered to nurse wounded soldiers. That experience inspired some of his finest poetry.

Song of the Truck

DORIS FRANKEL

This poem appeals to the sense of hearing. It creates a feeling of motion. As you read it, think of what makes the "song" the speaker describes.

This is the song that the truck drivers hear
In the grinding of brake and the shifting of gear,
From the noise of the wheel and the clarion horn,
From the freight and the weight—
          a song has been born: 5
Mohair and cotton and textiles and silk,
Chickens and onions and apples and milk,
Rubber and clothing and coffee and tires,
Harness and hay and molasses and wires,
Petroleum, vinegar, furniture, eggs,   10
Race horses, stoves, and containers and kegs,
Chemicals, cantaloupes, canned goods and seeds—
Song of the cargo America needs!
Song of the wheels in the well-traveled grooves—
Coastline to coastline—   15
          America moves!

Developing Comprehension Skills

1. The speaker names four sounds that truck drivers actually hear. What are they?

2. A song is usually associated with a positive feeling. How is this poem like a song?

3. "I Hear America Singing" and "Song of the Truck" both describe American life in terms of songs. How is the attitude toward America in the two poems similar?

4. The poem ends with the lines "Coastline to coastline—/America moves!" What is the literal meaning of these words? What is the figurative meaning?

5. Do you think the feeling about American life in this poem gives a true picture of what America is like? Explain your answer.

Freeway, 1966, VIJA CELMINS. Collection of Harold Cook, New York City. David McKee Gallery. Photograph by James Dee.

Reading Literature: Poetry

1. **Recognizing a Rhyme Scheme.** This poem is the first in this chapter that has rhyme. **Rhyme,** as you know, is the repetition of sounds at the ends of words, as in *true* and *blue.* When you look at the pattern of end rhyme in a poem, you look at the words at the ends of the lines. The pattern of end rhyme in a poem is called its **rhyme scheme.** To chart the rhyme scheme of a poem, use a different letter of the alphabet to stand for each rhyming sound. Here is an example from the poem.

> This is the song that the truck
>   drivers hear   *a*
> In the grinding of brake and the
>   shifting of gear,   *a*
> From the noise of the wheel and the
>   clarion horn,   *b*
> From the freight and the weight—   *c*
>   a song has been born.   *b*

On a sheet of paper, write out the rest of the poem. Write the rhyme scheme. Where are there repeated patterns?

2. **Examining Rhythm.** The pattern of rhythm in most lines of this poem is made up of one stressed syllable followed by two unstressed syllables with one stressed syllable at the end of the line. The first line is an example.

> This is the song that the truck drivers
>   hear.

How does this strong, regular rhythm sound like a moving truck? Does the rhythm also make the poem like a song? Explain.

3. **Understanding Mood.** In this poem the poet repeats the words *America* and *song.* She also uses exclamation points. These words and punctuation marks help to create a mood. What feelings are created by the poem?

Southbound on the Freeway

MAY SWENSON

In this poem an unusual visitor gives a different viewpoint on a familiar scene. Try to identify all the details that are described.

A tourist came in from Orbitville,
parked in the air, and said:

The creatures of this star
are made of metal and glass.

Through the transparent parts   5
you can see their guts.

Their feet are round and roll
on diagrams—or long

measuring tapes—dark
with white lines.   10

They have four eyes.
The two in the back are red.

Sometimes you can see a five-eyed
one, with a red eye turning

on the top of his head.   15
He must be special—

the others respect him
and go slow

when he passes, winding
among them from behind.   20

They all hiss as they glide,
like inches, down the marked

tapes. Those soft shapes,
shadowy inside

the hard bodies—are they   25
their guts or their brains?

May Swenson (*born 1919*) grew up and attended school in Utah. She taught at Purdue University where she later served as a Poet-in-Residence. Swenson's poems often are unusual shapes. She wants her readers to enjoy the sight as well as the sound of her poetry. Two of her well-known collections of poems are *A Cage of Spines* and *Half Sun Half Asleep*.

© Layle Silbert

Developing Comprehension Skills

1. Where is the tourist from? Where does this visitor park?

2. What does the visitor think he or she is seeing? What is the visitor actually seeing?

3. Explain what these phrases refer to:
   a. "diagrams—or long/measuring tapes"
   b. "four eyes"
   c. "a five-eyed/one"
   d. "their brains"

4. Do you think this poem is funny, serious, or both? Explain your answer.

Reading Literature: Poetry

1. **Understanding Theme.** As you know, **theme** is the writer's message about life. What does this poem say about the relationship between people and the "metal creatures"?

2. **Identifying Humor.** Part of the enjoyment of this poem comes from its humor. The humor results from the reader being aware of more than the tourist is. For instance, what is the tourist's view of a police car? What is the reader's view? Give two other examples of humor from the poem.

3. **Examining Stanzas.** A **stanza** is a group of lines in a poem. This poem has a regular pattern of stanzas. How many lines make up each stanza? Which stanzas contain complete sentences?

Developing Vocabulary Skills

Recognizing Borrowed Words. Many of the words in the four poems you have read so far are borrowed from other languages. Match the correct word from the poems with each word history described below.

voyage	textile	furniture
blithe	coffee	cantaloupe
plank	molasses	tourist
mohair		

1. This word came from the French word *fourniture*. It means "movable articles in a house."

2. This word came from the Latin word *textilis,* which means "woven."

3. This word came from the Indo-European base *bhlei-,* which means "to shine, gleam."

4. This word for a popular beverage was taken from the Turkish *kahve.* In turn, *kahve* came from the Arabic *qahwa.*

5. The origin of this word is the Greek word *phalanx,* which originally meant a "log."

6. This word for a summer fruit came from *Cantalupo,* an estate in Italy where the fruit was first grown in Europe.

7. This word came from the Old French word *torner,* meaning "to turn."

8. This word goes back to the Latin word *viaticum,* which means "provision for a journey."

9. This name for a kind of syrup came from the Portuguese word *melaco. Melaco* was based on the Latin word *mel,* for honey.

10. This name for a type of fabric was borrowed from an Arabic word, *mukhayyar.*

Developing Skills in Critical Thinking

Recognizing Faulty Logic. In "Southbound on the Freeway," the visitor from outer space makes some correct observations. For example, the objects the visitor sees really are made of metal and glass, and they do roll. However, the visitor also makes some faulty assumptions. When combining the correct observations with these faulty assumptions, the visitor jumps to illogical conclusions.

The following are several assumptions that the visitor makes. What is wrong with the logic of each one? Where in the poem does the visitor make each of these assumptions?

1. If something moves, it is alive.

2. If something cannot be seen clearly, it is unimportant.

3. If two things are alike in one way, they are the same.

What illogical conclusion does each of these assumptions lead to?

Developing Skills in Speaking and Listening

Interpreting a Poem Orally. Work with three classmates. Each student should choose a different poem from the four you have read so far in this chapter. Have each group member prepare a poem and read it for the rest of the group. Here are some suggestions for preparing, reading, and listening to these poems.

Choosing the Poem. Three of the poems in this section use a conversational rhythm. Those poems are "Discovery," "I Hear America Singing," and "Southbound on the Freeway." When you read these poems aloud, pause where there are commas, periods, or other breaks in the ideas. Do not automatically pause at the end of each line. Think about the meaning of the words as you read them. Then put stress on the words that are most important.

The fourth poem, "Song of the Truck," has strong, regular rhythm. In addition, it includes a list of items. To avoid reading the poem in a singsong, or monotonous, way, you must make some choices. Which words in the first four lines and the last four lines are more important and deserve more stress? Which words in the list do you want to emphasize? Which parts of the list should move faster? Which should move more slowly?

Preparing the Poem. After you have chosen a poem, read it aloud to yourself at least twice. Put stress on the important words. Pause where a pause makes sense. Listen to yourself, both for the meaning of the words and for the sounds. Make sure that you are pronouncing every word correctly. Make sure that you are not reading too quickly and blurring words.

Presenting the Poem. When you read the poem to your group, try to keep in mind the things you have practiced. Also try to make your voice loud enough for everyone in the group to hear.

Listening to a Poem. When you are listening to another member of the group read a poem, keep your book closed. Concentrate on what the reader is saying. Be able to tell the reader whether you could understand the words and the ideas. Let the reader know whether his or her voice was at the right speed and volume.

Developing Writing Skills

1. **Explaining an Idea.** The poem "Discovery" encourages you to develop "new eyes" and to see the world and people differently. Choose one of the poems you have read so far. In one paragraph, explain how it helps you to look at some part of life with "new eyes."

   Prewriting. Reread the poem you have chosen. Make a chart listing words and phrases in the poem that help you to see something familiar with "new eyes." Next to each word or phrase on the chart, write what it is describing or referring to. Then note how the word or phrase helps you to see a familiar person, experience, place, or object in a new way.

   Drafting. Write a topic sentence naming the poem and explaining that the poem lets you see in a new way. Then tell how. Use details from your chart to support your ideas.

   Revising and Sharing. Read your paragraph aloud and work on stating your ideas as clearly as possible. Ask someone who has not read the poem to read your paragraph. Have the person tell you what is good about the paragraph and what could be improved. Revise your draft and make a final copy.

2. **Describing an Activity.** "Southbound on the Freeway" shows how a visitor from space might see a common modern activity. Write your own poem or paragraph from a space visitor's viewpoint. Show how the visitor might see some other activity, such as going to the laundromat or going to a dance. Be sure to present the visitor's viewpoint consistently throughout. Use the steps of the process of writing: prewriting, drafting, revising, and sharing. For more help, see the Guidelines for the Process of Writing, beginning on page 654 of the handbook.

To Look at Any Thing

JOHN MOFFITT

This poem is about a way of seeing the world. What does the speaker mean by "you must be the thing you see"?

The Great Piece of Turf, 1503, ALBRECHT DÜRER.
Graphische Sammlung Albertina, Vienna.

To look at any thing,
If you would know that thing,
You must look at it long:
To look at this green and say
'I have seen spring in these   5
Woods,' will not do—you must
Be the thing you see:
You must be the dark snakes of
Stems and ferny plumes of leaves,
You must enter in   10
To the small silences between
The leaves,
You must take your time
And touch the very peace
They issue from.   15

John Moffitt *(1908–1987)* had different careers in his life. After being a social worker, he became a monk. Later he was a copyeditor and then the poetry editor for the magazine *America.* During all of this time, Moffitt wrote poetry and published several collections. Poetry, he said, was something that just flowed from him, something he could not help but write. He was also interested in watercolor painting, gardening, and music.

Developing Comprehension Skills

1. What word is repeated three times in lines 1–4?

2. The speaker suggests that there is more than one way of looking. What is the literal meaning of *looking?* What does the speaker mean by looking at a thing "long"?

3. The speaker describes stems and leaves as "the dark snakes of/Stems and ferny plumes of leaves." What picture do you form in your mind when you read these lines?

4. Do you think that the speaker's advice to "be the thing you see" is easy to practice? How can you "be the thing you see"? Give some examples from everyday life of when you could "be" a thing.

Reading Literature: Poetry

1. **Understanding the Speaker.** Notice what the speaker of this poem chooses to describe. What can you tell about the speaker's relationship with nature?

2. **Explaining the Theme.** As you know, **theme** is the poet's message about life. This

poem, as you have explained in answering the previous questions, describes a deeper way of seeing. What is the theme of the poem?

3. **Recognizing Repetition.** By repeating words, a poet can emphasize an idea. The phrases "to look" and "you must be" are repeated in this poem. How do these phrases relate to the theme of the poem?

4. **Identifying Mood.** As you have learned, **mood** is the feeling that a poem creates. What is the mood of this poem? List words and phrases that help to create this mood.

5. **Analyzing Word Choice.** Poetry is a compact way of expressing ideas. A poet, therefore, chooses words that have the precise meanings that are needed. A poet may also use a word because of its sound. Reread the poem and think about the following words. What does each one mean in the poem? What sounds in the two words are similar?

   silences   (line 11)
   issue   (line 15)

Fueled

MARCIE HANS

This poem takes a look at two events that seem to be very unlike one another. The poet, however, finds similarities between them. As you read, look for comparisons and contrasts.

Fueled
by a million
man-made
wings of fire—
the rocket tore a tunnel   5
through the sky—
and everybody cheered.
Fueled
only by a thought from God—
the seedling   10
urged its way
through the thickness of black—
and as it pierced
the heavy ceiling of the soil—
and launched itself   15
up into outer space—
no
one
even
clapped.   20

Baby Carrot Top, 1974, WALTER CHAPPELL.
© Walter Chappell, El Rito, New Mexico.

Developing Comprehension Skills

1. What two things does this poem compare?

2. What two events does the poem compare? How do people react to each event?

3. The speaker says that a rocket is fueled "by a million/man-made/wings of fire." What is the speaker describing with this figurative language?

4. Reread the last four lines of the poem. Does the speaker literally want people to clap? In what figurative way could people applaud the event?

5. What criticism is the speaker making of people's attitude toward nature? Do you agree with the speaker's criticism?

Reading Literature: Poetry

1. **Understanding Structure.** This poem is written as one stanza, with no break between lines. However, the ideas in the poem are presented in two sentences. What word alerts the reader to the beginning of the second sentence? How is this word emphasized? What new idea is introduced in this sentence?

2. **Recognizing Rhythm.** Each of the sentences in the poem describes an action. Notice that the rhythms in the second sentence are slower than those in the first. How does the slower pace match the action being described in the second sentence? Note that each of the last four lines is a single word. How does this structure slow down the lines? What do these last lines emphasize?

3. **Evaluating Word Choice.** The poet uses precise and imaginative words to create vivid pictures in the reader's mind. For example, the phrase "pierced/the heavy ceiling" creates a clear picture of a tiny seedling laboring to push up through dense earth. Find two other examples of effective word choice. What kind of picture does each example create?

Unfolding Bud

NAOSHI KORIYAMA

The speaker in this poem compares a flower bud and a poem. How does looking at a bud help you understand a poem?

Pink Lily with Dragonfly, 1981, JOSEPH RAFFAEL.
Photograph: Van Stratten Gallery, Chicago.

One is amazed
By a water-lily bud
Unfolding
With each passing day,
Taking on a richer color   5
And new dimensions.

One is not amazed,
At a first glance,
By a poem,
Which is as tight-closed   10
As a tiny bud.

Yet one is surprised
To see the poem
Gradually unfolding,
Revealing its rich inner self,   15
As one reads it
Again
And over again.

Naoshi Koriyama (*born 1926*) is a professor of English literature in Japan. Although his native language is Japanese, he set himself the challenge of composing his poetry in English. His works can be found in anthologies, textbooks, and magazines. Koriyama was born on Kikai Island in Japan. He attended college in Japan and also received a degree from the New York State College for Teachers in Albany, New York.

Developing Comprehension Skills

1. What amazes the speaker? What surprises the speaker?

2. How does a water-lily bud take on "richer color" and "new dimensions"?

3. The words *tight-closed* and *unfolding* refer to both the flower and the poem. Are the words used literally or figuratively to refer to the flower? to refer to the poem? Explain.

4. What causes a poem to "gradually unfold"?

5. What advice do you think the speaker would give you about how to read a poem? How do you think the comparison in this poem will affect the way you read poems in the future?

Reading Literature: Poetry

1. **Understanding Theme.** A poem's message is its **theme.** In this poem, the poet is concerned about what poetry is. What general statement does he make about the subject? State the theme in your own words.

2. **Recognizing Structure.** A poet can create structure in a poem in several ways. One way is through repetition, such as the repetition of the word *singing* in "I Hear America Singing." Another way is through rhyme, as in "Song of the Truck." A third way is through the use of stanzas. The stanzas may be all the same length or of different lengths.

The writer of "Unfolding Bud" uses two of these ways of structuring a poem. Which two does he use? Point out where each is used in the poem. How do these elements of structure help to organize the ideas?

3. **Identifying Rhythm.** Rhythm refers not only to the stressed and unstressed syllables of a line but also to the pace of a poem. Is this poem fast-paced or slow-paced? How does the rhythm fit with the theme?

Developing Vocabulary Skills

Identifying Types of Compound Words. A new word can be created through the combining of two words to form compound words. Some compounds, called **closed compounds,** are written without any break between the two words that have been combined. Examples are *sundown* and *headphone.* Other compounds, such as *full-scale,* are written with a hyphen. Still other compounds, called **open compounds,** are written as if they are separate words. Examples are *steam shovel* and *bass drum.* Often the only way you can be sure of the correct spelling of a compound is by checking a dictionary.

Write the compounds that are described below.

1. In "Fueled," find the closed compounds.

2. In "Fueled" and "Unfolding Bud," find three compounds written with hyphens.

3. In "Fueled," find two open compounds.

Developing Skills in Critical Thinking

Comparing and Contrasting. One way to understand a poem better is to compare and contrast it with other poems. Reread the last three poems in this section. Make a chart in which you list the similarities and differences in the poems. Consider elements such as rhythm, rhyme, theme, metaphor, alliteration, and so on. Review the chart when you have finished to see in what ways the poems are similar and in what ways they are different.

Developing Writing Skills

1. **Comparing Development of Theme.** In "To Look at Any Thing," "Fueled," and "Unfolding Bud," the poets use nature to develop their ideas. Choose any two of these poems. In one paragraph, compare the use of nature to express theme.

   Prewriting. Choose two poems. Make a chart for each poem. Use these headings: Details of Nature and Relationship of Nature to Theme. After you fill in the charts, note the similarities between the poems.

   Drafting. Write a topic sentence stating the general similarity in the use of nature in the two poems. Use details from your chart to help you explain how both poets use nature to develop their themes.

   Revising and Sharing. Reread your paragraph. If necessary, make sentences clearer and more direct. Be sure that you have in-

cluded specific details from the poems. After a classmate reads your paragraph, ask if any sentences are confusing or vague. Make any necessary changes on your draft. Write out a final copy.

2. **Using Your Senses.** In "To Look at Any Thing," the speaker advises you to look at a thing long and to "be" the thing you see. Choose one object that you can look at and touch. Examine the object closely. Then in one paragraph write a description of it. Use details that appeal to the senses of sight, hearing, and touch. If possible, include details that appeal to smell and taste as well. Your description should be clear and detailed so that your reader can "be" the thing you describe. As you write, use the process of writing: prewriting, drafting, revising, and sharing. For more help, see the Guidelines to the Process of Writing beginning on page 654 in the handbook.

Relationships

In the poems in this section, the events that stand out are encounters with people. These poems explore different types of relationships and the feelings, such as regret or pride, that these relationships create. See if you have ever had the same feelings that these poets describe.

Ada and Vincent in the Car, 1972, ALEX KATZ. Joseph Hirshhorn Foundation. Photograph: Marlborough Gallery, Inc., New York City.

Reading Literature

More About Poetry

You know that poets choose words for meaning, feeling, and sound. Poets also put words together in interesting ways. In this section you will learn about several ways poets use words: sensory images, figures of speech, and sounds of language such as alliteration and assonance.

Sensory Images

Sensory images are words and phrases that appeal to the five senses. The senses are sight, hearing, touch, taste, and smell. "The juicy, sweet apple," for example, is an image that appeals to the senses of taste and sight. "Smooth, soft feathers" appeals to the senses of sight and touch. "Freshly baked bread" appeals to the senses of sight, smell, and taste. Sensory images help readers to experience the subject of a poem.

Here are a few sensory images from the poems you have read:

a red eye turning *(sight)*
> —May Swenson, "Southbound on the Freeway"

Chickens and onions and apples and milk *(hearing, sight, smell, and taste)* —Doris Frankel, "Song of the Truck"

grinding of brake *(hearing)* —Doris Frankel, "Song of the Truck"

through the thickness of black *(sight, touch)* —Marcie Hans, "Fueled"

Figures of Speech

As you know, **figures of speech** use ordinary words in unusual ways. The four most common figures of speech are simile, metaphor, personification, and hyperbole.

A **simile** is a comparison between unlike things using *like* or *as*.

> a poem,/Which is as tight-closed/As a tiny bud.
>> —Naoshi Koriyama, "Unfolding Bud"

A **metaphor** is a comparison between unlike things that does not use *like* or *as*.

> the heavy ceiling of the soil
>> —Marcie Hans, "Fueled"

Personification is the giving of human qualities to an object, animal, or idea.

> I hear America singing
>> —Walt Whitman, "I Hear America Singing"

Hyperbole is exaggeration for emphasis.

> the hundred universes/that each of them sees.
>> —Marcel Proust, "Discovery"

Sounds of Language

You know that poets consider the sounds of words when they are writing. Three important techniques of sound are alliteration, assonance, and onomatopoeia. **Alliteration** is the repetition of the same consonant sound at the beginnings of words.

> Chemicals, cantaloupes, canned goods and seeds—
>> —Doris Frankel, "Song of the Truck"

Assonance is the repetition of the same vowel sound within words.

> Singing with open mouths, their strong melodious songs
>> —Walt Whitman, "I Hear America Singing"

Onomatopoeia is the use of words that sound like what they mean.

> they all hiss as they glide
>> —May Swenson, "Southbound on the Freeway"

Faces

SARA TEASDALE

Have you ever wondered about the lives of people you see on the street? Read to find out what this speaker finds in the faces of strangers.

People that I meet and pass
   In the city's broken roar,
Faces that I lose so soon
   And have never found before,

Do you know how much you tell   5
   In the meeting of our eyes,
How ashamed I am, and sad
   To have pierced your poor disguise?

Secrets rushing without sound
   Crying from your hiding places—   10
Let me go, I cannot bear
   The sorrow of the passing faces.

—People in the restless street,
   Can it be, oh can it be
In the meeting of our eyes   15
   That you know as much of me?

Office Girls, 1936, RAPHAEL SOYER. Oil, 26″ x 24″. Collection of Whitney Museum of American Art, New York City, Purchase.

Sara Teasdale *(1884–1933),* a native of St. Louis, Missouri, was a shy, imaginative young woman. After she finished her formal education, she traveled all over the world. Teasdale's poetry often tells her personal feelings about love. She won a Pulitzer Prize for *Love Songs* in 1918. Other well-known works are *Rivers to the Sea* and *Strange Victories.* She lived much of her later life in semi-seclusion.

Developing Comprehension Skills

1. Where are the faces that the speaker sees?

2. The speaker refers to "Faces that I lose so soon." How does the speaker "lose" the faces?

3. What are the disguises that the strangers wear? Are the disguises literal or figurative ones?

4. The speaker tries to understand the people behind the faces passing in the street. What does the speaker think the strangers need to disguise?

5. What do you see in the faces of people that you pass in the street? Are your reactions similar to or different from those of the speaker in the poem? Explain.

Reading Literature: Poetry

1. **Examining Rhyme Scheme.** This poem has a regular rhyme scheme. Using letters of the alphabet, show the rhyme scheme for the entire poem.

2. **Understanding Sensory Images.** As you have learned, **sensory images** are words and phrases that appeal to the senses. The sensory images in a poem can help to describe things and also to convey the feeling of the poem. An example of imagery in this poem is "the city's broken roar." This image helps you to imagine the sound of a big-city crowd and to sense the sad feeling of the poem. Find two other examples of sensory images in the poem. Tell which of the five senses each image appeals to and what feeling the image helps to create.

3. **Identifying Assonance.** You have learned that **assonance** is the repetition of a vowel sound within words. An example of assonance is the repetition of the *i* sound in "Crying from your hiding." Another is the repetition of the *e* sound in "People that I meet." What are two other examples of assonance in the poem? What ideas does the assonance emphasize?

Eviction

LUCILLE CLIFTON

The speaker is looking back and remembering an earlier time. What is the speaker aware of as a child? as an adult?

What I remember about that day
is boxes stacked across the walk
and couch springs curling through the air
and drawers and tables balanced on the curb
and us, hollering,   5
leaping up and around
happy to have a playground;

nothing about the emptied rooms
nothing about the emptied family

Window of a Deserted House, 1917. CHARLES
BURCHFIELD. Private Collection, Photograph: Kennedy
Galleries, New York City.

© Layle Silbert

Lucille Clifton (*born 1936*) grew up in New York and attended Howard University and Fredonia State Teachers College. She is the author of several collections of poetry, including *Good Times* and *An Ordinary Woman*. Clifton writes with warmth and humor about the vitality of black life. She won the 1974 Emmy Award for co-authoring a television program, *Free to Be You and Me*.

Developing Comprehension Skills

1. What is stacked on the sidewalk? What is balanced on the curb?

2. What is the "playground" that the speaker mentions?

3. About how old is the speaker at the time of the event? How can you tell?

4. Reread the last two lines of the poem. What do "the emptied rooms" refer to? What does "the emptied family" refer to?

5. As a child the speaker is not aware of the "emptied rooms" and the "emptied family." As an adult the speaker does remember, however. How is a child's awareness different from an adult's?

Reading Literature: Poetry

1. **Examining Form.** This poem has two stanzas. Which stanza gives the child's memories? Which one gives the adult's understanding? The poet also repeats words in the second stanza. What are these words? What idea do they emphasize?

2. **Understanding Sensory Images.** Images give the reader a picture of what a poet is describing. They also convey feelings. In this poem, for example, the poet uses the image "couch springs curling through the air." You can picture a beat-up old couch with holes and exposed coils. However, the words "curling through the air" also suggest a happy feeling. Find at least two other images in this poem. What do these images communicate to you?

The Song of a Dream

AZTEC

This poem tells what was important to the Aztec people. As you read, think about what is important to you.

Now, my friends, please hear:
it is the song of a dream:
each spring the gold young corn
gives us life;
the ripened corn gives us refreshment;   5
to know that the hearts of our friends
are true is to put around us
a necklace of precious stones.

The Goddess Chicomecatl, 15th century. Volcanic stone. The Brooklyn Museum, New York City, A. Augustus Healy Fund.

Developing Comprehension Skills

1. Whom does the speaker address?

2. The speaker says that "each spring the gold young corn/gives us life." How can young corn give life?

3. This poem does not have a single author, but is a poem of the Aztec people. According to this poem, what aspects of life do you think were most important to the Aztecs?

4. What is most important in your life? How, are your values similar to or different from those of the Aztecs?

Reading Literature: Poetry

1. **Understanding Metaphor.** A **metaphor** is a comparison between two unlike things. A metaphor does not use the words *like* or *as*. In the last three lines of this poem, friends are compared to precious stones. How are they alike? What is being said in this metaphor?

2. **Analyzing Mood.** **Mood** is the feeling that a poem creates in the reader. Describe the mood of "The Song of a Dream." Find three words and phrases that help to create this mood.

The Story-Teller

MARK VAN DOREN

A talented story-teller makes an audience feel part of the action. How good is the story-teller in this poem? He is so good that . . . .

He talked, and as he talked
Wallpaper came alive;
Suddenly ghosts walked,
And four doors were five;

Calendars ran backward,   5
And maps had mouths;
Ships went tackward
In a great drowse;

Trains climbed trees
And soon dripped down   10
Like honey of bees
On the cold brick town.

He had wakened a worm
In the world's brain,
And nothing stood firm   15
Until day again.

Mark Van Doren *(1894–1972)* was from Illinois. A graduate of the University of Illinois and of Columbia University, Van Doren was the editor of the *Nation* magazine and helped found the Great Books organization. His best-known works include poetry, fiction, essays, and biographies.

Disintegration of the Persistence of Memory, 1952–54, SALVADOR DALI. Oil on canvas. The Salvador Dali Museum, St. Petersburg, Florida.

Developing Comprehension Skills

1. List at least five things that happen when the story-teller talks.

2. The poet uses many unusual happenings to suggest the power of the story-teller. Is the meaning of statements such as "Wallpaper came alive" and "Calendars ran backward" literal or figurative? Explain.

3. What kinds of stories does this story-teller tell? Give a reason for your answer.

4. The last lines say that "nothing stood firm/ Until day again." What can you infer about when the story-telling takes place? Why is this time appropriate for story-telling?

5. A good story-teller can seem to make the impossible happen. Does the story-teller in

this poem make the impossible seem real? Explain.

6. In your opinion, what makes a good story-teller? Give reasons for your answers.

Reading Literature: Poetry

1. **Charting Rhyme Scheme.** Write the rhyme scheme for all four stanzas of this poem. Does each stanza show a different pattern or the same pattern? How does the pattern of the rhyme scheme contrast with the events being described in the poem?

2. **Recognizing Alliteration and Assonance.** Alliteration and assonance help to create musical effects in poetry. As you have learned, **alliteration** is the repetition of a consonant sound at the beginnings of words. **Assonance** is the repetition of a vowel sound within words. The phrase "maps had mouths," for example, contains both alliteration (the *m* sound) and assonance (the *a* sound). Find three other examples of alliteration, assonance, or a combination of both in the poem.

3. **Identifying Personification and Hyperbole.** Giving human qualities to an object, animal, or idea is **personification. Hyperbole** is exaggeration for emphasis. In this poem the poet combines personification and hyperbole, as in "Trains climbed trees." Identify two other examples of this combination.

Developing Vocabulary Skills

Identifying Word Origins. Below are listed six words from the poems you have read.

Following the words are descriptions of how each word came into English. Finally there is a list of four kinds of word origins. On a separate piece of paper write the six words. After each word write the number of the correct description and the letter of the correct word origin. Use a dictionary if necessary.

disguise	necklace	holler
cry	tackward	brick

1. The poet coined, or created, this word by putting together a word meaning "zigzag" with a suffix meaning "toward."

2. This word comes from a word in the Dutch language that refers to a piece of baked clay.

3. This word is related to *hollo, hallo, holla,* and *hullo,* all of which sound like shouts.

4. This word is adapted from a word, *quis,* that imitates a squeal.

5. This word comes from two common English words.

6. In Old French, *desguiser,* the word that this word comes from, means "to change costume."
   a. borrowing
   b. combining word parts
   c. combining words
   d. imitating sounds

Developing Skills in Study and Research

1. **Locating Information.** The Aztec poem "The Song of a Dream" suggests that corn was important to the Aztec culture. You can find out about the importance of corn to the Aztecs by looking in books about the Aztecs.

Use the card catalog or the computer index in your library to locate books about the Aztecs. When you look for information on a specific topic, you must be prepared to look up alternate topics if necessary. If "Aztecs" is not listed in your library's card catalog, what other topics might refer you to information on the Aztecs?

Once you have found some books on the shelves, look for "corn" in the index of each book. (If "corn" is not listed in a book's index, under what other topic might the information be listed?) Refer to the pages indicated to find information on the meaning of corn to the Aztecs. Take notes on the information.

2. **Using Audio-Visual Resources.** Your library probably has a separate card catalog or computer index for audio-visual materials such as tapes and records. Look through the catalog or index to find recordings of poetry. Choose a poem or group of poems that you think your class would be interested in

hearing. Perhaps there is a recording of a famous actor or actress reading poems by an author whose poetry you have recently read. You may also want to choose a particularly dramatic or humorous poem. Check out the tape or record from the library to use during designated class time.

Developing Skills in Speaking and Listening

Interpreting Mood. Each of the four poems, "Faces," "Eviction," "The Song of a Dream," and "The Story-Teller," has a slightly different mood. Choose one poem, and practice reading it to convey its mood to your audience. Use a tone of voice that matches the poem's mood. Also pace your reading to communicate the mood. For example, you can suggest a happy mood with a quick pace and a sad mood with a slower pace. When you feel you have practiced your reading enough, present it to a group of classmates.

Developing Writing Skills

1. **Writing About Mood.** Each of the four poems you have just read has a different mood. Choose one of the poems. In one paragraph describe the mood and explain how it is developed in the poem.

   Prewriting. Decide which poem you would like to write about. Reread it and describe the mood briefly in a few words. Then make a chart with headings such as *word choice, rhythm, rhyme, techniques of sound, sensory images,* and *theme.* (You may have different headings for different poems.) Under each heading list the details in the poem that contribute to creating the mood of the poem.

   Drafting. In your topic sentence state what the mood of the poem is. Then, using the details from your chart, explain how the mood is developed. Make sure you use at least one example of each type of detail from your chart.

   Revising and Sharing. Ask a classmate to read your paragraph. Are the ideas clear? Are enough examples included? Are any important ideas missing? Revise and proofread your paragraph. Share it in a class discussion. Compare your ideas with others who wrote about the same poem you chose.

2. **Exploring Viewpoint.** The speaker in "Eviction" recalls a past event in light of mature understanding. Think of an experience you had some time ago that you now see with new understanding. Write two paragraphs telling how you saw it then and how you see it now. As you write, use the process of writing: prewriting, drafting, revising, and sharing. For more help, see the Guidelines for the Process of Writing, beginning on page 654 in the handbook.

Those Winter Sundays

ROBERT HAYDEN

This speaker remembers when houses were heated by coal furnaces. Every night the fire was banked, or covered. Every morning more coal had to be put on the fire. Why does the speaker think of these experiences now?

Sundays too my father got up early
and put his clothes on in the blueblack cold,
then with cracked hands that ached
from labor in the weekday weather made
banked fires blaze. No one ever thanked him.   5

I'd wake and hear the cold splintering, breaking.
When the rooms were warm, he'd call,
and slowly I would rise and dress,
fearing the chronic angers of that house,

Speaking indifferently to him,   10
who had driven out the cold
and polished my good shoes as well.
What did I know, what did I know
of love's austere and lonely offices?

1950—A No. 2, 1950. CLYFFORD STILL.
Hirshhorn Museum and Sculpture Garden,
Smithsonian Institution, Washington, D.C.

© 1984 Jill Krementz

Robert Hayden *(1913–1980)* won many awards for his poetry. His themes centered around black history and folklore. Born in Detroit, Michigan, Hayden attended Wayne State University and the University of Michigan. He taught English at Fisk University and edited *Kaleidoscope*, an anthology of black poetry. In 1976 he was appointed Poetry Consultant to the Library of Congress.

Developing Comprehension Skills

1. What did the speaker's father do on Sunday mornings?

2. What type of job might the father have had? What kinds of things did he do for his family? Use details from the poem to support your answers.

3. How did the speaker respond to his father's actions at the time they were happening? What does the speaker mean by "chronic angers of that house"?

4. In line 5 the speaker says, "No one ever thanked him." In the last two lines, the speaker says, "What did I know, what did I know/of love's austere and lonely offices?" Look up the words *austere* and *offices* in a dictionary. As the speaker looks back, what does he realize about his father?

5. In this poem the speaker regrets taking his or her father for granted. What other relationships might people take for granted? Explain your answer.

Reading Literature: Poetry

1. **Evaluating the Speaker.** In some ways, the speaker of this poem is like the speaker of "Eviction." About how old are the speakers when the events in the poems take place? From what point in time do the speakers look at the events in the poems?

2. **Understanding Theme.** The theme of this poem is suggested by the actions of the father and the reactions of the speaker. What is the poet's message about how some people show their love? What does the poem say about how some people react to the love of those around them?

3. **Identifying Uses of Sound.** Reread the quotations below. Identify which techniques of sound you find in each: alliteration, assonance, or onomatopoeia. The same quotation may involve more than one technique.

   a. cracked hands that ached/from labor in the weekday weather
   b. made/banked fires blaze
   c. When the rooms were warm, he'd call
   d. love's austere and lonely offices

Piñones

LEROY QUINTANA

Piñones are a kind of nut, some-times called the pine or pignoli nut. Read the poem to find out what special meaning piñones have for the speaker.

when i was young
we would sit by
an old firewood stove
watching my grandmother make candy,
listening to the stories   5
my grandparents would tell
about "the old days"
            and eat piñones

now we belong
to a supersonic age   10
and have college degrees.
we sit around color t.v. sets
watching the super bowl
listening to howard cosell,
stories of rioting, war, inflation   15
            and eat piñones

Tamalada, 1987,
CARMEN LOMAS GARZA.
Photograph by Wolfgang Dietze.

Leroy Quintana was born and raised in New Mexico. After serving in the Vietnam War, he attended the University of New Mexico, Denver University, and New Mexico State University. Quintana went on to become a college instructor. *Hijo del Pueblo (Son of the Village)* is his first book of published poetry.

Developing Comprehension Skills

1. List three details the speaker tells about his or her youth.

2. List three details the speaker tells about his or her present life. How has the speaker's life changed?

3. What detail is the same in the speaker's past and present life?

4. The speaker indicates that even though many things change as time passes, certain important values and traditions do not. What changes have occurred during your life? What important parts have remained the same?

Reading Literature: Poetry

1. **Understanding a Symbol.** A **symbol** is a person, place, or object that stands for something beyond itself. In this poem, piñones stand for something important to the speaker. What do piñones symbolize?

2. **Evaluating Punctuation Clues.** There are no capital letters in this poem. At the end of each stanza, where a sentence ends, there is no period. Think about the purposes of capital letters and periods. What might the poet be emphasizing about the connections between past and present?

3. **Examining Structure.** In this poem the structure of the second stanza mirrors that of the first stanza. Almost every part of the first stanza has a related part in the second stanza. For example, in the first stanza, the speaker talks about the time "when I was young." In the second stanza, the speaker talks about "now we belong/to a supersonic age/and have college degrees." Find two more sets of related details. Tell how they are different.

   One line is repeated exactly. How does this repetition connect the ideas in the two stanzas?

4. **Recognizing Mood.** How would you describe the mood in each stanza of this poem? What feeling does the mood in each give you? Is one mood more positive? Explain.

Lineage

MARGARET WALKER

Many people have traced their lineage. They are proud of their ancestors for a variety of reasons. Read to find out why this speaker is proud of her grandmothers.

My grandmothers were strong.
They followed plows and bent to toil.
They moved through fields sowing seed.
They touched earth and grain grew.
They were full of sturdiness and singing. 5
My grandmothers were strong.

My grandmothers are full of memories
Smelling of soap and onions and wet clay
With veins rolling roughly over quick hands
They have many clean words to say. 10
My grandmothers were strong.
Why am I not as they?

Woodbury County, Iowa, 1936, RUSSELL LEE. Library of Congress, Washington, D.C.

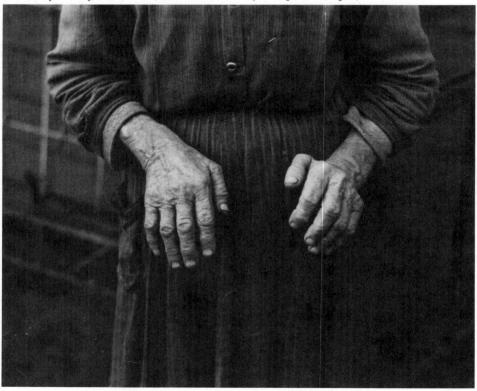

© 1984 Jill Krementz

Margaret Walker (*born 1915*) at the age of twenty-seven won the Yale Younger Poets award for her book of poetry *For My People.* She grew up in Birmingham, Alabama, lived in Mississippi and Louisiana, and earned a degree from the University of Iowa. Walker has held jobs as a newspaper reporter, a social worker, and an English teacher.

Developing Comprehension Skills

1. Name two of the activities in which the speaker's grandmothers took part.

2. The speaker's grandmothers were strong. In what literal ways were they strong? What figurative meaning of *strong* does the speaker mean as well?

3. What is the speaker's opinion of her grandmothers? What is her opinion of herself?

4. The speaker's grandmothers were strong in many ways. What kinds of strength are most important? Can every person be strong in some way? Explain.

Reading Literature: Poetry

1. **Analyzing Repetition.** In this poem one sentence is repeated three times. This repetition clearly emphasizes the theme. How does repetition organize the poem?

2. **Understanding Sensory Images.** As you recall, **sensory images** are words and phrases that appeal to the senses. In this poem, the sensory images call up specific ideas and feelings. For example, the image "They touched earth and grain grew" suggests a hopeful feeling and a nearly superhuman power, such as an ancient Greek goddess might have. In the lines below, explain the ideas and feelings that the images call up. What memories are these images connected to? What experiences?

   My grandmothers are full of memories
   Smelling of soap and onions and wet clay

3. **Identifying Uses of Sound.** Find at least three examples of alliteration in this poem. Find two examples of assonance. Tell where the poet uses rhyme. What effect do these techniques of sound create? Is the effect musical, harsh, disjointed, flowing?

Developing Vocabulary Skills

Recognizing Words with the Same Origins. Many words in English are related to each other. Related words may have come into the language in one form and then developed as separate forms. Or they may have come into the language separately but be based on the same word in another language.

Each of the following groups contains a word from the last three poems. In each group, three of the words come from the same base word in another language. The fourth word is not related. Use your knowledge of the words' meanings to decide which words come from a common base. On a sheet of paper, write the three related words. Tell how the meaning of each relates to the base word. Use a dictionary when you need help.

1. chronic, croon, chronicle, chronology—from the Greek word *chronos,* meaning "time"

2. cracker, crackle, crook, cracked—from an IndoEuropean base *ger,* that imitates the sound of a hoarse cry

3. indifferently, difficulty, difference, differ—from the Latin word *differens,* meaning "carried apart"

4. supersonic, resound, superior, sonic—from the Latin word *sonus,* meaning "sound"

5. granola, grain, grandmother, granule—from the Latin word *granum* meaning "grain"

6. lone, lonely, along, loner—derived from clipping the word *alone*

Developing Skills in Speaking and Listening

Interpreting the Speaker. In each of the last three poems, the speaker is a person with a clear attitude. To read any of these poems well, you must become the person. Choose one of the three poems and prepare to read it to a group.

To begin preparations, think about the age and circumstances of the speaker. Decide whether the speaker is excited, sad, thoughtful, happy, or feeling some other emotion. Try to suggest these aspects of the speaker with your tone of voice and gestures. Try reading at different speeds. Choose a pace that fits the personality of the speaker. Emphasize the words that convey the feelings of the speaker. See pages 390–391 for further suggestions on preparing to read poetry.

Developing Writing Skills

1. **Writing a Poem.** In the three poems you have just read, the speakers describe important memories of parents and grandparents. Think of a good memory you have of your grandparents, parents, or some other person or persons in your early childhood. Write a poem of one or two stanzas in which you describe the memory.

    Prewriting. To gather information for this assignment, you may wish to interview your parents or grandparents. Make a list of possible memories you would like to write about and decide on one. Write down the details that you remember most clearly. Then think about the kind of poem you want to write. It may be free verse or it may have regular rhyme and rhythm. It may tell a story or it may give a series of impressions. It may be about one happening or it may cover a longer period. List sensory images that you think you could use. Also think of figurative language, such as a simile or a metaphor, that would fit your subject.

    Drafting. Try two or three ways of beginning your poem. As you write you will figure out what works best. Try different arrangements of words, sensory details, and figures of speech. Look for ways to emphasize your meaning with patterns of sound such as alliteration, repetition, onomatopoeia, or rhyme.

    Revising and Sharing. After you have finished a draft, put it aside for a day or two. Then reread it. Does each word convey an exact meaning? Do the details and sensory images create vivid pictures? Does the form of the poem fit your subject? Are sound patterns used to help express meaning? Make any changes that will help the reader share your experience. Make a clean copy of the final form of your poem. Later, share your poem with the class. Work together to make a book of poems about memories. You may also want to illustrate the poems.

2. **Explaining an Opinion.** Which of the last three poems had the greatest effect on you? Which helped you to see your family in a different way? Which will you remember best? Write a paragraph explaining which poem meant the most to you and why. As a prewriting activity, list on a sheet of paper your reactions to the poem you chose. For each reaction, list the part of the poem that caused the reaction. Decide which part of the poem you will remember most clearly. Number your notes in order of importance. Organize your paragraph from your notes. Use the process of writing: prewriting, drafting, revising, and sharing. For more help, see the Guidelines for the Process of Writing, beginning on page 654 in the handbook.

Individuals

The poems in this section will help you to think about the uniqueness of every person. You will find ideas and attitudes that are interesting, important, amusing, and even puzzling. Who knows? These poems may help you to discover the individual inside yourself.

Untitled (Crowd), 1958, DAVID PARK. Collection of Mr. Harry Cohn, Hillsborough. Photograph: John Berggruen Gallery, San Francisco.

Thumbprint

EVE MERRIAM

What do you see when you look at your thumb? Read to discover what the speaker in this poem can see.

In the heel of my thumb
are whorls, whirls, wheels
in a unique design:
mine alone.
What a treasure to own!   5
My own flesh, my own feelings.
No other, however grand or base,
can ever contain the same.
My signature,
thumbing the pages of my time.   10
My universe key,
my singularity.
Impress, implant,
I am myself,
of all my atom parts I am the sum.   15
And out of my blood and my brain
I make my own interior weather,
my own sun and rain.
Imprint my mark upon the world,
whatever I shall become.   20

© Layle Silbert

Eve Merriam *(born 1916)* began writing as a child in Philadelphia, Pennsylvania. Her love of writing is shown in the volume and variety of work she has produced—more than thirty books, as well as television scripts, song lyrics, plays, and magazine articles. Merriam's book *Growing Up Female in America* reflects her interest in the issue of women's rights.

Developing Comprehension Skills

1. What makes the unique design of the thumbprint?

2. The speaker talks about "My signature," "My universe key," and "my singularity." In these phrases the speaker is referring to a thumb. What else do the phrases refer to?

3. The speaker refers to "my own interior weather,/my own sun and rain." Is this weather literal or figurative? What feelings would a person's "sun" and "rain" be?

4. How do you think the speaker feels about himself or herself? How do you think the speaker sees his or her future?

5. This poem emphasizes the uniqueness and individuality of every human being. How important is it for a person to recognize his or her uniqueness? Does the poem make you see yourself in a different way? Explain your answer.

Reading Literature: Poetry

1. **Relating Mood.** This is a poem of celebration. What is the speaker celebrating? What words and phrases create a mood of celebration?

2. **Recognizing Rhyme.** The rhymes in this poem appear in unexpected places. For example, look at the first five lines. What words rhyme with *design* and *alone?* In the rest of the poem, what are the rhymes for *singularity* and *brain?* Which two words rhyme with *thumb?* Do the irregular patterns of rhyme relate to the ideas of individuality and uniqueness? Explain.

3. **Appreciating Uses of Sound.** In this poem the poet uses alliteration and assonance frequently. As you know, **alliteration** is the repetition of a consonant sound at the beginnings of words. **Assonance** is the repetition of vowel sounds within words. In addition, the poem contains repetition of a consonant sound within words. An example is the repetition of the *ls* sound in "whorls, whirls, and wheels."

Identify at least two examples each of alliteration, assonance, and repetition of consonant sounds within words.

Macavity:
The Mystery Cat

This poem is about a most extraordinary cat! His crimes are many, but he always evades the law. As you read, look for qualities that make this cat almost believable.

T. S. ELIOT

Macavity's a Mystery Cat: he's called the Hidden Paw—
For he's the master criminal who can defy the Law.
He's the bafflement of Scotland Yard,[1] the Flying Squad's despair:[2]
For when they reach the scene of crime—*Macavity's not there!*

Macavity, Macavity, there's no one like Macavity,   5
He's broken every human law, he breaks the law of gravity.
His powers of levitation would make a fakir stare,
And when you reach the scene of crime—*Macavity's not there!*
You may seek him in the basement, you may look up in the air—
But I tell you once and once again, *Macavity's not there!*   10

Macavity's a ginger cat, he's very tall and thin;
You would know him if you saw him, for his eyes are sunken in.
His brow is deeply lined with thought, his head is highly domed;
His coat is dusty from neglect, his whiskers are uncombed.
He sways his head from side to side, with movements like a snake;   15
And when you think he's half asleep, he's always wide awake.

---

1. **Scotland Yard**–the London police department, especially the detective bureau.
2. **Flying Squad's despair**–Macavity is a problem even for the special emergency police unit.

Macavity, Macavity, there's no one like Macavity,
For he's a fiend in feline shape, a monster of depravity.
You may meet him in a by-street, you may see him in the square—
But when a crime's discovered, then *Macavity's not there!*   20

He's outwardly respectable. (They say he cheats at cards.)
And his footprints are not found in any file in Scotland Yard's.
And when the larder's looted, or the jewel-case is rifled,
Or when the milk is missing, or another Peke's[3] been stifled,
Or the greenhouse glass is broken, and the trellis past repair—   25
Ay, there's the wonder of the thing! *Macavity's not there!*

And when the Foreign Office find a Treaty's gone astray,
Or the Admiralty lose some plans and drawings by the way,
There may be a scrap of paper in the hall or on the stair—
But it's useless to investigate—*Macavity's not there!*   30
And when the loss has been disclosed, the Secret Service say:
'It *must* have been Macavity!'—but he's a mile away.
You'll be sure to find him resting, or a-licking of his thumbs,
Or engaged in doing complicated long division sums.

Macavity, Macavity, there's no one like Macavity,   35
There never was a Cat of such deceitfulness and suavity.
He always has an alibi, and one or two to spare:
At whatever time the deed took place—MACAVITY WASN'T THERE!
And they say that all the Cats whose wicked deeds are widely known
(I might mention Mungojerrie, I might mention Griddlebone)   40
Are nothing more than agents for the Cat who all the time
Just controls their operations: the Napoleon[4] of Crime!

---

3. **Peke**–clipped word for *Pekingese,* a small dog with long hair.
4. **Napoleon**–(nə pō′ lē ən)–Emperor of France (1804–15). As a military leader,
   Napoleon was powerful, clever, and seemed to be unconquerable.

T. S. Eliot *(1888–1965)* gained wide recognition for his work in modern poetry. Born in the Midwest, Eliot eventually studied at Harvard and in Europe, then settled in London. There he worked as a teacher, lecturer, banker, and editor. Eliot's humorous poems about cats are in contrast to his serious works which include most of his writing. His striking originality, shown in "The Love Song of J. Alfred Prufrock" and the long poem *The Waste Land,* was at first met with criticism as well as praise. Eliot's talent established him as a major poet, however, and in 1948 he won the Nobel Prize for literature.

Developing Comprehension Skills

1. What nickname is Macavity given in the first stanza?

2. List three details about Macavity in stanzas 1 and 2 that are not typical of a real cat. Then list three details about Macavity from stanza 3 that are typical of a real cat.

3. What are three of the crimes Macavity is accused of in lines 23 through 25? What do the crimes have in common with the ordinary behavior of cats?

4. The poem calls Macavity the "Napoleon of Crime." Napoleon was a powerful French emperor during the nineteenth century. What does this comparison suggest about Macavity?

5. How serious is this poem? What do you think is the poet's purpose? How well does he succeed? Explain your answer.

Reading Literature: Poetry

1. **Recognizing Personification.** In **personification,** an object, animal, or idea is given human qualities. Identify at least five lines that describe Macavity as if he were human.

2. **Understanding Hyperbole. Hyperbole** is exaggeration for emphasis. It is used to stress an idea or to create humor. An example of hyperbole about Macavity is "He's broken every human law, he breaks the law of gravity." Of course, this statement is not literally true. It is funny, however, and it makes the point that Macavity is a lawbreaker. Find two other examples of hyperbole in the poem.

3. **Analyzing Repetition.** What line is repeated several times in the poem? Where does the repeated line occur? What idea does it emphasize?

4. **Examining Humor.** The speaker's attitude toward the subject in this poem is playful and amused. Find three phrases or lines that you find humorous.

5. **Identifying Sensory Images.** The third stanza of the poem uses images to describe Macavity's appearance. One image, for in-

stance, is "His coat is dusty from neglect."
Find four other examples of sensory images
that describe details of how Macavity looks.
What impression of Macavity do these images create?

Developing Vocabulary Skills

Recognizing Word Origins. The underlined words in the following sentences are either taken from the last two poems or related to the poems. Each word belongs to one of the following groups:

words from names   borrowed words
words from sounds   combined words
clipped words   combined word parts

Use the clues that you see in the words and in the context to identify the origin of each underlined word. On a sheet of paper, write each underlined word and what you think is the origin of the word. Check your answers in a dictionary.

1. Although Hindu or Moslem <u>fakirs</u> claim to perform miracles, they would be astounded by Macavity's powers.
2. Each person <u>imprints</u> his or her <u>uniqueness</u> on the world.
3. Macavity, <u>unlike</u> other cats, rarely reveals himself with a <u>meow</u>.
4. The speaker in "Macavity" refers to a <u>Pekingese</u> dog as a <u>Peke</u>.
5. Your <u>thumbprints</u> and your signature are both <u>one-of-a-kind</u>.
6. Not even the <u>planes</u> of the Flying Squad can keep up with Macavity.

Developing Skills in Study and Research

Using a Thesaurus. Thesaurus, a word borrowed from Greek, means "treasure or storehouse." A **thesaurus** is a storehouse of information about words. It is a reference book

Idol for Housecats, 1924, PAUL KLÉE. Norton Simon Museum of Art, Pasadena, California, Blue Four Collection.

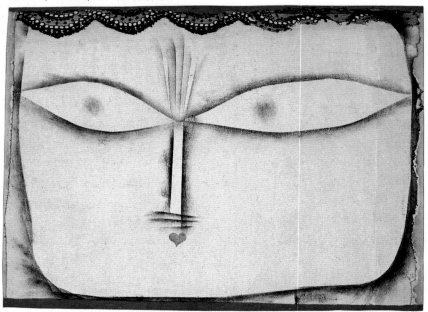

or computer program that lists words with their synonyms, antonyms, and related words. It may explain the slight differences in meaning among the words grouped together. Find a thesaurus, perhaps on your library's shelves or in its software file. Follow the directions in the thesaurus to find listings for three of the following words. For each of the three words, write on a sheet of paper at least four related words shown in the thesaurus.

design	mark	law	loot
grand	world	thought	wonder
base	scene	neglect	control

Developing Writing Skills

1. **Explaining an Idea.** "Thumbprint" celebrates the idea of being an individual, and Macavity is certainly described as an individual. What are the qualities of someone who is truly his or her own person? Write one paragraph defining and explaining individuality.

   Prewriting. Think about what the poems say about individuality. What makes some people stand out in a good way? List qualities these people have. Make notes about some special individuals you have known and how they behave differently from others. Then review your notes and decide what you mean by individuality. Arrange your notes in a clear order.

   Drafting. Begin by defining individuality. Then explain the characteristics of an individual. Use the ideas in your notes, and follow the order you decided on in prewriting. Include examples from the poems and from the lives of individuals you know or have read about.

   Revising and Sharing. First check the organization of your ideas. Is each idea related to the topic sentence? Is each idea stated clearly? Ask someone else to read your draft and to indicate where the writing is unclear. Then think about the language you used. Is every word precise? Are the verbs lively? Revise your draft where necessary. Finally, check the grammar, spelling, and punctuation. Make sure that no careless mistakes stand between your reader and your ideas. Mark any corrections on your draft. Make a clean copy.

2. **Analyzing Tone.** The tone of "Macavity: The Mystery Cat" is playful and amused. What creates this tone? Consider the following questions as you think about the tone. How is Macavity described? How does the speaker seem to feel about cats? What words and phrases help create the tone? How does exaggeration contribute? Write a paragraph explaining the tone in the poem. Use specific details from the poem to support your analysis. As you write, use the process of writing: prewriting, drafting, revising, and sharing. For more help, see the Guidelines for the Process of Writing, beginning on page 654 in the handbook.

Child on Top of a Greenhouse

THEODORE ROETHKE

Almost everyone likes a bird's-eye view of the world now and then. In this poem, a child climbs to a high place for a good view. As you read, try to decide how the child feels.

The wind billowing out the seat of my britches,
My feet crackling splinters of glass and dried putty,
The half-grown chrysanthemums staring up like accusers,
Up through the streaked glass, flashing with sunlight,
A few white clouds all rushing eastward,   5
A line of elms plunging and tossing like horses,
And everyone, everyone pointing up and shouting!

Night Greenhouse No. 3, 1982,
ROGER HOWRIGAN. Collection of
G. C. Janss.

Theodore Roethke *(1908–1963)* was a poet and a professor of English, as well as a fine athlete and coach. His love of nature developed from his childhood experiences growing up in Michigan where his family owned a greenhouse. Roethke was awarded a Pulitzer Prize in 1954 for his collection of poetry *The Waking*. His works include nonsense poems and serious verse.

Developing Comprehension Skills

1. Where is the speaker? Where are the other people? What are the other people doing?

2. Identify at least four things that the speaker sees. Name one thing that the speaker touches or feels. Name one thing that the speaker hears.

3. The speaker says that the chrysanthemums are "staring up like accusers." Flowers can't literally see or show attitudes. Why might the speaker think of the chrysanthemums as accusing? What connection might there be between the description of the flowers and what is happening in the last line?

4. The speaker is not afraid to take a risk. What do you think about his or her actions? Do you admire them? question them? disapprove of them? or have a mixture of feelings? Explain.

Reading Literature: Poetry

1. **Understanding the Speaker.** What can you tell from the poem about the speaker?
How do you think the speaker might feel about what is happening? Identify details from the poem to support your answer.

2. **Identifying Sensory Images.** This poem weaves together a series of brilliant images. **Sensory images,** as you recall, are words and phrases that appeal to the senses. One image, for example, is of "the streaked glass, flashing with sunlight." The glaring of the sun suggests the fear, thrill, and excitement that the child feels. Find two images that describe motion in lines 1 and 5. What senses do these images appeal to? What feeling does each image suggest?

3. **Recognizing Similes.** A **simile** is a comparison that uses *like* or *as*. There are two similes in this poem. You have already discussed the simile "chrysanthemums staring up like accusers." Find the second simile in the poem. What two things are being compared? What picture does the simile create? What feeling does it create?

Dreams

LANGSTON HUGHES

Are your dreams important to you? How does the speaker in this poem feel about dreams?

Hold fast to dreams
For if dreams die
Life is a broken-winged bird
That cannot fly.

Hold fast to dreams 5
For when dreams go
Life is a barren field
Frozen with snow.

Point of Tranquility, 1958, MORRIS LOUIS. Hirshhorn Museum and Sculpture Garden, Smithsonian Institution, Washington, D.C.

For information about **Langston Hughes,** see the biography that follows his short story "Thank You, M'am," on page 83.

Developing Comprehension Skills

1. What line is repeated in each stanza of the poem?

2. What does the speaker mean by "dreams"?

3. The speaker urges the reader to "Hold fast to dreams." How does the speaker view a life without dreams?

4. How important are dreams? Do you agree with the speaker's opinion?

Reading Literature: Poetry

1. **Understanding Structure.** Look at the form of this poem. Each stanza has a regular rhyme scheme and repeats key words and phrases. How do the rhyme scheme and repetition connect the ideas in the poem?

2. **Recognizing Alliteration and Assonance.** Besides using rhyme, stanza form, and repetition, the poet links the words of the poem with alliteration and assonance. Find two examples of each. Can you suggest reasons why the poet stresses those words?

3. **Interpreting Metaphor.** A **metaphor** is a comparison that does not use *like* or *as*. What are the two metaphors in this poem? What idea does the poet express through each metaphor?

Stopping by Woods on a Snowy Evening

ROBERT FROST

Listen for the conversational style of this poem. What are the speaker's thoughts and feelings? What choice does the speaker make?

Whose woods these are I think I know.
His house is in the village though;
He will not see me stopping here
To watch his woods fill up with snow.

My little horse must think it queer   5
To stop without a farmhouse near
Between the woods and frozen lake
The darkest evening of the year.

He gives his harness bells a shake
To ask if there is some mistake   10
The only other sound's the sweep
Of easy wind and downy flake.

The woods are lovely, dark and deep.
But I have promises to keep,
And miles to go before I sleep,   15
And miles to go before I sleep.

Robert Frost *(1874–1963)* had the honor of reading his poetry at the Presidential inauguration of John F. Kennedy. Frost's works, often set in rural New England, are noted for their conversational style and realism. Before he achieved fame for his poetry, Frost worked at a variety of jobs—mill hand, shoe salesman, and farmer. He wrote more than a dozen books of poetry and is the only American poet to win the Pulitzer Prize four times.

Winter Harmony, 1890–1900, JOHN H. TWACHTMAN. National Gallery of Art, Washington, D.C., Gift of the Avalon Foundation, 1964.

Developing Comprehension Skills

1. Where has the speaker stopped? Why does the speaker stop?

2. What sounds does the speaker hear? What time of day and year is it?

3. Why might the horse think that stopping might be "some mistake"?

4. What choice does the speaker make at the end of the poem?

5. The speaker says, "I have promises to keep." What might he or she be referring to? Do all people have "promises to keep"? Explain.

Reading Literature: Poetry

1. **Identifying Rhyme Scheme.** Write the rhyme scheme for the entire poem. How are the rhymes carried over from stanza to stanza? What variation is there in the fourth stanza?

2. **Recognizing Sensory Images.** Identify at least four sensory images used to describe the setting. To which sense does each image appeal?

3. **Examining Repeated Sounds.** Sometimes poets use words with sounds that suggest their meanings. Tell how the sounds of the words in these lines stress the meaning of the words:

> The only other sound's the sweep
> Of easy wind and downy flake.

4. **Thinking About Mood.** How would you describe the mood of this poem? How does the repetition in the last two lines reinforce the feeling of the poem?

Developing Vocabulary Skills

Reviewing Word Origins. On a sheet of paper, write each underlined word from the sentences below. Then tell how the word came into the English language. Use a dictionary if necessary.

borrowing   combining word parts
clipping   imitating a sound
combining words

1. The child standing on top of the greenhouse sees chrysanthemums, or mums, as many people call them, on the ground below.
2. The boy hears the sharp crackling of broken glass under his feet.
3. Life without dreams would be unthinkable.
4. In "Stopping by Woods on a Snowy Evening," the speaker stops the horse in an isolated spot, nowhere near a farmhouse.

Developing Skills in Speaking and Listening

Interpreting the Speaker. Review "Child on Top of a Greenhouse" and "Stopping by Woods on a Snowy Evening." Choose one of the poems, and prepare to read it for a group. Review the suggestions on page 391 for help in preparing the poem. Concentrate on making the speaker real to you, so that your face, voice, and gestures will make the speaker real for your audience.

Developing Writing Skills

1. **Creating Metaphors.** The speaker in "Dreams" uses two metaphors to describe what life would be like without dreams. In the first stanza, the speaker says that life without dreams "is a broken-winged bird/ That cannot fly." In the second stanza, life without dreams is compared to "a barren field/Frozen with snow." Think about some activity or aspect of life that means a great deal to you. Some examples are friends, family, music, or a favorite sport or form of exercise. Write a one-stanza or two-stanza poem using metaphors to express what life would be like without that activity or aspect of life.

Prewriting. Think about the activities and aspects of life that mean the most to you. Decide which one you would like to write a poem about. Make a list of the ways life would be different if this important part were taken away. What would change? How would you feel? Reread your list and think about what metaphors you might use to express some of your ideas and feelings. Decide how you want to organize your poem. Also decide whether you want to use regular rhythm and rhyme or free verse.

Drafting. Work on the opening lines of your poem. Keep in mind the ideas and organization you developed in prewriting. As you write, choose words carefully. Develop metaphors that clearly express your feelings and ideas to the reader. Use techniques of sound such as alliteration and assonance to add to the interest and meaning of the poem.

Revising and Sharing. Read over your draft. Look for places where words, images, or metaphors could be more precise. Read the poem aloud. Do the rhythm and any rhyme you have used work smoothly? Are the techniques of sound appropriate and effective? Be prepared to share your poem with the class. Ask for your listeners' responses to the metaphors you have used.

2. **Explaining Images.** "Child on Top of a Greenhouse" and "Stopping by Woods on a Snowy Evening" each use images of nature to express the feelings of the speaker. Choose one of the poems. Write one paragraph in which you identify at least three of the images of nature in the poem. Explain what feelings the images convey. You can organize your ideas according to order of importance or according to the order of the images in the poem. Include details from the poem in your discussion. Use the process of writing: prewriting, drafting, revising, and sharing. For more help, see the Guidelines for the Process of Writing, beginning on page 654 in the handbook.

Chapter 5 R*eview*

Using Your Skills in Reading Poetry

Read the following stanzas from the poem "The Challenge of Thor" by Henry Wadsworth Longfellow. Then follow the directions below.

I am the God Thor,
I am the War God,
I am the Thunderer!
Here in the Northland,
My fastness and fortress,
Reign I forever!

Here amid icebergs
Rule I the nations;
This is my hammer,
Miolner the might;
Giants and sorcerers
Cannot withstand it!

Viking silver amulet in the shape
of Thor's hammer, 11th century.
Statens Historiska Museer, Stockholm.

1. Identify the speaker.
2. Identify which of these sound techniques the stanzas use:

   rhyme   rhythm   alliteration   repetition of words

3. Tell how one of these techniques emphasizes the meaning of the stanzas.

Using Your Comprehension Skills

Here is a passage from "Place of Sorrows," a description of the battlefield at Little Big Horn, by Charles Kuralt. Identify in it at least one example of figurative language. Tell what you believe is the author's purpose in using figurative language rather than literal language.

> That's why this is the saddest place. For Custer and the Seventh Cavalry, courage only led to defeat. For Crazy Horse and the Sioux, victory only led to Wounded Knee.
> Come here sometime, and you'll see. There is melancholy in the wind and sorrow in the grass, and the river weeps.

Using Your Vocabulary Skills

Each underlined word is used in Chapter Six. Tell how each entered the English language: borrowed word, clipped word, word from combined word parts, word from combined words, word from a name, or word from a sound. Use a dictionary if necessary.

1. The child began to teach herself Braille.

2. The hiding place had a steep staircase.

3. Prospect comes from the Latin word *prospectus*, which means "lookout."

4. The other dogs yapped during the operation. The Doberman puppy simply ran away from the vet.

5. Anyone making a parachute jump should check the chute carefully ahead of time.

6. The coins were jingling in my pocket.

Using Your Skills in Speaking and Listening

In many of the poems you have read, the speaker is a person you can identify. Choose one of these poems and prepare a reading of it. Review the details about the speaker. Decide on the tone of voice and gestures you want to use to interpret the speaker. Choose a pace that suits the speaker. Practice so that your final reading will be natural and convincing.

Using Your Writing Skills

Complete one of the following assignments.

1. Choose any poem in this chapter. Think about the theme of the poem. Explain how two of the literary techniques used in the poem help to suggest the theme. Consider techniques such as rhythm, rhyme, sensory images, metaphor, and any others that apply.

2. Write a poem about a person, place, or animal. The poem should include the following: at least one sensory image, at least one simile or metaphor, and at least one use of alliteration. The lines of the poem may be rhymed or unrhymed.

CHAPTER SIX

Nonfiction

Quill in Inkwell, Book and Candle, 1899, JOHN PETO.
Private Collection. Photograph: Kennedy Galleries, New York City.

Reading Literature

Nonfiction

Nonfiction is writing about real people, places, times, and events. Like fiction, nonfiction may include elements such as characters, setting, and conflict. Unlike fiction, however, these elements are not made up or imagined. Every detail is from real life.

Nonfiction includes many types. Some of these are letters, reports, news stories, and magazine articles. You will read three types of nonfiction in the first part of this chapter:

1. An **autobiography** is the story of a person's own life, written by that person. Most often, the writer shares feelings and thoughts about the experiences of his or her own life.
2. A **diary** is a type of autobiographical writing. It is the day-by-day record a person keeps of his or her own activities and thoughts. A diary is meant for the writer alone.
3. A **biography** is the story of a person's life written by another person. The writer bases the biography on records of what the person did and said.

The History of Nonfiction

As long as writing has existed, people have written nonfiction. Examples include ancient law codes, government records, letters, biographies, and proverbs. Some kinds of nonfiction, though, have changed over the years. The first biographies, for example, were written to glorify heroes or leaders. These accounts told only good things about the subjects. In 1791, however, James Boswell published *The Life of Samuel Johnson* about his friend, the great English writer and creator of the first English dictionary. Boswell's biography describes Johnson's weaknesses and difficulties as well as his strengths and successes. Biographers since the time of Boswell have tried to be objective. They try to show the whole personality and history of their subjects.

The Elements of Nonfiction

Characters and Setting. The main character in an autobiography or biography is called the **subject.** The subject's words, thoughts, and actions are described. In the biography *Chief Sarah,* for example, the subject is Sarah Winnemucca. The selection presents Sarah's thoughts and actions during a conflict between Native American chiefs and an Army officer in 1857.

Tone and Mood. The writer's attitude toward his or her subject matter is called **tone.** A writer's tone may be comic, as in Bill Cosby's *Fatherhood.* It may be bitter, as in "The First Day of the War." It may be warm, hopeful, sad, or anything the writer likes.

The **mood** is the feeling that a piece of writing creates in the reader. In Lucy Ching's autobiography the mood is uplifting. In "Place of Sorrows" the mood is sad.

How to Read Nonfiction

1. As you read, try to separate facts from opinions. Keep in mind that the writer has chosen facts that present a certain picture of the subject. Think about what might be missing as well as what is included.
2. Think about the writer's purpose. What is he or she trying to explain? Is the writer trying to win you over to his or her opinion of an action or a person?
3. Be aware of the writer's tone. Often a writer tells something about himself or herself by the tone he or she uses. An admiring tone, for example, reveals what the writer values.

Comprehension Skills

Fact and Opinion

Most nonfiction presents both facts and opinions. A **fact** is a statement that can be proved. An **opinion** is a statement that cannot be proved true. Note the difference between these two sentences:

My cousin wrote me a letter.
My cousin wrote me a funny letter.

The first sentence is a fact. Another person could prove the truth of that statement. The second sentence is an opinion. The word *funny* shows what the speaker thinks of the letter. Another person might disagree.

Recognizing Opinions. There are two possible approaches to the subject matter in nonfiction. A writer can report facts with as few personal opinions as possible. Or, a writer can present his or her personal opinions about the facts. Even in highly factual writing, though, it is impossible to leave out opinions altogether. After all, the writer must begin by deciding which facts to use. This choice is based on opinions. The reader must be able to identify opinions in all kinds of nonfiction writing.

Evaluating Opinions. One guideline for evaluating opinions is the relationship between the opinion and the facts. Does the writer support each opinion with facts? Can you think of other facts that do not support the opinion?

Another guideline is the qualifications of the writer. Is the writer likely to know what he or she is talking about?

A third guideline is the writer's purpose. Is the writer trying to inform or to persuade?

Recognizing Slanted Writing. As you know, the **connotation** of a word refers to the feelings and ideas the word suggests. Writers can use words with strong negative or positive connotations to try to influence a reader's opinion. For example, if a writer says that a person is *skinny,* the reader will have a negative impression. If a writer says that a person is *slender,* the reader will have a positive impression.

Exercises: Recognizing Fact, Opinion, and Slanted Writing

A. Each of the following statements is from a selection in this chapter. Identify each statement as fact or opinion.

1. Every day I feel that I am developing inwardly.

    —from *The Diary of a Young Girl* by Anne Frank

2. [Maggie Walker] spent her last years in a wheelchair and died December 15, 1934.   —"Banker Maggie Walker" by Olive Burt

3. Such grief, Sarah thought, was enough to make the very mountain weep.

    —from *Chief Sarah* by Dorothy Nafus Morrison

4. Columbus got Spanish backing and sailed westward.

    —"The Uses of Error" by Isaac Asimov

B. Read this passage. Then follow these instructions. (a) Identify one fact and one opinion. (b) Identify three words with strong connotations. (c) State what you think the writer wants the reader to believe.

When Maggie was nineteen, she married Armstead Walker, a young businessman of Richmond. . . . Maggie had become a tall, stately woman with clear, dark eyes and a kind expression. Her voice was low and rich, and she was an excellent speaker. She was enthusiastic about any project she undertook, and she had the energy to carry it out.

    —"Banker Maggie Walker" by Olive Burt

Vocabulary Skills

The Dictionary

As you know, there are several ways to figure out the meaning of an unfamiliar word. First, look at the word itself for familiar word parts. Next, examine the context for clues. Third, check whether word origins might help you. Last, turn to a dictionary or glossary.

As you know, a **dictionary** is a book that gives the spellings, definitions, and sources of words. The words are listed in alphabetical order. A **glossary** is a form of dictionary. It appears within another book, as at the back of this book. A glossary lists words from the book in which it is found.

You should be familiar with the following features of each dictionary entry.

Entry Word. Each word listed is printed in boldface, or heavy, letters. The breaks between syllables are indicated by spacing, hyphens, or dots: **glo·ry.** The entry word tells you the correct spelling and where to break the word.

Respelling. The respelling of the word appears next, usually in parentheses. It uses symbols that show how to pronounce the word:

glo·ry (glôr′ ē)

In a dictionary, the symbols are explained in a key at the front and on every page or every second page. The symbols in this example are explained in the Glossary Key on page 661. Boldface accent marks show which syllable gets the most stress when you say the word. A lighter accent mark indicates a syllable with a lighter stress.

Parts of Speech. Each entry word is used as at least one part of speech. The definitions in an entry are grouped by part of speech. The part of speech used most often is usually listed first.

Notice the additional information given about the part of speech:

glo·ry (glôr′ ē) *n., pl.* **-ries**

The *n.* stands for "noun." The *pl.* stands for "plural." The **-ries** shows that the plural form of the noun *glory* is spelled *glories*. (Note: The plural spelling is given only when the plural is not formed by adding an *s* to the singular.)

Word Origin. Some dictionaries give the word origin after the part of speech. Others give it at the end of the entry. This information is usually set off by brackets. The abbreviations and symbols inside the brackets trace the history of the word. The abbreviations and symbols are explained in the dictionary, usually at the front.

glo·ry (glôr′ ē) *n., pl.* **-ries** [OFr. <L. *gloria*]

The example shows that *glory* came from Old French and before that from the Latin word *gloria*.

Definitions. The entry may list many definitions, grouped by parts of speech. To find the right definition of a word, first find the part of speech that fits the use of the word in the sentence. Then search for the definition that fits best.

Exercise: Using a Dictionary

Use this dictionary entry to answer the questions below.

ap·pe·tite (ap′ə tīt′) *n.* [<ME. & OFr. <L. *appetitus*] **1.** a desire for food or for a specific food **2.** any strong desire or craving [an *appetite* for learning]

1. How is *appetite* divided into syllables?
2. Which syllable is given the most stress?
3. From which language did Middle English and Old French take this word?
4. Tell which definition fits this sentence:
   The adventurers had an appetite for excitement.

Diaries

Most **diaries** are written for personal reasons. They are a form of autobiographical writing, but are not meant to be published. Sometimes, however, someone other than the writer has an opportunity to read a diary. Once in a great while, that reader believes that everyone should have a chance to read the diary. Here are excerpts from two such diaries. As you read them, decide why their publishers wanted to share them with you.

Birthplace: Douglas, Ariz., 1979, MANNY FARBER. Collection of Douglas Simay. Photograph by Roy Porello, San Diego.

From

The Life of Davy Crockett by Himself

DAVY CROCKETT

From the first entry in this diary to the last, Davy Crockett shows a fearless attitude toward his enemies. As you read, look for passages that reveal his courage.

February 19, 1836. San Antonio

We are all in high spirits, though we are rather short of provisions, for men who have appetites that could digest anything but oppression; but no matter, we have a prospect of soon getting our bellies full of fighting, and that is victuals and drink to a patriot any day. . . .

February 22

The Mexicans, about sixteen hundred strong, with their President Santa Anna at their head, aided by Generals Almonte, Cos, Sesma, and Castrillon, are within two leagues of Bexar. . . . Some of the scouts came in and bring reports that Santa Anna has been endeavoring to excite the Indians to hostilities against the Texans, but so far without effect. The Comanches, in particular, entertain such hatred for the Mexicans, and at the same time hold them in such contempt, that they would rather turn their tomahawks against them and drive them from the land, than lend a helping hand. We are up and doing and as lively as Dutch cheese in the dog days. . . .

February 23

Early this morning the enemy came in sight, marching in regular order and displaying their strength to the greatest advantage, in order to strike us with terror. But that was no go; they'll find that they have to do with men who will never lay down their arms as long as they can stand on their legs. We held a short council of war, and, finding that we should be completely surrounded and overwhelmed by numbers if we remained in town, we concluded to withdraw to the fortress of Alamo and defend it to the last extremity. We accordingly filed off, in good order, having some days before placed all the surplus provisions, arms, and ammunition in the fortress. We have had a large national flag made; it is composed of thirteen stripes, red and white, alternately, on a blue ground, with a large white star of five points, in the centre, and between the points the letters TEXAS. As soon as all our little band, about one hundred and fifty in number, had entered and secured the fortress in the best possible manner, we set about raising our flag on the battlements.

The enemy marched into Bexar, and took possession of the town, a blood-red flag flying at their head, to indicate that we need not expect quarters if we should fall into their clutches. In the afternoon a messenger was sent from the enemy to Colonel Travis, demanding an unconditional and absolute surrender of the garrison, threatening to put every man to the sword in case of refusal. The only answer he received was a cannon shot, so the messenger left us with a flea in his ear, and the Mexicans commenced firing grenades at us, but without doing any mischief. . . .

February 24

Very early this morning the enemy commenced a new battery on the banks of the river, about three hundred and fifty yards from the fort, and by afternoon they amused themselves by firing at us from that quarter. Our Indian scout came in this evening, and with him a reinforcement of thirty men from Gonzales, who were just in the nick of time to reap a harvest of glory; but there is some prospect of sweating blood before we gather it in. . . .

February 25

The firing commenced early this morning, but we haven't lost a single man, and our outworks have sustained no injury. Our sharpshooters have brought down a considerable number of stragglers at a long shot. . . . The enemy have been busy during the night, and have thrown up two batteries on the opposite side of the river. The battalion of Matamoras is posted there, and cavalry occupy the hills in the east and on the road to Gonzales. They are determined to surround us, and cut us off from reinforcement, or the possibility of escape by a sortie. Well, there's one thing they cannot prevent; we'll still go ahead, and sell our lives at a high price.

February 26

Colonel Bowie has been taken sick from over-exertion and exposure. He did not leave his bed today until twelve o'clock. He is worth a dozen common men in a situation like ours. . . .

February 27

The cannonading began early this morning, and ten bombs were thrown into the fort, but fortunately exploded without doing any mischief. So far it has been a sort of tempest in a teapot, not unlike a pitched battle in the Hall of Congress, where the

The Alamo, March 6, 1836, 1967, DONALD M. YENA. Collection of Frank Horlock. Photograph by Ronald Randolf, Corpus Christi, Texas.

parties array their forces, make fearful demonstrations on both sides, then fire away with loud-sounding speeches, which contain about as much meaning as the report of a howitzer charged with a blank cartridge. Provisions are becoming scarce, and the enemy are endeavoring to cut off our water. If they attempt to stop our grog in that manner, let them look out, for we shall become too wrathy for our shirts to hold us. We are not prepared to submit to an exercise of that nature, and they'll find

it out. This discovery has created considerable excitement in the fort.

February 28

Last night our hunters brought in some corn, and had a brush with a scout from the enemy beyond gunshot of the fort. They put the scout to flight and got in without injury. They bring accounts that the settlers are flying in all quarters, in dismay, leaving their possessions to the mercy of the ruthless invader, who is literally engaged in a war of extermination more brutal than the untutored savage of the desert could be guilty of. Slaughter is indiscriminate, sparing neither sex, age, nor condition. Buildings have been burnt down, farms laid waste, and Santa Anna appears determined to verify his threat and convert the blooming paradise into a howling wilderness. For just one fair crack at that rascal, even at a hundred yard's distance, I would bargain to break my Betsey[1] and never pull trigger again. My name's not Crockett if I wouldn't get glory enough to appease my stomach for the remainder of my life. . . .

The enemy, somewhat emboldened, draws nigher to the fort. So much the better. There was a move in General Sesma's division toward evening.

February 29

Before daybreak, we saw General Sesma leave his camp, with a large body of cavalry and infantry, and move off in the direction of Goliad. We think that he must have received news of Colonel Fanning's coming to our relief. We are all in high spirits at the prospect of being able to give the rascals a fair shake on the plain. . . .

March 1

The enemy's forces have been increasing in numbers daily, notwithstanding they have already lost about three hundred men in the several assaults they have made upon us. I neglected to mention in the proper place that, when the enemy came in sight, we had but three bushels of corn in the garrison but have since found eighty bushels in a deserted house. Colonel Bowie's illness still continues, but he manages to crawl from his bed every day, that his comrades may see him. His presence alone is a tower of strength. The enemy becomes more daring as his numbers increase.

March 2

This day the delegates meet in general convention at the town of Washington (Texas), to frame our (Texan) Declaration of Independence. That the sacred instrument may never be trampled on by the children of those who have freely shed their blood to establish it, is the sincere wish of David Crockett. Universal independence is an almighty idea, far too extensive for some brains to comprehend. . . .

March 3

We have given over all hopes of receiving assistance from Goliad or Refugio. Colonel Travis harangued the garrison, and concluded by exhorting them, in case the enemy should carry to fort, to fight to the last gasp and render their victory even more serious to them than to us. This was followed by three cheers.

---

1. **Betsey**—Frontier name for a gun.

March 4

Shells have been falling into the fort like hail during the day, but without effect. . . .

March 5

Pop, pop, pop! Bom, bom, bom! throughout the day. No time for memorandums now. Go ahead! Liberty and independence forever!

Here ends Colonel David Crockett's manuscript. Before the sun set again he was dead, as were all of his comrades of the Alamo.

The Alamo today. © Bill Benoit/Nawrocki Stock Photo, Chicago.

David "Davy" Crockett *(1786–1836)* was a famous frontiersman who became a folk hero during his lifetime. He was known not only for his marksmanship, but also for his humorous, exaggerated stories. After representing Tennessee in Congress, Crockett went to Texas in 1835. He fought at the Alamo to establish an independent Texas, and it is assumed that he died there.

Developing Comprehension Skills

1. Who are Crockett and the others fighting against? Who is the leader of the enemy forces?

2. The diary presents Crockett's opinions. Identify two personal feelings that Crockett includes in his diary.

3. After Crockett describes the enemy's positions, he writes, "Well, there's one thing they cannot prevent; we'll still go ahead, and sell our lives at a high price." What does he mean?

4. During the time he is writing this diary, Crockett is living with danger and uncertainty. What kind of attitude does Crockett seem to have? What type of person do you think he is? Use details from the diary to support your answers.

Reading Literature: Diaries

1. **Understanding Setting.** The **setting** is the time and place in which actions happen. The setting for the events in this diary is important. What aspects of the setting does Crockett describe? How does the setting contribute to the events described?

2. **Identifying Tone.** In this diary, Crockett's **tone,** or attitude, is primarily one of enthusiasm for an independent Texas. Select three passages where his choice of words suggests this enthusiasm.

   Two of the diary entries, February 26 and March 1, mention Colonel Jim Bowie. What is the tone of these entries?

3. **Examining Figurative Language.** As you know, **figurative language** is language that communicates ideas beyond the literal meanings of words. Crockett uses figurative language that makes his descriptions lively and vivid. Identify the figurative language in these sentences from the selection, and explain the meaning of each sentence.

   a. We have a prospect of soon getting our bellies full of fighting.

   b. [The] thirty men from Gonzales . . . are just in the nick of time to reap a harvest of glory; but there is some prospect of sweating blood before we gather it in.

   c. [Bowie's] presence alone is a tower of strength.

   d. Shells have been falling into the fort like hail during the day.

Developing Vocabulary Skills

1. **Using a Pronunciation Key.** A dictionary or glossary tells you how to pronounce a word by giving a respelling of the word. The **respelling** uses letters and symbols to stand for the sounds of each syllable in the spoken word. To find out what each letter and symbol stands for, refer to the pronunciation key of the dictionary or glossary. The **pronunciation key** lists the symbols that are used in the respellings. For each symbol, the key shows a sample word that uses that sound. These sample words are called **key words.** You already know how to pronounce them. For example, look at the pronunciation key in the glossary of this book. Find the symbol ə, called *schwa*. The key tells you that ə is pronounced like the *a* in *alive.*

   Find each of the following words from the diary in the glossary of this book.

   a. assault   c. contempt   e. victuals
   b. commence   d. harangue

Look at the respelling of each word. Match each part of the respelling with a key word in the pronunciation key. For example, the respelling for *sortie* is (sôr′ tē). The key words that match the respelling are *corn,* for the ô sound, and *equal,* for the ē sound. Write each word, its respelling, and its key words on a sheet of paper.

2. **Using Accent Marks.** The respelling also includes **accent marks.** A heavy accent mark is called the **primary accent.** If a word has more than two syllables, it may have more than one accent. The lighter accent mark is called the **secondary accent.** The word *indiscriminate* has two accents: (in′ dis krim′ ə nit).

Add the accent marks to the respellings you wrote for the words in question 1. Then try to say each word by using the accent marks, respelling, and key words.

Developing Skills in Critical Thinking

1. **Recognizing Subjective Statements.** A nonfiction selection often mixes facts and opinions. Sometimes a writer may not realize that some of his or her statements are opinions. He or she is looking at an event or an idea subjectively, that is, with a personal view. A reader must be alert to such statements in order not to confuse them with facts.

Reread the entry in Davy Crockett's diary for February 22, 1836. What reason does he give for the Comanches' refusal to fight with the Mexicans? Can you tell whether this reason is a fact? What other reasons might the Comanches have had?

Review the entries for March 1 and March 2. Find the following sentences in context. Explain how each sentence is subjective.

a. The enemy becomes more daring as his numbers increase.
b. Universal independence is an almighty idea.

2. **Identifying Slanted Writing.** **Slanted writing** is writing that favors one side of an issue. In slanted writing, a writer may use many words with strong connotations. **Connotations** are the feelings and ideas that words suggest. The connotations may lead readers to feel strongly for or against a subject.

In his diary, Davy Crockett presents his view of events. Read the following passage from the diary. Find at least three words with strong negative connotations. What does Crockett believe about his enemy? What response are readers likely to have to this passage?

Last night our hunters brought in some corn, and had a brush with a scout from the enemy beyond gunshot of the fort. They put the scout to flight and got in without injury. They bring accounts that the settlers are flying in all quarters, in dismay, leaving their possessions to the mercy of the ruthless invader, who is literally engaged in a war of extermination more brutal than the untutored savage of the desert could be guilty of.

Developing Writing Skills

Describing a Place. Suppose that Davy Crockett's diary is going to be made into a film. It would be important for the filmmaker to understand the setting and the mood. Imagine what the Texans' fort was like. Write a one-paragraph description of the fort. Use words that suggest the feeling of the place.

Prewriting. Make a list of the details of the setting as you imagine it. Include objects, the weather, trees or other plants, the structures of the fort, and supplies. Then think about the **mood,** or feeling, you want to create. Make lists of nouns, adjectives, verbs, and adverbs you could use to suggest the mood.

Decide how you will present the information about the setting. Figure out the order you will use to describe the details. On your paper, number your details or put them into an outline form.

Drafting. Follow your prewriting notes as you write your description. Use words and phrases that make the arrangement of details in the setting clear. Remember that you want your description to express the mood of the setting. Select words from your lists to create the specific mood.

Revising and Sharing. Read your description carefully. Ask yourself the following questions.

1. Is the topic sentence interesting?
2. Do the words give the reader a good picture of the Texans' fort?
3. Are the details arranged in a way that makes sense?
4. Do the words help create the mood I had in mind?

Change any part of your description that does not present a clear picture. Share your description with the class. How does it differ from the settings imagined by your classmates?

From

Anne Frank: The Diary of a Young Girl
Part One

This diary was written by a teen-age Jewish girl who was forced to live in hiding with her family during World War II. As you read, you will discover Anne Frank's honesty, humor, and courage.

ANNE FRANK
Translated by B. M. Mooyaart

Because of persecution from the Nazis in Germany in the 1930's, many Jews moved to Holland. The Nazi army invaded Holland during World War II, however. Jews again had to flee or go into hiding. Those who did not escape were sent to concentration camps in Germany, Poland, and Austria. There, millions of Jews and others who opposed the Nazis were killed or died of disease and starvation.

The Frank family moved to Holland in 1933. As the threat of being captured increased, friends helped them arrange a hiding place in the top floors of an office building in Amsterdam. They moved there in July 1942 and remained for more than two years before being discovered. Anne Frank was thirteen when the family went into hiding. She kept a diary during the whole time. The following excerpts are from that diary. They begin a short time before the family moved to the office building, which Anne called the "Secret Annexe."

Saturday, 20 June, 1942

I haven't written for a few days, because I wanted first of all to think about my diary. It's an odd idea for someone like me to keep a diary; not only because I have never done so before, but because it seems to me that neither I—nor for that matter anyone else—will be interested in the unbosomings of a thirteen-year-old schoolgirl. Still, what does that matter? I want to write, but more than that, I want to bring out all kinds of things that lie buried deep in my heart.

There is a saying that "paper is more patient than man"; it came back to me on one of my slightly melancholy days, while I sat chin in hand, feeling too bored and limp even to make up my mind whether to go out or stay at home. Yes, there is no doubt that paper is patient and as I don't intend to show this cardboard-covered notebook, bearing the proud name of "diary," to anyone, unless I find a real friend, boy or girl, probably nobody cares. And now I come to the root of the matter, the reason for my starting a diary: it is that I have no such real friend.

Let me put it more clearly, since no one will believe that a girl of thirteen feels herself quite alone in the world, nor is it so. I have darling parents and a sister of sixteen. I know about thirty people whom one might call friends—I have strings of boy friends, anxious to catch a glimpse of me and who, failing that, peep at me through mirrors in class. I have relations, aunts and uncles, who are darlings too, a good home, no—I don't seem to lack anything. But it's the same with all my friends, just fun and joking, nothing more. I can never bring myself to talk of anything outside the common round. We don't seem to be able to get any closer, that is the root of the trouble. Perhaps I lack confidence, but anyway, there it is, a stubborn fact and I don't seem to be able to do anything about it.

Hence, this diary. In order to enhance in my mind's eye the picture of the friend for whom I have waited so long, I don't want to set down a series of bald facts in a diary like most people do, but I want this diary itself to be my friend, and I shall call my friend Kitty. No one will grasp what I'm talking about if I begin my letters to Kitty just out of the blue, so, albeit unwillingly, I will start by sketching in brief the story of my life.

My father was thirty-six when he married my mother, who was then twenty-five. My sister Margot was born in 1926 in Frankfort-on-Main, I followed on June 12, 1929, and, as we are Jewish, we emigrated to Holland in 1933, where my father was appointed Managing Director of Travies N.V. This firm is in close relationship with the firm of Kolen & Co. in the same building, of which my father is a partner.

The rest of our family, however, felt the full impact of Hitler's anti-Jewish laws, so life was filled with anxiety. In 1938 after the pogroms,[1] my two uncles (my mother's brothers) escaped to the U.S.A. My old grandmother came to us, she was then seventy-three. After May 1940 good times rapidly fled: first the war, then the capitulation, followed by the arrival of the Germans, which is when the sufferings of us Jews really began. Anti-Jewish decrees followed each other in quick succession. Jews must wear a yellow star,[2] Jews must hand

---

1. **pogrom** (pō grăm')–An official organized persecution and killing of a minority group.
2. **yellow star**–This refers to the Star of David, the universal symbol of Judaism. It is made from two triangles interwoven to form a six-pointed star. In the countries the Nazis dominated, they forced all Jews to wear the star for easy identification.

Anne (right) playing with her friend. © 1984 by ANNE FRANK-Fonds/COSMOPRESS, Geneva.

in their bicycles, Jews are banned from trams and are forbidden to drive. Jews are only allowed to do their shopping between three and five o'clock and then only in shops which bear the placard "Jewish shop." Jews must be indoors by eight o'clock and cannot even sit in their own gardens after that hour. Jews are forbidden to visit theaters, cinemas, and other places of entertainment. Jews may not take part in public sports. Swimming baths, tennis courts, hockey fields, and other sports grounds are all prohibited to them. Jews may not visit Christians. Jews must go to Jewish schools, and many more restrictions of a similar kind.

So we could not do this and were forbidden to do that. But life went on in spite of it all. Jopie[3] used to say to me, "You're scared to do anything, because it may be forbidden." Our freedom was strictly limited. Yet things were still bearable.

Granny died in January 1942; no one will ever know how much she is present in my thoughts and how much I love her still. . . .

So far everything is all right with the four of us and here I come to the present day.

---

3. **Jopie**—Anne's best girl friend.

Sunday morning, 5 July, 1942

Dear Kitty,

Our examination results were announced in the Jewish Theater last Friday. I couldn't have hoped for better. My report is not at all bad, I had one *vix satis,*[4] a five for algebra, two sixes, and the rest were all sevens or eights. They were certainly pleased at home, although over the question of marks my parents are quite different from most. They don't care a bit whether my reports are good or bad as long as I'm well and happy, and not too cheeky: then the rest will come by itself. I am just the opposite. I don't want to be a bad pupil; I should really have stayed in the seventh form in the Montessori School, but was accepted for the Jewish Secondary. When all the Jewish children had to go to Jewish schools, the headmaster took Lies and me conditionally after a bit of persuasion. He relied on us to do our best and I don't want to let him down. My sister Margot has her report too, brilliant as usual. She would move up with *cum laude*[5] if that existed at school, she is so brainy. Daddy has been at home a lot lately, as there is nothing for him to do at business; it must be rotten to feel so superfluous. Mr. Koophuis has taken over Travies and Mr. Kraler the firm Kolen & Co. When we walked across our little square together a few days ago, Daddy began to talk of us going into hiding. I asked him why on earth he was beginning to talk of that already. "Yes, Anne," he said, "you know that we have been taking food, clothes, furniture to other people for more than a year now. We don't want our belongings to be seized by the Germans, but we certainly don't want to fall into their clutches ourselves. So we shall disappear of our own accord and not wait until they come and fetch us."

"But, Daddy, when would it be?" He spoke so seriously that I grew very anxious.

"Don't you worry about it, we shall arrange everything. Make the most of your carefree young life while you can." That was all. Oh, may the fulfillment of these somber words remain far distant yet!

Yours, Anne

Wednesday, 8 July, 1942

Dear Kitty,

Years seem to have passed between Sunday and now. So much has happened, it is just as if the whole world had turned upside down. But I am still alive, Kitty, and that is the main thing, Daddy says.

Yes, I'm still alive, indeed, but don't ask where or how. You wouldn't understand a word, so I will begin by telling you what happened on Sunday afternoon.

At three o'clock (Harry[6] had just gone,

---

4. **vix satis** (viks sa′tis)–*Latin*, hardly enough.
5. **cum laude** (koom lou′de)–*Latin*, with praise.
6. **Harry**–A friend of Anne's.

but was coming back later) someone rang the front doorbell. I was lying lazily reading a book on the veranda in the sunshine, so I didn't hear it. A bit later, Margot appeared at the kitchen door looking very excited. "The S.S.[7] have sent a call-up notice for Daddy," she whispered. "Mummy has gone to see Mr. Van Daan already." (Van Daan is a friend who works with Daddy in the business.) It was a great shock to me, a call-up; everyone knows what that means. I picture concentration camps and lonely cells—should we allow him to be doomed to this? "Of course he won't go," declared Margot, while we waited together. "Mummy has gone to the Van Daans to discuss whether we should move into our hiding place tomorrow. The Van Daans are going with us, so we shall be seven in all." Silence. We couldn't talk any more, thinking about Daddy, who, little knowing what was going on, was visiting some old people in the Joodse Invalide;[8] waiting for Mummy, the heat and suspense, all made us very overawed and silent.

Suddenly the bell rang again. "That is Harry," I said. "Don't open the door." Margot held me back, but it was not necessary as we heard Mummy and Mr. Van Daan downstairs, talking to Harry, then they came in and closed the door behind them. Each time the bell went, Margot or I had to creep softly down to see if it was Daddy, not opening the door to anyone else.

Margot and I were sent out of the room.

Van Daan wanted to talk to Mummy alone. When we were alone together in our bedroom, Margot told me that the call-up was not for Daddy, but for her. I was more frightened than ever and began to cry. Margot is sixteen; would they really take girls of that age away alone? But thank goodness she won't go, Mummy said so herself; that must be what Daddy meant when he talked about us going into hiding.

Into hiding—where would we go, in a town or the country, in a house or a cottage, when, how, where . . . ?

These were questions I was not allowed to ask, but I couldn't get them out of my mind. Margot and I began to pack some of our most vital belongings into a school satchel. The first thing I put in was this diary, then hair curlers, handkerchiefs, schoolbooks, a comb, old letters; I put in the craziest things with the idea that we were going into hiding. But I'm not sorry, memories mean more to me than dresses.

At five o'clock Daddy finally arrived, and we phoned Mr. Koophuis to ask if he could come around in the evening. Van Daan went and fetched Miep. Miep has been in the business with Daddy since 1933 and has become a close friend, likewise her brand-new husband, Henk. Miep came and took some shoes, dresses, coats, underwear, and stockings away in her bag, promising to return in the evening. Then silence fell on the house; not one of us felt

---

7. **S.S.**–A military unit of the Nazi party.
8. **Joodse Invalide**–Jewish hospital.

like eating anything, it was still hot and everything was very strange. We let our large upstairs room to a certain Mr. Goudsmit, a divorced man in his thirties, who appeared to have nothing to do on this particular evening; we simply could not get rid of him without being rude; he hung about until ten o'clock. At eleven o'clock Miep and Henk Van Santen arrived. Once again, shoes, stockings, books, and underclothes disappeared into Miep's bag and Henk's deep pockets, and at eleven-thirty they too disappeared. I was dog-tired and although I knew it would be my last night in my own bed, I fell asleep immediately and didn't wake up until Mummy called me at five-thirty the next morning. Luckily it was not so hot as Sunday; warm rain fell steadily all day. We put on heaps of clothes as if we were going to the North Pole, the sole reason being to take clothes with us. No Jew in our situation would have dreamed of going out with a suitcase full of clothing. I had on two vests, three pairs of pants, a dress, on top of that a skirt, jacket, summer coat, two pair of stockings, lace-up shoes, woolly cap, scarf, and still more; I was nearly stifled before we started, but no one inquired about that.

Margot filled her satchel with schoolbooks, fetched her bicycle, and rode off behind Miep into the unknown, as far as I was concerned. You see I still didn't know where our secret hiding place was to be. At seven-thirty the door closed behind us. Moortje, my little cat, was the only creature to whom I said farewell. She would have a good home with the neighbors. This was all written in a letter addressed to Mr. Goudsmit.

There was one pound of meat in the kitchen for the cat, breakfast things lying on the table, stripped beds, all giving the impression that we had left helter-skelter. But we didn't care about impressions, we only wanted to get away, only escape and arrive safely, nothing else. Continued tomorrow.

Yours, Anne

Thursday, 9 July, 1942

Dear Kitty,
So we walked in the pouring rain, Daddy, Mummy, and I, each with a school satchel and shopping bag filled to the brim with all kinds of things thrown together anyhow.

We got sympathetic looks from people on their way to work. You could see by their faces how sorry they were they couldn't offer us a lift; the gaudy yellow star spoke for itself.

Only when we were on the road did Mummy and Daddy begin to tell me bits and pieces about the plan. For months as many of our goods and chattels and necessities of life as possible had been sent away and they were sufficiently ready for us to have gone into hiding of our own accord on July 16. The plan had had to be speeded up ten days because of the call-up, so our quarters would not be so well organized, but we had to make the best of it. The hiding place itself would be in the building where Daddy has his office. It will be hard for outsiders to understand, but I shall explain that later on. Daddy didn't have many people working for him: Mr. Kraler, Koophuis, Miep, and Elli Vossen, a twenty-three-year-old typist who all knew of our arrival. Mr. Vossen, Elli's father, and two boys worked in the warehouse; they had not been told.

I will describe the building: there is a large warehouse on the ground floor which is used as a store. The front door to the house is next to the warehouse door, and inside the front door is a second doorway which leads to a staircase. There is another door at the top of the stairs, with a frosted glass window in it, which has "Office" written in black letters across it. That is the large main office, very big, very light, and very full. Elli, Miep, and Mr. Koophuis work there in the daytime. A small dark room containing the safe, a wardrobe, and a large cupboard leads to a small somewhat dark second office. Mr. Kraler and Mr. Van Daan used to sit here, now it is only Mr. Kraler. One can reach Kraler's office from the passage, but only via a glass door which can be opened from the inside, but not easily from the outside.

From Kraler's office a long passage goes past the coal store, up four steps and leads to the showroom of the whole building: the private office. Dark, dignified furniture,

The Secret Annexe. Culver Pictures, New York City.

linoleum and carpets on the floor, radio, smart lamp, everything first-class. Next door there is a roomy kitchen with a hot-water faucet and a gas stove. Next door the W.C.[9] That is the first floor.

A wooden staircase leads from the downstairs passage to the next floor. There

9. **W.C.**–A water closet, or bathroom.

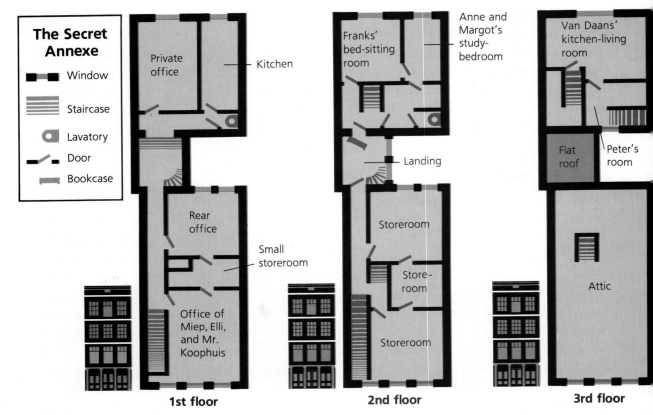

The Secret Annexe

Window

Staircase

Lavatory

Door

Bookcase

Private office

Kitchen

Rear office

Small storeroom

Office of Miep, Elli, and Mr. Koophuis

1st floor

Franks' bed-sitting room

Anne and Margot's study-bedroom

Landing

Storeroom

Store-room

Storeroom

2nd floor

Van Daans' kitchen-living room

Flat roof

Peter's room

Attic

3rd floor

Floor plan of the Secret Annexe.

is a small landing at the top. There is a door at each end of the landing, the left one leading to a storeroom at the front of the house and to the attics. One of those really steep Dutch staircases runs from the side to the other door opening on to the street.

The right-hand door leads to our "Secret Annexe." No one would ever guess that there would be so many rooms hidden behind that plain gray door. There's a little step in front of the door and then you are inside.

There is a steep staircase immediately opposite the entrance. On the left a tiny passage brings you into a room which was to become the Frank family's bed-sitting-room, next door a smaller room, study and bedroom for the two young ladies of the family. On the right a little room without windows containing the washbasin and a small W.C. compartment, with another door leading to Margot's and my room. If you go up the next flight of stairs and open the door, you are simply amazed that there could be such a big light room in such an old house by the canal. There is a gas stove in this room (thanks to the fact that it was used as a laboratory) and a sink. This is now the kitchen for the Van Daan couple, besides being general living room, dining room, and scullery.

A tiny little corridor room will become Peter Van Daan's apartment. Then, just as on the lower landing, there is a large attic. So there you are, I've introduced you to the whole of our beautiful "Secret Annexe."

Yours, Anne

Saturday, 11 July, 1942

Dear Kitty,

Daddy, Mummy, and Margot can't get used to the sound of the Westertoren clock yet, which tells us the time every quarter of an hour. I can. I loved it from the start, and especially in the night it's like a faithful friend. I expect you will be interested to hear what it feels like to "disappear"; well, all I can say is that I don't know myself yet. I don't think I shall ever feel really at home in this house, but that does not mean that I loathe it here; it is more like being on vacation in a very peculiar boardinghouse. Rather a mad idea, perhaps, but that is how it strikes me. The "Secret Annexe" is an ideal hiding place. Although it leans to one side and is damp, you'd never find such a comfortable hiding place anywhere in Amsterdam, no, perhaps not even in the whole of Holland. Our little room

looked very bare at first with nothing on the walls; but thanks to Daddy who had brought my film-star collection and picture postcards on beforehand, and with the aid of paste pot and brush, I have transformed the walls into one gigantic picture. This makes it look much more cheerful, and, when the Van Daans come, we'll get some wood from the attic, and make a few little cupboards for the walls and other odds and ends to make it look more lively.

. . . The four of us went to the private office yesterday evening and turned on the radio. I was so terribly frightened that someone might hear it that I simply begged Daddy to come upstairs with me. Mummy understood how I felt and came too. We are very nervous in other ways, too, that the neighbors might hear us or see something going on. We made curtains straight away on the first day. Really one can hardly call them curtains, they are just light, loose strips of material, all different shapes, quality, and pattern, which Daddy and I sewed together in a most unprofessional way. These works of art are fixed in position with drawing pins, not to come down until we emerge from here.

There are some large business premises on the right of us, and on the left a furniture workshop; there is no one there after working hours but even so, sounds could travel through the walls. We have forbidden Margot to cough at night, although she has a bad cold, and make her swallow large doses of codeine. I am looking for Tuesday when the Van Daans arrive; it will be much more fun and not so quiet. It is the silence that frightens me so in the evenings and at night. I wish like anything that one of our protectors could sleep here at night. I can't tell you how oppressive it is *never* to be able to go outdoors, also I'm very afraid that we shall be discovered and be shot. That is not exactly a pleasant prospect. We have to whisper and tread lightly during the day, otherwise the people in the warehouse might hear us.

Someone is calling me.

Yours, Anne

Friday, 14 August, 1942

Dear Kitty,

I have deserted you for a whole month, but honestly, there is so little news here that I can't find amusing things to tell you every day. The Van Daans arrived on July 13. We thought they were coming on the fourteenth, but between the thirteenth and sixteenth of July the Germans called up people right and left which created more and more unrest, so they played for safety, better a day too early than a day too late. At nine-thirty in the morning (we were still having breakfast) Peter arrived, the Van Daans' son, not sixteen yet, a rather soft, shy, gawky youth; can't expect much from his company. He brought his cat (Mouschi) with him. Mr. and Mrs. Van Daan arrived half an hour later. . . .

Yours, Anne

Friday, 21 August, 1942

Dear Kitty,

The entrance to our hiding place has now been properly concealed. Mr. Kraler thought it would be better to put a cupboard in front of our door (because a lot of houses are being searched for hidden bicycles), but of course it had to be a movable cupboard that can open like a door.

Mr. Vossen made the whole thing. We had already let him into the secret and he can't do enough to help. If we want to go downstairs, we have to first bend down and then jump, because the step is gone. The first three days we were all going about with masses of lumps on our foreheads, because we all knocked ourselves against the low doorway. Now we have nailed a cloth filled with wood wool against the top of the door. Let's see if that helps!

I am not working much at present; I'm giving myself holidays until September. Then Daddy is going to give me lessons; it's shocking how much I've forgotten already. There is little change in our life here. Mr. Van Daan and I usually manage to upset each other; it's just the opposite with Margot whom he likes very much. Mummy sometimes treats me just like a baby, which I can't bear. Otherwise things are going better. I still don't like Peter any more, he is so boring; he flops lazily on his bed half the time, does a bit of carpentry, and then goes back for another snooze.

What a fool!

It is lovely weather and in spite of everything we make the most we can of it by lying on a camp bed in the attic, where the sun shines through an open window.

Yours, Anne

Thursday, 25 March, 1943

Dear Kitty,

Yesterday Mummy, Daddy, Margot, and I were sitting pleasantly together when suddenly Peter came in and whispered something in Daddy's ear. I heard something about "a barrel fallen over in the warehouse" and "someone fumbling about at the door." Margot had heard it too; but when Daddy and Peter went off immediately, she tried to calm me down a bit, because I was naturally as white as a sheet and very jittery.

The three of us waited in suspense. A minute or two later Mrs. Van Daan came upstairs; she'd been listening to the wireless in the private office. She told us that Pim[10] had asked her to turn off the wireless and go softly upstairs. But you know what that's like, if you want to be extra quiet, then each step of the old stairs creaks twice as loudly. Five minutes later Pim and Peter appeared again, white to the roots of their hair, and told us their experiences.

They had hidden themselves under the stairs and waited, with no result at first. But suddenly, yes, I must tell you, they heard two loud bumps, just as if two doors were banged here in the house. Pim was upstairs in one leap. Peter warned Dussel[11] first, who finally landed upstairs with a lot of fuss and noise. Then we all went up in stockinged feet to the Van Daans on the next floor. Mr. Van Daan had a bad cold and had already gone to bed, so we all drew up closely around his bed and whispered our suspicions to him.

Each time Mr. Van Daan coughed loudly, Mrs. Van Daan and I were so scared that we thought we were going to have a fit. That went on until one of us got the bright idea of giving him some codeine, which soothed the cough at once. Again we waited and waited, but we heard no more and finally we all came to the conclusion that the thieves had taken to their heels when they heard footsteps in the house, which was otherwise so silent.

Now it was unfortunate that the wireless downstairs was still turned to England, and that the chairs were neatly arranged around it. If the door had been forced, and the air-raid wardens had noticed and warned the police, then the results might have been very unpleasant. So Mr. Van Daan got up and put on his coat and hat and followed Daddy cautiously downstairs, Peter took up the rear, armed with a large hammer in case of emergencies. The ladies upstairs (including Margot and me) waited

---

10. **Pim**—Nickname for Anne's father.
11. **Dussel**—A Jewish dentist who joined the Franks and Van Daans in the Secret Annexe.

The clocktower as seen out the window from the Secret Annexe. ©1984 by ANNE FRANK-Fonds/COSMOPRESS, Geneva.

in suspense, until the gentlemen reappeared five minutes later and told us that all was quiet in the house. . . .

When something like that happens, heaps of other things seem to come at the same time, as now. Number One was that the clock at the Westertoren, which I always find so reassuring, did not strike. Number Two was that, Mr. Vossen having left earlier than usual the previous evening, we didn't know definitely whether Elli had been able to get hold of the key, and had perhaps forgotten to shut the door. It was still evening and we were still in a state of uncertainty, although we certainly did feel a bit reassured by the fact that from about eight o'clock, when the burglar had alarmed the house, until half past ten we had not heard a sound. On further reflec-

tion it also seemed very unlikely to us that a thief would have forced open a door so early in the evening, while there were still people about in the street. Moreover, one of us got the idea that it was possible that the caretaker of the warehouse next door was still at work since, in the excitement, and with the thin walls, one can easily make a mistake, and what's more, one's imagination can play a big part at such critical moments.

So we all went to bed; but none of us could get to sleep. Daddy as well as Mummy and Mr. Dussel were awake, and without much exaggeration I can say that I hardly slept a wink. This morning the men went downstairs to see whether the outside door was still shut, and everything turned out to be quite safe. We gave everyone a detailed description of the nerve-racking event. They all made fun of it, but it is easy to laugh at such things afterwards. Elli was the only one who took us seriously.

Yours, Anne

Tuesday, 18 May, 1943

Dear Kitty,

I witnessed a terrific air battle between German and British planes. Unfortunately a couple of the Allies had to jump from burning machines. Our milkman, who lives in Halfweg, saw four Canadians sitting by the roadside, one of them spoke fluent Dutch. He asked the milkman to give him a light for his cigarette, and told him that the crew had consisted of six men. The pilot was burned to death, and their fifth man had hidden himself somewhere. The German police came and fetched the four perfectly fit men. I wonder how they managed to have such clear brains after that terrifying parachute trip.

Although it is fairly warm, we have to light our fires every other day, in order to burn vegetable peelings and refuse. We can't put anything in the garbage pails, because we must always think of the warehouse boy. How easily one could be betrayed by being a little careless!

All students who wish either to get their degrees this year, or continue their studies, are compelled to sign that they are in sympathy with the Germans and approve of the New Order. Eighty per cent have refused to go against their consciences. Naturally they had to bear the consequences. All the students who do not sign have to go to a labor camp in Germany. What will be left of the youth of the country if they have all got to do hard labor in Germany? . . .

Yours, Anne

Monday evening, 8 November, 1943

Dear Kitty,

If you were to read my pile of letters one after another, you would certainly be struck by the many different moods in which they are written. It annoys me that I am so dependent on the atmosphere here, but I'm certainly not the only one—we all find it the same. If I read a book that impresses me, I have to take myself firmly in hand, before I mix with other people; otherwise they would think my mind rather queer. At the moment, as you've probably noticed, I'm going through a spell of being depressed. I really couldn't tell you why it is, but I believe it's just because I'm a coward, and that's what I keep bumping up against.

This evening, while Elli was still here, there was a long, loud, penetrating ring at the door. I turned white at once, got a tummy-ache and heart palpitations, all from fear. At night, when I'm in bed, I see myself alone in a dungeon, without Mummy and Daddy. Sometimes I wander by the roadside, or our "Secret Annexe" is on fire, or they come and take us away at night. I see everything as if it is actually taking place, and this gives me the feeling that it may all happen to me very soon! Miep often says she envies us for possessing such tranquility here. That may be true, but she is not thinking about all our fears. I simply can't imagine that the world will ever be normal for us again. I do talk about "after the war," but then it is only a castle in the air, something that will never really happen. If I think back to our old house, my girl friends, the fun at school, it is just as if another person lived it all, not me.

I see the eight of us with our "Secret Annexe" as if we were a little piece of blue heaven, surrounded by heavy black rain clouds. The round, clearly defined spot where we stand is still safe, but the clouds gather more closely about us and the circle which separates us from the approaching danger closes more and more tightly. Now we are so surrounded by danger and darkness that we bump against each other, as we search desperately for a means of escape. We all look down below, where people are fighting each other, we look above, where it is quiet and beautiful, and meanwhile we are cut off by the great dark mass, which will not let us go upwards, but which stands before us as an impenetrable wall; it tries to crush us, but cannot do so yet. I can only cry and implore: "Oh, if only the black circle could recede and open the way for us!"

Yours, Anne

Developing Comprehension Skills

1. Who is Kitty?

2. Why is Anne starting a diary?

3. Why must the Frank family hide? What fate do they risk otherwise?

4. In what building do Anne and her family hide? What problems do they have to deal with?

5. In the diary entry dated Monday, 8 November, 1943, Anne states that she is a coward. Why does she think so? Do you agree with her opinion? Explain your answer.

6. How important is friendship to Anne? What does she think friendship is? State your own definition of a true friend.

7. The parts of the diary you have read go through the first sixteen months of Anne's being in hiding. She will be there for about one more year. What kinds of new problems might the residents of the Secret Annexe face? Do you think any of Anne's relationships will change? any of her attitudes? Explain your answers.

Reading Literature: Diaries

1. **Understanding Setting. Setting** is the time and place of the action. The setting of this selection is important to what happens. Identify three aspects of the setting. They may be related to time or to place. How do these aspects affect what happens to Anne? How do they affect her relationships? her activities? her feelings?

2. **Analyzing Figurative Language.** Reread the last paragraph of the entry dated 8 November, 1943. Notice the comparisons Anne uses to describe the situation of the people in the Secret Annexe. What could the clouds and darkness stand for? What does the wall that is trying to crush them represent?

3. **Examining a Diary.** In her diary Anne discusses her feelings and opinions. She also describes other people, everyday life, and the events of the war. Which parts of the diary do you find the most interesting and appealing? Use examples in your answer.

From

Anne Frank: The Diary of a Young Girl
Part Two

What will happen to the Franks and to those who share the Secret Annexe with them? How will Anne's feelings change as the war goes on? Read to learn more about Anne and her family.

ANNE FRANK
Translated by B. M. Mooyaart

Thursday, 6 January, 1944

Dear Kitty,

My longing to talk to someone became so intense that somehow or other I took it into my head to choose Peter.

Sometimes if I've been upstairs in Peter's room during the day, it always struck me as very snug, but because Peter is so retiring and would never turn anyone out who became a nuisance, I never dared stay long, because I was afraid he might think me a bore. I tried to think of an excuse to stay in his room and get him talking, without it being too noticeable, and my chance came yesterday. Peter has a mania for crossword puzzles at the moment and hardly does anything else. I helped him with them and we soon sat opposite each other at his little table, he on the chair and me on the divan.

It gave me a strange feeling each time I looked into his deep blue eyes, and he sat

Anne Frank, 1941. © 1984 by ANNE FRANK-Fonds/ COSMOPRESS, Geneva.

there with that mysterious laugh playing round his lips. I was able to read his inward thoughts. I could see on his face that look of helplessness and uncertainty as to how

Anne Frank: The Diary of a Young Girl   469

to behave, and, at the same time, a trace of his sense of manhood. I noticed his shy manner and it made me feel very gentle; I couldn't refrain from meeting those dark eyes again and again, and with my whole heart I almost beseeched him: oh, tell me, what is going on inside you; oh, can't you look beyond this ridiculous chatter?

But the evening passed and nothing happened. . . .

Yours, Anne

Saturday, 12 February, 1944

Dear Kitty,

The sun is shining, the sky is a deep blue, there is a lovely breeze and I'm longing—so longing—for everything. To talk, for freedom, for friends, to be alone. And I do so long . . . to cry! I feel as if I'm going to burst, and I know that it would get better with crying; but I can't, I'm restless, I go from one room to the other, breathe through the crack of a closed window, feel my heart beating, as if it is saying, "Can't you satisfy my longings at last?"

I believe that it's spring within me, I feel that spring is awakening, I feel it in my whole body and soul. It is an effort to behave normally, I feel utterly confused, don't know what to read, what to write, what to do, I only know that I am longing . . . !

Yours, Anne

Sunday, 13 February, 1944

Dear Kitty,

Since Saturday a lot has changed for me. It came about like this. I longed—and am still longing—but . . . now something has happened, which has made it a little, just a little, less.

To my great joy—I will be quite honest about it—already this morning I noticed that Peter kept looking at me all the time. Not in the ordinary way, I don't know how, I just can't explain.

I used to think that Peter was in love with Margot, but yesterday I suddenly had the feeling that it is not so. I made a special effort not to look at him too much, because whenever I did, he kept on looking too and then—yes, then—it gave me a lovely feeling inside, but which I mustn't feel too often.

I desperately want to be alone. Daddy has noticed that I'm not quite my usual self, but I really can't tell him everything. "Leave me in peace, leave me alone," that's what I'd like to keep crying out all the time. Who knows, the day may come when I'm left alone more than I may wish!

Yours, Anne

Friday, 18 February, 1944

Dear Kitty,

Whenever I go upstairs now, I keep on hoping that I shall see "him." Because my life now has an object, and I have something to look forward to, everything has become more pleasant.

At least the object of my feelings is always there, and I needn't be afraid of rivals, except Margot. Don't think I'm in love, because I'm not, but I do have the feeling all the time that something fine can grow up between us, something that gives confidence and friendship. If I get half a chance, I go up to him now. It's not like it used to be when he didn't know how to begin. It's just the opposite—he's still talking when I'm half out of the room.

Mummy doesn't like it much, and always says I'll be a nuisance and that I must leave him in peace. Honestly, doesn't she realize that I've got some intuition? She looks at me so queerly every time I go into Peter's little room. If I come downstairs from there, she asks me where I've been. I simply can't bear it, and think it's horrible.

Yours, Anne

Wednesday, 23 February, 1944

Dear Kitty,

It's lovely weather outside and I've quite perked up since yesterday. Nearly every morning I go to the attic where Peter works to blow the stuffy air out of my lungs. From my favorite spot on the floor I look up at the blue sky and the bare chestnut tree, on whose branches little raindrops shine, appearing like silver, and at the seagulls and other birds as they glide on the wind.

He stood with his head against a thick beam, and I sat down. We breathed the fresh air, looked outside, and both felt that the spell should not be broken by words. We remained like this for a long time, and when he had to go up to the loft to chop wood, I knew that he was a nice fellow. He climbed the ladder, and I followed; then he chopped wood for about a quarter of an hour, during which time we still remained silent. I watched him from where I stood. He was obviously doing his best to show off his strength. But I looked out of the open window too, over a large area of Amsterdam, over all the roofs and on to the horizon, which was such a pale blue that it was hard to see the dividing line. "As long as this exists," I thought, "and I may live to see it, this sunshine, the cloudless skies, while this lasts, I cannot be unhappy." . . .

Oh, who knows, perhaps it won't be long before I can share this overwhelming feeling of bliss with someone who feels the way I do about it.

Yours, Anne

Tuesday, 7 March, 1944

Dear Kitty,

If I think now of my life in 1942, it all seems so unreal. It was quite a different Anne who enjoyed that heavenly existence from the Anne who has grown wise within these walls. Yes, it was a heavenly life. Boyfriends at every turn, about twenty friends and acquaintances of my own age, the darling of nearly all the teachers, spoiled from top to toe by Mummy and Daddy, lots of sweets, enough pocket money, what more could one want? . . .

Now I look back at that Anne as an amusing, but very superficial girl, who has nothing to do with the Anne of today. Peter said quite rightly about me: "If ever I saw you, you were always surrounded by two or more boys and a whole troupe of girls. You were always laughing and always the center of everything!"

What is left of this girl? Oh, don't worry, I haven't forgotten how to laugh or to answer back readily. I'm just as good, if not better, at criticizing people, and I can still flirt if . . . I wish. That's not it though, I'd like that sort of life again for an evening, a few days, or even a week; the life which seems so carefree. But at the end of that week, I should be dead beat and would be only too thankful to listen to anyone who began to talk about something sensible. I don't want followers, but friends, admirers who fall not for a flattering smile but for what one does and for one's character. . . .

The first half of 1943: my fits of crying, the loneliness, how I slowly began to see all my faults and shortcomings, which are so great and which seemed much greater then. During the day I deliberately talked about anything and everything that was farthest from my thoughts, tried to draw Pim to me; but couldn't. Alone I had to face the difficult task of changing myself, to stop the everlasting reproaches, which were so oppressive and which reduced me to such terrible despondency.

Things improved slightly in the second half of the year, I became a young woman and was treated more like a grownup. I started to think, and write stories, and came to the conclusion that the others no longer had the right to throw me about like an India-rubber ball. I wanted to change in accordance with my own desires. But *one* thing that struck me even more was when I realized that even Daddy would never become my confidant over everything. I didn't want to trust anyone but myself any more.

At the beginning of the New Year: the second great change, my dream. . . . And with it I discovered my longing, not for a girl friend, but for a boy friend. I also discovered my inward happiness and my defensive armor of superficiality and gaiety. In due time I quieted down and discovered my boundless desire for all that is beautiful and good.

And in the evening, when I lie in bed and end my prayers with the words, "I thank you, God, for all that is good and dear and beautiful," I am filled with joy. Then I think about "the good" of going into hiding, of my health and with my whole being of the "dearness" of Peter, of that which is still embryonic and impressionable and which we neither of us dare to name or touch, of that which will come sometime; love, the future, happiness and of "the beauty" which exists in the world;

the world, nature, beauty and all, all that is exquisite and fine.

I don't think then of all the misery, but of the beauty that still remains. This is one of the things that Mummy and I are so entirely different about. Her counsel when one feels melancholy is: "Think of all the misery in the world and be thankful that you are not sharing it!" My advice is: "Go outside, to the fields; enjoy nature and the sunshine; go out and try to recapture happiness in yourself and in God. Think of all the beauty that's still left in and around you and be happy!"

I don't see how Mummy's idea can be right, because then you would have to behave as if you are going through the misery yourself. Then you are lost. On the contrary, I've found that there is always some beauty left—in nature, sunshine, freedom, in yourself; these can all help you. Look at these things, then you find yourself again, and God, and then you regain your balance.

And whoever is happy will make others happy too. He who has courage and faith will never perish in misery!

Yours, Anne

Friday, 17 March, 1944

Dear Kitty,

. . . [Margot and I] are treated as children over outward things, and we are much older than most girls of our age

Anne (center), with Father (left), Margot (far right), and family friends attending Miep's wedding, July 16, 1941. Copyright © Anne Frank-Fonds/COSMOPRESS, Geneva.

inwardly.

Although I'm only fourteen, I know quite well what I want, I know who is right and who is wrong, I have my opinions, my own ideas and principles, and although it may sound pretty mad from an adolescent, I feel more of a person than a child. I feel quite independent of anyone.

I know that I can discuss things and argue better than Mummy; I know I'm not so prejudiced, I don't exaggerate so much, I am more precise and adroit and because of this—you may laugh—I feel superior to her over a great many things. If I love anyone, above all I must have admiration for them, admiration and respect. Everything would be all right if only I had Peter, for I do admire him in many ways. He is such a nice, good-looking boy!

Yours, Anne

Sunday, 19 March, 1944

Dear Kitty,

Yesterday was a great day for me. I had decided to talk things out with Peter. Just as we were going to sit down to supper I whispered to him, "Are you going to do shorthand this evening, Peter?" "No," was his reply. "Then I'd just like to talk to you later!" He agreed. After the dishes were done, I stood by the window in his parents' room awhile for the look of things, but it wasn't long before I went to Peter. He was standing on the left side of the open window, I went and stood on the right side, and we talked. It was much easier to talk beside the open window in semidarkness than in bright light, and I believe Peter felt the same.

We told each other so much, so very much, that I can't repeat it all, but it was lovely; the most wonderful evening I have ever had in the "Secret Annexe." I will just tell you briefly the various things we talked about. First we talked about the quarrels and how I regard them quite differently now, and then about the estrangement between us and our parents.

I told Peter about Mummy and Daddy, and Margot, and about myself.

At one moment he asked, "I suppose you always give each other a good night kiss, don't you?"

"*One,* dozens, why, don't you?"

"No, I have hardly ever kissed anyone."

"Not even on your birthday?"

"Yes, I have then."

We talked about how we neither of us confide in our parents, and how his parents would have loved to have his confidence, but that he didn't wish it. How I cry my heart out in bed, and he goes up in the loft and swears. How Margot and I really only know each other well for a little while, but that, even so, we don't tell each other everything, because we are always together. Over every imaginable thing—oh, he was just as I thought!

Then we talked about 1942, how different we were then. We just don't recognize ourselves as the same people any more. How we simply couldn't bear each other in the beginning. He thought I was much too talkative and unruly, and I soon came to the conclusion that I'd no time for him. I couldn't understand why he didn't flirt with me, but now I'm glad. He also mentioned how much he isolated himself from us all. I said that there was not much difference between my noise and his silence. That I love peace and quiet too, and have nothing for myself alone, except my diary. How glad he is that my parents have children here, and that I'm glad he is here. That I understand his reserve now and his relationship with his parents, and how I would love to be able to help him.

"You always do help me," he said. "How?" I asked, very surprised. "By your cheerfulness." That was certainly the loveliest thing he said. It was wonderful, he must have grown to love me as a friend, and that is enough for the time being. I am so grateful and happy, I just can't find the words. I must apologize, Kitty, that my style is not up to standard today.

I have just written down what came into my head. I have the feeling now that Peter and I share a secret. If he looks at me with those eyes that laugh and wink, then it's just as if a little light goes on inside me. I hope it will remain like this and that we may have many, many more glorious times together!

Your grateful, happy Anne

Wednesday, 3 May, 1944

Dear Kitty,

. . . Since Saturday we've changed over, and have lunch at half past eleven in the mornings, so we have to last out with one cupful of porridge; this saves us a meal. Vegetables are still very difficult to obtain: we had rotten boiled lettuce this afternoon. Ordinary lettuce, spinach, and boiled lettuce, there's nothing else. With these we eat rotten potatoes, so it's a delicious combination!

As you can easily imagine, we often ask ourselves here despairingly: "What, oh, what is the use of the war? Why can't people live peacefully together? Why all this destruction?"

The question is very understandable, but no one has found a satisfactory answer to it so far. Yes, why do they make still more gigantic planes, still heavier bombs and, at the same time, prefabricated houses for reconstruction? Why should millions be spent daily on the war and yet there's not a penny available for medical services, artists, or for poor people?

Why do some people have to starve, while there are surpluses rotting in other parts of the world? Oh, why are people so crazy?

I don't believe that the big men, the politicians and the capitalists alone, are guilty of the war. Oh no, the little man is just as guilty; otherwise the peoples of the world would have risen up in revolt long ago! There's in people simply an urge to destroy, an urge to kill, to murder and rage, and until all mankind, without exception, undergoes a great change, wars will be waged, everything that has been built up, cultivated, and grown will be destroyed and disfigured, after which mankind will have to begin all over again.

I have often been downcast, but never in despair; I regard our hiding as a dangerous adventure, romantic and interesting at the same time. In my diary I treat all privations as amusing. I have made up my mind now to lead a different life from other girls and, later on, different from ordinary house-

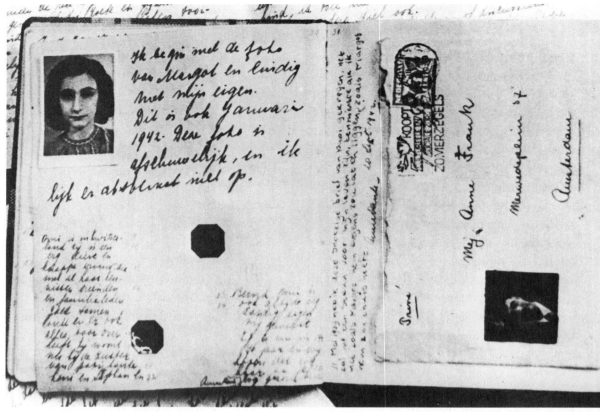

Anne Frank's diary. UPI/Bettmann, New York City.

wives. My start has been so very full of interest, and that is the sole reason why I have to laugh at the humorous side of the most dangerous moments.

I am young and I possess many buried qualities; I am young and strong and am living a great adventure. I am still in the midst of it and can't grumble the whole day long. I have been given a lot, a happy nature, a great deal of cheerfulness and strength. Every day I feel that I am developing inwardly, that the liberation is drawing nearer and how beautiful nature is, how good the people are about me, how interesting this adventure is! Why, then, should I be in despair?

Yours, Anne

Friday, 26 May, 1944

Dear Kitty,

. . . This evening at eight o'clock I had to go to the downstairs lavatory all alone; there was no one down there, as everyone was listening to the radio; I wanted to be brave, but it was difficult. I always feel much safer here upstairs than alone downstairs in that large, silent house; alone with the mysterious muffled noises from upstairs and the tooting of motor horns in the street. I have to hurry for I start to quiver if I begin thinking about the situation.

Again and again I ask myself, would it not have been better for us all if we had not gone into hiding, and if we were dead now and not going through all this misery, especially as we shouldn't be running our protectors into danger any more. But we all recoil from these thoughts too, for we still love life; we haven't yet forgotten the voice of nature. We still hope, hope about everything. I hope something will happen soon now, shooting if need be—nothing can crush us *more* than this restlessness. Let the end come, even if it is hard; then at least we shall know whether we are finally going to win through or go under.

Yours, Anne

Saturday, 15 July, 1944

Dear Kitty,

. . . I have one outstanding trait in my character, which must strike anyone who knows me for any length of time, and that is my knowledge of myself. I can watch myself and my actions, just like an outsider. The Anne of every day I can face entirely without prejudice, without making excuses for her, and watch what's good and what's bad about her. This "self-consciousness" haunts me, and every time I open my mouth I know as soon as I've spoken whether "that ought to have been different" or "that was right as it was." There are so many things about myself that I condemn; I couldn't begin to name them all. I understand more and more how true Daddy's words were when he said: "All children must look after their own upbringing." Parents can only give good advice or put them on the right paths, but the final forming of a person's character lies in their own hands.

In addition to this, I have lots of courage, I always feel so strong and as if I can bear a great deal, I feel so free and so young! I was glad when I first realized it, because I don't think I shall easily bow down before the blows that inevitably come to everyone. . . .

Anyone who claims that the older ones have a more difficult time here certainly doesn't realize to what extent our problems weigh down on us, problems for which we are probably much too young, but which thrust themselves upon us continually, until, after a long time, we think we've found a solution, but the solution doesn't seem able to resist the facts which reduce it to nothing again. That's the difficulty in these times: ideals, dreams, and cherished hopes rise within us, only to meet the horrible truth and be shattered.

It's really a wonder that I haven't dropped all my ideals, because they seem so absurd and impossible to carry out. Yet I keep them, because in spite of everything

I still believe that people are really good at heart. I simply can't build up my hopes on a foundation consisting of confusion, misery, and death. I see the world gradually being turned into a wilderness. I hear the ever approaching thunder, which will destroy us too. I can feel the sufferings of millions and yet, if I look up into the heavens, I think that it will all come right, that this cruelty too will end, and that peace and tranquility will return again.

In the meantime, I must uphold my ideals, for perhaps the time will come when I shall be able to carry them out.

Yours, Anne

Tuesday, 1 August, 1944

Dear Kitty,

. . . I've already told you before that I have as it were, a dual personality. One half embodies my exuberant cheerfulness, making fun of everything, my high-spiritedness, and above all, the way I take everything lightly. This side is usually lying in wait and pushes away the other, which is much better, deeper and purer. You must realize that no one knows Anne's better side and that's why most people find me so insufferable.

Certainly I'm a giddy clown for one afternoon, but then everyone's had enough of me for another month. Really, it's just the same as a love film is for deep-thinking people, simply a diversion, amusing just for once, something which is soon forgotten, not bad, but certainly not good. I loathe having to tell you this, but why shouldn't I, if I know it's true anyway? My lighter superficial side will always be too quick for the deeper side of me and that's why it will always win. You can't imagine how often I've already tried to push this Anne away, to cripple her, to hide her, because after all, she's only half of what's called Anne: but it doesn't work and I know, too, why it doesn't work.

I'm awfully scared that everyone who knows me as I always am will discover that I have another side, a finer and better side. I'm afraid they'll laugh at me, think I'm ridiculous and sentimental, not take me seriously. I'm used to not being taken seriously, but it's only the "lighthearted" Anne that's used to it and can bear it; the "deeper" Anne is too frail for it. Sometimes, if I really compel the good Anne to take the stage for a quarter of an hour, she simply shrivels up as soon as she has to speak, and lets Anne number one take over, and before I realize it, she has disappeared.

Therefore, the nice Anne is never present in company, has not appeared one single time so far, but almost always predominates when we're alone. I know exactly how I'd like to be, how I am too . . . inside. But, alas, I'm only like that for myself. And perhaps that's why, no, I'm sure it's the reason why I say I've got a happy nature within and why other people think I've got a happy nature without. I am guided by the pure Anne within, but outside I'm nothing but a frolicsome little goat who's broken loose.

As I've already said, I never utter my real feelings about anything and that's how I've acquired the name of chaser-after-boys, flirt, know-all, reader of love stories. The cheerful Anne laughs about it, gives cheeky answers, shrugs her shoulders indifferently, behaves as if she doesn't care, but, oh dearie me, the quiet Anne's reactions are just the opposite. If I'm to be quite honest, then I must admit that it does hurt me, that I try terribly hard to change myself, but that I'm always fighting against a more powerful enemy.

A voice sobs within me: "There you are, that's what's become of you: you're uncharitable, you look supercilious and peevish, people dislike you, and all because you won't listen to the advice given you by your own better half." Oh, I would like to listen, but it doesn't work; if I'm quiet and serious, everyone thinks it's a new comedy and then I have to get out of it by turning it into a joke, not to mention my own family, who are sure to think I'm ill, make me swallow pills for headaches and nerves . . . and criticize me for being in a bad mood. I can't keep that up: if I'm watched to that extent, I start by getting snappy, then unhappy, and finally I twist my heart round again, so that the bad is on the outside and the good is on the inside and keep on trying to find a way of becoming what I would so like to be, and what I could be, if . . . there weren't any other people living in the world.

Yours, Anne

Anne's diary ends here. On August 4, 1944, the police made a raid on the "Secret Annexe." All the occupants, together with their protectors Kraler and Koophuis, were arrested and sent to German and Dutch concentration camps. The "Secret Annexe" was plundered by the Gestapo.[12] Friends found Anne's diary among a pile of old books and newspapers left lying on the floor.

Of all the occupants of the "Secret Annexe," Anne's father alone returned from the concentration camps. Koophuis was released for medical care after a short imprisonment. Kraler withstood the hardships of the Dutch camp and was able to go home to his family.

In March 1945, three months before her sixteenth birthday and two months before the liberation of Holland, Anne died of typhus in the concentration camp of Bergen-Belsen.

---

12. **Gestapo**—Secret police in Nazi Germany.

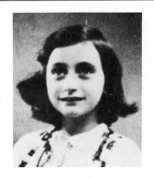

Anne Frank (Anneliese Marie) *(1929–1945)* was born in Frankfurt, Germany, to a respected Jewish family. Her father, Otto, was a successful businessman. In 1933 the Franks moved to the Netherlands to avoid Nazi persecution of the Jews. Mr. Frank's Dutch employees enjoyed four-year-old Anne, who was shy, well-mannered, and inquisitive. The Nazis invaded Holland in 1940, and in 1942 Anne and her family went into hiding at Prinsengracht 263 in Amsterdam. While there Anne, who wanted to be a writer, wrote stories and sketches as well as her diary.

After more than two years, the Franks were betrayed—probably by either a worker in the warehouse or a neighbor—and arrested. They were sent to Auschwitz, where Mr. Frank was separated from his family and Mrs. Frank died in the infirmary. Margot and Anne were moved to Bergen-Belsen. There Anne found her old friend Lies. Typhus had spread throughout the camp, however. Margot died first and Anne shortly after.

Developing Comprehension Skills

1. Why does Anne decide to talk to Peter?

2. Peter says that Anne always helps him. In Peter's opinion, how does she help him? How does Anne feel about Peter's comment?

3. Anne's mother and Anne have different ways of coping with sadness. Explain how their ways differ.

4. Reread the entries for 20 June 1942, 18 May 1943, 8 November 1943, and 3 May 1944. In these entries Anne writes about events happening in the world. Do you think the reader can trust her observations? Explain your answer.

5. What is Anne's idea about the basic nature of human beings? Give examples from the diary to support your answer.

6. Anne Frank's diary expresses thoughts, feelings, and experiences all people share, even though their circumstances may differ widely. Explain how Anne's comments on one of the following aspects of life apply to everyone. You may use examples from your own life or the lives of people you know.

> friendship
> fear
> relationships with parents
> change
> self-understanding

Reading Literature: Diaries

1. **Evaluating a Minor Character.** One minor character is Peter Van Daan. At first, Anne's attitude toward Peter is not very positive. However, her attitude changes as time passes. How does Anne's view of Peter change? Why? Does Peter change?

2. **Understanding Character.** Anne writes on 7 March 1944, "If I think now of my life in 1942, it all seems so unreal. It was quite a different Anne who enjoyed that heavenly existence from the Anne who has grown wise within these walls." In the last entry, Anne describes herself as being two different people. How does Anne change?

3. **Inferring Theme.** As you know, **theme** refers to a writer's message about life. At the beginning of her diary, Anne says, "I want to bring out all kinds of things that lie buried deep in my heart." Reread the diary entries for 7 March 1944, 15 July 1944, and 1 August 1944. In these entries, Anne tries to explain her outlook on life. In your own words, state the theme Anne is expressing in these entries.

4. **Determining Mood.** Select two passages in the diary that you think create two different **moods,** or feelings in the reader. On a sheet of paper, write the date and the first and last sentences of each passage (a passage may be less than an entire entry). Identify the mood that each passage creates. Then list the words and phrases in the passage that create the mood. Look for words with strong connotations.

5. **Recognizing Conflict.** A **conflict** is the struggle that a character faces. An **external conflict** takes place between a character and some outside person or force. An **internal conflict** takes place within a character. What are three conflicts that Anne experiences? Explain how she does or does not resolve each conflict.

Developing Vocabulary Skills

Determining Correct Pronunciation. Some dictionary entry words may be used as more than one part of speech. For example, sometimes the same word can be used as a noun and as a verb. Some of these words are pronounced differently when they are used as different parts of speech; for example:

A permit (pur' mit) is required to use the beach.

The town does not permit (pər mit') parking on all streets.

The following sentences use words from this selection. First decide if the underlined word is used as a noun, a verb, or an adjective. Then locate the word in a dictionary. On a sheet of paper, write the word, its part of speech in the sentence, and the correct respelling.

1. The family felt the impact of Hitler's anti-Jewish laws.

2. Anne's diary reveals that her grandmother was present in her thoughts.

3. They heard a sound downstairs and a minute or two later the wireless radio had to be turned off.

4. Anne fears that the Nazis will separate the members of her family.

5. Peter became the object of Anne's thoughts and feelings.

Developing Skills in Study and Research

Researching Historical Background. You have learned how to use the resources of a library to find facts. Choose either of the two diaries you have read. Write at least three questions about the events or people in the diary that are not answered by the diary. For each question, list at least two ways of locating an answer. Then use your school or local library to answer your questions. Report both the answers and the sources you used. For each source, note the information that applies: the title, the author, the volume number or issue date, and the page numbers of the article or chapter that you used.

Developing Writing Skills

1. **Making Comparisons and Contrasts.** Both Davy Crockett and Anne Frank experience war. One volunteers to be part of war; the other has no choice. Compare and contrast how they write about war in their diaries. Write two paragraphs about the similarities and differences you find.

   Prewriting. Make two lists: one for Anne Frank and one for Davy Crockett. On each list, include at least three subtopics. *Facts, Opinions, Conflicts, Relationships,* and *Tone* are possible subtopics you could use. Review each diary for details about each subtopic. List the information you find.

   Then look over your lists. Are there any general statements you can make about how the two writers write about war? What similarities are there? What differences? Decide how you want to organize your paragraphs. You can discuss similarities in one paragraph and differences in the other, or you may discuss one selection in the first paragraph and the other in the second.

   Drafting. Open your first paragraph with a topic sentence stating what you are writing about. Then develop your paragraphs according to the organization you decided on in prewriting. Use details from your lists to support your ideas.

   Revising and Sharing. Read your paragraph to a classmate. The ideas should be clear and supported with details. Be prepared to share your paragraphs with the class. Discuss the ideas that your classmates present in their writing.

2. **Writing a Diary.** If you have not already done so, begin a personal diary. Make daily entries for at least three weeks. Comment on the events of your life. Describe things that interest you. Discuss your opinions and feelings. These entries are for your information only.

   At the end of three weeks, review your entries. If you want, select three to share with others. Revise them as you like, to make them understandable to others. Then make a clean copy of those three entries.

Autobiographies

A diary is written soon after events take place. An **autobiography,** in contrast, may describe events that took place far in the past. Writers of autobiographies have taken the time to think about the people and events in their lives. They have looked for the most important experiences that shaped them as persons. They write their accounts to share what they have learned.

Self Portrait, 1930–35, WILLIAM H. JOHNSON. National Museum of American Art, Smithsonian Institution, Washington, D.C., Gift of the Harmon Foundation.

From

One of the Lucky Ones

LUCY CHING

It has been said that a handicap is a handicap only if you allow it to be so. Read to discover how Lucy Ching finds a way to read in spite of being blind.

We held our breath. Had we heard a voice through the static? Perched tense and still on the edge of the bed, we strained our ears. It came again, this time more clearly, in Mandarin but with an accent.

"Hello CY . . . Hello CY . . . This is DU . . . I am in Manila. Are you receiving me?"

"I am receiving you DU . . . ," said my brother into his microphone.

"I am a doctor of medicine and I think I can help you. I know what your sister needs. I will write to some people in America and ask them to send some things to help her. Tell me where to send them."

My brother gave our address as clearly as he could and then asked, "Where do you come from?"

"From New York, but I know Mandarin because I've always hoped to work in China."

Then he said, "Goodbye—and good luck!" and his voice was gone. We sat listening to the crackling static, wondering if it had really happened.

I was eight at that time. Three years before, when I was five, I had discovered that I was blind. Never having seen, I did not know until the day my mother told me. It came out when I grumbled about not being able to keep up with my brothers and sisters in a game. "You'll never be able to beat them," she said, "because they can see and you can't. You are blind."

Later I asked why they went to school.

"To learn to read and write so they can become useful people when they grow up."

"Can I go to school with them?"

"That's impossible. You can't go because you are blind." Mother sounded sorry but very definite. She said I would not be able to see the blackboard or read books.

When plans were being made for family visits or treats, I sometimes asked if I could go.

"No, you can't go; you are blind."

I soon learned not to ask.

One day I heard on the radio that blind

children in America and England learned to read in some special way with their fingers. Some went to special schools, others went to ordinary schools and studied alongside sighted children. I thought and thought about this and determined to find out somehow.

My older brother, who was sixteen, was very keen on electronics. In his spare time he built himself a transmitter and kept it on a small table beside his bed. After getting his license as a ham operator, he spent hours sending out call signals and talking to people in far-away places. I would sit beside him, listening, and that was when an idea came into my mind: suppose he were to ask if anyone listening knew how blind children could learn to read . . . someone might know . . . and answer. . . . He agreed to try. He spoke in Mandarin and English. He knew only the little of these languages that he had learned at school, but he did his best. He tried for three weeks but nothing happened. We were nearly giving up—it seemed hopeless. And then DU in Manila answered.

Two months later, soon after breakfast one morning, the doorbell rang. I went and called out to know who it was. It was the postman so I opened the door. He said there was a package for "Ching" and added that he thought it must be for me because he could read enough English to see that it said "Reading Material for the Blind." It suddenly dawned on me that the doctor in Manila must have kept his promise and this package was the result. I called my parents who were doubtful about accepting it, but in the end Father signed the receipt.

I stood in the hall with it in my hands. I could hear my father putting on his shoes, and a moment later my mother's sewing machine start up. Then Father called goodbye to everybody and went off to work. I knew the kitchen door was open because I could hear running water and knew that our amah, Ah Wor, was washing up. I took the parcel into the living room and set about opening it. The string would not come off, so I found some scissors and cut it in so many places that it fell off in bits. All the edges of the paper were stuck down and I could not start pulling it open anywhere. Impatiently I attacked it with the scissors and cut away what felt like wrappings until I came to something that felt like a flat envelope. Inside this I found some very thick, small-sized papers with raised dots all over them and some larger papers, several pages bound together, each page covered in hundreds of raised dots. With growing excitement, I realized that these must be the things that enabled blind children to learn by touch.

But I had no idea what to do with them. I wished I could get my parents to help me, but my father had gone to work and my mother would not want to be bothered with me. I knew Ah Wor would love to help me, but she had housework to do and she could not read anyway. There was nothing for it but to see what I could find out on my own.

I explored further. There was a small box; in it was a little metal strip with holes in it on one side and tiny knobs on the other. And there was a strange little round thing that felt like a spinning top with the point of a knitting needle sticking out of it. I turned these mysterious things over and over in my hands and felt every inch of them. I could make nothing of them. Then I dropped the metal strip. It landed with a clatter on the floor. I groped about for it and found that it had become twice as long as before. I realized that it was a double strip, hinged at one end so that it opened and shut like a book. I sat at the desk where my brother and sister did their homework, my strange new treasures in front of me, and kept feeling the cards with the dots and opening and shutting the metal thing. I ran my fingers again and again along the line of holes. I was called to lunch but I did not go. I was terrified that if I went away and left my mysterious new things, they might disappear. Nobody came and insisted. My parents—and therefore Ah Wor—often indulged me where they would be strict with the other children, and I was allowed to have my way so long as it did not inconvenience anyone. Perhaps it was a small effort to compensate me for my handicap.

Anyway, on this day I sat on in the living room, pushing my fingers into the holes and wondering. Ah Wor came in with a bowl of rice. I pushed it away and in doing so my hand touched the little round thing. I picked it up. I found I could push it right into the holes—it seemed to fit. Suddenly I wondered what would happen if I put a piece of paper between the two halves of the metal. I ran to the bathroom for some toilet paper and laid it on one half and carefully closed the other half on top of it. Then I tried pushing the point of the round thing into the holes to see if I could make raised dots like those on the cards. I pushed and pushed and then took the bit of paper out. It was full of holes, not dots. I examined the cards and my piece of toilet paper again and realized that the cards were much thicker and stronger, so I went and found a piece of my sister's drawing paper. I checked with Ah Wor that there was no drawing on it and then tried again. This time, to my surprise and delight, there were raised dots.

I waited impatiently for my brother and sister to come home from school. I was so excited I could hardly wait to show them what I had got. They looked very carefully at the papers and told me that one card had all the letters of the English alphabet, which they had learned at school, printed beside different groups of dots. So I asked them to take my hand and show me how to do them. Luckily I had often heard them doing their English lessons aloud, so I did at least know the names and the order of the English letters.

And so I started to teach myself Braille—although I never heard this name until two more years had passed. When I was familiar with the letters, I switched my attention to another card where there were several letters written close together, and the first word I spelled out was b-o-o-k. I asked my sister what it meant and how to pronounce it and she told me. Another group of letters was p-e-n-c-i-l, and I was surprised to hear my sister muttering the same word in her own homework. This was marvelous—I felt the world was opening up for me. It was just coincidence that we happened both to be learning the same word at the same moment, but I had been told ever since I was old enough to understand that it was no use a blind child trying to study because blind children and sighted children do not live in the same world or understand the same things.

At that moment, on that evening, I suddenly knew that this was not so. I knew in a flash that it was up to me—that I could do whatever I had the determination to do,

Lucy Ching instructing a blind student. Souvenir Press, Ltd., London.

and I was not limited by arbitrary, preset boundaries in the way that my family had brought me up to believe.

Lucy Ching was born in China in the 1930's. She was totally blind. Though blind people were often treated like outcasts and sold into slavery during that time, Ching's family kept her at home. She was fortunate in the care she received from an illiterate servant woman, her "amah," who taught Ching common sense and love. Determined to survive despite her blindness, Ching taught herself Braille and was eventually able to go to school with sighted children. She won a scholarship to the Perkins School for the Blind in Boston. Today she is a social worker in Hong Kong working with blind people.

Developing Comprehension Skills

1. How does Lucy first hear about blind children reading "with their fingers"?

2. When Lucy asks to go to school, her mother states, "You can't go because you are blind." Is her mother's statement a fact or an opinion?

3. How does Lucy get the materials for learning Braille?

4. Notice how Lucy patiently explores the parcel and tests it. What do her actions show about the kind of learner she might be?

5. Lucy is not allowed activities like the other children. What is her parents' attitude toward blindness? How do her brothers' and sisters' attitudes seem to differ from the attitude of the parents?

6. Lucy's attitude helps her overcome her disability. Suggest two or three qualities any person needs in order to overcome serious problems.

Reading Literature: Autobiographies

1. **Understanding Character.** What qualities does Lucy Ching have as a child? How does she relate to her family? How does she both accept and go beyond the limitations her mother imposes? How does she view herself?

2. **Examining Autobiography.** In this selection the writer is talking about herself as a child. How does she convey the feelings and thoughts she had as a child? What details does she use to draw the reader into her experiences? Give examples to support your answers.

3. **Exploring Theme.** The writer is physically blind, but she sees in ways that those around her do not. What does Lucy see about herself and her life? State the theme of this selection in your own words.

Developing Vocabulary Skills

Choosing the Correct Dictionary Definition. For most entry words a dictionary lists more than one definition. If a word is used as more than one part of speech, there will be at least one definition for each part. Several words in the selections you have read have more than one definition listed in the dictionary. For example, here is how the word *grumble* is used in this autobiography:

I *grumbled* about not being able to keep up with my brothers and sisters in a game.

In the dictionary, the definitions listed for the word *grumble* used as a verb are "to growl," "to mutter," and "to rumble." The definition that best fits the sense of the sentence above is "to mutter."

In a dictionary find the underlined word from each sentence below. On a sheet of paper, write each word and the part of speech and the definition that best fit the context of the sentence.

1. The hunters brought in some corn and had a <u>brush</u> with an enemy scout.

2. Anne had to hurry, for she would <u>quiver</u> if she began thinking about the situation.

3. Anne's father was the only one who took Anne into his <u>confidence</u>.

4. Anne says she has a happy <u>nature</u>.

5. Lucy and her brother sat listening to the crackling <u>static</u>.

6. Lucy's parents often <u>indulged</u> her where they would be strict with the other children.

7. Lucy knew in a <u>flash</u> it was up to her.

Developing Skills in Critical Thinking

Evaluating Assumptions. Lucy Ching and her mother have different views of Lucy's blindness. Each of them has different assumptions about blindness and how it will affect Lucy's life. Look at the statements each makes concerning blindness. What kind of assumptions does the mother make? What assumptions does Lucy make? Are the assumptions made by each person supported by any facts? Do Lucy and her mother test their assumptions to see if they are true? Support your answers with evidence from the selection.

Developing Skills in Speaking and Listening

Reading Dialogue. The scene that opens this selection is dramatic; it portrays the beginning of a great change for Lucy Ching. Present an oral reading of the dialogue in the first seven paragraphs of the selection. If you work with two other students, one student can read the doctor's words, one can read the brother's words, and one can read the narration. Practice reading the dialogue to convey the characters' feelings and the drama of the moment. When you are satisfied with your reading, present it to the class.

Developing Writing Skills

Analyzing a Character Trait. What do you think is Lucy Ching's most important quality? In two paragraphs, explain how this quality is revealed in this chapter from her autobiography and why the quality is important.

Prewriting. Think about Lucy's outstanding qualities. Decide which one you think is the most important. Jot down incidents and quotations from the autobiography that show this quality. List reasons why the trait is important for Lucy to have.

Drafting. Write an opening sentence identifying Lucy's most important quality. Use your lists as you tell how the quality is shown in the autobiography. Be sure to use examples and quotations. Then explain why this trait is important for Lucy to have.

Revising and Sharing. Check the topic sentence in each paragraph. Notice whether you have used details and quotations to develop each paragraph. Read your paragraphs aloud to a group of students. Ask them about your main idea and if you have supported your ideas fully. Make final revisions based on your classmates' responses and suggestions.

From
A Precocious Autobiography

YEVGENY YEVTUSHENKO
Translated by Andrew R. MacAndrew

Yevgeny Yevtushenko (yev gen' ē yev' too sheng' kō) is a famous Soviet poet. Here he writes about the summer during World War II when he was eleven. Read about the important lesson he learns.

In 1944 I was living alone in an empty apartment in a small, quiet Moscow street, Chetvertaya Meshchanskaya (chet vyer' tä yä mesh chän' skä yä).

My parents were divorced. My father was somewhere in Kazakhstan (kə zäk' stän) with his new wife and their two children. I seldom received letters from him.

My mother was at the front. She had given up her work as a geologist to become a singer and was giving concerts for the troops.

My education was left to the street. The street taught me to swear, smoke, spit elegantly through my teeth, and keep my fists up, always ready for a fight—a habit which I have kept to this day.

The street taught me not to be afraid of anything or anyone—this is another habit I have kept.

I realized that what mattered in the struggle for existence was to overcome my fear of those who were stronger.

The ruler of our street, Chetvertaya Meshchanskaya, was a boy of about sixteen who was nicknamed Red.

Red's shoulders were incredibly broad for a boy of his age.

Red walked masterfully up and down our street, his legs wide apart and with a slightly rolling gait, like a seaman on the deck of his ship.

From under his peaked cap, always worn back to front, his forelock tumbled down in a fiery cascade, and out of his round, pockmarked face, green eyes, like a cat's, sparkled with scorn for everything and everyone crossing his path. Two or three lieutenants, in peaked caps back to front like Red's, trotted at his heels.

Red could stop any boy and say impressively the one word "money." His lieutenants would turn out the boy's pockets, and if he resisted, they gave him a real beating.

Everyone was afraid of Red. I too was afraid. I knew he carried heavy brass knuckles in his pocket.

I wanted to conquer my fear of Red.

Azerbaijan, Baku, U.S.S.R., the Old Town and the New Baku, 1972–73, HENRI CARTIER-BRESSON. Magnum Photos, New York City.

So I wrote a poem about him.

This was my first piece of journalism in verse.

By the next day, the whole street knew the piece by heart and relished it with triumphant hatred.

One morning on my way to school, I suddenly came upon Red and his lieutenants. His eyes seemed to bore through me. "Ah, the poet," he drawled, smiling crookedly. "So you write verses. Do they rhyme?"

Red's hand darted into his pocket and came out armed with its brass knuckles; it flashed like lightning and struck my head. I fell down streaming with blood and lost consciousness.

This was my first payment as a poet.

I spent several days in bed.

When I went out, with my head still bandaged, I again saw Red. I struggled with instinctive fear but lost and took to my heels.

I ran all the way home. There I rolled on my bed, biting my pillow and pounding it with my fists in shame and impotent fury at my cowardice.

But then I made up my mind to vanquish it at whatever cost.

I went into training with parallel bars and weights, and after every session I would feel my muscles. They were getting harder, but slowly. Then I remembered something I had read in a book about a miraculous Japanese method of wrestling which gave an advantage to the weak over the strong. I sacrificed a week's ration card[1] for a textbook on jujitsu.

For three weeks I hardly left home—I trained with two other boys. Finally I felt I was ready and went out.

---

1. **ration card**–A card used to get food and other necessary supplies during wartime. A person could not buy larger quantities than the ration card allowed.

Red was sitting on the lawn in our yard, playing Twenty-one with his lieutenants. He was absorbed in the game.

Fear was still in me and it ordered me to turn back. But I went up to the players and kicked the cards aside with my foot.

Red looked up, surprised at my impudence after my recent flight.

He got up slowly. "You looking for more?" he asked menacingly.

As before, his hand dived into his pocket for the brass knuckles. But I made a quick, jabbing movement, and Red, howling with pain, rolled on the ground. Bewildered, he got up and came at me, swinging his head furiously from side to side like a bull.

I caught his wrist and squeezed slowly, as I had read in the book, until the brass knuckles dropped from his limp fingers. Nursing his hand, Red fell down again. He was sobbing and smearing the tears over his pockmarked face with his grimy fist. His lieutenants discreetly withdrew.

That day Red ceased to rule our street.

And from that day on I knew for certain that there is no need to fear the strong. All one needs is to know the method of overcoming them. There is a special jujitsu for every strong man.

What I also learned that day was that, if I wished to be a poet, I must not only write poems but also know how to stand up for what I have written.

Yevgeny Yevtushenko *(born 1933)* lived in Siberia as a child. His parents were both geologists. After studying at the Gorky Literary Institute, Yevtushenko began his career as a poet and writer. He has often used his writing to speak out against political events in the USSR. As a result, his poetry readings and plays have been cancelled and his work censored. He is well known in the United States for his dramatic readings in English of his work.

Developing Comprehension Skills

1. How does Red bully other boys?

2. Yevtushenko writes, "I wanted to conquer my fear of Red. So I wrote a poem about him." Does writing the poem help him get over his fear? Explain.

3. How does Yevtushenko overcome Red? What does he use besides physical force? In what way is Yevtushenko stronger than Red?

4. What effect does Red's defeat have on Red? What effect does it have on Yevtushenko?

5. Reread the last paragraph of the selection. What does Yevtushenko mean by "I must not only write poems but also know how to stand up for what I have written"?

6. Yevtushenko uses physical violence in solving his problem. Does he have other choices? Should he have found another way? Explain.

Reading Literature: Autobiographies

1. **Examining Autobiography.** In this selection, Yevtushenko writes about a difficult period in his life when his parents are absent and a war is going on. What can you tell about him from the way he describes himself and his problems? Give examples from the selection to support your ideas.

2. **Evaluating Setting.** The **setting** is the time and place of the action in a piece of writing. What is the setting for this chapter from Yevtushenko's autobiography? What aspects of the setting determine, at least in part, what happens to Yevtushenko?

3. **Understanding Conflict.** The **conflict** is a struggle that a character faces. An **external** conflict is a struggle with someone or something outside the character. An **internal conflict** is a struggle between opposing forces within a character. Nonfiction, like fiction, can portray conflicts. This selection shows Yevtushenko experiencing both external and internal conflicts. What are these conflicts? How is each resolved?

4. **Analyzing Theme.** Choose one of the following statements of theme and explain how the selection communicates this message.

> It is important to learn to conquer fear of those who are stronger.
>
> It is important to stand up for yourself and what is important to you.
>
> There are many ways of being strong other than being physically strong.

Developing Vocabulary Skills

Defining Idioms. An **idiom** is a phrase that means something different from what the words appear to say literally. An example is "break down," which means "to stop working," as in, "Did the car *break down?*" In a dictionary, an idiom is listed under an important word from the idiom. The idiom is usually shown in dark type at the end of the entry for the word. (See examples under *break* in a dictionary.)

The following sentences are taken from the selections you have read. The underlined phrases are idioms. Find each idiom in a dictionary. On a sheet of paper, write the idiom and its definition.

1. We are all in high spirits, though we are rather short of provisions.

2. But that was <u>no go</u>.

3. I do talk about "after the war," but then it is only a <u>castle in the air</u>.

4. He was obviously doing his best to <u>show off</u> his strength.

5. I struggled with instinctive fear but lost and <u>took to my heels</u>.

6. But then I <u>made up my mind</u> to vanquish it at whatever cost.

7. The whole street knew the piece <u>by heart</u>.

8. I must not only write poems but also know how to <u>stand up for</u> what I have written.

Developing Skills in Critical Thinking

Interpreting Levels of Meaning. In his autobiography, Yevtushenko communicates on more than one level at the same time. For example, when he writes, "There is no need to fear the strong," the word *strong* has more than one meaning. Yevtushenko is not referring to just physical power. He is also referring to political power.

In this selection you can infer different levels of meaning from knowing who the writer is and the kinds of conflicts he has faced as an adult. You can also infer other levels of meaning by relating your own life to the writing. You know from your experiences, for instance, that a person can be strong in several different ways.

Reread paragraph 5 on page 490 and paragraph 8 on page 492. In what ways is Yevtushenko in a "struggle"?

Developing Writing Skills

Comparing Characters. Both Lucy Ching and Yevgeny Yevtushenko have to overcome obstacles. Write two paragraphs comparing how each character handles his or her main problem.

Prewriting. Identify the major obstacle each character faces and explain how each tries to overcome his or her difficulty. List similarities in the characters' approaches and in the qualities the characters show. Then list differences in their approaches and character traits. Decide how to organize these ideas into paragraphs, perhaps using an outline. You can write about similarities in one paragraph and differences in another or you can write about one character in the first paragraph and the other in the second.

Drafting. For each paragraph, write a topic sentence stating the main idea. Use information from your lists to develop your paragraphs. Follow the organization you decided on in prewriting.

Revising and Sharing. Reread your paragraphs. Check to see if specific details support each topic sentence. Make sure all sentences are clear and understandable. Ask a classmate to read your paragraphs aloud. What do you hear that could be improved? Does your classmate understand your main points about Ching and Yevtushenko? Make any necessary revisions and write a final copy.

The First Day of the War

MAIA WOJCIECHOWSKA

Anne Frank in Holland and Maia Wojciechowska (mī' ä voi che hôv' skä) in Poland both experience the invasion of German troops. Read this selection from Wojciechowska's autobiography to see how the war affects her life.

It started like the best of all mornings. I woke up from a dream to the sound of the plane.

He would often come early in the morning, and I always knew he would not land before I got out of bed and ran outside. While waiting, he would make lazy circles in the sky. And as I rushed out, there would always be an unasked question in my mind: did he love fear more than freedom or freedom more than fear? For he always did something frightening that might end his freedom: rolls and spins and that horrible, inevitable climb into the infinity of the sky. Each time I saw him go vertically away from me, I thought he wouldn't *want* to come down.

But he always did. And that descent, straight down, the nose of the plane an arrow shooting the earth, falling, gaining in loudness as he lost altitude, made me catch my breath and forced my eyes to close. Would he straighten up in time? Would a wing catch a treetop as it once did? But he

was immortal. The plane might lose a wing or even burn, but nothing would happen to him. Not to my hero, my flying knight, my father.

Even as I raced against the landing plane, trying to reach it before he cut the engine, hoping that he would have time to take me up, trying not to be blown down by the great gusts of wind from the propeller blades, even as I climbed up to the cockpit, I was afraid. Afraid that he would be alone, unreachable, private in that world of his where I couldn't even be a trespasser. Even flying with him, beside him, even then he was still a fugitive from me.

Today was different. The sound of the plane was gone by the time I rushed outside. Then I heard another. Not just one but several planes were flying overhead. Next to me was my newest possession, one he had not yet seen—a Doberman puppy. The dog had no name yet. He was brand new, and I loved him. Yesterday, when I got him, he had run away from the vet who was going to trim his ears and cut his tail to a stump. The litter of five submitted yappingly to the operation, but not he. He tore himself away from me, and I chased him through a swamp, across what I was afraid was a bed of quicksand, wanting to catch him and yet also wanting him to get away. Now his black glistening body, for he had fallen into a puddle, was jumping over weeds and disappearing into the tall grass.

Now there was another plane. I looked up, but it wasn't his—it did not have white and red squared under the wings. The plane dipped down and flew low, parallel with my running dog. It slid down even lower, and there was a sound—a sound I didn't understand, a sound I had never heard before. As my dog leaped up, I saw him for a brief moment over the grass, shadowed by the plane's wing. Then the plane rose and flew away.

I stood in that field not moving, waiting for my dog to continue running in that sunlit place, which was at the edge of my summer world, but I couldn't see him anywhere. And there were no sounds—not one single sound since that sound that I was now beginning to understand. As I started to walk forward, I already knew what I would see, and knowing was evil and I wanted to take back what I knew.

I did not bury my dog. I did not touch him. I turned away from him because he did not move. He would never have a name.

I climbed a tree and sat there, trying not to think of anything, trying not to hate.

But trying did no good, and I hated—everything I knew and everything that I didn't understand. I hated everyone, especially those who now were making noises inside my house. I hated the car that had pulled in front of the house and its running, sputtering engine. And most of all I hated my mother's voice calling my name and the slamming of the doors. And I hated the summer for having so suddenly ended.

When I got tired of hating, I came down off the tree and swore to myself that nobody would ever know what had happened to my dog. I promised not to say anything to anyone, not until I understood why and who had done it. Not until I found a way of paying them back. Not until after I killed the one who had killed him.

A man I never liked, a friend of my mother's, was yelling at me that I was lucky I wasn't being left behind. I stuck my tongue out at him when he turned his back and told my mother there was no time to pack anything. He pulled her and pushed me toward the car, where my brothers were already seated, both of them sleepy and angry. I didn't dare protest against this kidnapping of my person because I was afraid that if I opened my mouth, I'd cry.

I remembered from way back that every time I felt hurt, I had to do something mean, as if being mean could in itself cure the hurt. I took away a roll my little brother Krzys (kris) was eating and threw it out of the car window. And when he, aged six, began to cry, I placed my hand over his mouth. He knew better than to struggle against me. But I could feel his tears on my hand, for he was crying over his loss while I couldn't cry over mine. I consoled myself with the thought that I have a devil inside me and that I would go straight to hell when I die.

The car was taking me away from the field where my dog was lying dead and would be eaten by buzzards before noon.

There was a loud argument in the car about the war. Zbyszek (zbi′ shək), my fourteen-year-old brother, was insisting that we were certainly going to win and especially because he planned to enlist in the Polish Air Force. The man at the wheel was of the opinion that Poland had no chance to defend itself against Germany. And my mother, pulling on a pair of white gloves, expressed her disbelief that the war should

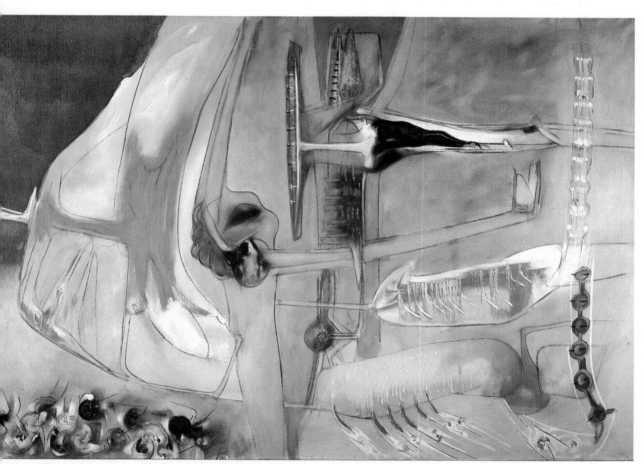

Untitled (Prime Ordeal). 1945, ROBERTO MATTA ECHAURREN. Collection of the Museum of Contemporary Art, Chicago, Gift of Mr. and Mrs. Joseph P. Shapiro.

have started at such an inconvenient time. We were going to go back to France next week. And I began to laugh. I laughed loud and hard because at twelve I was glad my country was at war with people who shot down dogs.

I realized it would be hard to find him, the one who actually did kill my dog. Maybe I could advertise. "Wanted: The German pilot who shot down a Doberman pup on September 1, 1939. Important reward." He'd answer the ad and I'd be ready for him. I had stolen a book from a Paris bookstore about medieval tortures. It was behind in the house, but I remembered most of them. He would be a long time dying. Water dripping first, then bamboo spikes, or better still nails, rusty and long, under the fingernails. Hot coals and scalding water. I could pull out his hair by the handfuls, or maybe I could even build a rack or a pendulum. What would be nicest of all would be to have him die behind a horse and be dragged around for miles, face down, across fields stubby with weeds, coarse with stones. Or maybe I could find a mad dog and let him be bitten to death. That would be poetic justice.

We were in a sixth-floor apartment in Warsaw. The view from here was fantastic. It was too good to be true. People down below on the street were running in circles; cars, buses, and trolleys were piling up, being abandoned; furniture and suitcases were all over the sidewalks. And in the distance there were several fires. The sirens went on again—I was getting used to their shrieks—and all activities stopped as the sound of the planes came into the apartment through the windows I flung open.

"Why did he leave us here?" My mother kept repeating the question, although my brother had told her several times that the reason her friend locked us in this place was that he wanted to steal from us. Especially the new car, the one my father had just brought into Poland from France—a splendid, new, custom-made Delage. I hated to listen to them, so I leaned farther out of the window and was glad when the bombs began to fall. I grabbed Krzys by the hand and dragged him to the window, and we began to imitate the sounds of the bomb. First the plane's engine, then the whistle of the falling bomb, and then its great triumphant explosion. "BOOM!" We laughed like crazy, and Mother suddenly realized we were in "mortal danger" and ordered us to hide under the sofa. I accused her of "sudden senility," which had recently become my favorite expression of disdain, and explained as haughtily as possible that if we were going to be hit, I'd feel much safer falling down six floors than having a sofa come on my head.

"We should be in a shelter," she answered with little logic since she'd tried the door several times and found it locked. Her friend assured us we'd be safe here. She always had a hard time coming to grips with reality and a harder time distrusting people or seeing herself being taken advantage of.

But I couldn't be bothered with her now. The view out of the window was fascinating. Houses collapsed, churches crumbled. Someone, maybe God Himself, had started the biggest game in the world, and I couldn't wait to get involved.

While Zbyszek attacked the door, trying to break it down, I invented a game for Krzys. We broke everything we could get our hands on, and what we couldn't break, we threw out of the window. My mother was carrying on a semi-hysterical monologue and didn't even notice when the house across the street, almost as tall as the one we were in, was hit directly, collapsed in slow motion and in a great cloud of dust as we were flung down by the explosion. There was broken glass all over the floor now, and the bookcase had fallen not two feet away from my mother. Krzys began to cry, and I hit him because I didn't want to give the Germans the satisfaction of making any of us cry. For suddenly I knew something else—I knew about wars. It started with the killing of dogs, but then it all became a matter of pride, of winning over fear.

The door opened, and the man who had locked us in was back telling us that he had seen my father. I tried to hear every word he said about him, but Zbyszek was yelling at him accusations of thievery, and my mother was asking silly questions about danger from bombs. I pieced together the information about my father; he had been ordered to go to London and Paris to ask for reinforcements for the Polish Air Force.

He had taken a plane and was piloting it himself. We were to get a train, go through Rumania to France, where we were to join him because he was ordered not to come back to Poland.

My father had done it again—abandoned us, freed himself from us! Not even a war could stop him from flying away. I hit my fist against the doorframe and wished everyone dead so that I could cry in peace over this news, over life's inhumanity to me.

How many times have I cried over my father without anyone's knowing about it? Each birthday and each name day because he was never there. And whenever it rained. I cried for him inside the dark movie houses when I watched sad films and over books that were not even sad. Only once—how old was I, nine or eight?—I cried in front of him. I had torn up a dress my mother had made for me. A horrid taffeta dress, loud with noises, full of ribbons and bows and laced petticoats. I had hated being a girl and wished to have nothing to do with dresses like that. I tore it off, tore it apart, threw it at her, and went to hide my anger over her attempts to brand me a girl. He had found me in the garden on a swing. He had his belt in his hands, and he hit me with it half a dozen times. Not hard, but he hit me. For the first and only time. And I had cried. Then he talked to me, for the first time, about being cruel to my mother and thoughtless. And I cried. Not because he had hit me. Not because of what he said. Not because of what

I was, and I was cruel and thoughtless. I cried because he did not know this first-hand but had learned it just then—from his wife.

He didn't know anything about me. He didn't know that I had always wanted to be a boy because being a boy would have made me closer to being like him when I grew up. He did not know about the time Zbyszek's friends had tied me to a tombstone and left me overnight in the cemetery. He didn't know that once the same boys tied me up to a tree, built a pile of sticks under my feet, and dared me to scream as they lit it. He did not know that I told them that not only would I not scream, but also that I would, if they untied my hands, light the fire myself so that they would not get into trouble. He did not know that I had been scared the time he finally allowed me to jump from an airplane, and that I had been lying to him that day, for I had changed my mind and didn't want to jump. He did not know that for a moment, before the chute opened, I wished that God would not let me die before I told my father than I loved him more than life. He didn't know my hates or my longings or my loves, or the fact that I could not fall asleep without reading to myself under the covers. He didn't know that I was jealous of everyone he had time for. He didn't know that I always wanted him to be proud of me. He didn't know my dog had been killed that morning. He didn't know he shouldn't have left us.

Maia Wojciechowska *(born 1927)* is a native of Warsaw, Poland. She has lived in many countries and is fluent in French, Spanish, Russian, English, and Portuguese, as well as in Polish. Wojciechowska has worked as a detective, bullfighter, translator, editor, and literary agent. Her novel *Shadow of a Bull* won the Newbery medal in 1965.

Developing Comprehension Skills

1. What happens to Maia's dog?

2. What forces Maia and her family to flee from their home?

3. As Maia and her family are being driven away from their home after the invasion has started, she writes, "I laughed loud and hard because at twelve I was glad my country was at war with people who shot down dogs." What feelings is she expressing? Why do you think she laughs at such a moment?

4. The writer describes her mother as "carrying on a semi-hysterical monologue" and "asking silly questions." Are these descriptions fact or opinion? Identify any slanted language.

5. Maia makes this statement about her father: "He didn't know he shouldn't have left us." What does she mean? What kind of relationship does Maia have with her absent father?

6. In the middle of the bombing, Krzys begins to cry. Maia writes, "I hit him because I didn't want to give the Germans the satisfaction of making any of us cry. For suddenly I knew something else—I knew about wars. It started with the killing of dogs, but then it all became a matter of pride, of winning over fear." What connection is she making between what happened to her dog and the reasons for war? Do you agree with her ideas? Explain your answers.

7. Maia expresses many feelings in her description of the first day of the war. Think about the kinds of experiences she has during that day. What has she lost by the end of the day? Are her feelings appropriate? Explain.

Reading Literature: Autobiographies

1. **Understanding Characterization.** In the first three paragraphs of the selection, Maia does not identify her father. He is also not directly involved in the experiences Maia is describing in the rest of the selection. He is, however, the central figure in Maia's account. Why is he so important in the selection? How does Maia focus on him even though he is absent?

2. **Analyzing Autobiography.** An autobiography often gives historical facts along with personal recollections. What facts does this autobiography tell you about World War II? What personal results of war are described in this autobiography?

3. **Examining Repetition.** An important part of Wojciechowska's writing style is repetition of key words and phrases. For example, in one paragraph about her father, she begins sentences with the following words:

> How many times have I cried over my father . . . .
> I cried for him inside . . . .
> I cried in front of him . . . .
> I cried because he did not know this firsthand . . . .

This repetition of the words "I cried" emphasizes the intensity of her feelings. Select two other passages in which the writer uses repetition. On a sheet of paper write the subject of each passage and the repeated words or phrases it contains. Then explain the effect of the repetition in the passage.

4. **Identifying Tone.** As you know, **tone** is the writer's attitude toward the subject. Tone is

suggested by the words the writer chooses. In this selection, what do you think is the writer's tone regarding the war? List at least three words or phrases from the selection that express this tone.

5. **Explaining Theme.** In this selection the writer talks about many subjects, including hero worship, war, anger, love, and fear of death. All of these subjects are connected to the relationship between the writer and her father. Review your answer to question 5 in Developing Comprehension Skills. Then explain the writer's understanding of what is most important in life to her.

Developing Vocabulary Skills

Identifying Word Origins. Many English words are based on words in other languages. Most dictionaries include information on the origin, or source, of each word.

The following English words are from "The First Day of the War." In the dictionary, locate the origin for each word. On a sheet of paper, write the word and the language or languages of its origin. Refer to the beginning of the dictionary for an explanation of the abbreviations used.

1. infinity
2. knight
3. gust
4. buzzard
5. abandon
6. taffeta

Developing Skills in Critical Thinking

1. **Recognizing Slanted Writing.** When a writer has strong feelings or opinions, he or she will often use slanted language. It is important to be able to recognize slanted language so that you can clearly evaluate what you are reading. In this selection the writer is dealing with many strong emotions: fear, love, disappointment, anger, grief. Reread the last three paragraphs of the selection. Identify three examples of slanted language, and explain how each reflects the writer's feelings and opinions.

2. **Evaluating an Action.** In this selection Maia learns that her father has flown to London and Paris for the Polish government. She and the rest of the family will have to get out of Poland on their own. Do you think Maia's father should have tried to stay with his family to help them escape? What factors do you think he had to consider in making his decision?

Developing Skills In Study and Research

Using Encyclopedias and a Library Indexing System. This autobiography is set in 1939 during the German invasion of Poland. Knowing about the setting can help you to understand the selection better. Look up information in an encyclopedia, using topic headings such as "World War II" and "Poland." Take notes on the information about the German invasion of Poland. Then use your library's indexing system to find a book on the subject. If your library has a computerized indexing system, type in your topic at the terminal, and look over the titles to find several that seem appropriate. If your library has no computerized system, use the card catalog. Look up your topic in the subject index and find several appropriate titles. Locate at least one of the books on the shelves. Make notes on the information it contains about the invasion of Poland in 1939.

Developing Writing Skills

Analyzing an Experience. In this selection the writer tells about experiences she has during a time of crisis. Think about what happens to her during this first day of the war. What kinds of things does she do? What feelings and reactions does she have? In a paragraph analyze, or explain, some aspect of Maia's experiences. Possibilities might be how she relates to the other people involved, her fears, her thoughts about what is happening, or her memories.

Prewriting. Review the selection as well as your answers to the study questions in Developing Comprehension Skills and to questions 1, 2, and 5 in Reading Literature. Identify the main experiences Maia describes and choose one aspect of them to write about. On a sheet of paper list details that convey the aspect of her experiences that you are explaining. Decide how you want to organize your material.

Drafting. In your topic sentence, present the aspect of Maia's experiences that you are analyzing. As you write the paragraph, explain how this aspect is developed in the selection. Give examples to make your explanation clear and specific.

Revising and Sharing. Read over your paragraph. Make sure that your topic sentence is clear and that your examples support your analysis. Eliminate any details or examples that are not related to the aspect you are writing about. Share your paragraph in a class discussion. Compare your views of Maia's experiences with those of your classmates.

From
Report from Part One

GWENDOLYN BROOKS

When poet Gwendolyn Brooks was a child, Christmas was not an ordinary holiday. Like the star on the tree, the day shone with the brightness of fun and giving. What were some of her favorite traditions of the season?

Home. Checker games. Dominoes. Radio (Jack Benny, Ben Bernie, and Kate Smith; "Amos and Andy"; Major Bowes' "Amateur Hour"; Wayne King, the Waltz King; and "Ladies and Gentlemen: Ea-sy Aces"). Christmases. I shall stop right here to tell about those. They were important.

The world of Christmas was firm. Certain things were done. Certain things were not done.

We did not put Christmas trees outdoors.

We did not open Christmas presents on Christmas Eve.

And we had *not* made fruitcakes two or three months ahead of time.

A Christmas tree, we felt—my mother, my father, my brother, and I—belonged in the living room. Green, never silver or gold or pink. Full-branched and aspiring to the ceiling.

Christmas presents were wrapped and hidden on Christmas Eve. Oh, the sly winks and grins. The furtive rustle of tissue, the whip of ribbon off the spool, semiheard. The trippings here and there in search of secure hiding places. Our house had nooks and crannies, a closet, a pantry, alcoves, "the little room," an extensive basement. There were hiding places aplenty.

Fruitcakes were made about a week before Christmas. We didn't care what the recipe books said. We liked having all the Christmas joy as close together as possible. Mama went downtown, as a rule, for the very freshest supplies, for then, as now, distributors sent their *worst* materials to "the colored neighborhood." Candied cherries and pineapple but no citron. Mama didn't like citron (*I* did and do), so that was out. Candied orange and lemon, however. Figs galore. Dates galore. Raisins, raisins, raisins.

We children had the bake-eve fun of cutting up the candied fruit, shelling and chopping the nuts, and mixing everything together. Our fingers got tired, our teeth and tongues never. We tasted and tasted and took tummy aches to bed. Next day, the house was rich with the aroma of brandied fruit and spice. How wonderful. How happy I was.

It was the baking of the fruitcakes that opened our Christmas season. After that, there was the merriest playing of Christmas carols on the piano by my mother and me, with everybody singing: mysterious shopping jaunts: the lingering, careful purchase of Christmas cards: the visit to Santa Claus: the desperately scrupulous housecleaning: for my mother and myself, the calls at the beauty shop for Christmas hairdos (you had to look your very best on Christmas Day): the Christmas hunt, undertaken by all, with the marvelous pungent symbol *found* and borne back triumphantly through the dusk of the third or fourth day before Christmas.

All this. So much more that fades and fades. I almost forgot the high, high angel food cake, made a day or two before Christmas. We were, somehow, not great Christmas cookie advocates, but there would be a few frosted cookies about. We had Christmas candy. And filled candies and Christmas mints. Some of those dates, too, were stuffed with nuts and sugared over, to make another sort of confection.

On Christmas Eve we decorated the Christmas tree. So much silver tinsel. And ropes of fringed gold, and red, silver, blue, and gold balls, and a star on top. We children hung our stockings on the mantel—in the morning they would ache with apples, oranges, nuts, and tiny toys—over

our, yes, *real* fireplace! That night we were allowed to "sample the sample"—that is, "test" fruitcake that my mother always made in a shallow pan, along with the proper proud giants—and with it we had eggnog with nutmeg on top.

With what excited pleasure my brother and I went to bed, trying to stay awake to hear Santa Claus come down our chimney, but always failing, for Santa was a sly old soul. We went to sleep with radio carols in our ears or to the sweet sound of Mama playing and singing "Silent Night," or "Hark! The Herald Angels Sing," or "O Little Town of Bethlehem."

Next day it was so hard to wait for the sky to turn on its light. As soon as it did, out of bed we children threw ourselves and rushed into the living room. There we found, always, that Papa had turned on the Christmas tree lights, and under the tree shone *just about* everything we had asked of Santa Claus. (Of course, Mama *always* "helped" us with our letters to Santa Claus.) My brother remembers trains and tracks, baseball equipment, wagons, skates, games. Various Christmases brought me dishes, a rocking chair, a doll house, paper dolls, which I liked better than hard dolls because so much more could be done with the paper ones. My most delicate and exquisite Christmas gift memory is of a little glass deer, dainty antlered, slender legged, and filled with perfume.

Of course, there were clothes—"secondary" gifts.

And BOOKS.

About books. My "book Christmas" had already begun, on Christmas Eve, soon after the Christmas tree was strung with lights. It was for long my own personal tradition to sit behind the tree and read a paper book I still own: *The Cherry Orchard* by Marie Battelle Schilling and published by the David C. Cook Publishing Company. It had been given me by Kayola Moore, my Sunday school teacher. I don't know why I enjoyed reading that book, Christmas Eve after Christmas Eve, to the tune of black walnut candy crunching.

And back I went—to the back of the Christmas tree—with my new books. Late, late. After the relatives, after the Christmas turkey, after the cranberries—fresh!— none of your canned cranberries for us— and the mashed potatoes and gravy and baked macaroni and celery and candied sweet potatoes and peas and carrots, and the fruitcake and angel cake and eggnog. Back, while the rest of the family forgot it all in bed, to the else-dark room. The silence. The black walnut candy. And the books that began the giving again.

Gwendolyn Brooks *(born 1917),* Poet Laureate of Illinois, grew up in Chicago. Her early experiences have inspired much of her writing. Brooks's poetry is popular and has received many awards including a Guggenheim Fellowship and a Pulitzer prize. In addition to poetry, her works include a novel, *Maud Martha,* and her autobiography, *Report from Part One.* Brooks graduated from Wilson Junior College. She has taught at many colleges in the Chicago area, as well as at the University of Wisconsin and the City College of New York.

Developing Comprehension Skills

1. What are the three things Gwendolyn Brooks's family did *not* do to celebrate Christmas?

2. What are some of the Brooks's Christmas traditions? List at least four.

3. Parts of this selection are fact and parts are opinion. Name one fact about the family's preparations for Christmas. Name one opinion presented about the family's preparations for Christmas.

4. How have the traditions in the Brooks family developed? Did the parents make them up? Did the traditions come from the whole family? Support your answer with examples and details from the selection.

5. One of Brooks's favorite Christmas gifts is books. Books, she writes, "began the giving again." How do books begin "the giving again"? Tell how a book has "given" to you.

Reading Literature: Autobiographies

1. **Describing Mood.** As you know, **mood** is the feeling that a piece of writing creates in the reader. Overall, what mood do Brooks's descriptions of Christmas activities create? Which passage in the selection creates a more peaceful and quiet mood than the rest?

2. **Identifying Sensory Images.** As you have learned, **sensory images** are words and phrases that appeal to the five senses: sight, hearing, touch, taste, and smell. For example, Brooks describes the sounds of "the furtive rustle of tissue, the whip of ribbon off the spool." Find at least one sensory image in the selection for each of the five senses.

3. **Understanding Character.** In an autobiography, the way the writer narrates events and the details he or she chooses can tell you a great deal about the person. In this selection, notice the activities that seem important to Brooks and the way she talks about her family. What kind of person does Brooks seem to be? Identify three of her qualities, and explain how she shows each quality.

4. **Analyzing Style.** In this selection the writer conveys the warmth and excitement of her family's holiday traditions. Explain how three of the following techniques are used to create the feeling of celebration.

   a. sentence fragments (including single words used as sentences)
   b. word choice
   c. details
   d. repetition
   e. imagery
   f. punctuation

Developing Vocabulary Skills

Using a Dictionary to Determine Word Origins. Some English words are clipped, or shortened, versions of longer words. Other English words come from the name of a person or place. The following words are used in the nonfiction selections you have read or are based on names from the selections. Look up each word in a dictionary. Write the word on a sheet of paper. Next to it, write the longer word or the name from which the word came.

1. bowie knife   4. Braille
2. Saturday   5. vet
3. plane   6. eve

Developing Skills in Study and Research

Becoming Familiar with Books in a Library. Choose a general subject—such as holidays, cooking, or music—that is in some way related to this autobiography. Locate the section of the library that has books on that subject. To find the section, you can refer to the card catalog or to the computerized indexing system. Look over the shelves and notice the books available. Choose at least three books on the subject, and write down their titles, authors, and call numbers.

Developing Skills in Speaking and Listening

Introducing a Guest Speaker. Imagine that your class has invited the six writers from these first two sections of this chapter to speak at your school. You have the job of introducing one of the guests. Select information from the writer's diary or autobiography, as well as from the writer's biography following the selection. Make notes organizing the information you want to use. Prepare and practice a short introductory speech. Then present the introduction to a small group.

Developing Writing Skills

1. **Describing a Tradition.** Every culture has its own holiday celebrations, and every family has its own traditions. In two or three paragraphs, describe a holiday celebration or family tradition that you know well. Use specific details to explain the tradition fully and to help the reader imagine it.

    Prewriting. Think about a celebration or tradition you have been part of. You may want to interview family members or friends to collect information. List the important activities, objects, and people involved. Then list details that appeal to the five senses. Decide how you want to organize your description. If you want to use time order, you may want to make a time line showing the order of events.

    Drafting. In your topic sentence introduce the celebration or tradition. Then describe it in detail. Follow the type of organization you decided on. Be sure to include sensory images to help your readers visualize the event.

    Revising and Sharing. Ask a classmate to read your description and tell you if your account is interesting. Ask if he or she has questions about the event. Make any necessary revisions.

2. **Explaining an Idea.** The traditions that Gwendolyn Brooks writes about involve many details that are unique to her family. What do you think traditions give a family? In one paragraph, state your idea and support it with reasons and examples. You may want to review your answer to question 4 in Developing Comprehension Skills. Follow the process of writing: prewriting, drafting, revising, and sharing. For more help see the Guidelines for the Process of Writing beginning on page 654.

Biographies

A good **biography** presents a person's character fairly. It reports the events of that person's life accurately. In order to accomplish these goals, a writer must learn all he or she can about the subject. The biographer uses interviews, letters, diaries, and other writing by or about the subject.

The biographies in this section describe three people who met challenges and overcame obstacles with determination and courage. As you read, see how the writers used the facts to develop a picture of each subject.

Portrait, 1984, CONSTANCE MALLINSON. © Constance Mallinson.

From

Alexander the Great

JOHN GUNTHER

Alexander the Great conquered and unified huge portions of the ancient world. As you read this selection, notice that even as a young boy he shows unusual daring and cleverness.

In the fifth century B.C., Greece was a center for government, art, and learning in the ancient world. The country became divided by warring factions, however, and as a result was conquered in 338 B.C. by King Philip of Macedon. Macedon was a country just north of Greece. When Alexander, Philip's son, began to build his great empire, he not only ruled Greece, but also spread Greek civilization throughout the known world. This spreading of civilization was one of Alexander's most enduring achievements.

This selection begins with a brief description of the world of Greece and Macedonia at the time when Alexander was born. The account continues with a famous story about Alexander as a young boy.

In those days the Eastern Mediterranean was the center of the universe. Athens, the chief city of Greece, had a position, geographically and culturally, something like that of New York today.

But the Greeks did not know much of what lay beyond. They knew their own seacoast well, their own rivers, islands, valleys, and steep mountains. They had crossed the Aegean Sea and built colonies along the coast of Asia Minor, and they had penetrated westward into Sicily. The Greek world was a kind of luminous circle, but beyond its outer fringes all was darkness.

If a Greek looked north, he would know that Macedonia and Thrace existed, but beyond those countries there were only the barbarians—savage marauders who lived in the Danube area. Looking west and southwest, he would know about the great trading city of Carthage, on the African coast. Daring explorers had even reached the Straits of Gibraltar, which were called the Pillars of Hercules. But when Alexan-

The Empire of Alexander the Great, 323 B.C.

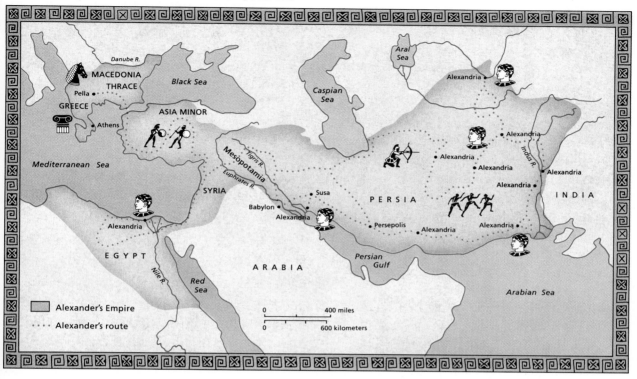

der was born, even Rome was little known outside Italy.

To the south, the Greeks had some knowledge of Egypt, and to the east, they had good reason to know a great deal about Persia and the huge and dangerous Persian Empire. Beyond that was India of which the Greeks had heard, although few of them had ever been there. Beyond India was China, a land unknown to the Greeks even by name.

Yet most of the world that was known at that time to the Greeks and Macedonians was eventually conquered by Alexander. This is what makes him so important to

history. China he never reached, and he did not go westward (toward Italy) at all. But he conquered practically everything else.

This was an achievement so remarkable, so extraordinary, that it has challenged the minds of people ever since. Alexander was the first of those titans like Caesar and Napoleon who, partly by accident and partly by design, set out to gather the whole world into their fists, unify it, rule it, and enlighten it.

He sought to make the entire world his own, and almost succeeded. Hence, even though his career was short-lived, it is one of the most dazzling landmarks of all time. . . .

The boy stood out there in the hot sun. He was of medium height, with ruddy blond hair, a straight nose, blue eyes, and a handsome figure. He had great physical courage and energy, and his mind was packed with dreams—such dreams as few people have ever had. His name was Alexander, and he was the son of Philip, King of Macedon.

The boy waited out in the sunshine, watching.

Soon there was a commotion, and Alexander saw his father, Philip, approach. Philip was a powerful, burly man, who was blind in one eye and walked with a limp. The boy was fond of him.

The sun is very hot in Greece and Macedonia in April. Alexander, who was about fourteen and who loved to watch everything that went on around the palace, squinted up at the burning sun.

King Philip saw Alexander across the courtyard and waved to him cheerfully. Surrounding Philip were courtiers, attendants, and horsemen. The Macedonians could ride like demons; they were practically centaurs.

The town where this took place was called Pella, and it was the capital of Macedonia. Really it was not a town at all, in our sense, but a mountain village—consisting mostly of stone huts, barracks for the fierce soldiery, and temples. There were multitudes of gods in those days, and peo-ple took them seriously, which is why so many temples were always being built. The time was about 342 B.C. . . .

King Philip's scouts had just returned from a foray into the neighboring hills, and they had bought some horses in the market. One after another these new horses were galloped around in the courtyard, while Philip, with his expert eye, looked them over.

Alexander, fascinated by the excitement of this spectacle and the beauty of the horses, watched eagerly from across the court. He got up on a fence to see better. None of the horses had ever been saddled before, and even the hard-riding Macedonian cavalrymen found them hard to mount and break in.

Then a horse was brought in whom nobody, not even King Philip himself, could master. This horse, Bucephalus by name, was destined to become one of the most famous horses in history.

Bucephalus was an enormous animal. This black giant, the scouts told Philip, had been extremely expensive; the price paid for him had been thirteen talents. It is very difficult to calculate what a talent would be worth in American dollars, but it was considered to be an imposing sum. One talent was probably equal to $6,000, so that Bucephalus had cost the equivalent of $78,000, a lot of money for a horse.

Now as he watched the animal, Alexander noticed something peculiar, and his muscles became taut. Bucephalus, snorting with rage and acting like a wild beast (which indeed he was), refused to be mounted. He would shy violently each time he heard a voice. No one could get near him, much less swing up on his naked back.

King Philip, who had a hasty temper, saw that Bucephalus was indeed unmanageable. In disgust, he shouted an order to have the horse taken away and returned to the market.

Alexander leapt down from the fence. "No, no!" he cried. He rushed toward Philip and the horse, muttering excitedly to himself, "What a wonderful beast they are turning away! They don't know how to handle him!"

With youthful eloquence the boy appealed to his father not to send Bucephalus back to the market.

Philip looked at Alexander with cool appraisal, and then at the wildly plunging horse. "Who could ride him?" Philip asked.

"I can," said Alexander.

Philip, who liked to treat his son like an adult, exclaimed, "And if you do not, what will you forfeit for your rashness?"

"I will pay the whole price of the horse," replied Alexander.

Thirteen talents, the price of Bucephalus, was much more money than Alexander had in the world. If he were to lose, he would have to mortgage his future to pay his father back.

"All right," said Philip. "Agreed."

The boy ran up to the giant horse, from whose eyes fury and terror were still darting. Grasping the bridle quickly, Alexander turned the animal full-face into the burning sun and kept him pointed in that direction.

The tough old courtiers around Philip were still laughing at the boy's bet. However, Philip, who tried to be a good father whenever he had time, had become alarmed lest his son be thrown and hurt. Now, as he watched the scene before him, the king's fears began to leave him and pride took their place.

Alexander was speaking gently to Bucephalus, clapping him on the back with a reassuring gesture. After a few minutes the horse's rapid panting began to slow down—a sign that he had become less agitated. He lowered his majestic head for the fraction of a second, and Alexander, with one bound, took advantage of this movement to leap up on the animal's back.

Alexander continued to keep Bucephalus pointed steadily toward the sun and soon this huge, ferocious beast walked as tamely as a faithful dog. Yet Alexander did not even strike him. He held the reins hard, eased his mount into a canter, and finally spurred him to a full gallop. The courtiers watched in amazement, hardly believing what their eyes reported.

Alexander then returned to where Philip stood open-mouthed. When the boy dismounted, his father clutched him with pride and happiness.

To master Bucephalus was easy, Alexander explained. He had noticed that when the animal was first led out into the open

Alexander the Great Riding Bucephalus, 1st century A.D. Greco-Roman bronze sculpture from Herculaneum. National Archaeological Museum, Naples.

courtyard his back was to the sun. Thus, his body cast a shadow that terrified him. The more he plunged and danced, the more frightening was the movement of the shadow. The boy shrewdly watched for his chance and turned the horse around, so that the shadow was not before him. Then he waited till Bucephalus tamed down.

Philip kissed Alexander on the head. "My son," he declared, with great emotion, "Macedonia will not be big enough for you. You will need a kingdom of your own!"

For years and years Alexander loved Bucephalus, and Bucephalus loved him in return. Almost always Bucephalus was the horse that he chose to ride in battle, and the gallant, flying figure of the blond young man on the huge black horse became a symbol of certain victory to the Macedonians. In time, Bucephalus became too old to fight, but Alexander always kept him with him. In fact, when Bucephalus was so aged that he could hardly walk, Alexander would nevertheless mount him before a battle and ride in sight of his troops for a few moments. This would encourage and stimulate them. Then he would change to another horse.

Bucephalus died sixteen years after that sunny spring morning in Pella when Alexander was the first human being ever to ride him. Alexander gave him a solemn funeral and even named a city after him. The ruins of this city still exist today, in Kashmir, one of the far-off countries conquered by Alexander.

John Gunther *(1901–1970)* was born in Chicago and attended the University of Chicago. He worked as a journalist, first in Chicago and then as a foreign correspondent for the *Daily News* in London. He covered many parts of the world, and in 1936 he published his first book, *Inside Europe.* It was a great success, and Gunther left journalism to research and write other books about life in different parts of the world. He eventually wrote a series, including *Inside Asia, Inside Africa,* and *Inside Russia Today.* The biography *Death Be Not Proud* is about his son, who struggled with cancer and died as a young man.

Developing Comprehension Skills

1. What country does Alexander's father rule? What important country lies just to the south?

2. How does Alexander's father respond to his son's request to ride Bucephalus? Does his father have any mixed feelings? Explain.

3. How do the king's men react to Alexander's wanting to ride the horse? What assumptions are they making about Alexander?

4. Alexander succeeds in riding Bucephalus. How does he manage to change the horse's behavior?

5. Decide whether each of these statements is a fact or an opinion.

   a. The Macedonians could ride like demons; they were practically centaurs.

   b. The price paid for him had been thirteen talents.

   c. "Macedonia will not be big enough . . . You will need a kingdom of your own!"

6. In this selection, the boy Alexander shows characteristics that will eventually make him a great leader. What are these characteristics? Are they still important characteristics for leaders to have? Explain your answers.

Reading Literature: Biography

1. **Evaluating Biography.** This selection is part of a book-length biography about Alexander the Great. In the book the writer tries to give a fair picture of Alexander, telling about his mistakes and weaknesses as well as his great triumphs. In the early part that you have read, however, the writer focuses only on Alexander's positive qualities. What is the purpose of this opening section? Does it make you want to know more about Alexander? Why would the writer emphasize Alexander's strengths rather than his weaknesses in the beginning of the biography?

2. **Analyzing Character.** Alexander shows great self-confidence and courage in his certainty that he can ride Bucephalus and in his promise to pay the price of the horse if he fails. Alexander's father, however, speaks of Alexander's "rashness." Is Alexander's behavior rash, or reckless, in any way? Explain your answer.

3. **Understanding Suspense.** The excitement and tension that readers feel as they become involved in a story is called *suspense.* In this selection suspense builds swiftly after Alexander first sees Bucephalus because so much depends on Alexander's ability to tame the horse. What has Alexander promised he will do if he fails? In what way is Alexander in danger? How do bystanders rate his chances for success?

4. **Examining Word Choice.** In this selection the writer chooses words that convey exactly the feeling or idea he wants to express. Choose three of the words from the following list. Find them in the story. Then tell how each one creates a clear, specific picture for the reader.

> ruddy (page 512, col. 1)
> burly (page 512, col. 1)
> foray (page 512, col. 2)
> taut (page 512, col. 1)
> hasty (page 513, col. 1)
> canter (page 513, col. 1)

Developing Vocabulary Skills

Multiple Meanings of Words. As you know, many words have more than one meaning. The following words are from the selection you have just read. Look up each word in a dictionary. On a sheet of paper write the meaning that fits the word as it is used in the selection. Then write a sentence using the word with one of its other meanings.

> talent (page 512, col. 2)
> shy (page 513, col. 1)
> handle (page 513, col. 1)
> cool (page 513, col. 1)
> danced (page 514, col. 1)

Developing Skills in Critical Thinking

Analyzing Conclusions. In this selection Alexander figures out why Bucephalus is acting so wildly when the courtiers try to ride him. Answer the following questions to analyze how Alexander approaches and solves the problem of Bucephalus's behavior.

What conclusion does Alexander reach about Bucephalus's behavior? How does he reach this conclusion? How does he test his conclusion? What assumptions do his father and the courtiers make about the horse's behavior? What do they fail to do in evaluating the situation?

Developing Writing Skills

1. **Supporting an Opinion.** When Alexander decides to ride Bucephalus, he takes a great risk. There is a real danger that he will be badly injured or even killed. Do you think Alexander should have taken this risk? Write a paragraph in which you explain your opinion.

   Prewriting. Make a chart like the one shown below. In one column write reasons against Alexander trying to ride Bucephalus. In the other write reasons in favor of his taking the risk. For each reason give one or two supporting facts or examples from the selection. Review your chart and form your opinion about Alexander's action.

   Drafting. State your opinion in your topic sentence. Then explain the reasons for your opinion. Support your reasons with facts and examples from the selection.

   Revising and Sharing. Reread your paragraph. Make sure that you support your opinion with specific reasons and accurate facts and examples. Check to be sure that your sentences are clearly connected. Read your paragraph in class and listen to your classmates' paragraphs. Compare your opinions in a class discussion.

2. **Describing an Event.** Alexander's first experience with Bucephalus is an important event. It reveals strong elements in Alexander's character and points to the kind of daring leader he will become. While few people will become famous like Alexander, everyone has experiences that are milestones in some way. Talk to an older relative or friend and ask that person to tell you about an important event from his or her childhood. The event may be something ordinary, but it should have a special meaning for the person. Learn as many details as you can. Then write a paragraph telling about the event. If possible, try to indicate how the incident shows something of the person's character or personality as an adult. Follow the steps in the process of writing: prewriting, drafting, revising, and sharing. For more help, see the Guidelines for the Process of Writing beginning on page 654.

Reasons For	Reasons Against	Facts and Examples
Riding Bucephalus would be a great victory.		Alexander would be conquering a wonderful but dangerous animal.
	Alexander might be injured or killed.	Bucephalus is huge and wild. The king's men have not been able to ride the horse.

Banker Maggie Walker

OLIVE W. BURT

Maggie Walker faced many obstacles as she worked to achieve her goals in life. What were some of these obstacles? How did she deal with them? Read this selection to find out.

Wrapped in an old, patched quilt, ten-year-old Maggie Mitchell sat up in bed. With the stub of a pencil and a bit of yellow paper, she was doing her arithmetic problems for school. Maggie enjoyed working with numbers.

She looked across the room to where her mother was bent over a wooden tub. Mrs. Mitchell was scrubbing a shirt on the corrugated wooden washboard. As she straightened up to wring out the garment, her eyes met Maggie's. "Feeling better, child?"

Maggie nodded. "Pain's all gone now, Ma. And I haven't coughed for a long time."

Her mother tossed the shirt into a basket filled with other laundry. "I'll just get these on the line," she said, "so they'll be dry before dark." She lifted the basket and went out. Left alone, Maggie put down her homework, slid down onto the pillow, and closed her eyes. Soon she was asleep.

She didn't hear her mother come back into the room but was awakened later by a sharp knock on the door. Mrs. Mitchell dried her hands on her apron as she crossed the room and opened the door. A tall, neatly dressed man stood there. He was the collector for the Independent Order of St. Luke, and he had come to get the ten cents a week that Mrs. Mitchell managed to save. She went to a shelf above the scrubbed pine table and took down a small bowl. From it she took two nickels and a small, dog-eared notebook which she handed to the collector. He put the money in his pocket and wrote in the book.

"You've done very well, Mrs. Mitchell," he said as he handed back the book. "Never missed a week. You'll be glad some day when you need the money for something special."

Maggie's mother looked at the little book and sighed. "It's mighty hard sometimes. And it takes so long!" She put the book back into the bowl and placed them on the shelf.

The St. Luke Bank. Valentine Museum, Richmond, Virginia.

"I know," the man said. "But keep up the good work, and I'll see you next week." He turned toward Maggie and waved. Then he left.

Maggie closed her eyes again. She was not sleeping now; she was thinking. Every week, no matter what—whether she had lots of washing to do or none at all—her mother always had ten cents for the collector. The money was being kept safe in the St. Luke bank, and, if they ever needed it, they could get it.

The St. Luke bank—the Independent Order of St. Luke—had been started by a group of black men in Richmond. When they saw that the black people lacked social clubs and a place to turn to for business advice, they decided to provide these services. St. Luke's was a bank, an insurance company, and a social club combined into one organization. It was the first business undertaking to benefit the freed blacks in the United States. Although it was planned to help men only, when Maggie's father died, the directors of the company permitted Mrs. Mitchell to continue with her husband's account.

Maggie Mitchell was born in Richmond, Virginia, on July 15, 1867. Since her father had died, her mother supported the two of them by taking in washing. Maggie helped as much as she could, but her mother wanted her to get an education rather than do odd jobs for pennies.

Maggie studied hard and worked hard, and every week she saved some of the money she earned. When she was sixteen, she graduated from the Richmond Normal and Colored School.[1] She was now considered ready to leave school and go to work, but the jobs open to blacks, especially black women, were those that required hard work and earned little pay. Maggie thought of the possibilities. She could do laundering, as her mother did. She could get a job as a servant in some white family's

1. **Richmond Normal and Colored School**—Normal schools were schools to train teachers. The students were often teen-agers. *Colored* was an accepted term in Walker's time.

home. She could leave the city and do field work on a nearby farm. For Maggie, there was one other choice. At sixteen, she was considered educated enough to teach black children.

None of these things appealed to Maggie. All of her teachers had spoken of her knack with numbers. They had suggested that she find a way to use this skill after she left school. And that was what she aimed to do.

Walking along the street one day, her mind busy with such thoughts, she almost bumped into the St. Luke's man who had collected money from her mother for so many years. "You trying to knock me down, Maggie?" he joked, and was about to go on his way.

"Wait a minute, please!" Maggie called out. "I want to ask you something."

He stopped, and she began to explain her problem. "Are there any jobs for me?" she asked.

He frowned and shook his head. "Not for women. If you were a man you might get work in the bank down the street or maybe in a store. But no one hires women for work like that. They just don't think any woman can do that sort of thing."

"But I'm good with numbers, better than any boy in my classes. What about St. Luke's? Don't they use bookkeepers?"

The man laughed. "Of course they do. But there aren't any females working there."

"Well, I'm going down there this very minute and ask for a job!" She turned and quickly walked down the street to the office of the Independent Order of St. Luke.

Maggie was not surprised to find the outer office filled with men. They sat about in small groups chatting, playing checkers. She paid little attention to the men, but glanced around until she saw the door marked "Private Office." She knocked sharply, and when a voice called, "Come on in!" she entered, closing the door behind her.

Mr. Simpson, director of the Order, looked up from the work on his desk and was surprised to see Maggie. Not that she was a stranger to him. He had known her father, had helped her mother over bad times, and had watched Maggie grow up, but he did not rise or ask her to sit down. "Why, Maggie Mitchell! What are you doing here?" he said.

Maggie came straight to the point. She told him that she had finished school, was very good with numbers, and would like to come to work at St. Luke. The old man was surprised and amused. He had never thought of hiring a girl, and he did not think the board of directors, who ran the business, would like it.

Maggie found it was no use to argue with him. He was friendly and kind, but he didn't seem to understand. Finally, he said, "You get a job in some other office or get some experience somehow. There are business schools, aren't there? Go to one. When you've had some experience, know something about business, you can come back, and I'll see what I can do for you."

Maggie unhappily thanked him and left the office. Business school was out of the question. It cost too much. So in the end, she accepted a job teaching second grade in a school for black children. Her salary was twenty dollars a month. After buying a few clothes for herself and giving her mother some money to help with food, she still had some money left over. Maggie used most of it to buy books, crayons, and other things that were not provided for the students by the school. Nevertheless, each month she managed to save some money for business school. But at that rate, it would be years before she could realize her dream.

When Maggie was nineteen, she married Armistead Walker, a young businessman of Richmond. In time they had two sons, Russell, born in 1890, and Melvin, born in 1897. Maggie had become a tall, stately woman with clear, dark eyes and a kind expression. Her voice was low and rich, and she was an excellent speaker. She was enthusiastic about any project she undertook, and she had the energy to carry it out. All this made it possible for her to care for her family and yet continue teaching. She hadn't lost sight of her goal and was saving every cent possible toward the business education she was determined to have. For a time, she attended night school. Then finally she gave up teaching altogether and spent full time at Richmond Business College. By the time Melvin was two years old, Maggie had her degree in business. With her diploma in hand, she went to the St.

Luke office again and applied for work.

Meanwhile, Mr. Simpson had died. Another man now ran the office, and Maggie saw at once that he didn't know anything about running a business. The office was cluttered and dirty. Stacks of papers overflowed the chairs. Even the man's desk was a mess, covered with papers, empty mugs, ash trays, and a spittoon. He listened to Maggie and sighed.

"I do need help here, as you can see. But a woman! If I can't handle the work, how can I expect a woman to?"

Maggie had been prepared for a struggle, but she was determined to get a job at St. Luke's one way or another. Now she had a plan.

"I can at least keep house!" she said. "The first thing I'd do would be to clean up this office!"

The man's face brightened. "That's more like it. You're hired. You'll get eight dollars a month!"

Maggie gulped. That was twelve dollars a month less than she had been earning. But the job was what she wanted—a chance to show what she could do. She'd clean that office, but that wouldn't be all!

For a while, that was all she was permitted to do. But gradually, she began taking over other duties when her boss was out to lunch or in a board meeting. She collected dues in such a pleasant way that folks came in when they knew she was there. Then she took over the bookkeeping and checked applications for loans.

The more Maggie learned about St.

Luke's, the more she realized it was poorly run. The rent the Order was paying was much too high. There was no reserve fund, though having money set aside for emergencies was the very thing the Order was urging people to do. The money that came in was not wisely invested, and much was lost through careless handling. In fact, St. Luke was on the verge of bankruptcy. The director and his board of six men had no idea how matters stood.

Maggie knew something must be done at once. If the Order went bankrupt, the hundreds of members would lose all their hard earned savings. How could she change things? The men on the board would not welcome suggestions from a newcomer, especially a woman. She would have to move slowly but tactfully. She waited until her "newness" had somewhat worn off and asked for permission to attend a board meeting.

The Director hesitated. However, when Maggie told him that she had found things in the books that the board should know about, he was startled. He hadn't the faintest idea what was in the company's books, so he obtained the board's permission for Maggie to attend a meeting.

Maggie listened to the rambling reports and the useless suggestions made by these men. She managed to look interested and to smile approval, and gradually their attitude toward her warmed. When she thought the time was right, she started with the simplest problem: Why didn't they purchase the building in which they had

their offices instead of renting space? She had figures to show them how much they would save in a year. The men sat up and listened.

The Board did not follow Maggie's suggestions immediately. However, before too long she learned that the building had been purchased. She was ready now to suggest that they install a new system of bookkeeping. This took a bit longer, because the men could not see any advantage. In time, they gave Maggie free rein to try out the new system. And so it was with her other suggested improvements. Moving slowly and carefully, she got the business organized with the best and newest equipment. She was promoted from clerk to secretary, then to executive secretary with the right to meet regularly with the Board and to suggest improvements. Her salary was raised with each promotion.

However, Maggie was not content with just getting the Order working well. She wanted to see it prosper. She wanted it to reach thousands of people instead of hundreds. And, she wanted it to employ more women, especially black women. When she was in charge of interviewing and hiring employees, she chose women whenever possible. Once they were working, she encouraged them to save a part of their salary each week. To get them started, Maggie promised that as soon as a woman had saved fifty dollars, she would lend her whatever amount she needed to make the first payment on a home, shop, or training course. She did not limit their choices. If a woman was talented at sewing, she was helped to open a dressmaking shop. If she liked baking, then a pastry shop was suggested. The study of medicine, law, engineering, or construction was also encouraged.

It was not always possible for a woman to get into the business or career of her choice. People in the early 1900's would not accept the fact that women might be very good at jobs generally considered for men only. But Maggie did her best. She once hired a cleaning woman, only to discover that the woman was really interested in business. Maggie urged her to save one dollar a week toward a business course. When she had enough money, she went to school at night and worked during the day. When she finished with her course, she became a bookkeeper. With a good paying job, the woman was later able to own her own home and continue to save money. "That's what one dollar a week will do!" Maggie would tell people.

In the thirty-five years that Maggie worked for the Order of St. Luke, membership grew from 3,000 to more than 100,000, a large part of them women. Maggie had helped many to buy their own homes and businesses. She once figured that St. Luke had helped more than 700 black families become home owners.

Maggie wanted to help children, too. She knew that the younger they started saving, the easier it would be when they grew up. And the black children were workers. They took odd jobs as soon as they were able. Maggie opened a Penny Bank, which would accept any deposit, no matter how small. She went into the schools to explain to the children what a savings account could do for them. She told stories of successful business people, some they knew, who had got their start by saving a little regularly. Soon more than 20,000 black children had accounts in the Penny Bank.

Meanwhile, Maggie continued her own education. She enrolled in Virginia Union University to study the latest banking methods. She received her Master's degree in business administration in 1925, when she was nearly sixty years old. Soon after this, she founded a new bank, which she called the St. Luke Bank and Trust Company. That name and association had meant so much to her that she wanted to keep the name in her new venture. She was made the first president of this new institution and so became the only black woman bank president in the country. And, under Maggie's direction, it became one of the most successful banks in Richmond.

Though she was active in business, Maggie always had time for civic and social projects. She raised money for schools for black girls and served on the board of directors of the National Training School for Girls at Lincoln Heights, in Washington, D.C. She edited St. Luke's *Herald* for more than thirty years and founded several organizations for black women of her city. One of them was the Richmond Council of Women, whose members were dedicated

Maggie Lena Walker, 1925. Valentine Museum, Richmond, Virginia. Photograph by Scurlock.

to improving the lives of underprivileged citizens, especially women and girls. This group agitated for better working conditions, higher pay, and wider employment opportunities, in order to help raise the standard of living of thousands of black women and their families.

Maggie Walker's service to her city was recognized when Richmond gave a dinner in her honor. Hundreds of people came to express their gratitude to the woman who helped them in the struggle to improve the quality of their lives. Among the tributes was one by Governor Lee Trinkle, who declared that "the State of Virginia could never pay its debt to Mrs. Walker for what she had done for the black citizens of Richmond."

Maggie was at the height of success when tragedy struck the family. Coming home late one night, her husband was mistaken for a burglar and shot by one of their sons. It was an accident, and the youth was declared innocent by the court. But afterwards Maggie aged rapidly. Then she had a fall from which she never fully recovered. She spent her last years in a wheelchair and died December 15, 1934.

As a tribute to her memory, the St. Luke Bank and Trust Company established a ten thousand dollar educational fund to help young people who want a college education.

Olive Burt *(1894–1981)* grew up in Utah and had a lifelong interest in the Old West. *Petticoats West, First Woman Editor, Sarah J. Hale,* and *Negroes in the Early West* are historical books that reflect this interest. Burt was also a teacher and editor. For many years, she edited a column called "School News and Views" for a daily newspaper in Salt Lake City. Students from eighty local schools sent her news items for the column.

Developing Comprehension Skills

1. How old is Maggie at the beginning of the account? At what age does she graduate from Normal School? How old is she when she receives her Master's degree?

2. What three services are provided by the Independent Order of St. Luke?

3. Tell what you learn about Maggie from each of these facts.

   a. She hires women employees whenever possible.

   b. She opens a Penny Bank for children.

   c. She founds an organization dedicated to improving the lives of the poor.

4. When Maggie first tries to get a job as a bookkeeper, she is turned down. When she tries again later, the new director hires her but at first only to help keep order in his office. What inaccurate assumption is made by the two directors? Why are such assumptions unfair?

Reading Literature: Biography

1. **Analyzing a Character.** In this biography, the writer creates a clear picture of Maggie Walker. Read each of the following quotations from the biography. Explain in your own words the quality that each passage describes.

   a. Maggie studied hard and worked hard, and every week she saved some of the money she earned.

   b. "But I'm good with numbers, better than any boy in my classes. What about St. Luke's? Don't they use bookkeepers?"

   c. However, Maggie was not content with just getting the Order working well. She wanted to see it prosper.

d. In the thirty-five years that Maggie worked for the Order of St. Luke, membership grew from 3,000 to more than 100,000.

2. **Examining Setting.** The writer uses several settings in this selection. Describe the following settings and identify the problem or conflict Maggie faces in each one.
   a. Maggie's childhood home.
   b. The outer office at St. Luke's when Maggie first applies for a job.
   c. The office of the new director at St. Luke's when she applies for a job the second time.

3. **Learning History from Biography.** What information do you learn from this selection about the lives of the newly freed black people shortly after the Civil War? What do you learn about the roles played by women, especially black women?

Developing Vocabulary Skills

Determining Word Meaning. You have learned three methods for determining the meaning of an unfamiliar word:
   a. Using the meanings of word parts—prefixes, suffixes, and base words
   b. using context clues
   c. using a dictionary

Read the following sentences from the selections you have read. Figure out the definition of each underlined word by using one of the above methods. On a sheet of paper, write each word and its definition. Also note which method or methods you used to learn the word's meaning.

1. We have had a large national flag made; it is <u>composed</u> of thirteen stripes, red and white, alternately, on a blue ground, with a large white star of five points, in the centre.

2. In the afternoon a messenger was sent from the enemy to Colonel Travis, demanding an <u>unconditional</u> and absolute surrender of the <u>garrison</u>.

3. He <u>relied</u> on us to do our best and I don't want to let him down.

4. Nothing can crush us *more* than this <u>restlessness</u>.

5. Perhaps it was a small effort to <u>compensate</u> me for my handicap.

6. Red walked <u>masterfully</u> up and down our street.

7. Each time I saw him go <u>vertically</u> away from me, I thought he wouldn't *want* to come down.

8. We were, somehow, not great Christmas cookie <u>advocates</u>, but there would be a few frosted cookies about.

9. Mrs. Mitchell was scrubbing a shirt on the <u>corrugated</u> wooden washboard.

10. Nevertheless, each month she <u>managed</u> to save some money for business school.

Developing Skills in Critical Thinking

Evaluating an Opinion. The writer of "Banker Maggie Walker" has a definite opinion about her subject. What is this opinion? Give examples of words and phrases that show her opinion. What facts does the writer provide to support her opinion? Do you think the writer's opinion is trustworthy? Explain your answers.

Developing Writing Skills

1. **Explaining an Idea.** Maggie Walker became an extremely successful businesswoman. How did she achieve this success? In three paragraphs, explain what contributed to her becoming an outstanding businesswoman.

   Prewriting. Reread the selection. Make a chart with three columns for different categories. At the top of each column write the name of the characteristic that contributed to Maggie Walker's becoming successful. Examples might be *intelligence* or *determination*. In each column list some examples from the selection that illustrate the characteristic. Decide how you want to organize your information. For example, you may choose to discuss these characteristics in the order of importance, from least to most important. Supporting examples may be arranged in the order they occurred.

   Drafting. Begin your first paragraph with a clear topic sentence that tells the general categories that you think contributed to Maggie Walker's success. Then explain the first category, based on the organization you decided on in prewriting. Give examples from the selection to support your general idea. In the next two paragraphs, repeat the process. End the last paragraph with a brief summary statement.

   Revising and Sharing. Set your paragraphs aside and then reread them. Look for places that are confusing or too general. Check for clear connections between ideas. Add examples where necessary. Make a final copy and proofread for errors. Prepare to read your paragraphs in a class session. Compare your ideas with those of your classmates. What different ideas do people have about how Maggie Walker succeeded?

2. **Describing a Scene.** In this selection the writer describes a scene that made an impression on Maggie as a young girl: a visit by the collector from the Order of St. Luke. Choose a scene from your childhood that made an impression on you. Write a paragraph describing the scene. Include details about the setting and the people. You can use dialogue if you wish. Follow the process of writing: prewriting, drafting, revising, and sharing. For more help see the Guidelines to the Process of Writing beginning on page 654.

From
Chief Sarah

DOROTHY NAFUS MORRISON

The daughter of a Paiute chief, thirteen-year-old Sarah finds herself a witness to a life-or-death conflict. As you read, think about how respect, understanding, and cooperation might have changed the outcome of this conflict.

Princess Sarah Winnemucca, 1880's. Dillon Press, Minneapolis.

Sarah Speaks Out: 1857

Hoofbeats pounded the desert floor. They were faint at first but grew rapidly louder until they resounded from the nearby mountains and rolled through the single dusty street of the frontier town, Genoa, Nevada. Hearing them, Sarah Winnemucca—daughter of a chief, sister of a chief—knew there was going to be trouble. Two white men had been murdered, arrows had been found in the wounds, and Major Ormsby had sent for Sarah's people, the Paiutes.

Sarah and her sister Elma had lived in Genoa with Major Ormsby's family for a whole year, sent by their grandfather to learn the white man's ways. Still, Sarah was loyal to her tribe, and the thud of hoofs filled her with dread. It was September, 1857, when she was about thirteen years old.

She went outside the Ormsby house to watch the warriors draw close. Her brother

Natchez, the peace chief, and her cousin Numaga, the war chief, rode in the lead, and when they drew rein, with a shout from their followers, Major Ormsby stepped forward.

He was tall and excitable, with short, black chin whiskers, and as he spoke, Sarah's face burned with embarrassment, for he didn't follow the rules of Indian courtesy. He didn't inquire about the chief's health or offer to smoke together, giving each time to look into the other's face and see into his heart. He didn't even make a polite comment on the weather. Instead, he handed over the fatal arrows.

"Do you know what tribe these arrows belong to?" he demanded harshly in English, which Sarah understood well.

Numaga, tall and broad shouldered, with wary, deepset eyes, turned them over in his hand. "The Washoes," he replied in his deep voice.

"Will you help us get the Washoe chief to give up the men who killed the whites?" asked Ormsby, his tone making it a command.

Sarah gasped. Surely he knew that the Washoes and Paiutes were not friends, that the only reason they didn't go to war was because it took all their energy to find food in their dry land! Surely he knew better than to send chiefs as errand boys to their enemies!

But Numaga grimly overlooked the insult and chose five men to bring in the Washoe leader. This was his only honorable course, for the Paiutes and whites had made a treaty in which both promised to turn over wrong-doers of either race.

That night Sarah watched the first war dance she had ever seen performed by her peace-loving people. Yet peace seemed to be slipping away from them. Many white men were passing through the desert on the trail to the California gold fields, while others had come to stay. Some of them were kind. A few—the cruel ones—burned the Numa's caches of stored food and shot the Indians on sight. Sarah was in turmoil, loving her people, yet loving the Ormsbys too; frightened, yet thrilled as she tried to spot Natchez and Numaga among the painted warriors by the bonfire.

Several days later Captain Jim of the Washoes came in, an enormous man, bear-like in his rabbit skin robe, wearing a necklace of bones. "You ask me if these are my people's arrows. I say yes," rumbled Captain Jim in the Washoe tongue. Natchez was interpreter, but even without him Sarah could understand, for she was unusually quick at languages.

The major turned toward Natchez. "Tell Captain Jim that his people have killed two men, and he must bring them in. They shall not be hurt. All will be right."

"I know my people have not killed the men," Captain Jim protested. "None have been away; we are all at Pine-Nut Valley."

But the major brusquely told Captain Jim he must surrender the murderers, or the Paiutes would make war on them, for they and the whites were friends. "Now go and bring them in," he ordered.

Although Sarah pitied the Washoes as they walked away looking at the ground, Major Ormsby had promised they would not be hurt, and Natchez had repeated his words. Surely, as the major said, all would be right.

Captain Jim had no choice. Unless he surrendered someone—anyone—the whites would make a war that might wipe out his whole band. Therefore, in mid-October he again appeared, bringing three frightened young prisoners, along with their mothers, one young wife, and several others of his tribe. Quickly the whites bound the young men's wrists and locked them up, and the next morning, when they were led out, a crowd gathered. Sarah, her sister Elma, and the Ormsby family were there.

"Hang the red devils right off!" shouted someone in the crowd, while boys threw stones and jeered.

When thirty-one men appeared with guns on their shoulders, a Washoe woman began to scream, "Oh, they have come to kill them!"

All the women flung themselves on Natchez. "Oh, dear chieftain, they did not kill the white men—indeed they did not. They have not been away from our camp for over a month." They said Captain Jim had chosen these three because they had no fathers to protect them and no children to need them.

"Oh, Good Spirit, come!" prayed the young wife. "Come into the hearts of this people. Oh, whisper in their hearts that they may not kill my poor husband!" She spoke to Natchez. "Our cruel chief has given up my husband because he is afraid we will all be killed."

Bound by the treaty, Natchez folded his arms and explained that the men were going to be taken to California only to be tried. But the terrified prisoners had so little faith in the white man's justice that they tried to run away. Instantly the settlers raised their guns and fired, killing two and recapturing the third, who was wounded and soon died.

The young wife threw herself on the dead body of her husband; the mothers took their bleeding sons into their arms. "Oh, my sweet son—gone, gone!" wailed one.

Such grief, Sarah thought, was enough to make the very mountain weep. It was cruel and wrong, for the major had promised that the young warriors would not be harmed. Natchez, who had repeated the major's words, had been betrayed.

Brilliant, sensitive, with a scorching temper, Sarah was outraged at the broken promise. She turned toward Mrs. Ormsby.

"I believe those Washoe women. They say their men are all innocent," she exclaimed, as tears streamed down her face. "They say they were not away from their camp for a long time." She told Mrs. Ormsby all she had heard the women say and repeated many times, "I believe them, I believe them."

Mrs. Ormsby drew back. "How came the Washoe arrows there? And the chief

The Paiutes of Pyramid Lake in 1867. The man standing in the center with his hand in his pocket is believed to be Sarah's brother, Natchez. Photograph by Timothy Sullivan.

himself has brought them to us. My husband knows what he is doing." Gentle as she had been in the past, today she showed no pity.

Sarah then went to her brother and the Washoe chief. "It is I who have killed them," Captain Jim was saying, his voice heavy with sorrow. "Their blood is on my hands."

Slowly the crowd dispersed, leaving the Washoes with their dead.

For Sarah and Elma this was a shattering experience. Elma fell sick. Neither one could bear to stay in Genoa, nor did their family want them to. As soon as Elma was well enough, Natchez and several warriors took them to their own people, to live once

more in a brush karnee[1] and wander over the desert in search of food.

Several weeks later, on a cold winter day, a huge man stepped close to their fire, where melting snow dripped from his robe and ran down his broad face. It was Captain Jim, come to say the Washoes had not been guilty. Instead, two white men had done the killing and placed arrows in the wounds to throw blame onto the Indians.

"Who told you?" asked Natchez.

"Major Ormsby says so," Captain Jim replied, and explained that the men had been gambling, got into a fight, and

---

1. **karnee**–Cone-shaped house made of tree branches.

boasted about the murders. Drawing his robe around him Natchez then followed the Washoe chief out into the storm, to travel to the settlement and see for himself what had happened.

Left behind, Sarah thought about that autumn day at Genoa—the readiness of the settlers to shoot first and find out the truth afterward—Major Ormsby's rudeness—his promise broken as lightly as a man would snap a twig. Had the chiefs been right in keeping to their treaty? Or had they been wrong in helping capture innocent Washoes? Could they find any honorable course in these troubled days?

Sarah remembered how boldly she had thrown herself into the arms of Mrs. Ormsby and protested that the weeping Washoe women told the truth. Few Indians, and especially young Indian girls,

would talk so to the wife of a white man.

But Sarah belonged to a family of chiefs.

Sarah Winnemucca became a strong and tireless leader of her people. At various times she was an interpreter, teacher, war scout, warrior, lecturer, lobbyist, and writer. Again and again she struggled against impossible odds to seek justice and better conditions for the Paiute. In 1878 the Paiute declared her their chief, the first woman ever to be chosen. She established the first Native American school taught and run by Native Americans themselves, and she wrote the first book published in English by a Native American. Her lecture tours were popular, and she became known throughout the country as a champion and defender of her people. She died in 1891, at age forty-seven, probably of tuberculosis.

Dorothy Nafus Morrison received her education at the State University of Iowa and then moved to the West. After teaching music for twelve years, she became a writer. Morrison loves the West and the people who live there. She also enjoys history and research. She has combined these interests to write biographies for young adults of historical figures from the West. To make sure that her works are accurate, Morrison makes extensive use of letters and journals and takes all the dialogue in her books from these sources.

Developing Comprehension Skills

1. Who are Sarah and her sister living with at the time of this incident? What group of Native American people do Sarah and Elma belong to?

2. Major Ormsby blames the Washoes for the murders of two white men. What evidence does he base his conclusion on? Does he try to find out all the facts or does he act on assumptions? Explain your answer.

3. What is the relationship between the Paiutes and the Washoes? Why is it insulting for Natchez and Numaga, the Paiute chiefs, to be asked to bring in Captain Jim, the Washoe chief, for Major Ormsby?

4. How does Sarah feel about the Ormsbys at the beginning of this selection? at the end? How does she feel about the actions of Natchez, Numaga, and Captain Jim?

5. Major Ormsby promises the Washoes that their men will not be hurt. However, the three innocent young men are killed when they try to run away. Sarah is outraged that Major Ormsby has broken his promise. Does Major Ormsby break his promise or not? Could he have prevented the killing? Are Sarah's feelings justified? Explain. (Before answering these questions, reread the third paragraph from the end as well as the description of the killing itself.)

Reading Literature: Biography

1. **Understanding Biography.** The events in this selection help to show the reader what Sarah Winnemucca is like. The writer describes her subject as "brilliant, sensitive," and having "a scorching temper." What evidence of these qualities do you find in the biography? What words or actions show these qualities?

2. **Analyzing Conflict.** A **conflict,** as you know, is a struggle between opposing forces. An **internal conflict** is a conflict within a character. Sarah has loyalty to her own people as well as to the Ormsbys. What internal conflicts develop for her from these loyalties? Is she able to resolve these conflicts? Explain your answers.

Developing Vocabulary Skills

Reviewing Ways to Define Words. You have studied three ways to figure out the meaning of an unfamiliar word. One way is to use context clues. A second way is to use word parts—base words and affixes. A third way is to use a dictionary.

The following sentences use words from this selection. On a sheet of paper, write the word, its definition, and the method or methods you used to decide on the definition.

1. Sarah hears hoofbeats resounding from the nearby mountains.

2. Sarah is in turmoil because she loves her people, but she has come to love the Ormsbys too.

3. The major brusquely orders Captain Jim to surrender the Washoe men accused of murder.

4. Settlers jeer at the warriors, calling them names and throwing stones.

5. The Washoes are afraid that justice will not be done.

Chief Sarah 533

Developing Skills in Critical Thinking

Evaluating Decisions. At the end of this selection, Sarah asks, "Had the chiefs been right in keeping to their treaty? Or had they been wrong in helping capture innocent Washoes? Could they find any honorable course in these troubled days?" What difficult decisions do Natchez and Numaga have to make? What difficult choices do Major Ormsby and Captain Jim also face? What alternatives does each character have, and what would be the effect of each alternative? Do any or all of the characters find an "honorable course" in making their decisions? Give reasons for your conclusions.

Developing Writing Skills

1. **Telling an Incident.** Sarah takes a risk when she speaks out to Mrs. Ormsby. Write a paragraph about a time when you, someone you know, or someone you admire took the risk of speaking out in a difficult situation.

    Prewriting. Try to visualize the incident that you will write about. Answer these questions in your prewriting notes:

    What brought about the conflict?
    When and where did it take place?
    Who were the people involved?
    What risks did the person take?
    What did the person say and do?
    What were the results of speaking out?

    Look over your list. Cross out the details that don't belong. Arrange the remaining details in a clear order.

    Drafting. Use the notes that you prepared during prewriting. First explain the situation. Then, in time order, tell what happened. Be sure to include the risk that the person took in speaking out and the consequences of his or her actions. Use dialogue if you wish.

    Revising and Sharing. Reread your draft. Decide whether more details would make the incident clearer and more dramatic. If necessary, add details. Then, ask someone to read your paragraph. See if the reader can summarize how the person spoke out and what risk the person took.

2. **Analyzing a Character.** This selection concludes with the sentence, "But Sarah belonged to a family of chiefs." In one paragraph explain the characteristics that identify Sarah as a potential leader herself. Consider such qualities as her ability to see situations from another person's view, her compassion, and her understanding of complex problems. Follow the steps in the process of writing: prewriting, drafting, revising, and sharing. For more help, see the Guidelines for the Process of Writing beginning on page 654.

Humorous Sketches

Humor delights the reader because of its unexpectedness. It often surprises the reader with contrasts and exaggerations. Humor may make a serious point, too, about human weaknesses. The three humorous sketches that follow will amuse you as they relate some of life's funny situations.

Golconde, 1953, RENÉ MAGRITTE. © 1987 The Menil Foundation, Houston.

Reading Literature

More About Nonfiction: The Essay

The most common type of nonfiction is the essay. An **essay** is a short nonfiction work that deals with one subject, often in a personal way.

Essays can be either formal or informal. **Formal essays** examine a topic in a thorough, highly organized manner. They are serious and objective. **Informal essays** reflect a writer's feelings and personality. Some of these essays may seem like friendly conversations. Others can be more thoughtful and informative. The essays you will be reading are informal.

The History of the Essay

The first essay was written in sixteenth-century France by Michel de Montaigne. In 1580 he put down his thoughts and feelings about various subjects. He called his writings *essais,* or "attempts." In 1597 the British writer Francis Bacon published the first essays in English. By the 1700's, essays had become popular features in newspapers.

Today essays are still a popular kind of writing. Essays appear in newspapers, magazines, and books. The subject of an essay can be something as simple as a description of a spring morning. On the other hand, the subject can be as important as the prevention of nuclear war.

More About the Elements of Nonfiction

Purpose. Different essays have different purposes. Some are written to inform and some to persuade. Some express feelings or entertain. Often an essay combines purposes. "A Poet's Advice to Students," for example, both informs and tries to persuade. As you read an essay, keep in mind what the writer is trying to do.

Theme. In an essay, as in other kinds of writing, the **theme** is the writer's message about life. Most essays have a clear theme. For example, the theme of "Place of Sorrows" is that the battles between the Native Americans and the Army forces led to defeat on both sides.

Humor. In any kind of writing, including essays, **humor** expresses what is funny or amusing. A writer may create humor by using exaggeration or irony. When writers use **exaggeration,** they describe things as bigger, faster, smarter, or more than they really are. When writers use **irony,** they may contrast what is expected with what actually happens. For example, it would be ironic to leave an umbrella at home on the only rainy day of the month. Another kind of irony results from saying the opposite of what is meant. An ironic comment might be "What took so long?" when something happens quickly. These ways of creating humor are used in the three humorous essays in this chapter.

Structure. The **structure** of an essay is the way in which the essay is put together. Some essays use time order. The selection from *Life with Father* uses this kind of structure. Most essays, however, depend on other kinds of order, such as spatial order or order of familiarity. "The Uses of Error," for example, uses order of familiarity.

Style. The **style** of an essay is the way in which it is written. Every writer has an individual style. It includes his or her choice of words. It refers to the length of sentences and their arrangement. Humor and figurative language also may mark a writer's style. For example, Bill Cosby uses everyday words, quick rhythms, and humor. Charles Kuralt, on the other hand, uses more formal vocabulary, slow, quiet sentences, and figurative language.

Punch, Brothers, Punch

MARK TWAIN

Have you ever had a tune stuck in your mind? If so, you'll identify with the maddening experience Mark Twain relates. As you read this sketch, note how each new development is more absurd than the one before.

Will the reader please cast his eye over the following lines and see if he can discover anything harmful in them?

Conductor, when you receive a fare,
Punch in the presence of the passenjare!
A blue trip slip for an eight-cent fare,
A buff trip slip for a six-cent fare,
A pink trip slip for a three-cent fare,
Punch in the presence of the passenjare!

CHORUS
Punch, brothers! Punch with care!
Punch in the presence of the passenjare!

I came across these jingling rhymes in a newspaper, a little while ago, and read them a couple of times. They took instant and entire possession of me. All through breakfast they went waltzing through my brain, and when, at last, I rolled up my napkin, I could not tell whether I had eaten anything or not. I had carefully laid out my day's work the day before—a thrilling tragedy in the novel which I am writing. I went to my den to begin my deed of blood.

I took up my pen, but all I could get it to say was, "Punch in the presence of the passenjare." I fought hard for an hour, but it was useless. My head kept humming, "A blue trip slip for an eight-cent fare, a buff trip slip for a six-cent fare," and so on and so on, without peace or respite. The day's work was ruined—I could see that plainly enough. I gave up and drifted downtown and presently discovered that my feet were keeping time to that relentless jingle. When I could stand it no longer, I altered my step. But it did no good; those rhymes accommodated themselves to the new step and went on harassing me just as before. I returned home and suffered all the afternoon; suffered all through an unconscious and unrefreshing dinner; suffered, and cried, and jingled all through the evening; went to bed and rolled, tossed, and jingled right along, the same as ever; got up at midnight, frantic, and tried to read; but there was nothing visible upon the whirling page except "Punch! Punch in the presence of the passenjare." By sunrise I was out of my mind, and everybody marveled and was distressed at the idiotic burden of my ravings—"Punch! Oh, punch! Punch in the presence of the passenjare!"

Two days later, on Saturday morning, I arose, a tottering wreck, and went forth to fulfill an engagement with a valued friend, the Rev. Mr. ——, to walk to the Talcott Tower, ten miles distant. He stared at me but asked no questions. We started. Mr. —— talked, talked, talked—as is his wont. I said nothing; I heard nothing.

At the end of a mile, Mr. —— said, "Mark, are you sick? I never saw a man look so haggard and worn and absent-minded. Say something, do!"

Drearily, without enthusiasm, I said, "Punch, brothers, punch with care! Punch in the presence of the passenjare!"

My friend eyed me blankly, looked perplexed, and then said, "I do not think I get your drift, Mark. There does not seem to be any relevancy in what you have said, certainly nothing sad; and yet—maybe it was the way you *said* the words—I never heard anything that sounded so pathetic— What is——"

But I heard no more. I was already far away with my pitiless, heart-breaking "blue trip slip for an eight-cent fare, buff trip slip for a six-cent fare; pink trip slip for a three-cent fare; punch in the presence of the passenjare." I do not know what occurred during the other nine miles. However, all of a sudden Mr. —— laid his hand on my shoulder and shouted,

"Oh, wake up! Wake up! Wake up! Don't sleep all day! Here we are at the Tower, man! I have talked myself deaf and dumb and blind and never got a response. Just look at this magnificent autumn landscape! Look at it! Look at it! Feast your eyes on it! You have traveled; you have seen boasted landscapes elsewhere. Come, now, deliver an honest opinion. What do you say to this?"

I sighed wearily and murmured, "A buff trip slip for a six-cent fare, a pink trip slip for a three-cent fare, punch in the presence of the passenjare."

Rev. Mr. —— stood there, very grave, full of concern, apparently, and looked long at me. Then he said, "Mark, there is something about this that I cannot understand. Those are about the same words you said before; there does not seem to be anything in them, and yet they nearly break my heart when you say them. Punch in the—how is it they go?"

I began at the beginning and repeated all the lines.

My friend's face lighted with interest. He said, "Why, what a captivating jingle it is! It is almost music. It flows along so nicely. I have nearly caught the rhymes myself. Say them over just once more, and then I'll have them, sure."

I said them over. Then Mr. —— said them. He made one little mistake, which I corrected. The next time and the next he got them right. Now a great burden seemed to tumble from my shoulders. That torturing jingle departed out of my brain,

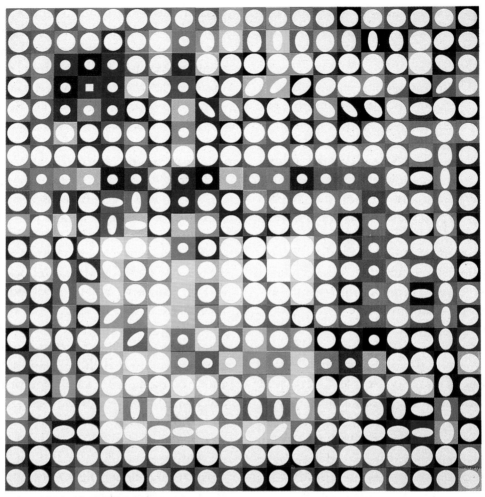

Orion, 1956–62, VICTOR VASARELY. Hirshhorn Museum and Sculpture Garden, Smithsonian Institution, Washington, D.C. © SPADEM, Paris/VAGA, New York City. Photograph by Lee Stalsworth, 1984.

and a grateful sense of rest and peace descended upon me. I was light-hearted enough to sing; and I did sing for half an hour, straight along, as we went jogging homeward. Then my freed tongue found blessed speech again, and the pent talk of many a weary hour began to gush and flow. It flowed on and on, joyously, jubilantly,

until the fountain was empty and dry.

As I wrung my friend's hand at parting, I said, "Haven't we had a royal good time! But now I remember, you haven't said a word for two hours. Come, come, out with something!"

The Rev. Mr. —— turned a lack-lustre eye upon me, drew a deep sigh, and said, without animation, without apparent consciousness, "Punch, brothers, punch with care! Punch in the presence of the passenjare!"

A pang shot through me as I said to myself, "Poor fellow, poor fellow! He has got it, now."

I did not see Mr. —— for two or three days after that. Then, on Tuesday evening, he staggered into my presence and sank dejectedly into a seat. He was pale, worn; he was a wreck. He lifted his faded eyes to my face and said, "Ah, Mark, it was a ruinous investment that I made in those heartless rhymes. They have ridden me like a nightmare, day and night, hour after hour, to this very moment. Since I saw you, I have suffered the torments of the lost. Saturday evening I had a sudden call, by telegraph, and took the night train for Boston. The occasion was the death of a valued old friend who had requested that I should preach his funeral sermon. I took my seat in the cars and set myself to framing the discourse. But I never got beyond the opening paragraph; for then the train started and the car wheels began their 'clack, clack—clack-clack-clack! clack-clack—clack-clack-clack!' and right away those odious rhymes fitted themselves to that accompaniment.

"For an hour I sat there and set a syllable of those rhymes to every separate and distinct clack the car wheels made. Why, I was as tired, then, as if I had been chopping wood all day. My skull was splitting with headache. It seemed to me that I must go mad if I sat there any longer; so I undressed and went to bed. I stretched myself out in my berth, and—well, you know what the result was. The thing went right along, just the same. 'Clack-clack-clack, a blue trip slip, clack-clack-clack, for an eight-cent fare; clack-clack-clack, a buff trip slip, clack-clack-clack, for a six-cent fare, and so on, and so on, and so on— *punch* in the presence of the passenjare!'

"Sleep? Not a single wink! I was almost a lunatic when I got to Boston. Don't ask me about the funeral. I did the best I could, but every solemn individual sentence was meshed and tangled and woven in and out with 'Punch, brothers, punch with care, punch in the presence of the passenjare.' And the most distressing thing was that my *delivery* dropped into the undulating rhythm of those pulsing rhymes, and I could actually catch absent-minded people nodding *time* to the swing of it with their stupid heads. And, Mark, you may believe it or not, but, before I got through, the entire assemblage were placidly bobbing their heads in solemn unison, mourners, undertaker, and all.

"The moment I had finished, I fled to the anteroom in a state bordering on frenzy. Of course it would be my luck to find a sorrowing and aged maiden aunt of the deceased there, who had arrived from Springfield too late to get into the church.

She began to sob and said, " 'Oh, oh, he is gone, he is gone, and I didn't see him before he died!'

" 'Yes!' I said, 'he *is* gone, he *is* gone, he

is gone—oh, *will* this suffering never cease!'

" 'You loved him, then! Oh, you too loved him!'

" 'Loved him! Loved *who?*'

" 'Why, my poor George! my poor, dear nephew!'

" 'Oh—*him!* Yes—oh, yes, yes. Certainly—certainly. Punch—punch—oh, this misery will kill me!'

" 'Bless you! bless you, sir, for these sweet words! *I,* too, suffer in this dear loss. Were you present during his last moments?'

" 'Yes. I—*whose* last moments?'

" '*His.* The dear departed's.'

" 'Yes! Oh, yes—yes—*yes!* I suppose so, I think so, *I* don't know! Oh, certainly—I was there—*I* was there!'

" 'Oh, what a privilege! what a precious privilege! And his last words—oh, tell me, tell me his last words! What did he say?'

" 'He said—he said—oh, my head, my head, my head! He said—he said—he never said *any*thing but Punch, punch, *punch* in the presence of the passenjare! Oh, leave me, madam! In the name of all that is generous, leave me to my madness, my misery, my despair!—a buff trip slip for a six-cent fare, a pink trip slip for a

three-cent fare—endu-rance *can* no further go!—PUNCH in the presence of the passenjare!' "

My friend's hopeless eyes rested upon mine a pregnant minute, and then he said impressively, "Mark, you do not say anything. You do not offer me any hope. But, ah me, it is just as well—it is just as well. You could not do me any good. The time has long gone by when words could comfort me. Something tells me that my tongue is doomed to wag forever to the jigger of that remorseless jingle. There—there it is coming on me again: a blue trip slip for an eight-cent fare, a buff trip slip for a—"

Thus murmuring faint and fainter, my friend sank into a peaceful trance and forgot his sufferings in a blessed respite.

How did I finally save him from an asylum? I took him to a neighboring university and made him discharge the burden of his persecuting rhymes into the eager ears of the poor, unthinking students. How is it with *them,* now? The result is too sad to tell. Why did I write this article? It was for a worthy, even a noble, purpose. It was to warn you, reader, if you should come across those merciless rhymes, to avoid them—avoid them as you would a pestilence!

Mark Twain *(1835–1910)* was the pen name of Samuel Clemens. He grew up in Hannibal, Missouri, where he had many boyhood adventures on the Mississippi River. He based his famous characters, Tom Sawyer and Huckleberry Finn, on people he knew in his childhood. In addition to his novels, Twain is also known for his humorous newspaper articles and lectures. One of his most successful books was *Innocents Abroad,* an account of his travels in Europe.

Developing Comprehension Skills

1. Where does Twain first read the jingle?

2. What is the jingle about?

3. How does Twain react to the jingle? Give at least three examples of how it affects him.

4. After the funeral, The Rev. Mr. —— speaks in a disordered way to the aunt. How does the aunt interpret his behavior? Is her reaction believable? Is his?

5. At the end of this essay Twain states why he wrote it. He claims he wants to warn readers to avoid the jingle. Do you believe him? Why or why not?

6. What is funny to one person may not be funny at all to another person. What parts of this essay do you find funny? Do you find any elements strange or puzzling? Explain your answer.

Reading Literature: Humorous Sketches

1. **Understanding Humor.** One way that a writer can create humor is to use exaggera-tion. When a person exaggerates, he or she stretches the truth to make something seem ridiculous. In this selection Twain exaggerates the common human experience of hearing a tune or jingle and not being able to forget it. Point out at least three examples from the selection in which the writer exaggerates events until they seem ridiculous.

2. **Analyzing Style.** Part of Twain's style in this selection is his use of figurative language. **Figurative language** is language that communicates ideas beyond the literal meanings of the words. In describing the lines of the jingle, Twain writes, "All through breakfast they went waltzing through my brain." Identify two other examples of figurative language in the sketch. In your own words, explain the meaning of each example.

3. **Recognizing Irony.** Humor can result from the use of irony. **Irony** is a contrast between what is expected and what actually happens or exists. In this selection irony occurs when Twain prepares to start his day's

work on the "thrilling tragedy" he is writing. In fact, all he can write is, "Punch in the presence of the passenjare." Something serious is expected, but instead the writer can produce only the silly rhymes. Explain the irony in one of the following situations from the selection.

a. Twain and his friend walk for ten miles to see a beautiful landscape. When the friend asks the writer to comment on the scene, the writer begins, "A buff trip slip for a six-cent fare. . . ."

b. The friend asks Twain to teach him the jingle. The friend says, "Say them over just once more, and then I'll have them, sure."

c. After the funeral the Rev. Mr. —— says "Oh, this misery will kill me!" The aunt replies, "Bless you! bless you, sir, for these sweet words! *I, too, suffer in this dear loss.*"

4. **Examining Purpose and Word Choice.** One purpose of this selection is to entertain and amuse. Twain often achieves this purpose by using grandiose or exaggerated language: for example, "burden of my ravings," "pitiless, heart-breaking," and "blessed respite." Reread the last three sentences of the selection, noticing the writer's use of words such as "worthy, even a noble, purpose," "merciless rhymes," and "a pestilence." What do these words describe? How does the use of these words create humor?

Developing Vocabulary Skills

Understanding Homographs. Some words are entered in the dictionary more than once. These entry words are called **homo-**

graphs. They are different words that are spelled the same way and have different origins. They may or may not have the same pronunciation. They always have different meanings. For example, locate the word *pound* in a dictionary. Notice the three separate entries. Each entry is numbered. Each has a different meaning. These are homographs.

Each of the following underlined words is a homograph. Locate each of these words in a dictionary. Be sure to read all the definitions of each word. On a sheet of paper, tell how many separate entries there are for the word. Then write the definition that best fits the sentence.

1. The jingle tended to <u>lead</u> the narrator away from his work.

2. When he tried to write, the narrator's <u>pen</u> would write only the jingle.

3. A blue trip <u>slip</u> indicated an eight-cent fare.

4. The jingle was the only <u>strand</u> of thought in the narrator's mind.

5. The narrator's friend gave him a <u>grave</u> look of concern.

Developing Skills in Study and Research

Using Biographical Reference Books. Mark Twain is one of America's most famous writers. You can find out about Twain's life and work by looking up information in special biographical reference books. Visit your school or public library. Look up the following titles of biographical reference books. They will be listed in either the card catalog or the library's computer indexing system. Find out which books the library owns and where they are located. Choose three of the books to look up information about Mark Twain.

American Authors 1600–1900
American Writers
Brief Lives
Cyclopedia of World Authors
Dictionary of American Biography
Dictionary of Literary Biography
Encyclopedia of American Biography
Encyclopedia of World Biography
Who Was Who

Write down the title of each book you used and the pages where you found the information. Take notes on important facts about Twain's life and career. Use your notes as the basis for an oral report to the class.

Developing Skills in Speaking and Listening

Reading Dialogue. Working with two other students, read aloud the dialogue between Twain and the Rev. Mr. —— on pages 539–540 (paragraphs 4 through 15). Assign the parts of the two characters and a narrator. The student who reads Twain's lines should try to convey his weariness. The student who reads the Rev. Mr. ——'s lines should try to convey his puzzlement. Remember that when you read, exaggeration can add to the humor. When your group is ready, present your reading to an audience.

Developing Writing Skills

Creating Humor. Many small problems in everyday life can seem humorous when they are exaggerated. A stubborn bottle cap, a broken vending machine, an ornery locker, a leaky pen—these are just a few examples. In one paragraph, write a humorous description of a small problem. Make it seem ridiculous by exaggerating it.

Prewriting. Pay attention to the little frustrations around you. Decide on one small problem that you would like to write about. Make a list of details about how the problem occurs. Then make a second list exaggerating the details on the first list. You may want to write a third list exaggerating the details on the second list, until you end up with funny descriptions.

Drafting. Use your lists to write a humorous description of an everyday problem. Begin by naming the problem you will be describing. For example, you might write, "Ketchup bottles and I don't get along well." Then, using the exaggerated details in your lists, describe a time when you experienced the problem. Conclude with a humorous comment that makes your opinion of the problem clear.

Revising and Sharing. Reread your draft, and make changes that add to the humor. Read your draft aloud to several people, and ask them if they can identify with the problem. If they laugh, you have succeeded in writing humor.

From
Fatherhood

BILL COSBY

As Bill Cosby tells it, being a father is a job that requires patience, wisdom, love—and a sense of humor. In these four essays, Cosby makes his way through some of the comic predicaments of fatherhood.

Good Morning, Opponents

If a family wants to get through the day with a minimum of noise and open wounds, the parents have to impose order on the domestic scene. And such order should start with breakfast, which we all know is the most important meal of the day. My wife certainly thinks so. A few weeks ago, she woke me at six o'clock in the morning and said, "I want you to go downstairs and cook breakfast for the children."

"But, dear," I said with an incredulous look at the clock, "it's six in the morning."

"You tell time very nicely. Now go down and cook breakfast for the children. They have to go to school."

"But to eat at six . . . isn't that bad for the stomach? I mean, they just ate twelve hours ago."

"Bill, get out of this bed and go downstairs and cook breakfast for your children!"

I would like to repeat a point I made before: I am not the boss of my house. I don't know how I lost it and I don't know where I lost it. I probably never had it to begin with. My wife is the boss, and I do not understand how she is going to outlive me.

"But here's the thing, dear," I said, now a desperate man, "I don't know what they want to eat."

"It's *down* there."

I went back to sleep. I dreamed I was with Scott in the Antarctic, perhaps because my wife was pouring ice water over my head.

"Have you given any more thought to cooking breakfast?" she said as I awoke again.

And so, downstairs I went, wondering about the divorce laws in my state, and I started slamming things around. I had bacon, sausages, and eggs all lined up when my four-year-old arrived, looking so adorable with her cute face and little braids.

"Morning, Daddy," she said.

"Okay," I said, "what do *you* want for breakfast?"

"Chocolate cake," she replied.

"Chocolate *cake?* For *breakfast?* That's ridiculous."

Then, however, I thought about the ingredients in chocolate cake: milk and eggs and wheat, all part of good nutrition.

"You want chocolate cake, honey?" I said, cutting a piece for her. "Well, here it is. But you also need something to drink."

And I gave her a glass of grapefruit juice.

When the other four children came downstairs and saw the four-year-old eating chocolate cake, they wanted the same, of course; and since I wanted good nutrition for them too, I gave each of them a piece.

So there my five children sat, merrily eating chocolate cake for breakfast, occasionally stopping to sing:

Dad is the greatest dad you can make!
For breakfast he gives us chocolate cake!

The party lasted until my wife appeared, staggered slightly, and said, "Chocolate cake for *breakfast?* Where did you all get *that?*"

"*He* gave it to us! *He* made us eat it!" said my five adorable ingrates in one voice; and then my eight-year-old added, "*We* wanted eggs and cereal."

A Law Newton Missed

My eight-year-old was given to me just for love because she certainly doesn't *do* anything. The new American father has more responsibilities than ever, but the children seem to have fewer. Ask any eight-year-old why she can never bring herself to do her chores and she will reply, "But I caaan't. I'm only a little person."

This little person who can jump rope nonstop for twenty-seven minutes says that her chores are too great a strain on her fragile little body. This little person who could ride a bicycle up Mount Washington cannot muster the strength to pick up the coat and sweater she dropped on her way to the kitchen. (To be fair, she may have left that trail of clothes so she could find her way *back* from the kitchen.)

One day, my eight-year-old was fooling around, undoubtedly because I had told her not to fool around, and she knocked over a big bucket of popcorn.

"You have to clean that up," I said.

"But it's so maaany, Dad."

"No, I'm afraid you have to clean it up. We're not leaving it down there for the birds."

And so, she began to pick up the popcorn. She was doing fine for five or six seconds, when she turned to me and said, "I'm so *tired,* Dad," and she started to walk away.

"Come back," I said, recognizing this approach to work from my days in the Navy. "Does that look cleaned up?"

"Well, I did the best I could. It's so maaany, Dad. And my arms got tired. I think I wanna go to bed now."

I am not a physicist, but I'm sure that

the theory of the conservation of energy was discovered while watching an eight-year-old pretend to work.

Who Dressed This Mess?

The father of a daughter, especially one in her teens, will find that she doesn't like to be seen walking with him on the street. In fact, she will often ask him to walk a few paces behind. The father should not take this outdoor demotion personally; it is simply a matter of clothes. His are rotten. Every American daughter is an authority on fashion, and one of the things she knows is that her father dresses like somebody in the Mummers Parade.[1]

In schools, you can always identify the children who were dressed by their fathers. Such children should have signs pinned on their strange attire that say:

Please do not scorn or mock me. I was dressed by my father, who sees colors the way Beethoven[2] heard notes.

Whenever I travel with my kids, the moment I open my suitcase in a hotel, I see the instructions from my wife:

The red blouse goes with the gray skirt.

Do not *let her wear the green striped shirt with the purple plaid pants.*

The pink paisley pants and pink paisley sweater go together.

They may jog or sleep in their sweat suits, but no *one is to wear a sweat suit into the hotel dining room.*

The problem is that men are less studied than women about the way they dress.

They never see what a woman sees—for example, that those khaki pants do not cover their ankles. Therefore, the child who goes out to be seen by the public represents the mother; and if this child is out of fashion, an observer will say, "Who dressed that little girl? Some woman at Ringling Brothers?"[3]

"No," will come the answer. "That is Mrs. Cosby's child."

"You're kidding! In spite of her choice of husband, I've always thought that woman had taste."

"It must have been Bill who dressed the child today."

"Oh no, he's not allowed to dress them."

Unless he happens to work for Halston,[4] the American father cannot be trusted to put together combinations of clothes. He is a man who was taught that the height of fashion was to wear two shoes that matched; and so, children can easily convince him of the elegance of whatever they do or don't want to wear.

"Dad, I don't want to wear socks today."

"Fine."

"Or a shirt."

"That's fine, too."

Mothers, however, are relentless in

---

1. **Mummers Parade**–An extravagant New Year's Day parade in which the participants dress in elaborate costumes.
2. **Beethoven**–A famous composer, German, 1770–1827, who became deaf.
3. **Ringling Brothers**–A circus.
4. **Halston**–A fashion designer.

dressing children and often draw tears.

"Young lady, you are not going to wear red leotards outside this house unless you're on your way to dance *Romeo and Juliet.*"

"But, Mom, everyone at *school* is wearing them."

"Then I'm helping you keep your individuality. You're wearing that nice gray skirt with the blue sweater and the white lace blouse."

"But, Mom, I *hate* that white lace blouse. It makes me look like a *waitress.*"

"Which is what you will be if you don't wear it 'cause you won't be leaving the house to go to school, and a restaurant job will be *it.*"

And now come the tears, which move a father deeply. His heart breaks for this child crying at seven in the morning, and he fears that this moment will leave a scar on her psyche. He wonders if Blue Cross covers psychiatry. Couldn't his wife back off a bit? After all, *he* would allow red leotards. He would *also* allow green combat boots.

However, a few minutes later at breakfast, where his darling little girl appears with swollen eyes, a runny nose, and the white lace blouse, she and her mother are getting along beautifully.

Of course, it is not hard to get along beautifully with my wife—certainly not for *me.* After twenty-two years of marriage, she is still as feminine as a woman can be; she has fine taste, especially in husbands; and we have many things in common, the

Bill Cosby, 1982. © Jim Britt/Shooting Star, Hollywood, California.

greatest of which is that we are both afraid of the children. (The sternness with which she disciplines them is just a front.) I am happiest when she is happy, which means I am happy most of the time.

Wheeler-Dealer

Buying a stereo is merely a father's practice for the Big Buy: a car. When his child requests a car, a father will wish that he were a member of some sect that hasn't gone beyond the horse.

"Dad, all my friends say I should have my own car," the boy says earnestly one day.

"Wonderful. When are they going to buy it?"

"No, Dad. They think that you and Mom should buy me the car."

"Is there any particular reason why we should?"

"Well, that's what parents *do.*"

"Not *all* parents. Did Adam and Eve get Abel a car? And he was the *good* one. Tell me this: why do you *need* a car?"

"To go places by myself."

"Well, you'd be surprised how many people manage to do that on public transportation. Elderly *ladies* do it every day. It's called a bus and I'd be happy to buy you a token. I won't even wait for your birthday."

"Dad, *you* know a bus isn't cool. My friends say I shouldn't have to ride on a bus now that I'm sixteen."

"They say that? Well, they couldn't be *good* friends because buses are so much fun. They expand your social circle. You meet new people every three blocks."

"That's cute, Dad."

"I know you don't go particularly deep in math, but do you happen to know what a car costs?"

"I'll get a *used* one."

"Terrific. And we'll have a family lottery to try to guess the day it will break down."

"Okay, *slightly* used."

"Which is slightly more or less than five thousand dollars, not counting insurance."

"Insurance?"

"You getting some used insurance too?"

"I'll drive it real carefully."

"And there's a chance you will," you say, suddenly picturing people all over town bouncing off your son's fenders.

"Dad, I just *have* to have a car. Say, what about *yours?* Then you could buy yourself a *new* one. Dad, you *deserve* a new car."

"That's very thoughtful, son," you say, now having heard the ploy you've been expecting.

"Think nothing of it, Dad."

And so, the moment has come for you to gently remind your son precisely how worthless he currently is—without bruising his ego, of course.

"You see," you tell him, "the thing is that unless a wonderful offer came in last night, you have no job. You are sixteen years old, you have no job, and you have an excellent chance of failing the eleventh grade."

"Not *Driver's Ed!* I'm *creaming* that!"

"I'm happy to hear it. You'll go on to college—if we can find one in Baja California—and you'll major in Driver's Ed. Maybe you'll get your M.A. in Toll Booths and even your Ph.D. in Grease and Lube."

"Dad, I wish you wouldn't keep bringing up school. I'm just not motivated."

"To improve your mind, that is. But you *are* motivated to get a car. The bus may not go to the unemployment office."

"Come on, Dad; *you* know what a car means. I need it to *go* places."

"Like the fast-food joint, where your career will be. Because with the grades you have right now, if you somehow *do* happen to be graduated from high school, which the Vatican[5] will declare a miracle, you'll be competing with only ten million others for the job of wrapping cheeseburgers."

"Dad, I'd love to talk more about my career, but I gotta tell you something really exciting that's gonna change your mind: I just saw an ad for a sensational sixty-nine Mustang."

"Really? How much?"

"Just two thousand dollars."

"Just two thousand dollars. Did you happen to ask if it had an engine? And are brakes optional?"

"Dad, I can't understand why you're being so unreasonable."

"That's what fathers are. It's one of the qualifications."

"But my friends keep saying I should *have* a car."

"And they certainly have the right to buy you one. I'll tell you what: how's *this* for reasonable? Bring your friends over here and we'll have a collection, a matching funds collection. Whatever you get from them, I'll match it."

The boy winds up with ninety-six cents.

---

5. **Vatican**–Vatican City, in Italy, home of the Pope, leader of the Roman Catholic Church.

William Henry (Bill) Cosby, Jr. *(born 1937)* is best known as a comedian, actor, and recording artist. He has created most of his own comedy material and has published several books. Cosby also has a Ph.D. in education and devotes much of his time to social organizations. He works for the National Council of Crime and Delinquency, the communications council at Howard University, and the American Sickle Cell Foundation. Winner of eight Grammy Awards and three Emmys, Cosby created and plays the main character in one of the most successful family shows in the history of television, *The Cosby Show.*

Developing Comprehension Skills

1. In "Good Morning, Opponents," what does Bill Cosby feed his children for breakfast? What reason do the children give their mother for their unusual breakfast?

2. In "A Law Newton Missed," why does the eight-year-old say she can't finish picking up the popcorn? What does Cosby think of her reason?

3. In "Who Dressed This Mess?" Cosby compares his attitude toward his children's clothes with his wife's attitude. What are the two attitudes? What opinion does he have of each attitude? How serious is he?

4. In "Wheeler-Dealer," Cosby's son gives reasons for buying a car, and Cosby gives reasons for not buying a car. The following sentences summarize some of the reasons given. Which statements are facts? Which are opinions?
   a. When you're sixteen, you should have your own car.
   b. A sixteen-year-old doesn't need a car.
   c. A used car could cost about five thousand dollars.
   d. The sixty-nine Mustang in the ad is sensational.
   e. The Mustang costs two thousand dollars.

5. Do you think that the family conflicts that Cosby describes are typical? Which of the incidents could you imagine happening in your own family or in your friend's families?

6. In these sketches, Cosby approaches everyday problems with humor. Explain how humor can help people deal with their conflicts. You may use examples from Cosby's sketches to illustrate your answer.

Reading Literature: Humorous Sketches

1. **Recognizing Exaggeration.** As you have learned, exaggeration helps to create humor. One example of exaggeration in *Fatherhood* is Cosby's description of his eight-year-old as a "little person who could ride a bicycle up Mount Washington." Find at least four more examples of exaggeration in these sketches.

2. **Understanding Humor.** The sketch about Cosby's eight-year-old daughter is called "A Law Newton Missed." Newton was a great physicist in the eighteenth century who figured out the laws of gravity and motion. At the end of the sketch, Cosby says, "I am not a physicist, but I'm sure that the theory of the conservation of energy was discovered while watching an eight-year-old pretend to work." What is unexpected about the references to Newton and physics in this sketch? Why is the unexpected comparison funny?

3. **Identifying Theme.** These four sketches are from the book *Fatherhood*. What picture does Cosby give of his relationship with his children? What do these sketches say about being a father?

4. **Analyzing Style.** For years, Bill Cosby has shared his humor with live audiences. In his writing, he uses the skills he first learned on stage. He helps readers "hear" his voice by emphasizing words. Look at the dialogue in these sketches. How does Cosby make it clear that certain words should be emphasized? Do you think the dialogue is realistic? Give two examples to support your answer.

Developing Vocabulary Skills

Finding Synonyms. A dictionary may list synonyms for an entry word. A **synonym,** as you recall, is a word that means the same or nearly the same as another word. Sometimes synonyms are listed at the end of an entry after an abbreviation for *synonymy,* such as SYN. The entry may also give information to help you understand the precise differences among synonyms. Here is an example:

in·con·stant (in kän′stənt) *adj.* [ME. < OFr. < L. *inconslans*] not constant; changeable; specif., *a)* not remaining firm in mind or purpose *b)* unsteady in affections or loyalties; fickle *c)* not uniform in nature, value, etc.; irregular; variable —**in·con′stan·cy** *n.* —**in·con′stant·ly** *adv.*
SYN.—**inconstant** implies an inherent tendency to change or a lack of steadfastness [an *inconstant* lover]; **fickle** suggests an even greater instability or readiness to change, especially in affection [spurned by a *fickle* public]; **capricious** implies an instability or irregularity that seems to be the product of whim or erratic impulse [a *capricious* climate]; **unstable,** in this connection, applies to one who is emotionally unsettled or variable [an *unstable* person laughs and cries easily] —*ANT.* **constant, reliable**

The synonyms listed for *inconstant* are *fickle, capricious,* and *unstable.* The entry tells exactly how these synonyms differ.

Use a dictionary to look up the following words from this selection. Find the definition that fits the use of the word in the selection. On a sheet of paper, write the word, its definition, and two synonyms.

1. noise
2. think
3. understand
4. work
5. strange
6. choice
7. surprise
8. ask

Developing Skills in Study and Research

Using Library Resources. Besides books, magazines, and pamphlets, a library's resources also include audio-visual materials. These materials may be films, videotapes, and records. In your school or local library, find the index for audio-visual materials, or use the computer indexing system. Look up listings for "Cosby, Bill." Locate any materials available at the library. After you have listened to records or watched films or tapes, compare these to the essays from *Fatherhood.* How is the subject matter similar? How is Cosby's tone similar? What are the most important differences?

Developing Skills in Speaking and Listening

Reading Dialogue. With two or three other students, work on reading dialogue from one of Cosby's sketches. Choose a passage of dialogue and assign parts for reading. Work on conveying the tone of the writing. Practice the reading until you are satisfied. Then present the dialogue to the class.

Developing Writing Skills

Writing a Humorous Sketch. In these sketches from *Fatherhood,* Bill Cosby brings out the funny side of everyday family life. Most families have experiences that have funny sides to them. Think of one such incident involving your family or a family you know. In one or more paragraphs describe the incident.

Prewriting. Decide on the incident you want to tell about. List the people involved, the setting, and the details of what happens. Note the order of happenings that make up the incident. Decide if you want to use dialogue. Think about how you can use exaggeration or irony to bring out the humor of the situation.

Drafting. Open the sketch with an interesting, funny sentence that will draw the reader into your story. Use your prewriting notes to write the sketch. As you describe the incident, make sure the order of events is clear.

Revising and Sharing. Ask a classmate to read your sketch. Ask him or her to identify any parts that are confusing. Does the reader respond to the humor? Make any necessary revisions to make your writing clear and to convey the humor of the incident. Be prepared to read your sketch in class. Your class may want to put together a book of humorous sketches.

From
Life with Father

CLARENCE DAY

This view of a family at the end of the nineteenth century is related by a child rather than a parent. In the selection you will read about the humorous dilemmas the Day family deals with.

Father made a great point of our getting down to breakfast on time. I meant to be prompt, but it never occurred to me that I had better try to be early. My idea was to slide into the room at the last moment. Consequently, I often was late.

My brothers were often late too, with the exception of George. He was the only thoroughly reliable son Father had. George got down so early, Father pointed out to me, that he even had time to practice a few minutes on the piano.

The reason George was so prompt was that he was in a hurry to see the sporting page before Father got hold of the newspaper, and the reason he then played the piano was to signal to the rest of us, as we dressed, which team had won yesterday's ball game. He had made up a code for this purpose, and we leaned over the banisters, pulling on our stockings and shoes, to hear him announce the results. I don't remember now what the titles were of the airs he selected, but the general idea was that if he played a lively air, it meant that the Giants had won, and when the strains of a dirge or lament floated up to us, it meant that Pop Anson[1] had beaten them.

As Father didn't approve of professional baseball, we said nothing to him about this arrangement. He led his life and we led ours, under his nose. He took the newspaper away from George the moment he entered the room, and George said good morning to him and stepped innocently into the parlor. Then, while Father watched him through the broad doorway and looked over the political headlines, George banged out the baseball news for us on the piano. Father used to admonish him with a chuckle not to thump it so hard, but George felt that he had to. We were at the top of the house, and he wanted to be sure that we'd hear him even if we were brushing our teeth. George always was

---

1. **Pop Anson**–A famous Chicago baseball player who won many batting championships and is thought to have batted over .400 in 1879 and 1887.

thorough about things. He not only thumped the piano as hard as he could, but he hammered out the tune over and over besides, while Father impatiently muttered to himself, *"Trop de zèle."*[2]

Upstairs, there was usually some discussion as to what kind of news George was sending. He had not been allowed to learn popular tunes, which it would have been easy for us to recognize, and the few classic selections which were available in his little music book sounded pretty much alike at a distance. George rendered these with plenty of good will and muscle but not a great deal of sympathy. He regarded some

of the rules of piano-playing as needlessly complicated.

The fact remained that he was the one boy who was always on time, and Father was so pleased by this that he bought a watch for him with "George Parmly Day, Always on Time" engraved on the back. He told me that as I was the eldest he had meant to give me a watch first, and he showed me the one he had bought for me. It was just like George's except that nothing had been engraved on it yet. Father

---

2. **Trop de zèle** (trō də zel)– *French,* Too much enthusiasm.

Father sharing some wisdom with two of his sons. From the Warner Brothers' 1947 film, *Life with Father,* starring William Powell. Phototeque, New York City.

explained that to his regret he would have to put it away for a while, until I had earned it by getting down early to breakfast.

Time went on, without much improvement on my part. Dawdling had got to be a habit with me. Sometimes my lateness was serious. One morning, when breakfast was half over and I had nothing on but a pair of long woolen drawers, Father called up from the front hall, napkin in hand, that he wouldn't stand it and that I was to come down that instant. When I shouted indignantly that I wasn't dressed yet, he said he didn't care. "Come down just as you are, confound it!" he roared. I was tempted to take him at his word, but thought there might be some catch in it and wouldn't, though I hurried, of course, all I could. Father ate his usual hearty breakfast in a stormy mood, and I ate my usual hearty breakfast in a guilty and nervous one. Come what might, we always ate heartily. I sometimes wished afterward that I hadn't, but it never seemed to hurt Father.

Mother told Father that if he would give me the watch, she was sure I'd do better. He said that he didn't believe it and that that was a poor way to bring a boy up. To prove to him that he was wrong, Mother at last unlocked her jewel box and gave me a watch which had belonged to one of her elderly cousins. It was really too valuable a watch for a boy to wear, she said, and I must be very careful of it. I promised I would.

The watch, however, turned out to be painfully delicate. It was old; I was young. We were not exactly made for each other. It had a back and front of thin gold, and as Mother had had the former owner's monogram shaved off the front cover, that cover used to sink in the middle when pressed. Also, the lid fitted so closely that there was barely room for the glass crystal over the face. Such a very thin crystal had to be used that any pressure on the lid broke it.

I didn't press on the lid, naturally, after the first time this happened. I was careful, and everything would have gone well enough if other boys had been careful, too. It was not practicable, however, for me to make them be careful enough. When I had a fight, friendly or otherwise, I used to ask my opponent if he would be so kind as not to punch me on the left side of my stomach.[3] He might or might not listen. If he and I were too excited and kept on long enough, the watch crystal broke anyway. There was never time to take off my watch first, and anyhow there was no place to put it. A watch that goes around the streets in a boy's pocket has to take life as it comes. This watch had never been designed for any such fate.

The first two crystals I broke Mother paid for, as Father disapproved of the whole business and would have nothing to do with it. Mother was always short of

3. The watch is a pocket watch, worn in a small pocket in a vest or trousers. Pocket watches were common before wristwatches.

small change, however, and I hated to trouble her—and she hated to be troubled, too. "Oh, Clarence, dear! You haven't broken your watch again?" she cried when I opened the cover the second time, to show her the shattered fragments. She was so upset that I felt too guilty to tell her the next time it happened, and from then on I was reduced to the necessity of paying for the damage myself.

My pocket money never exceeded a dollar a month. Every new crystal cost twenty-five cents. It was a serious drain.

Wrestling and rolling around on the floor with Sam Willets, my watch quite forgotten, I would suddenly hear a faint tinkle and know that I was once more insolvent. I would pick out the broken glass and leave the watch with no crystal till I had twenty-five cents on hand, but these delays made me nervous. I knew that Mother wanted to feel sure I was taking good care of the watch and that she might look at it any evening. As soon as I had the money, I hurried over to Sixth Avenue, where two old Germans kept a tiny watch shop, and left it there to be fixed. One of my most dismal memories is of that stuffy little shop's smell of sauerkraut, and how tall the glass counter then seemed, and the slowness of those two old Germans. When I got there late and they made me leave the watch overnight, I didn't have one easy moment until I got it back the next day. Again and again I argued with them that twenty-five cents was too much, especially for a regular customer, but they said it didn't pay them

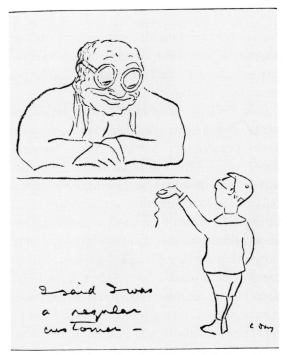

I said I was a regular customer —

Drawing by Clarence Day for this story's first printing, 1935. Alfred H. Knopf, New York City.

to do the work even for that, because those thin old-fashioned crystals were hard to get.

I gave up at last. I told Mother I didn't want to wear the watch anymore.

Then I found, to my amazement, that this way out of my troubles was barred. The watch was an heirloom. And an heirloom was a thing that its recipient must value and cherish. No good Chinese, I read later on in life, fails to honor his ancestors; and no good boy, I was told in my youth, fails to appreciate heirlooms.

I left Mother's room in low spirits. That night, as I wound up my watch with its slender key, I envied George. Father had selected the right kind for George; he knew what a boy needed. It had a thick nickel case, it had an almost unbreakable crystal, and it endured daily life imperturbably, even when dropped in the bathtub.

It seemed to me that I was facing a pretty dark future. The curse of great possessions became a living thought to me, instead of a mere phrase. The demands that such possessions made on their owners for upkeep were merciless. For months I had had no money for marbles. I couldn't even afford a new top. In some way that I didn't fully understand, I was yoked to a watch I now hated—a delicate thing that would always make trouble unless I learned to live gingerly.

Then I saw a way out. All this time I had kept on being late for breakfast at least once a week, out of habit, but it now occurred to me that if I could reform, perhaps Father might relent and give me that reliable nickel watch he had bought. I reformed. I occasionally weakened in my new resolution at first, but every time that crystal got broken, I was spurred on to fresh efforts. When I had at length established a record for promptness that satisfied Father, he had my name engraved on the watch he had bought and presented it to me. He was a little surprised at the intense pleasure I showed on this occasion, and as he watched me hopping around the room in delight, he said "There, there" several times. "Don't be so excited, confound it," he added. "You'll knock over that vase."

Mother said she couldn't see why Father should give me a nickel watch when I had a gold one already, but he laughed and told her that "that old thing" was no kind of a watch for a boy. She reluctantly laid it away again to rest in her jewel box.

Her parting shot at Father was that anyhow she had been right; she had said all along that a watch was what I needed to teach me how to be prompt.

Clarence Day (1874–1935) revealed much about his early life in three of his books: *God and My Father, Life with Father,* and *Life with Mother.* Day contracted crippling arthritis in his mid-twenties and was forced to run his stockbroking business from his New York apartment. Over the years he also wrote many book reviews, stories, and poems for major American magazines such as *Harper's* and *The New Yorker.* The details of his adult life are sketchy, and most of his later years remain a mystery.

Developing Comprehension Skills

1. Who insists that everyone in the Day family be on time for breakfast? Why is George always early for breakfast?

2. What are Mother's and Father's methods to try to make Clarence prompt for breakfast? What do these different methods show about Mother and Father?

3. Clarence says, "I was yoked to a watch I now hated." Why does Clarence hate the watch? Why won't Clarence's mother let him give it up?

4. Why does Clarence become prompt for breakfast? What does his mother think is the reason for the change?

5. This selection and the sketches by Bill Cosby deal with family life. What kinds of incidents do both writers use? Why do most readers enjoy reading about families?

6. Clarence Day gives readers a look at a nineteenth-century father. Bill Cosby shows readers a father of the twentieth century. In what ways are these fathers alike? In what ways do they differ? Tell which one you think is more effective and why.

Reading Literature: Humorous Sketches

1. **Understanding Irony.** The contrast between what is expected, or what appears to be true, and what actually happens or exists, is called **irony.** In this selection, Mother and Father are determined to make Clarence prompt. What is ironic about how Clarence becomes prompt? (You may want to refer to your answers to questions 3 and 4 in Developing Comprehension Skills.)

There are other kinds of irony. Irony occurs when the reader understands something that a character does not. At the end of this selection, Mother comments that she was right because a watch taught Clarence to be prompt. What does the reader understand about her comment that she does not?

2. **Contrasting Characters.** Clarence says of his father, "He led his life and we led ours, under his nose." His statement emphasizes the differences between Father and his children, especially Clarence. What differing ideas do the two have about George's piano playing? on how Clarence learns to be prompt? Find two other ways in which Father and his children differ.

3. **Identifying Theme.** As you have seen in the sketches by Bill Cosby, humorous writing often deals with an everyday experience retold as an entertaining story. Beneath the humor, however, you will find a message about family relationships. Think about what happens in this selection by Clarence Day. State a theme, or main idea about life, based on the story.

4. **Analyzing Humor.** Clarence's character contrasts with the well-behaved ideal that Mr. and Mrs. Day hold for their oldest son. This contrast creates humor in the sketch. What kinds of activities does Clarence prefer? Which of his attitudes would his parents disapprove of?

Developing Vocabulary Skills

Inferring Word Meaning. You have studied several types of context clues. Definition or restatement clues directly state the meaning of an unfamiliar word. Comparison and contrast clues tell what the unfamiliar word is like or unlike. Synonym and antonym clues provide words that mean the same as or the opposite of the unfamiliar word.

Sometimes the context does not give obvious clues to the meaning of an unfamiliar word. Often, however, the general idea of the entire passage or paragraph suggests the meaning. Whenever you use overall context to figure out a word, you **infer** the meaning of the word. Here is an example:

> He was an avid science fiction reader. Every spare moment he spent researching books about space travel. He had read all the latest scientific thrillers too.

From the surrounding ideas, you can conclude that *avid* means "eager and enthusiastic."

Each of the following passages is from this selection. Determine the meaning of the underlined word by using one of the following methods: definition or restatement clue, comparison clue, contrast clue, synonym clue, antonym clue, or by inferring the meaning from the overall context. On a sheet of paper, write the word and its definition. Briefly explain how you figured out the meaning.

1. Father made a great point of our getting down to breakfast on time. I meant to be prompt, but it never occurred to me that I had better try to be early. My idea was to slide into the room at the last moment. Consequently, I often was late.

2. Time went on, without much improvement on my part. Dawdling had got to be a habit with me. Sometimes my lateness was serious. One morning, when breakfast was half over and I had nothing on but a pair of long woolen drawers, Father called up from the front hall, napkin in hand, that he wouldn't stand it, and that I was to come down that instant.

3. I don't remember now what the titles were of the airs he selected, but the general idea was that if he played a lively air, it meant that the Giants had won, and when the strains of a dirge or lament floated up to us, it meant that Pop Anson had beaten them.

4. This watch, however, turned out to be painfully delicate. It was old; I was young. We were not exactly made for each other. It had a back and front of thin gold, and as Mother had had the former owner's monogram shaved off the front cover, that cover used to sink in the middle when pressed. Also, the lid fitted so closely that there was barely room for the glass crystal over the face. Such a very thin crystal had to be used that any pressure on the lid broke it.

5. He was a little surprised at the intense pleasure I showed on this occasion, and as he watched me hopping around the room in delight, he said "There, there," several times. "Don't be so excited, confound it," he added. "You'll knock over that vase."

Developing Skills in Study and Research

Using Multiple Resources. The type of gold pocket watch described in this sketch was once very popular. Over the centuries many kinds of watches and clocks have been invented and used. Choose two or more of the following resources to research some aspect of the history of timepieces:

1. encyclopedia articles
2. magazine articles
3. books
4. interview with a jeweler or clock repairer
5. visit to a museum collection
6. interview with a clock collector or antique dealer

Take notes on the information you find to share with your class. The class may want to make a book with illustrations about the history of timepieces.

Developing Skills in Speaking and Listening

Creating a Reading. Reread the last three paragraphs in the selection from *Life with Father.* Write a dialogue based on the part of the story in which Clarence finally gets his reward for promptness. In the dialogue, include the words of Father, Mother, and Clarence.

Read your dialogue aloud to a small group. Listen to their reactions and comments. Does your voice communicate the characters' feelings? Does your reading add to the humor of the dialogue? Are your words clear and understandable? Ask your listeners to tell you which parts of the dialogue they liked best and why.

Developing Writing Skills

Comparing Styles. The selections from *Fatherhood* and *Life with Father* are humorous portrayals of everyday family experiences. In two paragraphs compare and contrast how the writers create humor in these selections.

Prewriting. Reread the two selections. Make a list of the funny incidents and conversations in each sketch. Then list the ways humor is created in each. Consider techniques such as exaggeration, irony, unexpected comparisons or contrasts, and dialogue. Give at least one example for each technique you list. Review your lists. Note the similarities and the differences in the way humor is created in the two selections. Group the similarities together and the differences together.

Drafting. In your opening sentence state that you are comparing and contrasting the styles in these two humorous sketches. Present your comparisons, or similarities, in the first paragraph. Discuss the differences in the second paragraph. In both paragraphs, include examples or quotations from the selection.

Revising and Sharing. Reread your paragraphs. Make sure the sentences are clearly connected. Do you have enough examples of the techniques you discuss? Are the similarities and differences in the two styles clearly presented? Revise your paragraphs and make a final copy.

Essays

Some essays are written to make you laugh. Others, however, have a more serious tone. The essays in the following section are the more serious kind. They present subjects that are important to the writers. Each writer challenges the reader to think about new ideas and to try to understand them.

Lannis in the Mirror in the Garden, I, 1986, JOSEPH RAFFAEL. Oil on canvas. Photograph: Nancy Hoffman Gallery, New York City.

The Uses of Error

ISAAC ASIMOV

In this essay the writer corrects some mistaken ideas. He also shows that errors can lead to unexpected results.

In less than seven years we will be celebrating the 500th anniversary of the discovery of the American continents by Christopher Columbus. It's not too soon to try—once again—to set the record straight on that achievement.

In the first place, the common belief—which children pick up from elders who are as ignorant as they are—is that Columbus believed the world was round (the proper word is *spherical*) while everyone else thought it was flat.

This is ridiculous. To be sure, uneducated people in ancient and medieval times thought the world was flat, but so do uneducated people in most parts of the world today. Educated Europeans have known that the world is spherical ever since the time of Aristotle[1] in the fourth century B.C.

This, then, was not a matter of dispute between Columbus and his opponents. The point in question was this: Given that the earth is a sphere, how large is it?

The first person we know of who tried to determine the size of the earth was a Greek geographer named Eratosthenes (er′ ə täs′ thə nēz′). About 240 B.C. he noted that at noon at the summer solstice, the sun was directly overhead at Syene (sī ē′ nē) (now Aswan) in Egypt, while it was seven degrees from the zenith at Alexandria. From this, and by use of simple geometry, he decided the earth was 25,000 miles in circumference—and he was correct.

However, this seemed uncomfortably large to the Greeks. The land they knew of would fill only a small corner of such a huge world, and the thought of all that emptiness bothered them. About 150 years later, another Greek scholar, Poseidonius (pō′ sī dō′ nē əs), repeated Eratosthenes's work and came up with a circumference of 18,000 miles. This was wrong, but the lower figure was more comforting, and the Greeks accepted it.

What's more, the Greek geographers had estimated the Mediterranean Sea to be longer east and west than it really was, and

---

1. **Aristotle** (ar′ə stät′ ′l)–A Greek philosopher (384–322 B.C.), noted for works on logic, ethics, politics, etc.

based on that and the meticulous account of Marco Polo,[2] the eastern edge of Asia was considered to be substantially farther east than it really was.

In Columbus's time the Portuguese were trying to reach India by going around the African continent, a long and arduous voyage of some 10,000 miles. Columbus, assuming the small circumference of the world and the eastern overextension of Asia, maintained that one could achieve the same result by sailing 3,000 miles westward.

He approached the Portuguese with this idea, but the Portuguese geographers—the best in the world at that time—were convinced the earth was larger than Columbus thought and that the trip around Africa was the shorter route to India. Columbus, they said, would never reach any part of Asia.

Columbus got Spanish backing and sailed westward. What he didn't know, and what none of his European contemporaries knew, was that a vast, unknown continent blocked the way to Asia, and it was that new land that he reached—not India, even though we speak of native Americans as Indians to this day.

There are some other points.

First, Columbus did not prove that the earth was round. Those who wanted to believe it was flat could still do so, provided the flat earth was large enough to hold the Americas as well as Europe, Asia, and Africa. It wasn't until the voyage headed by Ferdinand Magellan (although he died en

Map (detail) from a 1675 sea atlas, *Tabulae Maritime*, by Frederick de Wit showing California as an island.
The Newberry Library, Chicago, Edward E. Ayer Collection.

route) forty years after Columbus that anyone actually sailed westward all the way to Asia and then continued onward back to Europe.

Second, Columbus did not truly discover America; he was not the first human being to set foot on it. Indeed, human beings met him on the shore. Human

2. **Marco Polo**–A Venetian explorer in East Asia (1254?–1324?).

beings had discovered the American continents when the first Siberian hunters crossed the Bering land bridge into North America about 25,000 years ago, and they settled the continents to the southern-most tip before Columbus arrived.

Columbus wasn't even the first European to arrive, since Norsemen had reached North America 500 years before him. Columbus was, however, the first person to publicize the discovery so effectively that Europeans explored and settled the new world and went on to dominate the whole world for a period of 450 years.

So you see the uses of error. If Columbus had known the truth—that 12,000 westward miles separated him from Asia—he would not have made the voyage, and the history of the world would have been different.

Who knows what mistaken scientific beliefs today may serve to lead us to great discoveries in the future?

Isaac Asimov (*born 1920*) came to America from Russia at the age of three. As a child, Asimov loved to read science-fiction magazines. He soon developed a deep interest in science. Asimov entered Columbia University at the age of fifteen. He eventually became a professor of biochemistry at Boston University's School of Medicine. He is the author of numerous professional books and hundreds of articles and science-fiction stories. Some of Asimov's popular writings include *I, Robot* and *The Caves of Steel.*

Developing Comprehension Skills

1. What two groups of people discovered the American continents before Columbus?

2. The writer notes the common belief "that Columbus believed the world was round . . . while everyone else thought it was flat." Then he says, "This is ridiculous." This statement is an opinion. Does he support this opinion with facts? Is "ridiculous" an example of slanted language? Explain.

3. The writer describes several different errors, or mistaken beliefs, in this essay. Identify three of these errors and the person or group who makes the errors.

4. Arrange the following ideas in the order in which they are presented in this essay.

   a. Columbus did not prove that the earth is round.

   b. Most of the educated people of Columbus's time did not believe that the world is flat. The main question for Columbus's time was "Given that the earth is a sphere, how large is it?"

   c. Columbus sailed westward because he thought he would find a shorter route to Asia from Europe.

   d. Columbus was the first to publicize his discovery of the American continents.

   e. Columbus did not know that a large unknown continent lay in his path.

   f. If Columbus had not been mistaken about the size of the earth's circumference, he would not have traveled west and landed in the Americas.

   g. Columbus did not discover the American continents first.

5. Why did the Portuguese refuse to back Columbus's venture? Were their ideas correct or was Columbus's view correct? Explain.

6. When Columbus sailed westward, he was trying to prove an idea. What is important about Columbus's questioning and stubborn attitude? Why is this attitude more useful than that of someone who refuses to question a belief or idea? Which attitude can lead to making discoveries? Explain.

7. The writer states, "So you see the uses of error. . . . Who knows what mistaken scientific beliefs today may serve to lead us to great discoveries in the future?" Is he recommending that people should have mistaken beliefs? Explain your answer.

Reading Literature: Essays

1. **Identifying Purpose.** The purpose of an essay may be to inform, to entertain, or to persuade. An essay often has more than one purpose. Identify the writer's purposes in this essay. How well does he succeed in carrying out his purposes?

2. **Analyzing Structure.** This essay is organized around widely-held errors of two kinds: mistaken beliefs about Columbus and mistaken beliefs held by Columbus. As the writer corrects or comments on each of these errors, he also explains what Columbus actually did or did not do.

   Each of the following statements describes one mistaken belief. Explain what the writer says about each error and how he then uses it to "set the record straight" about Columbus and his voyage. (You may want to refer to your answers to questions 3 and 4 in Developing Comprehension Skills.)

   a. Columbus believed the world was round while everyone else thought it was flat.

   b. Columbus thought that the circumference of the world was smaller than it is.

   c. Columbus proved that the earth was round.

   d. Columbus was the first human being to discover the American continents.

3. **Understanding Theme.** The theme is the writer's message about life. This essay discusses several ideas. Decide which of the following statements best expresses the theme. Be ready to explain why you chose the statement.

   a. Many people have mistaken beliefs about Columbus.

b. Columbus was wrong in some of his ideas.

c. Testing a belief or idea, even if the belief or idea is wrong, may lead to discovering a new idea or fact.

d. People do not always try to find out if their ideas and beliefs are true.

4. **Recognizing Tone.** The tone of the sketches you read in the previous section was humorous. What is the tone of this essay? How is this tone appropriate to the subject of the essay?

Developing Vocabulary Skills

Completing Analogies. You have learned that an analogy consists of two pairs of words related in the same way. Here is an example:

Dawn is to sunrise as dusk is to sunset. In each pair, the first term names a time and the second term names an event that occurs at that time. Sunrise occurs at dawn; sunset occurs at dusk. Other possible relationships in an analogy include synonyms, antonyms, relationships of properties, and parts of a whole.

Each of the following analogies uses at least one word from a selection you have read. Choose the word that will complete each relationship. Use a dictionary when necessary. Be ready to explain your reasoning.

1. Hesitate is to pause as ignorant is to _____.
   uneducated   stop   believable

2. Flat is to floor as spherical is to _____.
   round   square   ball

3. East is to west as ridiculous is to _____.
   silly   noticeable   reasonable

4. Future is to past as dispute is to _____.
   agreement   argument   estimate

5. Geometry is to mathematics as country is to _____.
   continent   city   solstice

6. Pride is to shame as meticulous is to _____.
   courage   sloppy   thoughtful

7. Zenith is to peak as arduous is to _____.
   difficult   funny   high

8. Journey is to voyage as dominate is to _____.
   separate   travel   rule

Developing Skills in Critical Thinking

Evaluating a Conclusion. The writer concludes that errors can result in great discoveries. How well does he support this conclusion? Does he base it on facts or opinions? Does he leave out any important possibilities? Does he consider what other consequences might result from errors? Decide, based on your answers to these questions, whether you agree with Asimov's conclusion.

Developing Skills in Study and Research

Using a Time Line. In this essay the writer refers to several dates. Often, the relationship between dates is difficult to understand. A time line can present time relationships so they can be understood at a glance.

Examine the following time line. Using the information you find there, decide if the statements above the time line are true or false.

1. Norsemen found America one thousand years before Columbus made his voyage to the Americas.

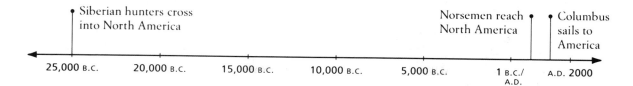

Siberian hunters cross into North America

Norsemen reach North America

Columbus sails to America

25,000 B.C.   20,000 B.C.   15,000 B.C.   10,000 B.C.   5,000 B.C.   1 B.C./A.D.   A.D. 2000

2. Siberian hunters, the ancestors of Native Americans, lived in America thousands of years before Columbus "discovered" America.

3. Midway between the Siberian crossing and Columbus's voyage, the Norse explorations occurred.

4. Less time has passed since Columbus's discovery and the present than between the Siberian crossing and the Norse explorations.

Developing Writing Skills

1. **Analyzing Theme.** The theme is one of the most important elements in this essay. In a paragraph explain what the theme is and how it is developed.

   Prewriting. Review your answer to Reading Literature question 3 in which you figured out the theme. Then review your answers to Developing Comprehension Skills questions 3, 6, and 7 and Reading Literature question 2. Based on your review of these answers and of the essay, write down the other main ideas in the essay. Decide which are most important for supporting the theme. Organize your ideas. You may want to use an outline.

   Drafting. State the theme in your topic sentence. Then explain how the main ideas in the essay develop the theme. Use the notes and organization you prepared in prewriting. Be especially careful to make clear connections between your ideas.

   Revising and Sharing. Ask a classmate to read your paragraph. Is your statement of theme clear to the person? Are there any confusing sentences or words? Have you supported your ideas adequately? Be prepared to talk about the ideas in your paragraph with your classmates in a class discussion.

2. **Using Your Imagination.** At the end of this essay Asimov writes, "If Columbus had known the truth . . . he would not have made the voyage, and the history of the world would have been different." How might the history of the world have been different if Columbus had not tested his idea and tried to sail to Asia by going west? In a paragraph describe how the world might be different. Follow the steps in the process of writing: prewriting, drafting, revising, and sharing. For more help see the Guidelines for the Process of Writing beginning on page 654.

A Poet's Advice to Students

e. e. cummings

In this brief essay, poet e. e. cummings writes about poetry and being yourself. How are the two related for him?

A poet is somebody who feels and who expresses his feeling through words.

This may sound easy. It isn't.

A lot of people think or believe or know they feel—but that's thinking or believing or knowing, not feeling. And poetry is feeling—not knowing or believing or thinking.

Almost anybody can learn to think or believe or know, but not a single human being can be taught to feel. Why? Because whenever you think or you believe or you know, you're a lot of other people: but the moment you feel, you're nobody-but-yourself.

To be nobody-but-yourself—in a world which is doing its best, night and day, to make you everybody else—means to fight the hardest battle which any human being can fight, and never stop fighting.

As for expressing nobody-but-yourself in words, that means working just a little harder than anybody who isn't a poet can possibly imagine. Why? Because nothing is quite as easy as using words like somebody else. We all of us do exactly this nearly all of the time—and whenever we do it, we're not poets.

If, at the end of your first ten or fifteen years of fighting and working and feeling, you find you've written one line of one poem, you'll be very lucky indeed.

And so my advice to all young people who wish to become poets is: do something easy, like learning how to blow up the world—unless you're not only willing, but glad, to feel and work and fight till you die.

Does this sound dismal? It isn't.

It's the most wonderful life on earth.

Or so I feel.

e. e. cummings (*1894–1962*) was born in Boston, Massachusetts, and was educated at Harvard University. He is one of the most unconventional of all American poets, shown by the fact that he preferred to write his name *e. e. cummings.* Cummings played with punctuation, capitalization, and arrangement of words in his poems to communicate the full force of his ideas and feelings. His unusual and unpredictable poetry drew criticism from some but praise from many. His collection of six hundred poems, *Poems: 1923–1954,* received a Special Citation from the National Book Awards Committee.

Developing Comprehension Skills

1. What definition of a poet does Cummings give at the beginning of the essay?

2. Cummings says that feeling is different from thinking, believing, or knowing. How is feeling different according to this essay?

3. What does Cummings mean when he says that "the moment you feel, you're nobody-but-yourself"?

4. Why does Cummings say that trying to be nobody-but-yourself is "to fight the hardest battle which any human being can fight"? How does the world try to "make you everybody else"?

5. If you wish to be a poet, you face the task of "expressing nobody-but-yourself in words." How hard is this task? Why? How do people use words most of the time according to Cummings?

6. After describing being a poet as a lifelong, demanding struggle, Cummings concludes that it is nevertheless "the most wonderful life on earth. Or so I feel." How can such

difficult work be wonderful? Is hard work usually rewarding? Explain your answer and give examples from your own experience or that of others.

Reading Literature: Essays

1. **Examining Structure.** One way that Cummings gives his essay structure is through repetition. Count how many times he uses the words *feel* and *feeling.* In which parts of the essay do these words appear? How does the repetition help to unify, or pull together, the essay?

2. **Understanding Style.** Cummings's style is known for its originality and inventiveness. Sometimes, Cummings creates new words. What hyphenated word does he make up for this essay? What does the word mean? How does the word relate to the main idea of the essay?

3. **Analyzing Contrast.** Near the end of this essay Cummings tells young people who want to become poets that they will have to work long and hard. He advises them to do

something easy—"like learning how to blow up the world"—if they are not willing to struggle. Most people would not consider learning to blow up the world easy or desirable. What does Cummings achieve by using this contrast? What comment is he making about violence and destruction?

4. **Evaluating Purpose.** The essay by Isaac Asimov is based mainly on facts. This essay by E. E. Cummings is based mainly on opinion. What is Cummings's purpose? Why are opinions more effective than facts in achieving this purpose?

Developing Vocabulary Skills

Using the Dictionary. You have learned that a dictionary can tell you not only a word's definition, but also its pronunciation, part of speech, and origin. The following words are from the essay you have just read. Look up each word in a dictionary and write down the pronunciation, part of speech, origin, and definition as it is used in the essay.

express   imagine
feel   dismal
moment

Developing Writing Skills

Analyzing Meaning. Study the following quotations from the essay. Choose one, and write a paragraph explaining what it means.

Poetry is feeling.

The moment you feel, you're nobody-but-yourself.

[The] world . . . is doing its best, night and day, to make you everybody else.

To be nobody-but-yourself . . . means to fight the hardest battle which any human being can fight.

Nothing is quite as easy as using words like somebody else.

Prewriting. Decide which quotation is most interesting to you. Rewrite the quotation in your own words. Then jot down your ideas about what the quotation means and examples you can use to make its meaning clear. You can use examples from the essay and from your own life.

Drafting. In your topic sentence, introduce the quotation from Cummings's essay. Then tell what you think it means. After explaining the quotation, give examples to clarify its meaning.

Revising and Sharing. Check for a clear topic sentence and specific examples. Ask a classmate to read your paragraph and tell you what he or she thinks the quotation means according to your explanation. Revise any parts of the paragraph that are unclear to the person.

Place of Sorrows

CHARLES KURALT

For Custer and his men, the Little Big Horn was a place of sorrows. Read to discover why this hill came to be a place of sorrows for the victorious Sioux and Cheyennes as well.

This is about a place where the wind blows and the grass grows and a river flows below a hill. Nothing is here but the wind and the grass and the river. But of all the places in America, this is the saddest place I know.

The Indians[1] called the river the Greasy Grass. White men called it the Little Big Horn. From a gap in the mountains to the east, Brevet Major General George A. Custer's proud Seventh Cavalry came riding, early in the morning of June 25, 1876, riding toward the Little Big Horn.

Custer sent one battalion, under Major Marcus Reno, across the river to attack what he thought might be a small village of hostile Sioux. His own battalion he galloped behind the ridges to ride down on the village from the rear. When at last Custer brought his two hundred and thirty-one troops to the top of a hill and looked down toward the river, what he saw was an encampment of fifteen thousand Indians stretching for two and a half miles, the largest assembly of Indians the plains had ever known—and a thousand mounted warriors coming straight for him.

Reno's men, meantime, had been turned, routed, chased across the river, joined by the rest of the regiment, surrounded, and now were dying, defending a nameless brown hill.

In a low, protected swale in the middle of their narrowing circle, the one surviving doctor improvised a field hospital and did what he could for the wounded. The grass covers the place now and grows in the shallow rifle trenches above, which were dug that day by knives and tin cups and fingernails.

Two friends in H Company, Private Charles Windolph and Private Julian Jones, fought up here, side by side, all that day

---

1. **Indians**–Term commonly used for native peoples in North and South America; now referred to as Native Americans. The misuse of the term *Indian* began with Columbus, who thought he had reached India when he landed in the Americas.

and stayed awake all that night, talking, both of them scared. Charles Windolph said: "The next morning when the firing commenced, I said to Julian, 'We'd better get our coats off.' He didn't move. I looked at him. He was shot through the heart." Charles Windolph won the Congressional Medal of Honor up here, survived, lived to be ninety-eight. He didn't die until 1950. And never a day passed in all those years that he didn't think of Julian Jones.

And Custer's men, four miles away? There are stones in the grass that tell the story of Custer's men. The stones all say the same things: "U.S. soldier, Seventh Cavalry, fell here, June 25, 1876."

The warriors of Sitting Bull, under the great Chief Gall, struck Custer first and divided his troops. Two Moon and the northern Cheyenne struck him next. And when he tried to gain a hilltop with the last remnants of his command, Crazy Horse rode over that hill with hundreds of warriors and right through his battalion.

The Indians who were there later agreed on two things: that Custer and his men fought with exceeding bravery; and that after half an hour, not one of them was alive.

The Army came back that winter—of course, the Army came back—and broke the Sioux and the Cheyenne and forced

Graves of unknown soldiers who fought with Custer at Little Big Horn.
© 1980 Jeff Apoian/Nawrocki Stock Photo, Chicago.

them back to the starvation of the reservations and, in time, murdered more old warriors and women and children on the Pine Ridge Reservation than Custer lost young men in battle here.

That's why this is the saddest place. For Custer and the Seventh Cavalry, courage only led to defeat. For Crazy Horse and the Sioux, victory only led to Wounded Knee.[2]

Come here sometime, and you'll see. There is melancholy in the wind and sorrow in the grass, and the river weeps.

---

2. **Wounded Knee**–Wounded Knee Creek, South Dakota, was the scene of the final battle in 1890 between the whites and the Sioux. The white soldiers killed two hundred Sioux men, women, and children.

Charles Bishop Kuralt (*born 1934*) was educated at the University of North Carolina and then began working on the *Charlotte News* as a reporter and columnist. He took a job with CBS news as a writer and correspondent and eventually created his own feature series "On the Road." Kuralt now combs the backwoods of America proving that many people "go on living in spite of the big, black headlines." He notes, "I've never heard calamity from the people. They seem to have a mystical confidence in themselves." Kuralt has earned a Peabody Award and an Emmy Award for his work.

Developing Comprehension Skills

1. Who won the battle at the Little Big Horn on June 25, 1876?

2. What was the battle at the Little Big Horn like for Custer and his soldiers? Support your answer with details from the essay.

3. Reread the sections in which the writer tells the story about Charles Windolph and describes the "stones in the grass." How do these two parts of the essay relate to the title?

4. The Native Americans who were at the Little Big Horn agree on two things, Kuralt says. What are these two things? Which is a fact, and which is an opinion?

5. "The Army came back that winter—of

course, the Army came back," Kuralt says. Why does he say "of course"? What is he suggesting about the relationship between the Army and the Native Americans in the West?

6. Why does Charles Kuralt think of the Little Big Horn as the saddest place he knows? What does the place lead to for Custer and the Seventh Cavalry? for Crazy Horse and the Sioux? Is the Little Big Horn a place of victory or defeat? Explain your answer.

7. If you were asked to write about a sad place where a tragic historic event took place, what place would you choose? Name the place and tell what happened there. List some of the details that you would use to convey the sadness of the place.

Reading Literature: Essays

1. **Recognizing Irony.** As you recall, the contrast between what is expected and what actually happens or exists is called **irony.** Irony can be used not only to create a humorous effect, but also to emphasize a point. Kuralt uses irony frequently in this essay. For example, in the first paragraph Kuralt introduces irony with his description of the Little Big Horn. It is ironic that a place with only wind, grass, and a river would be such a sad place. What is ironic about Custer's defeat at Little Big Horn? What is ironic about the victory of the Sioux and the Cheyenne?

2. **Examining Structure.** Kuralt uses time order to develop part of this essay. He tells the events in the order in which they happened. He also uses spatial order to tell about dif-ferent parts of the battlefield at the Little Big Horn. Note that as he writes he weaves the events and the place together to create a unified impression. Identify one paragraph that uses mainly time order and one that uses mainly spatial order. Find one example where he weaves time order and spatial description together.

3. **Understanding Theme.** The **theme** of an essay is the writer's message about life. Kuralt writes about the tragedy of war in this essay. State the theme in your own words.

4. **Identifying Mood.** The **mood** of an essay is the feeling it creates in the reader. What mood does this essay create? What details do you think are most important in creating this mood?

Developing Vocabulary Skills

Studying Names. Many place names in the United States come from Native American words and names. The dictionary can be a valuable resource to help you learn about these names. For example, a dictionary will tell you that the Missouri River is named for the Missouri tribe who lived on the river in North Dakota and that the name means "people of the big canoes." In a dictionary, look up the following place names. Write down each name, what it refers to, and how the name developed.

1. Dakotas   6. Tuscaloosa
2. Chicago   7. Okefenokee (Swamp)
3. Tucson   8. Oklahoma
4. Cheyenne   9. Minneapolis
5. Ontario   10. Mackinac (Island)

Developing Skills in Study and Research

Using a Topographical Map. A topographical map shows the surface features of a region. These include rivers, lakes, and land forms. The events that Kuralt describes occur at the Little Big Horn. Toward the end of the essay, he also mentions the battle at Wounded Knee. Topographical maps can help you to visualize the features of these two places. Use an atlas that has topographical maps of the western United States. On the map of Montana, locate the Little Big Horn River, and notice the land forms referred to in the essay. On a map of South Dakota, locate Wounded Knee. What kind of land features do you find there? Are they similar to or different from the features at Little Big Horn?

Developing Writing Skills

Writing an Essay. The essays in this section are informal essays about topics that are important to the writers. Write an informal essay on a topic that interests or concerns you. Structure your essay in three or more paragraphs.

Prewriting. Think about a topic you want to write about. You may want to look over current newspapers or news magazines for ideas. When you decide on a topic, read several newspaper and magazine articles on the topic. If possible, you can interview someone who knows something about your subject. Take notes on your reading and your interview. List your own ideas. Then write down your opinion on the topic. Also write down the reasons behind your opinion. Arrange these in order of importance or in another order that makes sense to you.

Drafting. In the introductory paragraph to your essay state your opinion on the topic and give any background information that a reader would need to know. Then develop each of your reasons in separate paragraphs. To support your reasons, use facts and examples from the articles you read, or conversations you have had. Be sure to tell where you got your information. Discuss your reasons in the order you decided on in prewriting.

Revising and Sharing. Reread your essay. If you have repeated yourself, work on structuring each paragraph around one main idea. Ask someone else to read your essay and tell you where the support for your main idea is strongest. Revise other parts of the essay to make them stronger.

Chapter 6 Review

Using Your Skills in Reading Nonfiction

Each of the two-page introductions titled Reading Literature is an example of nonfiction writing. Select one of the Reading Literature introductions in Chapters One through Six. Discuss these elements of nonfiction shown in the introduction: type of nonfiction, purpose, and structure.

Using Your Comprehension Skills

Here are two speeches from *Sherlock Holmes and the Stockbroker's Clerk* from Chapter Seven. Read the speeches. Identify two facts and two opinions.

Holmes. It is a case, Watson, that may prove to have something in it. There are certainly some very unusual features. And I shall be glad of the chance to hear the story again.

Pycroft. Well, then. I used to be a clerk in a stockbroking firm. I'd been with it five years and was doing very well, when the firm was forced to close. They gave me very good recommendations.

Using Your Vocabulary Skills

Read these sentences from *Sherlock Holmes and the Stockbroker's Clerk.* Then look up each underlined word in a dictionary. Write the following for each word: its pronunciation, its origin, and the definition that fits its use in the sentence.

1. My underlined funds were somewhat underlined depleted by my long underlined siege of unemployment.
2. I stood for a moment with my heart in my boots, wondering whether the whole thing was an underlined elaborate hoax, when someone suddenly underlined addressed me.

Using Your Skills in Critical Thinking

The following quotations from selections you have read contain examples of slanted writing. Identify each example of slanted writing. For each quotation, answer these questions:

a. What is the subject?

b. What words and phrases are slanted?

c. How does the writer feel about the subject?

1. Come here sometime, and you'll see. There is melancholy in the wind and sorrow in the grass, and the river weeps.

    —"Place of Sorrows" by Charles Kuralt

2. Mummy sometimes treats me just like a baby, which I can't bear. Otherwise things are going better. I still don't like Peter any more, he is so boring; he flops lazily on his bed half the time, does a bit of carpentry, and then goes back for another snooze. What a fool!

    —*Anne Frank: Diary of a Young Girl* by Anne Frank

3. Maggie had become a tall, stately woman with clear, dark eyes and a kind expression.   —"Banker Maggie Walker" by Olive W. Burt

Using Your Writing Skills

Complete one of the following assignments.

1. Choose one of the following pairs of selections from this chapter. Compare and contrast them in regard to two of the following elements: theme, tone, structure, or style.

    a. The excerpt from *Anne Frank: The Diary of a Young Girl* and "The First Day of the War"

    b. "Banker Maggie Walker" and the excerpt from *One of the Lucky Ones*

    c. The excerpts from *Life with Father* and *Fatherhood*

    d. "Place of Sorrows" and the excerpt from *Chief Sarah*

2. Write an essay of at least two paragraphs on any topic you like. You may wish to consider one of these topics suggested by selections in this chapter:

    a. a conflict of growing up

    b. breaking a bad habit

    c. solving a family conflict

    d. a pet peeve

    e. a difficult job

CHAPTER SEVEN

Drama

High Steppin' Strutter I, 1985, MIRIAM SCHAPIRO.
Collection of Jane and Robert Schecter. Photograph: Bernice
Steinbaum Gallery, New York City.

Reading Literature

Drama

Drama is literature that develops plot and characters through action and through dialogue, the words spoken by the characters. A drama, or play, is meant to be performed.

Some plays are acted on a stage in front of an audience. Others are filmed for movies or television. **Radio plays** are written for radio. The plays in this chapter are radio plays.

Like all plays, radio plays tell a story through the words of the characters. Radio plays also suggest action with sound effects, such as the sound of hoofbeats to suggest a rider on horseback.

The History of Drama

Drama began as a part of religious ceremonies in earliest times. By 500 B.C. plays were important in Greece. Later, they were also a prominent part of Roman culture. In other parts of Europe, however, drama did not develop until the Middle Ages. Then people started producing plays telling religious stories. In time, other subjects were used. By the 1500's, plays had become a favorite form of entertainment. The great English dramatist William Shakespeare wrote his plays during this period.

Drama continued to develop through the following centuries. In the twentieth century American dramatists such as Eugene O'Neill and Arthur Miller have produced important new plays. This century has also seen the development of drama for radio, television, and film.

The Elements of Drama

A play has many of the same elements as a short story. You know that some of these elements are plot, characters, setting, and theme. Plays and short stories develop the elements in different ways. For example, readers of short stories learn about events through description and explanation as well as through dialogue and action. For most plays, however, the audience finds out the plot through only dialogue and action. The audience of a radio play learns the plot from dialogue alone.

Dialogue. Most of a play is made up of **dialogue,** conversation between two or more characters. Dialogue gives insights into the personalities of the characters and unfolds the plot.

Characters. In plays, the audience learns about a character through his or her actions and words and through the reactions of other characters. The character's motivation, or reasons for acting, must be inferred from the dialogue and action.

Narrator. A **narrator** is a character who introduces or comments on the action. A narrator is more likely to be found in a radio play than in other kinds of plays. In *Sherlock Holmes and the Stockbroker's Clerk,* for example, Dr. Watson acts as narrator.

Scene and Act. In a play the action is divided into **scenes.** Each scene has a different setting, either in time or place. Usually the events are shown in the order they happen. Sometimes, however, one scene may be followed by another scene showing an earlier action. This kind of scene is called a **flashback.** In a long play, scenes are grouped in **acts.** The plays in this chapter are one-act plays, but many plays have two or more acts.

Stage Directions. The **stage directions** are the writer's instructions for performing the play. They tell the actors how to move and how to speak. Stage directions also describe the setting, stage set, lighting, music, props, and sound effects.

How to Read a Play

1. Read the play aloud, if possible. Imagine the sound effects.
2. Read all stage directions carefully. Try to picture the looks, movements, and tone of voice of each character.

Comprehension Skills

Evaluations

Evaluation is a process of examining something carefully and then deciding on its value. Here is an example of evaluation. You have decided to buy a bicycle. Before you buy, you look at all its parts. You ask yourself: Are the brakes new or worn out? Are the tires in good shape? Is the frame rusted? Only after you examine each part of the bicycle can you decide on its worth.

Evaluation involves comparing a subject with a standard. A standard is a completely satisfactory model. When you evaluate the bicycle, for example, you compare it to the best bicycle you can think of.

Evaluating a Literary Work. You are often asked to evaluate poems, short stories, nonfiction works, and plays. To evaluate these pieces of writing, you follow the same process as you do when you evaluate a bicycle. You look at each element of the selection. Then you compare that element with a standard. In evaluating a play, you may examine elements such as plot, setting, and characters. You may ask yourself questions such as these: Does the action move too slowly or too quickly? Does the setting add anything to the play? Does the dialogue sound realistic? Are the characters believable?

Supporting an Evaluation. Each person uses his or her own standards to evaluate. As a result, people don't always agree on their evaluations. To support an evaluation, you should base it on specific evidence and examples. In other words, you should try to be objective. Just saying that you like a play is not enough. You must explain what you like and why.

The following statements are evaluations. The first is not objective. It is not supported by any evidence. The second is objective. It gives reasons based on specific details.

This is a good play because I like it.

The dialogue in this play is fast-paced and kept me laughing all night. The mixed-up conversation between the maid and the butler in the first act is especially funny.

Evaluating a Writer's Purpose. Every piece of writing has one or more purposes. The writer may want to inform, entertain, or persuade. The writer may want to create suspense, humor, or romance. One way to evaluate a play is to decide whether the writer has achieved his or her purposes. To do that, you must first decide what the purposes are. Then study various parts of the play, and decide whether they help achieve the purposes. For example, one purpose of a detective play is to create suspense. When evaluating such a play, ask these questions: Does the play include clues that make you wonder about what will happen next? Does it have mysterious characters? Do events build tension?

Exercises: Making Evaluations

A. Identify which statements are objective evaluations. Then identify the statements that evaluate purpose. Be able to explain your decisions.

1. The nineteenth-century setting does not fit the modern dialogue.
2. This play was supposed to be funny, but the jokes fell flat and the characters were stilted and uninteresting.
3. Everyone will love this play.
4. The play is exciting because the suspense builds steadily. By the time the door slowly swings open, you can almost hear the audience holding its breath.

B. Read each evaluation below. Then identify the element that is evaluated.

1. The relationship between the events in the first act and the second act is unclear.
   a. dialogue   b. plot   c. character
2. The Yankee is appealing—bold and funny, but at the same time, warm and friendly.
   a. mood   b. character   c. purpose

$\mathcal{V}$ocabulary Skills

Levels of Language

How you speak depends to a certain degree on where you are and whom you are talking to. For example, if you were talking with friends after school, you would be casual and informal. If you were speaking to a school assembly, however, you would use a different level of language. You would probably use more difficult words and follow the rules of grammar more carefully.

Different situations call for different levels of language, both in real life and in plays. The two levels of English are standard and nonstandard. **Nonstandard English** refers to language that does not follow accepted grammatical rules. **Standard English** refers to language that does follow the rules of grammar. Standard English can be further divided into two additional levels, formal and informal.

Formal English

Formal English is appropriate in situations that are serious or dignified. In formal English, sentences may be long and complicated. Difficult words are used. Contractions and words found only in casual conversations are not used. Formal English always follows the rules of grammar, spelling, and punctuation. In the first play you will read, *Sherlock Holmes and the Stockbroker's Clerk,* Holmes often uses formal English.

> **Holmes.** And I hope that the cares of your medical practice, coupled with the joys of marriage, have not served to dampen the interest which you used to take in our little deductive problems.

Informal English

Informal English is used in everyday situations. It is the language of most magazines, newspapers, friendly letters, and conversation. Informal English follows the same rules of grammar as formal English. Informal English, however, is more personal and casual. It uses shorter words as well as contractions. Sentences are simpler. The following selection from *A Connecticut Yankee in King Arthur's Court* is an example of informal English.

> **Conn. Yankee.** Well, the King believed that I was a magician, right enough. But that old fake, Merlin, persuaded him that I was a humbug.

Idioms and Slang. Words and phrases used in special ways may be either idioms or slang. Both are classified as part of informal English. An **idiom** is an expression that has a meaning different from the literal meaning. For example, the expression "burning the midnight oil" means "working hard and long." **Slang** is used by members of a group. Slang words are usually popular only for a short time. Some examples of slang words of the past are *far out* and *square*.

Exercise: Recognizing Levels of Language

The following sentences are from the plays in this chapter. Identify each sentence as informal or formal English. Underline any idioms or slang expressions.

1. I stood for a moment with my heart in my boots.
2. Why, I knew Merlin seven hundred years ago, and he doesn't amount to shucks as a magician, not next to me!
3. I confess that I found Mr. Pycroft's story interesting, but it was not until he mentioned the detail of the gold tooth that I perceived the mystery in the affair.
4. And show him homage, high and low, rich and poor, for he is a great wizard and magician.
5. Sherlock Holmes, you old dog!

Sherlock Holmes and the Stockbroker's Clerk: Part One

One of the most famous detectives of all time is Sherlock Holmes. He is noted for his ability to use apparently meaningless details to arrive at accurate conclusions. As you read, try to solve the mystery as Holmes does.

SIR ARTHUR CONAN DOYLE
Dramatized by Lewy Olfson

CHARACTERS

Dr. Watson
Sherlock Holmes
Hall Pycroft
Arthur Pinner ⎱ *played by a*
Harry Pinner ⎰ *single actor*

Porter
Newsboy

Sound-Effects Person
Music-Effects Person

Watson. Most men, when they get married, retire from the world for a little while and allow their lives to become circumscribed by the four walls of their homes. But most men do not have an intimate acquaintance with the master detective, Sherlock Holmes. Therefore, I cannot admit to much surprise when, three weeks after my wedding, the bell of my town house door was rung, and I opened it to find my good friend, Sherlock Holmes.

Sound. *Doorbell, followed by a brief pause, then sound of door being opened.*

Holmes. My dear Watson, I am truly delighted to see you.

Watson *(Merrily).* Sherlock Holmes, you old dog! Come in, come in!

Holmes. I trust that Mrs. Watson has entirely recovered from all the little excitements connected with our adventure of the Sign of Four?[1]

Watson. Thank you, we are both well.

Holmes. And I hope that the cares of your medical practice, coupled with the joys

---

1. **Sign of Four**–Another Sherlock Holmes case.

of marriage, have not served to dampen the interest which you used to take in our little deductive problems.

Watson. On the contrary, it was only last night that I was discussing them with Mrs. Watson. That sad business of Pondicherry Lodge, for instance—and the curious mystery of the Beryl Coronet. I wouldn't mind seeing another case like that one.

Holmes. Then you don't consider your collection closed?

Watson. Not at all. I should wish nothing better than to have some more such experiences.

Holmes. Today, for example? Even though you have not been well lately?

Watson (*Taken aback*). How did you ever know that, Holmes?

Holmes. You know my methods, my dear Watson. I deduced it.

Watson. But from what?

Holmes. From your slippers.

Watson. How on earth ——?

Holmes. Your slippers are new. You could not have had them more than a few weeks—bought them for your wedding trip, I'd say. And yet the soles of them are slightly scorched. For a moment I thought they might have been wet and then burned in drying. But near the instep there is a small disc of paper with the shopman's marks on it. The damp would of course have removed this. You had, then, been sitting with your feet outstretched to the fire, which a man would hardly do in the middle of June if he were in full health.

Watson. You never cease to amaze me, Holmes. It's incredible!

Holmes. On the contrary, my dear Watson, it's elementary. I am afraid that I rather give myself away when I explain. Results without reasons are so much more impressive. But come, let us get to the business at hand. I have a case in Birmingham today. Will you come?

Watson. Certainly. What is the case?

Holmes. My client will tell it all to you on the train on our way down. Can you come at once?

Watson. In an instant. Let me just get my coat on and have a word with my wife.

Holmes. Very good. I shall meet you outside your door. I have some instructions for the cab driver, and I wish to take advantage of a few extra minutes in the sun.

Music. *Light theme, in and under.[2] Out.*

Watson. After telling my bride about the errand I was about to undertake, I donned my greatcoat and went out the

---

2. **in and under**–A musical direction that directs the music to swell and then fade into the background.

door, to find Holmes standing on my step, breathing in the fresh June air.

Sound. *Door closing.*

Holmes. Ah, here you are, Watson. I have been looking around. I see your neighbor is a doctor, too.

Watson. Yes, he bought an old practice just as I did. As a matter of fact, both our practices are of the same age—they have been here ever since the houses were built.

Holmes. Ah! Then you got hold of the better of the two.

Watson. I think I did. But how did you know?

Holmes. By the steps, my boy! Yours are worn three inches deeper than his. But we chat too long. My client is in the cab waiting for us. Come along and I'll introduce you.

Watson. With pleasure, Holmes.

Sound. *Cab door being slammed.*

Holmes. Dr. Watson, I should like to present to you a most interesting young man—Mr. Hall Pycroft.

Music. *Light theme, in and under. Out.*

Watson. The man whom I found myself facing was a well-built, fresh-complexioned young fellow with a frank, honest face. He wore a neat suit of sober black, which made him look like what he was—a smart young city man, probably employed somewhere as a junior clerk. It was not until we were all in a first-class railway carriage and well started upon our journey to Birmingham, however, that I was able to learn what trouble had driven him to Sherlock Holmes.

Sound. *Railroad wheels in softly in background and out.*

Holmes. We have a clear run here of seventy minutes. I want you, Mr. Pycroft, to tell Dr. Watson your very interesting experience, exactly as you told it to me.

Pycroft (*A pleasant-sounding young man*). With pleasure, Mr. Holmes.

Holmes. It is a case, Watson, which may prove to have something in it. There are certainly some very unusual features. And I shall be glad of a chance to hear the story again, so that I may review some of the particulars for myself.

Pycroft. Well, then. I used to be a clerk in a stockbroking firm. I'd been with them five years and was doing very well, when the firm was forced to close. They gave me very good recommendations, but that didn't help the fact that I was out of work. And so I began to look around. At last I saw a vacancy advertised at Mawson & Williams.

Watson. The firm on Lombard Street? It's the richest in London.

Pycroft. So it is, and I knew there'd be

many, many applicants for the post. But even though I had little chance of getting it, I sent in my letter of application. And, believe it or not, back came a letter saying that if I would appear the next Monday, I might take over my new duties at once. The pay was better than I had been earning before, and the duties were the same. You couldn't have found a happier man in London than I was when I got that position.

Watson. I can well believe it.

Pycroft. But now I come to the strange part of the business. I was living in a small boarding house in an out-of-the-way corner of London. It was more economical, you know, and my funds were somewhat depleted by my long siege of unemployment. I was sitting over my poor supper, thinking about my luck *(Fading)*, when the hall-porter brought in a card.

Sound. *Knock on door, door being opened.*

Porter. Mr. Pycroft? There's a gentleman below-stairs to see you, sir. Sent up this card.

Pycroft. A gentleman to see me? But nobody knows I live here. Let me see the card. Hmm. "Arthur Pinner, Financial

Agent." I don't know him. But still— why not? Show him up.

Porter. Very good, sir.

Pycroft (*Musing*). I wonder how on earth the fellow knows me. What does he want of me? And how did he find me?

Porter (*Off-mike, announcing*). Mr. Arthur Pinner, sir.

Pinner (*A sly, older man, fading on*). Mr. Hall Pycroft, I believe?

Pycroft. Yes, sir. Please come in.

Sound. *Door closing.*

Pinner. You were lately engaged at Coxon & Woodhouse's and are now to be on the staff at Mawson's?

Pycroft. Quite so. You seem to know a great deal about me, sir.

Pinner. Well, the fact is that I have heard some really extraordinary stories about your financial ability. You remember Parker, who used to be manager at Coxon's? He can never praise you enough. Among your strong points, I believe, is a good memory, is it not?

Pycroft. It's pretty fair, I must admit.

Pinner. You don't mind if I test you on that point, do you? I'm sure you read the stock quotations each day. What is the price of Ayrshires?

Pycroft (*Promptly*). A hundred and six and a quarter to a hundred and five and seven-eighths.

Pinner. And New Zealand Consolidated?

Pycroft. A hundred and four.

Pinner. British Broken Hills.

Pycroft. Seven to seven-and-six.

Pinner. Wonderful! This quite fits in with all I have heard. My boy, you are much too good to be a clerk at Mawson's.

Pycroft. I am very glad to have a position at Mawson's.

Pinner. Oh, pooh, man, you should be doing far better. Now I'll tell you how it is with me. What I have to offer is little enough for a man of your ability, but compared to Mawson's offer, it's a fortune. When do you start at Mawson's?

Pycroft. On Monday.

Pinner (*Laughing*). I'll wager you'll never go there at all. By Monday you will be the business manager of the Franco-Midland Hardware Company, Limited, with a hundred and thirty-four branches all over France, not counting one in Brussels and one in San Remo.

Pycroft. But—I've never heard of it!

Pinner. I daresay you haven't. It has been kept very quiet, because we don't want the word to get around until we have already started our operations in England. The competition, you know. Now, my brother—Harry Pinner—is managing director. He has asked me to find a good man to be business manager. I've heard a good deal about you and have decided that you're the man for me—although we're prepared to offer you only five hundred pounds a year to start.

Pycroft (*Amazed*). Five—five hundred pounds! But that's four times what Mawson's giving me.

Pinner. You're worth more, my boy. What do you say to my offer?

Pycroft. It's quite handsome, indeed, Mr. Pinner. But I must be frank. Mawson may not pay so handsomely, but it is a safe, secure company. I know so little about your company.

Pinner. Smart, smart. You are the very man for us. You are not to be talked over. I like that. Now, to answer your question, here's a hundred pounds for you, as an advance against your salary. That's security, isn't it?

Pycroft (*Firmly*). You have just hired yourself a business manager, Mr. Pinner. When shall I take over my duties?

Pinner. Be in Birmingham tomorrow at one. I have a note in my pocket which you will take to my brother, Harry Pinner. You will find him at this address, where the temporary offices of the company are located. He will explain your duties.

Pycroft. Really, sir, I hardly know how to express my gratitude.

Pinner. Not at all, my boy. But there are one or two small things—mere formalities—which much be arranged. You have a bit of paper beside you there. Kindly write upon it: "I am perfectly willing to act as the business manager of the Franco-Midland Hardware Company, Limited, at a minimum salary of five hundred pounds."

Sound. *Pen writing on paper.*

Pycroft (*Slowly*). "Minimum–salary, five–hundred–pounds." There you are.

Pinner. And one last thing. What do you intend to do about Mawson's?

Pycroft. I declare, I'd forgotten about them. I'll write and resign.

Pinner. Precisely what I don't want you to do. I had a row with Mawson's manager over you. I told him I was interested in you, and he was quite offensive, said that as he had hired you first, you'd no right to consider any other offer, no matter how much to your advantage. As a matter of fact, do you know what he said about you? "We picked Pycroft out of the gutter, and he's too grateful to us not to come to work here, no matter what you pay."

Pycroft. The impudence!

Pinner. Those were his very words. Don't

you think it would serve him right to give him no notice at all?

Pycroft. Imagine his talking about me like that—when I've never set eyes on him in my life. I shall certainly not write if you would rather I didn't.

Pinner. Good! That's a promise! Well, Mr. Pycroft, I'm delighted with our business transaction. We have a good man in you. Now don't forget to be in Birmingham tomorrow at one o'clock sharp and present this letter to my brother. He'll be expecting you. I must be off now, but we shall meet again.

Pycroft. Thank you, Mr. Pinner. I'm eternally grateful, you can be sure.

Pinner. Never you mind. *I'm* the one who is grateful. Goodbye now, and good luck. *(Fading)* May you have all the fortune that you deserve!

Music. *Lively theme, up and out.*

Watson. And was that the entire interview before you took your new position?

Pycroft. That is just about all that passed between us, as near as I can remember. You can imagine, Dr. Watson, how pleased I was at such an extraordinary bit of luck. I sat up half the night thinking about it, and the next day I was off to Birmingham. After settling in a hotel, I made my way straight to the address that had been given me.

Watson. And what sort of offices did you find?

Pycroft. That was the first thing that startled me. When I got to the building, I looked for the company name on the directory-board in the lobby, but it was not to be found.

Watson. How curious!

Pycroft. I stood for a moment with my heart in my boots, wondering whether the whole thing was an elaborate hoax,

when someone suddenly addressed me. I looked up, and there before me was a man very like the chap I had seen the night before. He was the same size, with the same voice, but he was clean-shaven, and his hair was of a lighter color. Clearly, the men were brothers. *(Fading)* If it hadn't been for the hair, one might have said they were twins.

Harry *(Fading on)*. Are you Mr. Hall Pycroft?

Pycroft. Yes, sir, I am.

Harry. I was expecting you, but you are a trifle before your time. I had a note from my brother this morning in which he sings your praises!

Pycroft. I was just looking for the offices when you came.

Harry. We have not put our name up yet, for we only secured these temporary premises last week. *(Fading)* Come up with me, and we'll talk the whole thing over.

Music. *Mysterious theme, in and under.*

Pycroft. I followed him to the top of a lofty staircase, and there, right under the roof, were two empty, dusty little rooms, uncurtained and uncarpeted. I had imagined a great office with shining tables and rows of clerks, such as I was used to, and I daresay I rather stared at the two rickety chairs and one little table which, with a ledger, made up the whole furniture.

Music. *Out.*

Harry *(Jovially)*. Come, Mr. Pycroft, don't be disheartened by humble appearances. Rome was not built in a day, and we have lots of money behind us, though we don't make much of a show with it. Pray sit down. From what my brother has written me of you, I know that you are the man we want. You may consider yourself definitely engaged.

Pycroft. What are my duties going to be, Mr. Pinner?

Harry. You will eventually manage the great depot in Paris, which will pour a flood of English crockery into the shops of a hundred and thirty-four agents in France. The purchases will be completed in a week. Meanwhile, you will remain here in Birmingham and make yourself useful.

Pycroft. How?

Harry. Here is a directory of Paris, with the trades listed after the names of the people. I want you to take it home with you and mark off all the hardware sellers, with their addresses. It would be of the greatest use to me to have them.

Pycroft. But surely, sir, there are classified lists available?

Harry. Not reliable ones. Their system is different from ours. Stick at it, and let me have the lists by Monday at twelve. If you continue to show zeal and intelligence, you will find us a good company. Good day, Mr. Pycroft.

Music. *In and under. Fades out.*

Pycroft. Well, gentlemen, what was I to think? The dingy offices—the lack of furniture—the absence of the company name upon the directory-board—all of these gave rise to my suspicions. And yet, Mr. Pinner had offered a good explanation for everything. Even the task he had set me to seemed reasonable, and so I gave it a try. All Sunday I was kept hard at work, and yet by Monday I had got only as far as the letter *H.* I went round to Mr. Pinner, found him in the same dismantled room, and was told to keep at it until Wednesday. On Wednesday it was still unfinished, so I hammered away until Friday—that is, yesterday. *(Fading)* Then I brought it round to Mr. Harry Pinner. *(Pause)*

Harry *(Fading on).* Thank you very much, Mr. Pycroft. I fear that I underrated the difficulty of the task. This list will be of very material assistance to me.

Pycroft. It took some time.

Harry. And now I want you to make a list of the furniture shops, for they all sell crockery.

Pycroft. Very good, sir, if that is what you want.

Harry. And you can come up tomorrow evening at seven and let me know how you are getting on. But don't overwork yourself, my boy. A couple of hours at a music hall in the evening would do you a world of good. *(Laughs evilly)* Yes, yes, Mr. Pycroft. Take your time. *(Fading)* There's no hurry. By all means, take your time.

Music. *Mysterious theme. Up and out.*

Pycroft. And that, Dr. Watson, is the whole story.

Watson. And you think there is some mystery in the business? It all sounds perfectly legitimate and straightforward to me.

Holmes. But that is because Mr. Pycroft neglected to tell you one interesting thing which he observed—a thing of a most peculiar nature.

Pycroft. By George, I did leave that out.

Watson. What is it, man?

Pycroft. As Harry Pinner discharged me last evening, he laughed—as I told you. And I saw that his second tooth upon the left-hand side had been very badly filled with gold.

Watson. And is that all? That doesn't sound like much to me.

Pycroft. You are quite right, Dr. Watson. There's much more to it. When I was speaking to the other chap in London—Mr. *Arthur* Pinner—I happened to notice that his same tooth was filled in the identical fashion. Of course you expect that two brothers will resemble each other, but not that they will have the same tooth filled in the same way. And then it suddenly occurred to me that the only differences in their appearances were such things as might be quickly altered with a razor and with dye. The things that *can't* be quickly changed—the voice, the figure, the teeth, the eyes—those were the same.

Holmes. An excellent observation, you will agree, Watson.

Watson. But if both men were the same, what is the meaning of it? Why had he sent you from London to Birmingham? Why had he gone there early to meet you? And why had he written a letter from himself to himself?

Pycroft. Those are the very questions I asked myself, Dr. Watson. And because I could not answer them, I went to the one man in all of England who could help me find the answers. That is precisely why I have called upon your good friend, Sherlock Holmes.

Music. *In, under, and out.*

Developing Comprehension Skills

1. What kind of work does Pycroft do? What company has hired him before Arthur Pinner arrives?

2. Where is the Pinner office located? Describe the office.

3. What task occupies Pycroft's time for several days after he is hired by Pinner?

4. What makes Pycroft so suspicious of Pinner that he goes to Sherlock Holmes for advice?

5. Contrast the characters of Holmes and Watson. Point out at least two differences.

6. Is Pycroft a believable character? Are his thoughts, words, and actions convincing? Support your evaluation with examples from this part of the play.

7. At the end of this part of the play, the characters realize that Pycroft has been given a useless job. They are puzzled about the reason. Can you suggest at least one possible reason why Pinner hired Pycroft?

Reading Literature: Drama

1. **Understanding a Narrator.** The **narrator** is a character who introduces or comments on the action. In this play, who is the narrator? How does he provide transitions between scenes? Why are his reactions and observations important to the audience?

2. **Analyzing Character Motivation.** Pycroft seems to be a careful and stable young man. Yet he accepts a position with a company he has never heard of from a man he has never met before. Why does he accept the position? At what point does he become nervous about his decision? What do his reactions tell about him?

3. **Recognizing Flashbacks.** A **flashback** is a scene or event that happened before the beginning of a story or play. During Pycroft's account in this first part of the play there are four flashbacks. Tell where each flashback begins and ends. What stage direction signals each one? What information do you get from each flashback?

4. **Examining Dialogue.** In the following lines of dialogue, what do the dashes suggest about the way Pycroft is speaking? What do they reveal about his frame of mind?

> **Pycroft.** Well, gentlemen, what was I to think? The dingy offices—the lack of furniture—the absence of the company name upon the directory-board—all of these gave rise to my suspicions.

Sherlock Holmes and the Stockbroker's Clerk: Part Two

You now have all the facts that Holmes has. Can you put them together in the same way he does? Continue to match wits with the great detective.

SIR ARTHUR CONAN DOYLE
Dramatized by Lewy Olfson

Watson. I confess that I found Mr. Pycroft's story interesting, but it was not until he mentioned the detail of the gold tooth that I perceived the mystery in the affair. Now, however, I could understand why Holmes had shown such enthusiasm for the case. The train had pulled into Birmingham Station just as Pycroft finished his narrative, and the three of us climbed down onto the platform. Both the young stockbroker's clerk and I turned upon Holmes with eager anticipation, anxious to know how he intended to proceed with the business.

Holmes (*Delightedly*). Rather fine, Watson, is it not? There are points in it which please me. I think you will agree with me that an interview with Mr. Arthur Harry Pinner—for we must call him by both names until we discover who he really is—in the temporary offices of the Franco-Midland Hardware Company,

Limited, would be a rather interesting experience for both of us.

Watson. But how can we manage it without his suspecting who we are?

Pycroft. Oh, easily enough. You can pretend to be two friends of mine who are in need of jobs. What could be more natural than that I should bring you both around to the managing director of my company?

Holmes. Quite so, quite so. I should like to have a look at the gentleman and see if I can make anything of his little game. I can't help but wonder, Mr. Pycroft, what it is about you that should have attracted him.

Watson. Shall we go right over to the offices now?

Pycroft. There is no use in that. He comes there only to see me, apparently, for the place is deserted up to the very hour he names.

Holmes. That is certainly suggestive of mischief.

Pycroft (*Suddenly*). I say! We are in luck. There he is ahead of us—the very man!

Watson. Which one? Where?

Pycroft. That one there, with his head lowered. He must have come down on the same train as we did.

Holmes. He's probably on his way to keep his appointment with you now, Mr. Pycroft. At least we will not be disappointed. I find myself quite anxious to have a good, long look at Mr. Arthur Harry Pinner.

Music. *Mysterious theme, in, under and out.*

Watson. The man Pycroft had pointed to was a smallish, well-dressed fellow, who seemed quite intent upon his own thoughts, for he never once looked up but went bustling along the streets with firm determination. Following him at a short distance, Holmes, Pycroft, and I never lost sight of him, and soon we found ourselves walking down the street of the company's offices. At the corner, there was a young urchin selling newspapers. (*Pause*)

Newsboy (*Off mike*). All the London papers here! Get your evening papers here!

Harry (*Off mike*). Here, boy. A *Standard*—and be quick about it! (*Pause*)

Watson. Pinner threw the boy a coin, and, clutching his newspaper tightly, he bustled off into the company's building, a worried look on his face. Following Pycroft's lead, we entered the same doorway and after climbing five flights of stairs, found ourselves outside a half-opened door, at which our client tapped. We entered a bare, unfurnished room such as had been described to us. At a single table sat the man whom we had seen in the street, with his evening paper spread out in front of him, and as he looked up, I saw an expression of grief, torment, and horror. His brow glistened with perspiration, his cheeks were dead white, his eyes glazed. He looked at his clerk as though he did not recognize him, so preoccupied was he with his own terrible thoughts.

Pycroft. You look ill, Mr. Pinner!

Harry (*Abstractedly, almost wildly*). Yes, I—I am not very well. Who are these gentlemen?

Pycroft. They are friends of mine, who are in need of work. I thought you might be able to make use of their experience in your enterprise.

Harry. Yes—yes—possibly, quite possibly. But I cannot talk about it now—I—please, please, leave me alone for a little bit. I—I must be alone.

Pycroft. You forget, Mr. Pinner, that I am here by appointment.

Harry. Appointment? Yes—yes, of course. I beg your pardon. You may wait here. You may all wait here. I must just slip away—if you will excuse me, I must go into the next room, only—only for a moment. *(Fading)* Excuse me—just for a moment. I—I must be alone—just for a moment.

Sound. *Door closing, off mike.*

Holmes. Is he trying to give us the slip?

Pycroft. It's impossible. There's no door in that second room except the one he entered by. It's an inside room—not so much as a window in it.

Holmes. Is it furnished?

Pycroft. It wasn't yesterday.

Watson. Then what on earth can he be doing in there? Probably went in merely to recover his composure. He did seem awfully upset. I say—do you suppose he suspects we are detectives? Is that what's upset him?

Holmes. No. He was already upset when we came in.

Sound. *Moans off mike.*

Pycroft. What's that?

Holmes. It's Pinner. See what he's up to.

Sound. *Footsteps running, then door being opened.*

Pycroft. Good grief!

Holmes. He's—he's hanged himself. How is he, Watson?

Watson. Dead, by Jove. He's made a good job of it. Dead as a doornail.

Holmes *(Regretfully).* I suppose we ought to call the police in. And yet I confess that I'd like to give them a complete case when they come.

Pycroft. It's a blessed mystery to me. Whatever did he want to bring me all the way up here for, when he—

Holmes *(Interrupting).* Pooh! All that is clear enough. It is just this last sudden move that has me confused.

Watson *(Incredulous).* You understand the rest, then? I must confess that I am out of my depth.

Holmes. Surely if you consider the events at first, they can only point to one conclusion. The whole thing hinges upon two points. The first is that he made Pycroft write a declaration by which he entered the services of this preposterous company. Do you not see how very suggestive it is?

Watson. No, I'm afraid I don't.

Holmes. Why did they want him to do it? It's not a usual business practice, you know. The only reason is that they were anxious to obtain a specimen of our young friend's handwriting.

Pycroft. But why should they need my handwriting?

Holmes. There can be only one adequate reason. Someone wished to learn to imitate it. And for the explanation of why, we must consider the second point: that you were specifically requested not to resign your position at Mawson's but to leave the manager there under the expectation that Mr. Hall Pycroft, whom he had never seen, was about to enter the office upon the next Monday morning.

Pycroft. Of course! What a blind fool I've been!

Holmes. Suppose that someone turned up in your place, writing in a hand identical to that in which your letter of application was written. How easy it would be for him to pass himself off as you. Of course, it was of the utmost importance to persuade you to accept the fake job offer, for it was essential that an impostor go to Mawson's in your place. That is why you were given the magnificent sum of a hundred pounds in advance; they wanted to make sure of you. And, of course, they very cleverly arranged for you to leave London, so that there would be no chance of your showing up at Mawson's on any pretext.

Pycroft. But why should this man pretend to have been his brother?

Holmes. That is pretty clear, also. There are evidently only two of them in on the scheme—whatever scheme it is. The other is impersonating you at the office. This one acted as your engager and then found it was wiser to pretend to be your Birmingham employer as well, rather than admit a third person into the plot. He changed his appearance and passed himself off as his own brother. But for the happy accident of the gold tooth, he would have succeeded.

Pycroft. But what scheme were they working? Why should one of them want to gain entrance to Mawson's under false pretenses?

Watson. And why should the other hang himself the minute we walk into the room?

Holmes. That is what I do not yet understand. (*Suddenly*) The paper! Of course! I should have thought of it before. The secret must lie there.

Pycroft. Here is the newspaper Pinner was reading. What do you make of it?

Sound. *Rustling newspaper pages.*

Holmes. It's an early edition of the *Evening Standard.* Let me see. Hmm . . . hmm. Aha, here it is. Look at this, Watson, and tell us what you think.

Watson. Ah! Listen to the headline of this story. "Murder at Mawson & Williams. Gigantic Robbery Attempted. Capture of the Criminal."

Pycroft. I begin to understand.

Holmes. By pretending to be you, the criminal managed to gain access to the safe. I gather from the newspaper article that he was discovered by a guard, whom he killed. But fortunately, the police caught him in time. And this fellow, when he learned that the jig was up, decided to kill himself.

Watson. Yes, Holmes, listen to this. "The criminal is lodged in Holloway Gaol.[1] His brother, however, who usually works with him, has not appeared in this job as far as we can presently ascertain, although the police are making energetic inquiries as to his whereabouts."

---

1. **Gaol** (jāl)–British spelling of *jail*.

Holmes. Well, we may save the police some little trouble in that direction.

Pycroft. It's ironic, isn't it? To think that this fellow really had a brother in London after all!

Watson. I must congratulate you, Holmes, on your splendid deductions.

Holmes. You could have done the same, Watson.

Watson. I disagree. You have pieced the thing together with uncanny skill. I don't know how you do it. It's amazing!

Holmes. On the contrary. It's elementary, my dear Watson. Elementary!

Music. *Full to finish.*

Sir Arthur Conan Doyle *(1859–1930)* was born in Scotland. He attended Edinburgh University and spent five years studying medicine. After leaving the university, he set up his medical practice in England. While waiting for patients, Doyle created Sherlock Holmes, a "scientific" detective who was modeled after an actual professor. Doyle's stories became so popular that he gave up his medical career to devote his time to writing.

Developing Comprehension Skills

1. Describe the expression on Pinner's face as Holmes, Watson, and Pycroft enter the office.

2. What has happened to Pinner's brother in the robbery attempt?

3. Pinner is so terrified that he hangs himself. Of what is he afraid?

4. Why had Arthur Pinner hired Hall Pycroft? Explain the plan devised by Pinner and his brother.

5. Dr. Watson calls Sherlock Holmes's skill in solving the case "uncanny" and "amazing." Holmes, on the other hand, dismisses the solution as "elementary." With whom do you agree, Watson or Holmes? To answer, consider questions such as these: Would every careful observer have come to the same conclusion as Holmes? How unusual is Holmes's ability to notice details? his ability to connect details logically? Are these skills beyond most people's powers?

6. The writer of this radio play tries to create suspense by withholding the solution until the end while providing clues throughout the play. Evaluate the suspense in the play. Think about your own reactions. Were you worried about any character's safety? Were you nervous at Pinner's look of terror? Were you puzzled by the strange events?

Reading Literature: Drama

1. **Analyzing Plot.** This play is a story within a story. The writer uses flashbacks of past events to help the audience understand the

present. Which of these events take place before the present action?

> Pycroft tells his story to Watson.
>
> Pinner visits Pycroft at Pycroft's room.
>
> Pycroft goes to Birmingham and begins to work for Pinner.
>
> Pycroft notices Pinner's gold tooth.
>
> Holmes, Watson, and Pycroft take the train to Birmingham.
>
> Pinner's brother attempts to rob Mawson's.

2. **Recognizing Scenes.** A new scene begins each time the action in a play shifts to a new place or time. In this radio play, how do you know when a scene changes? How many scenes are there in each part?

3. **Understanding Irony.** As you know, **irony** is a contrast between what is expected and what actually exists or happens. Pycroft points out an irony in this play when he comments, "It's ironic, isn't it? To think that this fellow really had a brother in London after all!" Explain why this statement is ironic. To do so, consider why Pycroft becomes suspicious of Pinner. At the beginning of Part Two of the play, does Pycroft believe that Pinner really has a brother?

4. **Interpreting Stage Directions.** Find each of these stage directions for the sound-effects person in Part Two. Explain which character each sound is related to and what the character is doing.

   a. *Sound. Door closing, off mike.*
   b. *Sound. Moans off mike.*
   c. *Sound. Footsteps running, then door being opened.*

5. **Examining Descriptions.** Because a radio play is only heard and not seen, the writer must include descriptions so the audience can picture the characters, action, and setting. Reread the long passages spoken by Watson on page 600. What do you learn about Pinner from each passage? What details do you learn about action and setting?

Developing Vocabulary Skills

Recognizing Formal and Informal English. To show that Holmes and Watson are members of the British upper class of the late 1800's, the writer usually has them use formal English. However, the dialogue in *Sherlock Holmes and the Stockbroker's Clerk* also includes informal English. Read the following sentences from the play. If the sentence is informal English, write the word or phrase that makes it informal. Explain any idioms or slang expressions. If the sentence is formal English, write *formal*. Then, rewrite the formal sentences in informal English. Use slang or an idiom in each sentence you rewrite.

1. After telling my bride about the errand I was about to undertake, I donned my greatcoat and went out the door, to find Holmes standing on my step, breathing in the fresh June air.

2. I wonder how on earth the fellow knows me.

3. Stick at it, and let me have the lists by Monday at twelve.

4. By George, I did leave that out.

5. Both the young stockbroker's clerk and I turned upon Holmes with eager anticipa-

tion, anxious to know how he intended to proceed with the business.

6. The man Pycroft had pointed to was a smallish, well-dressed fellow, who seemed quite intent upon his own thoughts, for he never once looked up but went bustling along the streets with firm determination.

7. Is he trying to give us the slip?

8. Dead, by Jove. He's made a good job of it. Dead as a doornail.

Developing Skills in Study and Research

Researching Biography. Read an article about Sir Arthur Conan Doyle, the creator of Sherlock Holmes, in an encyclopedia or a biographical reference book. Answer these questions.

1. How many stories about Sherlock Holmes did Arthur Conan Doyle write? how many novels?

2. Was Doyle's first major success a short story or a novel?

3. Did he write anything else?

4. How successful was he as a medical doctor?

Developing Skills in Speaking and Listening

Presenting a Dialogue. Work with a partner to present one of the following dialogues from *Sherlock Holmes and the Stockbroker's Clerk:* the dialogue between Holmes and Watson on pages 588–590 or the dialogue between Pinner and Pycroft on pages 592-594. Practice reading the lines with appropriate expression for each character. Pay special attention to any stage directions. Discuss with your partner your character's personality and mood. Practice creating a living, believable character. Then present your dialogue to a small group. If possible, read from the back of the room or from behind a screen so your audience can experience your reading as a radio play. Ask members of your audience to evaluate your performance.

Developing Writing Skills

1. **Writing a Scene.** This radio play is based on a short story by Arthur Conan Doyle. Choose a short story from Chapter One of this book and rewrite one scene from it as a scene in a radio play. Write dialogue for the characters and include sound effects and stage directions.

   Prewriting. Choose a short story from Chapter One that lends itself to adaptation as a radio play. The most appropriate stories are those that have many conversations between characters, such as "After Twenty Years," "A Man Who Had No Eyes," "The Weapon," and "Road to the Isles." Decide on the scene you will rewrite, and identify the characters. Plan how you can convey all the action through dialogue and sound effects. Figure out the stage directions you will need. Make notes on your ideas.

   Drafting. Write dialogue for the characters. You may be able to take some of the dialogue directly from the story. Be sure to indicate action and motives through the characters' words. Include sound effects and stage directions to make the actions seem real.

   Revising and Sharing. Ask a classmate to read your scene. Does the dialogue convey the action? Does the dialogue suggest the characters' motives? Get together with several classmates and read your scenes aloud.

2. **Analyzing Structure.** *Sherlock Holmes and the Stockbroker's Clerk* has several short scenes set in different places and times. To be sure that the audience knows where each scene takes place, the writer provides clear transitions, or shifts, from one scene to the next. Write one paragraph explaining how the writer makes transitions in this play. Follow the steps in the process of writing as you go about this assignment. For further help, see the Guidelines for the Process of Writing beginning on page 654 of the handbook.

A Connecticut Yankee in King Arthur's Court

In this play, the Connecticut Yankee goes back in time to Camelot, the legendary site of King Arthur's court, and tries to modernize sixth-century England. Read to see how successful he is.

MARK TWAIN
Dramatized by Lewy Olfson

CHARACTERS

Connecticut Yankee
Worker
Clarence
King Arthur
Merlin

Demoiselle Alisande de la Carteloise
  (dem' wə zel' al'ə sänd' də lä kär' tel waz')
First Woman
Second Woman
First Man
Second Man

Music. *Pastoral theme, in and under.*

Connecticut Yankee (*Elderly, as for all narrations*). I am an American, born and reared in Hartford, Connecticut. So, I am a Yankee of the Yankees—and practical. When I was little more than a lad, I went over to the great arms factory and learned my real trade; learned all there was to it. Why, I could make anything a body'd want—anything in the world. It didn't make any difference what; and if there wasn't any new-fangled way to make a thing quickly, I could invent one—and do it as easy as rolling off a log. I became head superintendent—had a couple of thousand men under me. Now with all those men, you can see how easy it would be to fall into an argument. Well, one day. . .

Music. *Reminiscent theme, in and under.*

Sound. *Factory noises softly in background.*

Conn. Yankee (*Younger than before, as for all dialogue sequences*). Is that so, now?

Well, sir, it just so happens that there *was* a total eclipse of the sun in the sixth century—matter of fact, it was on the twenty-first of June, in the year A.D. 528, and began at three minutes after twelve noon.

Worker. Now look here, just because you're the foreman of this plant doesn't mean that you know everything. Ah, the trouble with you thick-headed types is that you're sure you *do* know everything.

Conn. Yankee. And just who are you calling thick-headed, sir?

Worker. Just you, sir.

Conn. Yankee. Is that right, now? Well, let me tell you something. . .

Sound. *Angry voices fade off mike.*

Conn. Yankee (*Older voice*). Well, we argued and argued, and pretty soon we were taking off our shirts for a real fight. Everything was going along pretty smoothly, until he hit me a left under the chin that I didn't expect. The next thing I knew, I was floating through space. . .

Music. *Eerie, hypnotic dream theme, in and under.*

Sound. *Birds twittering happily.*

Clarence (*A young boy*). Faith, sir, be ye awake?

Conn. Yankee (*Yawning*). Wha . . . Hmmm? (*Alarmed*) Great green Johosophat! Who are you?

Clarence. Clarence is my name. I be a page, sir.

Conn. Yankee. A page? A little thing like you a page? Go 'long, you aren't more than a paragraph. Hey, what is this place anyway? Where am I? Bridgeport?[1]

Clarence. Camelot. You're in prison, sir.

Conn. Yankee. Prison! Then what are you doing all dressed up like you were going to a fancy ball?

Clarence. Marry,[2] sir, this is the latest thing for a page.

Conn. Yankee (*Suspiciously*). What's the date? This isn't April first, is it?

Clarence. No, sir. It's the twentieth of June, 528.

Conn. Yankee. Five twenty . . . look here. Is this a circus, maybe, or a lunatic asylum?

Clarence. No, sir, in faith it isn't.

Conn. Yankee. Well, then, either I am out of my mind, or something awful just happened. Now tell me, honest and true, where am I?

Clarence (*Simply*). Marry, sir, 'tis easy. You are in King Arthur's Court!

Music. *Delightful theme, in and under.*

---

1. **Bridgeport**—a city in Connecticut.
2. **Marry**—an exclamation of surprise used in Middle Ages.

A Connecticut Yankee in King Arthur's Court   609

Conn. Yankee (*Older voice*). Well, sir, there never was a man more dumbfounded than I was. I just couldn't get used to the idea. That's why, when I awoke again, I thought the whole thing a dream and, when I saw that page boy standing before me, I was more amazed than ever.

Clarence. Sir! Sir! Wake up!

Conn. Yankee. What? You here yet? Go along with the rest of the dream. Scat!

Clarence. Prithee, what dream?

Conn. Yankee. What dream? Why the dream that I am in Arthur's Court and that I talk to you, who are nothing but a work of the imagination.

Clarence. Indeed! And is it a dream that you're to be burned at the stake tomorrow? Answer me that!

Conn. Yankee (*Astounded*). What?

Clarence. Aye, by the command of the King. Merlin suggested it!

Conn. Yankee (*Nervously*). Now, Clarence, my boy, you're the only friend I've got. You must help me devise some way to escape from this place.

Clarence. Verily, sir, it is impossible. The corridors are filled with guards, and worse than that, Merlin has woven a spell about this dungeon, and there bides not a man in this kingdom who would dare attempt to escape!

Conn. Yankee. Merlin hath wrought a spell. *Merlin*, forsooth! That cheap old humbug, that maundering old fake. (*Laughs*)

Clarence (*Frightened*). Oh beware! Any moment these walls may crumble upon us if you say such things!

Conn. Yankee. Do you know why I laughed? Because I'm a magician myself. Why, I knew Merlin seven hundred years ago, and he doesn't amount to shucks as a magician, not next to me! Oh, he's all right for parlor magic and such, but he never learned the rudiments of the big stuff. Now listen to me. I want you to do me a favor; you said today is June twentieth, didn't you? Well, get word to the King that I am a magician myself, and if he dares to try burning me tomorrow, I will blot out the sun at noon, and it shall never shine again. The fruits of the earth shall rot for lack of light, and the peoples of the earth shall die. Do you understand?

Music. *Mischievous theme, in and under.*

Conn. Yankee (*Older voice*). Well, the King believed that I was a magician, right enough. But that old fake, Merlin, persuaded him that I was a humbug. And so, at twelve the next day, I found myself tied to a stake in the middle of the courtyard. That didn't bother me, though; I knew that in about a minute and a half, I could expect a total eclipse of the sun.

Sound. *Clamor of crowd in background.*

Conn. Yankee (*Older voice*). Sure enough, just as they were about to light the pile of wood at my feet, I saw the skies darken slightly. Majestically, I raised my arm, pointing at the sun. Then everyone noticed the darkness. Poor fools, they thought I was really going through with my threat. Suddenly, the King rose, and shouted. . .

Arthur (*Slightly off mike*). Stop the proceedings. I forbid the lighting of the stake!

Merlin (*An old, crackling voice*). But Your Majesty. . .

Arthur. Be quiet, Merlin. I, Arthur, King of England, command silence. But look you, the skies grow darker. (*Pleading*) Stranger, I am sorry! I beg of you: do not extinguish the sun!

Conn. Yankee. Stay where you are, all. If any man moves—even the King—before I give him leave, I will blast him with thunder and lightning.

Arthur. Be merciful, fair sir, and essay this peril no further, lest disaster follow. Name any terms, reverend sir, even to the halving of my Kingdom; but banish this calamity! Spare the sun!

Conn. Yankee (*Casually*). Give me time to consider.

Arthur. How long, oh, how long? Be merciful; look, it groweth darker, moment by moment. Prithee, how long?

Conn. Yankee. Oh, not long. Maybe an hour. For a lesson, I will let this darkness proceed and spread night in the world; but, whether or not I will blot out the sun for good shall rest with you. These are the terms: you shall remain King over all your dominions, but you shall appoint me your perpetual minister and executive, so that I'll be The Boss, and give me as payment, one percent of all revenue I raise for the state. Is it satisfactory?

Arthur. Away with his bonds, and set him free! And show him homage, high and low, rich and poor, for he is a great wiz-

Merlin (Murwyn Vye) and King Arthur (Sir Cedric Hardwicke). Photographs are from the 1949 Paramount Pictures film *A Connecticut Yankee in King Arthur's Court.* Culver Pictures, New York City.

ard and magician. Now, sir, banish, if you will, this awful night.

Conn. Yankee (*To himself*). Ah, at last the eclipse is total. Now is the time. (*Aloud majestically*) Let the enchantment dissolve and pass harmless away!

Sound. *Tumultuous cheers in background.*

Arthur (*Proclaiming*). Blessings upon thee, oh Great Wizard. I, Arthur, welcome thee to Camelot as my right-hand man. And from this day henceforward, shall thy name be called . . . The Boss!

Sound. *Crowd cheers.*

Arthur (*Shouting*). Make way! Make way! Make way for The Boss!

Music. *Fanfare into royal theme, in and under.*

Conn. Yankee (*Older voice*). Well that—miracle, shall we call it?—fixed things up as right as right could be. Soon news of it traveled throughout the Kingdom, and everybody knew what a wonderful person I was. Of course, I couldn't rest on my laurels. The Kingdom would get suspicious; besides, I was getting restless. I wanted some new glories. And so I began—inventing things.

Music. *Out.*

Conn. Yankee. Look, Your Majesty. My newest invention.

Arthur. It is a wondrous looking thing, but—but what is it?

Conn. Yankee. It's an artificial candle. It's cheaper to manufacture—I've already started a factory—and it'll give a hundred times the light that oil lamps give.

Arthur (*With awe*). Indeed! And what do you call your new miracle?

Conn. Yankee. I've given it the name . . . electric light bulb!

Music. *Low-pitched chord.*

Arthur. Another invention, Sir Boss?

Conn. Yankee. Yes. A collapsible sunshade—it'll protect you from rain, too. And when not in use, it can double as a walking-stick. I've got a factory producing twenty thousand of them a day. Do you like it?

Arthur (*In wonder*). Verily, I do. And what do you plan to call this wonderful device?

Conn. Yankee. How about—umbrella?

Music. *Higher chord.*

Conn. Yankee. Yes, Your Majesty, a new invention. It's a box that is capable of transfixing images of real things in miniature on paper. I call it a camera.

Music. *Higher chord.*

Conn. Yankee. It's a solution with which to get your skin much cleaner than with ordinary water. I plan to name it . . . soap.

Music. *Higher chord.*

Conn. Yankee. Yes, Your Majesty, I've just invented shoe polish. *(Pause)* That's right, Sire, it's my newest discovery: whipped cream. *(Pause)* Right again, King Arthur. Another invention: this one's the printing press.

Music. *A succession of chords mounting to a climax, then, fanfare.*

Arthur. I have sent for you, Sir Boss, to ask if you would like an adventure.

Conn. Yankee. An . . . an adventure?

Arthur. Yes. You must be tired of staying here in Camelot year after year, just working your humdrum miracles, so I thought—or, rather, Merlin thought—that you might like to go off on an adventure.

Conn. Yankee. Merlin did, did he?

Merlin. Yes, I did, did I.

Conn. Yankee. I'm awfully sorry, Sire, but much as I'd like to—well, I just couldn't. The factories have been going only a few months, and the Sunday schools have been in operation barely a week.

Merlin. You aren't afraid that I might get the upper hand while you're away, are you?

Conn. Yankee *(Not quite convincing)*. Of course not. It's just that—well, what adventure could I go on?

Arthur. Ah, that's all settled. This lady that you see on my right has just come to Camelot with a marvelous tale. It seems that her mistress is a captive in a vast and gloomy castle, along with forty-three other young and beautiful girls.

Alisande *(A sweet, innocent voice)*. Forty-four, an it please you, Sire.

Arthur. Ah yes; forty-*four* young ladies. The master of this castle is a giant, with four arms and one eye—in the center of his forehead. Your adventure is simply this: find the Princess and her ladies! Doesn't it sound exciting? I wish that I could go with you, but Guinevere would never hear of it. Oh, you must be thrilled!

Conn. Yankee *(Downheartedly)*. Yes, yes, Sire. Thrilled. I can hardly control myself. *(Weakly, limply)* Three cheers for adventure.

Music. *Pastoral theme, in and under.*

Sound. *Horses trotting leisurely on a dirt road.*

Conn. Yankee. I still don't understand why you insist upon accompanying me on this fool's errand, young lady.

Alisande. How else then should you find the castle, Sir Boss?

Conn. Yankee. Oh come, come; you don't mean to say that there really *is* such a place. Your name, please?

Alisande. I am called the Demoiselle Ali-

Alisande (Rhonda Fleming) with Connecticut Yankee (Bing Crosby). Culver Pictures, New York City.

sande de la Carteloise, if it please you.

Conn. Yankee. Now, Sandy—I'll call you that, for it's easier—have you brought any letters, any documents, any proofs that you are trustworthy and truthful?

Alisande. Of a surety, no; and wherefore should I? Have I not a tongue, and cannot I say all that by myself?

Conn. Yankee. But your saying it and someone else's saying it are different.

Alisande. Different? How might that be? I fear me I do not understand.

Conn. Yankee. Not understand? Can't you see the difference between you—why in Heaven's name do you look so innocent and idiotic?

Alisande (*Innocently*). I? In truth I know not, but it were the will of God.

Conn. Yankee. Oh, for the love of Heaven! (*Regaining his calm*) Now as to this castle—where is it?

Alisande. Oh, as to that, it lieth in a far country, many leagues away.

Conn. Yankee. Never mind the distance;

whereabout does the castle lie, in what direction?

Alisande. Ah, please you sir, it hath no direction from here, by reason that the road lieth not straight but turneth evermore.

Conn. Yankee. But have you not a map—a good map?

Alisande *(Puzzled).* Is that peradventure[3] the manner of thing which of late the unbelievers have brought from over the great seas, which being boiled in oil, *(Fading)* and an onion and salt added thereto, doth . . .

Music. *Pleasant theme, in and under.*

Conn. Yankee *(Older voice).* Ah, I knew right then that the poor girl was a liar from the word *Go,* and was only stalling for time. And here was I, a respectable Wizard of the Court of King Arthur, off gallivanting around the countryside with a beautiful young demoiselle named Sandy. Why, it was improper! It was indecent! It was scandalous! Especially since I was engaged to a telephone operator from East Hartford, Connecticut, named Kitty Flanagan. *(Sighs)* Ah, it was doubtful that I'd ever see her again or ever call her on the telephone, with a "Hello, Central."[4] At first, I did think that there might be some chance of my returning to the nineteenth century— but as time went on, I realized that such would never be the case. And so, after much wandering around the countryside, I finally decided that it was time that Sandy and I were married. Therefore, we returned briefly to Camelot.

Music. *Wedding March, in and under.*

Note. *The next six speeches overlap each other in sequence, in a montage effect.*

Arthur. Good health to you both! Good health and long life!

Clarence. Congratulations, Sir Boss.

First Woman. Long live Sir Boss and Lady Alisande!

First Man. The best of luck in the world to you both.

Second Woman. My heartiest congratulations and best wishes!

Second Man. Long live the happy bride and groom!

Music. *Wedding March, in and under.*

Conn. Yankee *(Older voice).* Although the first few months of our marriage were happy ones, in my dreams I still wandered thirteen centuries away. I could not get the face of that telephone operator—the one that I had been engaged to in Hartford—out of my mind. Night after night, I would toss upon my pillow

---

3. **peradventure**–perhaps; word not used in modern English.

4. **Central**–term used to address an operator at telephone switchboard.

and whisper fitfully in my sleep: *(Whispering)* Hello, Central! Hello, Central! Hello, Central! *(Pause)* In a little more than a year, Sandy presented me with a child, and, with great magnanimity, she saddled that cry of mine, uttered in my sleep, upon our little daughter, believing it to be the name of some lost darling of mine. It touched me to tears, and it nearly knocked me off my feet, too, when she smiled up at my face and said:

Alisande. The name of one who was dear to thee is here preserved, here made holy, and the music of it will abide always in our ears. Now thou'lt kiss me, as knowing the name I have given the child.

Conn. Yankee. Yes, I know, sweetheart— how dear and good it is of you, too! But I want to hear these lips of yours, which are also mine, utter it first. Then its music will be complete.

Alisande *(With deep feeling)*. I have called our baby . . . Hello-Central!

Music. *Lively theme, in and under.*

Conn. Yankee *(Older voice)*. After a year and a half of traipsing around the countryside in search of Sandy's mythical Princess, we returned once more to the Court of King Arthur. At first, I was worried about what I could tell His Majesty, but Sandy fixed that up just fine. She had lied me into the mess. Now, she lied me out again.

Music. *Lighthearted theme, in and under.*

Alisande. Yes, Your Majesty, we *did* find the forty-four maidens—*and* the Princess. But what do you think? They had been turned to swine! So we drove them back to the Kingdom from which they originally came, and the Sorcerer Glacklick turned them back into fair damsels.

Arthur. But why couldn't you turn them back into humans yourself, Sir Boss?

Conn. Yankee. Why, er . . . uh. . . .

Alisande *(Aghast)*. Surely you wouldn't have someone as mighty as The Boss associate with swine, Your Majesty?

Music. *Delightful theme, in and under.*

Conn. Yankee *(Older voice)*. Time marched on, and, I am pleased to say, England was altered. I had eradicated slavery, knight-errantry, serfdom, and ignorance. I had established schools everywhere and even colleges. Baseball was the national pastime—King Arthur was my prize shortstop! A number of pretty good newspapers were in operation, and I even had established a weekly magazine. Only one thing troubled me; that was Merlin. He seemed jealous and was always slinking around in corners, whispering to his friends in low tones, and sneering whenever I passed. No matter, though, I thought; I had more important business on my mind. Then one day . . .

Music. *Out.*

Alisande (*Breathless*). Sir! Sir Boss! Come quickly!

Conn. Yankee (*Kindly*). Easy, darling, easy. What is it?

Alisande. Hello-Central. She's sick—the doctor says it's mem . . . membraneous croup. I don't know what that is—it's a word he learned in one of your colleges. But I'm frightened!

Conn. Yankee (*Calling out*). Clarence! Fetch me my staff of physicians! And hurry!

Music. *Urgent theme, in and under.*

Conn. Yankee (*Older voice*). The doctors said we must take the child away if we would coax her back to health and strength again. And she must have sea air. Quickly, I had a yacht outfitted, and Sandy, the baby, and I took off for a cruise on the Mediterranean. I left Clarence in charge of things while I was away, and for three months I did not set foot on English soil.

Music. *Calm theme, in and under.*

Conn. Yankee (*Older voice; seriously, urgently*). The next time I saw Camelot, I knew at once that something was amiss. As I approached the gates of the Castle, Clarence ran out to greet me and, by the worried expression on his face, I knew that there was trouble.

Clarence (*Breathless*). Sir Boss, at last you have come!

Clarence, the page (William Bendix) and Connecticut Yankee (Bing Crosby). Phototeque, New York City.

Conn. Yankee. What is it, Clarence? Speak!

Clarence. It was a plot—all of it—all Merlin's idea. As soon as your sails were out of the harbor, he began a revolution.

Conn. Yankee (*Numb with shock*). A—revo . . . lution?

Clarence. He brought back slavery, nobility—everything that you worked for years to remove. The people were only too ready for things to go back to their old state. It was no good for you to try to change them.

Conn. Yankee (*Heartbroken*). My dreams . . . my dreams of a republic . . . all gone, all smashed. What of the King?

Clarence. Dead. It is no use, I say. No use at all!

Conn. Yankee (*Determined*). Come, Clarence. There is work to do.

Clarence. Work? Where?

Conn. Yankee. We must destroy the schools, the factories, the colleges, lest they fall into Merlin's hands. We must destroy them; else, they destroy England.

Music. *Dramatic theme, in and under.*

Sound. *Explosions in the background.*

Conn. Yankee (*Bitterly*). Look at them, Clarence. Factories, schools, everything—blown to smithereens. And by my own hand; that's the irony of it.

Clarence. The work of a lifetime gone, in one fell swoop. What took you three-and-thirty years to build, destroyed in three-and-thirty minutes.

Conn. Yankee. It was the only way. I knew it would come to this, I think; yes, I knew it all along. That's why I had the dynamite charges set under all the buildings as soon as they were completed—in preparation for an event such as this.

England simply wasn't ready for me, that's all.

Clarence. But it's not right, it's not fair.

Conn. Yankee. There can be no talk of right and fair. Go; see to the destruction of the newspaper office.

Clarence. The newspaper office? That too?

Conn. Yankee. That too. Go. I'll follow you in a moment.

Music. *Tense theme, in and under.*

Conn. Yankee (*To himself*). Just these last power lines to cut, and then it's finished. There . . . and . . . (*Exerting pressure*) . . . ugh! There! Now everything's done that must be done.

Merlin. Not everything, Sir Boss.

Conn. Yankee (*Surprised*). Wha . . . ? Who spoke? Merlin!

Merlin (*Maliciously*). Aye, Merlin. You see, Sir Boss, I win after all. I still have the upper hand here; I shall always have the upper hand here.

Conn. Yankee. Not as long as I am alive.

Merlin. Just so; and that is the one task that remains in the destruction of your Empire. I will not try magic with you; we understand each other too well for that. I shall only use—this dagger!

Conn. Yankee. Wha . . . ? Aggh!

Sound. *Body falling.*

Merlin. There now, Sir Boss! I, Merlin, am once again triumphant.

Alisande (*Fading on*). Husband, Clarence told me I might find you here . . . What's this? Merlin! Where is Sir Boss? (*Pause*) Stabbed!

Merlin. He's unconscious; aye, in my power at last!

Alisande (*Sobbing*). Husband!

Merlin. It is now *my* turn to work an enchantment—an enchantment to send Sir Boss back to wherever he came from. (*Calling aloud*) Thaglitch! Eerandabar! Sophoclus! Sophoclee!

Conn. Yankee (*A weird, echoing quality in his voice*). Goodbye, Alisande! Goodbye, Alisande! Goodbyyyyye, Aaaal-liiiiisaaaaaande!

Music. *Rapid succession of ascending chords.*

Sound. *Murmur of bewildered factory workers.*

Conn. Yankee (*Coming out of a coma*). Alisande! Alisande!

Worker (*Bewildered*). Alisande? Hey, who's Alisande? Come on, Boss, wake up. I didn't mean to hit you so hard, honest!

Conn. Yankee. Clarence . . . Merlin . . . eclipse.

Worker. Yeah, the eclipse, Boss. You were right about that. Now wake up, Boss. (*Pleading*) Please!

Conn. Yankee. Where . . . where am I?

Worker. You're in the factory, Boss. I was afraid you were never going to come around.

Conn. Yankee. Huh? What? You're sure this isn't Camelot?

Worker. It's the factory, the factory. Where did you think you were?

Conn. Yankee. Why in . . . oh, never mind. You'd probably never believe me, even if I told you. Besides, it was all just a dream.

Merlin (*Eerie and distant, speaking through miles and centuries*). It was the only way, Sir Boss. The only way.

Conn. Yankee (*Bewildered*). That voice. How can it be? It was only a dream. (*Pause*) Or . . . was it?

Music. *Full to finish.*

Developing Comprehension Skills

1. What causes the Connecticut Yankee to go back to A.D. 528 in England?

2. How does the Yankee escape from being burned at the stake in Camelot?

3. Name three inventions that the Yankee introduces into Arthur's kingdom.

4. Why does the Yankee distrust Merlin? Why does Merlin dislike the Yankee?

5. Explain how the Yankee's daughter comes to be called Hello-Central.

6. Why does the Yankee destroy all that he has created in England?

7. Assume that the Yankee can actually get back to sixth-century England. Does he behave realistically? Does he do and say what you would expect a modern person to do and say in such circumstances? Are the things he does, such as inventing a light bulb, really possible? Explain your answers.

Reading Literature: Drama

1. **Examining Differences in Dialogue.** This play uses dialogue to show differences in characters and time periods. How does the Yankee's style of speech differ from that of the characters he finds in Camelot? Give examples of both styles from the early part of the play. Find an example in the play of the Yankee talking in the same way the people of Camelot speak. Why does he use the older form of speech at this point?

2. **Evaluating Dramatic Technique.** Look back at the stage directions for times when music is used. Notice that different musical themes, described in ways such as "delightful" and "mischievous" are used. The musical themes reflect what is taking place in the play. Below are three types of musical themes used. Find an example of each one and explain what has just taken place, or is taking place, in the play.

   a. mischievous theme
   b. royal theme
   c. urgent theme

3. **Understanding Conflict.** An **external conflict** is a struggle between a character and an outside force. The Yankee's major external conflict is with Merlin. This conflict results in several struggles between the two characters. What are two of these struggles? How is each resolved?

4. **Identifying Theme.** Although this play is more humorous than serious, it still conveys a theme, or message, about life. In fact, like most other pieces of literature, it conveys several themes. One theme involves the results of ignorance and prejudice. Another concerns social change and how people react to it. A third theme may be the power of some inventions. Think about the play. State one theme that seems clear to you. Point out events or details in the play that develop that theme.

5. **Recognizing Fantasy.** This play contains elements of fantasy, or make-believe. In a fantasy, characters are involved in events that are too far-fetched to be realistic. Name two impossible events that take place in this play.

6. **Analyzing Humor.** In this play, humor arises from the clash of modern and medieval cultures. Find two examples of humor-

Tragedy and Comedy, 1951–52, JACOB LAWRENCE. Seattle Art Museum. Photograph by Paul Macapia.

ous situations that are created when one culture confronts the reality of the other culture. For example, what is the Yankee's reaction when Arthur invites him to rescue ladies from a giant? How do Arthur's feelings contrast with the Yankee's?

7. **Explaining Time Relationships.** This play takes place in three time periods: the present time when the narrator speaks; the time of the events in the factory; and the time of the events in sixth-century England. What

is the function of the narrator? What contrasts are there between the time periods in the factory and in sixth-century England? How are time periods mixed during the events at King Arthur's Camelot?

Developing Vocabulary Skills

Recognizing Levels of Language. Decide whether each of the following sentences from the play is written in formal English or informal English.

1. Well, sir, it just so happens that there *was* a total eclipse of the sun in the sixth century—matter of fact, it was on the twenty-first of June, in the year A.D. 528.

2. Be merciful, fair sir, and essay this peril no further, lest disaster follow.

3. For a lesson, I will let this darkness proceed and spread night in the world; but, whether or not I will blot out the sun for good shall rest with you.

4. You must be tired of staying here in Camelot year after year, just working your humdrum miracles.

5. And here was I, a respectable Wizard of the Court of King Arthur, off gallivanting around the countryside with a beautiful young demoiselle named Sandy.

6. The name of one who was dear to thee is here preserved, here made holy, and the music of it will abide always in our ears.

Developing Skills in Critical Thinking

Relating Character and Purpose. King Arthur has been the subject of stories, poems, and plays for centuries. He is usually pictured as heroic, noble, and brave. In this play, however, he is well-meaning but not too smart. He is a humorous character. Why does the writer portray a traditional hero in this way? How does this portrayal fit in with the author's purpose to entertain?

Developing Skills in Speaking and Listening

Giving a Dramatic Reading. Work with a group to present a portion of *A Connecticut Yankee in King Arthur's Court.* Each group member should select a role, study that character, and practice reading that character's lines aloud. Remember that two readers may be needed for the Connecticut Yankee—an older voice for the narrator and a younger voice for the dialogue. Several group members should prepare music and produce background noises. Perhaps your music teacher can suggest melodies for the various musical themes asked for in the play.

The group should practice reading the selection together at least once. Make sure that every speaker talks loudly enough to be heard. Try to make your dialogue sound as much like natural conversation as possible. Also, rehearse at least once with sound effects if you plan to use them. Finally, present your reading to the other groups in your class.

Developing Writing Skills

1. **Explaining an Opinion.** Some people enjoy fantasies such as *A Connecticut Yankee in King Arthur's Court,* while others do not. In one paragraph, state your opinion about fantasies and explain why you like or dislike them.

   Prewriting. Think about *A Connecticut Yankee in King Arthur's Court* and any other fantasies you have read. List the things you like about the stories. Then list the things you don't like about them. Decide whether you like or dislike fantasies. Next plan your paragraph. Study your list of reasons and arrange them in order of importance.

   Drafting. Begin your paragraph by stating your opinion about fantasies. Then state your reasons for your opinion. Use examples from this play and any other fantasies you have read to support your reasons. Be sure that your reasons are arranged in clear order.

   Revising and Sharing. Share your writing with a classmate who has expressed the opposite opinion. Have him or her read your argument. Ask your classmate whether your reasons make sense. Revise your draft if your classmate cannot understand your opinion.

2. **Predicting Outcomes.** Go beyond the ending of the play. Predict what would happen if the Yankee attempted to explain his experiences in Camelot to his fiancée and the factory employees. How would others react to his story? Would anyone believe him? Write two paragraphs explaining what you think might happen. If you prefer, express your ideas in play form. Follow the steps in the writing process as you go about planning and writing your prediction. For further help, see the Guidelines for the Process of Writing beginning on page 654 of the handbook.

Chapter 7 Review

Using Your Skills in Reading Drama

The myth of Pandora tells about how evil came into the world when she opened a box given her by the gods. The following scene is a dramatization based on the myth. Read the scene, which describes the gifts Pandora received from the gods. Then answer the questions that follow.

> **Pandora** (*In tone of wonder*). My earliest memories are of a large room filled with light. I was surrounded by beings much like me but far more beautiful.
>
> **Zeus** (*Murmur of voices in background*). Our creation is complete. What gifts shall we bestow upon her?
>
> **Aphrodite.** I can give her beauty.
>
> **Apollo.** I shall offer her the love of music.
>
> **Pandora.** With every gift the gods and goddesses gave me, I felt myself grow more beautiful and intelligent. At last one god limped forward, carrying an exquisite box of gold (*Cries of awe*).
>
> **Zeus.** Pandora, please accept this box which Hephaestus has fashioned. It is our gift for Man, whom you shall marry. We must ask you not to open the box; it is for Man alone.
>
> **Pandora** (*With dignity*). I thank you, mighty Zeus. And I thank all these great and kind gods and goddesses.

1. Who acts as the narrator of the scene?

2. What do you learn about the setting?

3. Identify a line of dialogue, a sound effect, and a stage direction other than a sound effect.

4. What do you learn about the characters? State at least one detail about each of two characters.

Using Your Skills in Comprehension

Decide which selection from Chapter Seven is the subject of each evaluation below. For each evaluation, list details that support it.

1. The play makes impossible events seem believable.
2. The writer builds suspense slowly and carefully so that the reader never loses interest.
3. The writer effectively uses humor to communicate the themes of the play.

Using Your Skills in Vocabulary

The scene about Pandora is written in formal English. Reread the fifth and sixth speeches. Explain why each is an example of formal English. Then rewrite one of the speeches in informal English.

Using Your Skills in Speaking and Listening

From one of the plays in this chapter choose a brief passage of dialogue that shows two characters coming into conflict. With one other student, practice reading the dialogue to show the characters' opposing feelings and ideas. Follow any stage directions that tell how the characters should speak or act. Present your dialogue to an audience.

Using Your Skills in Writing

1. Choose one of the plays in this chapter. Write one paragraph explaining how the writer informs the audience about the setting. Refer to various techniques used for different scenes.
2. Use the scene on page 624 as the introduction to a play on Pandora. Write a second scene in which Pandora goes to earth with the box for Man. In the scene portray what happens when Pandora arrives on earth with the box she is not supposed to open.

Handbook for Reading and Writing

Act. An act is a major unit of action in a play. Each act may contain several scenes, and each scene may have a different setting.

See also *Drama* and *Scene.*

Alliteration. Alliteration is the repetition of consonant sounds at the beginnings of words. Alliteration is found in prose, poetry, and everyday speech. The phrases "<u>r</u>ed <u>r</u>ose" and "<u>b</u>ouncing <u>b</u>aby <u>b</u>oy" contain alliteration. Notice how alliteration emphasizes certain words in the following example.

Fueled
by a <u>m</u>illion
<u>m</u>an-<u>m</u>ade
wings of fire
　　—"Fueled," page 394

For more about alliteration, see pages 218–219.

Assonance. Assonance is the repetition of a vowel sound within words. The phrases "h<u>i</u>gh and m<u>i</u>ghty" and "<u>sea</u> br<u>ee</u>ze" contain this kind of repetition. Assonance can help reinforce meaning and create mood in prose or poetry. The repetition of the *oo* sound in this line from "Faces" (page 402) suggests a feeling of loneliness.

Faces that I l<u>o</u>se so s<u>oo</u>n

For more about assonance, see page 220.

Autobiography. An autobiography is the story of a person's life, written by that person. Although it is a form of nonfiction, an autobiography contains elements also found in fiction including character, setting, conflict, and theme. An example of autobiography is "One of the Lucky Ones" by Lucy Ching (page 484).

For more about autobiography, see pages 440 and 483.

See also *Nonfiction* and *Biography.*

Biography. A biography is the story of a person's life, written by another person. Even though it is a form of nonfiction, a biography contains elements also found in fiction, such as character, setting, conflict, and suspense. An example of a biography is "Banker Maggie Walker" (page 454).

For more about biography, see pages 440 and 509.

See also *Nonfiction* and *Autobiography.*

Character. A character is a person or animal who takes part in the action of a work of literature. Generally, the plot of a short story focuses on the main character. A story also may have one or more minor characters. They may keep the plot moving or help the reader learn more about the main character. In "Raymond's Run" (page 104), Squeaky is the main character, while Raymond and Gretchen are minor characters.

For more about character, see pages 2–3 and 70.

See also *Characterization*.

Characterization. Characterization is the use of literary techniques to reveal the nature of a character. One way in which a writer reveals a character is through physical description. Another way is through a character's words and actions. A third way is through a narrator's direct comments about a character. Still another way is through the words, actions, and feelings of other characters.

For more about characterization, see pages 70–71.

Climax. The climax, or turning point, is the high point of interest or suspense in a story or play. Generally, at the climax the outcome of the story becomes clear. In "A Spark Neglected Burns the House" (page 9), the climax comes when Ivan realizes that he could have put out the fire if he had not wanted revenge.

For more about climax, see page 3.

See also *Plot, Exposition, Rising Action, Falling Action,* and *Resolution.*

Conflict. Conflict is a struggle between opposing forces. Conflict creates tension and suspense in a story or play. The two types of conflict are internal and external.

An internal conflict takes place inside the mind of a character. For example, in "The Third Wish" (page 151), Mr. Peters must decide whether to let Leita return to her former life.

An external conflict takes place between a character and another character or force. Sometimes one character struggles against another character, as do Gabriel and Ivan in "A Spark Neglected Burns the House" (page 9). At other times, a character struggles against an outside force. For example, in "Anne Frank: The Diary of a Young Girl" (page 455), Anne Frank and her family struggle against the Nazis.

For more about conflict, see pages 70 and 235.

Description. Description is writing that creates a picture of a scene, event, or character. Notice how the details in the following passage help you see the character.

> Instead of the great white bird, there was a little man all in green with a golden crown and long beard, standing by the water. He had fierce glittering eyes and looked by no means friendly.—"The Third Wish," page 152

Descriptions often include details that appeal to the senses of sight, hearing, smell, touch, and taste. Sometimes a description provides details about the actions or attitudes of a character.

See also *Sensory Images*.

Detective Story. A detective story is one in which the main character puts together clues to solve a crime. In most detective stories, the main character is observant, intelligent, and logical. The important clue may be something that the other characters overlook. *Sherlock Holmes and the Stockbroker's Clerk* (page 588) is a detective story written as a play.

Dialogue. A dialogue is a conversation between two or more characters. Dialogue can make the characters seem real, and it can give hints about their personalities. No quotation marks are used for dialogue in plays. In other writing, however, quotation marks set off the exact words of characters.

For more about dialogue, see page 583.

Diary. A diary is a daily record a person keeps of activities and thoughts. "The Life of Davy Crockett by Himself" (page 447) is an example of a diary.

For more about diaries, see pages 440 and 446.

Drama. Drama is writing that tells a story through dialogue and action. A drama, or play, is meant to be performed by actors and actresses. Like other types of fiction, drama has the elements of character, setting, plot, theme, and conflict.

Generally, a script for a play includes stage directions that tell the actors and actresses how to move or speak their lines. These directions also provide suggestions for sound effects, music, lighting, and scenery.

A play is made up of one or more acts. Each act may contain several scenes that may have different settings.

For more about drama, see pages 582–583.

See also *Act, Dialogue, Scene,* and *Stage Directions.*

Essay. An essay is a brief nonfiction work that deals with one subject, often in a personal way. "Place of Sorrows" (page 573) by Charles Kuralt is an example of an essay. It describes the writer's thoughts and feelings during a visit to the Little Big Horn, the site of a famous battle.

For more about the essay, see pages 536–537 and 563.

Exposition. The exposition is the part of a plot that provides background information and that introduces the setting and, possibly, the main character or characters. The following passage from the short story "The Weapon" (page 47) is the exposition.

The room was quiet in the dimness of early evening. Dr. James Graham, key scientist of a very important project, sat in his favorite chair, thinking. It was so still that he could hear the turning of pages in the next room as his son leafed through a picture book.

For more about exposition, see page 3. See also *Plot* and *Rising Action.*

External Conflict. See *Conflict.*

Falling Action. The falling action is the part of a plot in which the story begins to draw to a close. The falling action comes after the climax and before the resolution. In the short story "The Third Wish" (page 151), the climax comes when Mr. Peters changes Leita back into a swan. In the falling action the writer reveals that Leita often accompanies Mr. Peters as he grows older.

Some plots have no falling action since the resolution immediately follows the climax.

See also *Plot, Climax,* and *Resolution.*

Fantasy. A fantasy is a story that is set in an imaginary world. "The Third Wish" (page 151) is a fantasy.

Fiction. Fiction is writing about imaginary people, places, and events. Some works of fiction come entirely from the writer's imagination. Others may be based partly on facts, to which the writer adds imaginary details.

See also *Nonfiction.*

Figurative Language. Figurative language is language that communicates ideas beyond the literal, or actual, meanings of words. Writers use figurative language to describe familiar things in new ways.

Special types of figurative language, called figures of speech, include hyperbole, metaphor, personification, and simile.

For more about figurative language, see pages 376–377 and 400–401.

See also *Hyperbole, Metaphor, Personification,* and *Simile.*

Flashback. A flashback is a part of a story that interrupts the sequence of events to relate an earlier conversation, scene, or event. Generally, a plot moves forward in time. Sometimes, though, a writer interrupts this movement to tell the reader something that happened previously. This information may help you understand the present actions of a character.

For example, in *Sherlock Holmes and the Stockbroker's Clerk* (page 588), a flashback shows the earlier meeting between Pycroft and Arthur Pinner. Pinner's unusual behavior at the meeting helps to explain Pycroft's later uneasiness.

Foreshadowing. Foreshadowing is the technique of hinting about something that will occur in a story. Foreshadowing creates suspense and makes readers eager to find out what will happen. An example of foreshadowing can be found in "The Third Wish" (page 152). The King of the Forest gives Mr. Peters three wishes but, at the same time, claims, "Well, I have yet to hear of the human being who made any good use of his three wishes—they mostly end up worse off than they started." This statement hints that the wishes may not bring Mr. Peters happiness.

Free Verse. Free verse is poetry without patterns of rhyme and meter. Generally, free verse is more rhythmic than ordinary language. Much modern poetry is written in free verse. An example is "I Hear America Singing" (page 383) by Walt Whitman.

Hero. In a literary work the hero is a character who exhibits extraordinary powers such as strength, courage, and intelligence. Example of heroes are Odin, Perseus, and Odysseus.

Humor. Humor is the quality that makes writing funny or amusing. Two ways in which writers can create humor are through exaggeration and irony.

For more about humor, see pages 535 and 537.

See also *Irony*.

Hyperbole. Hyperbole is an exaggeration for emphasis. An example is the expression "I'm so tired, I could sleep for a week." In "Raymond's Run" (page 105), Squeaky uses hyperbole when she states that Cynthia "won the spelling bee for the millionth time."

For more about hyperbole, see pages 228–229.

See also *Figurative Language*.

Imagery. See *Sensory Images*.

Internal Conflict. See *Conflict*.

Irony. Irony is a contrast between what is expected and what actually exists or happens. The irony in "The Weapon" (page 47) is the contrast between Graham's concern for his son's safety and his work on the ultimate weapon.

For more about irony, see page 192.

Legend. A legend is a story passed down through many generations and popularly believed to have a historic basis. While the main character in a legend actually may have lived, many of the stories about him or her are fictitious. Legends often suggest the values and ideals of the people who originated them. An example of a legend is "The Trojan War" (page 334).

For more about legends, see pages 288–289 and 331.

Line. A line is a basic unit in a poem. Lines vary in length, from a single word to several words. Often lines are grouped into stanzas.

See also *Stanza.*

Main Character. See *Character.*

Metaphor. A metaphor is a comparison between two unlike things that have something in common. Unlike a simile, a metaphor does not contain the words *like* or *as.* Margot's poem from "All Summer in a Day" (page 170) contains a metaphor in which the sun is compared to a flower.

> I think the sun is a flower,
> That blooms for just one hour.

For more about metaphor, see pages 224–225.

See also *Figurative Language* and *Simile.*

Minor Character. See *Character.*

Mood. Mood is the feeling that the writer creates for the reader. The writer may develop a mood through descriptions of settings or the words of characters. Mood is also created by a careful choice of words in sensory images and figures of speech. For example, in "Those Winter Sundays" (page 412), such words as "No one ever thanked him" suggest a mood of melancholy.

For more about mood, see pages 375 and 441.

Myth. A myth is a traditional story, usually about a superhuman being or unlikely event. Generally, myths attempt to answer basic questions about nature, such as how the world began or why the seasons change. Several examples of myths can be found in Chapters Three and Four.

For more about myths, see pages 234–235 and 288–289.

Narrator. The narrator is the teller of a story. The narrator may be a character in the story, as in "Little Dog Lost" (page 37), or an outside voice created by the writer, as in "The Weapon" (page 47).

For more about the narrator, see pages 71 and 583.

See also *Point of View.*

Nonfiction. Nonfiction is writing about real people, places, and events. Nonfiction presents factual information. Types of nonfiction include diaries, autobiographies, biographies, humorous sketches, and essays.

Nonfiction may contain elements found also in fiction, such as character, setting, conflict, and theme.

For more about nonfiction, see pages 440–441.

See also *Autobiography, Biography, Diary, Essay,* and *Fiction.*

Onomatopoeia. Onomatopoeia is the use of words to imitate sounds. Examples of onomatopoeia include words such as *crash, splash,* and *creak.* Notice the words that imitate sounds in the following sentence from "Raymond's Run" (page 110).

> And I lean down to catch my breath and here comes Gretchen walking back, for she's overshot the finish line too, *huffing* and *puffing* with her hands on her hips.

For more about onomatopoeia, see pages 216–217.

Oral Tradition. Oral tradition refers to the body of literature passed by word of mouth from generation to generation. Myths and legends belong to the oral tradition.

For more about oral tradition, see page 234.

See also *Legend* and *Myth.*

Personification. Personification is the technique of giving human qualities to an object, animal, or idea. The following lines from "Macavity: The Mystery Cat" (page 423) contain personification.

> He's outwardly respectable. (They say he cheats at cards.)
> And his footprints are not found in any file in Scotland Yard's.

For more about personification, see pages 226–227.

See also *Figurative Language.*

Play. See *Drama.*

Plot. Plot is the sequence of events in a story. It is the writer's plan for what happens and when and to whom it happens.

Generally, a plot includes exposition, rising action, climax, falling action, and resolution. The plot centers on a conflict, a struggle faced by the main character. The actions taken by that character build toward the climax, or turning point. At this point, or shortly after, the conflict is resolved. The story then draws to a close, and the loose ends are tied up.

For more about plot, see pages 3, 235, and 289.

See also *Climax, Conflict, Exposition, Falling Action, Resolution,* and *Rising Action.*

Poetry. Poetry is an expression of ideas and feelings in compact, imaginative, and musical language. In most poems, words are arranged in lines and grouped in stanzas. Poetry depends heavily on sensory images, figurative language, and sound devices such as rhythm and rhyme.

For more about poetry, see pages 374–375.

See also *Figurative Language, Line, Rhyme, Rhyme Scheme, Rhythm, Sensory Images,* and *Stanza.*

Point of View. Point of view is the perspective from which a story is told. A story is told from the first-person or the third-person point of view.

In stories told from the first-person point of view, such as "Lather and Nothing Else" (page 97), the narrator is a character in the story. He or she uses pronouns such as *I, me,* and *we.* In stories told from the third-person point of view, such as "A Spark Neglected Burns the House" (page 9), the narrator is outside the story. This kind of narrator uses pronouns such as *he, she,* and *they.*

The third-person point of view can be limited or omniscient. If a story is told from the third-person limited point of view, such as "Just Try to Forget" (page 54), the narrator tells what only one character sees, thinks, and feels. If a story is told from the third-person omniscient point of view, such as "All Summer in a Day" (page 169), the narrator sees into the minds of all the characters.

For more about point of view, see page 71.

See also *Narrator.*

Prose. Prose is writing that is organized into sentences and paragraphs. Prose includes all fiction and nonfiction writing.

Repetition. Repetition is the technique of using a sound, word, phrase, sentence, or line again for emphasis. In the following line from "Macavity: The Mystery Cat" (page 423), the repetition emphasizes the name of the cat and gives rhythm and a musical quality to the line.

Macavity, Macavity, there's no one like
    Macavity.

See also *Alliteration* and *Rhyme.*

Resolution. The resolution is the point in a plot in which the conflict ends and the loose ends are tied up. The resolution comes after the falling action. In "After Twenty Years" (page 23), the resolution occurs when Bob reads the letter from Patrolman Wells.

For more about resolution, see page 3. See also *Conflict* and *Plot.*

Rhyme. Rhyme is the repetition of syllable sounds at the ends of words. In the following lines from "Song of the Truck" (page 386), the rhyming words come at the ends of lines.

This is the song that the truck drivers *hear*
In the grinding of brake and the shifting
    of *gear.*

Occasionally, one or more rhyming words fall in the middle of a line. That is called internal rhyme. Here is an example from "Song of the Truck."

From the *freight* and the *weight*—
    a song has been born.

For more about rhyme, see pages 212–213 and 375.

See also *Rhyme Scheme.*

Rhyme Scheme. The rhyme scheme of a poem is the pattern of rhymes at the ends of lines. To chart this pattern, use letters of the alphabet to show which lines end with the same sounds. Notice the rhyme scheme for these lines from "The Storyteller" (page 407).

He talked, and as he talked   *a*
Wallpaper came alive;   *b*
Suddenly ghosts walked,   *a*
And four doors were five.   *b*

For more about rhyme scheme, see page 213.
See also *Rhyme.*

Rhythm. Rhythm is the pattern of stressed and unstressed syllables in a sentence, a paragraph, or a line of poetry. Stressed syllables may be marked with / and unstressed syllables with ˘. Notice the rhythm in these lines from "Faces" (page 402).

> / ˘ / ˘ / ˘ /
> People that I meet and pass
> ˘ ˘ / ˘ / ˘ /
> In the city's broken roar,
> / ˘ / ˘ / ˘ /
> Faces that I lose so soon
> ˘ ˘ / ˘ / ˘ /
> And have never found before,

For more about rhythm, see pages 214–215 and 374.

Rising Action. The rising action is the part of a plot that introduces and develops the conflict, or struggle. The rising action builds toward the climax. In "Charles" (page 72), the rising action begins when Laurie reports on his first day in kindergarten.

For more about rising action, see page 3.
See also *Climax, Conflict, Exposition, Falling Action,* and *Plot.*

Scene. In a play a scene is a unit of action that takes place in one setting. Most plays consist of several scenes.

For more about scenes, see page 583.
See also *Act.*

Science Fiction. Science fiction is writing based on real or imagined scientific developments. Science fiction often presents an imagined view of the future or the past. "All Summer in a Day" (page 169) is an example of a science fiction story.

For more about science fiction, see page 150.

Sensory Images. Sensory images are words and phrases that appeal to the five senses: sight, hearing, touch, taste, and smell. Another term for sensory images is *imagery.* Notice how the words and phrases in the following passage from "A Man Who Had No Eyes" (page 30) appeal to the sense of sight.

> He was a shaggy, thick-necked fellow; his coat was greasy about the lapels and pockets, and his hand splayed over the cane's crook with a futile sort of clinging.

For more about sensory images, see page 400.
See also *Description.*

Setting. Setting is the time and place of the action of a story. The setting includes details that describe customs, clothing, scenery, weather, buildings, rooms, furnishings, and methods of transportation. In some stories, the setting is central to the action, as in "All Summer in a Day" (page 169). In other stories the setting is less important, as in "A Man Who Had No Eyes" (page 30).

For more about setting, see page 2.

Shape. Shape is the way that the words in a poem look on the page. The arrangement of words may suggest something about the subject of a poem. For example, in the last stanza of "Unfolding Bud" (page 396), the poet emphasizes the importance of rereading a poem by putting the word *again* on a line by itself.

Short Story. A short story is a work of fiction that generally can be read in one sitting. A short story usually develops one major conflict and produces a single effect on the reader. Elements of a short story include character, setting, plot, and theme. "The Trout" (page 63) is an example of a short story.

For more about the short story, see pages 2–3.

See also *Fiction*.

Simile. A simile is a comparison using the words *like* or *as*. Familiar examples of similes are "sly as a fox" and "bright as a penny." Notice the simile in the following sentence from "Little Dog Lost" (page 39).

I tried to shrink small, like a rat in a corner,

as the Old Man jammed gears and wheeled the car around.

For more about simile, see pages 222–223.

See also *Figurative Language* and *Metaphor*.

Sound Effects. Sound effects are sounds made as part of a play. In a radio play, sound effects help listeners picture the action. Instructions for sound effects are given in the stage directions.

Speaker. The speaker in a poem is the voice that talks to the reader. The speaker is not necessarily the poet. In "Child on Top of a Greenhouse" (page 428), for example, the speaker is a child in danger.

For more about speaker, see page 375.

Stage Directions. Stage directions are notes included in plays to help readers picture the action. Stage directions may describe stage sets, lighting, music, and sound effects. Also, these notes may tell actors and actresses how to move and speak their lines. Generally, stage directions are given in parentheses and printed in italics. Notice this stage direction from *A Connecticut Yankee in King Arthur's Court* (page 618).

Conn. Yankee *(Bitterly)*. Look at them, Clarence. Factories, schools, everything—blown to smithereens.

For more about stage directions, see page 583.

Stanza. A stanza is a group of lines that form a unit in a poem. Stanzas are similar to paragraphs in prose writing. "Stopping by Woods on a Snowy Evening" (page 432) is an example of a poem with four stanzas.

For more about stanzas, see page 374. See also *Line*.

Structure. Structure refers to the way in which a story, poem, play, or nonfiction selection is put together. For example, "Anne Frank: The Diary of a Young Girl" (page 455) consists of diary entries by a Jewish girl in Holland during the Nazi occupation. The poem "Piñones" (page 414) is divided into two stanzas that end with the same three words.

Style. Style is the way in which a work of literature is written. Style is made up of many elements including sentence length, vocabulary, imagery, and figurative language.

For more about style, see page 537.

Surprise Ending. A surprise ending is an unexpected twist in the plot at the end of a story. For example, in "After Twenty Years" (page 23), Bob finds out that the patrolman is his old friend Jimmy.

Suspense. Suspense is the feeling of growing tension and excitement felt by a reader. A writer creates suspense by raising questions in the reader's mind. For example, in "Little Dog Lost" (page 37) the reader wonders whether Jim will find his lost dog.

Symbol. A symbol is a person, place, or object that stands for something beyond itself. For example, a skull and crossbones on a bottle stands for poison.

In literature, symbols often reinforce ideas. For example, in "A Spark Neglected Burns the House" (page 9), the spark represents a minor disagreement that grows into a major problem.

Tale. A tale is a simple story told in prose or poetry. Examples include fairy tales, folk tales, and legends. "The Tale of the Superman" (page 255) is a tale.

For more about tales, see pages 234–235.

Theme. The theme is the message about life that the writer shares with the reader. Sometimes the writer states the theme directly. At other times, the reader must infer the theme. For example, one theme of "A Man Who Had No Eyes" (page 30) is that self-pity can destroy a person.

For more about theme, see page 70.

Tone. Tone is the writer's attitude toward a subject. The tone can be described as serious, bitter, humorous, sympathetic, angry, casual, or passionate, among many other possibilities. The tone of "The Man Who Was a Horse" (page 86) is admiring. The tone of "Place of Sorrows" (page 509) is pensive.

For more about tone, see page 441.

Summary of Comprehension and Thinking Skills

Analysis. Analysis means breaking something into its elements and examining each one. When you analyze a short story, you focus on individual elements such as character, setting, and plot. As you study each element, you understand the entire work better.

Throughout this book, study questions in Developing Comprehension Skills, Reading Literature, and Developing Writing Skills focus on important elements and how they function in literary works. In addition, questions under Critical Thinking develop skills of analysis.

Cause and Effect. Cause and effect describes one relationship between events in a story, poem, or play. In this type of relationship, one event brings about another event. The first event is the cause, and the second event is the effect.

Sometimes clue words signal cause and effect relationships. Among these clue words are *because, since, so that, in order that,* and *if/then.*

For more about cause and effect, see page 290.

Classification. Classification means sorting ideas, people, animals, places, objects, or some other group of items on the basis of something that they have in common. For example, you might classify short stories as serious or humorous. You might classify poems according to the century in which they were written.

For more about classification, see pages 310 and 368.

Comparison. Comparison is the process of showing that people, animals, places, things, or ideas have something in common. As a reader, you often make comparisons within a work or between works. For example, you might point out how two characters in a story are alike or how the plots in two stories are similar.

For more about comparison, see pages 236–237.

See also *Contrast.*

Conclusions. See *Inferences.*

Connotation. The connotation of a word is its suggested meaning. For example, to most readers the connotation of the word *friend* is positive. Connotations can make readers or listeners feel positive or negative about a subject.

For more about connotation, see page 249.

See also *Slanted Writing.*

Contrast. Contrast means pointing out differences. For example, in *A Connecticut Yankee in King Arthur's Court* (page 608), the writer contrasts medieval and modern life.

Sometimes readers contrast elements within a work or in several works. For example, you might notice the differences between two characters in a story or between the settings of two stories.

For more about contrast, see pages 236–237. See also *Comparison*.

Denotation. Denotation is the dictionary meaning of a word.

See also *Connotation* and *Slanted Writing*.

Evaluation. To evaluate means to judge the worth of something. To evaluate anything, you must apply standards, or measures of quality or value.

One way to evaluate a work of literature is to consider each element separately and then to judge how well the elements work together. For example, when judging a poem, you would think about the standards of a good poem, such as striking images, true emotions, skillful effects of sound, and new ways of looking at things. You would make a judgment and support your evaluation with evidence from the work.

Another way to evaluate a work of literature is to identify one or more purposes, and then decide whether the writer has achieved them. For example, you might evaluate how well a writer sustains suspense and develops the character of the detective in a mystery story.

For more about evaluation, see pages 584–585.

See also *Analysis, Comparison, Contrast,* and *Purpose*.

Fact and Opinion. A fact is a statement that can be proved, such as "Some squirrels are gray and some are brown." An opinion, on the other hand, is a statement that expresses a writer's belief and cannot be proved. An example of an opinion is "Brown squirrels are more attractive than gray ones."

Writers often present facts that lead the reader to accept their opinions, as in the example below. The opinion is underlined. Supporting the opinion are two sentences that state facts.

> <u>Hawaii is the most beautiful of our fifty states.</u> Its islands have both mountains and beaches. Many parts of Hawaii are covered with lush, green forests.

As you read, watch for opinions that are not supported by facts. Remember that a writer's opinions may influence his or her choice of facts. Also be aware that a writer may state facts using words with positive or negative connotations.

For more about fact and opinion, see pages 442–443.

See also *Slanted Writing*.

Figurative Language. Figurative language is language that communicates ideas beyond the literal meanings of the words. Figurative language helps you look at familiar things in new ways.

For example, if someone tells you that you see the world through rose-colored glasses, it does not mean that you wear glasses with a reddish tint. It means that you tend to see things optimistically. To understand this example of figurative language, you have to go beyond the literal meaning of the words.

For more about figurative language, see pages 376–377 and 400–401.

Generalization. A generalization is a statement made about a group. An example is "All short stories contain plot, character, and setting."

Sometimes generalizations are too broad, as in the following example: "All poems contain rhyme." In reality, some poems do not rhyme. The word *all* makes the statement too broad. You can correct this faulty generalization by using a qualifier such as *some, often, many,* or *most.* The statement "many poems contain rhyme" is a true generalization.

For more about generalizations, see pages 46 and 126.

Inferences. An inference is a logical conclusion based on evidence. As you read, you often make inferences. You infer, or figure out, more than the words say. For example, you may read a sentence such as this one: The woman brushed dust off her clothes and stiffly climbed down from the stagecoach. From the information given, you can infer that the time is long ago. The woman probably has completed a long journey.

For more about inferences, see pages 4–5.

Opinion. See *Fact and Opinion.*

Predicting Outcomes. An outcome is the result or consequence produced by the events in a story. When you make a reasonable guess about what will happen in a story, you are predicting an outcome. While some outcomes are easy to predict, others are more difficult.

When you predict outcomes, use the clues that the writer gives. Consider what you know about the characters, the plot, the setting, and human nature to help you in your inferences.

For more about predicting outcomes, see page 5.

Purpose. A writer's purpose is his or her reason for writing. Some purposes of works of literature include the following: to entertain, to inform, to express feelings, and to persuade. Writers may combine these purposes, but generally one is most important. A writer's purpose influences the treatment of elements such as character, setting, and theme.

For more about purpose, see page 585. See also *Evaluation*.

Slanted Writing. Slanted writing presents only one side of an issue or one view of an event. Even though slanted writing may appear to report facts, it actually presents the writer's opinions.

One way to slant writing is to give only the facts that support a particular opinion. For example, a writer might try to convince you that a certain actor is the best by mentioning only his or her successful performances.

Another way to slant writing is to use words that lead the reader to feel a particular way about the subject. A writer may use words with strong connotations, or suggestions. For example, a writer might call a candidate a *statesman,* a word with positive connotations, or a *hack,* a word with negative suggestions.

For more about slanted writing, see page 443.

See also *Connotation* and *Fact and Opinion*.

Stereotype. A stereotype is a character who conforms to a simplified, common type. For example, the wicked stepmother, the strong silent cowboy, and the absent-minded professor are familiar stereotypes.

For more about stereotypes, see page 185.

Time Order. Time order is the presentation of events in the order in which they take place. Words and phrases that signal time order relationships include the following: *then, next, gradually, while, finally,* and *the following day.*

For more about time order, see page 290.

See also *Cause and Effect*.

Word Choice. A writer's choice of words depends on several concerns. These include the purpose for writing and the intended audience. The setting of a story also influences the choice of words. Characters must sound as if they belong to the time and place described. For example, if the story takes place in ancient Greece, the characters might use terms such as *chariot, galley, Zeus,* and *Apollo.*

1. Word Parts

Studying word parts can help you figure out the meanings of unfamiliar words. The two kinds of word parts are base words and affixes. The two kinds of affixes are prefixes and suffixes.

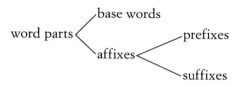

Base Word. A word to which word parts are added is called a base word. For example, the base word in *recover* is *cover*. The base word in *powerful* is *power*. Sometimes the spelling of the base word changes when a word part is added. For example, the *y* in *beauty* is changed to *i* when the suffix *-ful* is added to make the word *beautiful*.

For more about changes in base words, see *Spelling Changes*.

Prefix. A prefix is a word part added to the beginning of a base word. The addition of a prefix to a base word changes the meaning of the word.

Prefix	+	**Base Word**	=	**New Word**
mis-	+	spell	=	misspell

For a list of prefixes, see page 238.

Suffix. A suffix is a word part added to the end of a base word. The addition of a suffix changes the meaning of the word.

Base Word	+	**Suffix**	=	**New Word**
home	+	-less	=	homeless

For a list of suffixes, see page 239.

Spelling Changes. Before suffixes can be added, one of the following changes may be needed.

1. When a suffix beginning with a vowel is added to a word ending in silent *e*, the *e* is usually dropped.

    leave + -ing = leaving

    The *e* is not dropped when the suffix begins with a consonant.

    time + -ly = timely

2. When a suffix is added to a word ending in *y* preceded by a consonant, the *y* usually becomes an *i*.

mercy + -ful = merciful

The *y* does not change when preceded by a vowel.

enjoy + -able = enjoyable

3. Words of one syllable, ending in one consonant preceded by one vowel, double the final consonant before adding *-ing*, *-ed,* or *-er.*

skip + -ed = skipped

When two vowels appear in a one-syllable word, the final consonant is not doubled.

dream + -ing = dreaming

---

2. Context Clues

The context of a word is the sentence or paragraph in a prose work, or the line or stanza in a poem, in which you find the word. Clues to the meaning of a word can often be found in the context. Look for the following kinds of context clues.

Antonyms. An antonym, or a word opposite in meaning to a new word, may be found in the same sentence or in a nearby sentence. Often the antonym appears in the same position in its sentence as does the new word.

> The Gettysburg Address is well-known for its brevity. Other speeches are famous for their great length.

In the first sentence, the word *brevity* follows the preposition *for.* In the second sentence, the preposition *for* is followed by *great length. Brevity* means "the opposite of great length."

For more about antonyms, see page 52.

Comparison and Contrast. Writers often compare one idea with another. One part of the comparison may give a clue to the meaning of an unfamiliar word. The following words signal that a word is being compared to something similar: *like, as, similar to,* and *than.*

Here is an example of a comparison clue.

> Before the tryouts for the play, Beth felt anxious. Other students felt just as nervous.

The comparison suggests that *anxious* means "nervous."

Contrast clues also give hints about the meanings of unfamiliar words. A contrast clue suggests what the unfamiliar word is not. The following words signal contrast clues: *although, but, however, yet, on the other hand, different from,* and *in contrast.*

> Sean usually is loquacious. However, today he has been very quiet.

The contrast suggests that *loquacious* is the opposite of *quiet*.

For more about comparison and contrast clues, see page 7.

Definition or Restatement. A definition or restatement tells the meaning of an unfamiliar word. The following words and punctuation marks signal this kind of clue: *is, who is, which is, that is, in other words, or,* dashes, commas, and parentheses.

> The byline to the article was printed in tiny letters. A byline is a line that states the writer's name.
>
> Jeffrey is a somnambulist. That is, he walks in his sleep.

For more about definition or restatement clues, see page 6.

Example Clue. In an example clue, an unfamiliar word is related to a familiar word or phrase. The unfamiliar word may be an example of a familiar term, or the familiar term may be an example of the unfamiliar word.

The following key phrases signal examples in a sentence: *an example, for example, one kind, for instance, some types,* and *such as.*

> The class examined one-celled animals such as amoebas under the microscope.

For more about example clues, see page 7.

Inferring Meaning. Sometimes you can infer the meaning of an unfamiliar word from other words in a sentence or paragraph. For example, clues to the meaning of the word *lyre* are in the following sentence.

> The lyre made harp-like music.

You can infer that a lyre is a musical instrument.

The following paragraph suggests the meaning of the word *polo.*

> Michael had never played polo before. The other three players on his team showed him how to drive the small ball through the other team's goal with the long-handled mallet. The hard part was hitting the ball while on horseback.

From the paragraph, you can infer that polo is a game played on horseback by two teams with four members each. The object of the game is to hit a ball through the opponent's goal by using a mallet.

For more about inferring meaning from context, see pages 6–7.

Synonyms. Synonyms are words that have the same or almost the same meaning. You can figure out the meaning of an unfamiliar word by recognizing a nearby word as its synonym. Look for the synonym for the word *din* in this sentence.

> The blastoff made a terrific din. The noise could be heard for miles across the desert.

The word *din* means almost the same as its synonym *noise*.

For more about synonyms, see page 6.

Words in a Series. All of a series of words in a sentence may belong to the same group. If one of the words in the series is unfamiliar to you, you might guess its meaning by relating it to the familiar words. In the following example, you can guess that a *torte* is a kind of pastry.

The bakery sells <u>tortes</u>, cakes, and pies.

For more about words in a series, see page 102.

3. Word Origins

The English language comes from a prehistoric language called Indo-European. For more than a thousand years, England was invaded by warriors from different regions of Europe. Each group of invaders left behind words that became part of the English language. Large numbers of words also were added when English settlers took their language to other places. Words can enter the language in the following ways:

Borrowed Words. Throughout its history, the English language has taken words from other languages, such as French, Spanish, Italian, Latin, Greek, American Indian, African, and Arabic. For example, the word *barbecue* comes from Spanish.

Clipped Words. New words can be made by shortening existing words. For example, the word *math* is a clipped form of the word *mathematics*.

Combined Words. A word may be made by combining two existing words or word parts. For example, the word *lifeguard* combines the words *life* and *guard*. *Predawn* is a combination of the base word *dawn* and the prefix *pre-*.

Words from Names. A word may come from the name of a person or a place. For example, the word *Braille*, which means "a system of printing for the blind that uses a pattern of raised dots," comes from Louis Braille, the blind French teacher who invented the system.

Words from Sounds. Some words imitate sounds. These words are called echoic. Some examples are *cluck, hoot,* and *zoom*.

For more about word origins, see pages 378–379.

4. Reference Books: The Dictionary and Glossary

Dictionary. Sometimes context clues and word parts do not give enough information to figure out the meanings of unfamiliar words. Then you must use a dictionary, an alphabetical listing of words that gives definitions, origins, pronunciations, and other information about the words.

The dictionary definitions, or denotations, of a word probably will be grouped by parts of speech. To choose the correct definition, test each one in the sentence in which you found the word.

Glossary. A glossary, often found at the back of a nonfiction book, is an alphabetical listing of difficult or unfamiliar words used in the book. The definition given for a glossary word reflects its meaning in a particular selection.

For more about the dictionary, see pages 444–445.

See also *The Dictionary* under Guidelines for Study and Research.

5. Levels of Language

Standard English is language that strictly follows all grammatical rules and guidelines. Standard English can be formal or informal.

Formal standard English generally is used in speeches and in serious literature. This type of standard English often contains long sentences and difficult words. Informal standard English is used in conversations, diaries, magazines, and newspapers. It often contains short sentences and easy words. Informal standard English may include **slang,** expressions that are popular for a while, and **idioms,** expressions that mean something different from their literal meanings.

Nonstandard English is language that does not always follow grammatical rules. Writers sometimes use nonstandard English for special effects. For example, characters who are close friends might use some nonstandard words and expressions.

For more about levels of language, see pages 586–587.

Guidelines for Study and Research

1. Using the Library

Arrangement of Books

Library books are divided into two groups: fiction and nonfiction.

Fiction books are stories about imaginary happenings. These books are arranged alphabetically according to the last name of the author. This name generally appears on the spine of the book.

Nonfiction books contain factual information. These books are grouped according to subject. For example, all the books about American history are grouped together. Most libraries arrange nonfiction books according to the **Dewey Decimal System.** Every book is assigned a number in one of ten categories. This **call number** is displayed on the spine of the book. The books are then arranged in numerical order on the library shelves. Biographies are usually in a separate section of the library. They are arranged according to the last name of the subject.

<table>
<tr><td colspan="3">The Dewey Decimal System</td></tr>
<tr><td>000–099</td><td>General Works</td><td>encyclopedias, almanacs, handbooks</td></tr>
<tr><td>100–199</td><td>Philosophy</td><td>conduct, ethics, psychology</td></tr>
<tr><td>200–299</td><td>Religion</td><td>the Bible, mythology, theology</td></tr>
<tr><td>300–399</td><td>Social Science</td><td>law, education, government, folklore, legend</td></tr>
<tr><td>400–499</td><td>Language</td><td>languages, grammar, dictionaries, almanacs</td></tr>
<tr><td>500–599</td><td>Science</td><td>mathematics, chemistry, physics</td></tr>
<tr><td>600–699</td><td>Useful Arts</td><td>farming, cooking, sewing, radio, nursing, engineering, television, business, gardening, cars</td></tr>
<tr><td>700–799</td><td>Fine Arts</td><td>music, painting, drawing, acting, games, sports</td></tr>
<tr><td>800–899</td><td>Literature</td><td>poetry, plays, essays</td></tr>
<tr><td>900–999</td><td>History</td><td>biography, travel, geography</td></tr>
</table>

The Card Catalog

The best way to locate a book in the library is to use the card catalog. The **card catalog** is an alphabetical file that lists every book in the library. This file is kept in a cabinet of narrow drawers or it may be stored in a computer.

Generally, a cabinet-style card catalog has three cards for every nonfiction book: an author card, a title card, and a subject card. Each card contains the same information, but in a different order. The **author card** lists the author's name on the top line. The **title card** lists the title of the book on the top line. The **subject card** lists the subject or topic of the book on the top line. On the top left corner of the cards for nonfiction books, you will find the call number. By using the call number, you can locate the book.

A computerized card catalog stores the same information. Books can be located by authors, titles, or subjects. The type of computer varies with the library. Usually, directions near the computer show how to use it. Ask a librarian for help if you are unfamiliar with the computer.

Author Card

973.7
K19   **Katz, William Loren**

An album of the Civil War. Illustrated with original prints and photos. N.Y.C.: F. Watts. © 1974.

Title Card

973.7
K19   **An Album of the Civil War**

Katz, William Loren

An album of the Civil War. Illustrated with original prints and photos. N.Y.C.: F. Watts. © 1974.

Subject Card

973.7
K19   **U.S. History—Civil War**

Katz, William Loren

An album of the Civil War. Illustrated with original prints and photos. N.Y.C.: F. Watts. © 1974.

2. Using Reference Materials

The Nonfiction Book

For detailed information about a topic, your best source may be a nonfiction book. To judge the usefulness of a particular book, examine these parts:

The Title Page. Does the title mention your topic?

The Copyright Page. If you need up-to-date information, check to see that the copyright date is recent.

The Table of Contents. Do any sections or chapters deal with your topic?

The Index. Does the index list any terms you need information about?

The Encyclopedia

An **encyclopedia** is a collection of articles on a wide variety of topics. The articles are listed in alphabetical order according to their titles. Many encyclopedias are several volumes long. Generally, an index in the last volume lists the volumes and pages that give information on various topics.

For more about encyclopedias, see page 35.

Readers' Guide to Periodical Literature

Magazines can be sources of recent information. To find magazine articles on particular topics, use the *Readers' Guide to Periodical Literature*. The *Readers' Guide* is an alphabetical index of articles that have appeared in popular magazines. Articles are listed alphabetically by subject and by author. Each entry gives the title of the article, the name of the author, the title of the magazine in which the article appeared, and the month and year of its publication.

For more on the *Readers' Guide,* see page 78.

The Dictionary

A **dictionary** is an alphabetical listing of words, called entry words. The dictionary gives definitions, origins, pronunciations, and other information.

How to Find a Word. **Guide words** help you find the page on which an entry word appears. Generally, guide words are printed at the top of each page. They show the first and last entry words on the page.

For example, here are the guide words for two pages of a dictionary. On which page will *superficial* be listed?

suave—superior   *supervise—sustain*

Since *f* comes before *i, superficial* will appear between *suave* and *superior.*

What the Entry Word Tells You. The **entry word,** printed in dark type, tells how to spell the word and where to break it into syllables.

How to Find the Pronunciation. Use the **respelling** that follows the entry word to determine the pronunciation of the word. The respelling appears within parentheses. It uses letters and symbols to represent the sounds of the spoken word. You must refer to the pronunciation key to find out what each letter or symbol stands for.

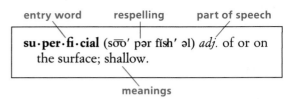

Accent marks in the respelling show which syllable or syllables to stress when pronouncing the word. Words with more than one syllable may have more than one accent. The **primary accent,** or heavy accent, is printed in dark type. The **secondary accent** is a lighter stress.

secondary accent   primary accent

competition (käm′ pə tish′ ən)

How to Find the Part of Speech and the Meaning. An abbreviation following the respelling tells the **part of speech** of the word. The **definition,** or statement of meaning, of the word follows. Some words have several definitions listed. In addition, many words can be used as more than one part of speech. All the definitions for one part of speech are grouped together.

After some entries, subentries are listed in dark, or bold, type. **Subentries** are familiar phrases in which the entry word appears. The special meaning of each phrase is then listed.

For more on the use of the dictionary, see pages 444–445.

Other Reference Sources

Almanac. An almanac provides up-to-date information and statistics about many subjects. Almanacs are published annually.

Atlas. An atlas is a book of maps. An index at the front or the back lists countries, cities, and physical features such as rivers, deserts, and mountain ranges alphabetically. Some atlases give additional information such as populations and capital cities.

To find a specific place, first look it up in the index. The index tells you which page contains the map that you need. After you turn to that page, use the coordinates listed in the index to pinpoint the location.

For more about atlases, see pages 148–149.

Nonprint Resources. These resources include films, slides, records, tapes, compact discs, and computer software. In some libraries, **picture files** contain posters, photos, pamphlets, and copies of works of art. These resources are often cataloged separately from the rest of the library's collection.

Thesaurus. A thesaurus is a book of synonyms. It can help you find a lively substitute for an overused word. For example, if you need a synonym for *happy,* the thesaurus would list *contented* or *glad.* It might also list antonyms such as *dejected* or *morose.* Look in the front of the thesaurus for directions. The index at the back of the book also will help you find a particular word.

For more about the thesaurus, see pages 426–427.

3. Studying

Three Types of Reading

You will find three types of reading useful in your studying. Each type is appropriate for a particular purpose.

Skimming. This type of fast reading gives you a quick overview of the material. Skimming also helps you become familiar with important facts. To skim, move your eyes rapidly over the material. Look for titles, subtitles, and illustrations that give you hints about the content of the material.

Scanning. A second type of fast reading is scanning. It helps you to locate a piece of information quickly. To scan, move your eyes quickly over the page. Look for key words that will lead you to the facts and ideas you need.

In-depth Reading. In-depth reading is slower than scanning or skimming. When you want to understand and remember what you read, you must do in-depth reading. To read this way, first look for main ideas in titles, subheadings, and first sentences of paragraphs. Then, carefully read about each main idea, noting details such as names, dates, numbers, and reasons. Try to see the connections among facts and ideas.

The SQ3R Study Method

The SQ3R method is an efficient way to improve your reading and study skills. SQ3R stands for five steps: Survey, Question, Read, Record, and Review.

Survey. Try to get a general idea of what the material is about. Read titles and subtitles. Look at pictures, maps, graphs, or tables. Read the introduction or the first few paragraphs.

Question. Some books may provide study questions or your teacher may assign them. Read these questions. They will help you identify important points to look for when you read the material.

Read. Read the material. Identify main ideas as you keep the study questions in mind.

Record. Write the answers to the study questions. Note any other important ideas not covered by the questions.

Review. Look at the study questions. Try to answer them without referring to your notes. If necessary, review the material to find the answers. Finally, study your notes so that you will remember the information.

4. Organizing Information

Note Taking

You will probably recognize main ideas and important facts as you read. Write them in a notebook or on cards.

Taking notes helps you in two ways: it forces you to concentrate on the material, and it identifies the important points to review for tests and assignments.

Write your notes clearly so that you can study from them later. Notes do not need to be written in sentences. Be sure to note where your information comes from. You may need to refer to that source again.

Sample Note Card

Title of book — *The Warrior Goddess Athena*, Copyright date — 1972

Author — *Doris Gates* Page number — *page 13*

Athena was the Goddess of Wisdom as well as the Goddess of War. She taught women the art of weaving and other crafts.

Outlining

One way of organizing your notes for study and research is to make an outline. An outline helps you identify the main ideas and the supporting details. An outline also gives you a graphic summary of the information.

To make an outline, label the main ideas with Roman numerals. Indent and label less important ideas with capital letters. These are subtopics. Use the format below when you outline.

I. Main Idea
   A. Subtopic
      1. Detail
      2. Detail
   B. Subtopic

II. Main Idea
   A. Subtopic
      1. Detail
      2. Detail
   B. Subtopic
      1. Detail
      2. Detail

Guidelines for the Process of Writing

Most writers develop their work by taking it through certain stages. Together, these stages are called the **process of writing.** This process includes **prewriting, drafting, revising,** and **sharing.**

Prewriting

In prewriting, writers prepare to write. During this stage they think, plan, and make several important choices.

Deciding on a Topic. List ideas that you find interesting. Think about what you might say about each idea and choose the one that is most appealing. That idea is your subject for writing. Then narrow the subject to a topic, or guiding idea. For example, if Greek myths is the subject, you might narrow it to this topic: the role of the gods in "The Beginning of the World" and "The Flood."

Determining a Purpose. Decide what you want to accomplish with your writing. You may want to express an idea or emotion, to inform, to persuade, or to entertain. How and what you write depends on the purpose for your writing.

Choosing a Form. Sometimes, an assignment specifies the form for your writing, such as a paragraph, a short story, a poem, or an essay. At other times, you must choose a form that suits your topic and purpose. For example, if you want to inform your readers about the role of the gods in two Greek myths, you might choose to write a paragraph.

Knowing the Audience. Decide who will read your writing. When you know who your readers are, you can choose the details to include. For example, you may need to give a great deal of background information if your audience is unfamiliar with your topic.

Gathering Information. First, reflect on what you know about your topic. Then analyze your topic to find out the kind of information you need to gather. Next, make a list of questions that you must answer. Consult reference sources such as an encyclopedia to find the answers.

Take notes on what you find. For example, in gathering information about the gods in the two Greek myths you have chosen, you might take notes similar to the following.

Prewriting Notes

"The Beginning of the World"

Prometheus was a god.
He shaped a human form from clay.
He put the seed of life in it.
The first man was alive.
Prometheus gave fire to humans.

"The Flood"

Two humans were left alive after a flood.
Goddess Themis told them to throw
  stones.
Stones turned into men and women.

Organizing Ideas. Review your notes. Cross out the details that seem unrelated to the topic. Choose an order for presenting the remaining details. For example,

you may choose time order for events. For a description, you may list details in the order you might notice them.

Make an informal outline or plan showing the order in which you will present your ideas. Here is an informal outline for a paragraph about the role of the gods in "The Beginning of the World" and "The Flood."

Main Idea: Greek myths show that the gods created and sustained human life.

Important details:

A. Prometheus, a god, created first human.
   1. Used clay
   2. Put seed of life in the clay
B. Themis, a goddess, helped humans survive after the flood.
   1. Two humans were left alive.
   2. They were told to throw stones.
   3. Stones turned into people.

Drafting

Drafting means putting words on paper or into a word processor. Try to get your ideas down in sentence form. Now is not the time to worry about errors in spelling and punctuation. You can correct them later when revising the draft.

Follow your prewriting plan, but feel free to change it if you think of better ideas. Leave space between the lines of your draft for later corrections and changes.

Notice how rough the writing is in the following first draft of a paragraph.

First Draft

Some myths says humans are alive because of the
gods. The god Prometheus made the first human
from clay he put the seed of life into the first man.
Another myth tells about how the godess Themis
after a great flood helped humans survive. She told
them to throw some stones the stones turned into
other humans

Revising

After you have completed the first draft, revise it to make your writing stronger and clearer. Ask yourself these questions:

1. Is the topic well developed? Should any details be added or dropped?
2. Is the organization clear?
3. Are the words exact?
4. Is the writing interesting and enjoyable?

Mark your corrections and notes on the draft. Cross out the words that you want to drop. Write in the words, phrases, and sentences that you want to add. If you are using a word processor, revise your work on the screen. You may need to write several drafts before you are satisfied.

Proofreading. Take time now to make your writing technically correct. Read your draft again. This time look for errors in grammar, usage, capitalization, punctuation, and spelling. Use proof-

Proofreading Symbols

Symbol	Meaning	Example
∧	insert	godĕss
≡	capitalize	he
/	make lower case	M̄yths
∿	transpose (trade positions)	pepole
ℓ	omit letters, words	some e
¶	make new paragraph	¶Greek
⊙	insert a period	humans⊙

reading symbols to correct any errors. Consult a dictionary and the Guidelines for Capitalization, Punctuation, and Spelling (page 654), if necessary.

Study the revised draft on page 657. Notice how the writer has improved the paragraph by changing the order of words, crossing out unnecessary words and adding precise ones. The writer also has corrected errors in capitalization, punctuation, grammar, and spelling. Compare the revised draft with the final draft on page 658. The final draft reflects the changes marked on the revised draft.

First Draft—Revised

~~Some~~ A Greek myths says that humans are alive because of the gods, created humans and a named formed a the of the earth. helped them ~~The~~ god Prometheus ~~made the first~~ human from clay he human shape and made the to survive. In put the seed of life into the first man. ~~Another myth~~ "The Beginning "The Flood" d of the World," tells about how the godess Themis after a great flood, the two people left alive helped humans survive. She told them to throw ~~some~~ living stones the stones turned into other humans

Preparing a Final Copy. When you are satisfied with the quality and correctness of your writing, write or type the draft one last time. If you have used a word processor, look over your writing, make a printout, and then proofread the final copy.

Sharing. Your writing reflects the care and effort you have given it. Share your writing with your audience. Let your friends, family, or teachers read it and comment on it. You also might wish to display your writing on a bulletin board or in a booklet.

Final Copy

Greek myths say that humans are alive because the gods created humans and helped them to survive. In "The Beginning of the World," a god named Prometheus formed a human from the clay of the earth. He put the seed of life into the human shape and made the first man. "The Flood" tells how the goddess Themis helped humans survive after a great flood. She told the two people left alive to throw stones. The stones turned into living humans.

Checklist for the Process of Writing

Prewriting

1. Decide on a topic.
2. Determine a purpose.
3. Choose a form.
4. Consider the audience.
5. Gather information.
6. Organize ideas.

Drafting

1. Follow your plan. Keep your topic, purpose, and audience in mind.
2. Write about your information, ideas, and feelings in sentence form.
3. Let your writing flow. Do not worry about errors at this time.

Revising

1. Read your draft. Ask yourself these questions:
   a. Is the writing interesting? Will others want to read it?
   b. Is the writing organized well? Are the details arranged in a sensible order?
   c. Should any details be omitted? Should any be added?
   d. Is every word the best possible choice?
2. Proofread your draft. Consider these questions as you look for errors:

Grammar and Usage

a. Is every word group a sentence rather than a fragment?
b. Does every verb agree with its subject?
c. Is the form of each pronoun, adjective, and adverb correct?

Capitalization

a. Is the first word in every sentence capitalized?
b. Are all proper nouns and proper adjectives capitalized?
c. Are titles capitalized correctly?

Punctuation

a. Does each sentence have the correct end mark?
b. Are marks such as commas, periods, apostrophes, hyphens, colons, semicolons, question marks, quotation marks, and underlining used correctly?

Spelling

a. Have unfamiliar words been checked in a dictionary?
b. Are plural and possessive forms spelled correctly?

3. Prepare the final copy. Make all changes and correct all errors. Finally, proofread your writing again and read it aloud as a final check.

Sharing

Let your family, friends, and teachers read your writing. Make your writing available on a bulletin board or in a booklet. You also might consider trying to publish your work in a student newspaper or literary magazine. Another way to share your writing is to read it onto a tape so that others can listen to it. If you have written a poem, a play, or a short story, you might have others present an oral reading of your work.

The **glossary** is an alphabetical listing of words from the selections, with meanings. The glossary gives the following information:

1. **The entry word broken into syllables.**

2. **The pronunciation of each word.** The **respelling** is shown in parentheses. The most common way to pronounce a word is listed first. The Pronunciation Key below shows the symbols for the sounds of letters and key words that contain those sounds.

   A **primary accent** ′ is placed after the syllable that is stressed the most when the word is spoken. A **secondary accent** ′ is placed after a syllable that has a lighter stress.

3. **The part of speech of the word.** These abbreviations are used:
   n. noun   *v.* verb   *adj.* adjective   *adv.* adverb

4. **The meaning of the word.** The definitions listed in the glossary apply to selected ways a word is used in these selections.

5. **Related forms.** Words with suffixes such as *-ing, -ed, -ness,* and *-ly* are listed under the base word.

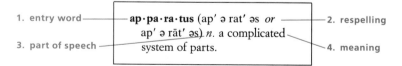

1. entry word — **ap·pa·ra·tus** (ap′ ə rat′ əs *or* — 2. respelling
   ap′ ə rāt′ əs) *n.* a complicated
3. part of speech — system of parts. — 4. meaning

Pronunciation Key

Symbol	Key Words	Symbol	Key Words	Symbol	Key Words	Symbol	Key Words
a	fat	o͞o	tool		a in ago	ch	chin
ā	ape	oo	look		e in agent	sh	she
ä	car, lot	yo͞o	use, cute, few	ə	i in sanity	th	thin
e	elf, ten	yoo	united, cure		o in comply	t͟h	then
ē	even	oi	oil		u in focus	zh	leisure
i	hit	ou	out			ŋ	ring
ī	bite, fire	u	up	ər	perhaps, murder	′	able (ā′b'l)
ō	go	ur	fur, bird				
ô	law, horn						

A

a·bate (ə bāt′) *v.* to become less; subside.

a·bom·i·na·ble (ə bäm′ə nə b'l) *adj.* very unpleasant; nasty.

a·brupt (ə brupt′) *adj.* **1.** curt or brusque in speech. **2.** sudden. —**abruptly** *adv.*

ab·surd·i·ty (əb sʉr′də tē *or* ab sʉr′də tē) *n.* the quality of being clearly unreasonable; foolishness.

a·can·thus (ə kan′ thəs) *n.* a thistlelike Mediterranean plant with lobed, often spiny leaves.

ac·cu·sa·tion (ak′yə zā′shən) *n.* an accusing or being accused.

ac·cuse (ə kyo̅o̅z′) *v.* to find fault, blame.

ac·quaint·ance (ə kwānt′′ns) *n.* the state of being acquainted or familiar with someone.

ac·quit·tal (ə kwit′′l) *n.* a setting free or being set free by a court.

ad·mon·ish (əd män′ish *or* ad män′ish) *v.* **1.** to caution against specific faults; warn. **2.** to criticize mildly.

a·droit (ə droit′) *adj.* skillful and clever.

ad·vo·cate (ad′və kit *or* ad′və kāt′) *n.* a person who speaks or writes in support of something.

af·ter·deck (af′tər dek′) *n.* the part of a ship's deck toward the stern.

a·ghast (ə gast′) *adj.* feeling great horror or dismay; horrified.

ag·i·tate (aj′ə tāt′) *v.* **1.** to stir up support through speeches and writing so as to produce changes. **2.** to move violently. —**agitated** *adj.*

air (er) *n.* a song or melody.

al·cove (al′kōv) *n.* a section of a room that is set back from the main part, such as a breakfast nook.

a·lert (ə lʉrt′) *v.* to warn to be ready.

al·ien (āl′yən *or* āl′ē ən) *n.* an outsider; one from another planet.

Al·lah (al′ə *or* ä′lə *or* ä lä′) *n.* the Moslem name for God.

al·lot (ə lät′) *v.* to give or assign as one's share.

al·ter (ôl′tər) *v.* to make different in detail; modify.

a·mah (ä′mə) *n.* in the Orient, a woman servant, especially one who serves as a baby's nurse.

am·bro·sia (am brō′zhə) *n.* **1.** the food of the gods and immortals. **2.** anything that tastes or smells delicious.

a·mends (ə mendz′) *n. pl.* something given or done to make up for injury or loss that one has caused.

am·i·ca·ble (am′i kə b'l) *adj.* friendly in feeling; showing good will; peaceable. —**amicably** *adv.*

a·miss (ə mis′) *adj.* wrong, faulty, improper.

am·ple (am′p'l) *adj.* enough; adequate.

an·gu·lar (aŋ′gyə lər) *adj.* with bones that jut out; gaunt.

an·nexe (an′eks) *n.* something added on; especially an addition built on or near a building.

an·te·room (an′ti ro̅o̅m′) *n.* a room leading to a more important one; waiting room.

anx·i·e·ty (aŋ zī′ə tē) *n.* a state of being uneasy or worried about what may happen.

anx·ious (aŋk′shəs *or* aŋ′shəs) *adj.* uneasy in mind; worried. —**anxiously** *adv.*

ap·pall (ə pôl′) *v.* to fill with horror or dismay; shock.

ap·pa·ra·tus (ap′ə rat′əs *or* ap′ə rāt′əs) *n.* instruments or equipment for a specific use.

ap·par·ent (ə per′ənt *or* ə par′ənt) *adj.* appearing to be true; seeming. —**apparently** *adv.*

ap·pease (ə pēz′) *v.* to make peaceful or quiet by giving in to the demands of.

ap·pre·hen·sive (ap′rə hen′siv) *adj.* uneasy or fearful about the future.

ap·pren·tice (ə pren′tis) *n.* a learner or beginner.

apt (apt) *adj.* tending or inclined; likely.

ar·bi·trar·y (är′bə trer′ē) *adj.* not fixed by rules but left to one's own choice.

arc (ärk) *n.* a bowlike curved line or object.

ar·che·ol·o·gy *or* **ar·chae·ol·o·gy** (är′kē äl′ə jē) *n.* the study of the life and culture of ancient peoples, as by excavation of ancient cities and objects.

arch·er·y (är′chər ē) *n.* the practice, art, or sport of shooting with bow and arrow.

ar·du·ous (är′joo wəs) *adj.* difficult to do; laborious.

ar·mor·er (är′mər ər) *n.* formerly, one who made or repaired armor.

ar·o·mat·ic (ar′ə mat′ik) *adj.* having a pleasant, often spicy odor or fragrance.

ar·rest (ə rest′) *v.* to stop or check.

art·ful (ärt′f'l) *adj.* done with much skill.

as·cer·tain (as′ər tān′) *v.* to find out in such a way as to be certain.

ash (ash) *n.* a timber and shade tree of the olive family, having tough, elastic, straight-grained wood.

as·pire (ə spīr′) *v.* to rise high; tower.

as·sail·ant (ə sāl′ənt) *n.* attacker.

as·sas·sin (ə sas′ 'n) *n.* a murderer who strikes suddenly.

as·sault (ə sôlt′) *n.* a violent attack, either physical or with words.

as·sem·blage (ə sem′ blij) *n.* a group of persons or things gathered together; assembly.

as·sume (ə soom′ *or* ə syoom′) *v.* to put on the appearance of.

asth·ma (az′ mə) *n.* a chronic disorder that causes wheezing, coughing, and difficulty in breathing.

a·stir (ə stur′) *adj.* in motion.

as·ton·ish (ə stän′ ish) *v.* to fill with sudden wonder or great surprise; amaze. —**astonishment** *n.*

as·tron·o·my (ə strän′ə mē) *n.* the science of stars, planets, and other heavenly bodies.

a·sy·lum (ə sī′ ləm) *n.* an old term for a place for the care of the mentally ill, or of the aged or poor.

a·tro·cious (ə trō′shəs) *adj.* very cruel or evil.

at·tach·ment (ə tach′ mənt) *n.* a legal document taking a person or his property into custody.

at·tire (ə tīr′) *n.* clothes.

aus·tere (ô stir′) *adj.* having a stern manner; forbidding.

av·a·lanche (av′ə lanch′) *n.* anything that comes suddenly in overwhelming numbers or large masses.

a·venge (ə venj′) *v.* to get revenge for an injury or a wrong. —**avenger** *n.*

a·vert (ə vurt′) *v.* to keep from happening; prevent.

awe (ô) *v.* to fill with deep respect mixed with fear and wonder. —**awesome** *adj.* —**in awe** respecting and fearing.

B

bab·ble (bab′ 'l) *v.* **1.** to say indistinctly or in a confused way. **2.** to say foolishly or inadvisedly.

babe (bāb) *n.* [Slang] a girl or young woman.

back·bite (bak′ bīt′) *v.* to speak falsehoods that harm a person's character or reputation.

---

at, āte, fär; pen, ēqual; sit, mīne; sō, côrn, join, took, fool, our; us, turn; chill, shop, thick, *th*ey, sin; **zh** *in* measure; **'l** *in* idle; ə *in* alive, cover, family, robot, circus.

bade (bad *or* bād) *v.* commanded; asked.

baf·fle (baf''l) *v.* to confuse so as to keep from understanding or solving; puzzle; confound. —**bafflement** *n.*

ban·ish (ban' ish) *v.* to send or put away; get rid of.

ban·is·ter (ban' əs tər) *n.* a railing and the balusters supporting it, as on a staircase.

bank (baŋk) *n.* **1.** a stretch of rising land at the edge of a stream. **2.** a large mound or ridge; steep rise or slope. *v.* to cover a fire with ashes and fuel so that it will burn longer. —**banked** *adj.*

bar (bär) *v.* **1.** to keep out; exclude. **2.** to obstruct; shut off; close.

bar·bar·i·an (bär ber' ē ən) *n.* a foreigner; one who was non-Greek.

bard (bärd) *n.* a poet.

bar·ra·cu·da (bar' ə kōō'də) *n.* a fierce, pikelike fish found in tropical seas.

bar·ren (bar'ən) *adj.* **1.** empty. **2.** not productive; unprofitable.

base (bās) *adj.* **1.** with little or no honor, courage, or decency; mean; contemptible. **2.** inferior in quality.

bat·tal·ion (bə tal'yən) *n.* a large group of soldiers arrayed for battle.

bat·ter·y (bat' ər ē *or* bat' rē) *n.* **1.** an emplacement or fortification equipped with heavy guns. **2.** the basic unit of artillery, like an infantry company.

bat·tle·ment (bat' 'l mənt) *n.* a low wall, as on top of a tower, with open spaces for shooting.

bead·y (bē' dē) *adj.* small, round, and glittering.

bear·ing (ber' iŋ) *n.* way of carrying and conducting oneself.

bed (bed) *n.* the bottom of a river or sea.

beech (bēch) *n.* a tree with smooth bark, hard wood, dark-green leaves, and edible nuts.

be·fell (bi fel') *v.* happened to.

bel·low (bel' ō) *v.* to cry out loudly.

bel·ly·ache (bel' ē āk') *v.* to complain.

be·reave (bi rēv') *v.* to leave in a sad or lonely state, as by death. —**bereavement** *n.*

berth (bʉrth) *n.* a built-in bed or bunk on a ship or train.

be·seech (bi sēch') *v.* to ask someone earnestly; implore.

be·spec·ta·cled (bi spek' tə k'ld) *adj.* wearing eyeglasses.

be·stir (bi stʉr') *v.* to stir to action.

be·stow (bi stō') *v.* present as a gift.

be·trothed (bi trōthd' *or* bi trôtht') *adj.* engaged to be married.

be·wil·der (bi wil' dər) *v.* to confuse hopelessly, as by something complicated. —**bewildered** *adj.*

bib (bib) *n.* the front upper part of overalls.

bick·er (bik' ər) *v.* to have a petty quarrel; squabble.

bid·dy (bid' ē) *n.* a hen.

bide (bīd) *v.* to dwell; reside.

bil·low (bil' ō) *v.* to surge, swell, or cause to swell.

bin (bin) *n.* a box or crib for storing grain.

bit·ters (bit'ərz) *n.* a liquor containing bitter herbs and roots.

bleak (blēk) *adj.* not cheerful; gloomy.

blithe (blīth) *adj.* cheerful; carefree.

blow (blō) *n.* a hard hit or stroke, as with the fist.

blurt (blʉrt) *v.* to say suddenly, without stopping to think.

blush (blush) *v.* to become red or rosy in color. —**blushing** *n.*

boar (bôr) *n.* a male hog or pig.

boast (bōst) *v.* to talk about one's deeds with too much pride and satisfaction; brag.

bod·ice (bäd'is) *n.* the upper part of a woman's dress.

bond (bänd) *n.* anything that binds, fastens, or unites; shackles.

bon·go (bäŋ′ gō) *n.* either of a pair of small joined drums, of different pitch, struck with the fingers.

boom (bōōm) *v.* to make a deep, hollow, resonant sound.

boor·ish (boor′ ish) *adj.* rude; ill-mannered.

boot·jack (bōōt jak) *n.* a device shaped like the letter *V* and used to pull off a boot.

bor·der (bôr′ dər) *n.* the dividing line between two countries.

bore[1] (bôr) *v.* past tense of **bear,** carried.

bore[2] (bôr) *v.* to make a hole or tunnel as by drilling.

borne (bôrn) *v.* tolerated.

bos'n (bōs′'n) *n.* a ship's officer in charge of the deck crew.

bouf·fant (bōō fänt′) *adj.* puffed out; full.

bound (bound) *adj.* **1.** confined by being tied. **2.** obliged. *n.* a jump; leap.

Braille (brāl) *n.* a system of printing and writing for the blind, using raised dots felt by the fingers.

brand (brand) *v.* to mark with a hot iron to show ownership of cattle.

bre·vet (brə vet′) *n.* a military commission giving an officer a higher honorary rank without more pay.

brib·er·y (brī′bər ē) *n.* the giving, offering, or taking of anything to get a person to do something illegal or wrong or something that he or she does not want to do.

brisk (brisk) *adj.* quick in manner or movement. —**briskly** *adv.*

britch·es (brich′ iz) *n.* trousers reaching to the knees.

broad (brôd) *adj.* of large extent from side to side; wide.

broth (brôth) *n.* a clear, thin soup made by boiling meat in water.

brusque (brusk) *adj.* rough and abrupt in manner or speech; curt. —**brusquely** *adv.*

brute (brōōt) *n.* an animal.

bulk (bulk) *n.* mass or body.

bunk·house (buŋk′ hous′) *n.* a large building for housing workers on a ranch.

buoy (boi *or* bōō′ e) *v.* to keep afloat.

bur·den (burd′ 'n) *n.* a heavy load.

bur·ly (bur′ lē) *adj.* big and strong; heavy and muscular.

bus·tle (bus′ 'l) *v.* to hurry busily or with much fuss and bother. *n.* busy, noisy activity.

C

cache (kash) *n.* a place in which stores of food or supplies are hidden.

cack·le (kak′ 'l) *v.* to laugh, making the shrill, unbroken, vocal sounds of a hen.

ca·lam·i·ty (kə lam′ə tē) *n.* any great misfortune that brings loss and suffering; disaster.

cal·cu·late (kal′ kyə lāt′) *v.* to determine by reasoning.

cal·lous (kal′ əs) *adj.* lacking pity or mercy; unfeeling; insensitive. —**callously** *adv.*

cam·o·mile (kam′ə mīl′ *or* kam′ə mēl′) *n.* a plant with strong-smelling leaves, whose dried flower heads have been used in medicinal tea.

can·non·ade (kan′ə nād′) *v.* to fire artillery.

can·teen (kan tēn′) *n.* a small metal container, usually covered with canvas, for carrying drinking water.

can·ter (kan′ tər) *v.* to ride a horse at a smooth, easy pace.

---

at, āte, fär; pen, ēqual; sit, mīne; sō, côrn, join, took, fōol, our; us, turn; chill, shop, thick, *th*ey, siŋ; zh *in* measure; 'l *in* idle; ə *in* alive, cover, family, robot, circus.

ca·pac·i·tor (kə pas′ ə tər) *n.* a device consisting of two or more conducting plates separated by insulating material and used for storing an electric charge.

cap·i·tal·ist (cap′ə t′l ist) *n.* **1.** a person who is in favor of an economic system in which the means of producing and distributing goods are privately owned and operated for profit, originally with full competition in a free market. **2.** an owner of wealth used in business.

ca·pit·u·la·tion (kə pich′ ə lā′ shən) *n.* surrender on certain conditions.

cap·ti·vate (kap′ tə vāt′) *v.* to capture the attention or affection of, as by beauty or excellence; fascinate; charm.

ca·ress (kə res′) *n.* a gentle touch.

car·ol (kar′əl) *n.* a song of joy or praise.

car·pet·bag·ger (kär′ pit bag′ ər) *n.* a Northern politican or adventurer who went South after the Civil War to profit from the confusion there.

car·tridge (kär trij) *n.* a metal container holding the bullets for a firearm.

cas·cade (kas kād′) *n.* a rippling fall of hair.

case·ment (kās′mənt) *n.* a hinged window frame that opens outward.

cas·sia (kash′ ə) *n.* a tree whose bark is used as a source of cinnamon.

cast (kast) *v.* **1.** to throw out or drop a net at the end of a rope or cable. **2.** to throw with force; fling; hurl. **3.** to cause to fall or turn; direct. **4.** to throw away.

cast off (kast ôf) *v.* to free a ship from a dock by releasing the lines.

cav·ern (kav′ ərn) *n.* a cave, especially a large cave.

cav·i·ty (kav′ ə tē) *n.* a hole or hollow place.

ce·les·tial (sə les′ chəl) *adj.* of heaven; divine.

cell (sel) *n.* a small room or cubicle.

cen·taur (sen′ tôr) *n.* from Greek mythology, any of a race of monsters with a man's head, trunk, and arms, and a horse's body and legs.

cha·os (kā′ äs) *n.* **1.** extreme confusion or disorder. **2.** the disorder of matter and space thought to have existed before the ordered universe.

char·i·ot (char′ ē ət) *n.* a horse-drawn, two-wheeled cart used in ancient times for war and racing.

chat·tel (chat′ ′l) *n.* a movable item of personal property, rather than real estate or other real property; a slave or other bound person.

check (chek) *v.* **1.** to stop suddenly. **2.** to block or restrain.

cheek·y (chēk′ ē) *adj.* saucy; impudent; insolent.

cher·ish (cher′ish) *v.* to take good care of; protect; foster.

chief·tain (chēf′tən) *n.* a leader, especially of a clan or tribe.

chor·tle (chôr′ t′l) *v.* to make, or utter with, a gleeful chuckling or snorting sound.

chron·ic (krän′ik) *adj.* lasting a long time or coming back again and again.

chron·i·cle (krän′ i k′l) *n.* a record or tale of things that happened.

churn (churn) *v.* **1.** to make foam by stirring vigorously. **2.** to stir up violently.

churr (chur) *v.* to make a low, trilled sound.

cir·cum·fer·ence (sər kum′ fər əns *or* sər kum′ frəns) *n.* **1.** the line bounding a circle or other rounded surface or area. **2.** the distance measured by this line.

cir·cum·scribe (sur′ kəm skrīb′ *or* sur′ kəm skrīb′) *v.* to limit; bind; restrict in scope or activity. —**circumscribed** *adj.*

cir·cum·stance (sur′ kəm stans′ *or* sur′ kəm stəns) *n.* the conditions affecting a person.

cit·ron (si′ trən) *n.* a yellow, thick-skinned

fruit resembling a lemon but larger and less acidic.

civ·i·li·za·tion (siv'ə lə zā' shən) *n.* a social organization of a high order, in which the arts, sciences, and government are developed; the total culture of a people, nation, or period.

clam·ber (klam' bər) *v.* to climb clumsily or with effort, using both hands and feet.

clar·i·on (klar' ē ən) *adj.* clear, sharp, and ringing like the sound of a clarion, a trumpet of the Middle Ages.

clash (klash) *n.* a conflict; struggle.

clas·si·fi·ca·tion (klas' ə fi kā' shən) *n.* an arrangement according to some systematic division into classes or groups.

cleave (klēv) *v.* to split; separate.

clutch (kluch) *v.* to grasp and hold tightly.

coax (kōks) *v.* to persuade or urge by soothing words or flattery.

cock (käk) *v.* to tip to one side; tilt.

co·deine (kō' dēn) *n.* a substance gotten from opium and resembling morphine: used for relieving pain and in cough medicines.

coin·age (koi' nij) *n.* a system of metal currency.

co·in·ci·dence (kō in' sə dəns) *n.* an accidental and remarkable occurrence of events or ideas at the same time, without one seeming to cause the other.

col·on·nade (käl' ə nād') *n.* a series of columns set at regular intervals, usually supporting a roof or series of arches of a building. —**colonnaded** *adj.*

colt (kōlt) *n.* a young horse.

co·ma (kō' mə) *n.* a condition like a deep, long sleep, when one is made unconscious by injury or disease.

com·man·deer (käm' ən dir') *v.* to take by force.

com·mence (kə mens') *v.* to begin; start.

com·merce (käm' ərs) *n.* the buying and selling of goods, as between cities, states, or countries.

com·mo·tion (kə mō' shən) *n.* a noisy rushing about; confusion.

com·pan·ion (kəm pan' yən) *n.* a good friend; comrade. —**companionable** *adj.*

com·pa·ny (kum' pə nē) *n.* the people who are one's companions.

com·pel (kəm pel') *v.* to get or bring about by force.

com·pen·sate (käm' pən sāt') *v.* to make up for; repay for a loss.

com·po·sure (kəm pō' zhər) *n.* calmness; self-control.

com·pound (käm pound' for verb; käm' pound for noun) *v.* to make greater by adding new elements. *n.* an enclosed space with a building or group of buildings in it.

con·ceit·ed (kən sēt' id) *adj.* having an exaggerated opinion of oneself or one's merits; vain.

con·cern (kən surn') *n.* a matter of interest.

con·course (kän' kôrs *or* käŋ' kôrs) *n.* a crowd; throng.

con·cus·sion (kən kush' ən) *n.* a violent shaking or jarring.

con·duct (kän' dukt') *n.* passage; travel.

con·duit (kän' dit *or* kän' doo wit) *n.* a pipe or channel for carrying fluids.

con·fec·tion (kən fek' shən) *n.* any candy or other sweet preparation.

con·fi·dant (kän' fə dant' *or* kän' fə dänt' *or* kän' fə dant' *or* kän' fə dänt') *n.* a close, trusted friend to whom one confides personal secrets.

---

at, āte, fär; pen, ēqual; sit, mīne; sō, côrn, join, took, fool, our; us, turn; chill, shop, thick, *th*ey, siŋ; **zh** *in* measure; 'l *in* idle; ə *in* alive, cover, family, robot, circus.

con·fi·dence (kän′ fə dəns) *n.* a relationship as confidant.

con·fla·gra·tion (kän′ flə grä′ shən) *n.* a big fire that does great damage.

con·found (kän′ found) *v.* to damn; used as a mild oath. [Confound it!]

con·quest (käŋ′ kwest *or* kän′ kwest) *n.* the act of conquering or overcoming by physical force.

con·sci·en·tious (kän′ shē en′ shəs *or* kän′ shē en′ chəs) *adj.* showing care and exactness.

con·scious (kän′ shəs) *adj.* self-conscious; ill-at-ease.

con·se·quence (kän′ sə kwens′ *or* kän′ sə kwəns) *n.* a result of an action.

con·sole (kən sōl′) *v.* to make feel less sad or disappointed; comfort. —**consoling** *adj.*

con·spir·a·cy (kən spir′ə sē) *n.* an unlawful or harmful plot.

con·struc·tive (kən struk′ tive) *adj.* leading to improvements. —**constructively** *adv.*

con·sult (kən sult′) *v.* to ask the advice of.

con·sume (kən soom′ *or* kən syoom′) *v.* to destroy, as by fire.

con·tem·po·rar·y (kən tem′ pə rer′ ē) *n.* a person or thing of the same time period or about the same age as another or others.

con·tempt (kən tempt′) *n.* the condition of being despised or scorned.

con·tent (kən tent′) *adj.* happy enough with what one has or is; satisfied. —**contentment** *n.*

con·tin·gent (kən tin′ jənt) *n.* a group forming part of a larger group.

con·tri·bu·tion (kän′ trə byoo′ shən) *n.* money given for charity or other fund.

con·trive (kən trīv′) *v.* to plan.

con·vey·ance (kən vā′əns) *n.* a means of transportation; vehicle.

con·viv·i·al (kən viv′ ē əl) *adj.* having to do with a feast or festive activity.

co·quette (kō ket′) *n.* a girl or woman who tries to get men to notice and admire her; flirt. —**coquettish** *adj.*

cor·mo·rant (kôr′ mə rənt) *n.* a large sea bird that is greedy for food and dives for the fish it eats.

cor·ru·gate (kôr′ ə gāt′ *or* kär′ ə gāt′) *v.* to put grooves and ridges in, so as to make look wavy; make wrinkles in. —**corrugated** *adj.*

cor·rupt (kə rupt′) *adj.* spoiled; rotten.

coun·cil (koun′ s′l) *n.* a group of people called together to plan or discuss something or give advice.

coun·ter·act (koun′ tər akt′) *v.* to act against; undo the effect of something with opposing action.

cou·pling pin (kup′ liŋ pin) *n.* a mechanical device for joining parts together.

course (kôrs) *v.* to run through; traverse. *n.* **1.** the direction taken, as by a ship or plane. **2.** way of behaving; mode of conduct.

court (kôrt) *n.* an uncovered space wholly or partly surrounded by buildings or walls.

cour·te·ous (kʉr′ tē əs) *adj.* polite and gracious; well-mannered. —**courteously** *adv.*

cour·ti·er (kôr′ tē ər *or* kôr′ tyər) *n.* an attendant at a royal court.

cow·er (kou′ ər) *n.* to crouch or huddle up, as from fear.

crack·pot (krak′ pät′) *n.* a crazy or unbalanced person.

cran·ny (kran′ ē) *n.* a small, narrow opening; crack, as in a wall.

craze (krāz) *v.* to make mentally ill or insane. —**crazed** *adj.*

crew-cut (kroo′ kut) *n.* a style of man's haircut in which the hair is cut close to the head.

crib (krib) *v.* to pass off another's ideas as one's own; do school-work dishonestly.

crim·son (krim′ z′n) *adj.* deep-red.

crock·er·y (kräk′ ər ē) *n.* earthenware pots, jars, and dishes.

crook (krook) *n.* a hooked, bent, or curved part; hook.

crouch (krouch) *v.* to stoop low with the limbs close to the body.

croup (kroop) *n.* an inflammation of the breathing passages that causes hard breathing and hoarse coughing.

cru·cial (kroo′ shəl) *adj.* of supreme importance.

cru·el (kroo′ əl) *adj.* causing pain.

crush (krush) *v.* to press forward; crowd.

cul·ti·vate (kul′ tə vāt′) *v.* to prepare and use land for growing crops.

curb (kurb) *n.* the stone or concrete edging forming a gutter along a street.

curt (kurt) *adj.* so short or abrupt as to seem rude; brusque. —**curtly** *adv.*

cus·tom (kus′ təm) *n.* a usual practice or habitual way of behaving; habit.

cut (kut) *v.* to separate. —**cut a figure** to attract attention or make a certain type of impression.

cyn·i·cal (sin′ i k'l) *adj.* doubting the sincerity of people's motives and actions. —**cynically** *adv.*

D

dab·ble (dab′ 'l) *v.* to dip lightly in and out of water.

damp·en (dam′ pən) *v.* to deaden, depress, reduce, or lessen.

dam·sel (dam′ z'l) *n.* a girl; maiden.

dank (daŋk) *adj.* disagreeably damp; moist and chilly.

dap·pled (dap′ 'ld) *adj.* marked with spots.

dash (dash) *v.* to smash.

daw·dle (dôd′ 'l) *v.* to waste time in pointless activity or by being slow; loiter.

de·cline (di klīn′) *v.* to refuse politely.

de·cree (di krē′) *n.* an official order or decision, as of a government or court.

ded·i·ca·tion (ded′ ə kā′ shən) *n.* devotion to a sacred purpose.

de·duce (di doos′ *or* di dyoos′) *v.* to figure out by logical reasoning; conclude from known facts or general principles.

de·duc·tion (di duk′ shən) *n.* reasoning from known facts or general principles to a logical conclusion. —**deductive** *adj.*

de·fect (dē′ fekt) *n.* an imperfection; fault.

de·fi·ant (di fī′ ənt) *adj.* openly and boldly resisting; opposing. —**defiantly** *adv.* —**defiance** *n.*

de·i·ty (dē′ ə tē) *n.* a god or goddess.

de·ject·ed (di jek′ tid) *adj.* in low spirits; depressed; disheartened; sad. —**dejectedly** *adv.*

de·lib·er·a·tion (di lib′ ə rā′ shən) *n.* consideration; carefulness.

de·liv·er·y (di liv′ ər ē) *n.* the act or manner of giving a speech.

dem·oi·selle (dem′ wə zel′) *n.* a damsel.

de·mote (di mōt′) *v.* to reduce to a lower grade; lower in rank. —**demotion** *n.*

de·plete (di plēt′) *v.* to make less by gradually using up.

de·pot (dē′ pō) *n.* a storehouse; warehouse.

de·prav·i·ty (di prav′ə tē) *n.* corruption, wickedness.

de·press (di pres′) *v.* to press down.

de·prive (di prīv′) *v.* to keep from using or enjoying.

der·e·lict (der′ ə likt′) *adj.* deserted by the owner; abandoned.

---

at, āte, fär; pen, ēqual; sit, mīne; sō, côrn, join, took, fool, our; us, turn; chill, shop, thick, they, siŋ; zh *in* measure; '1 *in* idle; ə *in* alive, cover, family, robot, circus.

de·ri·sion (di rizh′ ən) *n.* contempt or ridicule.

de·rive (di rīv′) *v.* to get or receive.

de·scent (di sent′) *n.* a descending; coming or going down.

des·e·crate (des′ ə krāt′) *v.* to violate or insult the sacredness of.

des·o·la·tion (des′ ə lā′ shən) *n.* grief, misery.

de·spair (di sper′) *n.* loss of hope; hopelessness. *v.* to lose hope; be without hope.

des·per·ate (des′ pər it) *adj.* extreme; drastic.

de·spoil (di spoil′) *v.* to deprive of something by force; rob; plunder.

de·spond·en·cy (di spän′ dən sē) *n.* loss of courage or hope; dejection.

de·spond·ent (di spän′ dənt) *adj.* dejected; discouraged. —**despondently** *adv.*

des·tine (des′ tin) *v.* to set apart for a certain purpose; intend.

des·tin·y (des′ tə nē) *n.* what will necessarily happen to a person.

de·tect (di tekt′) *v.* to discover; notice.

de·ter·mi·na·tion (di tur′ mə nā′ shən) *n.* a firm intention; firmness of purpose.

de·vour (di vour′) *v.* to eat hungrily or greedily.

dex·ter·i·ty (dek ster′ ə tē) *n.* skill in using one's hands or body; adroitness.

di·a·gram (dī′ə gram′) *n.* a drawing, plan, or chart that explains a thing, as by showing its parts and their relationships and workings.

dig·ni·ty (dig′ nə tē) *n.* loftiness of appearance or manner; stateliness.

di·men·sion (də men′shən) *n.* size or importance.

dim·ple (dim′ p'l) *n.* a small, natural, hollow spot, as on the cheek or chin. *v.* to show or form dimples.

din (din) *n.* a loud, continuous noise; confused clamor or uproar.

din·gy (din′jē) *adj.* dismal; shabby.

dirge (durj) *n.* a slow, sad song or poem expressing grief, especially for the dead.

dis·con·cert (dis kən surt′) *v.* to upset the calmness of.

dis·course (dis′ kôrs) *n.* a formal treatment of a subject, in speech or writing.

dis·cred·it (dis kred′ it) *v.* to damage the reputation of; disgrace.

dis·creet (dis krēt′) *adj.* careful about what one says or does; prudent. —**discreetly** *adv.*

dis·cus (dis′ kəs) *n.* a heavy disk of metal and wood thrown for distance in a contest of strength and skill.

dis·dain (dis dān′) *n.* aloof contempt or scorn.

dis·heart·en (dis här′ t'n) *v.* to discourage; depress.

dis·in·fect·ant (dis in′ fekt′ ənt) *n.* a substance that destroys harmful bacteria or viruses.

dis·mal (diz′ m'l) *adj.* gloomy; miserable. —**dismally** *adv.*

dis·man·tle (dis man′t'l) *v.* to strip of furniture or equipment. —**dismantled** *adj.*

dis·may (dis mā′) *n.* a loss of courage when faced with trouble or danger. *v.* to make discouraged at the prospect of trouble; fill with alarm; daunt.

dis·mount (dis mount′) *v.* to get off a horse.

dis·perse (dis purs′) *v.* to break up and move in different directions; scatter.

dis·pute (dis pyo͞ot′) *v.* to argue or debate.

dis·tort (dis tôrt′) *v.* to twist out of its usual shape. —**distorter** *n.*

dis·tract (dis trakt′) *v.* to draw the mind away in other directions; divert. —**distracting** *adj.*

dis·tress (dis tres′) *v.* to cause sorrow, worry, or suffering to; pain; trouble.

dis·tressed (dis trest′) *adj.* worried; anxious.

di·van (dī′ van *or* di van′) *n.* a large, low couch or sofa, usually without armrests or back.

dive (dīv) *n.* a cheap, disreputable bar or nightclub.

di·vert (də vʉrt′) *v.* to turn aside; deflect.

dog days (dôg dāz *or* däg dāz) *n.* the hot, humid days in July and August.

do·mes·tic (də mes′ tik) *adj.* of the home or family.

dom·i·nate (däm′ ə nāt′) *v.* to rule or control by superior power or influence.

do·min·ion (də min′ yən) *n.* a governed territory or country.

don (dän) *v.* to put on a garment.

doom (do͞om) *v.* to pass judgment on; condemn.

dot·age (dōt′ ij) *n.* feeble and childish state due to old age; senility.

down·cast (doun′ kast′) *adj.* unhappy or discouraged; dejected.

down·heart·ed (doun här′ tid) *adj.* sad or discouraged; dejected. **—downheartedly** *adv.*

down·y (doun′ ē) *adj.* of or covered with soft, fine feathers or hair; soft and fluffy, like down.

draw (drô) *v.* to bring up from a well.

drawl (drôl) *v.* to speak slowly, drawing out the vowels.

drought (drout *or* drouth) *n.* a long period of dry weather; lack of rain.

drowse (drouz) *n.* the act or an instance of drowsing; doze; sleeping lightly.

dumb·found (dum′ found′) *v.* to make speechless by shocking; amaze; astonish. **—dumbfounded** *adj.*

dun (dun) *n.* a horse of dull grayish brown color.

dupe (do͞op *or* dyo͞op) *v.* to deceive or cheat.

dusk (dusk) *n.* twilight; the time near evening.

dusk·y (dus′ kē) *adj.* somewhat dark in color.

dwelt (dwelt) *v.* resided; lived.

E

eaves (ēvz) *n. pl.* the lower edge or edges of a roof, usually projecting beyond the sides of a building.

ech·o (ek′ ō) *v.* to repeat or reflect sound.

é·clair (ā kler′ *or* ē kler′ *or* i kler′) *n.* a small oblong pastry shell filled with flavored custard or whipped cream and covered with frosting.

e·clipse (i klips′ *or* ē klips′) *n.* a partial or total covering of the sun when the moon comes between it and the earth.

ed·it (ed′ it) *v.* to prepare an author's work for publication by arranging and revising.

ee·rie (ir′ ē) *adj.* weird in a frightening way.

e·go·tism (ē′ gə tiz′m) *n.* too high an opinion of oneself; self-conceit.

e·lab·o·rate (i lab′ ər it) *adj.* **1.** developed in great detail. **2.** painstaking; very careful. **—elaborately** *adv.*

e·lect (i lekt′) *v.* to choose or decide.

el·e·men·tal (el′ ə ment′ t'l) *adj.* having to do with the four elements of nature; basic.

el·e·men·ta·ry (el′ ə men′ tər ē *or* el′ ə men′ trē) *adj.* of first principles or fundamentals; introductory; basic.

elm (elm) *n.* a tall, hardy shade tree.

e·lope (i lōp′ *or* ə lōp′) *v.* to run away secretly in order to get married.

el·o·quence (el′ ə kwəns) *n.* speech or writing that can stir people's feelings or influence their thinking.

---

at, āte, fär; pen, ēqual; sit, mīne; sō, côrn, join, to͞ok, fo͞ol, our; us, tʉrn; chill, shop, thick, *th*ey, siŋ; **zh** *in* measure; **'l** *in* idle; ə *in* alive, cover, family, robot, circus.

e·man·ci·pate (i man′ sə pāt′) *v.* to set free; release from bondage. —**emancipator** *n.*

em·bark (im bärk′) *v.* to go aboard a ship.

em·bry·on·ic (em′ brē än′ ik) *adj.* in an early stage; undeveloped.

e·merge (i mʉrj′) *v.* to come forth into view; become visible.

e·mit (i mit′) *v.* to send out; give forth.

en·camp·ment (in kamp′ mənt) *n.* a camp or campsite.

en·chant (in chant′) *v.* to cast a spell over, as by magic; bewitch. —**enchanted** *adj.*

en·chant·ment (in chant′ mənt) *n.* a magic spell or charm.

en·coun·ter (in koun′ tər) *v.* to meet unexpectedly; come upon.

en·deav·or (in dev′ ər) *v.* to try to do something.

en·dow (in dou′) *v.* to provide with some talent or quality.

en·dure (in door′ *or* in dyoor′) *v.* to hold up under great pain.

en·dur·ing (in door′ iŋ *or* in dyoor′ iŋ) *adj.* lasting; permanent.

en·gage (in gāj′) *v.* to hire; employ.

en·list (in list′) *v.* to get the help or services of.

e·nor·mous (i nôr′ məs) *adj.* very large. —**enormously** *adv.*

en·rage (in rāj′) *v.* to make angry; infuriate.

en·tan·gle (in taŋ′ g'l) *v.* to make tangled or twisted; trap.

en·ter·prise (en′ tər prīz′) *n.* a business venture.

en·twine (in twīn) *v.* to twine or twist together or around.

en·vel·op (in vel′ əp) *v.* to wrap up; cover completely.

e·ra (ir′ ə *or* er′ ə) *n.* a period of time considered in terms of noteworthy and typical events or people.

e·rad·i·cate (i rad′ ə kāt′) *v.* to get rid of; wipe out; destroy.

e·rase (i rās′) *v.* to wipe out; obliterate.

es·cort (i skôrt′) *v.* to go with; accompany.

es·say (e sā′) *v.* to try; attempt.

es·trange (ə strānj′) *v.* to turn a person from an affectionate or friendly attitude to an indifferent, unfriendly, or hostile one; alienate the affections of. —**estrangement** *n.*

e·ter·nal (i tʉr′ n'l) *adj.* never stopping or ending; perpetual.

e·ter·ni·ty (i tʉr′ nə tē) *n.* **1.** the quality or state of being everlasting; continuance without end. **2.** infinite time; time without beginning or end.

ev·i·dent (ev′ ə dənt) *adj.* easy to see or perceive; obvious. —**evidently** *adv.*

ew·er (yōo′ ər) *n.* a large pitcher with a wide mouth.

ex·al·ta·tion (eg′ zôl tā′ shən) *n.* a feeling of great joy and pride; elation; rapture.

ex·as·per·ate (ig zas′ pə rāt′) *v.* to make angry; annoy very much. —**exasperation** *n.*

ex·ceed·ing·ly (ik sēd′ iŋ lē) *adv.* very; extremely.

ex·cep·tion (ik sep′ shən) *n.* a case to which a rule or principle does not apply.

ex·e·cute (ek′ sə kyōot′) *v.* to carry out; perform.

ex·e·cu·tion·er (ek′ sə kyōo′ shən ər) *n.* a person who carries out a death sentence.

ex·ert (ig zʉrt′) *v.* to apply oneself with great energy or effort.

ex·er·tion (ig zʉr′ shən) *n.* the use of power and strength; effort.

ex·haus·tion (ig zôs′ chən) *n.* the state of being very tired; great weariness.

ex·hi·bi·tion (ek′ sə bish′ ən) *n.* a public show or display.

ex·hort (ig zôrt′) *v.* to urge strongly by advice or warning; entreat.

ex·panse (ik spans') *n.* a large area.

ex·pe·di·tion (ek' spə dish' ən) *n.* a journey or voyage as for exploration or battle.

ex·ploit (eks' ploit *for noun;* ik sploit' *for verb*) *n.* a daring act or bold deed. *v.* to profit from the labor of others in an unethical way. —**exploitation** *n.*

ex·qui·site (eks' kwi zit *or* ik skwiz' it) *adj.* very beautiful, especially in a delicate or carefully wrought way.

ex·tin·guish (ik stiŋ' gwish) *v.* to put an end to; destroy.

ex·tol (ik stōl') *v.* to praise highly; laud.

ex·tra·ter·res·tri·al (ek' strə tə res' trē əl) *adj.* originating or existing outside the earth.

ex·trem·i·ty (ik strem'ə tē) *n.* the outermost or utmost point or part; end.

ex·tri·cate (eks' trə kāt') *v.* to set free; disentangle.

ex·u·ber·ant (ig zoo' bər ənt) *adj.* full of life, vitality, or high spirits.

F

fa·kir (fə kir') *n.* a member of a Moslem holy sect who lives by begging.

fal·ter (fôl' tər) *v.* to act hesitantly; show uncertainty.

fan·cy (fan' sē) *n.* a liking or fondness.

fare (fer) *n.* money paid for a trip in a train, bus, or plane.

fan·fare (fan' fer') *n.* a loud flourish of trumpets.

fast (fast) *adv.* firmly; fixedly.

fa·tal (fāt' 'l) *adj.* **1.** very destructive. **2.** resulting in death.

feat (fēt) *n.* an act showing unusual skill. —**featly** *adv.* [Archaic]

feath·er (fe*th*' ər) *v.* to move or look like feathers.

fee·ble (fē' b'l) *adj.* weak; not strong.

fe·line (fē'līn) *adj.* of a cat or the cat family.

fern (furn) *n.* any of a group of nonflowering plants having roots, stems, and fronds, and reproducing by spores instead of by seeds. —**ferny** *adj.*

fe·ro·cious (fə rō' shəs) *adj.* fierce; savage; violently cruel.

fer·tile (fur' t'l) *adj.* producing abundantly; rich in resources; fruitful.

fes·tiv·i·ty (fes tiv' ə tē) *n.* merrymaking; gaiety.

fetch (fech) *v.* **1.** to go after and come back with; bring. **2.** to deliver or deal a blow.

fe·ver·ish (fē' vər ish) *adj.* greatly excited.

fiend (fēnd) *n.* an inhumanly wicked or cruel person.

fiend·ish (fēnd' ish) *adj.* inhumanly wicked or cruel; devilish. —**fiendishly** *adv.*

fi·er·y (fī' ər ē) *adj.* like fire; hot.

fire·brand (fīr' brand') *n.* a piece of burning wood.

fixed (fikst) *adj.* not movable.

flail (flāl) *v.* to move one's arms about in a wild, free-swinging motion.

flake (flāk) *n.* a small, thin mass.

flank (flaŋk) *n.* the fleshy side of a person or animal between the ribs and the hip.

flare (fler) *v.* **1.** to blaze up brightly or burn unsteadily. **2.** to burst out suddenly in anger.

fleck (flek) *n.* a particle; flake.

fleet·ing (flēt' iŋ) *adj.* passing swiftly; not lasting.

flick·er (flik' ər) *n.* a quick, wavering motion.

---

at, āte, fär; pen, ēqual; sit, mīne; sō, côrn, join, took, fool, our; us, turn; chill, shop, thick, they, siŋ; zh in measure; 'l in idle; ə *in* alive, cover, family, robot, circus.

flinch (flinch) *v.* to draw back or wince with pain.

flog (fläg *or* flôg) *v.* to beat or whip.

flour·ish (flʉr′ ish) *v.* to grow vigorously; thrive; prosper. —**flourishing** *adj.*

flus·ter (flus′ tər) *v.* to make or become confused or nervous.

fol·ly (fäl′ ē) *n.* a lack of sense or sensible conduct; foolishness.

foot (foot) *v.* to dance.

for·ay (fôr′ ā) *n.* a sudden attack or raid.

ford (fôrd) *v.* to cross a stream or river at a shallow place.

fore·bod·ing (fôr bōd′iŋ) *n.* a warning or a feeling that something bad is about to happen.

fore·leg (fôr′ leg′) *n.* either of the front legs of an animal with four or more legs.

for·est·er (fôr′ is tər *or* fär′ is tər) *n.* a person whose work is taking care of trees.

for·feit (fôr′ fit) *v.* to give up as a penalty for losing.

forge (fôrj) *v.* to shape metal by heating and pounding.

for·lorn (fər lôrn′ *or* fôr lôrn′) *adj.* wretched; miserable; pitiful. —**forlornly** *adv.*

for·mal·i·ty (fôr mal′ ə tē) *n.* a formal or conventional act or requirement; ceremony or form.

for·sooth (fer sooth′ *or* fôr sooth′) *adv.* [Archaic] in truth; no doubt; indeed.

for·tress (fôr′ trəs) *n.* a fortified place; fort.

for·tune (fôr′ chən) *n.* luck.

foul (foul) *adj.* **1.** unpleasant; disagreeable. **2.** extremely dirty; disgustingly filthy.

frail (frāl) *adj.* slender and delicate; weak.

frank·in·cense (fraŋ′ kən sens′) *n.* a gum resin from Arabian and African trees that is burned for its aroma.

fran·tic (fran′ tik) *adj.* wild with worry, fear, or other emotion. —**frantically** *adv.*

fraud (frôd) *n.* something said or done to cheat or trick.

fren·zy (fren′ zē) *n.* a wild outburst of feeling or action; brief period of strong emotion that is almost like madness. —**frenzied** *adj.*

fringe (frinj) *n.* an outer edge; border; margin.

friv·o·lous (friv′ ə ləs) *adj.* not properly serious or sensible; silly.

frol·ic·some (fräl′ ik səm) *adj.* full of fun or high spirits; playful; merry.

front (frunt) *n.* the most forward area, where actual fighting is going on in a war.

fu·el (fyoo′əl *or* fyool) *v.* to supply with power.

fu·gi·tive (fyoo′ jə tiv) *n.* **1.** a person who flees or has fled from danger. **2.** a fleeting or elusive thing.

fun·da·men·tal (fun′ də men′ t'l) *adj.* basic. —**fundamentally** *adv.*

fu·ri·ous (fyoor′ ē əs) *adj.* full of anger. —**furiously** *adv.*

fur·row (fʉr′ ō) *n.* a narrow groove made in the ground by a plow.

fur·tive (fʉr′ tiv) *adj.* done or acting in a sly, sneaky way.

fu·tile (fyoot′ 'l) *adj.* useless; vain; ineffective.

G

gait (gāt) *n.* manner of walking or running.

gal·ler·y (gal′ ə rē) *n.* a platform or projecting upper floor in a building, with seats for watching an event.

gal·ley (gal′ ē) *n.* a long, low, usually single-decked ship moved along by oars and sails.

gal·li·vant (gal′ ə vant′) *v.* to go in search of amusement or excitement.

gaol (jāl) *n.* British spelling of *jail*.

gap (gap) *n.* an opening; breach.

gar·ri·son (gar′ə s'n) *n.* a military post or station.

gas plate (gas plāt) *n.* a small gas burner for cooking.

gaud·y (gôd' ē) *adj.* bright and showy, but in bad taste; cheaply ornate.

gaunt (gônt) *adj.* thin and bony; hollow-eyed and haggard.

gawk·y (gô' kē) *adj.* awkward; clumsy; ungainly.

gaze (gāz) *n.* a steady look.

ge·ol·o·gy (jē äl' ə jē) *n.* the science dealing with the physical nature of the earth, including the structure and development of its crust and interior, types of rocks, and fossil forms. —**geologist** *n.*

gin·ger (jin' jər) *n.* a reddish-brown color.

gin·ger·ly (jin' jər lē) *adv.* very carefully or cautiously.

glass (glas) *n.* a mirror.

glock·en·spiel (gläk' ən spēl' *or* gläk' ən shpēl') *n.* a percussion instrument with flat metal bars set in a frame, that produce bell-like tones of the scale when struck with small hammers.

glo·ry (glôr' ē) *v.* to exult in.

gnaw (nô) *v.* to cut, bite, and wear away bit by bit.

goose pim·ples (gōōs pim' p'lz) *n. pl.* a bumpy condition of the skin caused by fear.

gos·sa·mer (gäs' ə mər) *n.* a very thin, soft, filmy cloth. *adj.* light, thin, and filmy.

gram·mat·i·cal (grə mat' i k'l) *adj.* conforming to the rules for speaking and writing in a given language.

gran·ite (gran' it) *n.* a very hard, crystalline rock.

grat·i·fi·ca·tion (grat' ə fi kā' shən) *n.* satisfaction and pleasure.

grat·i·tude (grat' ə tōōd' *or* grat' ə tyōōd') *n.* a feeling of thankful appreciation for favors received; thankfulness.

great·coat (grāt' kōt') *n.* a heavy overcoat.

green·horn (grēn' hôrn') *n.* a young, inexperienced person.

grieve (grēv) *v.* to feel grief; sadden or distress.

grim·y (grī' mē) *adj.* covered with grime; very dirty.

grit·ty (grit' ē) *adj.* containing sand or stones. —**grittiness** *n.*

grog (gräg) *n.* any alcoholic liquor, such as rum, especially when diluted with water.

grope (grōp) *v.* to feel or search about blindly or uncertainly.

gro·tesque (grō tesk') *adj.* having a twisted, strange, unreal appearance or shape; bizarre.

ground (ground) *v.* pressed down and rubbed together harshly or gratingly.

grove (grōv) *n.* a small wood or group of trees without undergrowth.

grum·ble (grum' b'l) *v.* to complain in low sounds that cannot be understood.

guise (gīz) *n.* the way a person seems to be, but is not.

guts (guts) *n. pl.* the stomach and intestines.

gut·ter (gut' ər) *n.* a narrow channel along the side of a swimming pool to carry off water.

H

ha·bit·u·al (hə bich' ōō wəl) *adj.* done in a typical or usual way; customary.

hack (hak) *adj.* stale; worn out by constant use.

hag·gard (hag' ərd) *adj.* having a wasted, worn look from grief or exhaustion.

---

at, āte, fär; pen, ēqual; sit, mīne; sō, côrn, join, took, fōōl, our; us, turn; chill, shop, thick, they, siŋ; zh in measure; 'l in idle;
ə *in* alive, cover, family, robot, circus.

half nel·son (haf nel′ s'n) *n.* a wrestling hold in which one arm is placed under the opponent's arm from behind with the hand pressing the back of the neck.

ha·rangue (hə raŋ′) *v.* to give a long blustering or scolding speech.

har·ass (hə ras′ *or* har′ əs) *v.* to trouble, worry, or torment repeatedly.

har·row (har′ ō) *n.* a heavy frame with spikes or disks, pulled by a horse, and used for breaking up and leveling plowed ground.

has·ten (hās′ 'n) *v.* to move swiftly; hurry.

haugh·ty (hôt′ ē) *adj.* showing great pride in oneself and contempt or scorn for others; arrogant. —**haughtily** *adv.*

head·y (hed′ ē) *adj.* tending to affect the senses; intoxicating.

heark·en (här′ kən) *v.* to pay careful attention; listen carefully.

heave (hēv) *n.* the act of raising or lifting with effort.

heir·loom (er′ loom′) *n.* a treasured possession handed down from generation to generation.

hel·ter-skel·ter (hel′ tər skel′ tər) *adv.* in haste and confusion; in a disorderly and hurried manner.

her·ald (her′ əld) *n.* an official who made proclamations, carried state messages, and took charge of tournaments.

hes·i·ta·tion (hez′ ə tā′ shən) *n.* a halting or pausing for a moment because of fear or uncertainty.

hig·gle·dy-pig·gle·dy (hig′ 'l dē pig′ 'l dē) *adv.* in disorder; in jumbled confusion.

hilt (hilt) *n.* the handle of a sword, dagger, or knife.

hoax (hōks) *n.* a trick or a fraud, especially one meant as a practical joke.

hob·ble (häb′ 'l) *v.* to hinder the movement of a horse by tying two legs together.

hoist (hoist) *v.* to raise aloft; lift, especially by means of a pulley or crane.

hol·low (häl′ ō) *n.* an empty space; cavity. *adj.* deep-toned and muffled, empty. —**hollowly** *adv.*

hom·age (häm′ ij *or* äm′ ij) *n.* anything given or done to show respect or honor.

home stretch (hōm′ strech′) *n.* the part of a race track between the last turn and the finish line.

hone (hōn) *v.* to sharpen.

hoot (hoot) *v.* to shout, especially in scorn or disapproval.

hos·pi·ta·ble (häs′ pi tə b'l *or* häs pit′ə b'l) *adj.* showing or characterized by friendliness, kindness, and generosity toward guests. —**hospitably** *adv.*

hos·pi·tal·i·ty (häs′ pə tal′ ə tē) *n.* the act, practice, or quality of being friendly, kind, and generous toward guests.

hos·tile (häs′ t'l) *adj.* having or showing dislike or ill will; unfriendly; antagonistic.

hos·til·i·ties (häs til′ ə tēz) *n. pl.* warlike acts.

hov·er (huv′ ər *or* häv′ ər) *v.* to stay fluttering in the air near one place.

how·itz·er (hou′ it sər) *n.* a short cannon, firing shells in a relatively high curve.

howl (houl) *n.* a long, wailing cry.

hud·dle (hud′ 'l) *v.* to draw or hunch oneself up.

hu·man·i·ty (hyoo man′ ə tē *or* hyoo man′ ə tē *or* yoo man′ ə tē) *n.* the human race.

hu·man·oid (hyoo′ mən oid′ *or* yoo′ mən oid′) *n.* a nearly human creature of another planet.

hum·bug (hum′ bug′) *n.* a person who is not what he claims to be; imposter.

hum·drum (hum′ drum′) *adj.* lacking variety; dull; monotonous.

hunch (hunch) *v.* to sit, stand, or squat with the back arched. —**hunched** *adj.*

hurl (hurl) *v.* to throw with force.

hus·tle (hus′ 'l) *v.* **1.** to work or act rapidly or energetically. **2.** [Slang] to obtain money by aggressive or dishonest means.

hy·a·cinth (hī′ ə sinth′) *n.* a plant of the lily family with spikes of fragrant bell-shaped flowers.

hys·te·ri·a (his tir′ ē ə *or* his ter′ ē ə) *n.* an outbreak of wild, uncontrolled excitement or other feeling, with fits of laughing and crying. —**hysterical** *adj.*

I

ice·box (īs′ bäks′) *n.* a cabinet with ice in it for keeping food cold.

i·de·al·is·tic (ī′ dē ə lis′ tik *or* ī dē′ ə lis′ tik) *adj.* having the characteristics of an impractical dreamer.

i·den·ti·ty (ī den′ tə tē *or* i den′ tə tē) *n.* the condition or fact of being a specific person; individuality.

id·i·ot·ic (id′ ē ät′ ic) *adj.* very foolish or stupid.

i·dle (ī′ d'l) *adj.* unemployed; not busy.

il·lus·tri·ous (i lus′ trē əs) *adj.* very distinguished; famous; outstanding.

im·mac·u·late (i mak′ yə lit) *adj.* perfectly clean; spotless.

im·mense (i mens′) *adj.* vast; huge; very large.

im·mor·tal (i môr′ t'l) *adj.* living or lasting forever.

im·pen·e·tra·ble (im pen′ i trə b'l) *adj.* that cannot be penetrated or passed through.

im·per·ti·nent (im pur′ t'n ənt) *adj.* not showing proper respect; insolent.

im·per·turb·a·ble (im′ pər tur′ bə b'l) *adj.* not easily perturbed or excited; impassive; calm. —**imperturbably** *adv.*

im·pi·e·ty (im pī′ ə tē) *n.* a lack of loyalty and devotion to parents and family.

im·plant (im plant′) *v.* to fix firmly in the mind; instill.

im·plore (im plôr′) *v.* to ask for with much feeling; beseech.

im·pose (im pōz′) *v.* to force oneself on another.

im·pos·ing (im pō′ zing) *adj.* impressive in size.

im·pos·tor (im päs′ tər) *n.* a person who deceives or cheats others by pretending to be someone or something that he is not.

im·po·tent (im′ pə tənt) *adj.* ineffective, powerless, or helpless.

im·press (im pres′) *v.* to arouse the approval of.

im·pres·sion·a·ble (im presh′ ən ə b'l) *adj.* capable of being influenced; sensitive.

im·pres·sive (im pres′ iv) *adj.* tending to have a strong effect on the mind or emotions. —**impressiveness** *n.*

im·print (im print′) *v.* to fix in the memory.

im·pu·dence (im′ pyoo dəns) *n.* the quality of being impudent, without thought of the consequences; rash; indiscreet.

im·pulse (im′ puls) *n.* a surge in one direction of voltage or energy.

in·cen·di·ar·y (in sen′ dē er′ ē) *adj.* designed to cause fires, as certain bombs.

in·cense (in′ sens) *n.* any substance burned for a pleasant odor.

in·cred·i·ble (in kred′ ə b'l) *adj.* so great or unusual as to seem impossible. —**incredibly** *adv.*

in·cred·u·lous (in krej′ oo ləs) *adj.* showing doubt or disbelief. —**incredulously** *adv.*

---

at, āte, fär; pen, ēqual; sit, mīne; sō, côrn, join, took, fool, our; us, turn; chill, shop, thick, *th*ey, siŋ; **zh** *in* measure; **'l** *in* idle; ə *in* alive, cover, family, robot, circus.

in·del·i·ble (in del′ ə b'l) *adj.* that cannot be erased or blotted out.

in·dif·fer·ence (in dif′ ər əns *or* in dif′ rəns) *n.* a lack of concern or interest.

in·dig·nant (in dig′ nənt) *adj.* angry about something that seems unjust, unfair, or mean. —**indignantly** *adv.* —**indignation** *n.*

in·dis·crim·i·nate (in′ dis krim′ ə nit) *adj.* not based on careful selection; confused or random.

in·dis·tin·guish·a·ble (in′ dis tiŋ′ gwish ə b'l) *adj.* that cannot be recognized as different or separate.

in·dulge (in dulj′) *v.* to gratify the wishes of; humor.

in·ef·fec·tu·al (in′ i fek′ choo wəl) *adj.* not being able to produce the desired effect or outcome.

in·ev·i·ta·ble (in ev′ ə tə b'l) *adj.* that cannot be avoided; certain to happen.

in·fi·nite (in′ fə nit) *adj.* extending beyond measure or comprehension. —**infinitely** *adv.*

in·fin·i·ty (in fin′ ə tē) *n.* endless or unlimited space.

in·fla·tion (in flā′shən) *n.* an increase in the amount of money in circulation that causes a fall in its value and a rise in prices.

in·gen·ious (in jēn′ yəs) *adj.* clever, resourceful, and inventive.

in·grate (in′ grāt) *n.* an ungrateful person, one who expresses no thanks.

in·hu·man·i·ty (in′ hyoo man′ ə tē) *n.* a state of being inhuman or unmoved by the suffering of others; cruel, brutal, or unkind.

ink·ling (iŋk′ liŋ) *n.* a vague notion or idea; a hint.

in·lay (in′ lā′) *n.* a decoration or design added to an object, usually level with the surface.

in·quis·i·tive (in kwiz′ ə tiv) *adj.* inclined to ask many questions; unnecessarily curious.

in·sane (in sān′) *adj.* very foolish; senseless. —**insanely** *adv.*

in·so·lent (in′ sə lənt) *adj.* boldly disrespectful in speech or behavior; rude. —**insolently** *adv.*

in·sol·vent (in säl′ vənt) *adj.* unable to pay debts; bankrupt.

in·stinc·tive (in stiŋk′ tiv) *adj.* caused or done by instinct.

in·sti·tu·tion (in′ stə too′ shən *or* in′ stə tyoo′ shən) *n.* a person long established in a place.

in·suf·fer·a·ble (in suf′ ər ə b'l) *adj.* not sufferable; hard to put up with; unbearable.

in·tense (in tens′) *adj.* occurring or existing in a high degree; very strong.

in·tent (in tent′) *adj.* having the mind or attention firmly fixed. —**intently** *adv.*

in·ter·mix (in′ tər miks′) *v.* to mix together; blend. —**intermixed** *adj.*

(at) in·ter·vals (at in′ tər v'lz) now and then.

in·ti·mate (in′ tə mit) *adj.* very close.

in·tri·cate (in′ tri kit) *adj.* full of elaborate and complicated details.

in·tu·i·tion (in′ too wish′ ən *or* in′ tyoo wish′ ən) *n.* the direct knowing or learning of something without the conscious use of reasoning; instant understanding.

in·vin·ci·ble (in vin′ sə b'l) *adj.* that cannot be defeated or overcome; unconquerable.

in·vo·ca·tion (in′ və kā′ shən) *n.* a prayer to the gods for blessing or help.

i·o·ta (ī ōt′ ə) *n.* a very small quantity.

ir·ri·ta·tion (ir′ ə tā′ shən) *n.* the act of annoying or causing anger.

J

jade (jād) *n.* a woman of low morals.

jaunt (jônt *or* jänt) *n.* a short trip; excursion.

jav·e·lin (jav′ lin *or* jav′ ə lin) *n.* a pointed spear thrown for distance as a field event in track and field meets.

jeer (jir) *v.* to make fun of a person or thing in a rude, sarcastic manner; mock; scoff at. *n.* a jeering, sarcastic, or derisive remark.

Jer·sey (jʉr′ zē) *n.* a small reddish-brown dairy cow.

jet·ty (jet′ ē) *n.* a landing pier.

jibe (jīb) *n.* a jeering remark; scoff.

jig is up, the [Slang] all chances for success are gone; said of a risky or improper activity.

jig·ger (jig′ ər) *n.* a fast, gay, bouncy dance.

jit·ter (jit′ ər) *v.* to be nervous. **—jittery** *adj.*

jos·tle (jäs′ ′l) *v.* to bump or push, as in a crowd.

jounce (jouns) *v.* to shake; bounce.

jo·vi·al (jō′ vē əl *or* jō′ vyəl) *adj.* full of hearty, playful good humor; genial and jolly. **—jovially** *adv.*

ju·bi·lant (jōō′ b′l ənt) *adj.* joyful and triumphant; elated. **—jubilantly** *adv.*

ju·jit·su (jōō jit′ sōō) *n.* a Japanese system of wrestling in which the strength and weight of an opponent are used against him.

jum·ble (jum′ b′l) *n.* a confused mixture.

jus·ti·fy (jus′ tə fī′) *v.* to free from blame or guilt.

jut (jut) *v.* to stick out.

K

keel (kēl) *n.* the chief timber or steel piece along the entire length of the bottom of a ship or boat.

keen (kēn) *adj.* **1.** sharp and quick in seeing, hearing, or thinking. **2.** eager, enthusiastic. **—keenness** *n.*

key (kē) *adj.* essential.

kick·er (kik′ ər) *n.* a surprise ending.

kin·dred (kin′ drid) *n.* family.

kir·tle (kʉr′ t′l) *n.* a dress or skirt.

knack (nak) *n.* a special ability or skill.

knight-er·rant (nīt′ er′ ənt) *n.* a person who is chivalrous or idealistic but impractical. **—knight-errantry** *n.*

L

la·bor (lā′ bər) *v.* to exert oneself to do something.

lab·y·rinth (lab′ ə rinth′) *n.* a structure containing an intricate network of winding passages hard to follow without losing one's way; maze.

la·ment (lə ment′) *n.* a song or poem mourning a loss or death.

lank·y (laŋ′ kē) *adj.* awkwardly tall and lean.

lapse (laps) *n.* a passing away of time.

lard·er (lär′ dər) *n.* a supply of food.

lash (lash) *v.* to fasten or tie.

latch on·to (lach än′ tōō) *v.* to get or obtain.

lau·rel (lôr′ əl *or* lär′ əl) *n.* **1.** an evergreen tree or shrub with glossy leaves. **2.** fame; honor. **—rest on one's laurels** to be satisfied with what one has already achieved.

lav·a·to·ry (lav′ ə tôr′ ē) *n.* a room equipped with a washbowl and toilet.

lav·ish (lav′ ish) *adj.* very great.

league (lēg) *n.* an old measure of distance, usually about three miles.

ledg·er (lej′ ər) *n.* the book of final entry, in which a record of debits, credits, and all money transactions is kept.

leg·end (lej′ ənd) *n.* stories about a notable person.

---

at, āte, fär; pen, ēqual; sit, mīne; sō, côrn, jȯin, tŏŏk, fōōl, ȯur; us, tʉrn; chill, shop, thick, *th*ey, siŋ; **zh** *in* measure; **′l** *in* idle; ə *in* alive, cover, family, robot, circus.

le·git·i·mate (lə jit′ ə mit) *adj.* staying or being within the law.

lest (lest) *conj.* for fear that; in case.

lev·i·ta·tion (lev′ ə tā′ shən) *n.* the illusion of raising and keeping a heavy body in the air with little or no support.

lib·er·a·tion (lib′ ə rā′ shən) *n.* a release from slavery or enemy occupation.

light·some (līt′ səm) *adj.* well-lighted, bright.

lin·ger (liŋ′ gər) *v.* to continue to stay because of an unwillingness to leave.

lin·i·ment (lin′ ə ment) *n.* a medicated liquid to be rubbed on the skin to sooth sore, sprained, or inflamed areas.

lin·tel (lin′ t′l) *n.* the horizontal crosspiece over a door or window carrying the weight of the structure above it.

loathe (lōth) *v.* to feel intense dislike or disgust for; detest.

loath·ing (lōth′ iŋ) *n.* intense dislike; disgust.

log·ic (läj′ ik) *n.* correct reasoning; valid induction or deduction.

loot (lōot) *n.* goods stolen or taken by force.

lot·ter·y (lät′ ər ē) *n.* a form of gambling in which people buy numbered chances on prizes, the winning numbers being drawn by lot.

lo·tus-eat·er (lōt′ əs ēt′ ər) *n.* one of a people who ate the fruit of the lotus and became lazy, dreamy, and forgetful of duty.

louse (lous) *n.* a small, wingless insect that lives in the hair or on the skin of man and some other mammals.

lu·mi·nous (lōo′ mə nəs) *adj.* very clear; easily understood.

lu·na·tic (lōo′ nə tik) *n.* an insane person. *adj.* insane.

lure (loor) *n.* anything having the power to attract or entice.

lus·ter (lus′ tər) *n.* the metallic appearance of glazed pottery.

lyre (līr) *n.* a small stringed instrument of the harp family, used by the ancient Greeks to accompany singing and reciting.

M

mag·is·trate (maj′ is trāt′ *or* maj′ is trāt) *n.* a civil officer empowered to administer the law.

mag·na·nim·i·ty (mag′ nə nim′ ə tē) *n.* a generous state of overlooking injury or insult; a rising above pettiness or meanness.

mag·pie (mag′ pī′) *n.* a noisy bird related to the crows and jays.

mal·ice (mal′ is) *n.* ill will; desire to harm another.

ma·li·cious (mə lish′ əs) *adj.* showing ill will; spiteful. —**maliciously** *adv.*

mam·moth (mam′ əth) *adj.* very big; huge.

ma·neu·ver (mə nōo′ vər *or* mə nyōo′ vər) *v.* to move in a planned, skillful manner toward a goal.

ma·ni·a (mā′ nē ə *or* mān′ yə) *n.* an enthusiasm for something that seems unreasonably great.

ma·nip·u·late (mə nip′ yə lāt′) *v.* to manage or control, often in an unfair or fraudulent way. —**manipulative** *adj.*

ma·raud (mə rôd′) *v.* to raid; plunder. —**marauder** *n.*

mare (mer) *n.* a fully mature female horse.

mar·i·ner (mar′ ə nər) *n.* a sailor; seaman.

mark (märk) *n.* **1.** the starting line of a race. **2.** an object aimed at, target.

mar·ry (mar′ ē) *interj.* an exclamation of surprise or anger.

mar·tyr (mär′ tər) *n.* a person who assumes an attitude of self-sacrifice in order to arouse feelings of pity in others.

mar·vel (mär′ v′l) *n.* a wonderful or astonishing thing.

mass (mas) *n.* a piece or an amount of indefinite shape or size.

mast (mast) *n.* a tall, vertical pole used to support the sails of a ship.

mas·ter·mind (mas′ tər mīnd′) *n.* a very intelligent being with the ability to plan a group project. —**masterminded** *adj.*

ma·te·ri·al (mə tir′ ē əl) *adj.* important; essential.

ma·tron·ly (ma′ trən lē) *adj.* mature and dignified.

maun·der (môn′ dər) *v.* to move or act in a confused, aimless way.

maw (mô) *n.* the opening; the mouth.

me·chan·i·cal (mə kan′ i k′l) *adj.* automatic, as if from force of habit. —**mechanically** *adv.*

me·di·e·val (mē′ dē ē′ v′l *or* med′ ē′ v′l *or* mid′ ē′ v′l) *adj.* of, like, or suggestive of the Middle Ages—the period in European history between ancient and modern times, about A.D. 476–A.D.1450.

med·ley re·lay (med′ lē rē′ lā) *n.* a swimming race in which a different stroke must be used for each length of the pool.

meg·a·phone (meg′ ə fōn′) *n.* a large funnel-shaped device for increasing the volume of the voice or other sound.

mel·an·chol·y (mel′ ən käl ē) *adj.* sad and depressed; gloomy. *n.* sadness and depression of spirits.

mel·low (mel′ ō) *adj.* genial or convivial. —**mellowness** *n.*

me·lo·di·ous (mə lō′ dē əs) *adj.* containing or producing melody; tuneful.

mem·brane (mem′ brān) *n.* a thin, soft layer of animal or plant tissue that covers or lines an organ or part. —**membranous** *adj.*

mem·o·ran·dum (mem′ ə ran′ dəm) *n.* a record, as of events, to help remember something in the future.

men·ace (men′ is) *v.* to threaten or be a danger to. —**menacingly** *adv.*

men·tal·ly ar·rest·ed (men′ t′l ē ə rest′ əd) *n.* the condition of being below normal in intelligence.

mere (mir) *adj.* nothing more or other than; only.

me·ringue (mə raŋ′) *n.* egg whites mixed with sugar, beaten until stiff, spread over pies or cakes, or used as a shell.

me·sa (mā′ sə) *n.* a small, high plateau or flat tableland with steep sides.

mess (mes) *n.* the place where a group of people regularly have their meals together.

met·a·phor (met′ ə fôr′ *or* met′ ə fər′) *n.* a figure of speech that suggests a likeness by speaking of one thing as if it were another.

me·tic·u·lous (mə tik′ yoo ləs) *adj.* very careful or too careful about details; scrupulous or finicky.

mi·grate (mī′ grāt) *v.* to move from one place to another, especially to another country.

mill (mil) *v.* to move slowly in a circle.

mim·ic (mim′ ik) *v.* to imitate in speech or action, as in making fun of someone.

mi·nute (mī noot′ *or* mī nyoot′) *adj.* very small; tiny. —**minutely** *adv.*

mi·nu·ti·ae (mi noo′ shi ē′ *or* mi nyoo′ shi ē′) *n. pl.* small or relatively unimportant details.

mi·rac·u·lous (mi rak′ yoo ləs) *adj.* having the nature of an event or action that seems to be against known scientific laws and is thus thought of as caused by God or a god.

mis·giv·ing (mis giv′ iŋ) *n.* a disturbed feeling of fear, doubt, or worry.

---

at, āte, fär; pen, ēqual; sit, mīne; sō, côrn, join, took, fool, our; us, turn; chill, shop, thick, *th*ey, siŋ; **zh** *in* measure; ′l *in* idle;
ə *in* alive, cover, family, robot, circus.

mis·tress (mis′ tris) *n.* a woman who rules others or has control over something.

mock (mäk) *v.* to make fun of; ridicule.

mode (mōd) *n.* a manner or way of doing something.

mod·er·ate (mäd′ ər it) *adj.* **1.** within reasonable limits. **2.** of average quality; avoiding extremes. —**moderately** *adv.*

mod·est (mäd′ ist) *adj.* having or showing a moderate opinion of one's own value or abilities; not vain. —**modesty** *n.*

mo·hair (mō′her) *n.* yarn or fabric made from the hair of the Angora goat.

mole (mōl) *n.* a barrier to break the force of the waves before they enter a harbor.

mo·lest (mə lest′ *or* mō lest′) *v.* to annoy or meddle with so as to trouble or harm.

mon·o·gram (män′ ə gram′) *n.* the initials of a name, combined in a single design.

mon·o·log (män′ ə lôg′ *or* män′ ə läg′) *n.* a long speech, especially one that keeps anyone else from talking.

mon·o·tone (män′ ə tōn′) *n.* the saying of a series of words without change of pitch or key.

mor·al (môr′ əl *or* mär′ əl) *adj.* teaching the principles of right and wrong.

mo·rose (mə rōs′ *or* mô rōs′) *adj.* gloomy; sullen. —**morosely** *adv.*

mor·sel (môr′ s′l) *n.* a small amount; bit.

mor·tal (môr′ t′l) *adj.* **1.** extreme; very great. **2.** of man as a being who must eventually die. —**mortally** *adv.*

moss·y (môs′ ē *or* mäs′ ē) *adj.* full of or covered by very small green plants called moss, growing in velvety clusters usually on rocks, trees, and moist ground.

mo·ti·vate (mōt′ ə vāt′) *v.* to cause one to act in a certain way; incite or impel.

mourn (môrn) *v.* to grieve for someone who has died. —**mournful** *adj.*

mouth (mouth) *v.* to form words without making sounds.

muf·fle (muf′ ′l) *v.* to deaden or quiet a sound. —**muffled** *adj.*

mul·ti·tude (mul′ tə tōōd′ *or* mul′ tə tyōōd′) *n.* a large number of persons.

mum·mer (mum′ ər) *n.* one who wears a mask or disguise for fun.

mur·der (mur′ dər) *n.* something very hard to do or deal with. *adj.* extraordinarily difficult or dangerous.

mus·tang (mus′ taŋ) *n.* a small wild horse of the Southwestern plains of the United States.

mus·ter (mus′ tər) *v.* to gather up, collect.

mu·ti·late (myōōt′ ′l āt′) *v.* to cut off or damage a limb or other important part of a person.

mut·ter (mut′ ər) *v.* to speak or say in low tones with the lips almost closed, often in an angry or complaining way; grumble.

muz·zle (muz′ ′l) *n.* the part of an animal's head including the mouth, nose, and jaws.

myr·tle (mur′ t′l) *n.* a shrub with evergreen leaves, white or pink flowers, and dark berries.

N

na·ïve (nä ēv′) *adj.* simple in an unaffected, or sometimes foolish, way; unsophisticated.

nape (nāp *or* nap) *n.* the back of the neck.

nau·se·ate (nô′ shē āt′ *or* nô′ zē āt′ *or* nô′ zhē āt′) *v.* to cause to feel sick to one's stomach. —**nauseatingly** *adv.*

nav·i·ga·tor (nav′ ə gāt′ ər) *n.* a person who steers or directs a ship.

nec·tar (nek′ tər) *n.* a very delicious beverage; the drink of the gods.

new·fan·gled (nōō′ faŋ′ g'ld *or* nyōō′ faŋ′

g'ld) *adj.* new; novel; a term showing mild contempt.

nigh (nī) *adv.* almost.

non·de·script (nän′ di skript′ *or* nän′ di skript′) *adj.* without distinctive qualities or features.

nook (nook) *n.* a corner, especially of a room, or a part cut off from the main part.

nymph (nimf) *n.* a minor nature goddess, thought of as a beautiful maiden living in a river, a tree, or the sea.

O

ob·scu·ri·ty (əb skyoor′ə tē *or* äb skyoor′ə tē) *n.* the quality or condition of being hidden; not famous or well-known.

ob·sti·nate (äb′ stə nit) *adj.* unreasonably determined to have one's own way; stubborn. —**obstinately** *adv.*

ob·vi·ous (äb′ vē əs) *adj.* easy to see or understand; evident.

o·di·ous (ō′ dē əs) *adj.* arousing or deserving hatred or loathing; disgusting.

of·fice (ôf′is *or* äf′is) *n.* something done for another; service.

off·spring (ôf′ sprin′) *n.* a child or animal as related to its parents.

o·le·an·der (ō′ lē an′ dər *or* ō′ lē an′ dər) *n.* a poisonous evergreen shrub with fragrant white, pink, or red flowers.

op·ti·cal (äp′ tik ′l) *adj.* having to do with the sense of sight; visual.

op·tion·al (äp′ shən ′l) *adj.* left to one's option, or choice; elective.

or·a·cle (ôr′ ə k′l *or* är′ ə k′l) *n.* a person through whom the ancient Greeks and Romans believed the gods spoke.

or·deal (ôr dēl′ *or* ôr dē′ əl *or* ôr′ dēl) *n.* a painful or severe test or experience.

ord·nance (ôrd′ nəns) *n.* all military weapons together with ammunition, vehicles, and equipment.

or·na·ment (ôr′ nə mənt′) *v.* to decorate.

out·land·ish (out lan′ dish) *adj.* very odd.

out·rage (out′ rāj′) *n.* a deep insult or offense.

o·ver·alls (ō′ vər ôlz′) *n. pl.* loose-fitting trousers, often with a part coming up over the chest.

o·ver·haul (ō′ vər hôl′) *v.* to catch up with or overtake.

P

pa·cif·ic (pə sif′ ik) *adj.* peaceful; calm.

pad (pad) *v.* to walk or run with a very soft step.

pains·tak·ing (pānz′ tā′ kin) *adj.* very careful and diligent.

pal·pi·tate (pal′ pə tāt′) *v.* to beat rapidly or flutter: said of the heart. —**palpitation** *n.*

pal·try (pôl′ trē) *adj.* very small and almost worthless.

pan·de·mo·ni·um (pan′ də mō′ nē əm) *n.* wild disorder, noise, or confusion.

pang (pan) *n.* a sudden, sharp, brief pain, physical or emotional; sudden feeling of distress.

pant (pant) *v.* to breathe rapidly and heavily.

pan·try (pan′ trē) *n.* a small room off the kitchen, where cooking ingredients and utensils are kept.

par·a·sit·ic (par′ ə sit′ ik) *adj.* of or like a parasite; living at the expense of others.

par·cel (pär′ s′l) *n.* a small, wrapped bundle; package.

---

at, āte, fär; pen, ēqual; sit, mīne; sō, côrn, join, took, fool, our; us, turn; chill, shop, thick, they, sin; zh in measure; ′l in idle; ə *in* alive, cover, family, robot, circus.

parch (pärch) *v.* to make hot and dry. —**parched** *adj.*

par·lor (pär′ lər) *n.* a room set aside for the entertainment of guests.

par·tic·u·lar (pər tik′ yə lər *or* pär tik′ yə lər) *n.* a detail; item.

pas·to·ral (pas′ tər əl) *adj.* of or characteristic of rural life, especially when thought of as being peaceful, simple, and natural.

pas·ture (pas′ chər) *v.* to graze. —**let out to pasture** to put out into a grassy field to graze.

pa·thet·ic (pə thet′ ik) *adj.* expressing or arousing pity or sympathy; pitiful.

pat·ter (pat′ ər) *n.* thin, quick, light sounds.

peal (pēl) *v.* to sound in a loud echoing way.

pe·cul·iar (pi kyool′ yər) *adj.* odd; strange.

peer (pir) *v.* to look closely.

pee·vish (pē′ vish) *adj.* irritable; fretful; cross.

pen·du·lum (pen′ joo ləm) *n.* an instrument of torture.

pen·e·trate (pen′ ə trāt′) *v.* to find or force a way into or through; enter as by piercing.

pent (pent) *adj.* held or kept in; penned.

per·ad·ven·ture (pur′ əd ven′ chər) *adv.* [Archaic] possibly; by chance.

per·ceive (pər sēv′) *v.* **1.** to become aware of through sight. **2.** to grasp or take in mentally.

per·i·scope (per′ ə skōp′) *n.* an optical instrument consisting of a tube equipped with lenses and mirrors arranged so that a person looking through one end can see objects reflected at the other end.

per·ish (per′ ish) *v.* to die; especially, to die a violent or untimely death.

per·pet·u·al (pər pech′ oo wəl) *adj.* lasting forever or for an indefinitely long time.

per·se·cute (pur′ sə kyoot′) *v.* to annoy constantly.

per·spi·ra·tion (pur′ spə rā′ shən) *n.* sweat.

pes·ti·lence (pes′ t'l əns) *n.* any disease that is fatal or very harmful and that spreads rapidly. —**pestilential** *adj.*

pe·tit four (pet′ ē fôr′ *or* pə tē foor′) *n.* a small cake cut from spongecake and decorated with icing.

pet·ri·fy (pet′ rə fī′) *v.* to replace the normal cells of organic matter with silica; re-form as a stony substance.

pho·to·graph·ic (fōt′ ə graf′ ik) *adj.* able to remember in exact detail.

phys·ics (fiz′ iks) *n. pl.* the science dealing with matter and energy. —**physicist** *n.* a specialist in the science of physics.

pi·ñon (pin′ yən *or* pin′ yōn; *Spanish*, pē nyōn′; *plural* pē nyō′ nes) *n.* any of the edible seeds of several small pine trees found in western North America.

pitch (pich) *v.* to hurl or toss something.

plac·ard (plak′ ärd *or* plak′ ərd) *n.* a notice for display in a public place; poster.

pla·cate (plā′ kāt *or* plak′ āt) *v.* to stop from being angry; appease. —**placatingly** *adv.*

plac·id (plas′ id) *adj.* undisturbed; tranquil; calm. —**placidly** *adv.*

plague (plāg) *n.* anything that causes suffering or trouble.

plain·tive (plān′ tiv) *adj.* expressing sorrow or melancholy; mournful; sad. —**plaintively** *adv.*

plod (pläd) *v.* to work steadily and monotonously; drudge. —**plodder** *n.*

plonk (plänk *or* pluŋk) *v.* to put down.

plot (plät) *v.* to plan secretly; scheme.

ploy (ploi) *n.* an action or maneuver intended to outwit and get the better of another person.

plume (ploom) *n.* something like a feather in shape and lightness.

plun·der (plun′ dər) *v.* to rob a person or place by force, especially in warfare.

plunge (plunj) *v.* **1.** to dive or rush, as into water, or a fight. **2.** to thrust or throw suddenly. **3.** to move violently and rapidly downward or forward.

pock·mark (päk′ märk′) *n.* a scar or pit left by an infected pimple, as of smallpox. —**pockmarked** *adj.*

po·et·ic jus·tice (pō et′ ik jus′ tis) *n.* justice, especially in which good is rewarded and evil punished.

po·grom (pō gräm′ *or* pō grum′ *or* pō′ grəm) *n.* an organized persecution and massacre of a minority group, especially of Jews.

poise (poiz) *v.* to balance; keep steady. —**poised** *adj.*

pome·gran·ate (päm′ gran′ it *or* päm′ ə gran′ it *or* pum′ gran′ it) *n.* an edible round fruit with a thick, red rind and many seeds covered with red, juicy pulp.

pore (pôr) *n.* a tiny opening in the skin through which fluids may go in or come out.

por·ridge (pôr′ ij *or* pär′ ij) *n.* a soft food made of cereal or meal boiled in water or milk until thick.

por·ter (pôr′ tər) *n.* a man who sweeps, cleans, and carries luggage for guests in a hotel.

por·ti·co (pôr′ tə kō′) *n.* a porch or covered walk, consisting of a roof supported by columns.

por·tion (pôr′ shən) *n.* a helping of food.

pound (pound) *n.* the monetary unit of the United Kingdom equal to 100 pennies or, in the earlier system, to 20 shillings.

prac·ti·ca·ble (prak′ ti kə b'l) *adj.* that can be used; usable.

pre·cious (presh′ əs) *adj.* dear; cherished.

pre·dict (pri dikt′) *v.* to state what one believes will happen; foretell.

pre·dom·i·nate (pri däm′ ə nāt′) *v.* to have controlling influence or power.

preen (prēn) *v.* to clean and trim the feathers with the beak.

pre·fab·ri·cate (prē fab′ rə kāt′) *v.* to make in standardized sections for shipment and quick assembly.

preg·nant (preg′ nənt) *adj.* full of meaning, significance.

prem·is·es (prem′ is ez) *n. pl.* real estate; buildings and land.

pre·pos·ter·ous (pri päs′ tər əs) *adj.* so contrary to nature or common sense as to be laughable; absurd.

pre·sent·a·ble (pri zen′ tə b'l) *adj.* properly groomed and dressed.

pre·side (pri zīd′) *v.* to have authority or control.

pres·tige (pres tēzh′ *or* pres tēj′) *n.* the power to impress or influence because of success or wealth.

pre·sump·tu·ous (pri zump′ choo wəs) *adj.* too bold or forward; overstepping proper bounds or limits.

pre·text (prē′ tekst) *n.* a false reason or motive put forth to hide the real one; excuse.

prey (prā) *v.* to hunt other animals for food.

prick (prik) *v.* to pierce with something loud, such as a sound.

prick·le (prik′ 'l) *v.* to feel a tingling sensation.

prim·rose (prim′ rōz′) *n.* a plant having variously colored, tubelike flowers.

prith·ee (prith′ ē) *interj.* [Archaic] I pray thee; please.

pri·va·tion (prī vā′ shən) *n.* a lack of the ordinary necessities of life; want.

priv·i·lege (priv′ 'l ij *or* priv′ lij) *n.* an advantage or favor specially granted to certain persons.

---

at, āte, fär; pen, ēqual; sit, mīne; sō, côrn, join, took, fool, our; us, turn; chill, shop, thick, *th*ey, sing; *zh* in measure; ′l in idle; ə *in* alive, cover, family, robot, circus.

probe (prōb) *n.* an instrument for exploring another planet.

pro·di·gious (prə dij′ əs) *adj.* enormous; huge.

prod·i·gy (präd′ ə jē) *n.* a child who is amazingly talented or intelligent.

pro·mot·er (prə mōt′ ər) *n.* a person who helps to organize an undertaking.

prompt (prämpt) *v.* to remind a person of something that has been forgotten.

proph·e·cy (präf′ ə sē) *n.* a prediction of the future by a prophet, as supposedly influenced by the guidance of God or a god.

prop·o·si·tion (präp′ ə zish′ ən) *n.* a proposed plan.

prov·ince (präv′ ins) *n.* a field of knowledge or activity.

pro·vi·sions (prə vish′ ənz) *n. pl.* a stock of food.

psych (sīk) *v.* **1.** to figure out the motives of others in order to outwit or control them. **2.** to cause to be disturbed mentally or excited emotionally.

psy·che (sī′ kē) *n.* the mind as a complex functional entity.

pub (pub) *n.* an inn; tavern.

pum·mel (pum′ ′l) *v.* to beat or hit with repeated blows.

punc·tu·ate (puŋk′ choo wāt′) *v.* to break in on here and there.

pun·gent (pun′ jənt) *adj.* producing a sharp sensation of taste or smell.

pyre (pīr) *n.* a pile of wood for burning a corpse in a funeral rite.

Q

quake (kwāk) *v.* to shudder or shiver, as from fear or cold.

quar·an·tine (kwôr′ ən tēn′ *or* kwär′ ən tēn′) *n.* an isolation or restriction on travel to keep contagious diseases or insects from spreading.

quar·ter (kwôr′ tər) *n.* **1.** place to live in, often just for a while. **2.** mercy granted to a surrendering foe.

qua·ver (kwā′ vər) *v.* to shake or tremble. *n.* a tremulous quality in a voice.

quay·side (kē′ sīd′) *n.* a wharf or dock for loading and unloading ships.

queer (kwir) *adj.* differing from what is usual or ordinary; odd; strange.

quench (kwench) *v.* to extinguish; put out.

quest (kwest) *n.* a journey in search of adventure.

quiv·er (kwiv′ ər) *n.* a case for holding arrows. *v.* to shake; tremble.

quoit (kwoit) *n.* a ring of rope or metal thrown, in a game like horseshoes, at an upright peg in an attempt to encircle it.

R

rack (rak) *n.* an instrument of torture consisting of a frame on which a body is stretched.

raft·er (raf′ tər) *n.* any of the beams that slope from the ridge of a roof to the eaves and serve to support the roof.

ram·part (ram′ pärt *or* ram′ pərt) *n.* a defensive embankment around a castle or fort with a parapet at the top.

rash (rash) *adj.* too hasty and careless. —**rashness** *n.*

ra·tion (rash′ ən *or* rā′ shən) *n.* a fixed allowance of food or provisions during wartime.

ra·tion·al·ize (rash′ ən ə līz′) *v.* to explain on the basis of reason or logic. —**rationalization** *n.*

rau·cous (rô′ kəs) *adj.* loud and rowdy.

rav·age (rav′ ij) *v.* to destroy violently; devastate; ruin.

rav·ing (rā′ viŋ) *n.* delirious speech that does not make sense.

raw·boned (rô′ bōnd′) *adj.* having little fat; lean.

realm (relm) *n.* a kingdom.

reap (rēp) *v.* to harvest crops from a planted field.

rear (rir) *v.* to bring to maturity by educating and nourishing.

reb·el (ri bel′) *v.* to resist any authority or controls.

re·cede (ri sēd′) *v.* to go or move back.

re·cip·i·ent (ri sip′ ē ənt) *n.* a person or a thing that receives.

re·coil (ri kɔil′) *v.* to draw, start, or shrink back, as in fear, surprise, or disgust.

rec·on·cile (rek′ ən sīl′) *v.* to make friendly again.

re·form (ri fôrm′) *v.* to make better by removing faults; correct.

ref·or·ma·tion (ref′ ər mā′ shən) *n.* an improvement in character and conduct.

re·gal (rē′ gəl) *adj.* royal; splendid.

re·gime (rə zhēm′ *or* rā zhēm′) *n.* a form of government.

reg·i·ment (rej′ ə mənt) *n.* a military unit consisting of two or more battalions.

reign (rān) *v.* **1.** to rule as a king or queen. **2.** to prevail or predominate.

rein (rān) *n.* a means of guiding or controlling. —**give free rein to** to allow to act freely.

re·in·force·ment (rē′ in fôrs′ mənt) *n.* a strengthening with more troops, ships, or planes.

re·ju·ve·nate (re jōō′ və nāt′) *v.* to bring back to youthful strength or appearance.

re·lent (ri lent′) *v.* to become less harsh, strict, or stubborn; soften.

re·lent·less (ri lent′ lis) *adj.* going on without stopping; persistent.

rel·e·vant (rel′ ə vənt) *adj.* having to do with the matter at hand; pertinent; to the point. —**relevancy** *n.*

re·lin·quish (ri liŋ′ kwish) *v.* to give up; abandon.

rel·ish (rel′ ish) *v.* to enjoy; like.

re·luc·tant (ri luk′ tənt) *adj.* not wanting to do something; unwilling. —**reluctantly** *adv.*

re·me·di·al (ri mē′ dē əl) *n.* a student who is having difficulty with a particular subject.

re·mem·brance (ri mem′ brəns) *n.* a memory.

rem·i·nisce (rem′ ə nis′) *v.* to remember past experiences. —**reminiscence** *n.* —**reminiscent** *adj.*

rem·nant (rem′ nənt) *n.* a small remaining part, amount, or number.

re·morse (ri môrs′) *n.* pity. —**remorseless** *adj.*

re·mote (ri mōt′) *adj.* far off; distant.

ren·der (ren′ dər) *v.* **1.** to cause to be; make. **2.** to play music, recite a poem, or act a play.

re·new (ri nōō′ *or* ri nyōō′) *v.* to cause to exist again; reestablish.

re·nounce (ri nouns′) *v.* to refuse to have anything more to do with.

re·nown (ri noun′) *n.* great fame.

rep (rep) *n.* shortened form of reputation.

re·per·cus·sion (rē′ pər kush′ ən *or* rep′ ər kush′ ən) *n.* an effect of or reaction to some event or action.

re·proach (ri prōch′) *v.* to accuse of and blame for a fault to make someone feel ashamed. —**reproachfully** *adv.*

re·prove (ri prōōv′) *v.* to speak to in disapproval; scold.

---

at, āte, fär; pen, ēqual; sit, mīne; sō, côrn, join, took, fōōl, our; us, turn; chill, shop, thick, *th*ey, siŋ; **zh** *in* measure; **'l** *in* idle; ə *in* alive, cover, family, robot, circus.

rep·u·ta·tion (rep′ yŏŏ tā′ shən) *n.* **1.** fame; distinction. **2.** good name.

re·sem·blance (ri zem′ bləns) *n.* the state or fact of resembling; likeness.

re·sil·ient (ri zil′ yənt) *adj.* springing back into shape after being stretched or bent.

res·o·lute (rez′ ə lŏŏt′) *adj.* showing a fixed, firm purpose; determined. —**resolutely** *adv.*

re·sound·ing (ri zŏŏnd′ iŋ) *adj.* reverberating; echoing.

res·pite (res′ pit) *n.* a period of temporary relief or rest, as from pain or work.

re·spond (ri spänd′) *v.* to answer; reply.

re·spon·sive (ri spän′ siv) *adj.* reacting quickly and easily to a suggestion. —**responsiveness** *n.*

rest·less (rest′ lis) *adj.* never or seldom still; always moving.

re·strain (ri strān′) *v.* to hold back from action; check; curb.

re·tail (ri tāl′) *v.* to repeat.

re·tir·ing (ri tīr′ iŋ) *adj.* drawing back from being with others; reserved; shy.

rev·e·nue (rev′ ə nŏŏ′ *or* rev′ ə nyŏŏ′) *n.* the income of a government from taxes and licenses.

rev·er·end (rev′ ər ənd *or* rev′ rənd) *adj.* worthy of reverence, respect, or veneration.

rev·o·lu·tion·ar·y (rev′ ə lŏŏ′ shən er′ ē) *n.* a person who favors or takes part in the overthrow of a government.

rheu·ma·tism (rŏŏ′ mə tiz′m) *n.* a painful condition in which the joints and muscles become inflamed and stiff.

rick·et·y (rik′ it ē) *adj.* liable to fall apart or break down; shaky.

ridge (rij) *n.* a long, narrow elevation of land or similar range of hills or mountains.

ri·fle (rī′ f'l) *v.* to ransack in order to rob.

rim (rim) *n.* an edge.

rip·ple (rip′ 'l) *n.* a wavelike movement.

rite (rīt) *n.* an act or ceremony carried out according to fixed rules.

rit·u·al (rich′ ŏŏ wəl) *adj.* done as a formal act or ceremony with fixed rules.

ri·val (rī′ v'l) *adj.* acting as a competitor.

roan (rōn) *n.* a horse of a solid color with a thick sprinkling of white hairs.

ro·bust (rō bust′ *or* rō′bust) *adj.* strong and healthy; hardy.

ros·trum (räs′ trəm) *n.* a platform on which a person stands while making a public speech.

rouse (rŏuz) *v.* **1.** to cause to come out of a state of rest or sleep. **2.** to stir up, as to anger or action.

rout (rŏut) *v.* to force out.

row (rŏu) *n.* a noisy quarrel, dispute, or disturbance.

row·dy (rŏu′ dē) *adj.* loud, rough, and disorderly.

ru·di·ment (rŏŏ′ də mənt) *n.* something to be learned first, as any basic principle of a subject.

ru·in (rŏŏ′ in) *n.* downfall, destruction, or decay, as of a thing or person, or the cause of this.

rum·ble (rum′ b'l) *v.* to make a deep, heavy rolling sound, as thunder.

ruse (rŏŏz) *n.* a trick or plan to fool someone.

rush (rush) *n.* **1.** a sudden, intense feeling. **2.** a grasslike plant usually growing in wet places, having round stems and easily bent leaves used in making baskets and mats. *adj.* made of rushes.

rus·set (rus′ it) *n.* yellowish brown or reddish brown.

rus·tle (rus′ 'l) *v.* to make soft sounds by moving about. —**rustling** *n.*

ruth·less (rŏŏth′ lis) *adj.* showing no pity or

kindness as in seeking some goal. —**ruth-lessly** *adv.*

S

sa·cred (sā′ krid) *adj.* given the respect that holy things receive; venerated.

sage (sāj) *adj.* having or showing wisdom or good judgment.

sal·low (sal′ ō) *adj.* having an unhealthy, pale-yellow look.

salt·y (sôl′ tē) *adj.* highly critical or sarcastic.

sanc·tu·ar·y (saŋk′ cho͞o wer′ ē) *n.* a holy place set aside for worship.

sash (sash) *n.* a broad ribbon or scarf worn over one shoulder or around the waist as a decoration.

sass (sas) *v.* to talk back in a rude, impudent way.

satch·el (sach′ əl) *n.* a small bag for carrying clothes or books.

sate (sāt) *v.* to satisfy to the full. —**sated** *adj.*

sav·age (sav′ ij) *adj.* cruel; pitiless. —**savagely** *adv.*

sa·vor (sā′ vər) *v.* to dwell on with delight; relish.

scan (skan) *v.* to look at in a broad, searching way; scrutinize.

scant·y (skan′ tē) *adj.* barely enough or not enough.

scheme (skēm) *n.* a carefully arranged plan for doing something.

scold (skōld) *n.* a person who habitually finds fault or nags.

scoot (sko͞ot) *v.* to go quickly; hurry.

scorch (skôrch) *v.* **1.** to criticize very sharply. **2.** to burn slightly in a way that chars or discolors the surface. —**scorched** *adj.*

score (skôr) *v.* to win or achieve.

scorn (skôrn) *v.* to refuse or reject as wrong or disgraceful. *n.* a great contempt for someone or something, often with some indignation.

scorn·ful (skôrn′ fəl) *adj.* filled with or showing contempt for someone or something. —**scornfully** *adv.*

scowl (skoul) *v.* to draw the eyebrows together and lower the corners of the mouth in showing displeasure; look angry.

scratch (skrach) *v.* to withdraw from a contest.

screech (skrēch) *v.* to make a shrill, high-pitched shriek or sound.

scrimp (skrimp) *v.* to spend or use as little as possible.

scrub (skrub) *n.* short, stunted trees or bushes growing thickly together.

scru·pu·lous (skro͞o′ pyə ləs) *adj.* demanding or marked by precision, care, and exactness.

scul·ler·y (skul′ ər ē) *n.* a room adjoining the kitchen, where pots and pans are cleaned or where the rough, dirty kitchen work is done.

scur·ry (skʉr′ ē) *v.* to run quickly; scamper.

scut·tle (skut′ ′l) *v.* to run quickly; scurry or scamper.

sea·son (sē′ z′n) *v.* to make more fit for use, as by aging or drying.

sect (sekt) *n.* a religious denomination.

seed·ling (sēd′liŋ) *n.* a plant grown from a seed, rather than from a cutting.

seize (sēz) *v.* to grasp.

se·nile (sē′ nīl *or* sen′ īl) *adj.* showing the weaknesses, especially the mental confusion and memory loss often found in old people. —**senility** *n.*

---

at, āte, fär; pen, ēqual; sit, mīne; sō, côrn, join, took, fo͞ol, our; us, turn; chill, shop, thick, they, siŋ; zh *in* measure; ′l *in* idle; ə *in* alive, cover, family, robot, circus.

sen·sa·tion (sen sā′ shən) *n.* a conscious feeling.

se·rene (sə rēn′) *adj.* not troubled; calm; peaceful. —**serenely** *adv.*

serf (surf) *n.* a person in a slavelike condition under the feudal system, bound to his master's land and transferred with it. —**serfdom** *n.*

se·vere (sə vir′) *adj.* serious; grave.

sheathe (shēth) *v.* to enclose in or protect with a case or covering.

shin·gle (shiŋ′ g'l) *n.* pebbles and small stones on the beach.

shin·ny (shin′ ē) *v.* to climb by gripping with both hands and legs.

shoal (shōl) *n.* a large school of fish.

shod (shäd) *v.* furnished with shoes.

shot (shät) *adj.* streaked with a different color.

shrewd (shrōōd) *adj.* keen-witted, clever, sharp in practical affairs. —**shrewdly** *adv.*

shriek (shrēk) *n.* a loud, shrill cry or sound.

shrill (shril) *v.* to say with or make a high, thin, sharp sound.

shrine (shrīn) *n.* a place of worship.

shroud (shroud) *v.* to hide; cover.

shush (shush) *v.* to tell someone to be quiet.

sick·le (sik′ 'l) *n.* a tool consisting of a curved blade with a short handle, for cutting tall grass.

side·kick (sīd′ kik′) *n.* a close friend; companion.

siege (sēj) *n.* **1.** the surrounding of a city or fort by an enemy army trying to capture it by continued blockade and attack. **2.** a long, difficult period.

sieve (siv) *n.* a utensil having many small openings, used to strain liquids or to separate fine particles from coarser ones; strainer.

sig·ni·fy (sig′ nə fī′) *v.* **1.** to show; indicate. **2.** [Slang] to engage in verbal play involving boastful taunts and witty insults.

si·mul·ta·ne·ous (sī′ m'l tā′ nē əs *or* sī m'l tān′ yəs) *adj.* occurring at the same time. —**simultaneously** *adv.*

sin·ew·y (sin′ yoo we) *adj.* tough; strong.

sin·gu·lar (siŋ′ gyə lər) *adj.* being the only one of its kind; unique. —**singularity** *n.*

si·ren (sī′ rən) *n.* a mythological sea creature whose sweet singing lured sailors to their death on rocky coasts. *adj.* dangerously attractive.

sit·ter (sit′ ər) *n.* [Slang] the buttocks; part on which one sits.

skirt (skurt) *v.* to move along the edge of or pass around.

slack·en (slak′ 'n) *v.* to become less active or intense.

slan·der (slan′ dər) *v.* to say something that harms a person's character or reputation.

slight (slīt) *n.* an insult, snub, or discourteous act.

sliv·er (sliv′ ər) *n.* a thin, sharp piece that has been cut or broken off; splinter.

slop pail (släp pāl) *n.* a container for garbage mixed with water for feeding pigs.

slope (slōp) *n.* ground that slants up or down; hillside.

slosh (släsh) *v.* to splash or move clumsily through water.

sluice (sloos) *v.* to wash with water from an artificial channel.

smith (smith) *n.* a person who makes or repairs metal objects.

smith·er·eens (smith′ ə rēnz′) *n. pl.* small fragments; bits.

smudge (smuj) *n.* a fire producing dense smoke.

sneer (snir) *v.* to say in a scornful or sarcastic way.

snick·er (snik′ ər) *v.* to give a sly, partly held back laugh that shows a lack of respect.

snuf·fle (snuf′ ′l) *v.* to breathe noisily by constant sniffing.

so·ber (sō′ bər) *adj.* not bright or flashy; quiet; plain.

sol·emn (säl′ əm) *adj.* **1.** serious; deeply earnest. **2.** awe-inspiring; very impressive. —**solemnly** *adv.*

sor·cer·y (sôr′ sər ē) *n.* seemingly magical power or influence. —**sorcerer** a person who practices sorcery.

sor·rel (sôr′ əl *or* sär′ əl) *n.* a horse of light reddish brown color.

sor·tie (sôr′ tē) *n.* a sudden attack made by troops from a besieged place against the besiegers.

sow (sō) *v.* **1.** to scatter or plant seed for growing. **2.** to spread or scatter.

spare (sper) *adj.* lean.

spawn (spôn) *n.* the young produced by a fish.

spec·ta·cle (spek′ tə k′l) *n.* a foolish or shocking public show or display. —**to make a spectacle of oneself** to behave foolishly or improperly in public.

spec·u·la·tive (spek′ yə lāt′ iv *or* spek′ yə lə tiv) *adj.* pondering or wondering about the various aspects of a subject. —**speculatively** *adv.*

spell (spel) *n.* a power or control that seems magical; fascination.

spher·i·cal (sfer′ i k′l *or* sfir′ i k′l) *adj.* shaped like a sphere; globular.

spite (spīt) *v.* to show one's feelings by hurting or annoying someone.

splay (splā) *v.* to spread out; extend.

splin·ter (splin′ tər) *n.* a thin sharp piece.

sprint (sprint) *v.* to run at full speed for a short distance.

spur (spʉr) *v.* to urge; stir up; stimulate.

squab·ble (skwäb′ ′l *or* skwôb′ ′l) *v.* to quarrel noisily over a small matter.

squan·der (skwän′ dər *or* skwôn′ dər) *v.* to spend or use money or time wastefully.

squid (skwid) *n.* a sea mollusk having a long, thin body and ten arms, two arms being much longer than the others.

squint (skwint) *v.* to keep the eyes partly closed in peering.

staff (staf) *n.* a stick, rod, or pole used as a support in walking, or as a weapon, a symbol of authority, or a measure.

stake (stāk) *n.* a length of wood or metal pointed at one end for driving into the ground.

stal·wart (stôl′ wərt) *adj.* strong and well-built; sturdy.

stand·still (stand′ stil′) *n.* a stop or halt.

stat·ic (stat′ ik) *n.* electrical discharges in the atmosphere that disturb radio or TV reception.

staunch (stônch *or* stänch) *adj.* loyal; firm. *v.* to stop or check.

stay (stā) *v.* to stop; halt.

stealth·y (stel′ thē) *adj.* secret; sneaky. —**stealthily** *adv.*

steed (stēd) *n.* a high-spirited riding horse.

steep (stēp) *v.* to cause to be deeply involved, interested, or absorbed in a subject.

stench (stench) *n.* an offensive smell; stink.

stern (stʉrn) *adj.* unshakable; firm. *n.* the rear end of a ship or boat.

stiff (stif) *n.* a person who is formal and constrained in thought and action.

sti·fle (stī′ f′l) *v.* **1.** to suffocate; smother. **2.** to hold back; check; stop.

stim·u·late (stim′ yə lāt′) *v.* to stir up or spur on; excite.

---

at, āte, fär; pen, ēqual; sit, mīne; sō, côrn, join, took, fo͞ol, o͝ur; us, tʉrn; chill, shop, thick, *th*ey, siŋ; **zh** in measure; ′l in idle; ə *in* alive, cover, family, robot, circus.

stole (stōl) *v.* moved or passed secretly or quietly.

stoop (stōop) *n.* a small porch with steps, at the door of a house.

stout (stout) *adj.* strong in body; sturdy.

stow·a·way (stō′ ə wā′) *v.* to hide aboard a ship so as not to pay for passage or get caught.

stream·let (strēm′ lit) *n.* a very small river or stream.

stride (strīd) *n.* a long step.

strife (strīf) *n.* the act of fighting or quarreling; conflict.

strig·il (strij′ əl) *n.* an instrument used by Greeks to scrape the skin after athletic exercises.

strop (sträp) *v.* to sharpen on a thick leather band. *n.* a thick leather band used for putting a fine edge on razors.

strut (strut) *v.* to show off proudly.

stub·by (stub′ ē) *adj.* short and thick.

stud (stud) *v.* to set or decorate with a series of objects.

stud·ied (stud′ ēd) *adj.* planned beforehand; deliberate.

stun (stun) *v.* to shock deeply; astound. —**stunned** *adj.*

stu·pe·fy (stōo′ pə fī′ *or* styōo′ pə fī′) *v.* to make senseless, or daze; stun.

stur·dy (stur′dē) *adj.* strong; hardy. —**sturdiness** *n.*

sty (stī) *n.* a pen for pigs. —**sties** *pl.*

suav·i·ty (swä′ və tē) *n.* the quality of being gracious or polite in a smooth way.

sub·ject (sub′ jikt) *adj.* likely to; liable to.

sub·merge (səb murj′) *v.* to cover completely with water or another substance.

sub·mit (səb mit′) *v.* to give in to the control or power of another.

sub·side (səb sīd′) *v.* to sink to a lower level.

sub·stance (sub′ stəns) *n.* material posses-

sions; property; wealth.

suc·cu·lent (suk′ yōo lənt) *adj.* juicy, especially in a way that is tasty or delicious.

suede (swād) *n.* tanned leather with the flesh side rubbed until the nap is very soft and fine.

suit·or (sōot′ ər) *n.* a man courting a woman.

sulk (sulk) *n.* a sullen or pouting mood.

sul·len (sul′ ən) *adj.* gloomy; dismal; depressed.

sum·mer sol·stice (sum′ ər säl′ stis *or* sum′ ər sōl′ stis) *n.* the time in the Northern Hemisphere when the sun is farthest north of the celestrial equator; June 21 or 22.

sum·mon (sum′ ən) *v.* to call together.

sup (sup) *v.* to have supper.

su·per·cil·i·ous (sōo′ pər sil′ ē əs) *adj.* proud and scornful; looking down on others; haughty. —**superciliously** *adv.*

su·per·fi·cial (sōo′ pər fish′ əl) *adj.* concerned with and understanding only the obvious; shallow. —**superficiality** *n.*

su·per·son·ic (sōo′ pər sän′ ik) *adj.* designating, of, or moving at a speed in a surrounding fluid greater than that of sound in the same fluid.

sup·pli·cant (sup′ lə kənt) *n.* a person making a humble request.

sur·e·ty (shōor′ ə tē *or* shōor′ tē) *n.* a being sure; assurance.

surf (surf) *n.* wave.

surge (surj) *v.* to move in a sudden rushing motion.

sur·plus (sur′ plus *or* sur′ pləs) *n.* a quantity over and above what is needed or used; excess.

sus·pend (sə spend′) *v.* to hold in place as though hanging.

sus·pi·cious (sə spish′ əs) *adj.* showing distrust or doubt. —**suspiciously** *adv.*

swag·ger (swag′ ər) *n.* a bold, showy walk.

v. to walk with a bold, showy stride; strut.

swale (swāl) *n.* a hollow or low area of land; specifically such a place in a wet, marshy area.

swerve (swʉrv) *v.* to turn aside suddenly from a straight line or course.

switch (swich) *v.* to jerk or swing sharply.

sym·pa·thet·ic (sim′ pə thet′ ik) *adj.* showing understanding and compassion. —**sympathetically** *adv.*

T

taf·fe·ta (taf′ i tə) *n.* a fine, rather stiff fabric of silk, nylon, or acetate with a sheen.

taint (tānt) *n.* a trace of something that is spoiled.

take in (tāk in) *v.* to view; look at.

tat (tat) *v.* to tap repetitiously. —**tatting** *adj.*

tat·tered (tat′ ərd) *adj.* torn and ragged.

taunt (tônt *or* tänt) *v.* to make fun of in scornful or sarcastic language; jeer at.

taut·en (tôt′ ən) *v.* to stretch tight. —**taut** *adj.*

taw·ny (tô′ nē) *adj.* brownish-yellow; tan.

tax (taks) *v.* to put a burden or strain on.

tear (ter) *v.* to move with force or speed; rush.

tem·pest (tem′ pist) *n.* a violent outburst; tumult.

ten·der (ten′ dər) *adj.* affectionate; loving.

ten·don (ten′ dən) *n.* a cord of tough, fibrous tissue connecting muscle to bone.

tes·ty (tes′ tē) *adj.* easily angered or annoyed; irritable.

thatch (thach) *n.* a roof of straw or reeds or material for such a roof. —**thatched** *adj.*

the·o·ry (thē′ ə rē *or* thir′ ē) *n.* a plan as to how something might be done.

thick·et (thik′ it) *n.* a thick growth of shrubs, underbrush, or small trees.

thrash (thrash) *v.* to move or toss about violently. —**thrashing** *adj.*

thresh·old (thresh′ ōld *or* thresh′ hōld) *n.* the entrance of something.

throng (thrôŋ) *n.* a great number of people gathered together.

tim·id (tim′ id) *adj.* easily frightened or shy.

to·fu (tō′ fo͞o) *n.* a bland, custardlike food, rich in protein, made from soybeans.

tongue (tuŋ) *v.* to speak; make sounds.

tongue-tied (tuŋ′ tīd′) *adj.* not being able to speak because of embarrassment or fear.

tor·ment (tôr′ ment) *n.* great pain, physical or mental; agony.

tor·rent (tôr′ ənt *or* tär′ ənt) *n.* a very heavy fall of rain.

tot·ter (tät′ ər) *v.* to be unsteady on one's feet; stagger.

touched (tucht) *adj.* slightly unbalanced mentally.

traipse (trāps) *v.* to walk or wander in an aimless or lazy way.

tram (tram) *n.* a streetcar; trolley.

trance (trans) *n.* a stunned condition; daze; stupor.

tran·quil (traŋ′ kwəl *or* tran′ kwəl) *adj.* calm, quiet, peaceful.

tran·quil·i·ty (traŋ kwil′ə tē *or* tran kwil′ə tē) *n.* the quality or state of being tranquil; calmness.

trans·ac·tion (tran sak′ shən *or* tran zak′ shən) *n.* a business deal.

trans·mit·ter (trans mit′ ər) *n.* the device that produces and sends out radio waves.

trans·par·ent (trans per′ənt) *adj.* so fine in texture or open in mesh as to be seen through; sheer; gauzy.

---

at, āte, fär; pen, ēqual; sit, mīne; sō, côrn, join, took, fo͞ol, our; us, tʉrn; chill, shop, thick, *th*ey, siŋ; zh *in* measure; 'l *in* idle; ə *in* alive, cover, family, robot, circus.

tread (tred) *v.* to move on foot; walk.

trek (trek) *v.* to travel slowly or with difficulty.

trem·u·lous (trem′ yoo ləs) *adj.* trembling; quivering.

trench (trench) *n.* a long, narrow ditch with earth banked in front, used to protect soldiers in battle.

trib·ute (trib′ yoot) *n.* something given, done, or said that shows gratitude, honor, or praise.

tri·dent (trīd′ ′nt) *n.* a three-pronged spear.

tri·fle (trī′ f′l) *n.* **1.** something of little value or importance. **2.** a small amount; bit. —**trifling** *adj.*

tri·pod (trī′ päd) *n.* **1.** a three-legged kettle. **2.** any three-legged object.

tri·umph (trī′ əmf) *n.* great joy over a victory. —**triumphant** *adj.* —**triumphantly** *adv.*

trudge (truj) *v.* to walk in a tired way or with effort.

tu·mul·tu·ous (too mul′ choo wəs) *adj.* wild; excited. —**tumultuously** *adv.*

tu·nic (too′ nik *or* tyoo′ nik) *n.* a loose gown worn by men and women in ancient Greece.

turf (turf) *n.* a surface layer of earth containing grass.

twi·light (twī′ līt′) *n.* a growing darkness.

twinge (twinj) *n.* a sudden, brief feeling of remorse, shame, or jealousy.

U

ul·ti·mate (ul′ tə mit) *adj.* beyond which it is impossible to go; maximum.

un·ac·count·a·ble (un′ ə koun′ tə b′l) *adj.* that cannot be explained; strange. —**unaccountably** *adv.*

un·a·mi·a·ble (un ā′ mē ə b′l) *adj.* not pleasant or friendly; ill-natured. —**unamiably** *adv.*

un·can·ny (un kan′ ē) *adj.* so remarkable or keen as to seem unnatural.

un·der·rate (un′ dər rāt′) *v.* to rate, assess, or estimate too low.

un·du·late (un′ joo lāt′) *v.* to move in waves.

un·err·ing (un ur′ iŋ *or* un er′ iŋ) *adj.* free from error; not missing or failing. —**unerringly** *adv.*

un·furl (un′ furl′) *v.* to spread out or unfold.

un·heed·ing (un hēd′ iŋ) *adj.* not taking notice; unmindful.

u·ni·son (yoo′ nə sən *or* yoo′ nə zən) *n.* agreement; harmony.

un·set·tle (un set′ ′l) *v.* to make unstable; disturb.

un·wit·ting (un wit′ iŋ) *adj.* not done on purpose; not intended. —**unwittingly** *adv.*

up·roar (up′ rôr′) *n.* a noisy, confused condition; loud commotion.

ur·chin (ur′ chin) *n.* a small boy, or any youngster, especially one who is mischievous.

ut·most (ut′ mōst′) *n.* the most that is possible.

ut·ter (ut′ ər) *v.* to express with the voice. *adj.* complete, absolute.

V

vain (vān) *adj.* with little or no result; not successful; futile; fruitless.

val·or (val′ ər) *n.* great courage or bravery.

van·quish (vaŋ′ kwish *or* van′ kwish) *v.* **1.** to conquer or defeat in battle. **2.** to overcome a feeling or condition; suppress.

var·si·ty (vär′ sə tē) *n.* the main team representing a school. *adj.* designating or of a school team.

vast (vast) *adj.* very great in size, extent, or amount. —**vastness** *n.*

vat (vat) *n.* a large tub or tank for holding

liquids used in manufacturing.

Vat·i·can (vat' i k'n) *n.* the government or authority of the Pope.

veil (vāl) *v.* to cover with a piece of light fabric.

venge·ance (ven' jəns) *n.* the return of an injury for an injury, in punishment; an avenging; revenge.

ven·tril·o·quist's dum·my (ven tril' ə kwists dum' ē) *n.* a figure in human form to which a person talks in such a way that the voice seems to come from the dummy.

ve·ran·da (və ran' də) *n.* an open porch, usually roofed, along the outside of a building.

verge (vʉrj) *n.* the edge; brink.

ver·i·fy (ver' ə fī') *v.* to prove to be true by demonstration or evidence; confirm.

ver·i·ly (ver' ə lē) *adv.* [Archaic] in very truth; truly.

ver·sion (vʉr' zhən *or* vʉr' shən) *n.* an account given from a particular point of view.

ver·ti·cal (vʉr' ti k'l) *adj.* perpendicular to the plane of the horizon or to a level surface; upright; straight up or down. —**vertically** *adv.*

ves·sel (ves' 'l) *n.* a ship or large boat.

vi·bra·tion (vī brā' shən) *n.* rapid movement back and forth.

vi·cin·i·ty (və sin' ə tē) *n.* a nearby or surrounding region; neighborhood.

vict·uals (vit' 'lz) *n. pl.* articles of food or other provisions.

vie (vī) *v.* to compete as in a contest.

vile (vīl) *adj.* evil; wicked.

vi·tal (vīt' 'l) *adj.* necessary to life; essential; very important.

vo·tive (vōt' iv) *adj.* given or done in fulfillment of a solemn promise or pledge.

vow (vou) *n.* a solemn promise or pledge binding oneself to an act or way of life.

vul·ture (vul' chər) *n.* a large bird related to the eagle and hawk, with a naked head: vultures feed on the remains of dead animals.

W

wal·low (wäl' ō *or* wôl' ō) *v.* to roll about, as in mud or dust.

ward·robe (wôrd' rōb') *n.* a closet or tall cabinet with hangers for holding clothes.

war·i·ly (wer' ə lē) *adv.* in a cautious manner.

war·y (wer' ē) *adj.* cautious; on one's guard.

wa·ter-lil·y (wôt' ər lil' ē) *n.* any of various water plants having large, flat, floating leaves and showy flowers in many colors.

wa·ver (wā' vər) *v.* to show doubt or be uncertain.

wea·ry (wir' ē) *adj.* tired; worn out. —**wearily** *adv.*

weight (wāt) *v.* to burden; load down.

Welsh-rare·bit (welsh' rer'bit) *n.* a dish of melted cheese, often mixed with beer or ale, served on crackers or toast.

whee·dle (hwē' d'l *or* wē' d'l) *v.* to influence or persuade by flattery or coaxing.

wheel (hwēl *or* wēl) *v.* to turn so as to reverse direction. *n.* anything like a wheel in shape.

whim·per (hwim' pər *or* wim' pər) *v.* to make low, broken crying sounds.

whine (hwīn *or* wīn) *v.* to make a drawn-out, high-pitched sound.

whirl (hwʉrl *or* wʉrl) *v.* to move rapidly in a circular manner. *n.* something whirling or being whirled.

---

at, āte, fär; pen, ēqual; sit, mīne; sō, côrn, join, took, fo͞ol, our; us, tʉrn; chill, shop, thick, they, siŋ; zh *in* measure; 'l *in* idle; ə *in* alive, cover, family, robot, circus.

whoop (ho͞op, hwo͞op, wo͞op, *or* wo͞op) *v.* to shout; cry out loudly.

whorl (hwôrl, wôrl, hwʉrl, *or* wʉrl) *n.* anything arranged in a circle, or having a coiled or spiral appearance.

wil·ly-nil·ly (wil′ ē nil′ ē) *adv.* whether one wishes it or not.

wire·less (wīr′ lis) *n.* a radio.

wont (wōnt, wônt, wunt *or* wänt) *n.* a usual practice, habit.

wrath (rath) *n.* intense anger; rage.

wreck (rek) *n.* a person in very poor health.

wrench (rench) *v.* to twist, pull, or jerk violently.

wretch·ed (rech′ id) *adj.* very unhappy; miserable; unfortunate.

writ (rit) *n.* a formal legal document ordering or prohibiting some action.

writhe (rīth) *v.* to make twisting or turning movements; squirm.

wrung (ruŋ) *v.* squeezed or pressed so as to force out water or other liquid.

Y

yank (yaŋk) *v.* to jerk; pull suddenly.

yawn (yôn) *v.* to open wide; gape.

yelp (yelp) *v.* to utter a short, sharp cry.

yoke (yōk) *n.* a wooden frame with loops at either end that fits over the shoulders for carrying pails. *v.* to harness; to join together closely.

Z

zeal (zēl) *n.* very great enthusiasm, as in working for a cause; strong interest or devotion; fervor.

ze·nith (zē′ nith) *n.* the point in the sky directly overhead.

Guidelines for Capitalization, Punctuation, and Spelling

Capitalization

Punctuation

Spelling

Guidelines for Capitalization

1   Proper Nouns and Adjectives

> **Capitalize proper nouns and proper adjectives.**

A **common noun** is a general name of a person, place, thing, or idea. A **proper noun** is the name of a particular person, place, thing, or idea. A **proper adjective** is an adjective formed from a proper noun.

Common Noun	Proper Noun	Proper Adjective
person	Elizabeth	Elizabethan
country	Spain	Spanish
city	Paris	Parisian

There are many different proper nouns. The following rules and examples will help you solve the capitalization problems that proper nouns present.

> **Capitalize the names of persons and also the initials or abbreviations that stand for those names.**

J. R. R. Tolkien	John Ronald Revel Tolkien
Elizabeth M. Grant	Elizabeth Mason Grant

> **Capitalize titles used with names of persons and also the initials or abbreviations that stand for those titles.**

The titles *Mr., Mrs., Ms.,* and *Miss* are always capitalized.

Rev. M. R. Eaton	Judge Esther Falks
Lt. Patricia Smith	Dr. John J. DeBender
Mr. Edward Scott	Professor White

Do not capitalize titles used as common nouns:

Have you seen your doctor?
She is the company president.
The judge entered the courtroom.

Capitalize titles of very high importance, even when these titles are used without proper names.

the Pope   the President of the United States
a United States Senator   the Prime Minister of England

Capitalize such words as *mother, father, aunt*, and *uncle* when these words are used as names.

When the noun is modified by a possessive word, *a,* or *the,* it is not capitalized.

Hello, Mother. Is Dad home yet?
My aunt is going to visit my grandmother next week.

Capitalize the pronoun *I*.

Is he taller than I?   I am sure that he is.

Capitalize all words referring to God, the Holy Family, and religious scriptures.

the Gospel   Buddha   the Torah
God   the Lord   the Bible
Allah   the Virgin Mary   the Book of Exodus

Capitalize personal pronouns referring to God.

God spoke to His prophets.

> **In a geographical name, capitalize the first letter of each word except articles and prepositions.**

The article *the* appearing before a geographical name is not part of the geographical name and is therefore not capitalized.

Continents: Europe, Asia, Africa, Australia

Bodies of Water: the Pacific Ocean, Puget Sound, the Columbia River, Hudson Bay

Landforms: the Cape of Good Hope, the Mojave Desert, the Atlas Mountains

Political Units: Los Angeles, Commonwealth of Puerto Rico, Utah, Great Britain

Public Areas: Badlands National Monument, Grant Park, Shawnee National Forest

Roads and Highways: Lincoln Highway, Broad Street, 34th Avenue, Tri-State Tollway

> **Capitalize names of sections of the country.**

Industrial production was high in the North.
The first English settlements were along the East Coast.
The Southwest is our fastest-growing region.

> **Capitalize proper adjectives derived from names of sections of the country.**

Western dress   a New England town
Southern-style cooking Midwestern twang

Do not capitalize directions of the compass.

We headed south for our vacation.
The pioneers moved west over the Oregon Trail.
The school is southwest of our home.

Do not capitalize adjectives derived from words indicating direction.

a north wind   the east side of the building

> **Capitalize the names of organizations and institutions, including political parties, governmental bodies or agencies, schools, colleges, churches, hospitals, clubs, businesses, and abbreviations of these names.**

Gillette Company	Children's Hospital
Oakwood High School	St. Mark's Church
University of Southern California	U.S.C.

Do not capitalize such words as *school, college, church,* and *hospital* when they are not used as parts of names:

This fund drive benefits the hospital.

> **Capitalize the names of historical events, documents, and periods of time.**

Battle of Hastings	Treaty of Paris	Age of Discovery
World War II	Bill of Rights	Middle Ages

> **Capitalize names of months, days, holidays, but not the names of seasons.**

March	Labor Day	summer
Friday	Feast of the Passover	spring

> **Capitalize the names of races, languages, nationalities, and religions and adjectives derived from them.**

Caucasian	African	Lutheranism
French	Buddhism	Catholic

> **Do not capitalize the names of school subjects, except course names followed by a number.**

physical education	History of Civilization II
social studies	Algebra I

> **Remember that the names of languages are always capitalized.**

English   Spanish   Hebrew   German

> **Capitalize the names of ships, trains, airplanes, and automobiles.**

U.S.S. Constitution   Santa Fe Chief
Cutlass   *Spirit of St. Louis*

> **Capitalize the abbreviations B.C. and A.D.**

The first Olympic Games were held in 776 B.C.
The Norman Conquest took place in A.D. 1066.

2 First Words and Titles

> **Capitalize the first word of every sentence and the first word in most lines of poetry.**

My sister likes tennis. She is the captain of her team.

Listen my children, and you shall hear
Of the midnight ride of Paul Revere . . . .
          —*from* "Paul Revere's Ride" by Henry Wadsworth Longfellow

Sometimes, especially in modern poetry, the lines of a poem do not begin with capital letters.

> **Capitalize the first word of a direct quotation.**

When you write the exact words of a speaker or writer, you are giving a **direct quotation.**

Ralph Waldo Emerson said, "Hitch your wagon to a star."

Sometimes a direct quotation is interrupted by explaining words like *she said.* This is called a **divided quotation.** Do not capitalize the first word of the second part of a divided quotation unless it starts a new sentence.

"Well," he said, "what you say is quite true."
"I agree," he said. "What you say is quite true."

Capitalize the first word, words like *Sir* and *Madam*, and the name of the person addressed in the greeting of a letter.

Dear Mrs. Gomez   Dear Ms. Perkins   Dear Mr. Castillo

In the complimentary close, capitalize the first word only.

Yours very truly   Sincerely yours

Capitalize the letters and the first word of each line of an outline.

I. Improve your handwriting.
   A. Form letters carefully.
      1. Watch *a, e, r, l,* and *t.*
      2. Watch *u, v,* and *o.*
   B. Proofread your work.

Capitalize the first word and all important words in chapter titles; titles of magazine articles; titles of short stories, essays, or single poems; and titles of songs or short pieces of music.

Chapter: Chapter 5, "The Undersea World"
Magazine article: "Sleep and Dreams"
Short story: "The Last Leaf"
Essay: "Nature"
Poem: "O Captain! My Captain!"
Song: "America the Beautiful"

> **Capitalize the first word and all important words in titles of books, newspapers, magazines, plays, movies, television programs, works of art, and long musical compositions.**

Underline these titles. (When these titles are printed, they are *italicized*.)

Book Title: *The Call of the Wild*
Newspaper: *Miami Herald*
Magazine: *People*
Play: *The Glass Menagerie*
Movie: *The Last Emperor*
Television Program: *The Evening News*
Work of art: Gainsborough's *Blue Boy*
Long musical composition: *Peter and the Wolf*

Guidelines for Punctuation

1 The Period

> **Use a period at the end of a declarative sentence.**

A **declarative sentence** is a sentence that makes a statement. It is the kind of sentence you use when you want to tell something.

My brother plays the guitar.

> **Use a period at the end of most imperative sentences.**

An **imperative sentence** is a sentence that requests or orders someone to do something.

Please close the door.

If the imperative sentence also expresses excitement or emotion, an exclamation point is used after it.

Watch out!

> **Use a period at the end of an indirect question.**

An **indirect question** tells what someone asked. However, it does not give the exact words of the person who asked the question.

She asked us whether we liked strawberries.

> **Use a period after an abbreviation or after an initial.**

An **abbreviation** is a shortened form of a word. An **initial** is a single letter that stands for a word.

Dr. Marla E. Corona   Trenton, N. J.
Rev. John L. Haeger, Jr.   2:30 P.M.

Periods are omitted in some abbreviations. If you are not sure whether or not to use periods, look up the abbreviation in your dictionary.

FM (*frequency modulation*)
UN (*United Nations*)
FBI (*Federal Bureau of Investigation*)

Use a period after each number or letter that shows a division of an outline or that precedes an item in a list.

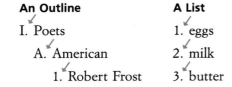

An Outline	A List
I. Poets	1. eggs
A. American	2. milk
1. Robert Frost	3. butter

Use a period in numerals between dollars and cents and before a decimal.

$18.98   2.853

2 The Question Mark and the Exclamation Point

Use a question mark at the end of an interrogative sentence.

An **interrogative sentence** is a sentence that asks a question.

Has anyone brought a flashlight?

The above sentence gives the exact words of the person who asked the question. It is called a **direct question.** A question mark is used only with a direct question.

> **Do not use a question mark with an indirect question. Instead use a period.**

Kelly asked whether anyone had brought a flashlight.

> **Use an exclamation point at the end of an exclamatory sentence.**

How great that looks!

> **Use an exclamation point after an interjection or after any other exclamatory expression.**

An **interjection** is a word or group of words used to express strong feeling. It may be a real word or simply a group of letters used to represent a sound. It is one of the eight parts of speech.

Hurrah!   Wow!   Ugh!

3 The Comma

Commas are used to separate words that do not belong together. In speaking, you can keep words apart by pausing. In writing, you must use commas.

> **Use a comma after every item in a series except the last.**

The items in a series may be single words, phrases, or clauses.

Words: The flag is red, white, and blue.

Phrases: The dog ran out the door, down the steps, and across the lawn.

Clauses: How kangaroos run, what jumps they can take, and how they live are explained in this book.

> **Use commas after the adverbs *first, second, third*, and so on, when these adverbs introduce a series of parallel items.**

There are three ways to get good marks: first, pay attention; second, take notes; third, study.

> **When two or more adjectives come before a noun, use a comma after each adjective except the last one.**

They drove away in a bright, shiny, expensive car.

Sometimes two adjectives are used together to express a single idea made up of two closely related thoughts. Adjectives so used are not usually separated by a comma.

Kim's dog is the small brown one.
Many young children go to that large elementary school.

> **Use a comma to separate an introductory word, phrase, or clause from the rest of the sentence.**

Yes, I will go.
After circling twice, the airplane landed.
Although Dick needed help, he said nothing.

The comma may be omitted if there would be little pause in speaking or if the phrase is very short.

At first I didn't know what to do.

> **Use commas to set off words or groups of words that interrupt the flow of thought in a sentence.**

Anne, to tell the truth, was quite happy.
The report, moreover, is altogether wrong.

Other examples of interrupters are *however, I think,* and *nevertheless.*

> **Use commas to set off nouns of direct address.**

The name of someone directly spoken to is a **noun of direct address.**

If you look, Peggy, you will see the book I mean.

Sarah, you won the election!

I'll be right back, Cathy.

> **Use commas to set off most appositives.**

An **appositive** is a word or group of words used directly after another word to explain it.

The speaker, a famous explorer, told about New Guinea.

An appositive phrase may have a prepositional phrase within it.

The leader, the person on horseback, moved away.

Nouns used as appositives are called **nouns in apposition.** When the noun in apposition is a short name, it is not usually set off by commas.

This is my friend Rhoda.

> **Use commas to set off the explaining words of a direct quotation.**

The explaining words used in giving a direct quotation are such brief statements as *Tina said, Christie answered,* or *Bill asked.*

The pilot said, "We will land in a few minutes."

In the sentence above, the explaining words come before the quotation. A comma is then placed after the last explaining word.

Now look at this quotation:

"We will land in a few minutes," the pilot said.

If the explaining words come *after* the quotation, as in the example above, place a comma within the quotation marks after the last word of the quotation.

Sometimes a quotation is separated into two parts by the explaining words. This is often done to add variety to the sentence construction. Here is an example:

"We will land," the pilot said, "in a few minutes."

The sentence above is an example of a divided quotation. A comma is used after the last word of the first part. Another comma is used after the last explaining word.

Do not confuse direct and indirect quotations. Indirect quotations are not set off from the rest of the sentence by commas.

The pilot said that the plane would land in a few minutes.

Use a comma before the conjunction that joins the two main clauses in a compound sentence.

Kimberly seemed to agree, and no one else objected.

Sometimes very short compound sentences have clauses joined by *and*. It is not necessary to use a comma if there is no change in the thought. Always use a comma before *or* or *but*. These words do change the direction of the thought.

Pete finally arrived *and* we started off.

Pete finally arrived, *but* it was too late to go anywhere.

Do not use a comma before the *and* that joins a compound subject or a compound predicate.

Sally turned on the radio *and* sat down to read a magazine.

In dates, use a comma between the day of the month and the year.

July 4, 1776   December 7, 1787

In a sentence, a comma follows the year.

The postmark read September 10, 1985, Chicago, Illinois.

> **Use a comma between the name of a city or town and the name of its state or country.**

Tucson, Arizona   Munich, Germany

In writing an address as part of a sentence, use a comma after each item.

Forward our mail to 651 Sentinel Drive, Milwaukee, Wisconsin 53203, where we will be moving next month.

Note that you do not place a comma between the state and the ZIP code.

> **Use a comma after the salutation of a friendly letter and after the complimentary close of a friendly letter or a business letter.**

Dear Tim,   Yours sincerely,

> **When no specific rule applies, but there is danger of misreading, use a comma.**

Who she is, is a mystery.   Inside, it was warm and cozy.

4 The Colon and the Semicolon

> **Use a colon after the greeting in a business letter.**

Dear Sir or Madam: Ladies and Gentlemen:

> **Use a colon between numbers indicating hours and minutes.**

10:00 P.M.   6:30 A.M.

> **Use a colon to introduce a list of items.**

If you are trying out for the team, bring the following things: a pair of gym shoes, your P.E. uniform, and your consent form.

Do not use a colon if the list immediately follows a verb or a preposition.

If you are trying out for the team, bring a pair of gym shoes, your P.E. uniform, and your consent form.

> **Use a semicolon to join the parts of a compound sentence when no coordinating conjunction is used.**

Dan has finished his homework; Darcy has not begun hers.

> **When there are commas in the first part of a compound sentence, use a semicolon to separate the main clauses.**

McCurdy of Illinois made the most spectacular shot of the game, a toss from mid-court; and Indiana, which had been favored to win, went down to defeat.

> **When there are commas within items in a series, use semicolons to separate the items.**

Hartford, New Haven, and Norwich, Connecticut; Springfield, Lowell, and Worcester, Massachusetts; and Pine Bridge, Mt. Kisco, and Chappaqua, New York, have all tried this experiment.

> **Use a semicolon before a word that joins the main clauses of a compound sentence.**

Such joining words are *therefore, however, hence, so, then, moreover, besides, nevertheless, yet,* and *consequently.*

It was a sunny day; however, it was quite cool.

5 The Hyphen and the Apostrophe

> **Use a hyphen if a syllable of a word must be carried over from one line to the next.**

In the library you will find several authorita-
tive books on solar energy.

Only words of two or more syllables can be divided at the end of a line. Never divide words of one syllable, such as *worse.*

A single letter must not be left at the end of a line. For example, this division would be wrong: *a-waken.* A single letter must not appear at the beginning of a line, either. This division would be incorrect: *dictionar-y.*

> **Use a hyphen in compound numbers from twenty-one through ninety-nine.**

twenty-three cents   forty-two students

> **Use a hyphen in fractions.**

We won a two-thirds majority.

> **Use a hyphen or hyphens in such compound nouns as *great-aunt* and *commander-in-chief.***

A Portuguese man-of-war stung the swimmer.

> **Use a hyphen or hyphens between words that make up a compound adjective used before a noun.**

It was a school-sponsored dance.
But: The dance was school sponsored.

When compound adjectives are used after the noun, they usually are not hyphenated. If you are unsure, look in a dictionary.

> **To form the possessive of a singular noun, add an apostrophe and an *s* after the apostrophe.**

girl + 's = girl's   man + 's = man's
boy + 's = boy's   Ross + 's = Ross's

> **To form the possessive of a plural noun that does not end in *s*, add an apostrophe and an *s* after the apostrophe.**

men + 's = men's   children + 's = children's

> **To form the possessive of a plural noun that ends in *s*, add only an apostrophe.**

drivers + ' = drivers'   pilots + ' = pilots'

> **Use an apostrophe and an *s* to form the possessive of indefinite pronouns.**

someone + 's = someone's   anybody + 's = anybody's

Never use an apostrophe in a possessive personal pronoun.

ours   yours   its   hers   theirs

The game reached *its* high point in the second quarter.

> **Use an apostrophe in a contraction.**

In a contraction, the apostrophe simply replaces one or more omitted letters.

he's = he is   aren't = are not   I'm = I am
it's = it is   isn't = is not   I've = I have
won't = will not   don't = do not   we've = we have

> **Use an apostrophe to show the omission of numbers in a date.**

the class of '84 (*the class of 1984*)

> **Use an apostrophe and s to form the plurals of letters, figures, and words used as words.**

two *m*'s   four *6*'s   *and*'s and *but*'s

6 Quotation Marks

> **Quotation marks tell your reader that you are quoting directly the exact spoken or written words of another person.**

Use quotation marks before and after the words of a direct quotation.

Sarah said, "My feelings were hurt."

Quotation marks are not used with indirect quotations:

Sarah said that her feelings were hurt.

Explaining words at the beginning of a sentence are followed by a comma before the quotation marks. At the end of a sentence a period is placed inside the quotation marks.

My sister announced, "There is someone to see you."

A quotation that begins the sentence is followed by a comma inside the quotation marks. A period follows the explaining words at the end of a sentence.

"There is someone to see you," my sister announced.

Sometimes the explaining words break into the middle of a direct quotation creating a **divided quotation.** Each part of the quotation is enclosed in quotation marks.

"Do you think," Don asked, "that you will like alfalfa sprouts?"

The second part of a divided quotation starts with a small letter, as in the last example. The only exceptions are the beginning of a new sentence and proper nouns or adjectives.

"We got drenched," said Sheila. "Our car roof leaks."

The first part of a divided quotation is followed by a comma inside the quotation marks.

"I want to see you," said Ms. Lazar, "before you leave."

The punctuation after the explanatory words in a divided quotation depends on the second part of the quotation. If the second part does not start a new sentence, a comma is used. If the second part does start a new sentence, a period is used.

"When you arrive," said Ben, "beep your horn."

"I can't go," said Janet. "I have to study."

Place question marks and exclamation points inside quotation marks if they belong to the quotation itself.

Dad asked, "Is Cindy working in the garage?"

"Look out!" Terry shouted.

Place question marks and exclamation points outside quotation marks if they do not belong to the quotation.

Did she say, "I'll be home at midnight"?

The man said, "You've won the contest"!

Occasionally, two or more sentences of a single speaker are quoted. Notice the punctuation of such a quotation:

"Is the council going to meet tomorrow?" asked Carly. "I wasn't sure whether we had decided to meet tomorrow or the next day. We have important things to discuss."

Dialogue is conversation between two or more people. Begin a new paragraph every time the speaker changes.

"Do you like horror movies?" asked Clyde.

"I don't," said Ted. "Real life can be horrifying enough. I don't understand why anyone needs any more fright."

"Well," said JoAnn, "maybe a few fake scares can help prepare you for real ones."

7 Punctuating Titles

> **Use quotation marks to enclose the titles of magazine articles, chapters, titles of short stories, essays, or single poems, songs, and short pieces of music.**

Chapter: Chapter 3, "Americans in London"
Magazine article: "Images of Youth Past"
Short story: "The Lottery"
Essay: "My First Article"
Poem: "The Raven"
Song: "The Star-Spangled Banner"

> **Underline the titles of books, newspapers, magazines, plays, television programs, movies, works of art, and long musical compositions.**

In writing or typewriting, these titles are underlined, like this: The Right Stuff.

In print, these titles appear in italics instead of being underlined.

Book: *Native Son*
Newspaper: *Des Moines Register*
Magazine: *Time*
Play: *You Can't Take It With You*
Television program: *Good Morning America*
Movie: *Casablanca*
Work of art: *Rembrandt's The Night Watch*
Long musical composition: *Nutcracker Suite*

Guidelines for Spelling

How to Become a Better Speller

1. Find out what your personal spelling enemies are and conquer them.

Go over your written assignments and make a list of the words you misspelled. Keep this list and master the words on it.

2. Pronounce words carefully.

Maybe you misspell words because you don't pronounce them carefully. For example, if you write *probly* for *probably,* you are no doubt mispronouncing the word.

3. Get into the habit of seeing the letters in a word.

Many people have never really looked at everyday words. As a result, they misspell even simple words.

Take a good look at unfamiliar words or difficult words. Copy their spellings several times.

4. Proofread everything you write.

Learn to examine carefully everything you write. To proofread a piece of writing, read it slowly, word for word. Otherwise, your eyes may play tricks on you and you may skip over misspelled words.

5. Use a dictionary to check troublesome words.

6. Study the rules for spelling.

Mastering Particular Words

1. **Look at the word and say it to yourself.**

Be sure you pronounce it correctly. If it has more than one syllable, say it again, one syllable at a time. Look at each syllable as you say it.

2. **Look at the letters and say each one.**

If the word has more than one syllable, divide the word into syllables when you say the letters.

3. **Write the word without looking at it.**

4. **Now look at your book or list and see whether you have spelled the word correctly.**

If you have, write it again and compare it with the correct form again. Do this once more.

5. **If you made a mistake, note exactly what it was.**

Then repeat steps 3 and 4 until you have written the word correctly three times.

Rules for Spelling

Adding Prefixes and Suffixes

Prefixes

When a prefix is added to a word, the spelling of the word remains the same.

re- + elect = reelect   mis- + direct = misdirect
mis- + spell = misspell   re- + enter = reenter
im- + moderate = immoderate   dis- + satisfy = dissatisfy
il- + legible = illegible   ir- + regular = irregular

The Final Silent e

When a suffix beginning with a vowel is added to a word ending in a silent e, the e is usually dropped.

create + -ion = creation   grieve + -ing = grieving
graze + -ing = grazing   relate + ive = relative
fame + -ous = famous   continue + -ing = continuing

When a suffix beginning with a consonant is added to a word ending in a silent e, the e is usually retained.

spite + -ful = spiteful   taste + -ful = tasteful
state + -ment = statement   move + -ment = movement
voice + -less = voiceless   wide + -ly = widely

The following words are exceptions:

truly   argument   ninth   wholly

Words Ending in y

When a suffix is added to a word ending in y preceded by consonant, the y is usually changed to i.

crazy + -ly = crazily   puppy + -es = puppies
seventy + -eth = seventieth   silly + -ness = silliness
hilly + -est = hilliest   marry + -age = marriage

Note the following exception: When -ing is added, the y does not change:

scurry + -ing = scurrying   carry + -ing = carrying
ready + -ing = readying   worry + -ing = worrying

When a suffix is added to a word ending in *y* preceded by a vowel, the *y* usually does not change.

employ + -ed = employed   stay + -ing = staying
play + -er = player   relay + -ing = relaying

The Suffixes *-ness* and *-ly*

When the suffix *-ly* is added to a word ending in *l*, both *l*'s are kept. When *-ness* is added to a word ending in *n*, both *n*'s are kept.

normal + -ly = normally   open + -ness = openness

Doubling the Final Consonant

In words of one syllable that end in one consonant preceded by one vowel, double the final consonant before adding *-ing*, *-ed*, or *-er*.

hit + -ing = hitting   spot + -ed = spotted
nod + -ed = nodded   rob + -er = robber

The following words do not double the final consonant because *two* vowels precede final consonant:

near + -ing = nearing   cool + -er = cooler
look + -ed = looked   meet + -ing = meeting

Words with the "Seed" Sound

Only one English word ends in *sede: supersede.*
Three words end in *ceed: exceed, proceed, succeed.*
All other words ending in the sound of *seed* are spelled *cede:*

concede   precede   recede   secede

Words with *ie* and *ei*

When the sound is long *e* (*ē*), the word is spelled *ie* except after *c*.

I before E

relieve   grieve   field   pierce
belief   piece   pier   reprieve

Except after C

conceit   conceive   perceive   deceive   receive

Or when sounded like A

weigh   eight   neighbor

The following words are exceptions:

either   weird   species   neither   seize   leisure

Words Often Confused

accept means to agree to something or to receive something willingly.

except means to keep out or leave out. As a preposition, *except* means "but" or "leaving out."

▶ My brother will *accept* the job the grocer offered him.
▶ Michelle likes every flavor of ice cream *except* pistachio.

capital means chief, most serious, or most important. It is also the official seat of government.

capitol is a building in which a state legislature meets.

the Capitol is the building in Washington, D.C., where the United States Congress meets.

▶ Murder is a *capital* crime.
▶ The state *capitol* building is in Springfield.
▶ The nation's laws are made in the *Capitol*.

des'·ert means a barren, dry region.
de·sert' means to leave or to abandon.

dessert (note the two *s*'s) is a sweet food, the last course of a meal.

▶ Lizards thrive in the *desert*.
▶ One soldier *deserted* his company.
▶ Order the cheesecake for *dessert*.

hear means to listen to or to take notice of.
here means in this place.

▶ Did you *hear* the news on the radio?
▶ The fire hose is kept *here*.

its is a word that shows possession by *it*.
it's is a contraction for *it is* or *it has*.

▶ The violin has *its* own case.
▶ *It's* time for a break.

loose means free, not fastened, not tight.
lose means to mislay or suffer the loss of something.

▶ Runners wear *loose* clothing.
▶ Did you *lose* track of time?

peace is calm or stillness or the absence of disagreement.
piece means a portion or part.

▶ After two years of war, *peace* was finally achieved.
▶ This statue was carved from a *piece* of jade.

principal refers to something which is chief or of highest importance.
It is also the name for the head of an elementary or high school.
principle is a basic truth, rule, or policy.

▶ The *principal* speaker is the mayor.
▶ The Bill of Rights states basic *principles*.

quiet means free from noise or disturbance.
quite means truly or almost completely.

▶ The only time our classroom is *quiet* is when it's empty.
▶ The aquarium tank is *quite* full.

stationary means fixed or unmoving.
stationery refers to paper and envelopes used for writing letters.

▶ The boat in the distance looks *stationary*.
▶ Cindy has *stationery* with her name on it.

their is a possessive word meaning belonging to *them*.
there means in that place.
they're is the contraction for *they are*.

▶ The children rode *their* bicycles.
▶ The trail begins *there*.
▶ Plants turn yellow when *they're* watered too often.

to means toward or in the direction of.
too means also or extremely.
two is the number.

▶ This bus goes *to* the civic center.
▶ Marla wears glasses, and Dave does *too*.
▶ We reserved *two* tickets.

weather refers to the state of the atmosphere, including temperature, wind, and moisture.
whether introduces choices or alternatives.

▶ Bad *weather* spoiled the picnic.
▶ The player must decide *whether* to pass or kick the ball.

who's is a contraction for *who is* or *who has*.
whose is the possessive form of *who*.

▶ *Who's* going to Sue's party?
▶ *Whose* locker is that?

your means belonging to *you*.
you're is the contraction for *you are*.

▶ Do *your* new boots feel comfortable?
▶ *You're* taking the bus, aren't you?

Index of Titles and Authors

Index of Skills

Reading Literature Skills

Fairy Tale, 234
  See also **Tale**
Falling Action, *See* **Plot**
Fantasy, 150, 158, 620, 631
Fiction, *See* **Drama, Fantasy, Folk Tale, Poetry, Short Story, Tale**
Figure of Speech/Figurative Language, 221–229, 309, 400, 452, 468, 543, 631
  See also **Hyperbole, Metaphor, Personification, Simile**
Flashback, 95, 583, 598, 604, 631
Folk Tale, 234, 263
  See also **Tale**
Foreshadowing, 76, 102, 157, 632
Free Verse, *See* **Poetry**
Greek Myth and Legend, 288–289
  elements of, 288–289, 329
  history of, 288
  purpose of, 289, 303, 350
  values reflected in, 289, 315, 350, 355, 361, 367
  See also **Character, Setting, Theme** *in Greek myths and legends*
Humor, 632
  in drama, 620
  in humorous sketches, 535, 543, 552, 560
  in nonfiction, 537
  in poetry, 389, 425
  in tales, 273
Hyperbole, 228, 632
  in poetry, 229, 401, 409, 425
  in prose, 228
  See also **Figure of Speech**
Imagery
  sensory images, 400, 403, 405, 417, 425, 429, 434, 507, 636
Irony, 192, 274, 543–544, 560, 576, 605, 632
Legend, 234, 288–289, 355, 632
  comparing and contrasting, 361

contrasted with myth, 331, 338, 345, 370
  See also **Greek Myth and Legend**
Metaphor, 224, 633
  in poetry, 225, 401, 406, 431
  in prose, 224
  See also **Figure of Speech**
Mood, 157, 633
  in nonfiction, 441, 481, 507, 576
  in poetry, 375, 385, 387, 393, 406, 415, 422, 434
Myth, 234–235, 633
  comparing and contrasting, 249, 303
  contrasted with legends, 331, 338, 345, 370
  contrasted with tales, 263
  diagraming setting in, 243, 323
  elements of, 235
  Greek, 288–289
  history of, 234
  purpose of, 235, 253, 284
  values reflected in, 253
  See also **Tale**
  See also **Character, Setting, Theme** *in myths*
Narrator, 70, 76, 184, 633
  in drama, 583, 598, 621
  See also **Point of View**
Nonfiction, 440–441, 633
  elements of, 441, 536–537
  history of, 440
  subject of, 441
  See also **Autobiography, Biography, Essay**
  See also **Setting, Theme** *in nonfiction*
Onomatopoeia, 216, 633–634
  in poetry, 216–217, 401
  in prose, 216
  See also **Sounds of Language**
Oral Tradition, 234, 288, 634
  See also **Legend, Myth, Tale**
Personification, 226, 634
  in poetry, 226–227, 401, 409, 425

Comprehension and Thinking Skills

Study and Research Skills

Outlining, 653
   elements of a story, 84
   plot, 355
Periodicals, 113
Readers' Guide to Periodical Literature, 77, 113, 650
Research Topic, Refining, 77
Short Story Index, 175
Symbols and Abbreviations, 113
Subject Heading, 113
Taking Notes, 304, 562, 653
Thesaurus, 426, 651
Time Line, 568

Writing Skills

Analysis, Writing an, 127
   of an experience, 503
   of meaning, 572
   of a relationship, 330
   of plot, 351
   of scene structure, 607
   of theme, 569
Character, Analyzing, 29, 362, 489, 534
   motivation, 317, 339
Character, Writing about, 29, 62, 114, 317, 362
   comparing and contrasting, 193, 265, 285, 310, 494
   describing what makes a hero, 251
Comparing and Contrasting, 193, 265, 285, 310, 482, 562, 579
Creating a Creature, 185, 283
Creating Humor, 545
Creating Metaphors, 435
Definition, Writing a, 149
Describing
   an activity, 391
   an event, 517, 534

   a place, 454
   a scene, 527
   a setting, 245
   a tradition, 508
Description, Writing a, 96, 176, 346
Developing an Argument, 53, 103
   See also Opinion
Dialogue, *See* Scene, Writing a
Diary, Writing a, 482
Drafting, 205–206, 655–656, 659
   See also Process of Writing
Essay, 577
Expanding a Myth, 304, 325
Experience, Writing about, 68, 149, 330
Explaining
   an expression, 339
   an idea or opinion, 46, 85, 391, 419, 427, 508, 527, 623
   a prediction, 251
   fantasy elements, 158
   images, 435
Explanation, Writing an, 304
   See also Explaining
Fantasy, *See* Explaining
Figures of Speech, Using, 221–229
   See also Figure of Speech in *Reading Literature Skills*
Humorous Sketch, Writing a, 554
Idea, *See* Explaining
Imagination, Using Your, 569
Mood, Writing about, 411
Narration, 168
Opinion, Supporting an, 62, 517
   See also Developing an Argument, Explaining
Plot, Analyzing, 351
Poem, Writing a, 419, 437
Point of View, Changing, 78, 103, 168
Prewriting, 200–204, 654–655, 659

Index of Fine Art

Art Credits

Cover

The Large Family, 1947. RENÉ MAGRITTE. Copyright for René Magritte © 1963 Charly Herscovici. Collection of Gustave Nellens, Knokke, Belgium.

Illustrations

David Cunningham, 204–205; Sarah Woodward, 332; Dale Bēda, 462; Candace Haught, 511; Troy Thomas, 591, 594–595, 603.

Photographs

Milton Ackoff: 500. The Bettmann Archive: 26, 83, 381, 385, 403, 543, 559. Angelou/Camera Press/Photo Trends: 492. © 1987 *Chicago Tribune,* all rights reserved, used with permission: 506. *Deseret News* photograph: 525. Dillon Press, from *Sarah Winemucca* by Doris Kloss: 528. Bob East/Photo Trends: 432. *El Tiempo:* 101. Alex Gottfryd: 156. Erich Hartmann/Magnum Photos: 76. © Heinemann/Camera Press/Photo Trends: 66. Historical Pictures Service: 20. Suzanne Lee Houfek: 191. Houghton Library, Harvard University: 571. Anthony Armstrong-Jones/Camera Press/Photo Trends: 425. Oil on canvas in two parts, overall, 10'2" x 12'8¼"; top panel: 6'9" x 12'8¼"; bottom panel, 41" x 12'8¼". Collection, The Museum of Modern Art, New York City. Acquired through the Carter Burden, Barbara Jakobson, Saidie A. May Funds and Purchase: 294. National Portrait Gallery, Smithsonian Institution: 451. Photo Researchers: 407. Photo Trends: 575. UPI/Bettmann: 480. AP/Wide World Photos: 33, 302, 515, 551, 566.

Acknowledgments

Agberg, Ltd. and Robert Silverberg: For "The Assassin" by Robert Silverberg, from *Travels Through Time;* copyright © 1957 by Greenleaf Publications, Inc. *American Way,* inflight magazine of American Airlines: For "The Uses of Error" by Isaac Asimov; copyright © 1985 by American Airlines. Atheneum Publishers, Inc., a division of Macmillan Publishing Company: For "Thumbprint" by Eve Merriam, from *It Doesn't Always Have to Rhyme;* copyright © 1954 by Eve Merriam. For an excerpt from *Chief Sarah* by Dorothy Nafus Morrison; copyright © 1980 Dorothy Nafus Morrison. Toni Cade Bambara: For "Raymond's Run," from *Gorilla, My Love* by Toni Cade Bambara; copyright © 1972 by Random House, Inc. Blackie & Son, Ltd.: For "The Story of the Fisherman and the Brass Bottle," from *The Arabian Nights,* retold by Amabel Williams-Ellis. Brandt and Brandt: For excerpts from "Daniel Boone," "Nancy Hanks," and "Johnny Appleseed" by Rosemary and Stephen Vincent Benét, from *A Book of Americans;* copyright 1933 by Rosemary and Stephen Vincent Benét; copyright renewed © 1961 by Rosemary Carr Benét. Broadside Press: For an excerpt from *Report From Part One* by Gwendolyn Brooks. John Ciardi: For an excerpt from "Speed Adjustments" by John Ciardi, from *The Monster Den;* reprinted by permission of the author and copyright holder. The Christian Science Publishing Society: For "Unfolding Bud" by Naoshi Koriyama, from *The Christian Science Monitor;* © 1957, all rights reserved. Collins Publishers, London: For an excerpt from "Narnian Suite" by C. S. Lewis, from *Poems of C. S. Lewis.* Don Congdon Associates, Inc.: For "All Summer in a Day" by Ray Bradbury; copyright © 1954 by Ray Bradbury, renewed 1982 by Ray Bradbury. Delacorte Press: For "Future Tense" by Robert Lipsyte, excerpted from *Sixteen Short Stories by Outstanding Writers for Young Adults,* edited by Donald R. Gallo; copyright © 1984 by Robert Lipsyte. Devin-Adair Publishers: For "The Trout" by Sean O'Faolain, from *The Man Who Invented Sin;* copyright © 1948 by Sean O'Faolain, renewed in 1976. Doubleday & Company, Inc.: For excerpts from *Fatherhood* by Bill Cosby; copyright © 1986 by William H. Cosby, Jr. For "After Twenty Years," from *The Four Million* by O. Henry; copyright 1904 by Press Publishing Co. For excerpts from *Anne Frank: The Diary of a Young Girl* by Anne Frank; copyright 1952 by Otto H. Frank. For "Child on Top of a Greenhouse" by Theodore Roethke and an excerpt from "Night Journey," from *The Collected Poems of Theodore Roethke;* copyright 1946 by Editorial Publications, Inc. For "The Third Wish" by Joan Aiken, from *Not What You Expected* by Joan Aiken; copyright © 1974 by Joan Aiken. E. P. Dutton, Inc.: For manuscript page from *My Side of the Mountain* by Jean George, all rights reserved. For pages of text (changing Roman names to Greek—the author chose to use Roman names in telling the stories) from *Stories of Gods and Heroes* retold by Sally Benson; copyright 1940, 1968 by Sally Benson, reprinted by permission of the publisher, Dial Books for Young Readers, a division of E. P. Dutton, Inc. For an excerpt from *A Precocious Autobiography* by Yevgeny Yevtushenko, translated by Andrew R. MacAndrew, English translation copyright © 1963 by E. P. Dutton, reprinted by permission of the publisher, E. P. Dutton, a division of NAL Penguin, Inc. For "All Cats are Gray" by Andre Norton, from *The Many Worlds of Science Fiction,* edited by Ben Bova; copyright © 1971 by Ben Bova, by permission of E. P. Dutton, a division of NAL Penguin, Inc. For "The Man Who Was a Horse," from *The Long Journey Home: Stories From Black History* by Julius Lester; copyright © 1972 by Julius Lester, by permission of Dial Books for Young Readers. Farrar, Straus & Giroux, Inc.: For an excerpt from "Lawnmower" by Valerie Worth, from *More Small Poems;* copyright © 1976 by Valerie Worth. For "The Storyteller" by Mark Van Doren, from *Collected and New Poems, 1924–1963;* copyright © 1963 by Mark Van Doren. For "The Song of a Dream," from *In the Trail of the Wind* by John Bierhorst; copyright © 1971 by John Bierhorst. For "Charles" by Shirley Jackson, from *The Lottery;* copyright 1948 by Shirley Jackson, renewed © 1976 by Laurence Hyman, Mrs. Sarah Webster, and Mrs. Joanne Schnurer. Richard Garcia: For an excerpt from "The City Is So Big" by Richard Garcia. Harcourt Brace Jovanovich, Inc.: For an excerpt from "Women" by Alice Walker, from *Revolutionary Petunias.* For excerpts from "Four Preludes on Playthings of the Winds," "Under a Hat Rim," "Jazz Fantasia," and "Sunsets" by Carl Sandburg, from *The Complete Poems of Carl Sandburg.* For "Macavity: the Mystery Cat," from *Old Possum's Book of Practical Cats* by T. S. Eliot; copyright 1939 by T. S. Eliot, renewed 1967 by Esme Valerie Eliot. For "To Look at Any Thing," from *The Living Seed* by John Moffitt; copyright © 1961 by John Moffitt. For "Fueled," from *Serve Me a Slice of Moon* by Marcie Hans; copyright © 1965 by Marcie Hans. For "Road to the Isles" by Jessamyn West, from *Cress Delahanty;* copyright 1948, 1976 by Jessamyn West. Harper & Row Publishers, Inc.: For an excerpt from "Where Would You Be" by Karla Kuskin, from *Dogs and Dragons, Trees and Dreams;* copyright © 1964 by Karla Kuskin. For an excerpt from "If You Should Go" by Countee Cullen, from *On These I Stand, An Anthology of the Best Poems of Countee Cullen;* copyright 1925 by Harper & Row, Publishers, Inc., renewed 1953 by Ida M. Cullen. For an excerpt from "Alms" by Edna St. Vincent Millay, from *Collected Lyrics.* Holiday House: For an excerpt from "A Circle of Seasons" by Myra Cohn Livingston. Holt, Rinehart and Winston: For an excerpt from "The Runaway" by Robert Frost and "Stopping by Woods on a Snowy Evening," from *The Poetry of Robert Frost,* edited by Edward Connery Lathem; copyright 1923, © 1969 by Holt, Rinehart and Winston; copyright 1951 by Robert Frost. Indiana University Press: For "Haiku" by José Juan Tablada, from *Anthology of Mexican Poetry* translated by Samuel Becket, compiled by Octavia Paz. J.C.A. Literary Agency as agents for the author: For "The Fish," from *Folk and Fairy Tales of Far-Off Lands,* edited and adapted by Eric and Nancy Protter; copyright © 1965 by Eric Protter and Nancy Protter. Little, Brown and Company: For Chapters 1 & 2 from

Staff Credits

Executive Editor, Literature: Susan D. Schaffrath
Senior Editor: Sherry A. Stansbury
Editors: Christine M. Iversen, Dennis Ryan
Associate Editor: Linda Williams

Production Coordinator: Mary Schafer
Production Editor: Ronald A. Rutkowski
Associate Production Editor: Teri L. Firmiss
Copyeditor: Elizabeth M. Garber

Designer: Linda Schifano FitzGibbon
Picture Editor: Carmine Fantasia